McGraw-Hill Ryerson

Principles of Mathematics 10

Authors

Barbara Canton
B.A., B.Ed., M.Ed.
Limestone District School Board

Chris Dearling
B.Sc., M.Sc.
Burlington, Ontario

Wayne Erdman
B.Math., B.Ed.
Toronto District School Board

Brian McCudden
M.A., M.Ed., Ph.D.
Toronto, Ontario

Fran McLaren
B.Sc., B.Ed.
Upper Grand District School Board

Roland W. Meisel
B.Sc., B.Ed., M.Sc.
Port Colborne, Ontario

Jacob Speijer
B.Eng., M.Sc.Ed., P.Eng.
District School Board of Niagara

Assessment Consultants

Chris Dearling

Brian McCudden

Technology Consultant

Roland W. Meisel

Literacy Consultant

Barbara Canton
Limestone District School Board

Special Consultants

John Ferguson
Lambton-Kent District School Board

Fred Ferneyhough
Caledon, Ontario

Jeff Irvine
Peel District School Board

Advisors

Becky Bagley
Greater Essex Catholic District School Board

John DiVizio
Durham Catholic District School Board

Derrick Driscoll
Thames Valley District School Board

David Lovisa
York Region District School Board

Anthony Meli
Toronto District School Board

Tess Miller
Queen's University
Kingston, Ontario

Colleen Morgulis
Durham Catholic District School Board

Larry Romano
Toronto Catholic District School Board

Carol Shiffman
Peel District School Board

Tony Stancati
Toronto Catholic District School Board

Toronto   Montréal   Boston   Burr Ridge, IL   Dubuque, IA   Madison, WI   New York
San Francisco   St. Louis   Bangkok   Bogotá   Caracas   Kuala Lumpur   Lisbon   London
Madrid   Mexico City   Milan   New Delhi   Santiago   Seoul   Singapore   Sydney   Taipei

The McGraw·Hill Companies

McGraw-Hill Ryerson
Principles of Mathematics 10

Copyright © 2007, McGraw-Hill Ryerson Limited, a Subsidiary of The McGraw-Hill Companies. All rights reserved. No part of this publication may be reproduced or transmitted in any form or by any means, or stored in a data base or retrieval system, without the prior written permission of McGraw-Hill Ryerson Limited, or, in the case of photocopying or other reprographic copying, a licence from the Canadian Copyright Licensing Agency (Access Copyright). For an Access Copyright licence, visit *www.accesscopyright.ca* or call toll free to 1-800-893-5777.

Any request for photocopying, recording, or taping of this publication shall be directed in writing to Access Copyright.

ISBN-13: 978-0-07-097332-9
ISBN-10: 0-07-097332-6

http://www.mcgrawhill.ca

1 2 3 4 5 6 7 8 9 0 TCP 6 5 4 3 2 1 0 9 8 7

Printed and bound in Canada

Care has been taken to trace ownership of copyright material contained in this text. The publishers will gladly take any information that will enable them to rectify any reference or credit in subsequent printings.

Microsoft® Excel is either a registered trademark or a trademark of Microsoft Corporation in the United States and/or other countries.

The Geometer's Sketchpad®, Key Curriculum Press, 1150 65th Street, Emeryville, CA 94608, 1-800-995-MATH.

PUBLISHER: Linda Allison
ASSOCIATE PUBLISHER: Kristi Clark
PROJECT MANAGERS: Maggie Cheverie, Janice Dyer
DEVELOPMENTAL EDITORS: Julia Cochrane, Jackie Lacoursiere, David Peebles
MANAGER, EDITORIAL SERVICES: Crystal Shortt
SUPERVISING EDITOR: Janie Deneau
COPY EDITORS: Julia Cochrane, Linda Jenkins, Red Pen Services
PHOTO RESEARCH/PERMISSIONS: Linda Tanaka
PHOTO RESEARCH/SET-UP PHOTOGRAPHY: Roland W. Meisel
EDITORIAL ASSISTANT: Erin Hartley
ASSISTANT PROJECT COORDINATOR: Janie Reeson
MANAGER PRODUCTION SERVICES: Yolanda Pigden
PRODUCTION COORDINATOR: Sheryl MacAdam
REVIEW COORDINATOR: Jennifer Keay
COVER DESIGN: Pronk & Associates
INTERIOR DESIGN: Pronk & Associates
ELECTRONIC PAGE MAKE-UP: Tom Dart and Kim Hutchinson/ First Folio Resource Group, Inc.
COVER IMAGE: Paul Rapson/Science Photo Library

COPIES OF THIS BOOK MAY BE OBTAINED BY CONTACTING:

McGraw-Hill Ryerson Ltd.

WEB SITE:
http://www.mcgrawhill.ca

E-MAIL:
orders@mcgrawhill.ca

TOLL-FREE FAX:
1-800-463-5885

TOLL-FREE CALL:
1-800-565-5758

OR BY MAILING YOUR ORDER TO:
McGraw-Hill Ryerson
Order Department
300 Water Street
Whitby, ON L1N 9B6

Please quote the ISBN and title when placing your order.

Acknowledgements

REVIEWERS OF *PRINCIPLES OF MATHEMATICS 10*

The publishers, authors, and editors of *McGraw-Hill Ryerson Principles of Mathematics 10* wish to extend their sincere thanks to the students, teachers, consultants, and reviewers who contributed their time, energy, and expertise to the creation of this textbook. We are grateful for their thoughtful comments and suggestions. This feedback has been invaluable in ensuring that the text and related teacher's resource meet the needs of students and teachers.

Andrea Clarke
Ottawa Carleton District School Board

Karen Frazer
Ottawa Carleton District School Board

Doris Galea
Dufferin Peel Catholic District School Board

Alison Lane
Ottawa Carleton District School Board

Paul Marchildon
Ottawa Carleton District School Board

David Petro
Windsor Essex Catholic District School Board

Anthony Pignatelli
Toronto Catholic District School Board

Sharon Ramlochan
Toronto District School Board

Julie Sheremeto
Ottawa Carleton District School Board

Robert Sherk
Limestone District School Board

Susan Siskind
Toronto District School Board (retired)

Victor Sommerkamp
Dufferin Peel Catholic District School Board

Joe Spano
Dufferin Peel Catholic District School Board

Carolyn Sproule
Ottawa Carleton District School Board

Maria Stewart
Dufferin Peel Catholic District School Board

Anne Walton
Ottawa Carleton District School Board

Contents

A Tour of Your Textbook vi

Chapter 1

Linear Systems 2

Get Ready 4
1.1 Connect English With Mathematics and Graphing Lines 8
1.2 The Method of Substitution 20
1.3 Investigate Equivalent Linear Relations and Equivalent Linear Systems 29
1.4 The Method of Elimination 34
1.5 Solve Problems Using Linear Systems 42
Chapter 1 Review 48
Chapter 1 Practice Test 50

Chapter 2

Analytic Geometry 52

Get Ready 54
2.1 Midpoint of a Line Segment 56
2.2 Length of a Line Segment 70
2.3 Apply Slope, Midpoint, and Length Formulas 80
2.4 Equation for a Circle 92
Chapter 2 Review 100
Chapter 2 Practice Test 104

Chapter 3

Geometric Properties 106

Get Ready 108
3.1 Investigate Properties of Triangles 110
3.2 Verify Properties of Triangles 117
3.3 Investigate Properties of Quadrilaterals 128
3.4 Verify Properties of Quadrilaterals 137
3.5 Properties of Circles 145
Chapter 3 Review 152
Chapter 3 Practice Test 154
Chapters 1 to 3 Review 156
Tasks 158

Chapter 4

Quadratic Relations 160

Get Ready 162
4.1 Investigate Non-Linear Relations 164
4.2 Quadratic Relations 168
4.3 Investigate Transformations of Quadratics 174
4.4 Graph $y = a(x - h)^2 + k$ 180
4.5 Quadratic Relations of the Form $y = a(x - r)(x - s)$ 189
4.6 Negative and Zero Exponents 194
Chapter 4 Review 202
Chapter 4 Practice Test 204

Chapter 5

Quadratic Expressions — 206

Get Ready — 208
5.1 Multiply Polynomials — 210
5.2 Special Products — 220
5.3 Common Factors — 228
5.4 Factor Quadratic Expressions of the Form $x^2 + bx + c$ — 236
5.5 Factor Quadratic Expressions of the Form $ax^2 + bx + c$ — 242
5.6 Factor a Perfect Square Trinomial and a Difference of Squares — 248
Chapter 5 Review — 256
Chapter 5 Practice Test — 258

Chapter 6

Quadratic Equations — 260

Get Ready — 262
6.1 Maxima and Minima — 264
6.2 Solve Quadratic Equations — 274
6.3 Graph Quadratics Using the x-Intercepts — 282
6.4 The Quadratic Formula — 292
6.5 Solve Problems Using Quadratic Equations — 304
Chapter 6 Review — 316
Chapter 6 Practice Test — 318
Chapters 4 to 6 Review — 320
Tasks — 322

Chapter 7

Trigonometry of Right Triangles — 324

Get Ready — 326
7.1 Investigate Properties of Similar Triangles — 330
Use Technology
    Create Designs With Similar and Congruent Figures Using Dynamic Geometry Software — 336
7.2 Use Similar Triangles to Solve Problems — 342
7.3 The Tangent Ratio — 352
7.4 The Sine and Cosine Ratios — 366
7.5 Solve Problems Involving Right Triangles — 378
Chapter 7 Review — 386
Chapter 7 Practice Test — 390

Chapter 8

Trigonometry of Acute Triangles — 392

Get Ready — 394
8.1 The Sine Law — 396
8.2 The Cosine Law — 405
8.3 Find Angles Using the Cosine Law — 412
Use Technology
    Program a Graphing Calculator — 420
Use Technology
    Program a TI-89 Calculator — 422
8.4 Solve Problems Using Trigonometry — 424
Chapter 8 Review — 430
Chapter 8 Practice Test — 432
Chapters 7 and 8 Review — 434
Tasks — 436
Course Review — 438

Challenge Problems Appendix — 448
Prerequisite Skills Appendix — 458
Technology Appendix — 476
Answers — 504
Glossary — 570
Index — 582

A Tour of Your Textbook

Chapter Opener

- This two-page spread introduces what you will learn in the chapter.
- The specific curriculum expectations that the chapter covers are listed.
- In the vocabulary lists are the mathematical terms that are introduced and defined in the chapter.
- The chapter problem is introduced. Questions related to the chapter problem occur in the Connect and Apply sections of the exercises throughout the chapter and are identified by a **Chapter Problem** descriptor.

Get Ready

Examples and practice questions review key skills from previous mathematics courses that are needed for success with the new concepts of the chapter.

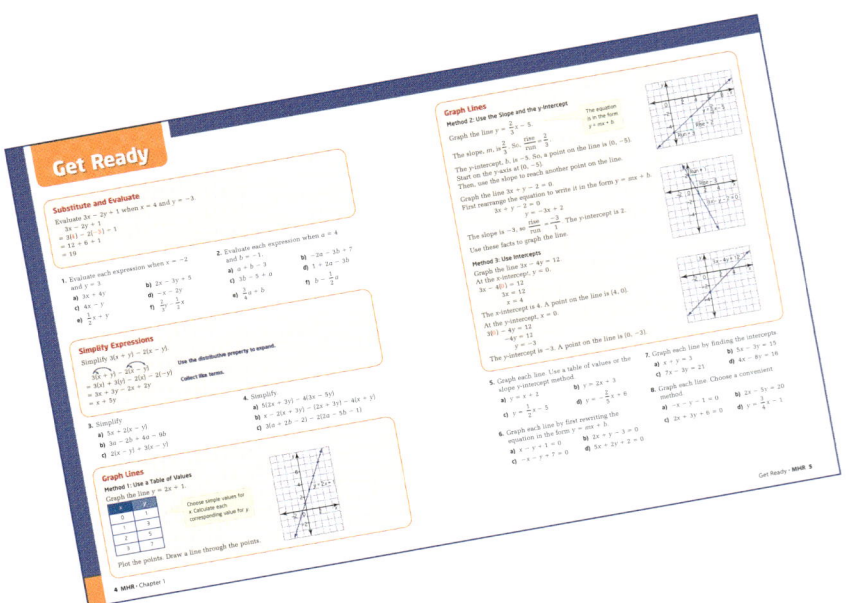

Numbered Sections

Lesson Opener
Many lessons start with a photograph and short description of a real-world setting to which the mathematical concepts relate.

Investigate
These are step-by-step activities, leading you to build your own understanding of the new concepts of the lesson. Many of these activities can best be done by working in pairs or small groups to share ideas.

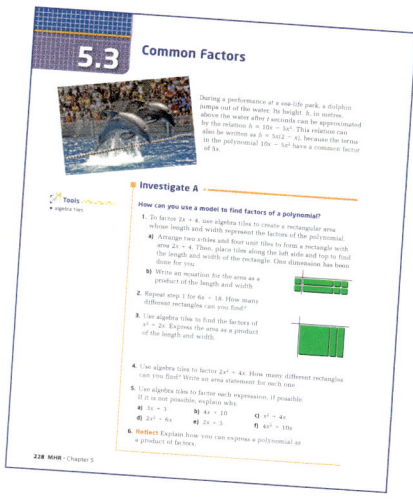

Examples
- Examples provide model solutions that show how the new concepts are used.
- The examples and their solutions include several tools to help you understand the work.
  – Notes in a thought bubble help you think through the steps.
  – Sometimes different methods of solving the same problem are shown. One may make more sense to you than the other. Often, alternative methods, using different technology tools, are shown.

- Some examples use the four-step problem solving model to remind you of a very helpful way of tackling problems.

A Tour of Your Textbook • MHR **vii**

Key Concepts
- This feature summarizes the concepts learned in the lesson.
- You can refer to this summary when you are studying or doing homework.

Communicate Your Understanding
These questions allow you to reflect on the concepts of the section. By discussing these questions in a group, you can see whether you understand the main points and are ready to start the exercises.

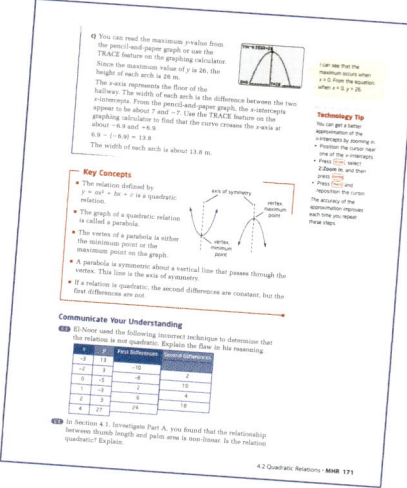

Exercises

Practise
- These questions provide an opportunity to practise your knowledge and understanding of the new concept.
- To help you, questions are referenced to the examples.

Connect and Apply
- These questions allow you to use what you have learned to solve problems and make connections among concepts. In answering these questions you will be integrating your skills with many of the math processes.
- There are many opportunities to use technology. If specific tools or materials are needed, these are noted and the question has a **Use Technology** descriptor.

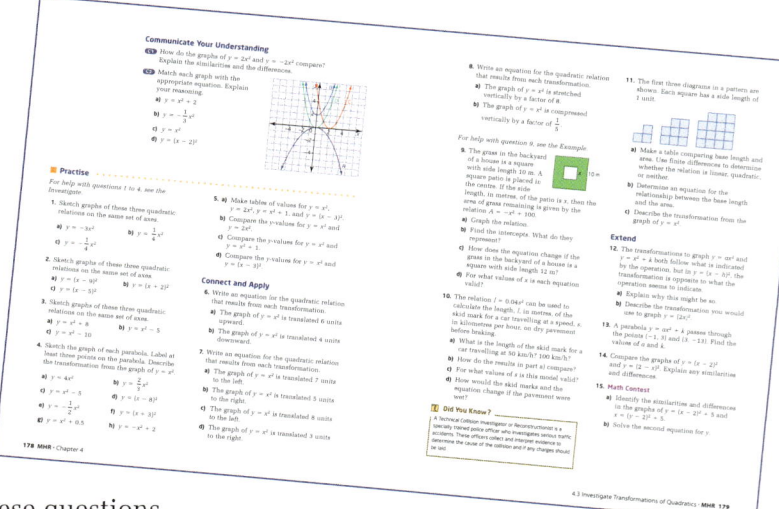

Extend
- These are more challenging and thought-provoking questions.
- Most sections conclude with a few **Math Contest** questions.

Technology

Scientific and graphing calculators are useful for many sections. Keystroke sequences are provided for techniques that may be new to you.

- A TI-83 Plus or TI-84 Plus graphing calculator is useful for some sections, particularly for graphing relations. In the analytic geometry chapters, alternative methods using Cabri® Jr are shown.

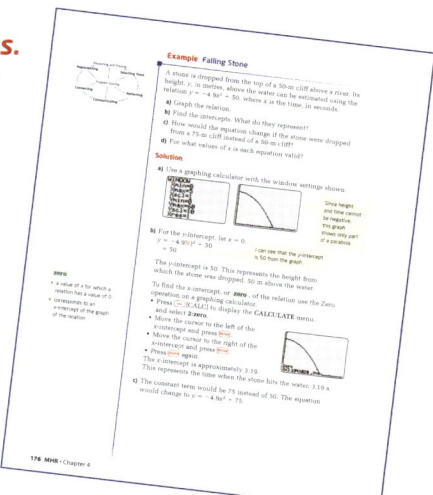

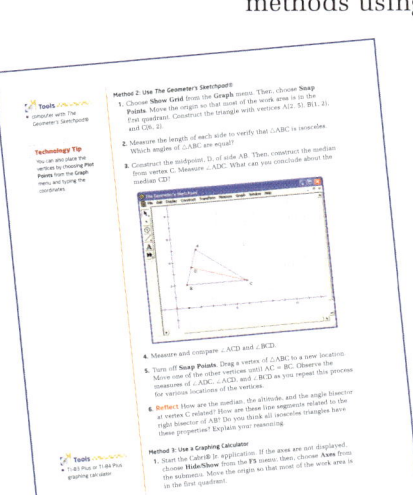

- *The Geometer's Sketchpad*® is used in several sections for investigating concepts related to analytic geometry. Alternative steps for doing investigations using pencil and paper are provided for those who do not have access to this computer software.

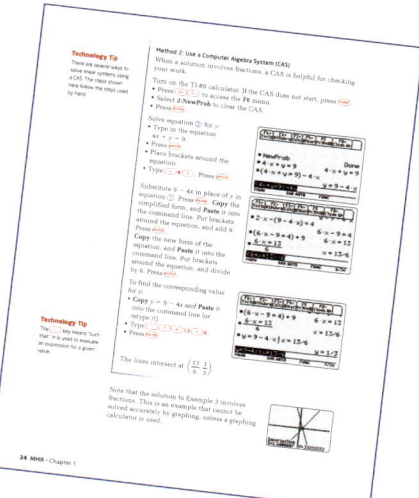

- Some sections show you how to use a computer algebra system (CAS) to explore algebraic processes or as an alternative tool to solve algebraic problems. This text uses the TI-89 calculator.

Technology Tip

- This margin feature points out helpful hints or alternative strategies for working with graphing calculators or *The Geometer's Sketchpad*®.

Technology Appendix

- The **Technology Appendix** provides detailed help with all the functions of the graphing calculators and *The Geometer's Sketchpad*® that are used in this course.

A Tour of Your Textbook • **MHR ix**

Assessment

Communicate Your Understanding

- These questions provide an opportunity to assess your understanding of the concepts before proceeding to use your skills in the Practise, Connect and Apply, and Extend questions.
- Through this discussion you can identify any concepts you need to study further.

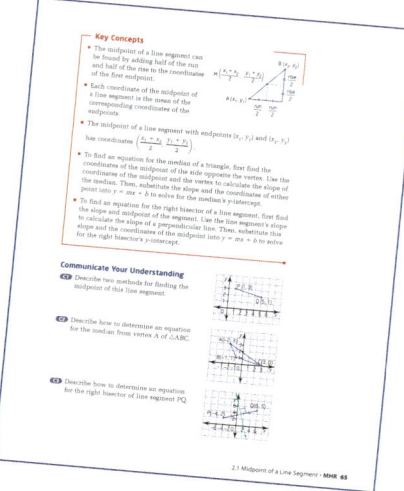

Special Connect and Apply Questions

- Some questions are related to the **Chapter Problem**.
- **Achievement Check:** The last Connect and Apply question of some sections provides an opportunity to demonstrate your knowledge and understanding and your ability to apply, think about, and communicate what you have learned. Achievement Check questions occur every two or three sections and are designed to assess learning of the key concepts in those sections.

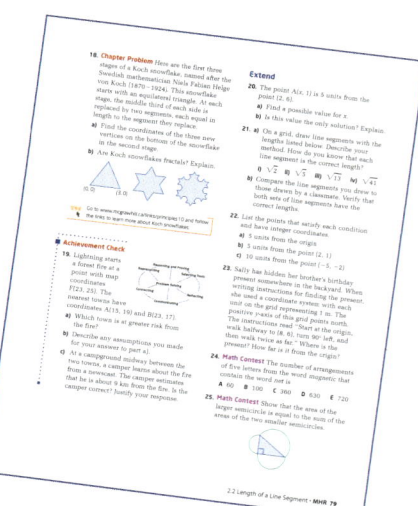

Chapter Problem Wrap-Up

This summary problem occurs at the end of the **Chapter Review**. The **Chapter Problem** may be assigned as a project.

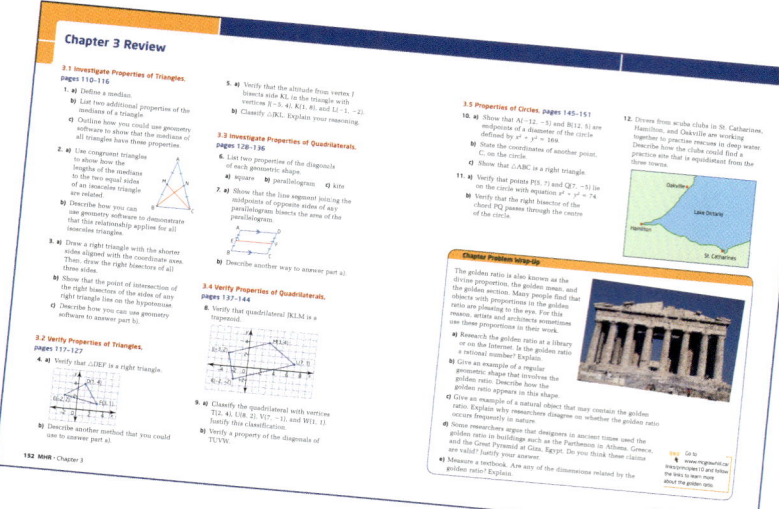

Practice Test

- Each chapter ends with a practice test.

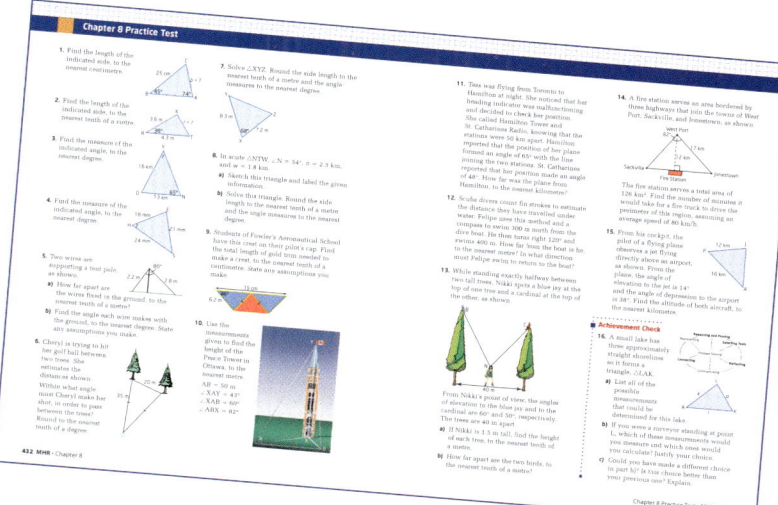

Tasks

- Tasks are presented at the end of Chapters 3, 6 and 8.
- These are more involved problems that require you to use several concepts from the preceding chapters. Each task has multi-part questions and may take about 20 min to complete.
- Some tasks may be assigned as individual or group projects.

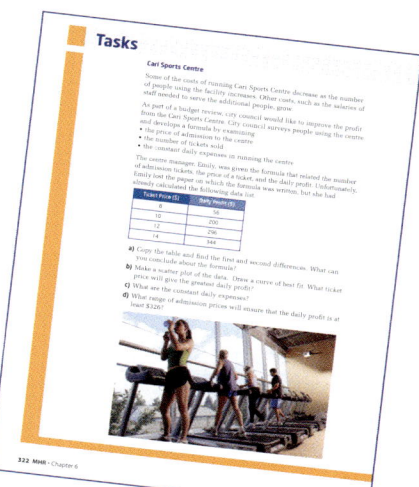

Chapter Review

- This feature appears at the end of each chapter.
- By working through these questions, you will identify areas where you may need more review or study before doing the Practice Test.

Cumulative Review

- A cumulative review occurs at the end of Chapters 3, 6, and 8. These questions allow you to review concepts you have learned in the chapters since the last cumulative review. They also help to prepare you for the tasks that follow.

Course Review

- A Course Review follows the tasks at the end of Chapter 8. This comprehensive selection of questions will help you to determine if you are ready for the final examination.

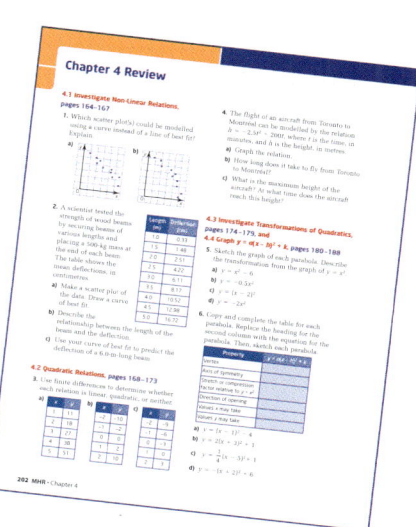

A Tour of Your Textbook • MHR xi

Other Features

The Mathematical Process

These seven mathematical processes are integral to learning mathematics:
- problem solving
- reasoning and proving
- reflecting
- selecting tools and computational strategies
- connecting
- representing
- communicating

These processes are interconnected and are used throughout the course. Some examples and exercises are flagged with a math processes graphic to show or remind you which of the processes are involved in solving the problem.

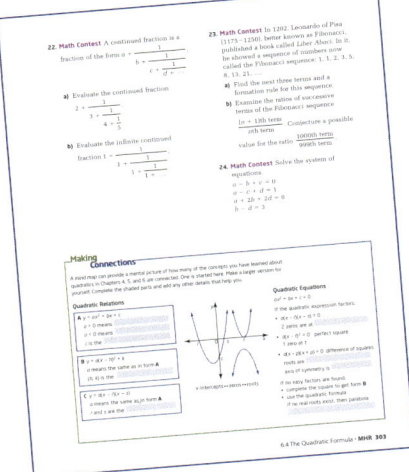

Making Connections

This feature points out some of the connections between topics in the course, or to topics learned previously.

Literacy Connections

This margin feature provides tips to help you read and interpret items in math.

Literacy Connections

It is a good idea to read a word problem three times.

Read it the first time to get the general idea.

Read it a second time for understanding. Express the problem in your own words.

Read it a third time to plan how to solve the problem.

Internet Links

This logo is shown beside questions in which it is suggested that you use the Internet to help solve the problem or to research or collect information. Some direct links are provided on our Web site www.mcgrawhill.ca/links/principles10.

Did You Know?

This feature provides interesting facts related to the topics in the examples or the exercises.

Did You Know?

Household white vinegar is 5% acetic acid. A 5% acetic acid solution means that 5% pure acid is mixed with 95% water. For example, 1 L of white vinegar contains 50 mL of pure acetic acid and 950 mL of water.

Appendices

Challenge Problems Appendix

A varied selection of more difficult problems is presented on pages 448–457. Some are directly related to the content of this course, while others are more general "puzzler" problems. These problems will provide new challenges and enrichment. They will help if you are planning to take the grade 11 university course to prepare for more difficult problems.

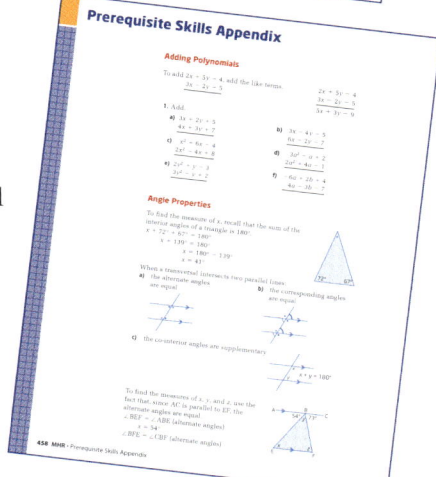

Prerequisite Skills Appendix

If you need help with any of the topics in the Get Ready for each chapter, refer to this appendix on pages 458–475. Examples and practice questions are provided. The topics are arranged in alphabetical order.

Technology Appendix

The **Technology Appendix**, on pages 476–503, provides detailed help for some basic functions of the TI-83 Plus or TI-84 Plus graphing calculator, the computer algebra system on the TI-89 graphing calculator, and *The Geometer's Sketchpad®*. These pages will be particularly helpful if you have not used these tools before.

Other Back Matter

Glossary

A complete illustrated glossary is included. All key terms of the text, as well as other mathematical terms, are listed on pages 570–581. This is a good resource if you want to check the exact meaning of a term.

Answers

Complete illustrated answers are provided for all questions in each Get Ready, numbered section, Chapter Review, and Practice Test. Refer to pages 504–569. Answers for the Achievement Check questions, the Chapter Problem Wrap-Up, the Investigate questions, and Communicate Your Understanding questions are provided in *Principles of Mathematics 10 Teacher's Resource*.

Index

A general index is included on pages 582–585.

CHAPTER 1

Linear Systems

You often need to make choices. In some cases, you will consider options with two variables. For example, consider renting a vehicle. There is often a daily cost plus a cost per kilometre driven. You can write two equations in two variables to compare the total cost of renting from different companies. By solving linear systems you can see which rental is better for you.

Analytic Geometry

- Solve systems of two linear equations involving two variables, using the algebraic method of substitution or elimination.
- Solve problems that arise from realistic situations described in words or represented by linear systems of two equations involving two variables, by choosing an appropriate algebraic or graphical method.

Vocabulary

linear system
point of intersection
method of substitution
equivalent linear equations
equivalent linear systems
method of elimination

Chapter Problem

The Clarke family is planning a summer holiday. They want to rent a car during the week they will be in Victoria, B.C., visiting relatives. They contact several car rental companies to obtain costs. In this chapter, you will see how to compare the costs and help the Clarkes decide which car to rent based on the distance they are likely to travel.

Get Ready

Substitute and Evaluate

Evaluate $3x - 2y + 1$ when $x = 4$ and $y = -3$.
$3x - 2y + 1$
$= 3(4) - 2(-3) + 1$
$= 12 + 6 + 1$
$= 19$

1. Evaluate each expression when $x = -2$ and $y = 3$.
   a) $3x + 4y$
   b) $2x - 3y + 5$
   c) $4x - y$
   d) $-x - 2y$
   e) $\frac{1}{2}x + y$
   f) $\frac{2}{3}y - \frac{1}{2}x$

2. Evaluate each expression when $a = 4$ and $b = -1$.
   a) $a + b - 3$
   b) $-2a - 3b + 7$
   c) $3b - 5 + a$
   d) $1 + 2a - 3b$
   e) $\frac{3}{4}a + b$
   f) $b - \frac{1}{2}a$

Simplify Expressions

Simplify $3(x + y) - 2(x - y)$.

$3(x + y) - 2(x - y)$ Use the distributive property to expand.
$= 3(x) + 3(y) - 2(x) - 2(-y)$
$= 3x + 3y - 2x + 2y$ Collect like terms.
$= x + 5y$

3. Simplify.
   a) $5x + 2(x - y)$
   b) $3a - 2b + 4a - 9b$
   c) $2(x - y) + 3(x - y)$

4. Simplify.
   a) $5(2x + 3y) - 4(3x - 5y)$
   b) $x - 2(x + 3y) - (2x + 3y) - 4(x + y)$
   c) $3(a + 2b - 2) - 2(2a - 5b - 1)$

Graph Lines

Method 1: Use a Table of Values

Graph the line $y = 2x + 1$.

x	y
0	1
1	3
2	5
3	7

Choose simple values for x. Calculate each corresponding value for y.

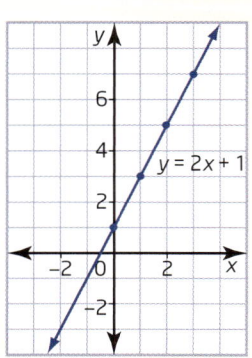

Plot the points. Draw a line through the points.

Graph Lines

Method 2: Use the Slope and the y-Intercept

Graph the line $y = \frac{2}{3}x - 5$.   *The equation is in the form $y = mx + b$.*

The slope, m, is $\frac{2}{3}$. So, $\frac{\text{rise}}{\text{run}} = \frac{2}{3}$.

The y-intercept, b, is -5. So, a point on the line is $(0, -5)$.
Start on the y-axis at $(0, -5)$.
Then, use the slope to reach another point on the line.

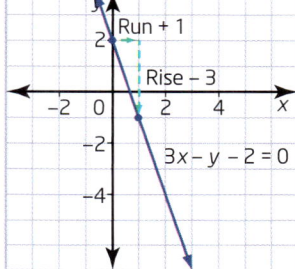

Graph the line $3x + y - 2 = 0$.
First rearrange the equation to write it in the form $y = mx + b$.
$$3x + y - 2 = 0$$
$$y = -3x + 2$$
The slope is -3, so $\frac{\text{rise}}{\text{run}} = \frac{-3}{1}$. The y-intercept is 2.
Use these facts to graph the line.

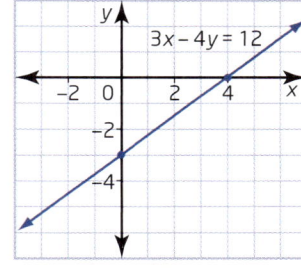

Method 3: Use Intercepts

Graph the line $3x - 4y = 12$.
At the x-intercept, $y = 0$.
$$3x - 4(0) = 12$$
$$3x = 12$$
$$x = 4$$
The x-intercept is 4. A point on the line is $(4, 0)$.

At the y-intercept, $x = 0$.
$$3(0) - 4y = 12$$
$$-4y = 12$$
$$y = -3$$
The y-intercept is -3. A point on the line is $(0, -3)$.

---

5. Graph each line. Use a table of values or the slope y-intercept method.
   a) $y = x + 2$
   b) $y = 2x + 3$
   c) $y = \frac{1}{2}x - 5$
   d) $y = -\frac{2}{5}x + 6$

6. Graph each line by first rewriting the equation in the form $y = mx + b$.
   a) $x - y + 1 = 0$
   b) $2x + y - 3 = 0$
   c) $-x - y + 7 = 0$
   d) $5x + 2y + 2 = 0$

7. Graph each line by finding the intercepts.
   a) $x + y = 3$
   b) $5x - 3y = 15$
   c) $7x - 3y = 21$
   d) $4x - 8y = 16$

8. Graph each line. Choose a convenient method.
   a) $-x - y - 1 = 0$
   b) $2x - 5y = 20$
   c) $2x + 3y + 6 = 0$
   d) $y = \frac{3}{4}x - 1$

Use a Graphing Calculator to Graph a Line

Graph the line $y = \frac{2}{3}x - 5$.

First, ensure that STAT PLOTs are turned off:
Press [2nd] [Y=] to access the STAT PLOT menu.
Select **4:PlotsOff**, and press [ENTER].
Press [Y=].
If you see any equations, clear them.
Enter the equation $y = \frac{2}{3}x - 5$:

Press 2 [÷] 3 [X,T,θ,n] [−] 5.
Press [GRAPH].

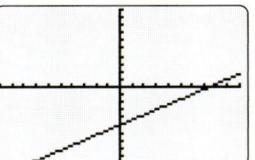

To change the scale on the x- and y-axes, refer to page 489 of the Technology Appendix for details on the window settings.

9. Graph each line in question 5 using a graphing calculator.

10. Use your rewritten equations from question 6 to graph each line using a graphing calculator.

Percent

Calculate the amount of salt in 10 kg of a 25% salt solution.
25% of 10 kg = 0.25 × 10 kg
          = 2.5 kg
The solution contains 2.5 kg of salt.

> 25% means $\frac{25}{100}$ or 0.25.

How much simple interest is earned in 1 year on $1000 invested at 5%/year?
Interest = $1000 × 0.05
        = $50
In 1 year, $50 interest is earned.

11. Calculate each amount.
   a) the volume of pure antifreeze in 12 L of a 35% antifreeze solution
   b) the mass of pure gold in 3 kg of a 24% gold alloy
   c) the mass of silver in 400 g of an 11% silver alloy

12. Find the simple interest earned after 1 year on each investment.
   a) $2000 invested at 4%/year
   b) $1200 invested at 2.9%/year
   c) $1500 invested at 3.1%/year
   d) $12 500 invested at 4.5%/year

> **Did You Know?**
> An alloy is a mixture of two or more metals, or a mixture of a metal and a non-metal. For example, brass is an alloy of copper and zinc.

Use a Computer Algebra System (CAS) to Evaluate Expressions

Evaluate $2x + 3$ when $x = 1$.

Turn on the TI-89 calculator. Press [HOME] to display the CAS home screen. Clear the calculator's memory. It is wise to do this each time you use the CAS.
- Press [2nd] [F6] to display the **Clean Up** menu.
- Select **2:NewProb**.
- Press [ENTER].

Enter the expression and the value of x:
- Press 2 [X] [+] 3 [|] [X] [=] 1.
- Press [ENTER].

This key means "such that".

13. Evaluate.

a) $2x + 1$ when $x = 3$

b) $4x - 2$ when $x = 1$

c) $3y - 5$ when $y = 1$

14. Use a CAS to check your answers in question 1. Hint: first substitute $x = -2$, and then substitute $y = 3$ into the resulting expression.

Use a CAS to Rearrange Equations

Rewrite the equation $5x + 2y - 3 = 0$ in the form $y = mx + b$.

Start the CAS and clear its memory using the **Clean Up** menu.
Enter the equation:
Press 5 [X] [+] 2 [Y] [−] 3 [=] 0.
Press [ENTER].

To solve for y, you must first isolate the y-term. Subtract $5x$ and add 3 to both sides. Use the cursor keys to put brackets around the equation in the command line. Then, press [−] 5 [X] [+] 3. Press [ENTER].
The $2y$-term will appear on the left, and all other terms will appear on the right.

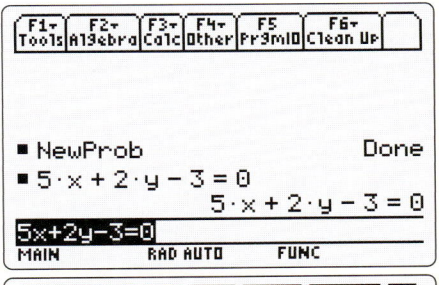
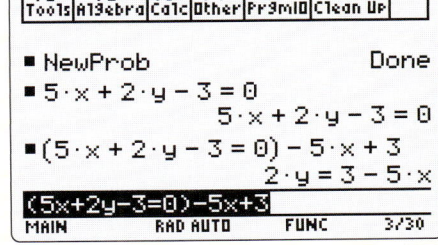

The next step is to divide both sides of the equation by 2. Use the up arrow key to highlight the new form of the equation. Press [♦] [↑] for [COPY]. Cursor back down to the command line. Press [♦] [ESC] for [PASTE] to copy this form into the command line. Use the cursor keys to enclose the equation in brackets. Press [÷] 2 to divide both sides by 2.

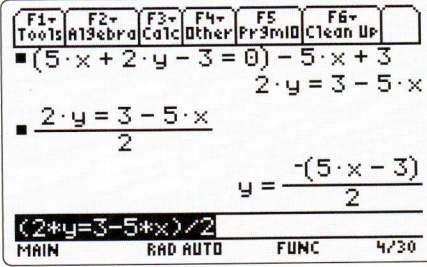

15. Use a CAS to check your work in question 6.

1.1 Connect English With Mathematics and Graphing Lines

The key to solving many problems in mathematics is the ability to read and understand the words. Then, you can translate the words into mathematics so that you can use one of the methods you know to solve the problem. In this section, you will look at ways to help you move from words to equations using mathematical symbols in order to find a solution to the problem.

Investigate

- placemat or sheet of paper

How do you translate between words and algebra?

Work in a group of four. Put your desks together so that you have a placemat in front of you and each of you has a section to write on.

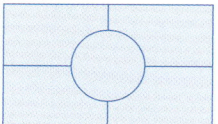

1. In the centre of the placemat, write the equation $4x + 6 = 22$.

2. On your section of the placemat, write as many word sentences to describe the equation in the centre of the placemat as you can think of in 5 min.

3. At the end of 5 min, see how many different sentences you have among the members of your group.

4. Compare with the other groups. How many different ways did your class find?

5. Turn the placemat over. In the centre, write the expression $\frac{1}{2}x + 1$.

6. Take a few minutes to write phrases that can be represented by this expression.

7. Compare among the members of your group. Then, check with other groups to see if they have any different phrases.

8. Spend a few minutes talking about what words you used.

9. **Reflect** Make a list of all the words you can use to represent each of the four operations: addition, subtraction, multiplication, and division.

Example 1 Translate Words Into Algebra

a) Write the following phrase as a mathematical expression:
the value five increased by a number

b) Write the following sentence as a mathematical equation.
Half of a value, decreased by seven, is one.

c) Translate the following sentence into an equation, using two variables. Mario's daily earnings are $80 plus 12% commission on his sales.

Solution

a) Consider the parts of the phrase.
- "the value five" means the number 5
- "increased by" means add or the symbol +
- "a number" means an unknown number, so choose a variable such as n to represent the number

The phrase can be represented by the mathematical expression $5 + n$.

b) "Half" means $\frac{1}{2}$
- "of" means multiply
- "a value" means a variable such as x
- "decreased by" means subtract or $-$
- "seven" is 7
- "is" means equals or =
- "seven" is 1

The sentence can be represented by the equation $\frac{1}{2}x - 7 = 1$.

c) Consider the parts of the sentence.
- "Mario's daily earnings" is an unknown and can be represented by E
- "are" means equals or =
- "$80" means 80
- "plus" means +
- "12% commission on his sales" can be represented by $0.12 \times S$

The sentence translates into the equation $E = 80 + 0.12S$.

Sometimes, several sentences need to be translated into algebra. This often happens with word problems.

> **Did You Know?**
>
> The airplane in Example 2 is a Diamond Katana DA40. These planes are built at the Diamond Aircraft plant in London, Ontario.

> **Literacy Connections**
>
> It is a good idea to read a word problem three times.
>
> Read it the first time to get the general idea.
>
> Read it a second time for understanding. Express the problem in your own words.
>
> Read it a third time to plan how to solve the problem.

Understand the Problem

Choose a Strategy

Carry Out the Strategy

linear system
- two or more linear equations that are considered at the same time

Example 2 Translate Words Into Algebra to Solve a Problem

Ian owns a small airplane. He pays $50/h for flying time and $300/month for hangar fees at the local airport. If Ian rented the same type of airplane at the local flying club, it would cost him $100/h. How many hours will Ian have to fly each month so that the cost of renting will be the same as the cost of flying his own plane?

Solution

Read the paragraph carefully.

> What things are unknown?
> • the number of flying hours
> • the total cost

> I'll choose variables for the two unknowns. I will translate the given sentences into two equations. Then, I can graph the two equations and find where they intersect.

Let C represent the total cost, in dollars.
Let t represent the time, in hours, flown.

The first sentence is information that is interesting, but cannot be translated into an equation.

The second sentence can be translated into an equation. Ian pays $50/h for flying time and $300/month for hangar fees at the local airport.
$C = 50t + 300$

The third sentence can also be translated into an equation. If Ian rented the same type of airplane at the local flying club, it would cost him $100/h.
$C = 100t$

The two equations form a **linear system**. This is a pair of linear relations, or equations, considered at the same time. To solve the linear system is to find the point of intersection of the two lines, or the point that satisfies both equations.

Graph the two lines on the same grid.

Both equations are in the form $y = mx + b$. You can use the y-intercept as a starting point and then use the slope to find another point on the graph.

The lines on the graph cross at one point, (6, 600). The **point of intersection** is (6, 600).

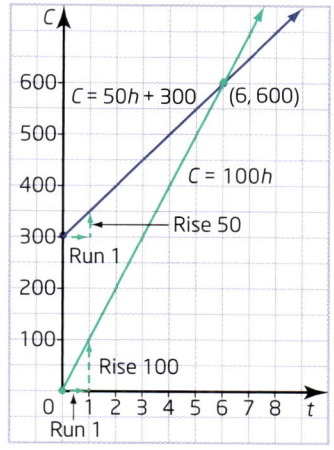

point of intersection
- a point where two lines cross
- a point that is common to both lines

Reflect

Check that the solution is correct.
If Ian uses his own airplane, the cost is $6 \times \$50 + \$300$. This is $600.
If he rents the airplane, the cost is $6 \times \$100$. This is $600.
So, the solution $t = 6$ and $C = 600$ checks.

Write a conclusion to answer the problem.

If Ian flies 6 h per month, the cost will be the same, $600, for both airplanes.

Linear equations are not always set up in the form $y = mx + b$. Sometimes it is easy to rearrange the equation. Other times, you may wish to graph using intercepts.

Example 3 Find the Point of Intersection

The equations for two lines are $x - y = -1$ and $2x - y = 2$. What are the coordinates of the point of intersection?

Solution

Method 1: Graph Using Slope and y-Intercept

Step 1: Rearrange the equations in the form $y = mx + b$.

Equation ①:
$$x - y = -1$$
$$x - y + y + 1 = -1 + y + 1$$
$$x + 1 = y$$
$$y = x + 1$$

Equation ① becomes $y = x + 1$. Its slope is 1 and its y-intercept is 1.

Equation ②:
$$2x - y = 2$$
$$2x - y + y - 2 = 2 + y - 2$$
$$2x - 2 = y$$
$$y = 2x - 2$$

Equation ② becomes $y = 2x - 2$. Its slope is 2 and its y-intercept is -2.

Step 2: Graph and label the two lines.

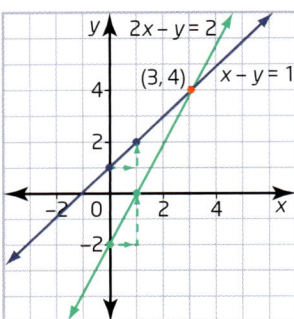

Step 3: To check that the point (3, 4) lies on both lines, substitute $x = 3$ and $y = 4$ into both original equations.

In $x - y = -1$:
L.S. $= x - y$ **R.S.** $= -1$
$= 3 - 4$
$= -1$
   L.S. = R.S.
So, (3, 4) is a point on the line $x - y = -1$.

In $2x - y = 2$:
L.S. $= 2x - y$ **R.S.** $= 2$
$= 2(3) - 4$
$= 6 - 4$
$= 2$
   L.S. = R.S.
So, (3, 4) is a point on the line $2x - y = 2$.

> If I don't get the same result when I substitute into both equations, I've made a mistake somewhere!

The solution checks in both equations. The point (3, 4) lies on both lines.

Step 4: Write a conclusion.
The coordinates of the point of intersection are (3, 4).

Method 2: Graph Using Intercepts

Step 1: Find the intercepts for each line.

Equation ①: $x - y = -1$

At the x-intercept, $y = 0$.   At the y-intercept, $x = 0$.
$x - 0 = -1$ $0 - y = -1$
$x = -1$ $-y = -1$
Graph the point $(-1, 0)$. $y = 1$
                                      Graph the point $(0, 1)$.

Equation ②: $2x - y = 2$

At the x-intercept, $y = 0$.   At the y-intercept, $x = 0$.
$2x - 0 = 2$ $2(0) - y = 2$
$2x = 2$ $-y = 2$
$x = 1$ $y = -2$
Graph the point $(1, 0)$.   Graph the point $(0, -2)$.

Step 2: Draw and label the line for each equation.

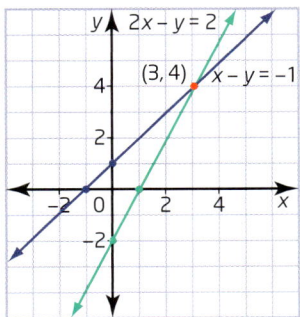

Step 3: Check by substituting $x = 3$ and $y = 4$ into both original equations.
See Method 1.

Step 4: Write a conclusion.
The coordinates of the point of intersection are (3, 4).

Example 4 Solve an Internet Problem

Brian and Catherine want to get Internet access for their home. There are two companies in the area. IT Plus charges a flat rate of $25/month for unlimited use. Techies Inc. charges $10/month plus $1/h for use. If Brian and Catherine expect to use the Internet for approximately 18 h/month, which plan is the better option for them?

Solution

Represent each situation with an equation. Then, graph to see where the two lines intersect to find when the cost is the same.

Let t represent the number of hours of Internet use.

Let C represent the total cost for the month.

IT Plus:
$C = 25$

This is a flat rate, which means it costs $25 and no more.

Techies Inc.:
$C = 10 + 1t$

The cost is $10 plus $1 for every hour of Internet use.

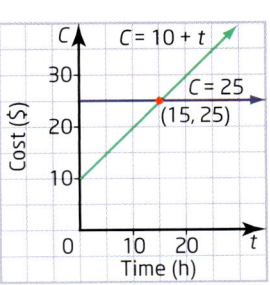

The two plans cost the same for 15 h of Internet use. The cost is $25. For more than 15 h, the cost for Techies Inc. Internet service is more than $25. If Brian and Catherine expect to use the Internet for 18 h/month, they should choose IT Plus.

Example 5 Use Technology to Find the Point of Intersection

Find the point of intersection of the lines $y = x - 12$ and $y = -3x + 20$ by graphing using technology.

Solution

Method 1: Use a Graphing Calculator

- First, make sure that all STAT PLOTS are turned off. Press [2nd] [Y=] for [STAT PLOT]. Select **4:PlotsOff**.

- Press [WINDOW]. Use window settings of -20 to 20 for both x and y.

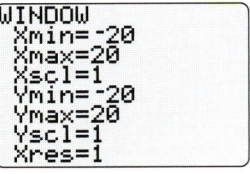

- Enter the two equations as Y1 and Y2 using the [Y=] editor.
  Note: use the [−] key when entering the first equation, but the [(−)] key at the beginning of the second equation.

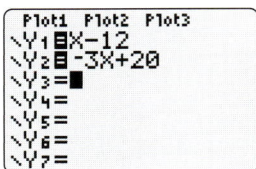

- Press [GRAPH].

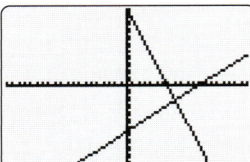

- Find the point of intersection using the Intersect function.
  Press [2nd] [TRACE] for the **Calc** menu.
  Select **5:intersect**.

Respond to the questions in the lower left corner.

- **First curve?** The cursor will be flashing and positioned on one of the lines. The calculator is asking you if this is the first of the lines for which you want to find the point of intersection. If this is the one you want, press [ENTER].

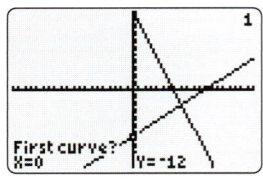

- **Second curve?** The cursor will be flashing and positioned on the second line. The calculator is checking to see if this is the second line in the pair. If this is the line you want, press [ENTER].

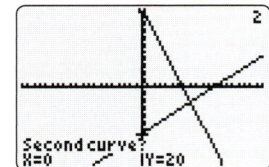

- **Guess?** Here, the calculator is giving you a chance to name a point that you think is the point of intersection. If you do not wish to try your own guess, then press (ENTER) and the calculator will find the point for you.

The point of intersection is (8, −4).

Another way to see the point of intersection is to view the table.

First, press (2nd) (WINDOW) for [TBLSET]. Check that both **Indpnt** and **Depend** have **Auto** selected.

Press (2nd) (GRAPH) for [TABLE].
Cursor down to $x = 8$.
Observe that the values of Y1 and Y2 are both −4 at $x = 8$. At other values of x, Y1 and Y2 have different values.

Method 2: Use *The Geometer's Sketchpad*®

Open *The Geometer's Sketchpad*®. Choose **Show Grid** from the **Graph** menu. Drag the unit point until the workspace shows a grid up to 10 in each direction.

Choose **Plot New Function** from the **Graph** menu. The expression editor will appear. Enter the expression $x - 12$, and click **OK**. Repeat to plot the second function.

Note the location of the point of intersection of the two lines. Draw two points on each line, one on each side of the intersection point. Construct line segments to join each pair of points. Select the line segments. Choose **Intersection** from the **Construct** menu. Right-click on the point of intersection and select **Coordinates**. The coordinates of the point of intersection are displayed.

The point of intersection is (8, −4).

> **Making Connections**
>
> Refer to the Technology Appendix for help with *The Geometer's Sketchpad*® basics.

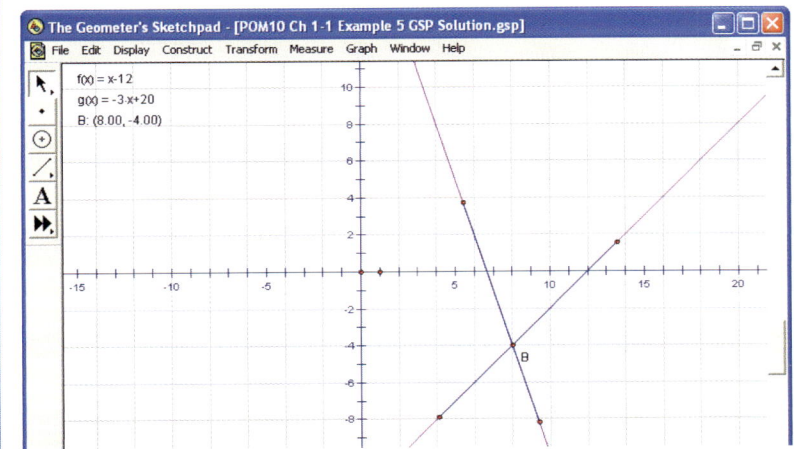

Key Concepts

- When changing from words into algebra, read each sentence carefully and think about what the words mean. Translate into mathematical expressions using letters and numbers and mathematical operations.

- There are many different word phrases that can represent the same mathematical expression.

- To solve a system of two linear equations means to find the point of intersection of the two lines.

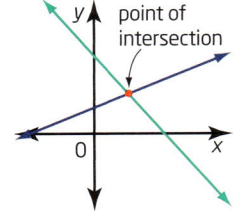

- A system of linear equations can be solved by graphing both lines and using the graph to find the point where the two lines intersect.

- If the two lines do not cross at a grid mark, or if the equations involve decimals, you can use technology to graph the lines and then find the point of intersection.

- Check an answer by substituting it into the two original equations. If both sides of each equation have equal values, the solution is correct.

Communicate Your Understanding

C1 Work with a partner. Make up at least eight sentences to be converted to mathematical equations. Exchange lists with another pair and translate the sentences into equations. As a group of four, discuss the answers and any difficulties.

C2 In a group of three, use chart paper to list different phrases that can be represented by the same mathematical symbol or expression. Post the chart paper around the classroom as prompts.

C3 Your friend missed today's class. She calls to find out what you learned. Explain, in your own words, what it means to solve a system of equations.

C4 Will a linear system always have exactly one point of intersection? Explain your reasoning.

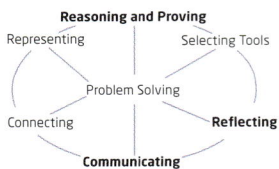

C5 Describe in words how you would solve the linear system $y = 3x + 1$ and $y = -2x + 3$.

Practise

For help with questions 1 to 6, see Example 1.

1. Translate each phrase into an algebraic expression.
   a) seven less than twice a number
   b) four more than half a value
   c) a number decreased by six, times another number
   d) a value increased by the fraction two thirds

2. Translate each phrase into an algebraic expression.
   a) twice a distance
   b) twenty percent of a number
   c) double a length
   d) seven percent of a price

3. Translate each sentence into an algebraic equation.
   a) One fifth of a number, decreased by 17, is 41.
   b) Twice a number, subtracted from five, is three more than seven times the number.
   c) When tickets to a play cost $5 each, the revenue at the box office is $825.
   d) The sum of the length and width of a backyard pool is 96 m.

4. For each of the following, write a word or phrase that has the opposite meaning.
   a) increased
   b) added
   c) plus
   d) more than

5. a) All of the words and phrases in question 4 are represented by the same operation in mathematics. What operation is it?
   b) Work with a partner. Write four mathematical words or phrases for which there is an opposite. Trade your list with another pair in the class and give the opposites of the items in each other's list.

6. Explain in your own words the difference between an expression and an equation. Explain how you can tell by reading whether words can be represented by an expression or by an equation. Provide your own examples.

For help with question 7, see Example 2.

7. Which is the point of intersection of the lines $y = 3x + 1$ and $y = -2x + 6$?
   A (0, 1) **B** (1, 1)
   C (1, 4) **D** (2, 5)

For help with questions 8 and 9, see Example 3.

8. Find the point of intersection for each pair of lines. Check your answers.
   a) $y = 2x + 3$
      $y = 4x - 1$
   b) $y = -x - 7$
      $y = 3x + 5$
   c) $y = \frac{1}{2}x - 2$
      $y = \frac{3}{4}x + 3$
   d) $y = 4x - 5$
      $y = \frac{2}{3}x + 5$

9. Find the point of intersection for each pair of lines. Check your answers.
   a) $x + 2y = 4$
      $3x - 2y = 4$
   b) $y + 2x = -5$
      $y - 3x = 5$
   c) $3x - 2y = 12$
      $2y - x = -8$
   d) $x - y = 1$
      $x + 2y = 4$

For help with question 10, see Example 5.

10. **Use Technology** Use a graphing calculator or *The Geometer's Sketchpad*® to find the point of intersection for each pair of lines. Where necessary, round answers to the nearest hundredth.
    a) $y = 7x - 23$
       $y = -4x + 10$
    b) $y = -3x - 6$
       $y = -6x - 20$
    c) $y = 6x - 4$
       $y = -5x + 12$
    d) $y = -3x + 4$
       $y = 4x + 13$
    e) $y = 5.3x + 8.5$
       $y = -2.7x - 3.4$
    f) $y = -0.2x - 4.5$
       $y = -4.8x + 1.3$

Connect and Apply

11. Fitness Club CanFit charges a $150 initial fee to join the club and a $20 monthly fee. Fitness 'R' Us charges an initial fee of $100 and $30/month.

   a) Write an equation to represent the cost of membership at CanFit.

   b) Write an equation to represent the cost of membership at Fitness 'R' Us.

   c) Graph the two equations.

   d) Find the point of intersection.

   e) What does the point of intersection represent?

   f) If you are planning to join for 1 year, which club should you join? Explain your answer.

12. LC Video rents a game machine for $10 and video games for $3 each. Big Vid rents a game machine for $7 and video games for $4 each.

   a) Write a linear equation to represent the total cost of renting a game machine and some video games from LC Video.

   b) Write a linear equation to represent the total cost of renting a game machine and some video games from Big Vid.

   c) Find the point of intersection of the two lines from parts a) and b).

   d) Explain what the point of intersection represents in this context.

13. Jeff clears driveways in the winter to make some extra money. He charges $15/h. Hesketh's Snow Removal charges $150 for the season.

   a) Write an equation for the amount Jeff charges to clear a driveway for the season.

   b) Write an equation for Hesketh's Snow Removal.

   c) What is the intersection point of the two linear equations?

   d) In the context of this question, what does the point of intersection represent?

14. **Use Technology** Brooke is planning her wedding. She compares the cost of places to hold the reception.

   Limestone Hall: $5000 plus $75/guest
   Frontenac Hall: $7500 plus $50/guest

   a) Write an equation for the cost of Limestone Hall.

   b) Write an equation for the cost of Frontenac Hall.

   c) Use a graphing calculator to find for what number of guests the hall charges are the same.

   d) In what situation is Limestone Hall less expensive than Frontenac Hall? Explain.

   e) What others factors might Brooke need to consider when choosing a banquet hall?

15. **Use Technology** Gina works for a clothing designer. She is paid $80/day plus $1.50 for each pair of jeans she makes. Dexter also works for the designer, but he makes $110/day and no extra money for finishing jeans.

   a) Write an equation to represent the amount that Gina earns in 1 day. Graph the equation.

   b) Write an equation to represent the amount that Dexter earns in 1 day. Graph this equation on the same grid as in part a).

   c) How many pairs of jeans must Gina make in order to make as much in a day as Dexter?

16. Ramona has a total of $5000 to invest. She puts part of it in an account paying 5%/year interest and the rest in a GIC paying 7.2% interest. If she has $349 in simple interest at the end of the year, how much was invested at each rate?

17. **Chapter Problem** The Clarke family called two car rental agencies and were given the following information.

    Cool Car Company will rent them a luxury car for $525 per week plus 20¢/km driven.

    Classy Car Company will rent them the same type of car for $500 per week plus 30¢/km driven.

    a) Let C represent the total cost, in dollars, and d represent the distance, in kilometres, driven by the family. Write an equation to represent the cost to rent from Cool Car Company.

    b) Write an equation to represent the cost to rent from Classy Car Company.

    c) Draw a graph to find the distance for which the cost is the same.

    d) Explain what your answer to part c) means in this context.

Extend

18. Alain has just obtained his flight instructor's rating. He is offered three possible pay packages at a flight school.

    i) a flat salary of $25 000 per year

    ii) $40/h of instruction for a maximum of 25 h/week for 50 weeks

    iii) $300/week for 50 weeks, plus $25/h of instruction for a maximum of 25 h/week

    a) For each compensation package, write an equation that models the earnings, E, in terms of the number of hours of instruction, n.

    b) Graph each equation, keeping in mind the restrictions on the flying hours.

    c) Use your graph to write a note of advice to Alain about which package he should take, based on how many hours of instruction he can expect to give.

19. Graph the equations $3x - y + 1 = 0$, $y = 4$, and $2x + y - 6 = 0$ on the same grid. Explain what you find.

20. a) Can you solve the linear system $y = 2x - 3$ and $4x - 2y = 6$? Explain your reasoning.

    b) Can you solve the linear system $y = 2x - 3$ and $4x - 2y = 8$? Explain your reasoning.

    c) Explain how you can tell, without solving, how many solutions a linear system has.

21. Solve the following system of equations by graphing. How is this system different from the ones you have worked with in this section?

    $y = x - 4$
    $y = -x^2 + x$

22. **Math Contest** A group of 15 explorers and two children come to a crocodile-infested river. There is a small boat, which can hold either one adult or two children.

    a) How many trips must the boat make across the river to get everyone to the other side?

    b) Write a formula for the number of trips to get n explorers and two children across the river.

23. **Math Contest** A number is called *cute* if it has four different whole number factors. What percent of the first twenty-five whole numbers are cute?

24. **Math Contest** The average of 13 consecutive integers is 162. What is the greatest of these integers?

    A 162   **B** 165   **C** 168   **D** 172   **E** 175

1.2 The Method of Substitution

You know how to use a graph to find the point of intersection of two linear equations. However, graphing is not always the most efficient or accurate method.

If you are graphing by hand, the point of intersection must be on the grid lines to give an exact answer.

If you use a graphing calculator or *The Geometer's Sketchpad®*, you can find the point of intersection to a chosen number of decimal places. However, the equations must be expressed in the form $y = mx + b$ first to enter them into the calculator or computer. Rearranging some equations is not easy.

method of substitution

- solving a linear system by substituting for one variable from one equation into the other equation

There are other ways to find the point of intersection of two linear relations. One of these is an algebraic method called the **method of substitution**.

Investigate

How can you use substitution to solve a linear system?

Did You Know?

"Canton" is a French word meaning portion. Switzerland is, like Canada, a confederation. It is formed of cantons, which are similar to our provinces. Switzerland has three levels of government: federal, canton, and local authorities. The capital of Switzerland, Berne, is in the canton of Berne.

Sometimes, at the beginning of geography class, Mrs. Thomson gives her students a puzzle to solve. One morning the puzzle is as follows.

The sum of the number of cantons in Switzerland and the states in Austria is 35. One less than triple the number of Austrian states is the same as the number of Swiss cantons. How many states are there in Austria and how many cantons are there in Switzerland?

Wesam wrote two equations to represent the information:

$S + A = 32$ ①
$3A - 4 = S$ ②

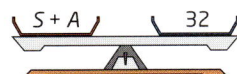 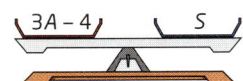

1. a) What does the S represent in the first equation?

b) What does the S represent in the second equation?

c) Do the S's in both equations represent the same value or different values?

2. a) What equation results if you substitute $3A - 4$ from the second equation into the first equation in place of S?

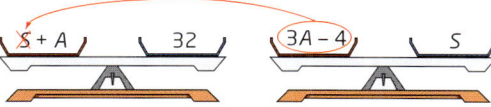

b) Solve the resulting equation for A.

c) What does this mean in the context of this question?

d) How can you find the value for S?

e) Find that value.

f) What did you do to find the values for A and S?

3. a) Solve the first equation for A.

b) Substitute that value for A into the second equation.

c) Solve for S.

d) Did you get the same answer as you found in step 2 part e)?

4. Reflect

a) Do you think that you have found the point of intersection of the linear system that Wesam wrote? Use a graph to check.

b) What is the answer to the geography puzzle?

Example 1 Solve Using the Method of Substitution

The lines $y = -x + 8$ and $x - y = 4$ intersect at right angles. Find the coordinates of the point of intersection.

Solution

Label the equations of the lines ① and ②.
$y = -x + 8$ ①
$x - y = 4$ ②

The phrase "intersect at right angles" is extraneous information. I don't need this fact to find the point of intersection of the two lines.

Step 1: Equation ① is $y = -x + 8$, so you can substitute $-x + 8$ in equation ② for y.

$$x - y = 4$$
$$x - (-x + 8) = 4$$
$$x + x - 8 = 4$$
$$2x - 8 = 4$$
$$2x = 4 + 8$$
$$2x = 12$$
$$x = 6$$

Now I have one equation in one variable. I can solve for x.

I still need to find the y-coordinate.

Step 2: Substitute $x = 6$ in equation ① to find the corresponding value for y.
$y = -x + 8$
$y = -(6) + 8$
$y = 2$

Making Connections

If lines intersect at right angles, they are perpendicular. You can check that these two lines are perpendicular using their slopes. In grade 9, you learned that the product of the slopes of perpendicular lines is –1. The line $y = -x + 8$ has slope –1. The line $x - y = 4$ can be rearranged to give $y = x - 4$; its slope is 1. The product of the two slopes, $(-1) \times 1$, is –1.

Step 3: Check by substituting $x = 6$ and $y = 2$ into both original equations.

In $y = -x + 8$:
L.S. $= y$ **R.S.** $= -x + 8$
     $= 2$ $= -(6) + 8$
                      $= 2$
L.S. = R.S.

In $x - y = 4$:
L.S. $= x - y$ **R.S.** $= 4$
      $= 6 - 2$
      $= 4$
L.S. = R.S.

The solution checks in both equations. This means that the point (6, 2) lies on both lines.

Step 4: Write a conclusion.
The point of intersection is (6, 2).

Example 2 Solve Using the Method of Substitution

Find the solution to the linear system
$x + y = 5$
$3x - y = 7$

Solution

Label the equations of the lines ① and ②.
$x + y = 5$ ①
$3x - y = 7$ ②

Step 1: Rearrange equation ① to obtain an expression for y.
Note: Here you could just as easily solve equation ① for x or equation ② for y.
$x + y = 5$
     $y = 5 - x$

Now substitute $5 - x$ into equation ② in place of y.
$3x - (5 - x) = 7$
$3x - 5 + x = 7$
    $4x - 5 = 7$
        $4x = 7 + 5$
        $4x = 12$
         $x = 3$

Step 2: Substitute $x = 3$ into equation ① to find the corresponding value for y.
$x + y = 5$
$3 + y = 5$
     $y = 5 - 3$
     $y = 2$

Step 3: Check by substituting $x = 3$ and $y = 2$ into both original equations.
In $x + y = 5$:
L.S. $= x + y$ **R.S.** $= 5$
$ = 3 + 2$
$ = 5$
**L.S. = R.S.**

In $3x - y = 7$:
L.S. $= 3x - y$ **R.S.** $= 7$
$ = 3(3) - 2$
$ = 9 - 2$
$ = 7$
**L.S. = R.S.**

The solution checks in both equations.

Step 4: Write a conclusion.
The solution is $x = 3$, $y = 2$.

Example 3 Solve Using the Method of Substitution

Where do the lines $2x - y = 4$ and $4x + y = 9$ intersect?

Solution

Method 1: Solve Algebraically by Hand

Label the equations of the lines ① and ②.
$2x - y = 4$ ①
$4x + y = 9$ ②

$4x + y = 9$ ②
$y = 9 - 4x$

> I can choose to isolate either of the variables. I'll look to see which will be less work. In equation ①, the *x* is multiplied by 2 and the *y* is negative. In equation ②, the *x* is multiplied by 4 and the *y* is positive. Isolating the *y* in equation ② will take fewer steps.

Next, substitute $9 - 4x$ in place of y in equation ①.

$2x - y = 4$
$2x - (9 - 4x) = 4$
$2x - 9 + 4x = 4$
$6x - 9 = 4$
$6x = 4 + 9$
$6x = 13$
$x = \dfrac{13}{6}$

> I am substituting $9 - 4x$ for *y*.

> Now I have only one variable, so I can solve for *x*.

Then, substitute back into equation ② to find the value for y.
$4x + y = 9$
$4\left(\dfrac{13}{6}\right) + y = 9$
$\dfrac{26}{3} + y = 9$
$y = \dfrac{27}{3} - \dfrac{26}{3}$
$y = \dfrac{1}{3}$

The lines intersect at $\left(\dfrac{13}{6}, \dfrac{1}{3}\right)$.

Technology Tip

There are several ways to solve linear systems using a CAS. The steps shown here follow the steps used by hand.

Method 2: Use a Computer Algebra System (CAS)

When a solution involves fractions, a CAS is helpful for checking your work.

Turn on the TI-89 calculator. If the CAS does not start, press [HOME].
- Press [2nd] [F1] to access the **F6** menu.
- Select **2:NewProb** to clear the CAS.
- Press [ENTER].

Solve equation ② for y:
- Type in the equation $4x + y = 9$.
- Press [ENTER].
- Place brackets around the equation.
- Type [−]4[x]. Press [ENTER].

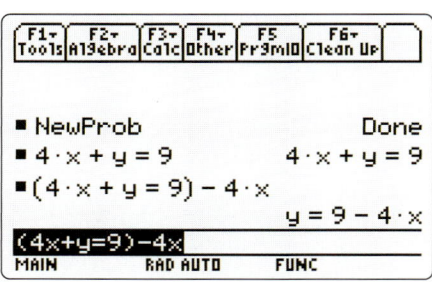

Substitute $9 - 4x$ in place of y in equation ①. Press [ENTER]. **Copy** the simplified form, and **Paste** it into the command line. Put brackets around the equation, and add 9. Press [ENTER].
Copy the new form of the equation, and **Paste** it into the command line. Put brackets around the equation, and divide by 6. Press [ENTER].

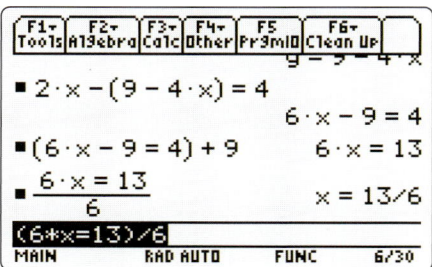

To find the corresponding value for y:
- **Copy** $y = 9 - 4x$ and **Paste** it into the command line (or retype it).
- Type [|][x][=]13[÷]6.
- Press [ENTER].

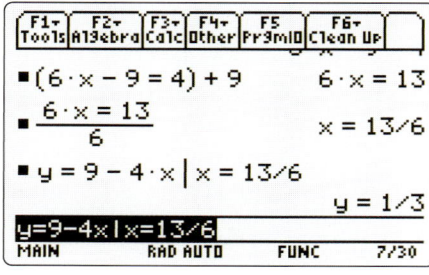

Technology Tip

The [|] key means "such that." It is used to evaluate an expression for a given value.

The lines intersect at $\left(\dfrac{13}{6}, \dfrac{1}{3}\right)$.

Note that the solution to Example 3 involves fractions. This is an example that cannot be solved accurately by graphing, unless a graphing calculator is used.

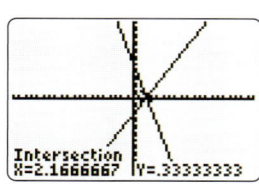

Example 4 A Fish Tale

Stephanie has five more fish in her aquarium than Brett has. The two have a total of 31 fish. How many fish does Stephanie have? How many fish does Brett have?

Solution

Model the information using equations.
Let S represent the number of fish that Stephanie has.
Let B represent the number of fish that Brett has.

From the first sentence,
$S = 5 + B$ ①

From the second sentence,
$S + B = 31$ ②

I have two linear equations in two unknowns, so this is a linear system.

Substitute $5 + B$ for S in ②.
$$S + B = 31$$
$$5 + B + B = 31$$
$$5 + 2B = 31$$
$$2B = 31 - 5$$
$$2B = 26$$
$$B = 13$$

Substitute 13 for B in ①.
$$S = 5 + B$$
$$S = 5 + 13$$
$$S = 18$$

Look back: Verify that this solution works in the original problem statements. Stephanie has 5 more fish than Brett has. 18 is 5 more than 13. The two have 31 fish altogether. $18 + 13 = 31$.
Make a final statement: Stephanie has 18 fish and Brett has 13 fish.

Key Concepts

- To solve a linear system by substitution, follow these steps:
  Step 1: Solve one of the equations for one variable in terms of the other variable.
  Step 2: Substitute the expression from step 1 into the other equation and solve for the remaining variable.
  Step 3: Substitute back into one of the original equations to find the value of the other variable.
  Step 4: Check your solution by substituting into both original equations, or into the statements of a word problem.

- When given a question in words, begin by defining how variables are assigned. Remember to answer in words.

Communicate Your Understanding

C1 Describe the steps you would take to solve this linear system using the method of substitution.
$y = 3x + 1$ ①
$x + y = 3$ ②

C2 Your friend was absent today. He calls to find out what he missed. Explain to him the idea of solving by substitution.

C3 Compare solving by graphing and solving by substitution. How are the two methods similar? How are they different?

C4 When is it an advantage to be able to solve by substitution? Give an example.

Practise

You may wish to check your work using a CAS.

For help with question 1, see Example 1.

1. Solve each linear system using the method of substitution. Check your answers.

a) $y = 3x - 4$
$x + y = 8$

b) $x = -4y + 5$
$x + 2y = 7$

c) $y = -2x + 3$
$4x - 3y = 1$

d) $2x + 3y = -1$
$x = 1 - y$

For help with questions 2 to 5, see Examples 2 and 3.

2. In each pair, decide which equation you will use first to solve for one variable in terms of the other variable. Do that step. Do not solve the linear system.

a) $x + 2y = 5$
$3x + 2y = 6$

b) $2x + y = 6$
$3x + 2y = 10$

c) $2x + 5y = 7$
$x - 3y = -2$

d) $3x - y = 5$
$7x + 2y = 9$

e) $2x - y = 2$
$4x + y = 16$

3. Is $(3, -5)$ the solution for the following linear system? Explain how you can tell.
$2x + 5y = -19$
$6y - 8x = 54$

4. Solve by substitution. Check your solution.

a) $x + 2y = 3$
$5x + 4y = 8$

b) $6x + 5y = 7$
$x - y = 3$

c) $2m + n = 2$
$3m - 2n = 3$

d) $3a + 2b = 4$
$2a + b = 6$

e) $2x + y = 4$
$4x - y = 2$

5. Find the point of intersection of each pair of lines.

a) $2x = y + 5$
$3x + y = -9$

b) $4x + 2y = 7$
$-x - y = 6$

c) $p + 4q = 3$
$5p = -2q + 3$

d) $a + b + 6 = 0$
$2a - b - 3 = 0$

e) $x - 2y - 2 = 0$
$3x + 4y - 16 = 0$

Connect and Apply

For help with questions 6 to 11, see Example 4.

6. Samantha works twice as many hours per week as Adriana. Together they work a total of 39 h one week.
   a) State how you will assign variables.
   b) Write an equation to represent the information in the first sentence.
   c) Write an equation to represent the information in the second sentence.
   d) Use the method of substitution to find the number of hours worked by each person.

7. Jeff and Stephen go to the mall. The two boys buy a total of 15 T-shirts. Stephen gets three less than twice as many T-shirts as Jeff.
   a) Write an equation to represent the information in the second sentence.
   b) Write an equation to represent the information in the third sentence.
   c) Solve the linear system by substitution to find the number of T-shirts each boy bought.
   d) If the T-shirts cost $8.99 each, how much did each boy spend before taxes?

8. Ugo plays hockey and is awarded 2 points for each goal and 1 point for each assist. Last season he had a total of 86 points. He scored 17 fewer goals than assists.
   a) Write a linear system to represent the information.
   b) Solve the system using the method of substitution.
   c) What does the solution represent in the context of this question?

9. Joanne's family decides to rent a hall for her retirement party. Pin Hall charges $500 for the hall and $15 per meal. Bloom Place charges $350 for the hall and $18 per meal.
   a) Write two equations to represent the information.
   b) Solve the linear system to find the number of guests for which the charges are the same at both halls.

10. Charlene makes two types of quilts. For the first type, she charges $25 for material and $50/h for hand quilting. For the second type, she charges $100 for material and $20/h for machine quilting. For what number of hours are the costs the same?

11. Pietro needs to rent a truck for 1 day. He calls two rental companies to compare costs. Joe's Garage charges $80 for the day plus $0.22/km. Ace Trucks charges $100/day and $0.12/km. Under what circumstances do the two companies charge the same amount? When would it be better for Pietro to rent from Joe's Garage?

12. Explain why the following linear system is not easy to solve by substitution.
    $3x + 4y = 10$
    $2x - 5y = 9$

13. Explain why it would be appropriate to solve the following linear system either by substitution or by graphing.
    $x + y = 4$
    $y = 2x + 4$

14. The following three lines intersect to form a triangle.
    $y = x + 1$
    $2x + y = 4$
    $x + y = 5$
    a) Find the coordinates of each vertex.
    b) Is this a right triangle? Explain how you know.

15. Sensei's Judo Club has a competition for the students. If you win a grappling match, you are awarded 5 points. If you tie, you are awarded 2 points. Jeremy grappled 15 times and his score was 48 points. How many grapples did Jeremy win?

> **Did You Know?**
>
> Grappling is the term used for wrestling in both judo and ju jitso. In judo you throw your opponent and grapple him or her on the ground.

16. Chapter Problem The Clarke family considers the option of renting a car for 1 day, rather than the full week. One agent recommends a full-size car for a flat fee of $90/day with unlimited kilometres. Another agent recommends a mid-size car that costs $40/day plus 25¢/km driven.
   a) Write an equation to represent the cost for the full-size car.
   b) Write an equation to represent the cost for the mid-size car.
   c) Solve to find when the costs of the two car are the same.
   d) In what circumstances will the mid-size car cost less?
   e) If the Clarkes want to drive to visit relatives in Parksville, about 120 km away, which option will cost less? Explain. Remember that they plan to return the car the same day.

■ **Achievement Check**

17. a) Solve this linear system using the method of substitution.
$$2y - x = -10$$
$$y = -\frac{3}{2}x - 1$$
   b) Verify your solution graphically.
   c) A blue spruce tree grows an average of 15 cm per year. An eastern hemlock grows an average of 10 cm per year. When they were planted, a blue spruce was 120 cm tall and an eastern hemlock was 180 cm tall. How many years after planting will the trees reach the same height? How tall will they be?

Extend

18. The Tragically Hip held a concert to help raise funds for local charities in their hometown of Kingston. A total of 15 000 people attended. The tickets were $8.50 per student and $12.50 per adult. The concert took in a total of $162 500. How many adults came to the concert?

19. a) What happens when you try to solve the following system by substitution?
$$4x - 2y = 9$$
$$y = 2x + 1$$
   b) Solve by graphing and explain how this is related to the solution when solving by substitution.

20. Simplify each equation, and then solve the linear system by substitution.
   a) $2(x - 4) + y = 6$
      $3x - 2(y - 3) = 13$
   b) $2(x - 1) - 4(2y + 1) = -1$
      $x + 3(3y + 2) - 2 = 0$

21. The following three lines all intersect at one point. Find the coordinates of the point of intersection and the value of k.
$$2x + 3y = 7$$
$$x + 4y = 16$$
$$4x - ky = 9$$

22. Math Contest Toni and her friends are building triangular pyramids with golf balls. Write a formula for the number of golf balls in a pyramid with n layers.

23. Math Contest In a magic square, the sum of the numbers in any row, column, or diagonal is the same. What is the sum of any row of this magic square?

A −6   **B** 0   **C** 10   **D** 15   **E** 18

x	−2	−3x
0		4

1.3 Investigate Equivalent Linear Relations and Equivalent Linear Systems

In these investigations, use the most convenient method to graph each linear relation:
- a table of values
- slope and y-intercept
- x- and y-intercepts
- a graphing calculator
- *The Geometer's Sketchpad®*

Investigate A

Tools
- grid paper, graphing calculators, or geometry software

What are equivalent linear equations?

1. **a)** On the same grid, graph the lines $x + 2y = 4$ and $2x + 4y = 8$.
   b) How are the graphs related?
   c) How are the equations related?

2. **a)** On the same grid, graph the lines $y = -\frac{1}{2}x + 3$ and $x + 2y = 6$.
   b) How are the graphs related?
   c) How are the equations related?

3. **a)** Without graphing, tell which two of the following are **equivalent linear equations**.
   $$y - x + 5 = 0 \qquad y = 3x + 15 \qquad 2y = 2x - 10$$
   b) Check your answer by graphing the three equations.

4. Which one of the following is *not* equivalent to the others?
   $$2x - 4y = 8 \qquad y = \frac{1}{2}x - 2 \qquad 2y - x - 4 = 0$$

5. Write two equivalent equations for each of the following. Check by graphing.
   a) $3x + 2y = 12$ **b)** $x + y = 4$ **c)** $y = \frac{2}{3}x + 1$

6. **Reflect**
   a) Describe how to obtain an equivalent equation for any linear relation.
   b) How many equivalent equations are there for a given linear relation?

equivalent linear equations
- equations that have the same graph

Investigate B

What are equivalent linear systems?

Tools
- grid paper, graphing calculators, or geometry software

1. Graph the linear system and find the point of intersection.
   $$y = x - 1$$
   $$y = -\frac{1}{2}x + 2$$

2. Graph the linear system and find the point of intersection.
   $$2x - 2y - 2 = 0$$
   $$2y + x = 4$$

3. **a)** Compare the solutions to questions 1 and 2. What do you notice?

   b) Compare the equations in questions 1 and 2. How are the equations related?

4. **a)** Graph the linear system and find the point of intersection.
   $$y = 2x + 1$$
   $$y + x = 7$$

   b) Choose a number. Multiply the first equation in part a) by the number. How is the new equation related to the first equation in part a)?

   c) Choose another number. Multiply the second equation in part a) by the number. How is the new equation related to the second equation in part a)?

   d) If you graphed the two new equations that you obtained in parts b) and c), what would you expect the point of intersection to be? Explain why. Check by graphing.

5. **Reflect** Explain how you can use equivalent linear equations to write an **equivalent linear system**. Use your own examples in your explanation.

equivalent linear systems
- pairs of linear equations that have the same point of intersection

6. **a)** Graph the linear system and find the point of intersection.
   $$x + 2y = 4$$
   $$x - y = 1$$

   b) If you add the left sides and the right sides of the two equations in part a), you obtain the equation $2x + y = 5$. Graph this equation on the same grid as in part a). What do you find?

   c) If you subtract the left sides and the right sides of the two equations in part a), you obtain the equation $3y = 3$. Graph this equation on the same grid as in part a). What do you find?

7. a) Graph the linear system and find the point of intersection.

$2x + 3y = -4$
$x + 2y = -3$

b) On the same coordinate grid, graph the equation $3x + 5y = -7$. What do you notice? How is this equation related to the two equations in part a)?

c) On the same coordinate grid, graph the equation $x + y = -1$. What do you notice? How is this equation related to the two equations in part a)?

8. a) Graph the linear system and find the point of intersection.

$3x - 2y = 18$ ①
$2x + y = 12$ ②

b) Obtain a new equation, ③, by adding the left sides and the right sides of the equations in part a). If you graphed the linear system formed by equations ① and ③, what result would you expect? Check by graphing.

c) If you graphed the linear system formed by equations ② and ③, what result would you expect? Check by graphing.

d) Obtain a new equation, ④, by subtracting the left sides and the right sides of the equations in part a). If you graphed the linear system formed by equations ① and ④, or by equations ② and ④, what result would you expect? Check by graphing.

e) Do you think the linear system formed by equations ③ and ④ will give the same result? Check by graphing.

9. Reflect Given a linear system of two equations in two variables, describe at least three ways in which you can obtain an equivalent linear system. Provide your own examples to illustrate.

Key Concepts

- Equivalent linear equations have the same graph.

- For any linear equation, an equivalent linear equation can be written by multiplying the equation by any real number.

- Equivalent linear systems have the same solution. The graphs of the linear relations in the system have the same point of intersection.

- Equivalent linear systems can be written by writing equivalent linear equations for either or both of the equations, or by adding or subtracting the original equations.

Communicate Your Understanding

C1 Rohan claims that the following linear equations will have the same graph. Is he correct? Explain why or why not.

$y = \dfrac{3}{4}x + 1$ and $4y = 3x + 4$

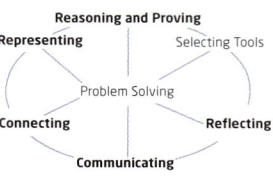

C2 If $y = 2x - 5$ and $3y = kx - 15$ are equivalent linear equations, what is the value of k?

C3 Are the linear systems A and B equivalent? Explain how you can tell from the equations. How could you check using a graph?

System A
$y = 2x - 2$
$y = x + 1$

System B
$y = 2x - 2$
$2y = 2x + 2$

C4 The graph of the following linear system is shown.

$y = x + 4$ ①
$y = -x + 2$ ②

The following is an equivalent linear system. Explain how you can tell from the graph. How can these equations be obtained from equations ① and ②?

$x = -1$
$y = 3$

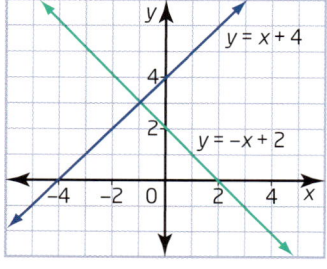

Practise

1. Which two equations are equivalent?

A $y = \dfrac{1}{2}x + 3$ **B** $y = x + 6$

C $2y = x + 6$

2. Which is *not* an equivalent linear relation?

A $8y = 12x + 4$ **B** $4y = 6x + 2$

C $2y = 3x + 4$ **D** $y = \dfrac{3}{2}x + \dfrac{1}{2}$

3. Write two equivalent equations for each.

a) $y = 3x - 2$ b) $3x + 6y = 12$

c) $y = \dfrac{3}{5}x + 2$ d) $8x + 4y = 10$

Connect and Apply

4. The perimeter of the rectangle is 24. Write an equation to represent this situation. Then, write an equivalent linear equation.

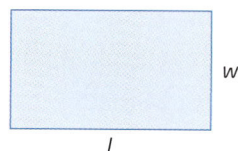

5. The value of the nickels and dimes in Tina's wallet is 70¢. Write an equation to represent this information. Then, write an equivalent linear equation.

6. A linear system is given.

$3x - 6y = 15$ ①
$x + y = 3$ ②

Explain why the following is an equivalent linear system.

$x - 2y = 5$
$2x + 2y = 6$

7. A linear system is shown on the graph.

$y = 2x$ ①
$y = 6 - x$ ②

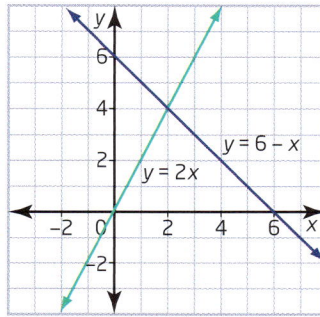

a) Use a graph to show that the following is an equivalent linear system.

$2y = x + 6$ ③
$0 = 3x - 6$ ④

b) How is equation ③ obtained from equations ① and ②?

c) How is equation ④ obtained from equations ① and ②?

8. A linear system is given.

$y = \frac{2}{3}x - 1$ ①
$y = -\frac{1}{3}x + 2$ ②

a) Explain why the following is an equivalent linear system.

$3y - 2x = -1$ ③
$3y + x = 2$ ④

b) If you graph the four equations, what result do you expect? Graph to check.

Extend

9. Work backward to build a more complicated linear system. Start with a solution, for example $x = 3$ and $y = -2$. Choose your own example.

a) Write an equivalent linear system by adding and then subtracting the two equations in your solution.

b) Multiply each equation from part a) by a different number to write another equivalent system.

c) Use other ways to write equivalent linear equations to transform your linear system.

d) Use graphing or substitution to check that your result in part c) has the same solution as you started with.

e) Exchange your linear system from part c) with that of another student. Solve the linear system.

10. Math Contest The self-taught Indian mathematician Srinvasa Ramanujan (1887−1920) discovered more than 3000 theorems. One of his challenge problems was to find the least number that can be written as the sum of two cubes in two different ways. Find the number.

11. Math Contest If the two spinners shown are each spun once, what is the probability that the sum of the two numbers is either even or a multiple of 3?

A $\frac{7}{13}$ **B** $\frac{2}{3}$ **C** $\frac{1}{3}$ **D** $\frac{9}{13}$ **E** $\frac{3}{4}$

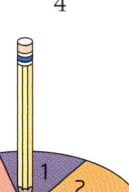

1.4 The Method of Elimination

You have now seen how to solve a linear system by graphing or by substitution. There is another algebraic method as well. With each new method, you have more options for solving the linear system.

Investigate

How can you solve a linear system by elimination?

Parnika and her mother, Mati, share a digital camera. They use two memory cards to store the photos. While on vacation, they took a total of 117 photos. There are 41 more photos on Parnika's memory card than on her mother's.

1. Read the situation described above. Let p represent the number of photos on Parnika's memory card and m represent the number of photos on Mati's memory card.

   a) Write an equation to represent the total number of photos on the memory cards.

   b) Write an equation to represent the difference in the number of photos on the memory cards.

2. **a)** Write your two equations below one another, so like terms align in columns. Add like terms on the left sides and add the right sides of the equations.

   b) Which variable has disappeared?

   c) Solve for the remaining variable.

   d) Substitute your answer from part c) into the first equation. Solve for the other variable.

   e) How many photos are on Parnika's memory card? on Mati's memory card?

3. **a)** Write the pair of equations from step 1 again. Put a line under the two equations and subtract the bottom equation from the top equation.

   b) Which variable has disappeared?

   c) Solve for the remaining variable.

d) Substitute your answer from part c) into the first equation. Solve for the other variable.

e) How many photos are on each person's memory card?

4. Reflect

a) Explain what you have done in order to find the number of photos on the memory cards.

b) How can you verify that you have obtained the correct solution?

In the Investigate above you solved a linear system by the **method of elimination**. This is another method for solving a system of linear equations.

method of elimination
- solving a linear system by adding or subtracting to eliminate one of the variables

Example 1 Solve a Linear System Using the Method of Elimination

Solve the system of linear equations.
$3x + y = 19$
$4x - y = 2$
Check your solution.

Solution

$3x + y = 19$ ①
$4x - y = 2$ ②   **Add columns vertically.**
$7x = 21$ ① + ②

I notice that I have +y in the first equation and −y in the second equation. If I add the two equations, y will be eliminated.

$x = \dfrac{21}{7}$

$x = 3$

Now I have one equation in one variable. I can solve for x.

Substitute $x = 3$ into equation ① to find the corresponding y-value.
$3x + y = 19$
$3(3) + y = 19$
$9 + y = 19$
$y = 10$

I can substitute back into either original equation.

Check by substituting $x = 3$ and $y = 10$ into both original equations.

In $3x + y = 19$:
L.S. $= 3x + y$ **R.S.** $= 19$
$ = 3(3) + 10$
$ = 19$
**L.S.** $=$ **R.S.**

In $4x - y = 2$:
L.S. $= 4x - y$ **R.S.** $= 2$
$ = 4(3) - 10$
$ = 2$
**L.S.** $=$ **R.S.**

The solution checks in both equations.

The solution to the linear system is $x = 3$ and $y = 10$.

Example 2 Solve Using Elimination

Solve the linear system.
$10x + 4y = -1$
$8x - 2y = 7$

Solution

$10x + 4y = -1$ ①
$8x - 2y = 7$ ②

> I can't eliminate either variable by adding or subtracting the equations given. If I multiply equation ② by 2, then I will have $-4y$ in the second equation. Then, I can add to eliminate the y-terms.

① $10x + 4y = -1$
$2 \times$ ② $16x - 4y = 14$
① $+ 2 \times$ ② $26x = 13$

$$x = \frac{13}{26}$$

$$x = \frac{1}{2}$$

Substitute $x = \frac{1}{2}$ in ② to find the corresponding y-value.

$8x - 2y = 7$
$8\left(\frac{1}{2}\right) - 2y = 7$
$4 - 2y = 7$
$-2y = 7 - 4$
$-2y = 3$
$y = \frac{3}{-2}$
$y = -\frac{3}{2}$

> I chose to substitute in ② because that equation looks simpler.

Check: Substitute $x = \frac{1}{2}$ and $y = -\frac{3}{2}$ into both original equations.

In $10x + 4y = -1$:
L.S. $= 10x + 4y$ **R.S.** $= -1$
$= 10\left(\frac{1}{2}\right) + 4\left(-\frac{3}{2}\right)$
$= 5 - 6$
$= -1$
        L.S. = R.S.

In $8x - 2y = 7$:
L.S. $= 8x - 2y$ **R.S.** $= 7$
$= 8\left(\frac{1}{2}\right) - 2\left(-\frac{3}{2}\right)$
$= 4 + 3$
$= 7$
        L.S. = R.S.

The solution to the linear system is $x = \frac{1}{2}$, $y = -\frac{3}{2}$.

You can check your work using a Computer Algebra System (CAS).
- Type in equation ①, in brackets.
- Add equation ②, in brackets, multiplied by 2.
- Press ENTER.
- Divide the resulting equation by 26.
- Substitute $x = \dfrac{1}{2}$ in equation ① and solve for y.

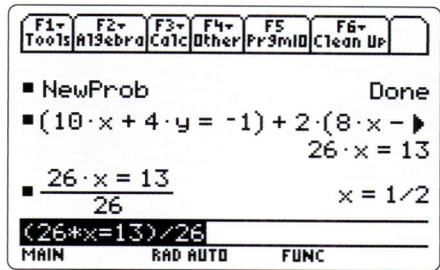

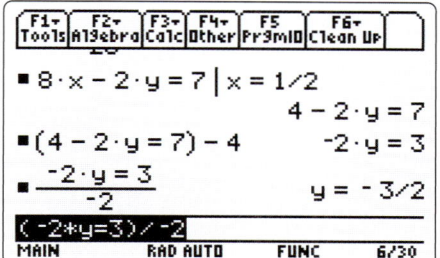

Example 3 Find a Point of Intersection Using Elimination

Find the point of intersection of the linear system.
$4x + 3y = 13$
$5x - 4y = -7$
Verify your answer.

Solution

$4x + 3y = 13$ ①
$5x - 4y = -7$ ②

> I'll need to multiply each of the equations to get the same coefficient in front of one of the variables. If I multiply equation ① by 5 and equation ② by 4, both equations will start with $20x$.

Method 1: Eliminate x

$5 \times$ ① $20x + 15y = 65$
$4 \times$ ② $20x - 16y = -28$
                 $31y = 93$
                 $y = \dfrac{93}{31}$
                 $y = 3$

> Now if I subtract, x will be eliminated.
> In the y-column, $15y - (-16y) = 15y + 16y$.
> On the right, $65 - (-28) = 65 + 28$.

Substitute $y = 3$ into ① to find the corresponding x-value.
$4x + 3y = 13$
$4x + 3(3) = 13$
$4x + 9 = 13$
$4x = 4$
$x = 1$

1.4 The Method of Elimination • MHR **37**

Method 2: Eliminate y

$4x + 3y = 13$ ①
$5x - 4y = -7$ ②

$4 \times$ ① $\quad 16x + 12y = 52$
$3 \times$ ② $\quad \underline{15x - 12y = -21}$
$\qquad\qquad\quad 31x = 31$
$\qquad\qquad\quad\;\; x = 1$

> If I multiply ① by 4 and ② by 3, one equation will have 12y and the other will have −12y. Then, if I add, y will be eliminated.

Substitute $x = 1$ into ① to find the corresponding y-value.
$\quad 4x + 3y = 13$
$4(1) + 3y = 13$
$\quad 4 + 3y = 13$
$\qquad\;\; 3y = 9$
$\qquad\;\;\; y = 3$

Verify by substituting $x = 1$ and $y = 3$ into both original equations.

In $4x + 3y = 13$:
L.S. $= 4x + 3y \qquad$ **R.S.** $= 13$
$\quad\;\; = 4(1) + 3(3)$
$\quad\;\; = 4 + 9$
$\quad\;\; = 13$
$\qquad$ **L.S. = R.S.**

In $5x - 4y = -7$:
L.S. $= 5x - 4y \qquad$ **R.S.** $= -7$
$\quad\;\; = 5(1) - 4(3)$
$\quad\;\; = 5 - 12$
$\quad\;\; = -7$
$\qquad$ **L.S. = R.S.**

The point of intersection of the lines is (1, 3).

Example 4 Solve a Problem Using the Method of Elimination

A small store sells used CDs and DVDs. The CDs sell for $9 each. The DVDs sell for $11 each. Cody is working part time and sells a total of $204 worth of CDs and DVDs during his shift. He knows that 20 items were sold. He needs to tell the store owner how many of each type were sold. How many CDs did Cody sell? How many DVDs did Cody sell?

Solution

Let c represent the number of CDs sold.
Let d represent the number of DVDs sold.

$c + d = 20$ ①
$9c + 11d = 204$ ②

> The number of CDs plus the number of DVDs is 20.

Multiply ① by 9.
$9c + \;\;9d = 180$
$\underline{9c + 11d = 204}$
$\qquad -2d = -24$
$\qquad\quad\; d = 12$

> $9 for each CD plus $11 for each DVD totals $204.

> I can also solve this system using substitution or graphing.

> If I subtract, c is eliminated.

Substitute $d = 12$ into one of the original equations to solve for c.
$$c + d = 20$$
$$c + 12 = 20$$
$$c = 8$$

Check in the original word problem:
Money: 8 CDs at \$9 is \$72, and 12 DVDs at \$11 is \$132. The total is \$204.
Number of items: 8 CDs and 12 DVDs is 20 items sold.

Cody sold eight CDs and twelve DVDs during his shift.

Key Concepts

- To solve a linear system by elimination, follow these steps:
  – Arrange the two equations so that like terms are aligned.
  – Choose the variable you wish to eliminate.
  – If necessary, multiply one or both equations by a value so that they have the same or opposite coefficient in front of the variable you want to eliminate.
  – Add or subtract (as needed) to eliminate one variable.
  – Solve for the remaining variable.
  – Substitute into one of the original equations to find the value of the other variable.
  – Check your solution by substituting into the original equations, or into the word problem.
  – If you are solving a word problem, write the answer in words.

Communicate Your Understanding

C1 Consider solving the linear system $x + y = 5$
$x - y = 7$

  a) To eliminate x, do you add or subtract the two equations?
  b) To eliminate y, do you add or subtract the two equations?
  c) Will you obtain the same solution if you add or subtract the two equations? Explain.

C2 Consider solving the linear system $4x + 3y = 15$ ①
$8x - 9y = 15$ ②

  a) Describe the steps you would use to eliminate x.
  b) The linear system can also be solved by first eliminating y. Describe the steps you would use if you chose this method.

C3 In what situations would you use the method of graphing? substitution? elimination? Consider the following linear systems. Which method would you use for each and why?

  a) $y = x - 9$
   $2x + 3y = 1$

  b) $3x + 2y = 8$
   $2x - 2y = 7$

  c) $y = -\dfrac{2}{3}x + 5$
   $3x - 2y = 6$

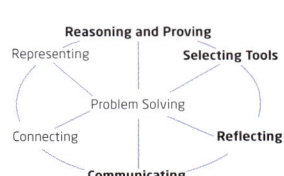

Practise

For help with questions 1 and 2, see Example 1.

1. Solve using the method of elimination.
   a) $x + y = 2$
      $3x - y = 2$
   b) $x - y = -1$
      $3x + y = -7$
   c) $x + 3y = 7$
      $x + y = 3$
   d) $5x + 2y = -11$
      $3x + 2y = -9$

2. Solve using the method of elimination. Check each solution.
   a) $2x + y = -5$
      $-2x + y = -1$
   b) $4x - y = -1$
      $-4x - 3y = -19$
   c) $2x + y = 8$
      $4x - y = 4$
   d) $3x + 2y = -1$
      $-3x + 4y = 7$

For help with questions 3 and 4, see Example 2.

3. Find the point of intersection of each pair of lines.
   a) $x + 2y = 2$
      $3x + 5y = 4$
   b) $3x + 5y = 12$
      $2x - y = -5$
   c) $3x + y = 13$
      $2x + 3y = 18$
   d) $6x + 5y = 12$
      $3x - 4y = 6$

4. Solve by elimination. Check each solution.
   a) $4x + 3y = 4$
      $8x - y = 1$
   b) $5x - 3y = 25$
      $10x + 3y = 5$
   c) $5x + 2y = 48$
      $x + y = 15$
   d) $2x + 3y = 8$
      $x - 2y = -3$

For help with questions 5 to 7, see Example 3.

5. Solve by elimination. Check each solution.
   a) $3x - 2y = 5$
      $2x + 3y = 12$
   b) $5m + 2n = 5$
      $2m + 3n = 13$
   c) $3a - 4b = 10$
      $5a - 12b = 6$
   d) $3h - 4k = 5$
      $5h + 3k = -11$

6. Find the point of intersection of each pair of lines. Check each solution.
   a) $3x + y = 13$
      $2x + 3y = 18$
   b) $2x + 3y = -18$
      $3x - 5y = 11$
   c) $3x - 2y + 2 = 0$
      $7x - 6y + 11 = 0$
   d) $2a - 3b = -10$
      $4a + b = 1$

7. Solve each system of linear equations by elimination. Check your answers.
   a) $4x - 9y = 4$
      $6x + 15y = -13$
   b) $2x + 9y = -4$
      $5x - 2y = 39$
   c) $3a - 2b + 4 = 0$
      $2a - 5b - 1 = 0$
   d) $2u + 5v = 46$
      $3u - 2v = 12$

Connect and Apply

For help with questions 8 and 9, see Example 4.

8. Mehrab works in a department store selling sports equipment. Baseball gloves cost $29 each and bats cost $14 each. One shift, he sells 28 items. His receipts total $647.
   a) How many bats did Mehrab sell?
   b) How many gloves did he sell?

9. Liz works at the ballpark selling bottled water. She sells 37 bottles in one shift. The large bottles sell for $5 each and the small bottles sell for $3 each. At the end of one game, she has taken in $131.
   a) How many large bottles did Liz sell?
   b) How many small bottles did she sell?

10. Consider the linear system $2x - 3y = 5$ and $4x + y = 8$.
    a) Solve by elimination.
    b) Solve by substitution.
    c) Which method do you prefer? Why?

11. Explain how you would solve the system $3x + 2y = 5$ and $4x + 5y = 11$ using the method of elimination. Do not actually solve the system.

12. Expand and simplify each equation. Then, solve the linear system.
    a) $2(3x - 1) - (y + 4) = -7$
       $4(1 - 2x) - 3(3 - y) = -12$
    b) $3(a - 1) - 3(b - 3) = 0$
       $3(a + 2) - (b - 7) = 20$
    c) $5(k + 5) - 2(n - 3) = 62$
       $4(k - 7) - (n + 4) = -9$

13. To solve the following linear system by elimination, Brent first multiplied each equation by 10. Explain why he did this step. Complete the solution.

    $0.3x - 0.5y = 1.2$
    $0.7x - 0.2y = -0.1$

14. Solve each linear system.

    a) $0.2x - 0.3y = 1.3$
       $0.5x + 0.2y = 2.3$

    b) $0.1a - 0.4b = 1.9$
       $0.4a + 0.5b = -0.8$

15. Bhargav stops in at a deli to get lunch for his crew. He buys five roast beef and three vegetarian sandwiches and the order costs $27.50. The next week, he pays $23.00 for two roast beef and six vegetarian sandwiches. How much does one roast beef sandwich cost?

16. Maria rented the same car twice in one month. She paid $180 the first time for 3 days and she drove a total of 150 km. The next time, she also paid $180 and had the vehicle for only 2 days, but travelled 400 km.

    a) What was the cost per day?

    b) What was the cost per kilometre?

17. **Chapter Problem** The Clarke's son suggests that they rent a car that costs $250 for the week plus 22¢/km. Their daughter does not want to drive far, so she suggests a car that is only $96 for the week but 50¢/km.

    a) Write an equation to represent the cost of the car suggested by the son.

    b) Write an equation to represent the cost of the car suggested by the daughter.

    c) When will the two cars cost the same? Use the method of elimination to solve.

    d) If the Clarkes plan to drive 500 km, which option is less expensive?

18. What happens when you solve the system $2x + 3y = 6$ and $6x + 9y = 0$ by elimination? Use a graph in your explanation.

Achievement Check

19. a) Nita's class visited a provincial site to view some ancient rock drawings. Two adults and five students in one van paid $77 for the visit. Two adults and seven students in a second van paid $95. What were the entry prices for a student and an adult? Verify your solution.

    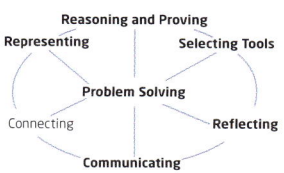

    b) Katie and Chris each solved a system of two linear equations as shown. Whose method is correct? Explain why.

    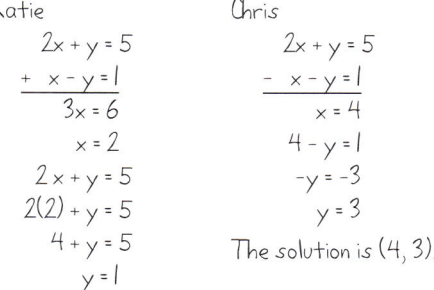

Extend

20. Solve by elimination.

    a) $\frac{1}{2}m + n = -4$
       $\frac{m}{2} - \frac{3n}{2} = 1$

    b) $\frac{4a}{3} - \frac{b}{4} = 6$
       $\frac{5a}{6} + b = 13$

    c) $\frac{t-5}{3} + \frac{w+1}{2} = 1$
       $\frac{t-1}{5} + \frac{w+2}{3} = 2$

21. Consider the linear system $ax + by = c$
    $dx + ey = f$

    Find a general solution for x and y. State any restrictions on the values of a, b, c, d, e, and f.

22. Solve the system of equations.

    $x + 3y - z = -14$
    $7x + 6y + z = 1$
    $4x - 2y - 5z = 11$

1.5 Solve Problems Using Linear Systems

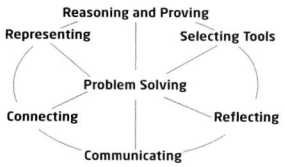

Now you know a number of different ways to solve a system of linear equations. You can solve
- graphically by hand
- graphically with a graphing calculator or graphing software
- algebraically by substitution
- algebraically by elimination

In this section, you will look at how to choose among these methods. You will also see how to apply the methods to some more challenging problems.

Investigate

Tools
- grid paper
- ruler

How do you choose a method for solving a linear system?

1. **a)** Graph the line $y = 3x + 1$.
   b) On the same set of axes, graph the line $y = 4x - 3$.
   c) What is the point of intersection of these two lines?

2. **a)** Graph the line $x + y = 101$.
   b) On the same set of axes, graph the line $300x - y = 200$.
   c) What is the point of intersection of these two lines?

3. Why was it easier to find the point of intersection of the two lines in step 1 than in step 2?

4. **a)** Use the method of substitution to find the intersection point of the lines $y = 3x + 1$ and $y = 4x - 3$.
   b) Did you get the same result you found in step 1 part c)?

5. **a)** Use the method of elimination to find the intersection point of the lines $y = 3x + 1$ and $y = 4x - 3$.
   b) Did you get the same result you found in step 1 part c)?

6. **a)** Find the solution to the linear system $x + y = 101$ and $300x - y = 200$ by substitution.
   b) Did you get the same result you found in step 2 part c)?

7. **a)** Find the solution to the linear system $x + y = 101$ and $300x - y = 200$ by elimination.
   b) Did you get the same result you found in step 2 part c)?

8. You have learned three methods for solving a linear system: graphing, substitution, and elimination.

   a) Which method was easiest to use for the lines $y = 3x + 1$ and $y = 4x - 3$? Explain.

   b) Which method was easiest to use for the lines $x + y = 101$ and $300x - y = 200$? Explain.

9. **Reflect** Consider pairs of equations that form a linear system.

   a) Describe the equations in a linear system that you would choose to solve by graphing.

   b) Describe the equations in a linear system that you would choose to solve by substitution.

   c) Describe the equations in a linear system that you would choose to solve by elimination.

Example 1 Graphing, Substitution, or Elimination?

Christian has a total of eight cars and trucks to play with. His birthday is soon. He hopes to double the number of cars he has now. If he does, he will have a total of 11 cars and trucks. How many cars does he have now? How many trucks?

Solution

Let c represent the number of cars Christian has now.
Let t represent the number of trucks he has now.
$c + t = 8$
$2c + t = 11$

For the line $c + t = 8$, the intercepts are at (8, 0) and (0, 8).
Rearrange the second equation as $t = -2c + 11$.
The t-intercept is 11 and the slope is -2.

The solution is $c = 3$, $t = 5$.

Check in the problem:

Christian's cars and trucks now:
3 cars + 5 trucks = 8 toys

Christian's cars and trucks after his birthday: 6 cars + 5 trucks = 11 toys
Also, 6 cars is double 3 cars.
This checks.
Christian has three cars and five trucks now.

> It doesn't make sense to have part of a car, so I expect whole-number answers. I will graph both equations. I'll put c on the horizontal axis and t on the vertical axis.

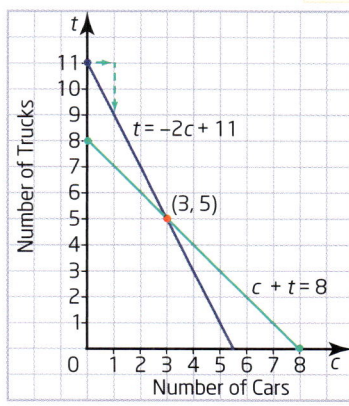

The problem in Example 1 was solved by graphing, but it can be solved by any of the three methods: graphing, substitution, or elimination.

Example 2 Solve a Distance, Speed, Time Problem

A canoeist took 2 h to travel 12 km down a river. The return trip, against the current, took 3 h. What was the average paddling rate of the canoeist? What was the speed of the current?

Solution

Let p represent the canoeist's average paddling speed, in kilometres per hour. Let c represent the speed of the current, in kilometres per hour. Draw a diagram to model the situation. Then, use a table to organize the given facts.

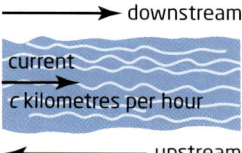

Going downstream, the current helps the canoeist. Going upstream, the current slows the canoeist down.

Direction	Distance (km)	Speed (km/h)	Time (h)
Downstream	12	$p + c$	2
Upstream	12	$p - c$	3

To write the equations, use the fact that distance = speed × time.
$12 = (p + c)2$ ①
$12 = (p - c)3$ ②

I can simplify each equation by dividing both sides of the first equation by 2, and both sides of the second equation by 3.

$6 = p + c$
$4 = p - c$
$\overline{10 = 2p}$
$p = 5$

I can solve this linear system directly using elimination. I will add.

Substitute $p = 5$ into equation ① to find c.
$12 = (5 + c)2$
$12 = 10 + 2c$
$2 = 2c$
$c = 1$

Verify in the original problem:
Downstream: Speed is $5 + 1$, or 6 km/h. So, in 2 h the distance is 12 km. This checks with the first sentence.
Upstream: Speed is $5 - 1$, or 4 km/h. So, in 3 h the distance is 12 km. This checks with the second sentence.
The canoeist's average paddling rate was 5 km/h. The speed of the current was 1 km/h.

Example 3 Solve a Mixture Problem

Marryam has a bottle of 5% acetic acid and a bottle of 10% acetic acid. How much of each should she use to make 250 mL of 8% acetic acid?

Did You Know?

Household white vinegar is 5% acetic acid. A 5% acetic acid solution means that 5% pure acid is mixed with 95% water. For example, 1 L of white vinegar contains 50 mL of pure acetic acid and 950 mL of water.

Solution

Let f represent the amount of 5% acid in the 8% mixture.
Let t represent the amount of 10% acid in the 8% mixture.

Use a table to organize the given information.

Volume (mL)	5% Acid	10% Acid	8% Mixture
Solution	f	t	250
Pure Acid	$0.05f$	$0.1t$	$0.08(250)$

$f + t = 250$ ①
$0.05f + 0.1t = 20$ ②

The sum of the two volumes is 250 mL.

These equations would not be easy to solve by graphing, unless I used a graphing calculator or multiplied equation ② by 20 first.

Consider the volume of pure acid. In the 8% mixture, $0.08(250) = 20$.

Rearrange equation ①: $f = 250 - t$
Substitute into equation ②.
$$0.05f + 0.1t = 20$$
$$0.05(250 - t) + 0.1t = 20$$
$$12.5 - 0.05t + 0.1t = 20$$
$$12.5 + 0.05t = 20$$
$$0.05t = 7.5$$
$$t = \frac{7.5}{0.05}$$
$$t = 150$$

I'll use the method of substitution because it is easy to solve equation ① for one variable.

Substitute $t = 150$ into equation ①.
$f + t = 250$
$f + 150 = 250$
$f = 100$

Marryam should mix 100 mL of the 5% acetic acid with 150 mL of the 10% acetic acid to make 250 mL of 10% acetic acid.

Key Concepts

- You can solve linear systems using any of the three methods: graphing, substitution, or elimination.
- Look at the equations carefully to see if there is an advantage to solving using a particular method.

Communicate Your Understanding

C1 In what situations would solving by graphing be your preferred choice? Give an example.

C2 In what situations would solving by substitution be your preferred choice? Give an example.

C3 In what situations would solving by elimination be your preferred choice? Give an example.

C4 Write a linear system that can be solved by any of the three methods.

Practise

For help with questions 1 to 6, see Example 1.

1. Leanne works at a greenhouse. She needs to plant a total of 32 bulbs. Two types of bulbs are available. She is asked to plant three times as many crocus bulbs as tulip bulbs. How many of each should she plant?

2. James looks in his TV cabinet and finds some old Beta and VHS tapes. He has 17 tapes in all. He finds that he has three more Beta tapes than VHS tapes. How many of each type does he have?

3. The girls' soccer team held a fundraising car wash. They charged $5 for each car and $8 for each van. They washed 44 cars and vans and collected $262. How many of each type of vehicle did they wash?

4. Rehman invests his summer earnings of $3050. He invests part of the money at 8%/year, and the rest at 7.5%/year. After 1 year, these investments earn $242 in simple interest. How much did he invest at each rate?

5. Why might it be more appropriate to solve questions 1 and 2 by graphing than questions 3 and 4?

6. Consider the linear system
$3x - y = 8$
$4x - y = -15$

   a) Which method would you choose to solve the linear system and why? Solve using the method you chose.

   b) Now solve using one of the other methods available to you.

Connect and Apply

For help with questions 7 and 8, see Example 2.

7. Tyler rows 10 km downstream in 2 h. On the return trip, it takes him 4 h to travel 8 km. Determine his average rowing speed and the speed of the current.

8. With a tailwind, a plane flew the 3000 km from Calgary to Montréal in 5 h. The return flight, against the wind, took 6 h. Find the wind speed and the speed of the plane.

For help with questions 9 and 10, see Example 3.

9. Milk and cream contain different percents of butterfat. How much 3% milk needs to be mixed with how much 15% cream to give 20 L of 6% cream?

10. Amy needs to make 10 L of 42% sulphuric acid solution. In the supply room, she finds bottles of 30% sulphuric acid solution and 60% sulphuric acid solution. What volume of each solution should she mix in order to make the 42% solution?

11. To join Karate Klub, David must pay a monthly fee of $25 and an initial fee of $200. If he chooses Kool Karate, he must pay an initial fee of only $100 but $35/month.
    a) After how many months is the cost the same at either karate club?
    b) If David plans to try karate for 6 months, which club should he join?
    c) If David decides to do karate for a year, which club should he join?

12. For a school band trip, Marcia decides to order T-shirts for all of the participants. It will cost $4 per shirt for the medium size, and $5 per shirt for the large size. Marcia orders a total of 70 T-shirts and spends $320. How many are medium shirts?

13. One type of granola has 30% nuts, by mass. A second type of granola has 15% nuts. What mass of each type needs to be mixed to make 600 g of granola that will have 21% nuts?

14. A metal alloy is 25% copper. Another metal alloy is 50% copper. How much of each should be used to make 500 g of an alloy that is 45% copper?

15. Some students at L.C.V.I. held a bake sale recently to raise money for a field trip. They charged $7 for fruit pies and $10 for meat pies. They sold a total of 52 pies and earned $424. How many of each type of pie did they sell?

16. A class trip is being planned. For one option, each student will pay $630. This includes two meals a day and accommodation for the 9-day trip. The other option offers three meals a day and accommodation for the 9 days. This second option costs $720. What is the cost per meal? What is the cost per day for accommodation?

Extend

17. Ian flew his airplane at best cruise speed for 2 h, then at economy cruise speed for 3 h, covering a total of 850 km. On the following day, he flew at best cruise speed for 3 h and at economy cruise speed for 2 h, covering a total of 900 km. Find the best cruise speed and the economy cruise speed for Ian's airplane.

18. A train leaves Toronto for Montréal at the same time as another train leaves Montréal for Toronto. The cities are 500 km apart. The trains pass each other 2 h later. The train from Montréal is travelling 50 km/h faster than the one from Toronto. At what distance away from Toronto do the trains pass each other?

19. Sam is a jewellery artist. She needs to mix metals to make her products. Pure gold is 24-karat and is very soft. It is usually mixed with other metals such as silver to make it harder. Sam has some 18-karat gold ($\frac{18}{24}$ pure gold) and some 9-karat gold ($\frac{9}{24}$ pure gold). What mass of each type of gold should she use to make 600 g of 15-karat gold?

20. **Math Contest** A chemist has one 30-L bottle of 15% hydrochloric acid and one 30-L bottle of 90% hydrochloric acid. She mixes 20 L of 60% hydrochloric acid and then pours 5 L of that solution back into the bottle containing the 90% hydrochloric acid. How strong is the acid in that bottle now?

Chapter 1 Review

1.1 Connect English With Mathematics and Graphing Lines, pages 8–19

1. Translate each sentence into an equation. Tell how you are assigning the two variables in each.
   a) John has nickels and dimes that total $2.50 in his pocket.
   b) Maggie's age increased by three is twice Janice's age, decreased by nine.
   c) Twice a number, decreased by nine, is half the same number, increased by six.

2. Use graphing to find the point of intersection of the lines
   $y = -2x + 5$ and $y = \frac{1}{2}x - 5$.

3. **Use Technology** Allison is planning her parents' 25th wedding anniversary dinner party. La Casa charges a fixed cost of $1500 plus $25 per guest. Hastings Hall charges $1000 plus $30 per guest.
   a) Write an equation for the cost at La Casa.
   b) Write an equation for the cost at Hastings Hall.
   c) Use a graphing calculator to find the number of guests for which the charge is the same at both locations.
   d) In what situation should Allison choose La Casa? Explain.
   e) In what situation should Allison choose Hastings Hall? Explain.

1.2 The Method of Substitution, pages 20–28

4. Solve each linear system using the method of substitution.
   a) $x + y = -2$
      $y = x + 6$
   b) $x - y = 9$
      $y = -x + 3$
   c) $y = -2x + 2$
      $3x + 2y = 5$
   d) $2x - 3y = 6$
      $2x - y = 7$

5. On Derwin farm there is a total of 50 chickens and cows. If there are 118 legs, how many chickens are there?

6. Josie wants to buy Internet access. One service provider charges a flat rate of $34.95/month. A second charges $25/month plus 33¢/h. For what number of hours per month should Josie choose the flat rate?

7. There are 35 people in a room. There are seven more males than females in the room. How many males are there? How many females?

1.3 Investigate Equivalent Linear Relations and Equivalent Linear Systems, pages 29–33

8. Which is *not* an equivalent equation for $9x - 3y = 18$?
   A $y = 3x - 6$ **B** $y = \frac{1}{3}x - 2$
   C $6x - 2y = 12$

1.4 The Method of Elimination, pages 34–41

9. Find the point of intersection of each pair of lines.
   a) $x - y = 3$
      $2x + y = 3$
   b) $3x + 2y = 5$
      $x - 2y = -1$
   c) $2x + 5y = 3$
      $2x - y = -3$
   d) $2x + y = 7$
      $x - y = -1$

10. Solve each linear system. Check each solution.
    a) $3x + 2y = 12$
       $2x + 3y = 13$
    b) $3x + 2y = 34$
       $5x - 3y = -13$
    c) $5a + 2b = 5$
       $2a + 3b = 13$
    d) $4k + 5h = -0.5$
       $3k + 7h = 0.6$

11. Make up your own problem to solve by elimination. Trade your question with one of your classmates and ask him or her to solve it. Check each other's work.

1.5 Solve Problems Using Linear Systems, pages 42–47

12. Solve each linear system. Justify your choice of method.

    a) $x + y = 7$
       $x = y + 3$

    b) $4x + 3y = -1.9$
       $2x - 7y = 3.3$

    c) $5x - 4y + 13 = 0$
       $7x - y + 9 = 0$

    d) $2(x - 1) - 3(y - 3) = 0$
       $3(x + 2) - (y - 7) = 20$

13. In one city, taxi company A charges $5 plus $0.35/km travelled. Taxi company B charges $3.50 plus 50¢/km.

    a) For what distance is the charge the same using either taxi company?

    b) In what situations would you choose company A?

14. Mengxi has $10 000 to invest. She invests part in a term deposit paying 5%/year, and the remainder in Canada Savings Bonds paying 3.5%/year. At the end of the year, she has earned simple interest of $413. How much did she invest at each rate?

15. A motor boat took 5 h to travel a distance of 60 km up a river, against the current. The return trip took 3 h. Find the average speed of the boat in still water and the speed of the current.

16. One type of fertilizer has 30% nitrogen and a second type has 15% nitrogen. If a farmer needs 600 kg of fertilizer that is 20% nitrogen, how much of each type should the farmer mix together?

17. Fran and Winston have a combined income of $80 000. One quarter of Winston's income is the same as one-sixth of Fran's income. How much does each person earn?

Chapter Problem Wrap-Up

The Clarke family will be leaving soon for Victoria. Mrs. Clarke suggests that they rent a car that costs $180 for the week plus 41¢/km. Mr. Clarke has found a car for $275 for the week plus 21¢/km.

a) Use your skills with linear systems to find the number of kilometres driven for which the cost will be the same for either of these cars.

b) The Clarkes want to go to Parksville and to visit an aunt who lives in Crofton. They would also like to go to Tofino. These trips will be a total of 628 km. Write a note to explain which of the two cars would cost less.

c) Look back at question 17 in Section 1.2, question 16 in Section 1.3, and question 17 in Section 1.4. Of the cars that the Clarkes have considered, which is the cheapest?

d) What other factors should they consider when choosing the car?

Chapter 1 Practice Test

1. Translate each sentence into an equation.
   a) In a group of 20 people, there are seven more men than women.
   b) The total of seven and twice a number gives the same result as three times that number.

2. Write a system of equations that can be solved by graphing and then show the solution.

3. a) Use graphing to find the point of intersection of the lines $y = 3x - 22$ and $y = 4x - 29$.
   b) What is the solution to the following linear system?
   $y = 3x - 22$
   $y = 4x - 29$

4. Solve each linear system using the method of substitution. Check each solution.
   a) $y = 2x - 13$
      $x + 2y = -6$
   b) $a + b = 5$
      $3a + 4b = 15$
   c) $x + 3y = 0$
      $3x - 6y = 5$
   d) $3m - 2n = -12$
      $m - 4n = 8$

5. A graph of a linear system is shown. Explain why each of the following is an equivalent linear system to the system shown in the graph.
   a) $y = 2x + 1$
      $2x - 3y = 9$
   b) $x = -3$
      $y = -5$
   c) $4x - 2y + 2 = 0$
      $4x - 6y - 18 = 0$

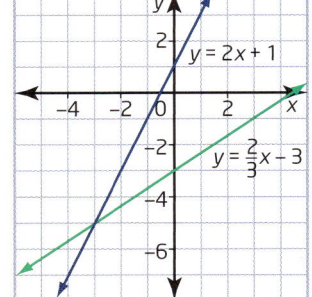

6. Use the method of elimination to solve each linear system. Check each solution.
   a) $3x + 2y = 19$
      $5x - 2y = 5$
   b) $4x - 3y = 15$
      $4x + 3y = 5$
   c) $6k + 5h = 20$
      $3k - 4h = 23$
   d) $4p - 2q = 6$
      $10p - 3q = -1$

7. Solve each linear system. Choose a method and explain why you chose that method. Check each solution.
   a) $y + 3x = 6$
      $y = 2x + 1$
   b) $2x - y = 3$
      $4x - y = -1$
   c) $2x - y = -6$
      $4x + y = -6$
   d) $6x - 5y = -1$
      $5x - 4y = -1$

8. Which is your preferred method for solving linear systems? Explain why. Give two advantages and two disadvantages of the method you prefer.

9. A triangle lies on a Cartesian plane. The sides are formed by the intersection of the lines $y = 3x - 1$, $2x + y - 4 = 0$, and $x - 2y = -7$. Find the coordinates of each vertex of the triangle.

10. Gregory works half as many hours per week as Paul. Between the two, they work a total of 48 h one week.
    a) Write an equation to represent the information in the first sentence.
    b) Write an equation to represent the information in the second sentence.
    c) Use the method of substitution to find the number of hours worked by each of them.

11. A physics contest has 30 multiple-choice questions. A correct answer gains 4 points, while a wrong answer loses 1 point. Rolly answered every question and scored 55 points. How many questions did he answer correctly?

12. A swimming pool has a perimeter of 96 m. The length is 3 m more than twice the width. Find the length and width of the pool.

13. A restaurant that serves a buffet lunch has one price for adults and another price for children under 12. The Jung group has two adults and three children and their bill is $48.95. The Harvey group has three adults and two children. Their bill is $52.05. What is the price of the buffet for an adult? for a child?

14. A total of 27 coins, in nickels and dimes, are in a wallet. If the coins total $2.15, how many of each type of coin are there?

15. Candice and Dino operate computer repair services. For a service call, Candice charges $40 and Dino charges $50. In addition, they each charge an hourly rate. Candice charges $35/h, and Dino charges $30/h. One day, their charges for two service calls were the same. What did they charge and how long did each person work?

16. Simplify and then solve each linear system.
    a) $3(x + 1) - 4(y - 1) = 13$
       $5(x + 2) + 2(y + 3) = 0$
    b) $3c + 0.8d = 1.4$
       $0.5c - 0.4d = 1.4$
    c) $x + y = 40$
       $\dfrac{x}{20} - \dfrac{y}{5} = 1$

17. Maya inherited $50 000. She invested part of it in a Guaranteed Investment Certificate (GIC) that paid 5%/year and the rest in a venture capital that returned 10%/year. The total simple interest after 1 year was $4000. How much did she invest at each rate?

18. Chemex Lab needs to make 500 L of a 34% acid solution for a customer. The lab has 25% and 50% acid solutions available to make the order. How many litres of each should be mixed to make the 34% solution?

19. Carl travelled the 1900 km from his home in Eastern Ontario to Winnipeg. He travelled by bus to Toronto at an average speed of 60 km/h and then flew to Winnipeg at an average speed of 700 km/h. His total travelling time was 7 h. How many kilometres did he travel by bus? How far did he travel by airplane?

Achievement Check

20. a) Choose an algebraic method to solve the following linear system. Explain why you chose this method.

    $$\dfrac{x}{2} - \dfrac{2y}{3} = \dfrac{7}{3}$$

    $$\dfrac{3x}{2} + 2y = 5$$

    b) Use the method you chose to solve the system. Check your solution.

    c) A fishing boat took 3 h to travel 36 km upstream, against the current, on the St. Lawrence River. The same trip downstream only took 2 h. What is the average speed of the fishing boat in still water? What was the speed of the river current?

CHAPTER 2

Analytic Geometry

Analytic Geometry

- Develop a formula for the midpoint of a line segment, and use this formula to solve problems.
- Develop a formula for the length of a line segment, and use this formula to solve problems.
- Develop an equation for a circle with centre (0, 0) and radius r.
- Determine the radius of a circle with centre (0, 0) given its equation, write an equation for a circle with centre (0, 0) given its radius, and sketch the circle given its equation in the form $x^2 + y^2 = r^2$.
- Solve problems involving the slope, length, and midpoint of a line segment.

Vocabulary

fractal
Cartesian grid
midpoint
median
equidistant
right bisector
altitude

A global positioning system (GPS) device uses signals from satellites to calculate its location. The GPS describes locations with three coordinates: latitude, longitude, and altitude. Coordinate systems are the basis of analytic geometry, the algebraic analysis of geometric shapes. This chapter uses coordinates to calculate distances, find halfway points, and analyse various shapes. The chapter also shows how to apply these skills to solve problems in design and construction.

Chapter Problem

A **fractal** is a geometric pattern that repeats infinitely with a smaller scale for each repetition. How can you use analytic geometry to create such patterns? How do fractals model natural processes?

Get Ready

Solving Equations

You can use opposite operations to isolate a variable in an equation.

1. Solve each equation.
   a) $3x + 2 = 14$
   b) $7y - 5 = 2y + 10$
   c) $\frac{1}{4}z = \frac{1}{3}z - 2$
   d) $\sqrt{t} = 0.5$

2. Convert each equation to the form $y = mx + b$.
   a) $x - y + 2 = 0$
   b) $3x + y - 5 = 0$
   c) $2x - 4y + 7 = 0$
   d) $\frac{1}{2}x - 3y + 5 = 0$

Slope of a Line

You can determine the slope, m, of a line from the coordinates of any two points, (x_1, y_1) and (x_2, y_2), on the line:

$$m = \frac{\text{rise}}{\text{run}}$$
$$= \frac{y_2 - y_1}{x_2 - x_1}$$

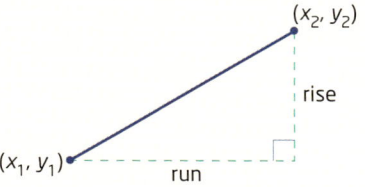

3. Find the slope of each line or line segment.

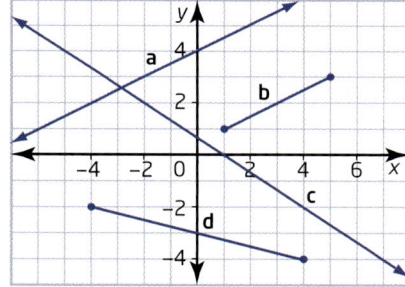

4. Find the slope of the line through each pair of points.
   a) $(4, 6)$ and $(12, 10)$
   b) $(-4, 6)$ and $(12, 2)$
   c) $(-5, -4)$ and $(3, -8)$
   d) $(2.5, 6.4)$ and $(9.8, 7.6)$

Equation for a Line

- If you know the slope and y-intercept of a line, substitute these values directly into $y = mx + b$ to get an equation for the line.

- If you know the slope and the coordinates of a point on the line, substitute into $y = mx + b$ and solve for the y-intercept, b.

- If you know the coordinates of two points on the line, use these coordinates to calculate the slope. Then, use the slope and the coordinates of either point to solve for the y-intercept, b.

5. Find an equation for the line that
   a) has slope -2 and y-intercept 4
   b) has slope $\dfrac{2}{7}$ and y-intercept -14
   c) has slope 4 and passes through $(6, 3)$
   d) has slope $-\dfrac{1}{2}$ and passes through $(-2, 4)$

6. Find an equation for the line that passes through each pair of points.
   a) A$(1, 1)$ and B$(5, 9)$
   b) C$(-1, 1)$ and D$(-3, -2)$
   c) E$(-4, 1)$ and F$(2, 4)$
   d) G$(5, -8)$ and H$(-1, 4)$

Parallel and Perpendicular Lines

- Parallel lines have equal slopes: $m_1 = m_2$.
- The slopes of perpendicular lines are negative reciprocals of each other: $m_2 = -\dfrac{1}{m_1}$.

7. Find the slope of a line with each property.
   a) parallel to the line defined by $y = 3x + 16$
   b) parallel to the line defined by $y = -\dfrac{1}{6}x + 5$
   c) perpendicular to the line defined by $y = -4x - 7$
   d) perpendicular to the line defined by $y = \dfrac{3}{4}x + 8$

8. Find an equation for the line that
   a) is parallel to the line defined by $y = -3x + 1$ and passes through A$(-3, 5)$
   b) is perpendicular to the line defined by $y = -\dfrac{3}{2}x - \dfrac{1}{2}$ and passes through B$(2, 3)$
   c) is parallel to the line defined by $y = -\dfrac{3}{4}x - \dfrac{1}{2}$ and passes through C$(-5, 1)$

Similar and Congruent Triangles

- Similar geometric figures have the same shape but may differ in size.
- Congruent geometric figures have exactly the same shape and size.

9. △ABC is similar to △EFD.
   a) Find the measure of ∠D.
   b) Find the length of side EF.

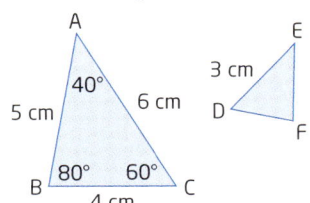

10. Use congruent triangles to show that any point on the **right bisector** of a line segment is the same distance from both endpoints.

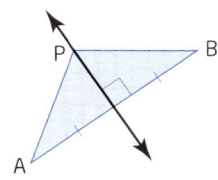

2.1 Midpoint of a Line Segment

Cartesian grid
- grid with perpendicular axes

Coordinates on a **Cartesian grid** are a simple and convenient way to specify a location. Such grids have many uses beyond graphs and maps. Machinists use coordinates to direct computer numerical control (CNC) machine tools that shape, drill, and weld parts. Similarly, coordinate systems are essential for programming industrial robots on automated assembly lines.

When you know the coordinates of a set of points, you can calculate the coordinates of related points, such as the **midpoint** between a pair of points.

midpoint
- point that divides a line segment into two equal line segments

Investigate

Tools
- grid paper

How can you determine the coordinates of a midpoint?

Method 1: Use Pencil and Paper

1. Use a Cartesian grid to plot the line segment defined by each pair of endpoints. Label the endpoints with their coordinates. What property do the line segments have in common?
   a) A(-4, 2) and B(6, 2)   b) C(-3, 0) and D(2, 0)
   c) E(5, -2) and F(-4, -2)

2. Count squares or use a ruler to determine the coordinates of the midpoint of each segment. Label each midpoint with its coordinates. How are the coordinates of the midpoint of each line segment related to the coordinates of its endpoints?

3. Plot and label the line segment defined by each pair of endpoints. What property do the line segments have in common?
   a) G(-4, 2) and H(-4, -6)   b) J(-1, 7) and K(-1, -2)
   c) L(5, -4) and N(5, 7)

4. Determine the coordinates of the midpoint of each line segment in step 3. Label each midpoint with its coordinates. How are the coordinates of the midpoint of each segment related to the coordinates of its endpoints?

5. Plot and label the line segment defined by each pair of endpoints.
   a) P(1, 1) and Q(7, 5)   **b)** R(−5, −4) and S(−1, 0)
   c) T(−3, −4) and U(6, 1)   **d)** V(−4, 6) and W(3, 4)

6. Determine the coordinates of the midpoint of each line segment in step 5. Describe how you calculated these coordinates.

7. Reflect How are the coordinates of the midpoint of a line segment related to the coordinates of the endpoints? Write an expression for the coordinates of the midpoint of a line segment that has endpoints at (x_1, y_1) and (x_2, y_2).

Method 2: Use *The Geometer's Sketchpad*®

Tools
- computer with *The Geometer's Sketchpad*®

1. Turn on automatic labelling of points. From the **Edit** menu, choose **Preferences**. Click on the **Text** tab. Ensure that **For All New Points** is checked.

To display a Cartesian grid, open the **Graph** menu and choose **Show Grid**.

From the **Edit** menu, choose **Preferences**; for distance, choose **cm** units and **hundredths** precision.

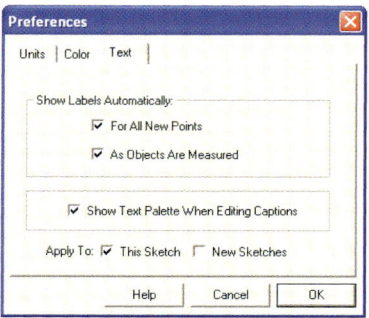
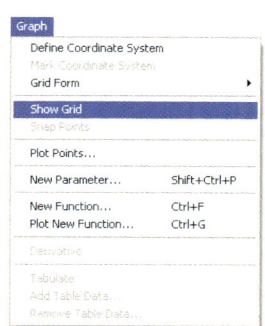
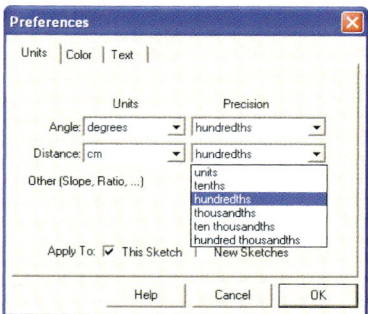

2. From the **Graph** menu, choose **Plot Points**. Enter the coordinates for the point A(−4, 2). Use the tab key to move from the *x*-coordinate to the *y*-coordinate. Then, plot the point B(6, 2). To display the coordinates of points A and B, select the points and choose **Coordinates** from the **Measure** menu.

3. Construct the line segment AB by selecting points A and B and then choosing **Segment** from the **Construct** menu. Predict the coordinates of the midpoint of this line segment.

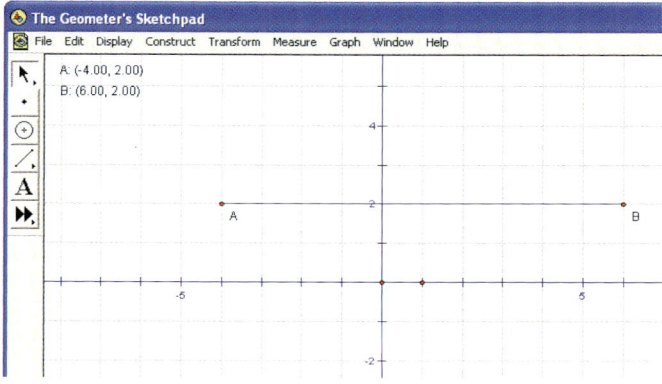

2.1 Midpoint of a Line Segment • MHR 57

4. Select line segment AB and choose **Midpoint** from the **Construct** menu. Then, select the midpoint and choose **Coordinates** from the **Measure** menu. Check whether the coordinates of the midpoint match your prediction.

5. Construct a line segment with endpoints D(-3, 0) and E(2, 0). Predict the coordinates of the midpoint of DE. Then, use *The Geometer's Sketchpad*® to determine these coordinates. Predict and then determine the coordinates of the midpoint of a line segment with endpoints G(5, -2) and H(-4, -2).

6. **Reflect** What property do line segments AB, DE, and GH have in common? How are the coordinates of their midpoints related to the coordinates of their endpoints?

7. Start a new sketch. Predict and then determine the coordinates of the midpoint of the line segment defined by each pair of endpoints.
   a) A(-4, 2) and B(-4, -6)   b) D(-1, 7) and E(-1, -2)
   c) G(5, -4) and H(5, 7)

8. **Reflect** What property do line segments AB, DE, and GH have in common? How are the coordinates of their midpoints related to the coordinates of their endpoints?

9. Start a new sketch. Predict and then determine the coordinates of the midpoint of the line segment defined by each pair of endpoints.
   a) A(1, 1) and B(7, 5)   b) D(-5, -4) and E(-1, 0)
   c) G(-3, -4) and H(6, 1)   d) J(-4, 6) and K(3, 4)

10. **Reflect** How are the coordinates of the midpoint of a line segment related to the coordinates of the endpoints? Write an expression for the coordinates of the midpoint of a line segment that has endpoints at (x_1, y_1) and (x_2, y_2).

Method 3: Use a Graphing Calculator

1. Press APPS, and choose **CabriJr**. Press ENTER when the title screen appears. If you need to clear the screen, press Y= to display the **F1** menu, and choose **New**.

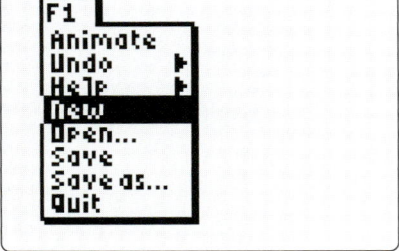

Tools
- TI-83 Plus or TI-84 Plus graphing calculator

Technology Tip
The position where **CabriJr** appears on the **APPS** screen depends on what other applications have been installed.

2. If the axes do not appear on the screen, press GRAPH to display the F5 menu. Highlight **Hide/Show**, press ▶, and choose **Axes**. Press ENTER and then CLEAR. Position the axes so that you can graph the points (−2, 2) and (6, 2). Move the cursor close to the axes. When the axes start flashing, press ALPHA. Then, use the cursor keys to move the axes to the desired position and press ALPHA again.

> **www** Go to
> www.mcgrawhill.ca/links/principles10 and follow the links to install or upgrade Cabri® Jr.

3. Press WINDOW to display the **F2** menu. Move the cursor up to **Point** if it is not already highlighted and press ENTER. Press GRAPH to display the **F5** menu, choose **Coord.&Eq.**, and press ENTER twice to show the coordinates of the plotted point. You can use the cursor keys to move the coordinates label. Press ENTER and then CLEAR. If the coordinates are not exactly (−2, 2), move the cursor to the point. When the point flashes, press ALPHA. Then, use the cursor keys to reposition the point and press ALPHA again.

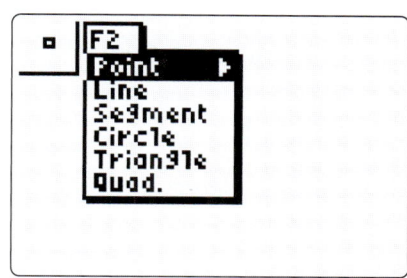

4. Plot and label a point at (6, 2). Press WINDOW to display the **F2** menu. Choose **Segment**, move the cursor to one of the points, and press ENTER. Move the cursor to the other point, press ENTER again, and press CLEAR. Predict the coordinates of the midpoint of the line segment joining the two points.

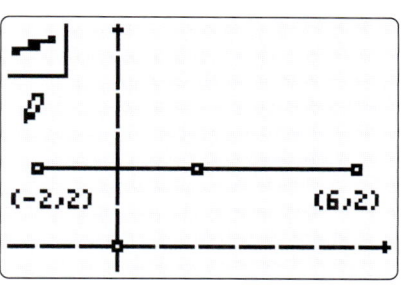

Technology Tip
Small gaps mark units along the axes.

5. Press ZOOM to display the **F3** menu. Choose **Midpoint** and press ENTER. Move the cursor to the line segment. When the line segment starts flashing, press ENTER again. Now, move the cursor to the midpoint of the segment. Press GRAPH to display the **F5** menu. Choose **Coord.&Eq.**, press ENTER twice, and press CLEAR. Check whether the coordinates of the midpoint match your prediction.

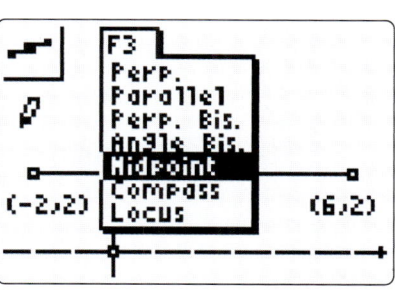

6. Construct a line segment with endpoints (−3, 0) and (2, 0). Predict the coordinates of the midpoint of this line segment. Then, use Cabri® Jr. to determine these coordinates. Predict and then determine the coordinates of the midpoint of a line segment with endpoints (5, −2) and (−2, −2).

7. **Reflect** What property do the three line segments on the screen have in common? How are the coordinates of their midpoints related to the coordinates of their endpoints?

8. To clear the screen, press `Y=` and choose **New**. Press `2nd` to highlight **NO**, and then press `ENTER`.

Technology Tip
You can also use the cursor keys to switch between options in a dialogue box.

9. Predict and then determine the coordinates of the midpoint of the line segment defined by each pair of endpoints.
    a) $(-4, 4)$ and $(-4, -2)$ b) $(-1, 3)$ and $(-1, -1)$
    c) $(5, -2)$ and $(5, 3)$

10. **Reflect** What property do the three line segments in step 9 have in common? How are the coordinates of their midpoints related to the coordinates of their endpoints?

11. Start a new graph. Predict and then determine the coordinates of the midpoint of the line segment defined by each pair of endpoints.
    a) $(-2, 2)$ and $(4, 4)$ b) $(1, 0)$ and $(5, 3)$
    c) $(-2, -1)$ and $(4, -2)$

12. **Reflect** How are the coordinates of the midpoint of a line segment related to the coordinates of the endpoints? Write an expression for the coordinates of the midpoint of a line segment that has endpoints at (x_1, y_1) and (x_2, y_2).

Example 1 Find a Midpoint

A city has two hospitals, shown on the city map at coordinates A(3, 5) and B(11, 14). The city wants to build a new ambulance station halfway between the two hospitals. Determine the coordinates of this location.

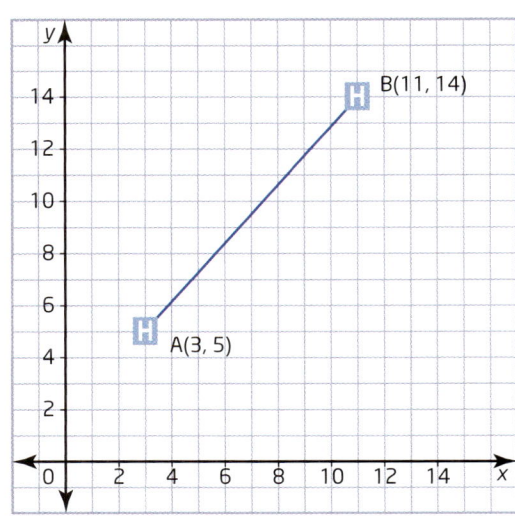

Solution

Method 1: Calculate the Rise and Run

The location of the new ambulance station is the midpoint of the line segment AB. The run between point A and the midpoint is half the run of AB. Similarly, the rise between point A and the midpoint is half the rise of AB.

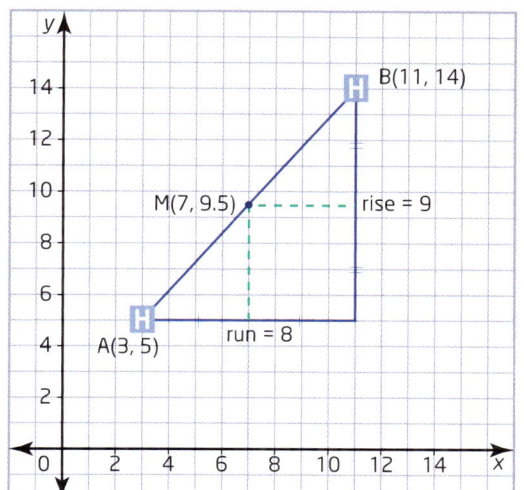

run $= x_2 - x_1$
$= 11 - 3$
$= 8$

rise $= y_2 - y_1$
$= 14 - 5$
$= 9$

Therefore, the coordinates of the midpoint are

$(x, y) = \left(x_1 + \dfrac{\text{run}}{2},\ y_1 + \dfrac{\text{rise}}{2} \right)$

$= \left(3 + \dfrac{8}{2},\ 5 + \dfrac{9}{2} \right)$

$= (3 + 4,\ 5 + 4.5)$

$= (7, 9.5)$

> I could use a similar method to divide a line segment into three or more equal parts.

> I can also subtract half the run and half the rise from the coordinates of the second point.

Method 2: Use a Formula

The *x*-coordinate of the midpoint is equal to the *x*-coordinate of point A plus half the difference between the *x*-coordinate of point B and the *x*-coordinate of point A. So, the *x*-coordinate of the midpoint is the mean of the *x*-coordinates of the endpoints of AB. Similarly, the *y*-coordinate of the midpoint is the mean of the *y*-coordinates of the endpoints.

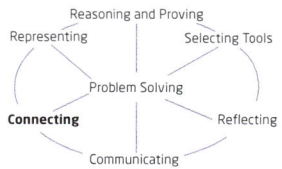

Therefore, the coordinates of the midpoint are

$(x, y) = \left(\dfrac{x_1 + x_2}{2}, \dfrac{y_1 + y_2}{2} \right)$

$= \left(\dfrac{3 + 11}{2}, \dfrac{5 + 14}{2} \right)$

$= \left(\dfrac{14}{2}, \dfrac{19}{2} \right)$

$= (7, 9.5)$

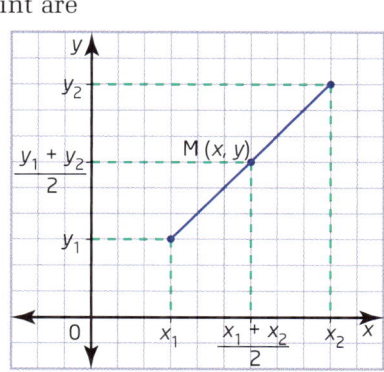

The coordinates of the new ambulance station are (7, 9.5).

2.1 Midpoint of a Line Segment • MHR 61

Example 2 Median of a Triangle

median
- line segment joining a vertex of a triangle to the midpoint of the opposite side

Determine an equation for the **median** from vertex C for the triangle with vertices C(5, 2), A(−3, 3), and B(2, −5).

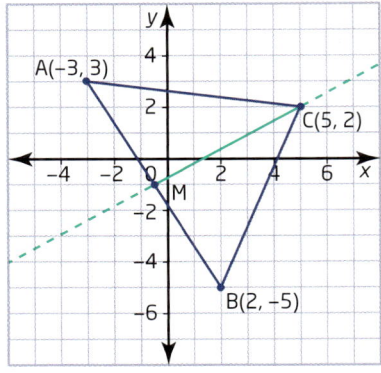

Solution

The median from C goes to the midpoint, M, of the opposite side, AB.

Use the formula from Example 1 to determine the coordinates of this midpoint.

$$(x, y) = \left(\frac{x_1 + x_2}{2}, \frac{y_1 + y_2}{2}\right)$$
$$= \left(\frac{-3 + 2}{2}, \frac{3 + (-5)}{2}\right)$$
$$= \left(\frac{-1}{2}, \frac{-2}{2}\right)$$
$$= \left(-\frac{1}{2}, -1\right)$$

Now, find the slope of CM.

$$\text{Slope, } m = \frac{\text{rise}}{\text{run}}$$
$$= \frac{y_2 - y_1}{x_2 - x_1}$$
$$= \frac{2 - (-1)}{5 - \left(-\frac{1}{2}\right)}$$
$$= \frac{3}{\frac{11}{2}}$$
$$= 3 \times \frac{2}{11}$$
$$= \frac{6}{11}$$

> If I extend the median on the graph, I can verify that its slope is $\frac{6}{11}$ by checking that the rise is 6 over a run of 11.

62 MHR • Chapter 2

Since the point C(5, 2) is on the median, $y = 2$ when $x = 5$. Use these coordinates and the slope to solve for the y-intercept, b.

$$y = mx + b$$
$$2 = \frac{6}{11}(5) + b$$
$$2 = \frac{30}{11} + b$$
$$\frac{22}{11} = \frac{30}{11} + b$$
$$\frac{22}{11} - \frac{30}{11} = b$$
$$\frac{-8}{11} = b$$

> I could use the coordinates of the midpoint, M, but the calculation with point A is easier since it has integer coordinates. I could use the coordinates of M to verify my answer.

> The median intersects the y-axis at $y = -\frac{8}{11}$.

The y-intercept of the median is $-\frac{8}{11}$.

Therefore, an equation for the median from vertex C is $y = \frac{6}{11}x - \frac{8}{11}$.

Example 3 Equation of a Right Bisector

Two schools are located at the points P(−1, 4) and Q(7, −2) on a town map. The school board is planning a new sports complex to be used by both schools. The board wants to find a location **equidistant** from the two schools. Use an equation to represent the possible locations for the sports complex.

equidistant
- equally distant

Solution

From the diagram, you can see that a point can be the same distance from both schools without being directly between them. In fact, any point on the **right bisector** of a line segment is equidistant from the endpoints of the segment. The possible locations for the athletic complex lie on the right bisector of PQ.

right bisector
- the line that passes through the midpoint of a line segment and intersects it at a 90° angle

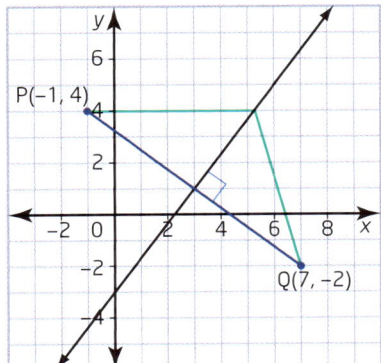

Literacy Connections

A *right bisector* is sometimes called a *perpendicular bisector*.

2.1 Midpoint of a Line Segment • MHR 63

To determine an equation for the right bisector, find the slope of the bisector and the coordinates of the midpoint of PQ. First, determine the slope of PQ.

$$m_{PQ} = \frac{y_2 - y_1}{x_2 - x_1}$$
$$= \frac{4 - (-2)}{-1 - 7}$$
$$= \frac{6}{-8}$$
$$= -\frac{3}{4}$$

Perpendicular lines have slopes that are the negative reciprocals of each other. So, the slope of any line perpendicular to PQ is

$$m_\perp = \frac{4}{3}$$

To find the negative reciprocal of a fraction, invert the fraction and use the opposite sign.

The right bisector passes through the midpoint of PQ. Use the midpoint formula to find the coordinates of the midpoint.

$$(x, y) = \left(\frac{x_1 + x_2}{2}, \frac{y_1 + y_2}{2}\right)$$
$$= \left(\frac{-1 + 7}{2}, \frac{4 + (-2)}{2}\right)$$
$$= \left(\frac{6}{2}, \frac{2}{2}\right)$$
$$= (3, 1)$$

Now, use the coordinates of the midpoint with the slope to solve for the y-intercept of the right bisector.

$$y = mx + b$$
$$1 = \frac{4}{3}(3) + b$$
$$1 = 4 + b$$
$$1 - 4 = b$$
$$-3 = b$$

I can use the graph to check that this value for the y-intercept is reasonable.

An equation for the right bisector of PQ is $y = \frac{4}{3}x - 3$. This equation represents the possible locations for the sports complex.

Key Concepts

- The midpoint of a line segment can be found by adding half of the run and half of the rise to the coordinates of the first endpoint.

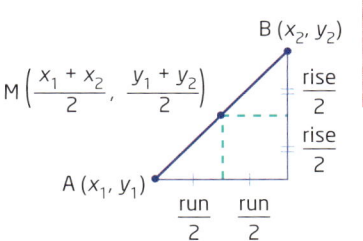

- Each coordinate of the midpoint of a line segment is the mean of the corresponding coordinates of the endpoints.

- The midpoint of a line segment with endpoints (x_1, y_1) and (x_2, y_2) has coordinates $\left(\dfrac{x_1 + x_2}{2}, \dfrac{y_1 + y_2}{2}\right)$.

- To find an equation for the median of a triangle, first find the coordinates of the midpoint of the side opposite the vertex. Use the coordinates of the midpoint and the vertex to calculate the slope of the median. Then, substitute the slope and the coordinates of either point into $y = mx + b$ to solve for the median's y-intercept.

- To find an equation for the right bisector of a line segment, first find the slope and midpoint of the segment. Use the line segment's slope to calculate the slope of a perpendicular line. Then, substitute this slope and the coordinates of the midpoint into $y = mx + b$ to solve for the right bisector's y-intercept.

Communicate Your Understanding

C1 Describe two methods for finding the midpoint of this line segment.

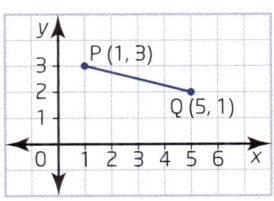

C2 Describe how to determine an equation for the median from vertex A of △ABC.

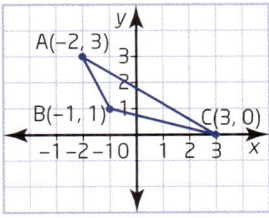

C3 Describe how to determine an equation for the right bisector of line segment PQ.

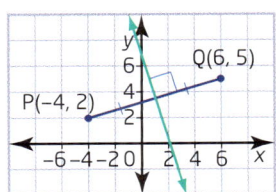

Practise

For help with questions 1 to 3, see Example 1.

1. Determine the coordinates of the midpoint of each line segment.

   a)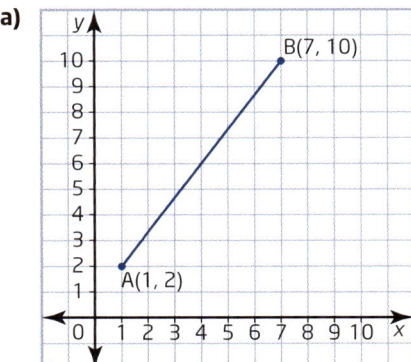

   b)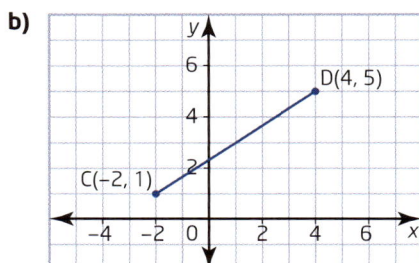

   c)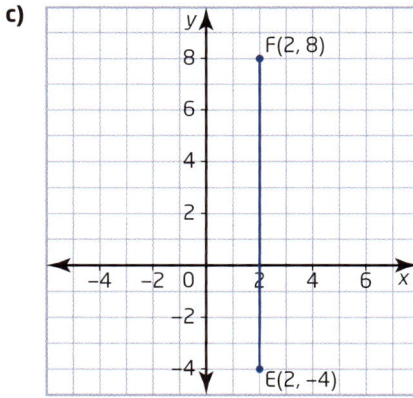

   d)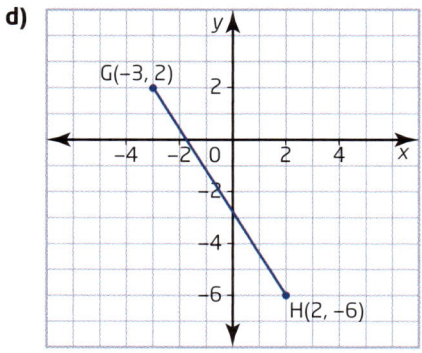

2. Determine the coordinates of the midpoint of the line segment defined by each pair of endpoints.
   a) J(5, 7) and K(3, 9)
   b) L(−1, 0) and M(1, −6)
   c) N(−2, −4) and P(−2, 8)
   d) Q(−3, −3) and R(−1, −7)

3. Determine the coordinates of the midpoint of the line segment defined by each pair of endpoints.
   a) J(0.2, 1.5) and K(3.6, 0.2)
   b) N(−1.4, −3.2) and P(0.6, −5.3)
   c) $L\left(\dfrac{1}{2}, \dfrac{5}{2}\right)$ and $M\left(\dfrac{3}{2}, -\dfrac{5}{2}\right)$
   d) $Q\left(-\dfrac{3}{8}, \dfrac{1}{8}\right)$ and $R\left(2, -\dfrac{7}{8}\right)$

For help with question 4, see Example 2.

4. Find the slope of each median shown.

   a)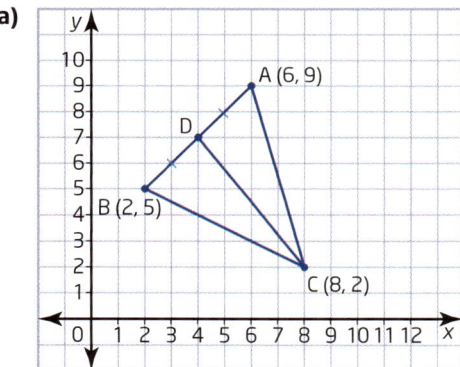

   b)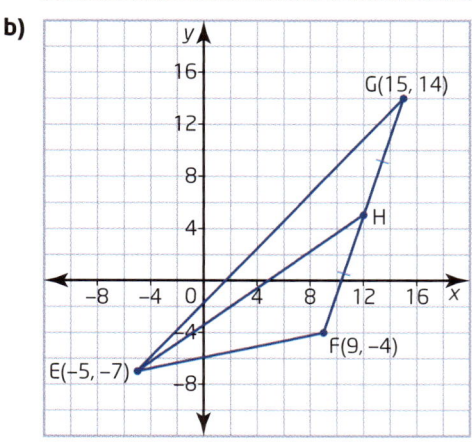

66 MHR • Chapter 2

Connect and Apply

5. A charity is organizing a fundraising run along a straight section of highway. On the grid of a roadmap, the starting point is at (23.6, 38.0) and the finish line is at (79.4, 43.8). The charity wants to set up a checkpoint table with water for the runners at the halfway point. Find the coordinates of this checkpoint.

6. The endpoints of the diameter of a circle are P(−7, −4) and Q(−1, 10). Find the coordinates of the centre of this circle.

7. **Use Technology** Use *The Geometer's Sketchpad*® or Cabri® Jr. to verify your answer to question 6. Describe the method you used.

8. The vertices of △ABC are A(4, 4), B(−6, 2), and C(2, 0). Find an equation in slope y-intercept form for the median from vertex A.

9. **Use Technology** Use *The Geometer's Sketchpad*® or Cabri® Jr. to verify your answer to question 8. Describe the method you used.

Technology Tip

You can use geometry software to display an equation for a line:
- With *The Geometer's Sketchpad*®, choose **Equation** from the **Measure** menu.
- With Cabri® Jr., choose **Coord.&Eq.** from the **F5** menu.

10. For the triangle with vertices P(−2, 0), Q(4, 6), and R(5, −3), find an equation for the median from
    a) vertex P   b) vertex Q

11. **Use Technology** Use geometry software to check your answer to question 10. Describe your method.

12. Write an expression for the coordinates of the midpoint of the line segment with endpoints P(a, b) and Q(3a, 2b). Explain your reasoning.

13. A line segment with one end at C(6, 5) has midpoint M(4, 2).
    a) Determine the coordinates of the other endpoint, D.
    b) Explain your solution.
    c) Describe a method you could use to check your answer to part a).

14. One endpoint of a diameter of a circle centred on the origin is (−3, 4). Find the coordinates of the other endpoint of this diameter.

15. One radius of a circle has endpoints D(2, 4) and E(−1, 2).
    a) Find a possible endpoint for the diameter that contains this radius.
    b) Explain why there are two possible answers in part a).

16. Determine an equation for the right bisector of the line segment with endpoints P(−5, −2) and Q(3, 6).

17. A telecommunications company wants to build a relay tower that is the same distance from two adjacent towns. On a local map, the towns have coordinates (2, 6) and (10, 0).
    a) Explain how you could use a right bisector to find possible locations for the tower.
    b) Find an equation for this bisector.

18. **Use Technology** Use *The Geometer's Sketchpad*® or Cabri® Jr. to verify your answer to question 17. Describe the method you used.

19. a) Draw △ABC with vertices A(−2, 0), B(8, 8), and C(4, −2).
    b) Draw the median from vertex A. Then, find an equation in slope y-intercept form for this median.
    c) Draw the right bisector of BC. Then, find an equation for this right bisector.
    d) Use your drawing to check your answers for parts b) and c).

20. a) Draw △PQR with vertices P(0, 0), Q(16, 0), and R(0, 16).

b) Construct the midpoints of PQ, QR, and PR, and label them S, T, and U, respectively.

c) Join the midpoints to form △STU. The length of a line segment joining the midpoints of two sides of a triangle is half the length of the third side. Use this property to show that △STU is congruent to all three of the other triangles inside △PQR.

d) Compare the area of △STU to the area of △PQR.

e) Shade △STU. Construct and label the midpoint of each side of the three other triangles inside △PQR. Join the midpoints to create a set of even smaller triangles.

f) Compare the area of one of these triangles to the area of △STU and to the area of △PQR.

21. Chapter Problem Question 20 uses a procedure developed by the Polish mathematician Waclaw Sierpinski in 1915. This procedure produces a fractal known as Sierpinski's triangle or Sierpinski's gasket.

a) Use a library or the Internet to learn more about Sierpinski's triangle.

b) Describe the procedure for producing this fractal. Does the procedure work with any shape of triangle? Explain.

c) Sketch the first four stages in shading a triangle using Sierpinski's method.

d) Explain why Sierpinski's triangle is a fractal.

 Go to www.mcgrawhill.ca/links/principles10 and follow the links to learn more about Sierpinski's triangle.

Extend

22. A is the midpoint of BC, D is the midpoint of AC, and E is the midpoint of AD. ED is 2 units in length. What is the length of BC?

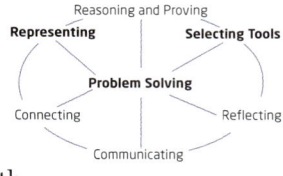

23. A line segment has endpoints A(2, 1) and B(11, 19).

a) Find the coordinates of the two points that divide the segment into three equal parts.

b) Describe the method that you used in part a).

24. In △ABC, P(0, 2) is the midpoint of side AB, Q(2, 4) is the midpoint of BC, and R(1, 0) is the midpoint of AC.

a) Find the coordinates of A, B, and C. (Hint: Use the properties of a line segment joining the midpoints of two sides of a triangle.)

b) Use the midpoint formula to check the coordinates you calculated in part a).

25. In three dimensions, the location of a point can be represented by the ordered triple (x, y, z).

a) Find the coordinates of the midpoint of the line segment with endpoints A(2, 3, 1) and B(6, 7, 5).

b) Write an expression for the coordinates of the midpoint of the line segment with endpoints (x_1, y_1, z_1) and (x_2, y_2, z_2).

26. Suppose that the relay tower in question 17 is to serve three towns instead of two. Describe how you could find a location that is equidistant from all three towns. Can there be more than one such location? Explain, using a diagram to support your answer.

27. Geographers and navigators use a spherical coordinate system with lines of latitude that are parallel to the equator and lines of longitude that are perpendicular to the lines of latitude and meet at Earth's poles.

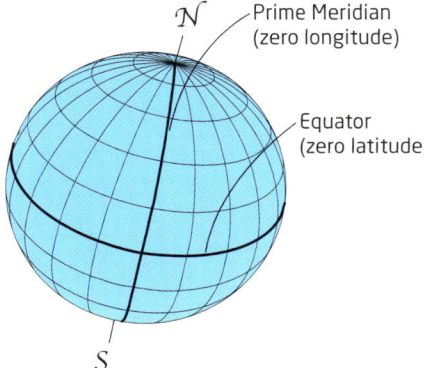

a) Explain why the formula for the midpoint of a line segment will not always give accurate results with the longitude-latitude coordinate system.

b) Search the Internet to find a Web site that calculates the distance between two points from their latitudes and longitudes. Use the site's calculator to show that the point at the mean of the latitudes and longitudes of two points is not actually equidistant from the two points.

 Go to www.mcgrawhill.ca/links/principles10 and follow the links to experiment with distance calculators.

28. Decide whether each statement is always true, sometimes true, or never true. Justify your answers.
a) Two line segments with the same midpoint have the same length.
b) Two parallel line segments have the same midpoint.
c) The midpoint of a line segment is the only point that divides it into two equal parts.
d) A point equidistant from the endpoints of a line segment is the midpoint of the line segment.

29. The endpoints of line segment PQ are P(3, −4) and Q(11, c). The midpoint of PQ is M(d, 3). Find the values of c and d.

30. Math Contest The number of arrangements of five letters from the word *magnetic* that end with a vowel is

A 360 **B** 420 **C** 840 **D** 2520 **E** 7560

31. Math Contest If $2^5 + 2^5 = 2^x$, the value of x is

A 3 **B** 5 **C** 6 **D** 8 **E** 10

Making Connections

The branch of mathematics known as analytic geometry started when French mathematician René Descartes (1596–1650) invented a system of numerical coordinates for describing locations on a rectangular grid. The Cartesian grid let mathematicians use algebra to analyse geometric shapes. Before Descartes, all geometric properties were proved using logical reasoning based on the work of the Greek mathematician Euclid (around 300 B.C.E.) and his followers. Analytic geometry is the basis of applications such as computer-aided design (CAD) and computer-generated imaging (CGI). These applications are widely used for engineering, architecture, medical tests, cartoon animation, and special effects in movies.

2.2 Length of a Line Segment

Most maps have a grid for locating places on the map. Maps that show a lot of detail usually have Cartesian grids with a scale that make it easy to estimate distances. For example, topographic maps commonly have grids where each side of a square represents 1 km. If you are planning a hiking or canoe trip, you can easily count squares to get a rough estimate of the length of possible routes. You can also use coordinates to calculate the exact distance between two points.

Investigate

How can you use coordinates to calculate distances?

Jan and Tara are planning a canoe trip in Georgian Bay. The dock where they will launch the canoe is at point A(2, 2) on their map. The campsite where they will stay the first night is at B(6, 5), and the campsite for the second night is at C(7, 1).

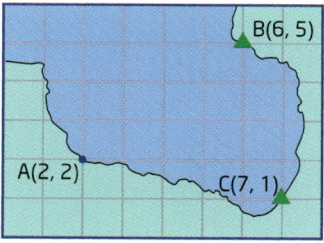

Tools
- grid paper

Method 1: Use Pencil and Paper

1. Plot points A and B on grid paper. Draw a line segment joining points A and B. What does this line segment represent?

2. Draw a right triangle below line segment AB to show its run and rise. How are the run and rise of AB related to the coordinates of its endpoints?

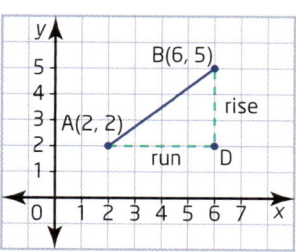

70 MHR • Chapter 2

3. Find the coordinates of the vertex of the right angle in the run-rise triangle. Label this vertex D. How are the coordinates of D related to the coordinates of points A and B?

4. Find the lengths of sides AD and BD. Then, use the Pythagorean theorem to determine the length of AB.

5. Each side of a grid square represents an actual distance of 4.0 km. How far will Jan and Tara have to paddle on the first day of their trip?

6. **Reflect** How is the length of line segment AB related to its run and rise? How is this length related to the coordinates of points A and B?

7. Calculate the distance from the campsite at B to the campsite at C. Do you have to change your method for calculating the length if the run or rise is negative? Explain.

8. Calculate the distance from the campsite at C back to the dock at A.

9. **Reflect** How is the length, d, of the line segment with endpoints (x_1, y_1) and (x_2, y_2) related to the run and rise of the segment? Write an equation showing how d is related to the coordinates of the endpoints.

Method 2: Use *The Geometer's Sketchpad*®

- computer with *The Geometer's Sketchpad*®

1. From the **Graph** menu, choose **Show Grid**. From the **Edit** menu, choose **Preferences**; for distance, choose **cm** units and **hundredths** precision. Check that automatic labelling of points is turned on.

2. From the **Graph** menu, choose **Plot Points**. Then, enter the coordinates for A(2, 2), B(6, 5), and C(7, 1). Display the coordinates by opening the **Measure** menu and choosing **Coordinates**. Construct line segment AB.

3. Construct a right triangle below line segment AB to show its run and rise. How are the run and rise of AB related to the coordinates of its endpoints?

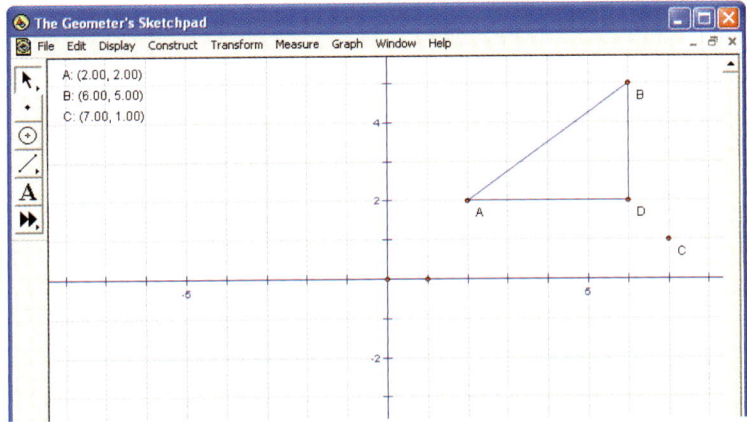

4. Display the coordinates of the vertex, D, of the right angle in the run-rise triangle. How are they related to the coordinates of points A and B?

5. Calculate the lengths of sides AD and BD. Then, use the Pythagorean theorem to determine the length of AB. Check your calculations by selecting the segments and choosing **Length** from the **Measure** menu.

6. Each side of a grid square represents an actual distance of 4.0 km. How far will Jan and Tara have to paddle on the first day of their trip?

7. **Reflect** How is the length of line segment AB related to its run and rise? How is this length related to the coordinates of points A and B?

8. Use the Pythagorean theorem to calculate the distance from the campsite at B to the campsite at C. Use the **Measure** menu to check your answer. Do you have to change your method for calculating the length if the run or rise is negative? Explain.

9. Calculate the distance from the campsite at C back to the dock at A. Use the **Measure** menu to check your answer.

10. **Reflect** How is the length, d, of the line segment with endpoints (x_1, y_1) and (x_2, y_2) related to the run and rise of the segment? Write an equation showing how d is related to the coordinates of the endpoints.

Method 3: Use a Graphing Calculator

Tools
- TI-83 Plus or TI-84 Plus graphing calculator

1. Press (APPS) and choose **CabriJr**. Press (ENTER) when the title screen appears. If you need to clear the screen, press (Y=) to display the **F1** menu and choose **New**.

2. Press (GRAPH) to display the **F5** menu. Choose **Hide/Show**, press (▶), and choose **Axes**. Press (ENTER) and then (CLEAR). Move the cursor close to the axes. When the axes start flashing, press (ALPHA). Then, use the cursor keys to move the axes to the lower left corner of the screen. Press (ALPHA) again.

3. Press (WINDOW) to display the **F2** menu. Choose **Point**. Use the cursor keys to move the pen cursor to (2, 2) and press (ENTER). Press (GRAPH) to display the **F5** menu, choose **Coord.&Eq.**, and press (ENTER) twice to show the coordinates of the plotted point. You can use the cursor keys to move the coordinates label. Press (ENTER) and then (CLEAR). If the coordinates are not exactly (2, 2), move the cursor to the point A. When the point flashes, press (ALPHA). Then, use the cursor keys to reposition the point and press (ALPHA) again.

4. To add a letter label to a point, choose **Alph-Num** from the **F5** menu. Move the cursor near the point. Press ENTER and then ALPHA followed by the key for the letter. Then, press ENTER to lock the label in place. To move the label, press CLEAR and move the cursor toward the letter until it starts flashing. Then, press ALPHA, use the cursor keys to move the label to the desired location, and press ENTER.

Technology Tip

When moving a label or geometric shape, you can press either ENTER or ALPHA to set the position.

5. Plot and label points B(6, 5) and C(7,1). Press WINDOW to display the **F2** menu. Choose **Segment**, move the cursor to A(2, 2), and press ENTER. Move the cursor to B(6, 5), press ENTER again, and then press CLEAR.

6. Use the **F2** menu to construct a point D and two line segments forming a right triangle that shows the run and rise of line segment AB. How are the run and rise of segment AB related to the coordinates of its endpoints? How are the coordinates of point D, the vertex of the right angle, related to the coordinates of points A and B?

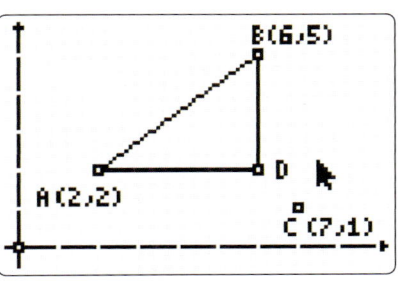

7. Find the lengths of sides AD and BD. Then, use the Pythagorean theorem to calculate the length of AB. To check this calculation, choose **Measure** from the **F5** menu and then choose **D.&Length**. Move the cursor toward segment AB until it flashes, and press ENTER. Use the cursor keys to position the measurement, if necessary; then, press ENTER again.

8. Each side of a grid square represents an actual distance of 4.0 km. How far will Jan and Tara have to paddle on the first day of their trip?

9. **Reflect** How is the length of line segment AB related to its run and rise? How is this length related to the coordinates of points A and B?

10. Use the Pythagorean theorem to calculate the distance from the campsite at B to the campsite at C. Measure the length as described above to check your answer. Do you have to change your method for calculating the length if the run or rise is negative? Explain.

11. Calculate the distance from the campsite at C back to the dock at A. Measure the length to check your answer.

12. **Reflect** How is the length, d, of the line segment with endpoints (x_1, y_1) and (x_2, y_2) related to the run and rise of the segment? Write an equation showing how d is related to the coordinates of the endpoints.

Example 1 Calculate a Length

Literacy Connections

A cam is a rotating mechanical part shaped to guide the motion of another part of a machine. Usually, the controlled part connects to the side of the cam or runs against its edge.

To make round parts, programmable machine tools often use a coordinate system with the origin at the centre of the part. How far apart are the centres of the mounting holes A and B in this cam? The coordinates are in centimetres. Round your answer to the nearest tenth.

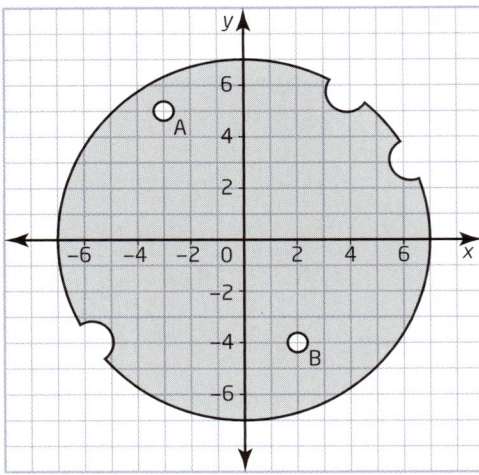

Solution

Applying the Pythagorean theorem gives $AB^2 = run^2 + rise^2$. The run of AB is equal to the difference between the x-coordinate of B and the x-coordinate of A. Similarly, the rise of AB is equal to the difference between the corresponding y-coordinates. Therefore,

$$\begin{aligned} AB &= \sqrt{(x_2 - x_1)^2 + (y_2 - y_1)^2} \\ &= \sqrt{(-3 - 2)^2 + [5 - (-4)]^2} \\ &= \sqrt{(-5)^2 + 9^2} \\ &= \sqrt{25 + 81} \\ &= \sqrt{106} \\ &\doteq 10.3 \end{aligned}$$

The centres of the mounting holes are about 10.3 cm apart.

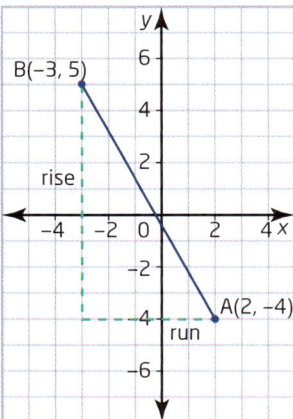

Example 2 Compare Distances

An air ambulance service uses a grid system to help estimate flying times and fuel requirements. Coordinates on this grid are distances in kilometres east and north of a reference point on the lower left corner of a map of northern Ontario. A helicopter ambulance picks up a patient at point P(96, 197). The nearest hospitals that can provide the treatment the patient needs are in Timmins at T(200, 296) and Sudbury at S(232, 80).

a) To which hospital should the helicopter take the patient?

b) List any assumptions you made for your answer.

Solution

a) First, find the distance to each hospital.

For the Timmins hospital:

$$PT = \sqrt{(x_2 - x_1)^2 + (y_2 - y_1)^2}$$
$$= \sqrt{(200 - 96)^2 + (296 - 197)^2}$$
$$= \sqrt{104^2 + 99^2}$$
$$= \sqrt{20\,617}$$
$$\doteq 144$$

For the Sudbury hospital:

$$PS = \sqrt{(x_2 - x_1)^2 + (y_2 - y_1)^2}$$
$$= \sqrt{(232 - 96)^2 + (80 - 197)^2}$$
$$= \sqrt{136^2 + (-117)^2}$$
$$= \sqrt{32\,185}$$
$$\doteq 179$$

The helicopter should go to the Timmins hospital because it is closer to the pick-up point.

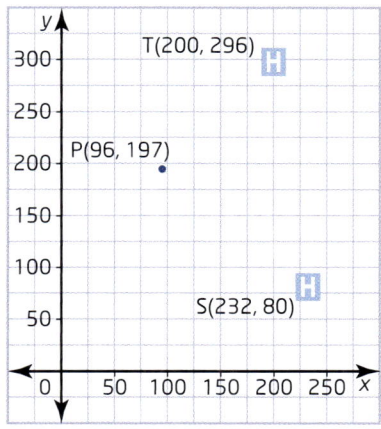

b) The decision to go to the closer hospital assumes that the helicopter can travel in a straight line to either hospital. The decision also assumes that weather will not affect the flying times or prevent a landing at the closer hospital.

Example 3 Find the Length of a Median

Find the length of the median from P for a triangle with vertices P(−2, −2), Q(7, −1), and R(1, 5).

Solution

The median is the line segment that joins P to the midpoint, M, of QR. To find the coordinates of M, substitute the coordinates of Q and R into the midpoint formula.

$$(x, y) = \left(\frac{x_1 + x_2}{2}, \frac{y_1 + y_2}{2}\right)$$
$$= \left(\frac{7 + 1}{2}, \frac{-1 + 5}{2}\right)$$
$$= \left(\frac{8}{2}, \frac{4}{2}\right)$$
$$= (4, 2)$$

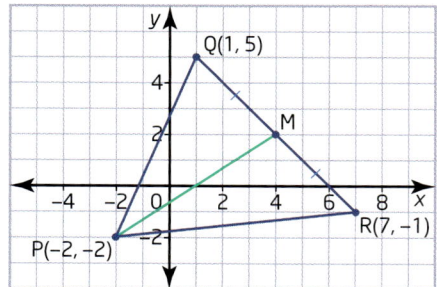

Now, substitute the coordinates of P(−2, −2) and M(4, 2) into the length formula.

$$PQ = \sqrt{(x_2 - x_1)^2 + (y_2 - y_1)^2}$$
$$= \sqrt{[4 - (-2)]^2 + [2 - (-2)]^2}$$
$$= \sqrt{6^2 + 4^2}$$
$$= \sqrt{36 + 16}$$
$$= \sqrt{52}$$

The length of the median from vertex P is $\sqrt{52}$.

Key Concepts

- You can calculate the length, d, of a line segment using its run and rise:
$$d = \sqrt{(\text{run})^2 + (\text{rise})^2}$$

- You can also determine the length of a line segment directly from the coordinates of its endpoints, (x_1, y_1) and (x_2, y_2):
$$d = \sqrt{(x_2 - x_1)^2 + (y_2 - y_1)^2}$$

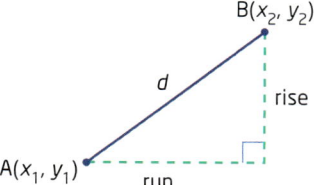

Communicate Your Understanding

C1 Describe how you can find the length of the line segment joining the points A(0, 1) and B(4, 3).

C2 When you use the formula for the length of a line segment, does it matter which point is represented by (x_1, y_1) and which point is represented by (x_2, y_2)? Use an example to explain your reasoning.

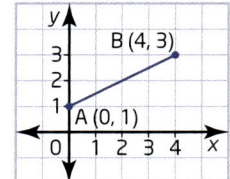

C3 Explain why the expression $(x_2 - x_1)^2 + (y_2 - y_1)^2$ never has a negative value.

Practise

For help with questions 1 to 3, see Examples 1 to 3.

1. Estimate the length of each line segment from its graph. Then, calculate the exact length.

    a)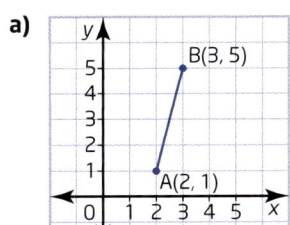

    b)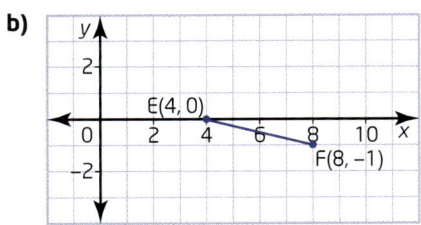

    c)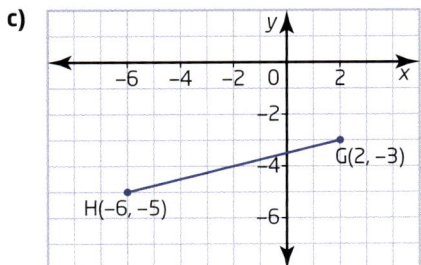

2. Calculate the length of the line segment defined by each pair of endpoints.

    a) A(−6, −2) and B(4, 3)
    b) C(−2, 0) and D(7, −3)
    c) E(−5, −6) and F(−1, −2)
    d) G(0, 5) and H(8, −1)

3. Calculate the length of the line segment defined by each pair of endpoints.

    a) J(2.1, 8.3) and K(−4.5, −4.7)
    b) L(−4.2, −5.1) and M(11.6, 9.2)
    c) $N\left(\dfrac{1}{2}, \dfrac{5}{2}\right)$ and $P\left(\dfrac{3}{2}, -\dfrac{5}{2}\right)$

Connect and Apply

4. On a city map, the coordinates of two department stores are (4, 3) and (1, 7). How far apart are the stores if each unit on the map represents 1 km?

5. On a street map of his town, Jordan's house has coordinates (8, 1). The town's two high schools are at (0, 5) and (6, 11).

    a) Which school is closer to Jordan's house?
    b) Describe a method you could use to check your answer to part a).

6. The vertices of △ABC are A(2, 5), B(−6, −1), and C(10, −1).

    a) Determine the length of each side of this triangle.
    b) Determine the perimeter of the triangle.
    c) Classify the triangle.

7. a) Show that the triangle with vertices D(−1, 0), E(1, 0), and F(0, $\sqrt{3}$) is equilateral.

    b) List the coordinates of the vertices of another equilateral triangle.

2.2 Length of a Line Segment • MHR 77

8. Determine the length of the median from vertex J in the triangle with vertices J(−2, −2), K(−3, 2), and L(1, 3).

9. **Use Technology** Use *The Geometer's Sketchpad*® or Cabri® Jr. to verify your answer to question 8.

10. Determine the area of the right triangle with vertices R(4, 4), S(−2, −2), and T(10, −2).

11. **Use Technology** Use *The Geometer's Sketchpad*® or Cabri® Jr. to verify your answer to question 10.

12. Use the length formula to verify that C(−5, −1) is the midpoint of the line segment joining A(−2, 5) and B(−8, −7).

13. A line segment has endpoints K(−2, 7) and L(4, −2).
    a) Find the coordinates of the midpoint of this line segment.
    b) Use the length formula to verify your answer to part a).

14. An architect's drawing shows a pipe running diagonally under a basement floor from a floor drain to a sewer connection. The floor drain is at a point 2 m east and 2 m north of the southwest corner of the basement. The sewer connection is 10 m east and 17 m north of the corner. The pipe costs $3.15 per metre, including taxes. How much should the builder budget for pipe for the floor drain?

15. a) Draw a triangle with vertices P(−3, −4), Q(5, 1), and R(2, 7).
    b) Determine the coordinates of the midpoints of PQ and PR. Label these midpoints S and T.
    c) Show that ST is half the length of QR.
    d) Show that ST is parallel to QR.
    e) Show that the triangle formed by joining the midpoints of the sides of △PQR is similar to △PQR.

16. **Use Technology** Use *The Geometer's Sketchpad*® or Cabri® Jr. to verify your answer to question 15.

17. The charges for most long-distance telephone calls used to be based on the distance between the two stations and the duration of the call. To determine the distance, telephone companies used a rectangular coordinate grid with its origin located off the northeast coast of Canada. The coordinates in this system indicate the horizontal and vertical distance from the grid's origin. This table lists the telephone coordinates, converted to kilometres, for four cities.

City	Coordinates
Edmonton	(3978, 2520)
Montréal	(1015, 2104)
Ottawa	(1142, 2232)
Toronto	(1268, 2540)

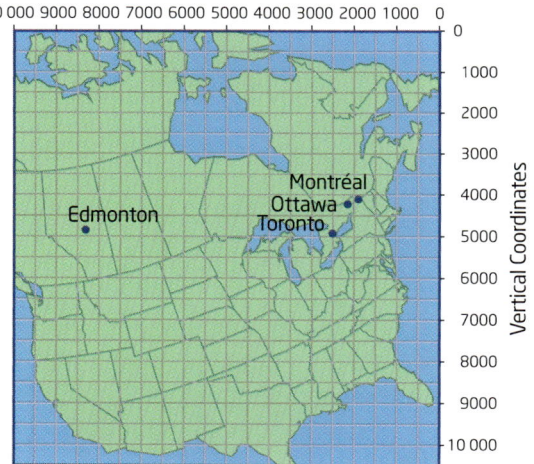

a) Calculate the distance, to the nearest kilometre, between Edmonton and Ottawa, between Montréal and Toronto, and between Edmonton and Toronto.

b) Research the flying distances between these cities. How accurate is the telephone coordinate system?

18. Chapter Problem Here are the first three stages of a Koch snowflake, named after the Swedish mathematician Niels Fabian Helge von Koch (1870–1924). This snowflake starts with an equilateral triangle. At each stage, the middle third of each side is replaced by two segments, each equal in length to the segment they replace.

a) Find the coordinates of the three new vertices on the bottom of the snowflake in the second stage.

b) Are Koch snowflakes fractals? Explain.

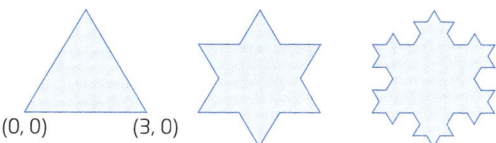
(0, 0)   (3, 0)

 Go to www.mcgrawhill.ca/links/principles10 and follow the links to learn more about Koch snowflakes.

Achievement Check

19. Lightning starts a forest fire at a point with map coordinates F(23, 25). The nearest towns have coordinates A(15, 19) and B(23, 17).

a) Which town is at greater risk from the fire?

b) Describe any assumptions you made for your answer to part a).

c) At a campground midway between the two towns, a camper learns about the fire from a newscast. The camper estimates that he is about 9 km from the fire. Is the camper correct? Justify your response.

Extend

20. The point A(x, 1) is 5 units from the point (2, 6).

a) Find a possible value for x.

b) Is this value the only solution? Explain.

21. a) On a grid, draw line segments with the lengths listed below. Describe your method. How do you know that each line segment is the correct length?

i) $\sqrt{2}$ **ii)** $\sqrt{5}$ **iii)** $\sqrt{13}$ **iv)** $\sqrt{41}$

b) Compare the line segments you drew to those drawn by a classmate. Verify that both sets of line segments have the correct lengths.

22. List the points that satisfy each condition and have integer coordinates.

a) 5 units from the origin

b) 5 units from the point (2, 1)

c) 10 units from the point (-5, -2)

23. Sally has hidden her brother's birthday present somewhere in the backyard. When writing instructions for finding the present, she used a coordinate system with each unit on the grid representing 1 m. The positive y-axis of this grid points north. The instructions read "Start at the origin, walk halfway to (8, 6), turn 90° left, and then walk twice as far." Where is the present? How far is it from the origin?

24. Math Contest The number of arrangements of five letters from the word *magnetic* that contain the word *net* is

A 60   **B** 100   **C** 360   **D** 630   **E** 720

25. Math Contest Show that the area of the larger semicircle is equal to the sum of the areas of the two smaller semicircles.

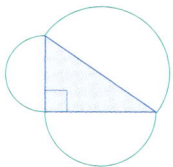

2.3 Apply Slope, Midpoint, and Length Formulas

Ideally, the route of a power line should be as short as possible. A shorter route reduces the construction cost as well as the energy losses due to the resistance of the wire. Engineers use analytic geometry to find the best route for the transmission lines that deliver electricity throughout the province. Analytic geometry is also a powerful tool for designing roads, buildings, pipelines, industrial machinery, and consumer products.

This section shows how to apply geometry and algebra to a variety of problems. Many of these problems involve several steps that require different skills. Developing a problem solving process is particularly important for dealing with such problems. These four steps can help you:

   1. Understand the problem.
   2. Choose a strategy.
   3. Carry out the strategy.
   4. Reflect.

Investigate

How can you construct the shortest line segment from a point to a line?

Method 1: Use Pencil and Paper

   1. Draw a line and any point P not on the line.

   2. Describe how you could draw a line segment from the point to the line so that the line segment is as short as possible.

Tools
- grid paper
- protractor or compasses

3. Draw a line segment from P to meet the line at a right angle. Label the vertex of the right angle Q. Choose any other point on the line and label it R.

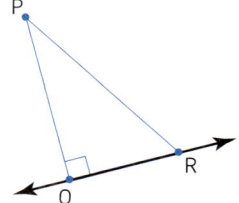

4. How are the lengths of PQ, QR, and PR related? Explain why the line segment PQ must be shorter than a line segment joining P to any other point on the line.

5. **Reflect** What property does the shortest line segment from a point to a line have?

Method 2: Use *The Geometer's Sketchpad*®

Tools
- computer with *The Geometer's Sketchpad*®

1. Plot two points, A and B, and construct the line through them. Plot a point C that is not on the line.

2. Describe how you could draw a line segment from point C to the line so that the segment is as short as possible.

3. Construct a point D anywhere on the line through points A and B. Then, construct the line segment CD.

4. With segment CD selected, choose **Length** from the **Measure** menu.

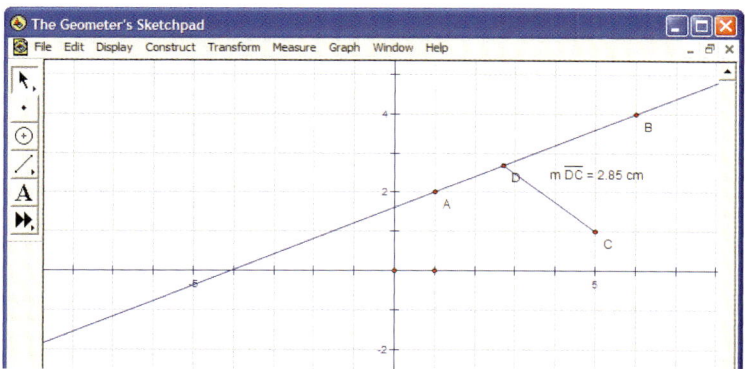

5. Slide the point D along the line until the distance is as small as possible. Estimate the measure of ∠ADC.

6. Measure ∠ADC. Was your estimate accurate?

7. **Reflect** What property does the shortest line segment from a point to a line have?

2.3 Apply Slope, Midpoint, and Length Formulas • MHR 81

Tools

- TI-83 Plus or TI-84 Plus graphing calculator

Method 3: Use a Graphing Calculator

1. Start the Cabri® Jr. application. Clear the screen, if necessary.

2. To construct a line, choose **Line** from the **F2** menu. Move the cursor to any convenient point A and press ENTER. Move the cursor to a second point, B. Press ENTER and then CLEAR.

3. From the **F2** menu, choose **Segment**. Move the cursor to a point C well away from the line, and press ENTER. Move the cursor to any point D on the line. Press ENTER and then CLEAR.

4. Highlight **Measure** on the **F5** menu, press ▶, and choose **D.&Length** from the sub-menu. Move the cursor until segment CD flashes, and press ENTER and then CLEAR. Press ALPHA, move the measurement to a corner of the screen, and press ALPHA again.

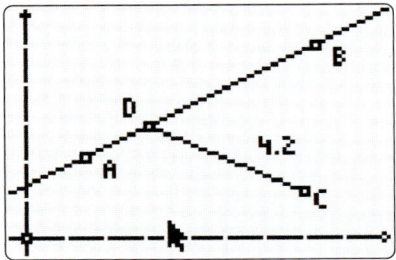

5. Move the cursor back to point D. Press ALPHA and use the cursor keys to slide point D along AB. Find the location that gives the shortest length for CD. To increase the precision displayed, move the cursor to the measurement and press +.

6. Estimate the measure of ∠ADC. To check your estimate, highlight **Measure** on the **F5** menu, press ▶, and choose **Angle**. Move the cursor toward point A until it flashes; then, press ENTER. Select point D and point C in the same way. Move the angle measurement to a convenient position and press ENTER. Was your estimate accurate?

7. **Reflect** What property does the shortest line segment from a point to a line have?

Example 1 Find the Shortest Route

A ranger cabin is to be built in a flat wooded area near the straight road that connects the two campgrounds in a park. A new side road will connect the cabin to the campground road. On the park map, the campgrounds have coordinates A(2.0, 8.5) and B(10.0, 4.5), while the site for the cabin is at R(6.0, 1.5). Each unit on the map grid represents 500 m.

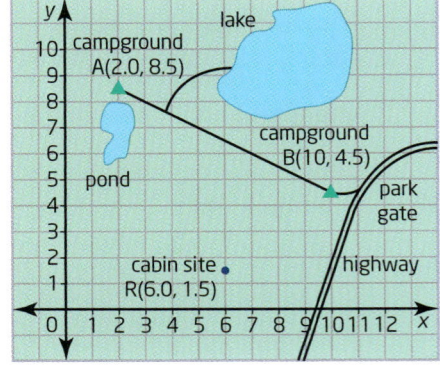

82 MHR • Chapter 2

a) Find the route that minimizes the cost and the number of trees that have to be cut down for the side road. Draw a diagram of this route.

b) Find the length of the side road, to the nearest tenth of a kilometre.

Solution

Since the area is level, the shortest route for the side road is the cheapest and easiest to build. The shortest route from the ranger cabin to the campground road is perpendicular to that road. To describe the route of the side road and to calculate its length, find the point where a perpendicular from R meets the line segment AB.

Understand the Problem

Use the coordinates of points A and B to calculate the slope of AB and find an equation for the line through A and B.

Choose a Strategy

The slope of the side road is the negative reciprocal of the slope of AB. Use this slope to determine an equation for the perpendicular line that passes through point R.

Use the equations for the two lines to find the point of intersection, D. Calculate the length of line segment RD from the coordinates of its endpoints. Then, use the map scale to find the length of the side road.

a) Calculate the slope of AB using the coordinates of the campgrounds, A(2.0, 8.5) and B(10.0, 4.5).

$$m = \frac{y_2 - y_1}{x_2 - x_1}$$
$$= \frac{4.5 - 8.5}{10.0 - 2.0}$$
$$= \frac{-4.0}{8.0}$$
$$= -0.5$$

Carry Out the Strategy

Since the slope of AB is -0.5, the slope of any line perpendicular to AB is $-\frac{1}{-0.5}$, or 2.

Perpendicular lines have slopes that are negative reciprocals of each other.

Now, find equations for AB and RD by substituting the slope and the coordinates of a point into $y = mx + b$.

For AB, use A(2.0, 8.5):
$y = mx + b$
$8.5 = -0.5(2.0) + b$
$8.5 = -1.0 + b$
$9.5 = b$

For RD, use R(6.0, 1.5):
$y = mx + b$
$1.5 = 2(6.0) + b$
$1.5 = 12.0 + b$
$-10.5 = b$

I can use the coordinates of point B to check the equation for AB.

An equation for AB is $y = -0.5x + 9.5$ and an equation for RD is $y = 2x - 10.5$.

Use the substitution method to find the point of intersection of AB and RD. At the point of intersection, the y-coordinates of the two lines are equal, so

$$-0.5x + 9.5 = 2x - 10.5$$
$$9.5 + 10.5 = 2x + 0.5x$$
$$20.0 = 2.5x$$
$$\frac{20.0}{2.5} = x$$
$$8.0 = x$$

Substitute $x = 8.0$ into the equation for either line to find the y-coordinate of the point of intersection.

$y = -0.5x + 9.5$	$y = 2x - 10.5$
$= -0.5(8.0) + 9.5$	$= 2(8.0) - 10.5$
$= -4.0 + 9.5$	$= 16.0 - 10.5$
$= 5.5$	$= 5.5$

The second equation shows that my calculation for the y-coordinate is correct.

The point of intersection of the two roads is D(8.0, 5.5). The best route for the side road to the ranger cabin is represented by the line segment joining (6.0, 1.5) to (8.0, 5.5).

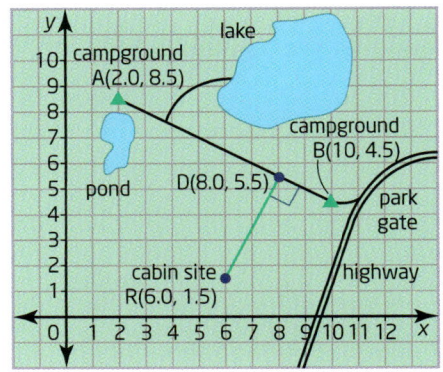

b) To calculate the length of line segment RD, substitute the coordinates of its endpoints into the length formula.

$$RD = \sqrt{(x_2 - x_1)^2 + (y_2 - y_1)^2}$$
$$= \sqrt{(8.0 - 6.0)^2 + (5.5 - 1.5)^2}$$
$$= \sqrt{2.0^2 + 4.0^2}$$
$$= \sqrt{4.0 + 16}$$
$$= \sqrt{20}$$
$$\doteq 4.5$$

I can use the graph to check that my answers are reasonable. It is hard to determine the exact coordinates or length from the graph.

Each unit on the map represents 500 m, so 4.5 units represents 4.5 × 500 m, or 2250 m.

The side road is 2.3 km long.

 **Reflect**

Algebraic methods are particularly useful for situations that involve non-integer coordinates or lengths.

Example 2 Determine a Geometric Property Algebraically

The vertices of △ABC are A(5, 5), B(−3, −1), and C(1, −3). Determine whether △ABC is a right triangle.

Solution

Draw a diagram to help visualize the problem.

Understand the Problem

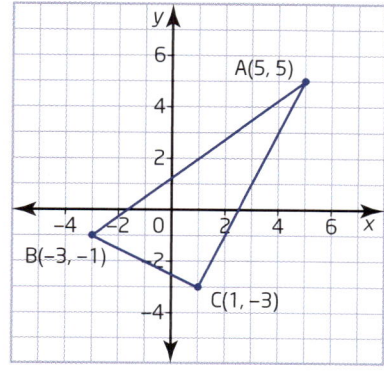

If △ABC is a right triangle, two of its sides are perpendicular to each other. Also, the Pythagorean theorem applies.

Choose a Strategy

Determine the slopes of the three sides of the triangle. Then, check if the product of any two of these slopes is −1.

Alternatively, calculate the lengths of all three sides, and check if the lengths satisfy the Pythagorean relation.

Method 1: Use Slopes

Carry Out the Strategy

Calculate the slope of each side of △ABC.

$$m_{AB} = \frac{y_2 - y_1}{x_2 - x_1}$$
$$= \frac{-1 - 5}{-3 - 5}$$
$$= \frac{-6}{-8}$$
$$= \frac{3}{4}$$

$$m_{BC} = \frac{y_2 - y_1}{x_2 - x_1}$$
$$= \frac{-3 - (-1)}{1 - (-3)}$$
$$= \frac{-3 + 1}{1 + 3}$$
$$= \frac{-2}{4}$$
$$= -\frac{1}{2}$$

$$m_{AC} = \frac{y_2 - y_1}{x_2 - x_1}$$
$$= \frac{-3 - 5}{1 - 5}$$
$$= \frac{-8}{-4}$$
$$= 2$$

Since $m_{AC} \times m_{BC} = -1$, ∠ACB is a right angle. Therefore, △ABC is a right triangle.

Method 2: Use the Pythagorean Theorem

Find the length of each side of △ABC by substituting the coordinates of the vertices into the length formula.

$$AB = \sqrt{(x_2 - x_1)^2 + (y_2 - y_1)^2}$$
$$= \sqrt{(-3 - 5)^2 + (-1 - 5)^2}$$
$$= \sqrt{(-8)^2 + (-6)^2}$$
$$= \sqrt{64 + 36}$$
$$= \sqrt{100}$$
$$= 10$$

$$BC = \sqrt{(x_2 - x_1)^2 + (y_2 - y_1)^2}$$
$$= \sqrt{[1 - (-3)]^2 + [-3 - (-1)]^2}$$
$$= \sqrt{(4)^2 + (-2)^2}$$
$$= \sqrt{16 + 4}$$
$$= \sqrt{20}$$

$$AC = \sqrt{(x_2 - x_1)^2 + (y_2 - y_1)^2}$$
$$= \sqrt{(1 - 5)^2 + (-3 - 5)^2}$$
$$= \sqrt{(-4)^2 + (-8)^2}$$
$$= \sqrt{16 + 64}$$
$$= \sqrt{80}$$

Check whether the square of the longest side equals the sum of the squares of the two shorter sides:

$$AB^2 = 10^2 \qquad AC^2 = \left(\sqrt{80}\right)^2 \qquad BC^2 = \left(\sqrt{20}\right)^2$$
$$= 100 \qquad\quad\; = 80 \qquad\qquad\; = 20$$

$$AC^2 + BC^2 = 80 + 20$$
$$= 100$$
$$= AB^2$$

> Squaring and taking the square root are opposite operations, so $\left(\sqrt{x}\right)^2 = x$.

Since the Pythagorean relationship applies, △ABC is a right triangle.

Reflect

There is often more than one way to solve a problem using analytic geometry.

Example 3 Median to a Hypotenuse

Show that the median from the right angle of the triangle in Example 2 is half as long as the hypotenuse.

Solution

Understand the Problem

You need to know the length of the hypotenuse and the length of the median from the right angle to the hypotenuse.

- A median joins a vertex of a triangle to the midpoint of the opposite side.
- From Example 2, you know that C is the vertex of the right angle and AB is the hypotenuse.
- Determine the coordinates of the midpoint of AB.
- Use these coordinates with the coordinates of vertex C to find the length of the median.
- Compare this length to the length of AB calculated in Example 2.

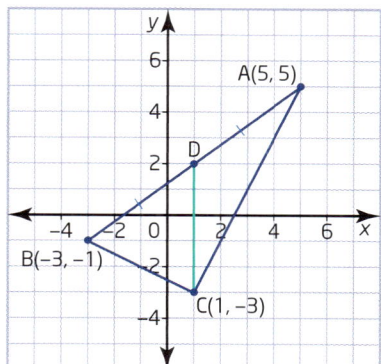

Carry Out the Strategy

Let point D be the midpoint of AB. Use the coordinates of vertices A and B to find the coordinates of D.

$$(x, y) = \left(\frac{x_1 + x_2}{2}, \frac{y_1 + y_2}{2}\right)$$
$$= \left(\frac{5 + (-3)}{2}, \frac{5 + (-1)}{2}\right)$$
$$= \left(\frac{2}{2}, \frac{4}{2}\right)$$
$$= (1, 2)$$

The endpoints of the median from vertex C are C(1, −3) and D(1, 2). Substitute these coordinates into the length formula.

$$CD = \sqrt{(x_2 - x_1)^2 + (y_2 - y_1)^2}$$
$$= \sqrt{(1 - 1)^2 + [2 - (-3)]^2}$$
$$= \sqrt{0^2 + 5^2}$$
$$= \sqrt{25}$$
$$= 5$$

Since CD is vertical, I can also find its length from the difference of the y-coordinates of points C and D.

As shown in Example 2, substituting the coordinates A(5, 5) and B(−3, −1) into the length formula gives AB = 10. Since $CD = \frac{AB}{2}$, the median from the right angle is half as long as the hypotenuse.

You could also use congruent triangles or geometry software to show the relationship between the length of the median and the length of the hypotenuse.

Reflect

Key Concepts

- You can use analytic geometry to determine properties of geometric shapes.
- These steps are helpful for solving multi-step problems:
  - Understand the Problem
  - Choose a Strategy
  - Carry Out the Strategy
  - Reflect
- A graph can be helpful for understanding a problem and for checking whether answers are reasonable.
- You can often use different methods to solve the same problem. Solving a problem in two different ways lets you check your calculations.

Communicate Your Understanding

C1 Describe how you would find an equation for the right bisector of line segment AB.

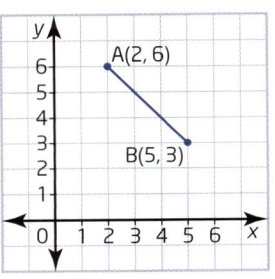

C2 Outline an algebraic method for showing that △CDE is an isosceles right triangle.

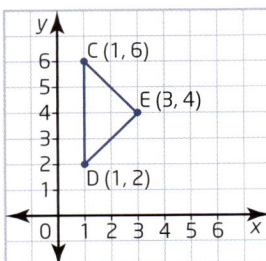

C3 Outline an algebraic method for finding the length of the **altitude** from vertex F of △FGH.

C4 Describe how you would find the coordinates of the point where the medians of △FGH intersect.

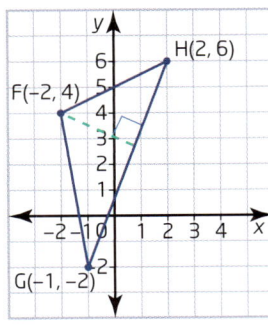

altitude

- height of a geometric shape

Practise

For help with question 1, see Example 1.

1. Find an equation for the line containing line segment AB.

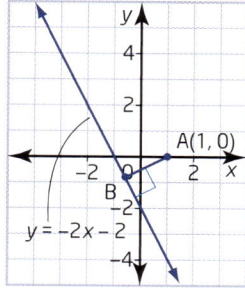

For help with questions 2 and 3, see Example 2.

2. List two properties you could use to show that a triangle contains a right angle.

3. A triangle has vertices C(1, 4), D(−2, 2), and E(3, 1).
   a) Draw △CDE.
   b) Use analytic geometry to verify that ∠C is a right angle.

For help with question 4, see Example 3.

4. Find the length of the median from vertex K.

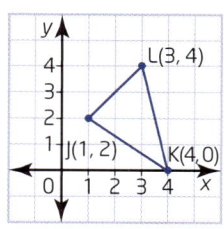

Connect and Apply

5. In △PQR, M is the midpoint of PQ and N is the midpoint of PR.
   a) Show that MN is parallel to QR.
   b) Show that MN is half the length of QR.

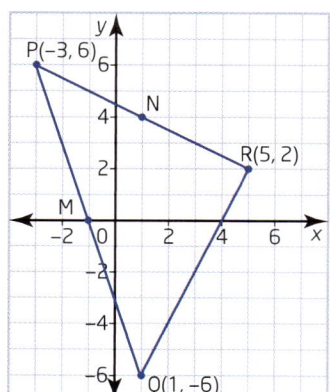

6. Determine whether the point T(2, −1) lies on the right bisector of the line segment with endpoints U(3, 5) and V(−3, −1). Explain your reasoning.

7. A quadrilateral has vertices O(0, 0), P(3, 5), Q(8, 6), and R(5, 1).
   a) Determine whether OPQR is a parallelogram.
   b) Describe how you could use geometry software to verify your answer to part a).

8. The endpoints of the diameter of a circle are M(−3, 5) and N(9, 7). Determine
   a) the coordinates of the centre of the circle
   b) the radius of the circle

9. Determine whether the triangle with vertices A(−3, 4), B(−1, −2), and C(3, 2) is isosceles.

10. Determine the shortest distance from the point (5, 2) to the line represented by $y = 2x + 1$. Use a diagram to check your answer.

11. Determine the shortest distance from the origin to the line represented by $y = \frac{1}{2}x - 2$.

12. Determine the shortest distance from the point D(5, 4) to the line represented by $3x + 5y - 4 = 0$.

13. Determine the shortest distance from the point E(1, −4) to the line through points F(−5, 2) and G(3, 4). Use a diagram to check your answer.

14. Determine the shortest distance from the point H(5, 2) to the line through points J(−6, 4) and K(−2, −4).

2.3 Apply Slope, Midpoint, and Length Formulas • MHR 89

15. Use Technology Use *The Geometer's Sketchpad®* or *Cabri® Jr.* to verify the solution to
   a) Example 1
   b) Example 2
   c) Example 3

16. The points A(5, −3), B(−2, 4), and C(−1, 7) are three vertices of a parallelogram ABCD. Find the coordinates of vertex D. Check your answer by using a different method.

17. A triangle has vertices E(2, −2), F(−4, −4), and G(0, 4).
   a) Determine an equation for the median from vertex E.
   b) Determine the length of the median from vertex E.

18. a) Draw △DEF with vertices D(−1, 6), E(4, 3), and F(0, −4). Then, draw the altitude from vertex D.
   b) Find an equation for the altitude from vertex D.

19. Use Technology Use *The Geometer's Sketchpad®* or *Cabri® Jr.* to verify your answer to question 18. Describe the method you used.

20. A quadrilateral has vertices P(−5, 4), Q(−2, 8), R(6, 2), and S(3, −2).
   a) Show that the quadrilateral is a rectangle.
   b) Determine the length of each diagonal.
   c) Determine the midpoint of each diagonal.
   d) What can you conclude about the diagonals of PQRS?

21. A triangle has vertices J(−2, 0), K(4, −3), and L(8, 8).
   a) Find an equation for the altitude from vertex L to side JK.
   b) Find the length of the altitude.
   c) Find the area of △JKL.

22. Use Technology Use *The Geometer's Sketchpad®* or *Cabri® Jr.* to verify your answer to question 20. Describe the method you used.

23. A cable company is connecting a new customer to its cable network. On a site plan, the customer's house has coordinates H(7, 17). The equation $y = \frac{1}{2}x + 4$ represents the existing trunk cable. The cable company wants to keep the branch to the customer's house as short as possible.
   a) Where should the cable company make the connection to the trunk cable?
   b) How long will the branch connection be if each unit on the grid of the site plan represents 10 m?

24. Dylan and Indira are hiking on the Caledon Hills section of the Bruce Trail. They have reached the point that has coordinates (6, 8) on their map of the trail. They want to hike out to the straight section of Hockley Road that joins points (4, 7) and (6, 5).
   a) At what point will they reach Hockley Road if they take the shortest possible route?
   b) Explain why the shortest route might not be the best route.

25. A utility company is running new power lines to two cottages. On a site plan, the cottages have coordinates A(6, 7) and B(13, 6) and the closest transformer is at T(13, 14). The utility will run a line straight from the transformer to one of the cottages and then connect the other cottage to that line using the shortest possible route.
   a) Draw a diagram on a grid to show the two possible ways to run the power lines.
   b) Determine which route will require the least cable.

26. Use Technology Use geometry software to verify your answer to question 25. Describe the method you used.

Achievement Check

27. a) Determine an equation for the median from vertex A of △ABC.

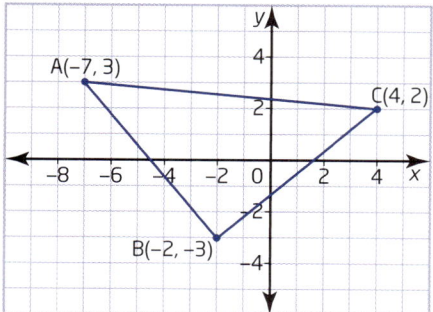

b) Determine an equation for the right bisector of BC.

c) Are the equations in parts a) and b) the same?

d) What property must a triangle have if the median to one of its sides coincides with the right bisector of that side?

Extend

28. a) Draw the triangle with vertices A(2, 1), B(4, −1), and C(−2, −5). Then, construct the median from each vertex.

b) Verify algebraically that the three medians intersect at a single point, the **centroid** of △ABC.

29. Use Technology Use *The Geometer's Sketchpad*® or Cabri® Jr. to determine whether the median to the hypotenuse of a right triangle is always half as long as the hypotenuse. Describe your method and your findings.

30. In three dimensions, the location of a point can be represented by the ordered triple (x, y, z).

a) Find the length of the line segment with endpoints P(2, 3, 1) and Q(6, 6, 5).

b) Write a formula for the distance between the points (x_1, y_1, z_1) and (x_2, y_2, z_2).

31. The municipal sewer line runs straight through a new subdivision from point A(20, 20) to point B(80, 60) on a survey map. Houses at C(30, 70) and D(85, 20) need connections to this sewer line. The developer calculates that connecting to the sewer line at points E(50, 40) and F(65, 50) will minimize digging and the length of pipe required.

a) Verify that the developer has found the shortest route from each house to the sewer line.

b) To the nearest metre, what length of pipe is needed for the two connections if the intervals between grid lines on the survey each represent 2 m?

c) The excavation contractor suggests digging a straight trench between the two houses and connecting to the sewer line at the point where the trench meets it. Find the coordinates of this point.

d) Should the developer use the contractor's suggestion? Justify your answer.

32. Math Contest In factorial notation, $n!$ represents the product $n(n − 1)(n − 2)…(3)(2)(1)$. If $x! = 3!5!7!$, the value of x is

A 10   **B** 8   **C** 11   **D** 9   **E** 12

33. Math Contest The perimeter of the smaller square is 96 cm and the shaded area is 100 cm². The perimeter of the larger square is

A 40 cm   **B** 72 cm   **C** 104 cm
D 144 cm   **E** 400 cm

2.4 Equation for a Circle

A licence is not required for portable two-way radios with a power of up to 2 W operating on the General Mobile Radio Service (GMRS) frequencies in Canada. GMRS radios are similar to Family Radio Service (FRS) radios, which are limited to 0.5 W and use different frequencies. Some radios are hybrids that can operate on both the GMRS and the FRS frequencies.

Investigate

How can you find an equation for a circle?

Near his home, Trevor's GMRS radios have a range of about 5 km.

Method 1: Use Pencil and Paper

Tools
- grid paper
- compasses

1. Draw a circle to represent the range of Trevor's radios. Let the origin represent Trevor's position.

2. Label the x- and y-intercepts of your circle. What do these intercepts have in common?

3. Find four other points on the circle that have integer coordinates. Label these points A, B, C, and D, and mark their coordinates on your drawing. Use the distance formula to verify that each of these points is exactly 5 units from the origin.

4. Mark a point P(x, y) anywhere on the circle. Construct a right triangle with OP as the hypotenuse and the rise and the run of OP as the other two sides.

5. Write an equation relating the length of OP to the length of the other two sides of the right triangle. Substitute OP = 5 into the equation.

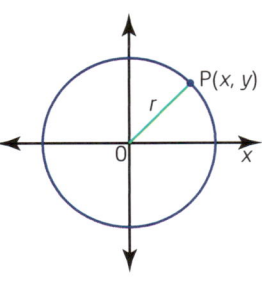

6. Verify that the coordinates of points A, B, C, and D satisfy the equation in step 5.

7. **Reflect** Will the coordinates of every other point on the circle also satisfy the equation? Explain your reasoning.

8. Away from built-up areas, Trevor finds that his GMRS radios have a range of about 7 km. Add a circle to your drawing to represent this larger range.

9. Write an equation for the larger circle.

10. **Reflect** Write an equation for the circle with centre (0, 0) and radius r. Then, use this equation to write an expression for the radius.

Method 2: Use *The Geometer's Sketchpad*®

Tools
- computer with *The Geometer's Sketchpad*®

1. Choose **Show Grid** from the **Graph** menu.

2. Construct a circle to represent the range of Trevor's radios. Let the origin represent Trevor's position. Use the **Compass Tool** to construct a circle with its centre at the origin and a radius of 5 units.

3. Label the x- and y-intercepts of the circle. What do these points have in common?

4. Use the **Point Tool** to construct a point on the circle. Select the point and choose **Coordinates** from the **Measure** menu. Then, drag the point around the circumference of the circle to find four other points that have integer coordinates. Construct these points and label them with their coordinates.

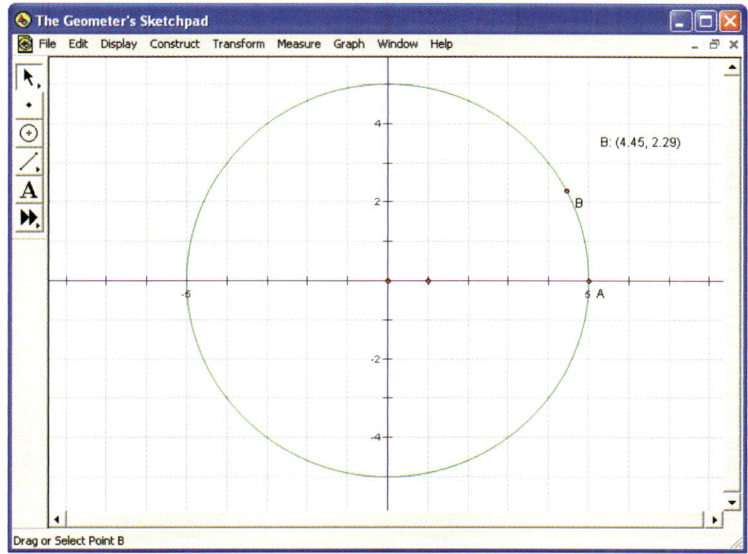

5. Verify that each of the points is 5 units from the origin. Select a point and the origin, and choose **Distance** from the **Measure** menu. Use the same method to measure the distance from the origin to each of the other points.

2.4 Equation for a Circle • MHR **93**

6. Construct a point anywhere on the circle. Label the point P. Construct a right triangle with OP as the hypotenuse and the rise and the run of OP as the other two sides.

7. Write an equation relating the length of OP to the length of the other two sides of the right triangle. Substitute OP = 5 into the equation.

8. Verify that the coordinates of the points in step 4 satisfy the equation in step 7.

9. **Reflect** Will the coordinates of every other point on the circle also satisfy the equation? Explain your reasoning.

10. Away from built-up areas, Trevor finds that his GMRS radios have a range of about 7 km. Add a circle to your drawing to represent this larger range.

11. Write an equation for the larger circle.

12. **Reflect** Write an equation for the circle with centre (0, 0) and radius r. Then, use this equation to write an expression for the radius.

Example 1 Equation for a Circle

Find an equation for the circle with centre (0, 0) and radius 4.

Solution

The distance from the origin to any point P(x, y) on the circle is the length of the radius. So,

OP = 4

The distance formula also gives an expression for the length of OP:

$OP = \sqrt{(x_2 - x_1)^2 + (y_2 - y_1)^2}$
$= \sqrt{(x - 0)^2 + (y - 0)^2}$
$= \sqrt{x^2 + y^2}$

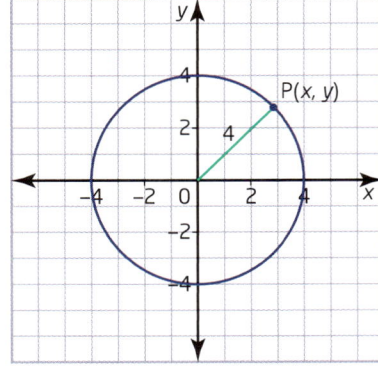

Therefore,
$\sqrt{x^2 + y^2} = 4$
$x^2 + y^2 = 16$

An equation for the circle is $x^2 + y^2 = 16$.

Example 2 Determine Whether a Point Lies Within a Circle

a) Determine an equation and the radius for the circle that has its centre at the origin and passes through the point A(6, −8).

b) Is the point B(−5, 9) inside this circle?

Solution

a) An equation for a circle centred at the origin has the form $x^2 + y^2 = r^2$.

> The point (6, −8) lies on this circle, so the coordinates of the point must satisfy the equation of the circle.

Substitute the coordinates of the point (6, −8) into the equation for the circle.

$$x^2 + y^2 = r^2$$
$$6^2 + (-8)^2 = r^2$$
$$36 + 64 = r^2$$
$$100 = r^2$$
$$\sqrt{100} = \sqrt{r^2}$$
$$10 = r$$

An equation for the circle is $x^2 + y^2 = 100$, and the radius of the circle is 10.

b) Consider a circle with its centre at the origin and with point B(−5, 9) on the circumference. Let r_1 be the radius of this circle. To find the length of the radius, substitute the coordinates of point B into the formula for the radius of a circle centred at the origin.

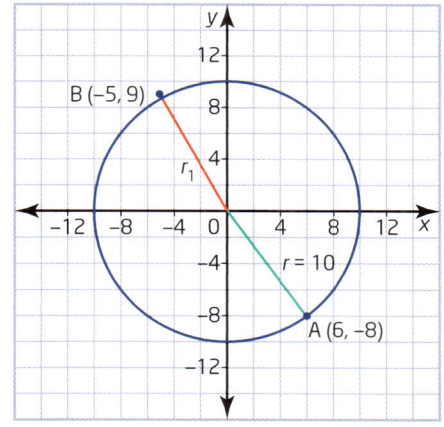

$$r_1 = \sqrt{x^2 + y^2}$$
$$= \sqrt{(-5)^2 + 9^2}$$
$$= \sqrt{25 + 81}$$
$$= \sqrt{106}$$
$$\doteq 10.3$$

Since $r_1 > 10$, point B lies outside the circle defined by $x^2 + y^2 = 100$.

If $r_1 > r$, then $r_1^2 > r^2$. So, the inequality $x^2 + y^2 > r^2$ defines the region *outside* the circle with centre (0, 0) and radius r.

Key Concepts

- An equation for the circle with centre at the origin and radius r is $x^2 + y^2 = r^2$.

- The radius of a circle centred at the origin is $r = \sqrt{x^2 + y^2}$.

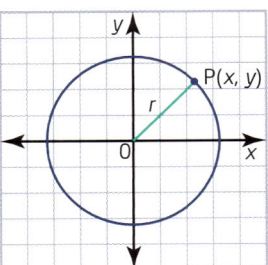

Communicate Your Understanding

C1 Outline how you would find an equation for the circle centred at the origin with a radius of 12.

C2 Describe how you would determine whether the point (3, 5) lies on the circle defined by $x^2 + y^2 = 35$.

C3 Explain how you would determine whether the point (8, 8) lies inside the circle defined by $x^2 + y^2 = 100$.

Practise

For help with question 1, see Example 1.

1. Determine an equation for each circle.

a)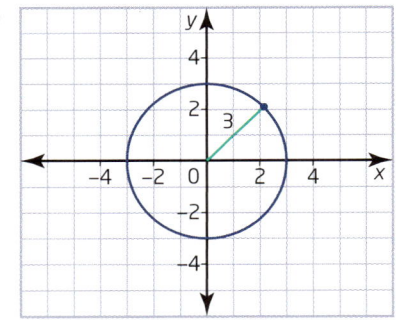

b)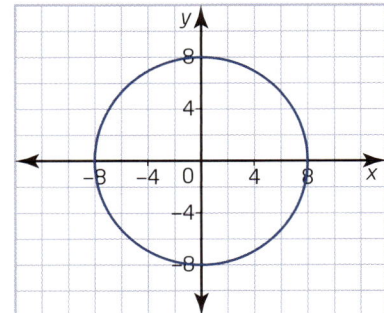

c)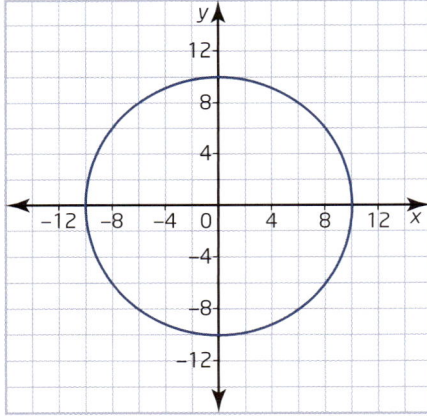

d)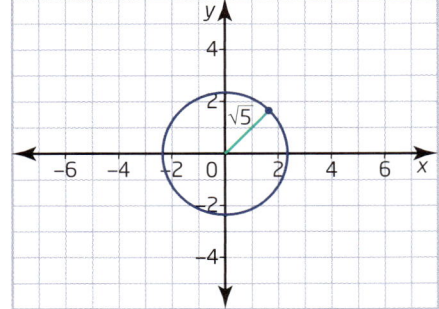

e)
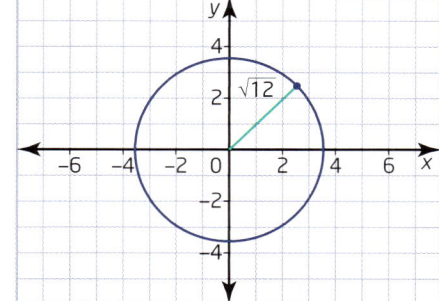

f)
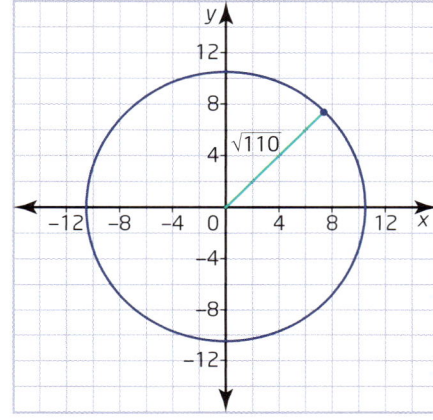

For help with questions 2 to 4, see Example 2.

2. For each equation, state the radius of the corresponding circle and give the coordinates of one point on the circle.

   a) $x^2 + y^2 = 36$ b) $x^2 + y^2 = 144$
   c) $x^2 + y^2 = 20$ d) $x^2 + y^2 = 50$
   e) $x^2 + y^2 = 1.69$

3. For each point, find an equation for the circle that is centred at the origin and passes through the point. Then, check your answer by graphing the circle and plotting the point.

   a) $(-4, 3)$ b) $(5, 2)$
   c) $(-3, -6)$ d) $(-7, 12)$

4. Determine whether each point is on, inside, or outside the circle defined by $x^2 + y^2 = 34$.

   a) $(5, -3)$ b) $(4, 4)$
   c) $(-6, 0)$ d) $(-3, -5)$
   e) $(2, -6)$ f) $(\sqrt{34}, 0)$

Connect and Apply

5. A satellite orbits Earth on a circular path with equation $x^2 + y^2 = 1.44 \times 10^8$, with distances measured in kilometres. Another satellite orbiting in the same plane passes through the point (8000, 9800). Is this satellite inside the orbit of the first one?

6. Determine an equation for the circle that has a diameter with endpoints A(−4, 3) and B(4, −3).

7. The point $(a, 8)$ lies on the circle defined by $x^2 + y^2 = 100$.
   a) Explain why there are two possible values for a. Find these values.
   b) Use a graph to check that the points corresponding to both values for a are on the circle.

8. A farmer is building a circular corral to hold livestock. With distances measured in metres, the shape of the corral is modelled by the equation $x^2 + y^2 = 64$.
   a) Find the length of fencing required for this corral.
   b) Find the area of the corral.

9. a) Graph the circle defined by $x^2 + y^2 = 100$.
   b) Verify algebraically that the points P(−8, 6) and Q(6, 8) are both on the circle.
   c) Find an equation for the right bisector of the **chord** PQ.
   d) Verify that the right bisector in part c) passes through the centre of the circle.
   e) Do you think that the right bisector of any chord of the circle passes through the centre of the circle? Explain your reasoning.

10. a) Graph the circle defined by $x^2 + y^2 = 40$.
   b) Verify algebraically that the line segment joining R(−6, 2) and S(2, −6) is a chord of this circle.
   c) Determine an equation for the line joining the centre O to the midpoint of this chord.
   d) Verify that this line is perpendicular to the chord.

11. a) Graph the circle defined by $x^2 + y^2 = 41$.
   b) Verify algebraically that the line segment joining U(−4, 5) and V(−5, −4) is a chord of this circle.
   c) Determine an equation for the line that passes through the origin and is perpendicular to the chord UV.
   d) Verify that this line passes through the midpoint of the chord.

12. Use Technology Use geometry software to determine whether the right bisector of any chord of a circle passes through the centre of the circle. Describe the method you used and your findings.

13. a) Graph the circle defined by $x^2 + y^2 = 25$.
   b) Verify algebraically that the point A(−3, −4) lies on the circle.
   c) Construct the line segment AO.
   d) Draw the line through A that is perpendicular to AO. This perpendicular line is a **tangent of a circle**.
   e) Determine an equation for the tangent in part d).
   f) Explain why A is the only point that is on both the circle and the tangent.

14. Brandon has three close friends who live in different parts of the city. Brandon wants to meet them for lunch at a restaurant that is roughly equidistant from their homes. How could Brandon use his knowledge of circles to help find a suitable restaurant? Explain your reasoning.

15. As part of the North American Free Trade Agreement (NAFTA), Canada, the United States, and Mexico are developing joint standards for highway trucks. One standard specifies a maximum width of 2.60 m and a maximum height of 4.15 m. Will a truck of this size fit through a semicircular tunnel with a maximum height of 4.50 m?

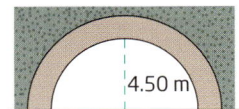

16. Lei is designing a construction set for small children. The set includes cylindrical cups with radii of 5 cm, 6 cm, and 7 cm as well as rectangular blocks that measure 7 cm by 8 cm by 9 cm. Will the blocks fit inside all of the cups?

17. A ship drops its anchor into the water and creates a circular ripple. The radius of this ripple increases at a rate of 50 cm/s.
   a) Find an equation for the circle 10 s after the anchor is dropped.
   b) A small rowboat is 50 m east and 75 m north of the point where the anchor was dropped. How long does the ripple take to reach the rowboat?
   c) Describe any assumptions you made for your answers to parts a) and b).

Extend

18. Describe the region defined by each inequality. Then, draw and label a diagram of the three regions.
   a) $x^2 + y^2 < 25$
   b) $x^2 + y^2 > 49$
   c) $25 < x^2 + y^2 < 49$

19. An equation for the small circle in this design is $x^2 + y^2 = 4$. Determine an equation for the larger circle.

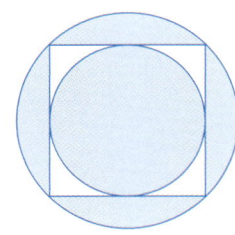

20. a) Write an equation for the circle in the diagram below.

b) Write the coordinates of points B and D.

c) Determine equations for the lines containing line segments AB and CD.

d) Determine the coordinates of point E.

e) Determine the area of the shaded portion of the circle.

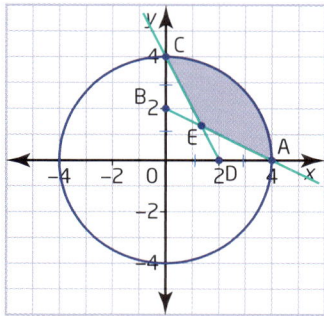

21. A boat moving east at 2 m/s creates circular waves that travel outward from the boat at a speed of 1 m/s.

a) How far does the wave produced by the boat travel in the time it takes the boat to move 10 m?

b) Plot the waves when the boat has moved 10 m. Draw circles at 1-m intervals from the origin to (8, 0).

c) Describe the pattern formed by the points of intersection of the waves. What does this pattern represent?

22. Find an equation for the circle centred at (4, 3) with a radius of 5.

23. Use a counterexample to show that this statement is false: "Every circle with a radius greater than 1 has at least one point with integer coordinates."

24. a) Draw the triangle with vertices Q(-2, 0), R(2, 8), and S(7, 3). Then, construct the right bisector of each side.

b) Verify algebraically that the three right bisectors intersect at a single point, the **circumcentre** of △QRS.

c) Find the distance from each vertex of △QRS to the circumcentre.

d) Describe the circle that passes through the vertices of △QRS.

e) Describe how you would use geometry software to answer parts a) to d).

25. Math Contest Find the radius of the circle represented by the equation $kx^2 + ky^2 = r^2$, where $k > 0$.

26. Math Contest Given that $a > 0$ and $b > 0$, describe the graph of the equation $ax^2 + by^2 = r^2$ if

a) $a < b$

b) $a > b$

Making Connections

You can use *The Geometer's Sketchpad*® to generate a variety of fractals. One of the easiest is a nest of circles.

- From the **Edit** menu, choose **Preferences**. Click on the **Text** tab. Ensure that **For All New Points** is checked.
- Construct a horizontal line segment AB. Select AB and choose **Midpoint** from the **Construct** menu. Construct a circle with centre C and radius CB. Hide line segment AB.
- Select points A and B, in that order. Choose **Iterate** from the **Transform** menu. Map A onto A and B onto C. Choose **Add New Map** from the **Structure** menu. Map A onto C and B onto B.
- Press the (+) key to add iterations and the (−) key to remove iterations. When you are satisfied with the image, click on **Iterate**.
- Clean up the sketch by hiding all visible points.

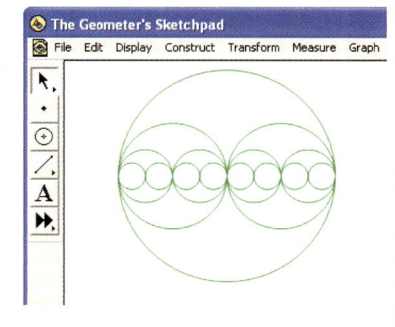

Chapter 2 Review

2.1 Midpoint of a Line Segment, pages 56–69

1. Find the midpoint of each line segment.

   a)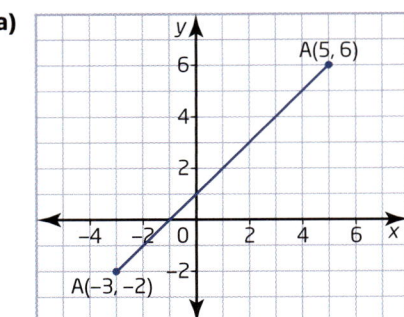

   b)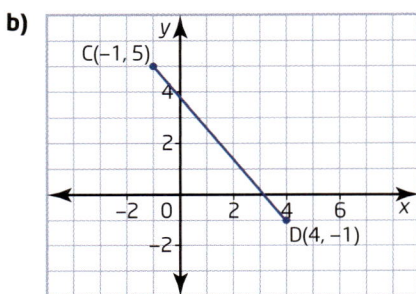

   c)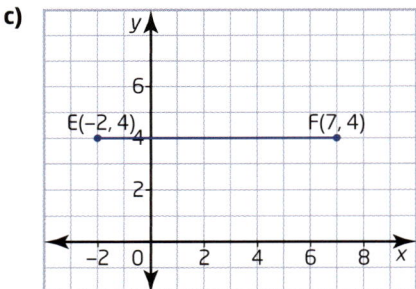

   d)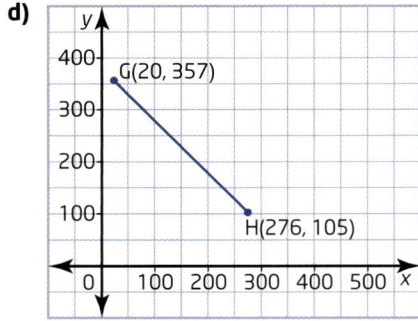

2. a) Determine the midpoint of the line segment with endpoints J(3, −5) and K(−5, −6).

   b) Determine the midpoint of the line segment with endpoints L(4, 8) and N(4, −2).

3. a) Draw the triangle with vertices P(−2, 5), Q(6, 5), and R(2, −7).

   b) Determine the midpoint of each side of the triangle algebraically.

   c) Join the midpoints to form a smaller triangle. Compare this triangle to the original triangle.

4. a) Draw the triangle with vertices T(−8, 6), U(2, 10), and V(4, −4).

   b) Draw the median from vertex U. Then, find an equation for this median.

   c) Draw the altitude from vertex T. Then, find an equation for this altitude.

   d) Draw the right bisector of TU. Then, find an equation for this right bisector.

5. The midpoints of the sides of △ABC are D(4, 1), E(−2, 3), and F(1, −4).

   a) Plot the midpoints. Use this plot to estimate the coordinates of the vertices of △ABC.

   b) Use analytic geometry to calculate the coordinates of the vertices of △ABC.

   c) Describe how to use geometry software to find the coordinates of the vertices.

2.2 Length of a Line Segment, pages 70–79

6. Find the length of each line segment.

a)

b)

c)

d)

7. Determine the length of the line segment defined by each pair of points.

a) J(4, 8) and K(4, −2)
b) M(−3, −12) and N(−15, −7)
c) P(−3, −2) and Q(5, 6)
d) R(−1, 5) and S(4, −1)
e) T(−2, 4) and U(7, 4)
f) V(3, −5) and W(−5, −6)

8. a) Determine the length of the median from vertex A of △ABC.

b) Determine the perimeter of the triangle.

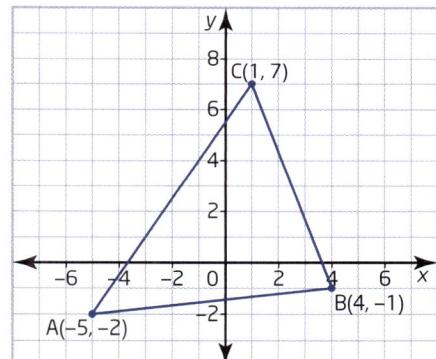

9. a) Draw the triangle with vertices D(5, 25), E(210, 1), and F(3, 210).

b) Use analytic geometry to classify △DEF.

c) Determine the area of △DEF.

d) Describe how to use geometry software to answer part c).

2.3 Apply Slope, Midpoint, and Length Formulas, pages 80–91

10. Show that this triangle is isosceles.

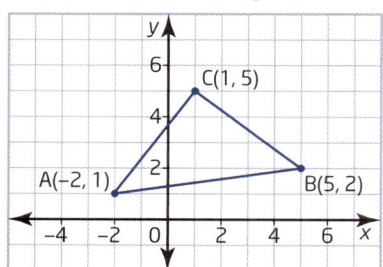

11. A triangle has vertices D(−2, 7), E(−4, 2), and F(6, −2).
   a) Show algebraically that this triangle is a right triangle.
   b) Find the midpoint of the hypotenuse.
   c) Show that this midpoint is equidistant from each of the vertices.

12. A map shows a main gas pipeline running straight from A(45, 60) to B(65, 40).
   a) How long is the section of pipeline from A to B if each unit on the map grid represents 1 km?
   b) A branch pipeline runs perpendicular to the main pipeline and meets it at a point halfway between A and B. Find the coordinates of this point.
   c) Is the point C(63, 54) on the branch pipeline? Explain your reasoning.
   d) What is the shortest route for connecting point C to the main pipeline? Explain.

13. Find the shortest distance from the origin to the line defined by $y = 3x - 10$.

2.4 Equation for a Circle, pages 92–99

14. Determine an equation for each circle.

a)

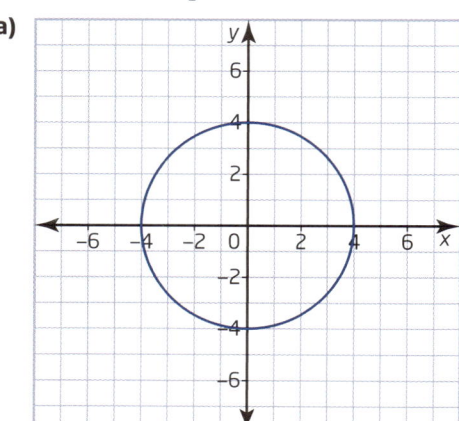

b)

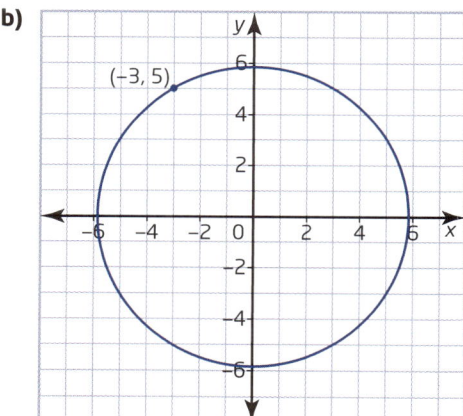

c)

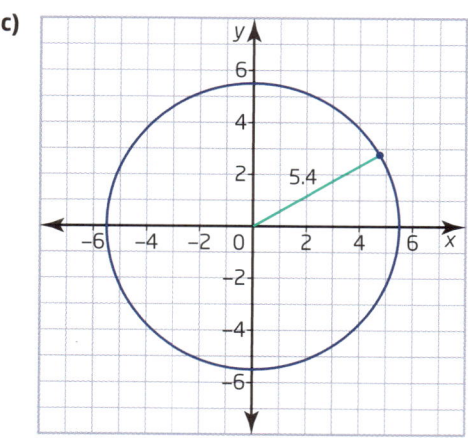

15. Find an equation for the circle that is centred on the origin and

   a) has a radius of $4\frac{1}{2}$

   b) has a diameter of 14

   c) has a radius of $\sqrt{12}$

   d) passes through the point $(4, 7)$

16. a) Determine whether the point $A(-2, -6)$ lies on the circle defined by $x^2 + y^2 = 40$.

   b) Find an equation for the radius from the origin O to point A.

   c) Find an equation for the line that passes through A and is perpendicular to OA.

   d) Use a graph to check your answers to parts a), b), and c).

   e) Explain why A is the only point on the line that also lies on the circle.

17. a) Show that the line segment joining $A(-3, 1)$ and $B(1, 3)$ is a chord of the circle defined by $x^2 + y^2 = 10$.

   b) Determine an equation for the right bisector of the chord AB.

   c) Show that the line in part b) passes through the centre of the circle.

18. A communication tower can send and receive signals from cell phones up to 20 km away. A cell phone user is 15 km east and 13 km south of the tower. Is this user able to receive a signal from the tower?

Chapter Problem Wrap-Up

Many natural systems, such as river deltas and tree branches, have patterns that look like fractals. Parts within a natural pattern usually vary somewhat, so they are not exactly similar. Nonetheless, fractals often provided the first reasonably accurate mathematical model for such complex systems.

Beginning with a discovery by the meteorologist Edward Lorentz in 1961, scientists and mathematicians found that fractal models revealed surprising patterns in data that had appeared to be completely random. The mathematics that describes this hidden order in complex systems is called chaos theory. Applications of chaos theory include models of ocean currents, population growth, commodity prices, and blood flow in veins and arteries.

a) Research fractals at a library or on the Internet. Describe how to create a fractal different from the ones mentioned in this chapter. Choose a fractal you learned about during your research or create one of your own. Explain how midpoints, lengths, or equations for circles are used to generate the fractal.

b) Make a poster of the fractal you described in part a). Draw the fractal by hand or by using technology. Describe any special features of the fractal.

c) Describe a specific application of fractals, such as a scientific model or computer-generated imaging (CGI).

Chapter 2 Practice Test

For questions 1 to 3, choose the correct answer.

1. The midpoint of the line segment with endpoints A(−3, −3) and B(1, 5) is at
   - **A** (−2, 2)
   - **B** (−4, −8)
   - **C** (−1, 1)
   - **D** (1, −1)

2. The length of the line segment with endpoints C(−5, 2) and D(1, −4) is
   - **A** $\sqrt{20}$
   - **B** $\sqrt{24}$
   - **C** $\sqrt{72}$
   - **D** $\sqrt{80}$

3. An equation for the circle with centre (0, 0) and radius 4 is
   - **A** $x^2 + y^2 = 2$
   - **B** $x^2 + y^2 = 4$
   - **C** $x^2 + y^2 = 8$
   - **D** $x^2 + y^2 = 16$

4. Determine the midpoint coordinates and the length of each line segment.

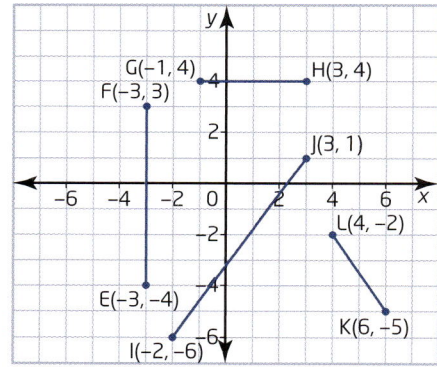

5. Write an equation for each circle.

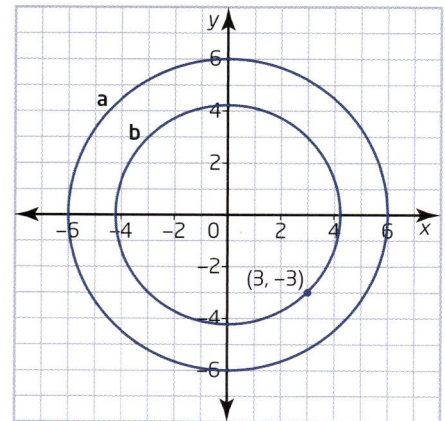

6. Rachel makes the following statement: "Since point A is the same distance from both B and C, A is the midpoint of BC." Is Rachel correct? Explain your reasoning.

7. Jason lives exactly halfway between the primary and secondary schools in his neighbourhood. The intervals between the grid lines represent 1 km.

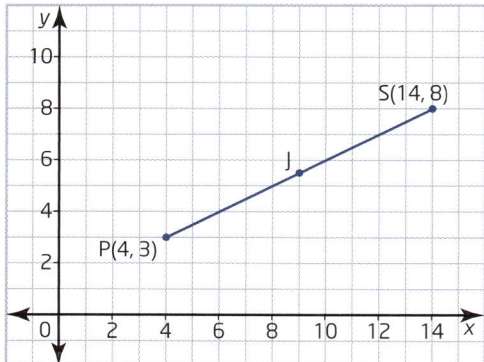

   a) How far apart are the schools?
   b) Determine the coordinates of Jason's home.
   c) What other locations are equidistant from the two schools? Explain your reasoning.
   d) Determine an equation that represents all locations that are equidistant from the two schools.

8. a) Plot the triangle with vertices A(−2, 1), B(2, −1), and C(0, 5).
   b) Determine the lengths of the sides of the triangle.
   c) Classify △ABC. Explain your reasoning.
   d) Find the area of △ABC.
   e) Describe how you could use geometry software to verify your answers to parts b), c), and d).

9. a) Plot the triangle with vertices P(3, 4), Q(−5, 2), and R(1, −4). Then, draw the median from vertex R.
   b) Determine an equation for this median.
   c) Is this median also an altitude for this triangle? Justify your answer.

10. a) Determine the coordinates of the other endpoint of the diameter shown.

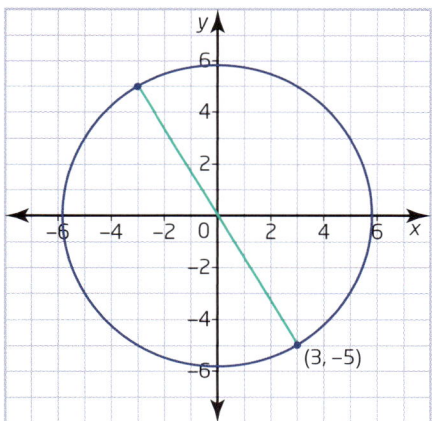

b) Does any other point on the circle have an *x*-coordinate of 3? Justify your answer.

c) Determine an equation for the circle.

d) Explain how you can use the equation of the circle to verify your answer to part b).

e) Determine the coordinates of four more points on the circle.

11. a) Determine the coordinates of the midpoints G and H.

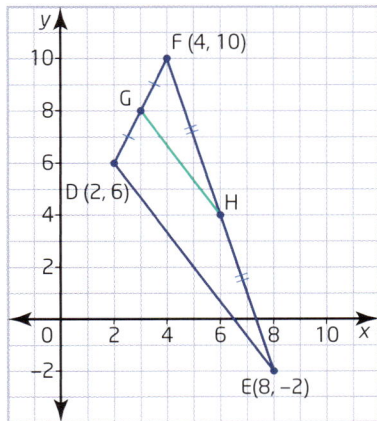

b) Verify that GH is parallel to DE.

c) Show that GH is exactly half the length of DE.

12. a) Show that the triangle with vertices U(4, 3), V(0, −5), and W(−4, −3) is a right triangle.

b) Verify that the median from the right angle to the hypotenuse is half as long as the hypotenuse.

c) Find an equation for the circle that passes through the vertices of △UVW.

d) Describe how you could use geometry software to verify your answers to parts a), b), and c).

13. Scott, Arif, and Diane run a small delivery company. For their business, they use licensed two-way radios with a 20-km range. Scott is at their office, which they have marked as the origin on their map of the town. The grid lines on the map are spaced 1 km apart. Arif is dropping off a package at (−8, 16) while Diane is making a pick-up at (4, 20).

a) Draw a diagram to represent the reception range for the radio at the office.

b) Find an equation that describes the boundary of this area.

c) Are Arif and Diane both within range of the radio at the office? Justify your answer.

d) Are Arif and Diane within radio range of each other? Justify your answer.

■ **Achievement Check**

14. A(9, 5) and B(5, −9) are two points on a circle centred at the origin.

a) Determine an equation for the circle.

b) Determine the midpoint, C, of chord AB.

c) Show that the right bisector of chord AB passes through the centre of the circle.

d) Give a different solution for part c).

CHAPTER 3
Geometric Properties

Analytic Geometry

- Determine, through investigation, some characteristics and properties of geometric figures.
- Verify, using algebraic techniques and analytic geometry, some characteristics of geometric figures.
- Plan and implement a multi-step strategy that uses analytic geometry and algebraic techniques to verify a geometric property.

Vocabulary

concurrent
centroid
collinear
chord

Artists and craftspeople use colour and simple geometric shapes to make images and patterns of striking beauty. You can find these shapes in paintings, quilts, carpets, tiles, and stained glass. This chapter shows how to apply analytic geometry to learn more about the properties of geometric shapes.

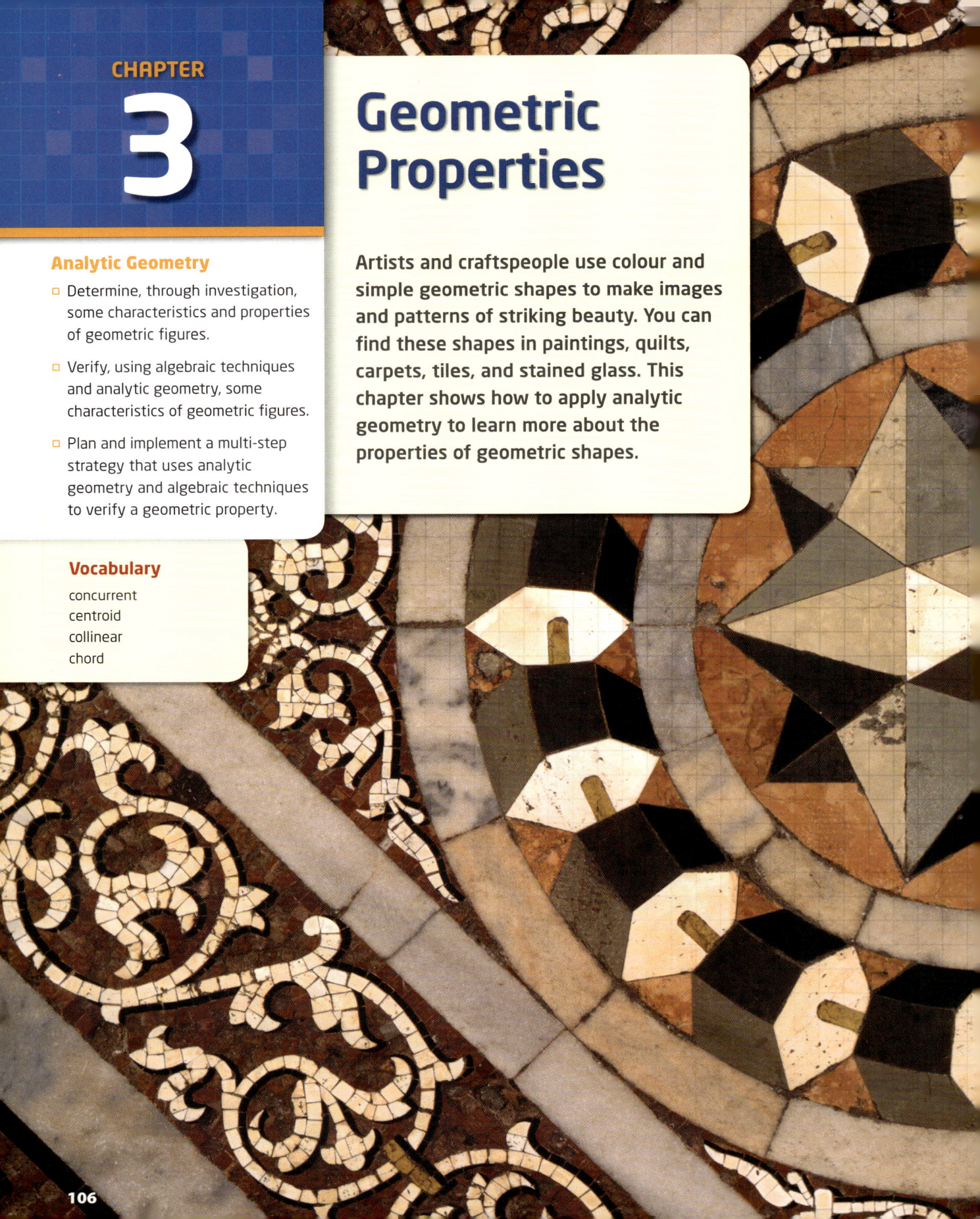

Chapter Problem

The quantities *a* and *b* are related by the golden ratio if $\frac{a}{b} = \frac{a+b}{a}$. Mathematicians have studied this ratio and its applications since ancient times. How is the golden ratio related to geometric shapes? What unusual properties does it have?

Get Ready

Length and Midpoint of a Line Segment

You can determine the midpoint and the length of a line segment from the coordinates of its endpoints.

Find the length and midpoint of the line segment joining A(−2, −3) and B(4, 4).

Midpoint of AB:

$$(x, y) = \left(\frac{x_1 + x_2}{2}, \frac{y_1 + y_2}{2}\right)$$
$$= \left(\frac{-2 + 4}{2}, \frac{-3 + 4}{2}\right)$$
$$= \left(1, \frac{1}{2}\right)$$

Length of AB:

$$d = \sqrt{(x_2 - x_1)^2 + (y_2 - y_1)^2}$$
$$= \sqrt{[4 - (-2)]^2 + [2 - (-3)]^2}$$
$$= \sqrt{6^2 + 5^2}$$
$$= \sqrt{36 + 25}$$
$$= \sqrt{61}$$

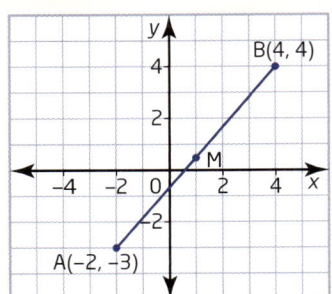

1. Find the midpoint of each line segment.
   a) CD with C(−1, 5) and D(4, −2)
   b) EF with E(−3, 0) and F(5, −2)
   c) GH with G(4, 6) and H(4, −3)
   d) JK with J(−8, 5) and K(2, 5)

2. Find the length of each line segment.
   a) LM with L(−2, 4) and M(3, −3)
   b) PQ with P(−4, 0) and Q(3, −2)
   c) RS with R(6, 5) and S(6, −4)
   d) TU with T(−6, 7) and U(4, 7)

Intersection of Lines

The coordinates of the point of intersection of two lines satisfy the equations of both lines.

Find the point of intersection of the lines defined by $y = -2x + 12$ and $2x - 3y = 12$.

Substitute from the first equation into the second equation.

$$2x - 3y = 12$$
$$2x - 3(-2x + 12) = 12$$
$$2x + 6x - 36 = 12$$
$$8x = 12 + 36$$
$$8x = 48$$
$$x = 6$$

Now, substitute $x = 6$ into the first equation.
$$y = -2x + 12$$
$$= -2(6) + 12$$
$$= 0$$

The point of intersection of the two lines is (6, 0).

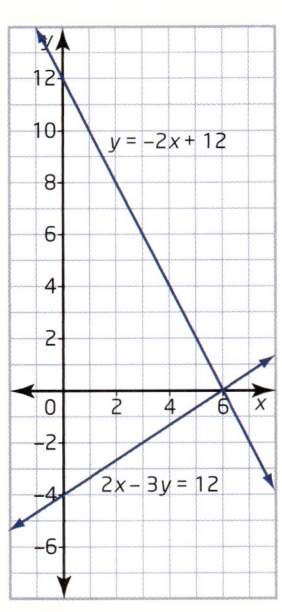

3. Find the point of intersection of the lines represented by each pair of equations.
   a) $y = x - 4$ and $y = -x + 2$
   b) $y = x + 4$ and $y = 2 - x$
   c) $y = 2x - 5$ and $y = x - 3$

4. Find the point of intersection of the lines represented by each pair of equations.
   a) $2x - 3y = 4$ and $3x - 4y = 5$
   b) $2x + y = 5$ and $x - 2y = 10$
   c) $2x + y = -5$ and $3x - y = -5$

Sum of the Angles in a Triangle

The sum of the angles in a triangle is 180°.

Find the measure of ∠C.

$\angle A + \angle B + \angle C = 180°$
$\angle C = 180° - \angle A - \angle B$
$= 180° - 40° - 65°$
$= 75°$

The measure of ∠C is 75°.

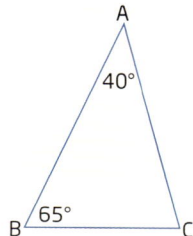

5. Find the measure of the third angle in each triangle.
   a)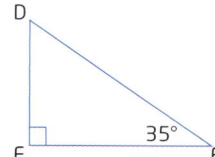
   b)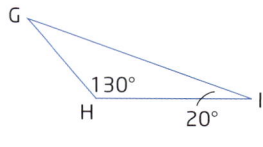

6. Find the measures of the unknown angles in each triangle.
   a)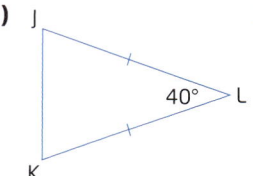
   b)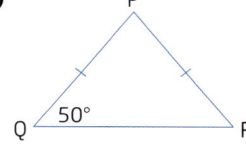

Types of Quadrilaterals

Quadrilaterals are classified by the properties of their sides and angles.

What are the key properties of a square?

A square has four equal sides and four right angles.

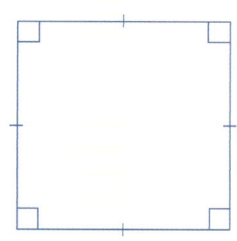

7. List the key properties of
   a) a rectangle
   b) a parallelogram
   c) a trapezoid

8. Draw an example of each shape and mark all equal sides and all parallel sides.
   a) a rhombus
   b) a parallelogram
   c) a kite

3.1 Investigate Properties of Triangles

The distribution of an object's mass around its balance point is such that no net force acts to tilt the object. In fact, the object acts like its entire mass is concentrated at a point directly above the balance point. Calculating a balance point accurately can be crucial in the design of aircraft, ships, lift bridges, cranes, and other machinery. Analytic geometry can help find balance points and other properties of geometric shapes.

Investigate

How can you find the balance point of a flat triangular object?

Tools
- ruler
- cardboard
- scissors
- compasses

Method 1: Use Pencil and Paper

1. Draw a large triangle on a sheet of paper. Then, draw an identical triangle on cardboard and cut out this triangle.

2. Move the cardboard triangle around on the tip of a pencil until you find the point where the triangle balances on the pencil. Mark this balance point. Then, mark the corresponding point on the triangle on the sheet of paper.

3. Fold the paper triangle along one of its medians. Where is the balance point relative to this fold?

4. Explain how you know that the median bisects the area of the triangle. Will the cardboard triangle balance on the edge of a ruler if the median is aligned with the edge? Explain your reasoning. Try balancing the cardboard triangle on the edge of a ruler.

5. Fold the paper triangle in half along a different median. What do you notice about the balance point?

6. Fold the paper triangle along the third median. What do you notice about the creases from the three folds? Check whether your classmates get the same result.

7. Reflect

a) Are the medians of your triangle **concurrent**? Do you think that all triangles have this property? Explain your reasoning.

b) How is the balance point of your triangle related to the **centroid** of the triangle? Do you think that this relationship applies for all triangles? Explain.

concurrent
- meeting at a single point

centroid
- the point where the three medians of a triangle intersect

Method 2: Use *The Geometer's Sketchpad*®

1. Construct any triangle. Then, construct the three medians of the triangle. Are the medians **concurrent**?

- computer with *The Geometer's Sketchpad*®

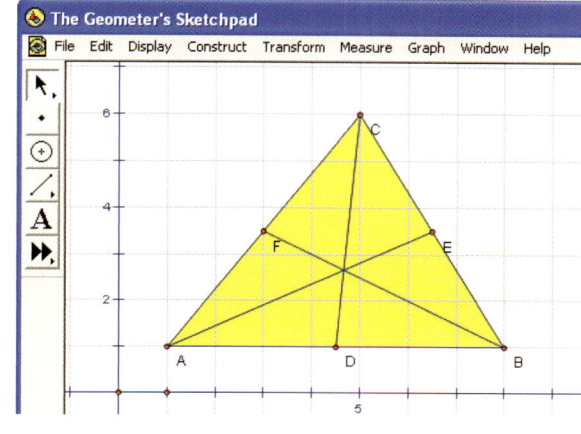

2. Observe the intersection of the medians while you drag each of the vertices of the triangle to change the shape of the triangle.

3. **Reflect** Does every triangle have a **centroid**, a single point where all three medians intersect? Explain your reasoning.

4. Construct and measure the areas of the two triangles that have median AE as their base. Compare these areas. Then, construct the altitude to AE for both triangles. Compare the lengths of these altitudes.

5. Compare the areas and altitudes of the two triangles that have median BF as their base. Then, compare the areas and altitudes of the two triangles that have median CD as their base.

6. Drag the vertices of the original triangle around the screen. Do the relationships among the areas and altitudes of the smaller triangles change?

Technology Tip

When there are overlapping triangles, you can change which interior is selected by clicking on it again.

7. Reflect

a) What property does the median of a triangle have? Explain how you know that all medians have this property.

b) Will a flat triangular object balance if it is placed with one of its medians along the edge of a ruler? Explain.

c) Where is the balance point of a flat triangular object? Explain your reasoning.

Tools
- TI-83 Plus or TI-84 Plus graphing calculator

Method 3: Use a Graphing Calculator

1. Start the Cabri® Jr. application. Choose **Triangle** from the **F2** menu, and draw a large triangle. Choose **Midpoint** from the **F3** menu, and construct the midpoint of each side of the triangle. Choose **Segment** from the **F2** menu, and draw the medians of the triangle by joining each vertex to the midpoint of the opposite side. Are the medians **concurrent**?

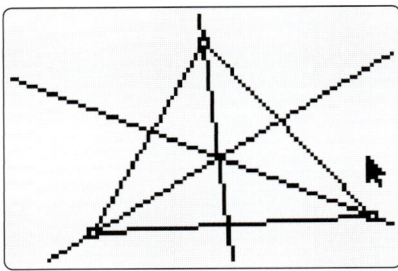

2. Move the cursor to one of the vertices of the triangle. Press [ALPHA]. Observe the intersection of the medians while you drag the vertex of the triangle to change the shape of the triangle. Try dragging the other vertices as well.

3. **Reflect** Does every triangle have a **centroid**, a single point where all three medians intersect? Explain your reasoning.

4. Construct a new triangle on top of the original triangle by selecting the endpoints of a median and one of the other vertices of the original triangle. Measure the area of the new triangle. Then, construct the other triangle that has the median as its base, and measure the area of this triangle. Compare the areas of the two smaller triangles. How are the altitudes to the common base of the two triangles related?

5. Compare the areas and altitudes of the two triangles that have the second median as their base. Then, compare the areas and altitudes of the two triangles that have the third median as their base.

6. Drag the vertices of the original triangle around the screen. Do the relationships among the areas and altitudes of the smaller triangles change?

7. **Reflect**
   a) What property does the median of a triangle have? Explain how you know that all medians have this property.
   b) Will a flat triangular object balance if it is placed with one of its medians along the edge of a ruler? Explain.
   c) Where is the balance point of a flat triangular object? Explain your reasoning.

Technology Tip
Measure the area of each triangle before constructing the next triangle on top of it. Once a triangle is covered, you cannot select it for measurement.

Example Median of an Isosceles Triangle

What are the properties of the median from the vertex between the equal sides of an isosceles triangle?

Solution

Draw any isosceles triangle. Label the equal sides AB and AC. Let D be the midpoint of BC.

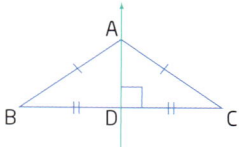

The right bisector of a line segment includes all points that are equidistant from the endpoints of the line segment. Since AB = AC, vertex A lies on the right bisector of BC. The midpoint, D, also lies on the right bisector of BC. So, AD is perpendicular to BC.

Since the median from vertex A is perpendicular to BC, this median is also the altitude from vertex A.

△ABC and △ACD have side AD in common. The other corresponding sides of these two triangles are equal since AB = AC and D is the midpoint of BC. Therefore, △ABD and △ACD are congruent, and ∠BAD = ∠CAD. So, AD bisects ∠BAC.

Therefore, the median from the vertex between the equal sides of an isosceles triangle coincides with the altitude to the vertex and bisects the angle at the vertex.

Key Concepts

- The medians of a triangle meet at a single point, the centroid.
- Each median bisects the area of the triangle.
- The median from the vertex between the equal sides of an isosceles triangle coincides with the altitude to the vertex and bisects the angle at the vertex.
- You can use both pencil-and-paper techniques and geometry software to investigate the properties of geometric shapes.

Communicate Your Understanding

C1 Describe two methods for drawing a median of this triangle.

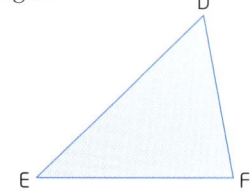

C2 Explain how you know that this diagram has three pairs of equal angles.

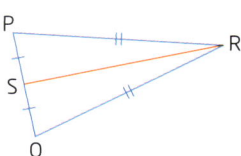

Practise

1. The area of △ABC is 12 square units. Find the area of △ABD.

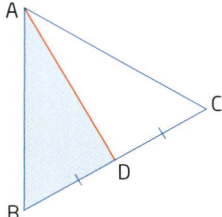

2. The area of △EFH is 30 square units. Find the area of △EFG.

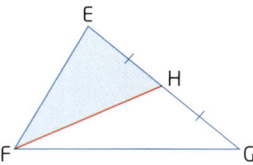

For help with questions 3 and 4, see the Example.

3. a) Which line segments are perpendicular in △JKL?
   b) Which angles are equal?

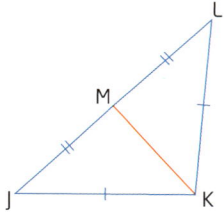

4. Which of the following coincide in △PQR?
   - the bisector of ∠P
   - the bisector of ∠R
   - the altitude from vertex Q
   - the altitude from vertex R
   - the right bisector of side PQ
   - the median from vertex P

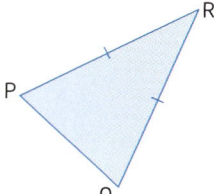

Connect and Apply

5. a) Draw any isosceles triangle. Then, construct the altitude from the vertex between the equal sides.
   b) List three properties of this altitude that an altitude of a scalene triangle does not have.
   c) Verify these properties by measuring your drawing.

6. Steve says, "If a median of a triangle is also an angle bisector, the triangle must be equilateral." Is he correct? Justify your answer.

7. a) Draw any right triangle. Find and label the midpoint of the hypotenuse.
   b) Measure the distance from this midpoint to each of the vertices of the triangle. How are these distances related?
   c) Investigate whether the same relationship applies for all right triangles. Describe your method and your findings.

8. List at least six properties of equilateral triangles. Explain how you know that every equilateral triangle has each of these properties.

9. Alana claims, "In an equilateral triangle, the angle bisectors and the right bisectors of the sides all meet at the same point." Do you agree with Alana's claim? Explain, using a diagram.

10. a) Draw any triangle and all three of its medians. The centroid divides each median into two sections. Compare the lengths of the sections of each median.
    b) Investigate whether the centroid in every triangle divides each median in the same ratio. Outline your method and describe your findings.
    c) Explain how you can use your findings in part b) to find the balance point of a flat triangular object.

11. Use Technology

a) Construct any △ABC. Then, construct the midpoint D of side AB and the midpoint E of side AC.

b) Compare the slope and the length of line segment DE to those of side BC.

c) Investigate whether the relationships between DE and BC depend on the shape of the triangle. Describe your findings.

12. a) Draw a large triangle on a sheet of paper. Then, draw the angle bisector at each vertex. Are the three angle bisectors of your triangle concurrent?

b) Repeat part a) with different types of triangles. Does every triangle have an **incentre**, a point where all three angle bisectors meet? Explain your reasoning.

c) Put the point of a set of compasses at the incentre of a triangle, and adjust the compasses so that the pencil just touches one side of the triangle. Draw a circle with this radius. What property does the incentre of this triangle have?

d) What property does the incentre of every triangle have? Justify your answer.

13. Use Technology Use geometry software to investigate the properties of the angle bisectors of a triangle. Outline your method and describe your findings.

14. a) Investigate whether every triangle has a **circumcentre**, a point where all the right bisectors of the sides meet. Describe your method and your results.

b) How are the distances from the circumcentre to the vertices related? Do all triangles have this property? Justify your answer.

c) A company with plants in Hamilton, Oshawa, and Barrie wants to set up a distribution centre that is roughly equidistant from the three plants. How can the company use the properties of triangles to find a suitable location?

15. In this triangle, the altitudes from the three vertices meet at a single point, called the **orthocentre**. Investigate whether the altitudes intersect at a single point in all triangles. Outline your method and describe your findings.

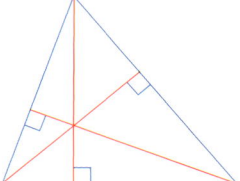

16. Use a triangle to estimate the geographical centre of Canada.

a) Trace the outline of Canada from a map onto a sheet of paper. Draw a triangle on your outline to approximate the shape of Canada as closely as you can.

b) Find the centroid of the triangle. Then, draw the angle bisectors of the triangle and find their point of intersection. Also find the point of intersection of the right bisectors of the sides and the point of intersection of the altitudes of the triangle. Which of these four points gives the best approximation for the geographic centre of Canada? Justify your choice.

c) Find the town or city closest to the centre you chose in part b). Compare your estimate with those made by your classmates.

17. a) Investigate how the areas of equilateral triangles constructed on the sides of a right triangle are related. Outline your method and describe your findings.

b) Describe another method that you could use to compare the areas of the triangles.

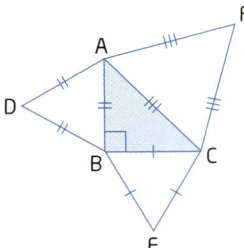

18. Chapter Problem

a) Let x represent the measure of the base angles of an isosceles triangle and let y represent the angle at the vertex between the two equal sides. Find the values of x and y when $x = 2y$.

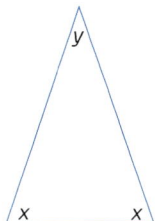

b) Draw a large triangle that has the angle measures that you calculated in part a). Measure the lengths of the sides of your triangle.

c) Calculate the ratio $\dfrac{a}{b}$, where a is the length of one of the equal sides and b is the length of the base of the isosceles triangle.

d) The golden ratio, denoted by the Greek letter φ (phi), is equal to $\dfrac{1 + \sqrt{5}}{2}$.

Compare the decimal value for φ to the ratio you calculated in part c).

e) A golden triangle is an isosceles triangle with side lengths that correspond to the golden ratio. Is the triangle you drew in part b) a golden triangle?

f) Draw an isosceles triangle with the angle at the vertex between the two equal sides three times as large as the base angles. Is this triangle a golden triangle? Explain.

g) Draw an isosceles triangle with the angle at the vertex between the two equal sides four times as large as the base angles. Is this triangle a golden triangle?

Extend

19. Does the point of intersection of the angle bisectors of a triangle (the incentre) always lie inside the triangle? Justify your answer.

20. When will the point of intersection of the right bisectors of the sides of a triangle (the circumcentre) lie

a) outside the triangle?

b) on a side of the triangle?

Justify your answers using diagrams.

21. Investigate how the locations of the centroid, the orthocentre, and the circumcentre of a triangle are related. Describe your method and your findings.

22. Investigate whether the point of intersection of the altitudes of a triangle (the orthocentre) can lie

a) outside the triangle

b) on the triangle

Outline your method and describe your findings.

23. Math Contest Show that the medians of △ABC and the medians of △DEF all meet at a single point.

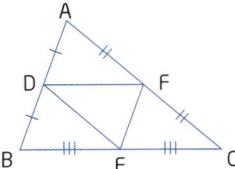

3.2 Verify Properties of Triangles

Since triangular frames are strong and simple to make, they are widely used to strengthen buildings and other structures. This section applies analytic geometry to verify the properties of specific triangles.

Investigate

- grid paper

How can you verify the properties of an isosceles triangle?

Method 1: Use Pencil and Paper

1. Draw the triangle with vertices A(2, 5), B(1, 2), and C(6, 2). Use the coordinates of the vertices to verify that △ABC is isosceles. Which angles of △ABC are equal?

2. Describe how you could fold your drawing of △ABC to confirm that it is isosceles.

3. Find the coordinates of the midpoint, D, of side AB. Draw the median from vertex C. Use slopes to verify that this median is perpendicular to AB.

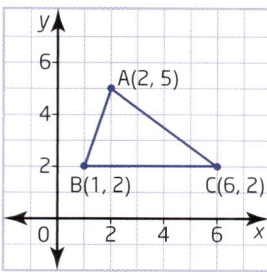

4. Explain how you can use congruent triangles to verify that CD is perpendicular to AB. Describe two different ways to show that △ADC and △BDC are congruent.

5. Use angle sums to verify that CD bisects ∠ACB.

6. Describe another way to show that CD bisects ∠ACB.

7. **Reflect** How are the median, the altitude, and the angle bisector at vertex C related? How are these line segments related to the right bisector of AB? Do you think all isosceles triangles have these properties? Explain your reasoning.

Tools
- computer with *The Geometer's Sketchpad*®

Technology Tip
You can also place the vertices by choosing **Plot Points** from the **Graph** menu and typing the coordinates.

Method 2: Use *The Geometer's Sketchpad*®

1. Choose **Show Grid** from the **Graph** menu. Then, choose **Snap Points**. Move the origin so that most of the work area is in the first quadrant. Construct the triangle with vertices A(2, 5), B(1, 2), and C(6, 2).

2. Measure the length of each side to verify that △ABC is isosceles. Which angles of △ABC are equal?

3. Construct the midpoint, D, of side AB. Then, construct the median from vertex C. Measure ∠ADC. What can you conclude about the median CD?

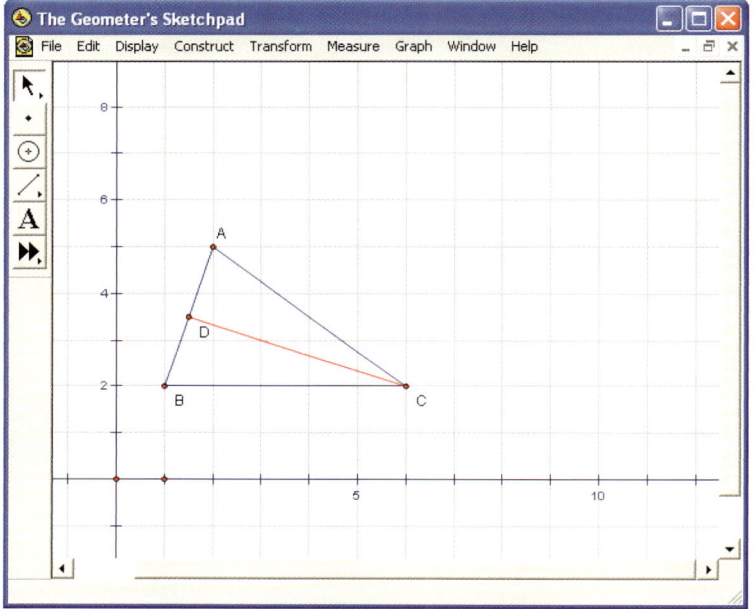

4. Measure and compare ∠ACD and ∠BCD.

5. Turn off **Snap Points**. Drag a vertex of △ABC to a new location. Move one of the other vertices until AC = BC. Observe the measures of ∠ADC, ∠ACD, and ∠BCD as you repeat this process for various locations of the vertices.

6. **Reflect** How are the median, the altitude, and the angle bisector at vertex C related? How are these line segments related to the right bisector of AB? Do you think all isosceles triangles have these properties? Explain your reasoning.

Tools
- TI-83 Plus or TI-84 Plus graphing calculator

Method 3: Use a Graphing Calculator

1. Start the Cabri® Jr. application. If the axes are not displayed, choose **Hide/Show** from the **F5** menu; then, choose **Axes** from the submenu. Move the origin so that most of the work area is in the first quadrant.

2. Draw the triangle with vertices A(2, 5), B(1, 2), and C(6, 2). Choose **Coord. & Eq.** from the **F5** menu. Then, select the vertices to display their coordinates. To adjust a vertex, move the cursor to it, press (ALPHA), and use the arrow keys to reposition the vertex.

3. Choose **Measure** from the **F5** menu, and then choose **D. & Length**. Measure the length of each side to verify that the triangle is isosceles. Which angles of △ABC are equal?

4. Choose **Midpoint** from the **F3** menu and construct the midpoint, D, of side AB. Then, choose **Segment** from the **F2** menu and construct the median from vertex C. Measure ∠ADC. What can you conclude about the median DC?

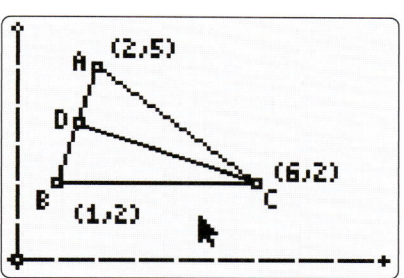

5. Measure and compare ∠ACD and ∠BCD.

6. Drag a vertex of △ABC to a new location. Move one of the other vertices until AC = BC. Observe the measures of ∠ADC, ∠ACD, and ∠BCD as you repeat this process for various locations of the vertices.

7. **Reflect** How are the median, the altitude, and the angle bisector at vertex C related? How are these line segments related to the right bisector of AB? Do you think all isosceles triangles have these properties? Explain your reasoning.

Example 1 Centroid of a Triangle

a) Verify that C(4, 0) is the centroid of △OPQ.

b) Verify that the centroid divides each median in a 2:1 ratio.

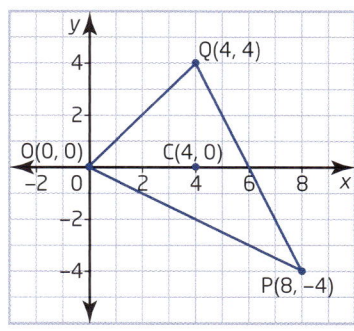

Solution

a) The centroid of a triangle is the point of intersection of the three medians. Verify that C(4, 0) is the centroid by showing that the coordinates of this point satisfy the equations for the lines that include the three medians.

Start by using the midpoint formula to find the coordinates of the midpoint, R, of side OQ.

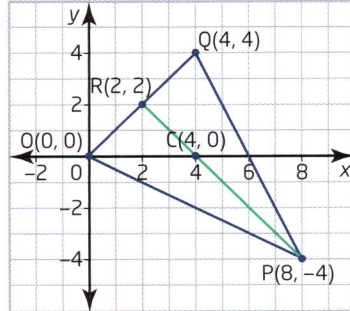

$$R(x, y) = \left(\frac{x_1 + x_2}{2}, \frac{y_1 + y_2}{2}\right)$$
$$= \left(\frac{0 + 4}{2}, \frac{0 + 4}{2}\right)$$
$$= (2, 2)$$

Use these coordinates to find the slope of the median from vertex P(8, −4).

$$m_{PR} = \frac{y_2 - y_1}{x_2 - x_1}$$
$$= \frac{2 - (-4)}{2 - 8}$$
$$= \frac{6}{-6}$$
$$= -1$$

> I could also substitute the coordinates of points P and R into $y = mx + b$ to get two equations with m and b as the unknowns. Solving this system of equations gives values for m and b.

Use this slope and the coordinates of point R to find the *y*-intercept.
$y = mx + b$
$2 = -1(2) + b$
$2 = -2 + b$
$4 = b$

An equation for the line that includes the median PR is $y = -x + 4$.

Now, substitute the coordinates of point C(4, 0) into each side of the equation.

L.S. $= y$ **R.S.** $= -x + 4$
$ = 0$ $ = -4 + 4$
$ = 0$

Since the coordinates of point C satisfy the equation and the point lies within the triangle, C(4, 0) lies on the median PR.

Next, find the midpoints, S and T, of sides OP and PQ.

$$S(x, y) = \left(\frac{x_1 + x_2}{2}, \frac{y_1 + y_2}{2}\right) \qquad T(x, y) = \left(\frac{x_1 + x_2}{2}, \frac{y_1 + y_2}{2}\right)$$
$$= \left(\frac{0 + 8}{2}, \frac{0 + (-4)}{2}\right) \qquad\qquad = \left(\frac{8 + 4}{2}, \frac{-4 + 4}{2}\right)$$
$$= (4, -2) \qquad\qquad\qquad\qquad = (6, 0)$$

The method used for the median PR will also show that point C lies on the medians OT and QS. However, examining the coordinates of the points and the diagram of △OPQ reveals a shortcut for the medians OT and QS.

Since S(4, −2), C(4, 0), and Q(4, 4) all have the same x-coordinate, these three points lie on the vertical line with equation $x = 4$. Therefore, point C lies on the median QS. Similarly, O(0, 0), C(4, 0), and T(6, 0) are **collinear** since these points all lie on the x-axis. So, point C also lies on the median OT.

collinear
- lying on the same line

Since the point C(4, 0) lies on all three medians, it is the centroid of △OPQ.

b) To find the ratio of the parts of a median on either side of the centroid, use the length formula to find the length of each part.

For the median PR, compare the lengths of PC and RC.

$$PC = \sqrt{(x_2 - x_1)^2 + (y_2 - y_1)^2} \qquad RC = \sqrt{(x_2 - x_1)^2 + (y_2 - y_1)^2}$$
$$= \sqrt{(8 - 4)^2 + (-4 - 0)^2} \qquad = \sqrt{(2 - 4)^2 + (2 - 0)^2}$$
$$= \sqrt{4^2 + (-4)^2} \qquad = \sqrt{2^2 + 2^2}$$
$$= \sqrt{4^2 \times 2} \qquad = \sqrt{2^2 \times 2}$$
$$= \sqrt{4^2} \times \sqrt{2} \qquad = \sqrt{2^2} \times \sqrt{2}$$
$$= 4\sqrt{2} \qquad = 2\sqrt{2}$$

To move a factor out from under a square root sign, I take the square root of the factor:
$\sqrt{nx} = \sqrt{n} \times \sqrt{x}$

PC is twice the length of RC.

Since the median OT is a horizontal line segment, find the lengths of OC and TC by simply comparing the x-coordinates of the endpoints. Subtract the lesser x-coordinate from the greater one.

$$OC = x_2 - x_1 \qquad TC = x_1 - x_2$$
$$= 4 - 0 \qquad = 6 - 4$$
$$= 4 \qquad = 2$$

Since QS is a vertical line segment, compare y-coordinates to find the lengths of QC and SC.

$$QC = y_1 - y_2 \qquad SC = y_2 - y_1$$
$$= 4 - 0 \qquad = 0 - (-2)$$
$$= 4 \qquad = 2$$

The centroid C(4, 0) divides each of the medians of △OPQ into a 2:1 ratio.

Example 2 Midpoints of the Sides of a Triangle

In △ABC, D is the midpoint of side AC and E is the midpoint of side BC.

a) Verify that line segment DE is parallel to side AB.

b) Verify that line segment DE is half the length of side AB.

c) Use geometry software to check your calculations in parts a) and b).

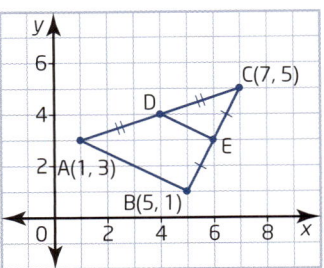

Solution

a) First, use the coordinates of the vertices to find the coordinates of the midpoints D and E.

$$D(x, y) = \left(\frac{x_1 + x_2}{2}, \frac{y_1 + y_2}{2}\right) \qquad E(x, y) = \left(\frac{x_1 + x_2}{2}, \frac{y_1 + y_2}{2}\right)$$

$$= \left(\frac{1 + 7}{2}, \frac{3 + 5}{2}\right) \qquad\qquad = \left(\frac{5 + 7}{2}, \frac{1 + 5}{2}\right)$$

$$= (4, 4) \qquad\qquad\qquad = (6, 3)$$

Now, use the coordinates of points A, B, D, and E to compare the slope of AB to the slope of DE.

$$m_{AB} = \frac{y_2 - y_1}{x_2 - x_1} \qquad m_{DE} = \frac{y_2 - y_1}{x_2 - x_1}$$

$$= \frac{1 - 3}{5 - 1} \qquad\qquad = \frac{3 - 4}{6 - 4}$$

$$= \frac{-2}{4} \qquad\qquad\qquad = -\frac{1}{2}$$

$$= -\frac{1}{2}$$

Since the slopes are the same, AB is parallel to DE.

b) Use the distance formula to compare the length of DE to the length of AB.

$$DE = \sqrt{(x_2 - x_1)^2 + (y_2 - y_1)^2} \qquad AB = \sqrt{(x_2 - x_1)^2 + (y_2 - y_1)^2}$$

$$= \sqrt{(6 - 4)^2 + (3 - 4)^2} \qquad\qquad = \sqrt{(5 - 1)^2 + (1 - 3)^2}$$

$$= \sqrt{2^2 + (-1)^2} \qquad\qquad\qquad = \sqrt{4^2 + (-2)^2}$$

$$= \sqrt{5} \qquad\qquad\qquad\qquad = \sqrt{16 + 4}$$

$$\qquad\qquad\qquad\qquad\qquad\qquad = \sqrt{20}$$

$$\qquad\qquad\qquad\qquad\qquad\qquad = \sqrt{4 \times 5}$$

$$\qquad\qquad\qquad\qquad\qquad\qquad = \sqrt{4} \times \sqrt{5}$$

$$\qquad\qquad\qquad\qquad\qquad\qquad = 2\sqrt{5}$$

Therefore, DE is half the length of AB.

c) Use either *The Geometer's Sketchpad*® or Cabri® Jr. to construct the triangle with vertices A(1, 3), B(5, 1) and C(7, 5). Construct the midpoint of AC and the midpoint of BC. Label these midpoints D and E, respectively. Then, construct the line segment DE. Use the software's measurement tools to find the slope and length of DE and of AB.

Comparing these measurements shows that the slopes are equal and AB = 2DE. Therefore, DE is parallel to AB and half the length of AB.

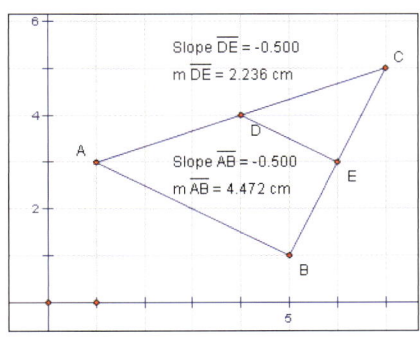
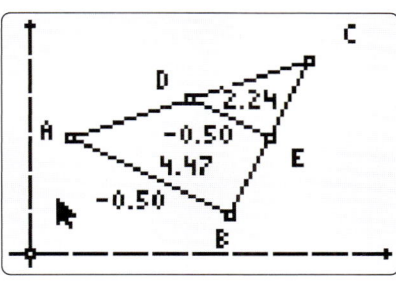

Key Concepts

- You can use the midpoint, length, and slope formulas to verify properties of specific triangles.
- Sometimes, there are several different ways to verify a property of a given triangle.
- Often, you can use a shortcut for calculations involving horizontal or vertical line segments.
- The centroid of a triangle divides each median into two parts, with one part twice the length of the other.
- The line segment joining the midpoints of two sides of a triangle is parallel to the third side and half its length.

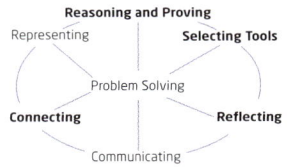

Communicate Your Understanding

C1 Describe two different ways to verify that △PQR is isosceles.

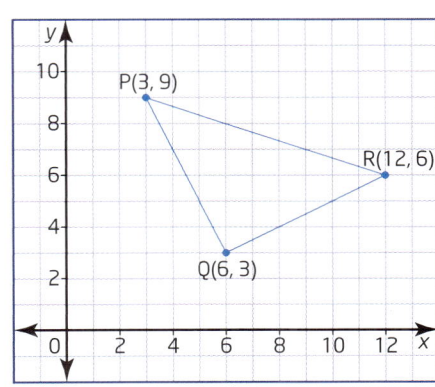

C2 Outline how to use analytic geometry to verify that the part of the median on one side of the centroid of △STU is twice the length of the part on the other side.

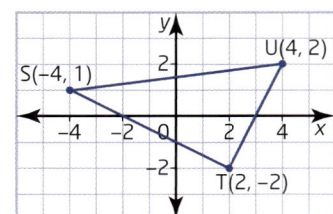

C3 Describe how to use geometry software to verify that each line segment within △VWX is parallel to one of the sides of the triangle.

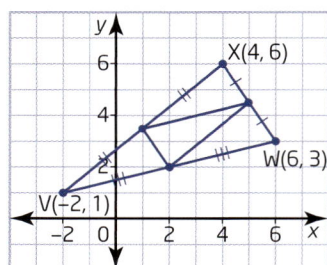

Practise

For help with question 1, see Example 1.

1. Determine an equation for the line shown with each triangle.

   a)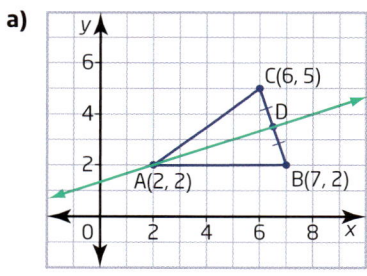

   b)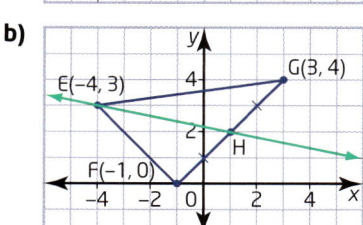

   c)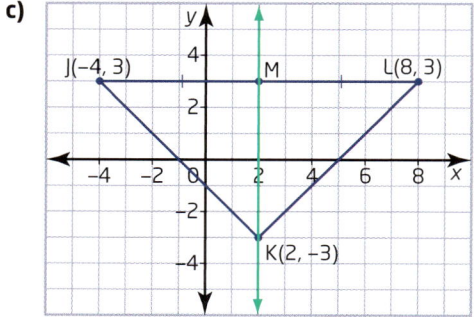

For help with questions 2 and 3, see Example 2.

2. a) Verify that DE and BC are parallel.

   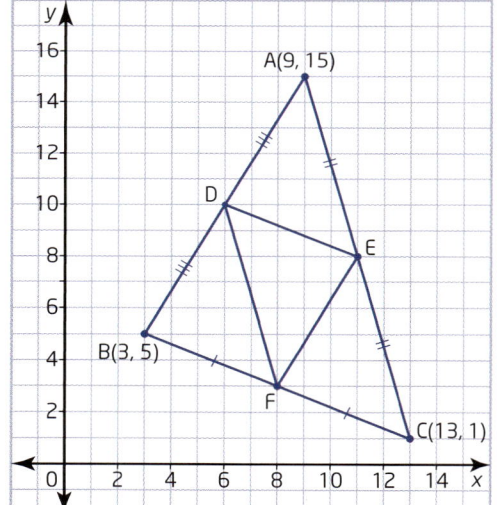

   b) List the other line segments that are parallel.
   c) Verify that DE = BF.
   d) List the other line segments that have equal lengths.

124 MHR • Chapter 3

3. Verify that PQ is twice the length of ST.

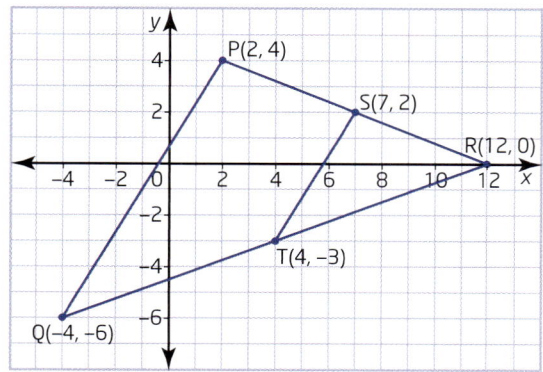

Connect and Apply

4. a) Verify that △ABC is isosceles.

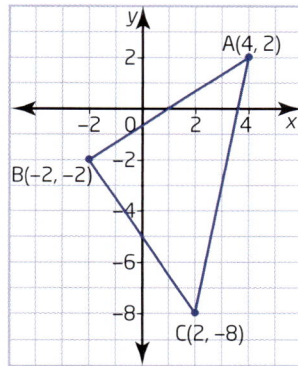

   b) Verify that the median from vertex B is also an altitude of the triangle.

5. **Use Technology** Use geometry software to verify your answers to question 4.

6. a) Find the lengths of the sides of △DEF.

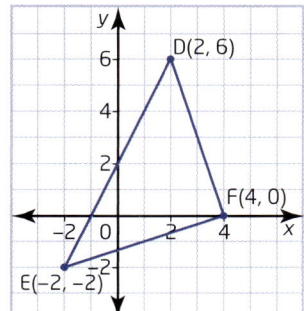

   b) Find the slopes of the sides of the triangle.

   c) Classify △DEF. Explain your reasoning.

7. a) Draw the triangle with vertices J(8, 8), K(−5, −5), and L(5, −7). What type of triangle does △JKL appear to be?

   b) Use analytic geometry to verify your classification of △JKL.

   c) Determine the perimeter of the triangle.

   d) Determine the area of the triangle.

8. **Use Technology** Use geometry software to verify your answers to question 7.

9. a) Draw the triangle with vertices P(−12, 6), Q(4, 0), and R(−8, −6).

   b) Determine the coordinates of S, the midpoint of PR, and T, the midpoint of PQ.

   c) Verify that ST is parallel to QR.

   d) Verify that ST is half the length of QR.

10. a) Draw the triangle with vertices A(3, 4), B(−2, 0), and C(5, 0). Find the midpoint of each side, and label these midpoints D, E, and F.

    b) Verify that △DEF is similar to △ABC. Find the ratio of the lengths of corresponding sides of these triangles.

    c) Verify that the area of △ABC is four times the area of △DEF.

    d) How is the ratio of the lengths of corresponding sides related to the ratio of the areas of △ABC and △DEF?

11. **Use Technology** Use geometry software to verify your answers to question 10.

12. A landscape architect is drawing plans for a rigid triangular canopy to provide shade in a courtyard. On the drawing, the vertices of the canopy are O(0, 0), P(10, 0), and Q(2, 12). A single pole will support the canopy.

    a) Verify that the triangular canopy has a centroid.

    b) Explain why the centroid is a good location for attaching the canopy to the support pole.

13. a) Verify that the triangle with vertices J(1, 2), K(−3, −1), and L(0, −5) is an isosceles right triangle.
    b) Describe another method that you could use to answer part a).

14. a) Determine the equations of the right bisectors of the sides of △OAB.

    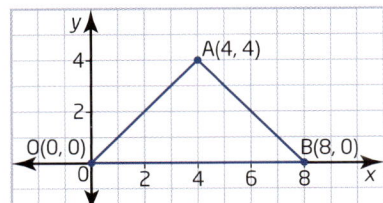

    b) Determine the coordinates of the circumcentre, the point of intersection of the right bisectors of the sides.
    c) What kind of triangle is △OAB? Justify your answer.
    d) Describe the location of the circumcentre of this triangle.

15. a) Show that the right bisectors of the sides of △DEF all intersect at point C(−4, 4), the circumcentre of the triangle.
    b) Verify that point C is equidistant from the three vertices of △DEF.

    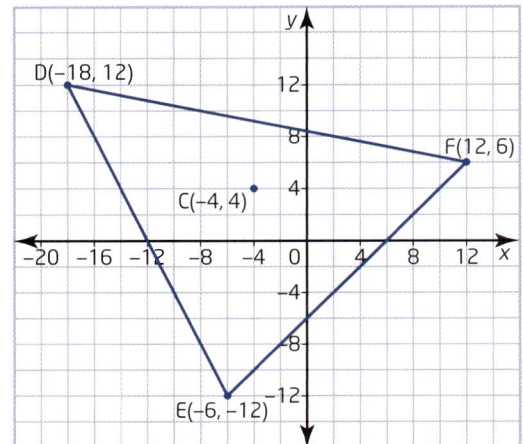

16. **Chapter Problem**
    a) Draw a large △ABC with ∠A = 36° and ∠B = ∠C = 72°. Bisect ∠B. Label the intersection of the angle bisector with side AC as point D.

    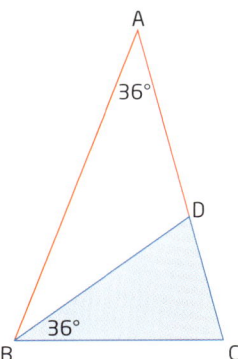

    b) Verify that both △ABC and △BCD are golden triangles. Explain how you know that these two triangles are similar.
    c) Construct the bisector of ∠C, and label the intersection with BD as point E. Then, bisect ∠CDE. Continue this process to produce a series of smaller and smaller golden triangles.
    d) Draw a smooth curve through points A, B, C, D, E, and so on. This curve is a golden spiral.
    e) Is this golden spiral a fractal? Explain.

Achievement Check

17. Verify that the points A(2, 1), B(8, 5), and C(−1, −1) are collinear using
    a) slopes
    b) an equation of a line
    c) lengths

Extend

18. A triangle has vertices P(a, b), Q(c, d), and R(e, f).
    a) Determine the coordinates of S and T, the midpoints of PQ and PR, respectively.
    b) Verify that ST is parallel to QR
    c) Verify that ST is half the length of QR.

19. A **cevian** is any line segment that joins a vertex of a triangle to a point on the opposite side. In 1678, the Italian mathematician Giovanni Ceva published a theorem about concurrent cevians in a triangle. Ceva's theorem states that $\frac{AD}{DB} \times \frac{BE}{EC} \times \frac{CF}{FA} = 1$, where AE, BF, and CD are concurrent cevians in $\triangle ABC$.

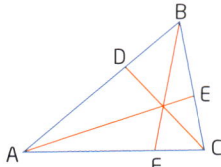

a) Draw any three concurrent cevians in a large scalene triangle. Measure the line segments to verify that Ceva's theorem applies for your triangle.

b) Verify that Ceva's theorem applies for the medians of any triangle.

c) **Use Technology** Use geometry software to verify that Ceva's theorem applies for all triangles. Outline your method.

20. ABCDE is a regular pentagon. Which of the triangles formed by the diagonals of pentagon ABCDE are golden triangles?

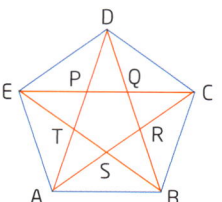

21. Math Contest The golden ratio is $\varphi = \frac{1 + \sqrt{5}}{2}$. Show that $\varphi^2 = \varphi + 1$.

22. Math Contest How many different three-letter arrangements can you make using the letters in the word *MOLLY*?

A 6
B 30
C 33
D 60
E 120

Making Connections

You can use *The Geometer's Sketchpad*® to generate nested golden triangles.

Construct a long line segment AB. Select point A, and choose **Mark Center** from the **Transform** menu. Select point B, and choose **Rotate** from the **Transform** menu. Change the rotation angle to 36°. Construct line segments from A to B' and B to B'.

Select points A and B, in that order. Choose **Iterate** from the **Transform** menu. Map A onto B and B onto B'. Press (+) or (−) to set the number of iterations to at least 5. Click on **Iterate**.

Drawing a smooth curve through the vertices of the nested golden triangles produces a golden spiral. You can draw this spiral by hand on a printout. There are Web sites with software for drawing golden spirals.

www Go to www.mcgrawhill.ca/links/principles10 and follow the links to find sites that generate golden triangles and golden spirals.

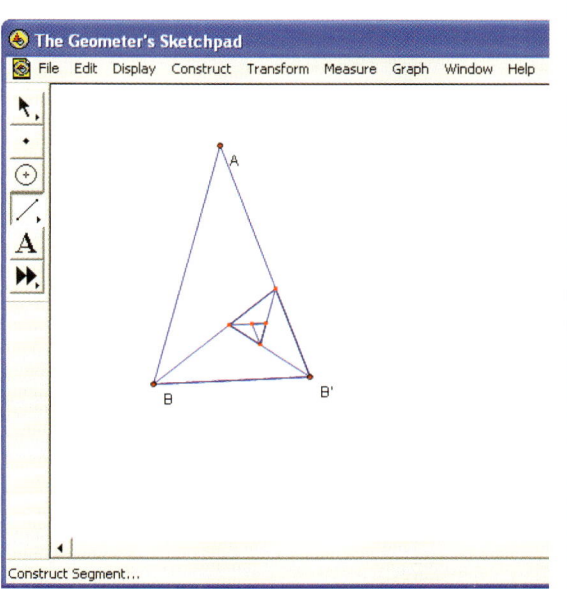

3.3 Investigate Properties of Quadrilaterals

Rectangular shapes dominate the skylines of most cities in North America. This section investigates the properties of rectangles and other types of quadrilaterals.

Investigate

What properties does a parallelogram have?

Tools
- grid paper
- ruler
- compasses
- protractor

Method 1: Use Pencil and Paper

1. Draw a large parallelogram on grid paper. Describe your method and explain how you know that it produces a parallelogram.

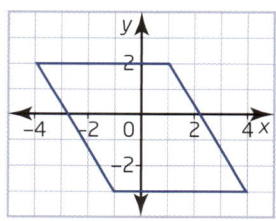

2. Draw the diagonals of the parallelogram. Describe the location of the point where the diagonals intersect.

3. Make a conjecture about how the point of intersection of the diagonals divides each diagonal.

4. Fold your parallelogram drawing to test your conjecture. Describe your findings. Compare your results with those of several classmates.

5. **Reflect** What can you conclude about the diagonals of the parallelograms drawn by you and your classmates? Do you think that this conclusion applies to all parallelograms? Explain your reasoning.

6. Mark the midpoint of each side of the parallelogram. Join the midpoints of adjacent sides to form a quadrilateral within the parallelogram. What properties does the new quadrilateral appear to have?

7. Make a conjecture about the type of quadrilateral formed by joining the midpoints of adjacent sides of a parallelogram.

8. Use measurements or paper-folding to determine whether your conjecture is true. Describe your findings, and compare them with those of several classmates.

9. Reflect What can you conclude about the midpoints of the sides of the parallelograms drawn by you and your classmates? Do you think that this conclusion applies to all parallelograms? Explain.

Method 2: Use *The Geometer's Sketchpad*®

Tools
- computer with *The Geometer's Sketchpad*®

1. Turn on the grid display and automatic labelling of points.

2. Construct line segment AB and point C above it. Connect B to C with a line segment. Select point C and line segment AB. Choose **Parallel Line** from the **Construct** menu. Select point A and line segment BC. Then, choose **Parallel Line** from the **Construct** menu again.

3. Select the two lines that you constructed, and choose **Intersection** from the **Construct** menu. Select the two lines again, and choose **Hide Parallel Lines** from the **Display** menu.

Technology Tip
The keyboard shortcut for the **Hide** option is Ctrl+H.

4. Construct line segments from C to D and from D to A.

5. Explain how you know that quadrilateral ABCD is a parallelogram.

6. Construct diagonals AC and BD. Select the two diagonals and choose **Intersection** from the **Construct** menu. Measure the distance from the intersection point E to each of the four vertices. What can you conclude from these measurements?

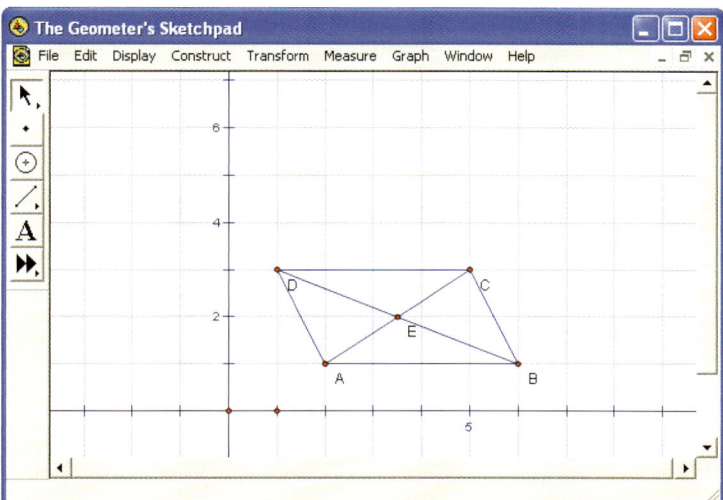

7. Drag each of the vertices of ABCD to various new locations. Does ABCD remain a parallelogram? What do you notice about the lengths of AE, BE, CE, and DE?

8. Reflect What property do the diagonals of parallelograms have? Explain your reasoning.

9. Hide or delete the diagonals and their measurements. Construct the midpoint of each side of the parallelogram. Construct line segments to join the midpoints of adjacent sides. What properties does the quadrilateral formed by these line segments appear to have?

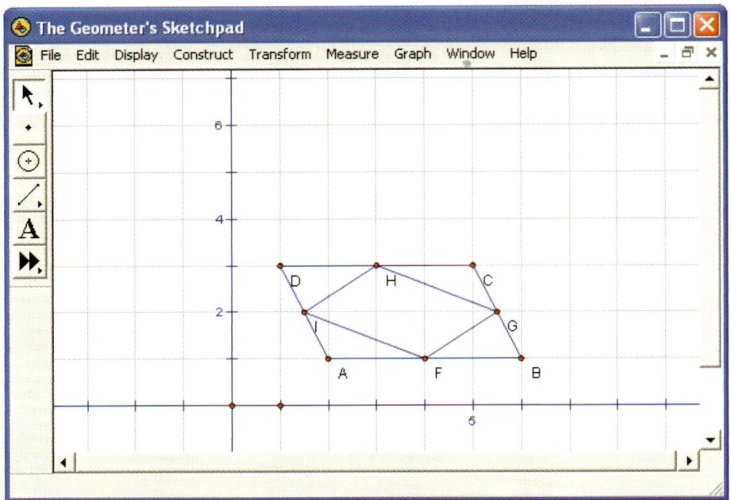

10. Make a conjecture about the type of quadrilateral formed by joining the midpoints of adjacent sides of a parallelogram.

11. Use measurements to determine whether your conjecture is true. Describe your findings.

12. Observe your measurements of quadrilateral FGHI as you drag the vertices of ABCD around the screen. Do any of the relationships among the measurements change?

13. **Reflect** What can you conclude about the midpoints of the sides of a parallelogram? Explain how you know that this conclusion applies to all parallelograms.

Method 3: Use a Graphing Calculator

Tools
- TI-83 Plus or TI-84 Plus graphing calculator

1. Start the Cabri® Jr. application. Use the **F5** menu to show the axes if they do not appear on the screen. Choose **Segment** from the **F2** menu, and draw a line segment AB near the bottom of the screen. Draw another segment from B to a point C above the segment AB. Choose **Alpha-Num** from the **F5** menu. Label the points A, B, and C.

2. Choose **Parallel** from the **F3** menu. Move the cursor to segment AB until it flashes, and press (ENTER). Select point C, segment BC, and point A in the same way.

3. Choose **Point** from the **F2** menu; then, choose **Intersection** from the submenu. Move the cursor to the line through point A and press (ENTER). Then, move the cursor to the line through point C and press (ENTER) again. Label the intersection as point D.

4. Choose **Segment** from the **F2** menu, and construct diagonal line segments from A to C and from B to D. Then, choose **Intersection** from the **F2** menu, and construct the intersection of the line segments. Label this intersection as point E.

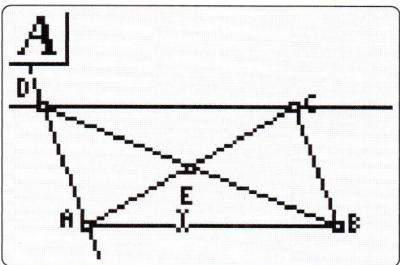

5. Choose **Measure** from the **F5** menu; then, choose **D. & Length**. Move the cursor to point A until it flashes and press ENTER. Select point E in the same way. Move the measurement to a convenient location. Press ENTER to lock the measurement in place. Use the same procedure to measure the lengths of BE, CE, and DE. What can you conclude from these measurements?

6. Press CLEAR. Move the cursor to point B and press ALPHA. Drag vertex B to various new locations. Does ABCD remain a parallelogram? What do you notice about the lengths of AE, BE, CE, and DE?

7. **Reflect** What property do the diagonals of parallelograms have? Explain your reasoning.

8. Press ALPHA. Choose **Hide/Show** from the **F5** menu; then, choose **Object**. Hide the diagonals and their measurements. Choose **Midpoint** from the **F3** menu. Select point A and then point B. Select point B again; then, select point C. Use the same procedure to construct the midpoints of CD and AD. Label the midpoints F, G, H, and I.

9. Construct line segments to join the midpoints of adjacent sides. What properties does the quadrilateral formed by these line segments appear to have?

10. Make a conjecture about the type of quadrilateral formed by joining the midpoints of adjacent sides of a parallelogram.

11. Use measurements to determine whether your conjecture is true. Describe your findings.

12. Observe your measurements of quadrilateral FGHI as you drag vertex B around the screen. Do any of the relationships among the measurements change?

13. **Reflect** What can you conclude about the midpoints of the sides of a parallelogram? Explain how you know that this conclusion applies to all parallelograms.

Example 1 Midpoints of a Quadrilateral

Draw any quadrilateral ABCD and find the midpoint of each side. Form a smaller quadrilateral EFGH inside the original one by drawing line segments joining the midpoints of adjacent sides. Investigate the properties of the smaller quadrilateral.

Solution

The inner quadrilateral EFGH appears to be a parallelogram. To test this conjecture, investigate the properties of the sides of EFGH.

Method 1: Use Pencil and Paper

Draw the diagonal from vertex A to vertex C. In △DAC, line segment GH joins the midpoints of sides AD and CD. Any line segment joining the midpoints of two sides of a triangle is parallel to the third side. Therefore, GH is parallel to CA. Similarly, EF joins the midpoints of two sides of △ABC, so EF is also parallel to CA. Therefore, EF is parallel to GH.

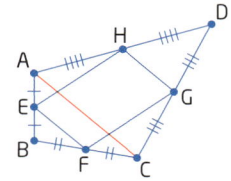

Applying the same properties in △ABD and △BCD shows that EH is parallel to FG. Since both pairs of opposite sides in quadrilateral EFGH are parallel, it is a parallelogram.

Method 2: Use Geometry Software

Construct any quadrilateral. Then, construct the midpoint of each side. Add line segments joining the midpoints of adjacent sides.

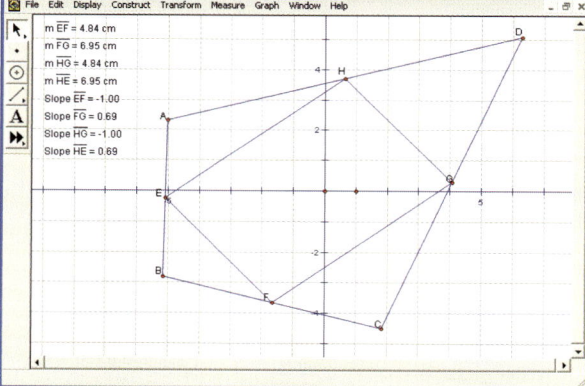

Measure the slope of each side of the inner quadrilateral. The measurements show that the opposite sides are parallel.

When the vertices of the original quadrilateral are dragged around the screen, the slopes of the opposite sides remain equal.

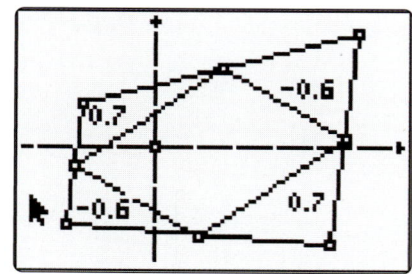

Therefore, the quadrilateral formed by joining the midpoints of adjacent sides of any quadrilateral is a parallelogram.

> **Did You Know?**
>
> The parallelogram formed by connecting the midpoints of adjacent sides of a quadrilateral is called a **Varignon parallelogram** after the French mathematician Pierre Varignon (1654–1722).

Example 2 Midpoints of a Trapezoid

Investigate the properties of the midpoints of the non-parallel sides of a trapezoid.

Solution

Method 1: Use Paper Folding

Draw a large trapezoid on a sheet of paper. Find the midpoint of each non-parallel side by folding your drawing so that one end is on top of the other.

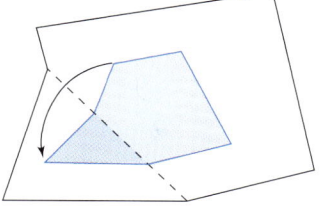

Then, draw a line segment joining the midpoints of the non-parallel sides. This line segment appears to be parallel to the parallel sides of the trapezoid.

Now, fold the trapezoid along the line segment joining the midpoints of the non-parallel sides. The parallel sides of the trapezoid line up perfectly.

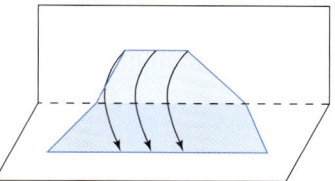

Therefore, the line segment joining the midpoints of the non-parallel sides is parallel to the other two sides and lies halfway between them.

Method 2: Use Analytic Geometry

Draw run-rise triangles on the two non-parallel sides. The sum of the runs of these sides is equal to the difference between the lengths of the parallel sides. So,

$QR = PS + \text{run}_{PQ} + \text{run}_{RS}$

Similarly, $TU = PS + \text{run}_{PT} + \text{run}_{US}$.

The run from the midpoint of a side to either endpoint is equal to half the run between the endpoints. So,

$TU = PS + \dfrac{\text{run}_{QP}}{2} + \dfrac{\text{run}_{RS}}{2}$

$= \dfrac{2PS + \text{run}_{QP} + \text{run}_{RS}}{2}$

$= \dfrac{PS + (PS + \text{run}_{QP} + \text{run}_{RS})}{2}$

$= \dfrac{PS + QS}{2}$

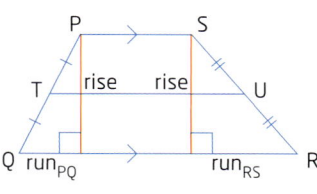

The length of the line segment joining the midpoints of the non-parallel sides is equal to the mean of the lengths of the parallel sides.

Key Concepts

- The diagonals of a parallelogram bisect each other.
- Joining the midpoints of adjacent sides of any quadrilateral forms a parallelogram.
- The line segment joining the midpoints of the non-parallel sides of a trapezoid is parallel to the parallel sides and has a length equal to the mean of the lengths of the parallel sides.

Communicate Your Understanding

C1 Describe how you could fold a drawing to investigate the properties of the diagonals of a rhombus.

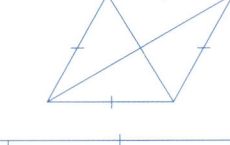

C2 Describe how you could use geometry software to investigate the properties of the diagonals of a rectangle.

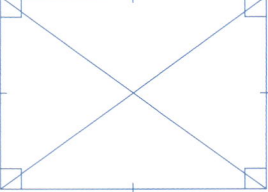

Practise

1. Which of the line segments inside each parallelogram are equal in length?

a)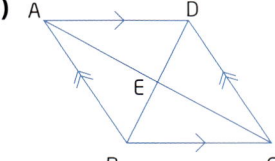

b)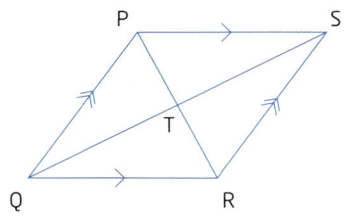

For help with questions 2 and 3, see Example 1.

2. Which of the line segments inside each quadrilateral are parallel?

a)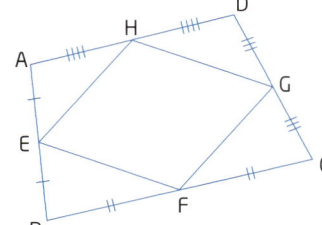

b)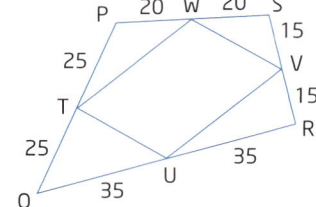

3. Which of the line segments inside each quadrilateral in question 2 are equal in length?

For help with questions 4 and 5, see Example 2.

4. a) Which line segments are parallel in the figure below?
   b) Find the length of EG.
   c) Find the length of FH.

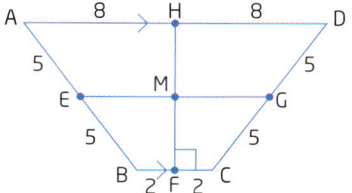

5. Find the length of QR.

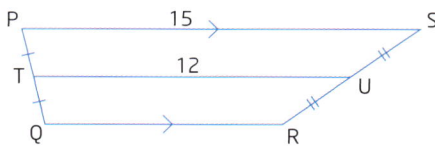

Connect and Apply

6. Fold a drawing of a square to investigate the properties of its diagonals. Describe your findings.

7. Describe how you can use geometry software to determine when the diagonals of a parallelogram are equal in length.

8. a) Draw two line segments, AC and BD, that bisect each other at right angles. Then, draw a quadrilateral that has AC and BD as its diagonals. Classify the quadrilateral. Justify this classification.
   b) Find the midpoints of AB, BC, CD, and DA, labelling these points E, F, G, and H, respectively. Draw line segments joining the midpoints of adjacent sides. Classify the quadrilateral EFGH. Justify this classification.

9. What properties make rectangles useful in the construction of buildings and other structures?

10. Sarah determines that the diagonals of a particular quadrilateral bisect each other and are equal in length. She concludes that the quadrilateral must be a square. Is Sarah correct? Explain your reasoning.

11. a) Investigate the properties of the diagonals of a rectangle. Describe your findings.
    b) Investigate the properties of the diagonals of a kite. Describe your findings.
    c) A rhombus is both a parallelogram and a kite. Make a conjecture about the properties of the diagonals of a rhombus.
    d) Describe how you could use geometry software to test your conjecture in part c).
    e) Make a table to summarize the properties of the diagonals of squares, rectangles, parallelograms, rhombi, and kites.

12. a) Predict the location of the balance point of a flat uniform rectangular object. Explain your reasoning.
    b) Describe how you could determine if your prediction is correct.

13. Use a rectangle to estimate the location of the geographical centre of Canada.
    a) Trace the outline of Canada from the map on page 115 onto a sheet of paper. Draw a rectangle on your outline to approximate the shape of Canada as closely as you can.
    b) Describe how to find the centre of this rectangle.
    c) Find the centre you described in part b). Then, find the town or city closest to this centre. Compare your estimate of the geographical centre of Canada with those made by your classmates.

Achievement Check

14. Use analytic geometry to verify that

    a) joining the midpoints of adjacent sides of quadrilateral JKLM forms a rhombus

    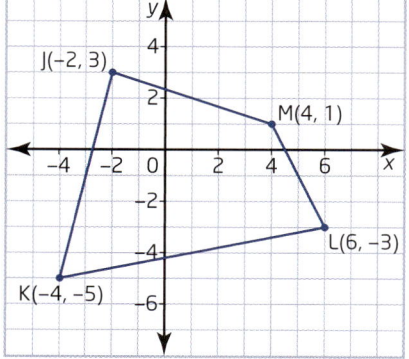

    b) the diagonals of the rhombus bisect each other at right angles

Extend

15. Investigate the Varignon parallelogram formed by joining the midpoints of adjacent sides of various types of quadrilaterals. Under what conditions is this parallelogram

    a) a rectangle?
    b) a square?
    c) a rhombus?

    Explain how you determined these conditions.

16. a) Can you draw a circle through all of the vertices of any rectangle? Justify your answer.

    b) Can you draw a circle through all of the vertices of any quadrilateral? Support your answer with a diagram.

17. Explain why a triangular brace is stronger than a rectangular brace made of the same materials.

    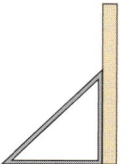 

18. The English mathematician and theoretical physicist Roger Penrose (b. 1931) has studied the patterns that can be made with tiles that have shapes based on the golden ratio.

    a) Use a library or the Internet to research Penrose tiles.

    b) Draw the two rhombus shapes that Penrose used for his tiles. Explain how each shape is made from golden triangles.

    c) Penrose tiles can cover a plane without any gaps, but the pattern is *aperiodic*. Explain what this term means.

    d) Describe another unusual property of Penrose tiles.

    e) Penrose also made aperiodic tilings using a particular kite and dart. Draw these two shapes, and explain how they are related to the golden ratio.

    f) Make your own tile pattern with Penrose rhombi. Use computer software, or cut the tile shapes out of paper or cardboard.

     Go to www.mcgrawhill.ca/links/principles10 and follow the links to learn more about Penrose tilings.

19. **Math Contest** The golden ratio is $\varphi = \dfrac{1 + \sqrt{5}}{2}$. Show that $\dfrac{1}{\varphi} = \varphi - 1$.

3.4 Verify Properties of Quadrilaterals

The new addition to the Royal Ontario Museum features a number of quadrilateral panels. This controversial design mimics the shape of mineral crystals.

Investigate

How can you verify properties of a parallelogram?

Tools

- grid paper

Method 1: Use Pencil and Paper

1. Calculate the slopes of the sides of quadrilateral ABCD. Explain how you can use these slopes to verify that ABCD is a parallelogram.

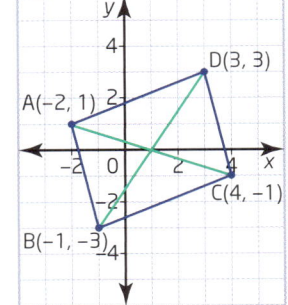

2. Calculate the length of each side of ABCD. Explain how you can use these lengths to show that ABCD is a parallelogram.

3. Explain how you can use angle measurements to show that ABCD is a parallelogram.

4. **Reflect** List the properties that you can use to determine whether a given quadrilateral is a parallelogram.

5. Verify that the diagonals, AC and BD, bisect each other.

6. Explain how you can use congruent triangles to verify that the diagonals of ABCD bisect each other.

7. **Reflect** Are all quadrilaterals with diagonals that bisect each other parallelograms? Can you use this property to determine whether a given quadrilateral is a parallelogram? Justify your answer.

- computer with *The Geometer's Sketchpad*®

Method 2: Use *The Geometer's Sketchpad*®

1. Construct the quadrilateral with vertices A(−2, 1), B(3, 3), C(4, −1), and D(−1, −3).

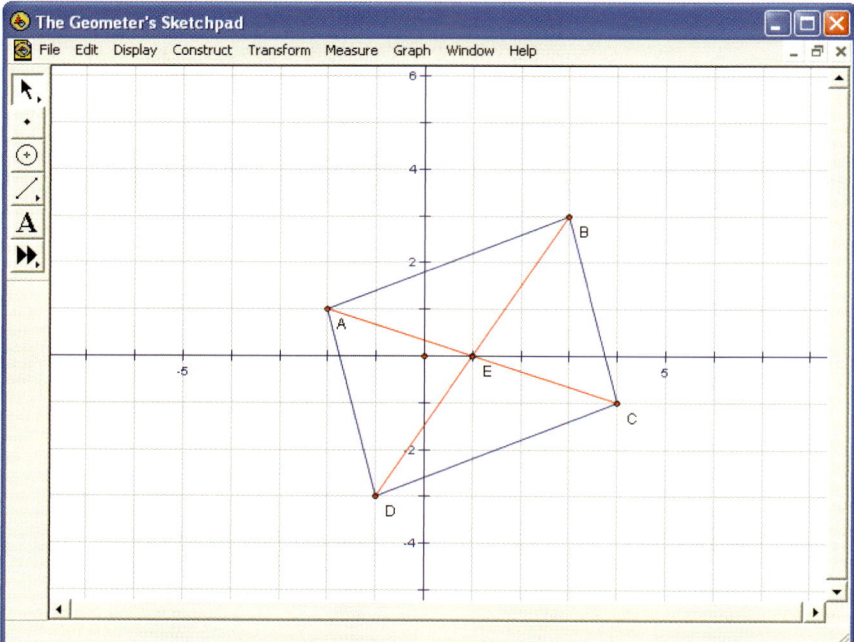

2. Measure the slope of each side of the quadrilateral. Explain how you can use these slopes to verify that ABCD is a parallelogram.

3. Measure the length of each side of ABCD. Explain how you can use these lengths to show that ABCD is a parallelogram.

4. Explain how you can use angle measurements to show that ABCD is a parallelogram.

5. **Reflect** List the properties that you can use to determine whether a given quadrilateral is a parallelogram.

6. Construct the diagonals AC and BD and their point of intersection. Verify that the diagonals bisect each other.

7. **Reflect** Are all quadrilaterals with diagonals that bisect each other parallelograms? Can you use this property to determine whether a given quadrilateral is a parallelogram? Justify your answer.

Method 3: Use a Graphing Calculator

- TI-83 Plus or TI-84 Plus graphing calculator

1. Start the Cabri® Jr. application. Check that the axes are displayed.

2. Construct the quadrilateral with vertices A(−2, 1), B(3, 3), C(4, −1), and D(−1, −3). Choose **Coord. & Eq.** from the **F5** menu. Then, select the vertices to display their coordinates. Reposition any vertices that are not at the right coordinates.

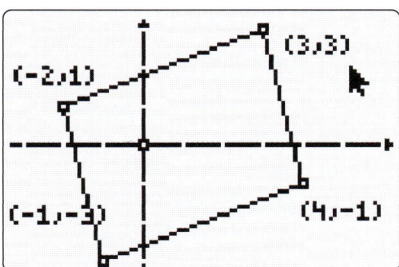

3. Choose **Measure** from the **F5** menu, and **Slope** from the submenu. Measure the slope of each side of the quadrilateral. Explain how you can use these slopes to verify that ABCD is a parallelogram.

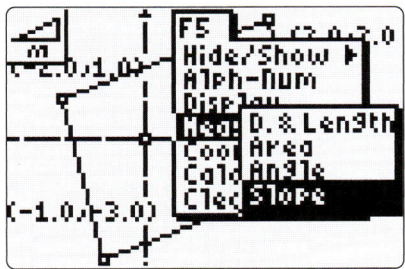

4. Measure the length of each side of ABCD. Explain how you can use these lengths to show that ABCD is a parallelogram.

5. Explain how you can use angle measurements to show that ABCD is a parallelogram.

6. **Reflect** List the properties that you can use to determine whether a given quadrilateral is a parallelogram.

7. Construct the diagonals AC and BD and their point of intersection. Verify that the diagonals bisect each other.

8. **Reflect** Are all quadrilaterals with diagonals that bisect each other parallelograms? Can you use this property to determine whether a given quadrilateral is a parallelogram? Justify your answer.

Example 1 Midpoints of a Parallelogram

Verify that quadrilateral EFGH, formed by joining the midpoints of adjacent sides of quadrilateral ABCD, is a parallelogram.

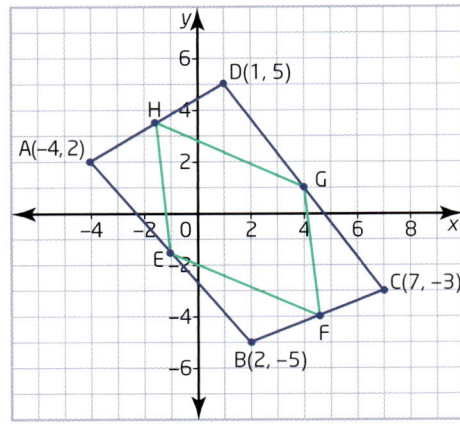

Solution

The simplest way to verify that EFGH is a parallelogram is to show that the slopes of the opposite sides are equal. First, find the coordinates of the midpoint of each side of ABCD.

$$E(x, y) = \left(\frac{x_1 + x_2}{2}, \frac{y_1 + y_2}{2}\right) \qquad F(x, y) = \left(\frac{x_1 + x_2}{2}, \frac{y_1 + y_2}{2}\right)$$

$$= \left(\frac{-4 + 2}{2}, \frac{2 + (-5)}{2}\right) \qquad = \left(\frac{2 + 7}{2}, \frac{-5 + (-3)}{2}\right)$$

$$= (-1, -1.5) \qquad = (4.5, -4)$$

$$G(x, y) = \left(\frac{x_1 + x_2}{2}, \frac{y_1 + y_2}{2}\right) \qquad H(x, y) = \left(\frac{x_1 + x_2}{2}, \frac{y_1 + y_2}{2}\right)$$

$$= \left(\frac{7 + 1}{2}, \frac{-3 + 5}{2}\right) \qquad = \left(\frac{1 + (-4)}{2}, \frac{5 + 2}{2}\right)$$

$$= (4, 1) \qquad = (-1.5, 3.5)$$

Use these coordinates to find the slope of each side of EFGH.

$$m_{EF} = \frac{y_2 - y_1}{x_2 - x_1} \qquad m_{FG} = \frac{y_2 - y_1}{x_2 - x_1}$$

$$= \frac{-4 - (-1.5)}{4.5 - (-1)} \qquad = \frac{1 - (-4)}{4 - 4.5}$$

$$= \frac{-2.5}{5.5} \times \frac{2}{2} \qquad = \frac{5}{-0.5}$$

$$= -\frac{5}{11} \qquad = -10$$

$$m_{GH} = \frac{y_2 - y_1}{x_2 - x_1} \qquad m_{HE} = \frac{y_2 - y_1}{x_2 - x_1}$$

$$= \frac{3.5 - 1}{-1.5 - 4} \qquad = \frac{-1.5 - 3.5}{-1 - (-1.5)}$$

$$= \frac{2.5}{-5.5} \times \frac{2}{2} \qquad = \frac{-5}{0.5}$$

$$= -\frac{5}{11} \qquad = -10$$

Sides EF and GH have the same slope, so they are parallel. Similarly, FG is parallel to EH. Therefore, quadrilateral EFGH is a parallelogram.

Example 2 Properties of a Rhombus

a) Verify that the quadrilateral with vertices P(3, 3), Q(0, 1), R(3, −1), and S(6, 1) is a rhombus.

b) Verify that the diagonals of PQRS bisect each other at right angles.

Solution

a) Find the length of each side of PQRS.

$PQ = \sqrt{(x_2 - x_1)^2 + (y_2 - y_1)^2}$
$= \sqrt{(0 - 3)^2 + (1 - 3)^2}$
$= \sqrt{(-3)^2 + (-2)^2}$
$= \sqrt{13}$

$QR = \sqrt{(x_2 - x_1)^2 + (y_2 - y_1)^2}$
$= \sqrt{(3 - 0)^2 + (-1 - 1)^2}$
$= \sqrt{3^2 + (-2)^2}$
$= \sqrt{13}$

$RS = \sqrt{(x_2 - x_1)^2 + (y_2 - y_1)^2}$
$= \sqrt{(6 - 3)^2 + (1 - (-1))^2}$
$= \sqrt{3^2 + 2^2}$
$= \sqrt{13}$

$PS = \sqrt{(x_2 - x_1)^2 + (y_2 - y_1)^2}$
$= \sqrt{(6 - 3)^2 + (1 - 3)^2}$
$= \sqrt{3^2 + (-2)^2}$
$= \sqrt{13}$

All four sides are equal in length. Therefore, PQRS is a rhombus.

b) If the diagonals have the same midpoint, they bisect each other.
Find the coordinates of the midpoint of each diagonal.

For PR:
$(x, y) = \left(\dfrac{x_1 + x_2}{2}, \dfrac{y_1 + y_2}{2}\right)$
$= \left(\dfrac{3 + 3}{2}, \dfrac{3 + (-1)}{2}\right)$
$= (3, 1)$

For QS:
$(x, y) = \left(\dfrac{x_1 + x_2}{2}, \dfrac{y_1 + y_2}{2}\right)$
$= \left(\dfrac{0 + 6}{2}, \dfrac{1 + 1}{2}\right)$
$= (3, 1)$

> I could show that the diagonals bisect each other by calculating and comparing the lengths PT, QT, RT, and ST.

Since the midpoints of the diagonals have the same coordinates, the diagonals bisect each other.

Now, calculate the slopes of the diagonals.

$m_{PR} = \dfrac{y_2 - y_1}{x_2 - x_1}$
$= \dfrac{-1 - 3}{3 - 3}$
$= \dfrac{-4}{0}$

$m_{QS} = \dfrac{y_2 - y_1}{x_2 - x_1}$
$= \dfrac{1 - 1}{6 - 0}$
$= 0$

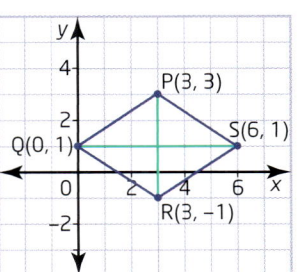

> The graph of PQRS confirms that PR is vertical and QS is horizontal.

Since m_{PR} is undefined, PR is a vertical line segment. The zero value for m_{PR} indicates that QS is a horizontal line segment. So, PR and QS are perpendicular.

Therefore, PR and QS bisect each other at right angles.

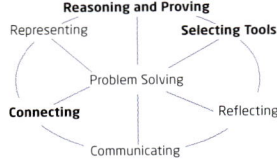

Key Concepts

- You can use the formulas for lengths, midpoints, and slopes to verify properties of quadrilaterals.
- Often, there is more than one way to verify a property of a geometric shape.

Communicate Your Understanding

C1 Describe how to use analytic geometry to verify that quadrilateral ABCD is a trapezoid.

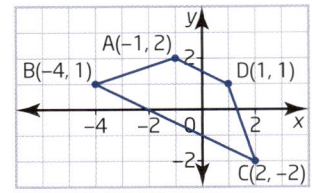

C2 Describe how to verify that the point of intersection of the diagonals of kite EFGH bisects only one of the diagonals.

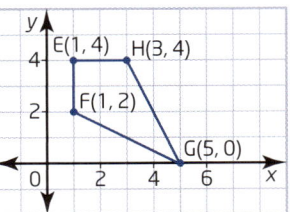

C3 Describe two methods for verifying that quadrilateral JKLM is a parallelogram. Which method is easier to use?

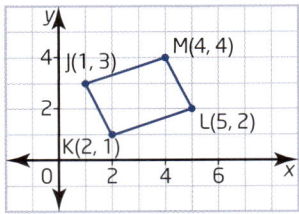

Practise

For help with question 1, see Example 1.

1. Verify that quadrilateral ABCD is a trapezoid.

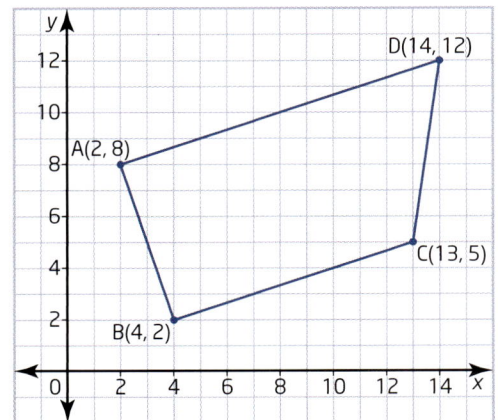

For help with questions 2 and 3, see Example 2.

2. Verify that quadrilateral EFGH is a rhombus.

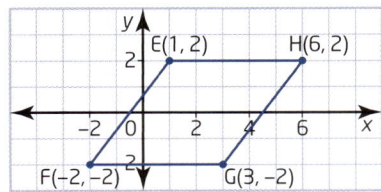

3. Verify that quadrilateral JKLM is a kite.

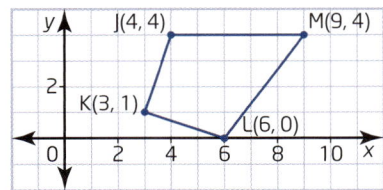

142 MHR • Chapter 3

Connect and Apply

4. a) Verify that quadrilateral ABCD is a rectangle.

b) Verify that the diagonals of ABCD are equal in length and bisect each other.

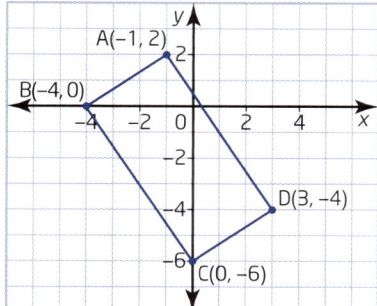

5. a) Draw the quadrilateral with vertices P(0, 7), Q(−2, 1), R(4, −1), and S(6, 3).

b) Find the midpoint of each side. Join the midpoints of adjacent sides to form a new quadrilateral TUVW.

c) Verify that opposite sides of TUVW are parallel.

d) Verify that opposite sides of TUVW are equal in length.

6. Use Technology Use geometry software to answer question 5. Outline your method.

7. a) Draw the trapezoid with vertices A(−2, −2), B(2, −2), C(4, 1), and D(2, 4).

b) Verify that the line segment joining the midpoints of the non-parallel sides of the trapezoid is parallel to the other two sides.

8. Use Technology Use geometry software to answer question 7. Outline your method.

9. a) Verify that the diagonals of the rectangle with vertices J(−2, 1), K(2, 3), L(4, −1), and M(0, −3) bisect each other at right angles.

b) Do all rectangles have this property?

c) What can you conclude about the lengths of the sides of JKLM? Explain your reasoning.

10. a) Verify that PR bisects QS at right angles.

b) Verify that QS does not bisect PR.

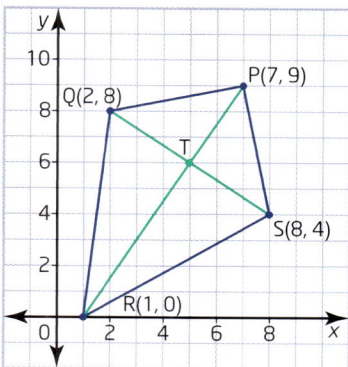

11. a) Draw the quadrilateral with vertices A(3, 4), B(−1, 2), C(−3, −4), and D(5, −6). Then, join the midpoints of the adjacent sides of ABCD to form a new quadrilateral, EFGH.

b) Verify that EFGH is a rhombus.

c) Describe another method for verifying that EFGH is a rhombus.

12. a) Draw the quadrilateral with vertices P(−3, −1), Q(3, 1), R(7, 5), and S(1, 3). Then, draw the diagonals of PQRS.

b) Verify that the diagonals bisect each other.

c) What kind of quadrilateral is PQRS? Justify your answer.

13. Use Technology Use geometry software to answer question 12. Outline your method.

14. a) Draw the rhombus with vertices A(−5, 2), B(−1, 3), C(−2, −1), and D(−6, −2).

b) Verify that joining the midpoints of the adjacent sides of ABCD produces a rectangle.

15. Use Technology Use geometry software to answer question 14. Outline your method.

16. **Chapter Problem**

a) A rectangle with $\dfrac{\text{length}}{\text{width}} = \varphi$ is called a golden rectangle. On grid paper, draw a large rectangle, making the ratio of the length to the width as close to φ:1 as you can. The golden ratio, φ, equals 1.618….

b) Divide your golden rectangle into a square and a smaller rectangle, with the sides of the square equal to the width of the original rectangle. Measure the width and length of the smaller rectangle. Calculate the ratio of these dimensions.

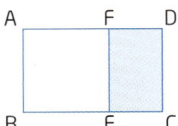

c) Divide the smaller rectangle into a square and a third rectangle. Predict the ratio of the length and the width of the third rectangle. Measure these dimensions, and calculate their ratio. Do the measurements confirm your prediction?

d) Divide the third rectangle in the same way as the others to produce a fourth rectangle. Find the length-to-width ratio of this rectangle.

e) **Use Technology** Use *The Geometer's Sketchpad*® to construct a golden rectangle. Divide this rectangle into a square and a smaller rectangle. Divide the smaller rectangle in the same way. Continue the process, producing progressively smaller rectangles. Compare the length-to-width ratios of these rectangles. What can you conclude about these ratios?

f) Is the series of nested rectangles a fractal? Justify your answer.

g) Describe how you could use the nested rectangles to generate a golden spiral.

Extend

17. Let P(a, b), Q(c, d), R(e, f), and S(g, h) represent the coordinates of the vertices of a quadrilateral.

a) Determine the coordinates of the midpoints T, U, V, and W of sides PQ, QR, RS, and SP, respectively.

b) Verify that TUVW is a parallelogram.

18. **Math Contest** How are ∠BAD and ∠BCD related?

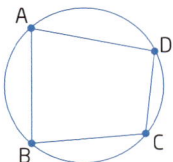

19. **Math Contest** How many four-digit numbers with no repeated digits can you make using the digits from 1 to 8?

A 7
B 8
C 1680
D 3584
E 4096

3.5 Properties of Circles

From the Canadian Arctic to Southern Africa, people have developed ingenious circular structures to use as homes or temporary shelters. The materials available and the climate greatly influence the design of these structures.

Investigate

What properties do circles have?

Method 1: Use Pencil and Paper

1. Draw a circle on a sheet of paper by tracing around a circular object such as a juice can.

2. Find the centre of the circle by folding your drawing. Explain how you know where the centre is.

3. **Reflect** What property do diameters of a circle have?

4. Mark any two points on the circle and label them A and B. Join the points to form a **chord** of the circle. Draw the right bisector of this chord. What property does this right bisector have? Check whether the right bisectors drawn by your classmates have the same property.

5. Choose any point on a blank sheet of paper, but do not mark this point. Instead, mark three points that are all about the same distance from the first point. Label these three points P, Q, and R. Exchange your set of points with a classmate.

6. Find the centre of the circle that passes through the three points that your classmate marked. Explain your method. Draw the circle that passes through the points.

7. **Reflect** What property do the chords of a circle have?

Tools
- circular object such as a juice can
- compasses
- ruler

chord
- line segment joining two points on a curve

- computer with *The Geometer's Sketchpad*®

Method 2: Use *The Geometer's Sketchpad*®

1. Turn on the grid display. Construct a point at the centre of the grid and a second point near the edge. Using the first point as the centre, construct a circle by choosing **Circle by Centre and Point** from the **Construct** menu.

2. Construct any two points on the circle. Construct a **chord** by joining these two points with a line segment.

3. Construct the right bisector of the chord.

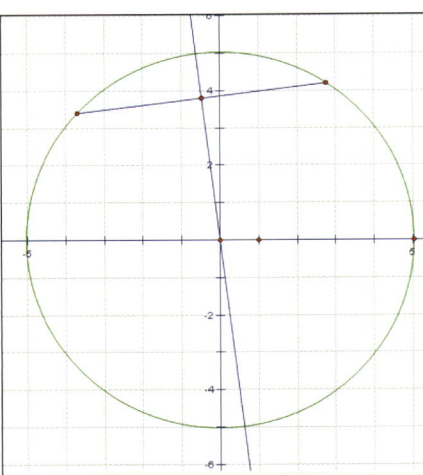

4. Select one of the endpoints of the chord. From the **Display** menu, choose **Animate Point**. As the endpoint of the chord moves around the circle, watch the right bisector of the chord. What property does this bisector have?

5. **Reflect** What property do the chords of a circle have? How you could use this property to find the centre of a circle given three points on the circumference?

- TI-83 Plus or TI-84 Plus graphing calculator

Method 3: Use a Graphing Calculator

1. Start the Cabri® Jr. application. Check that the axes are displayed. Choose **Circle** from the **F2** menu. Place the centre near the middle of the screen, and place the end of the radius close to the top of the screen.

2. Choose **Segment** from the **F2** menu. Construct a **chord** by using a line segment to join any two points on the circle.

3. Choose **Perp. Bis.** from the **F3** menu, and construct the right bisector of the chord.

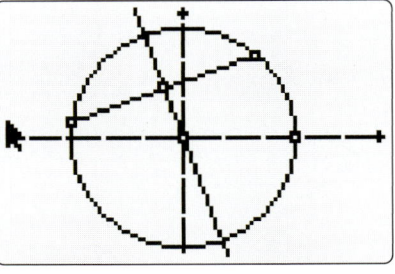

4. Move the cursor to one endpoint of the chord, and press ALPHA. Watch the right bisector of the chord as you move the endpoint around the circle. What property does this bisector have?

5. **Reflect** What property do the chords of a circle have? How could you use this property to find the centre of a circle given three points on the circumference?

Example 1 Right Bisector of a Chord

Verify that the centre of this circle lies on the right bisector of the chord AB.

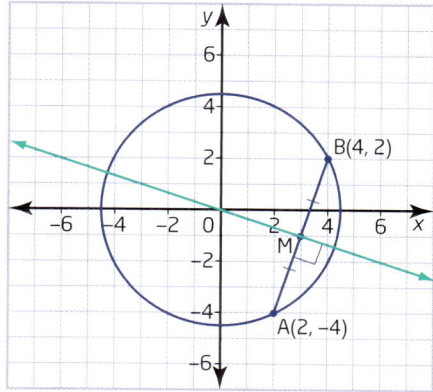

Solution

The centre lies on the right bisector of AB only if the coordinates (0, 0) satisfy the equation of the right bisector. **‹ Understand the Problem**

The midpoint of AB is on the right bisector. Use the coordinates of A and B to find the midpoint and the slope of AB. Then, calculate the slope of a line perpendicular to AB. Use this slope and the coordinates of the midpoint, M, to determine the equation of the right bisector of AB. **‹ Choose a Strategy**

Find the midpoint coordinates and the slope of AB. **‹ Carry Out the Strategy**

$$M(x, y) = \left(\frac{x_1 + x_2}{2}, \frac{y_1 + y_2}{2}\right) \qquad m_{AB} = \frac{y_2 - y_1}{x_2 - x_1}$$

$$= \left(\frac{2 + 4}{2}, \frac{-4 + 2}{2}\right) \qquad \qquad = \frac{2 - (-4)}{4 - 2}$$

$$= (3, -1) \qquad \qquad \qquad \quad = \frac{6}{2}$$

$$\qquad \qquad \qquad \qquad \qquad \qquad \quad = 3$$

Since the right bisector is perpendicular to AB, the slope of this bisector is the negative reciprocal of m_{AB}.

$$-\frac{1}{m_{AB}} = -\frac{1}{3}$$

Use this slope and the coordinates M(3, −1) to find the y-intercept.
$y = mx + b$

$-1 = -\frac{1}{3}(3) + b$

$-1 = -1 + b$
$0 = b$

All lines with a y-intercept of 0 pass through the origin.

The equation of the right bisector is $y = -\frac{1}{3}x$. The coordinates (0, 0) satisfy this equation. Therefore, the centre of the circle lies on the right bisector of the chord PQ. **‹ Reflect**

Example 2 Points on a Circle

a) Show that the points P(9, −3), Q(8, 6), and R(−1, 5) lie on a circle with its centre at C(4, 1).

b) Does any other circle pass through points P, Q, and R? Explain.

Solution

a) If the three points lie on a circle centred at (4, 1), each point must be the same distance from (4, 1). Compare the lengths of CP, CQ, and CR.

$$CP = \sqrt{(x_2 - x_1)^2 + (y_2 - y_1)^2}$$
$$= \sqrt{(9 - 4)^2 + (-3 - 1)^2}$$
$$= \sqrt{5^2 + (-4)^2}$$
$$= \sqrt{41}$$

$$CQ = \sqrt{(x_2 - x_1)^2 + (y_2 - y_1)^2}$$
$$= \sqrt{(8 - 4)^2 + (6 - 1)^2}$$
$$= \sqrt{4^2 + 5^2}$$
$$= \sqrt{41}$$

$$CR = \sqrt{(x_2 - x_1)^2 + (y_2 - y_1)^2}$$
$$= \sqrt{(-1 - 4)^2 + (5 - 1)^2}$$
$$= \sqrt{(-5)^2 + 4^2}$$
$$= \sqrt{41}$$

Since CP = CQ = CR, the points P, Q, and R all lie on a circle centred at C(4, 1).

b) The right bisector of PQ includes all points that are equidistant from P and Q. Similarly, the right bisector of QR includes all points that are equidistant from Q and R. These two lines meet only at point C(4, 1). There is no other point equidistant from P, Q, and R.

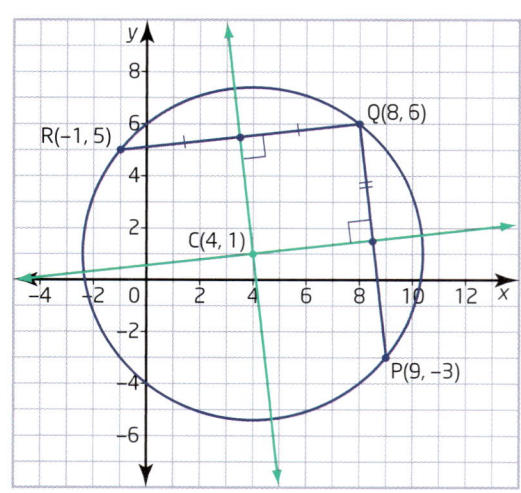

Therefore, the circle with centre C(4, 1) and radius $\sqrt{41}$ is the only circle that passes through the points P, Q, and R.

You cannot determine the centre of a circle from just two points on the circumference. The centre can lie anywhere on the right bisector of the chord between the two points.

> Reflect

Key Concepts

- The diameters of a circle intersect at the centre of the circle.

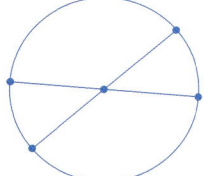

- The right bisector of a chord of a circle passes through the centre of the circle.

- The right bisectors of two chords of a circle intersect at the centre of the circle.

- There is only one circle that passes through three given non-collinear points.

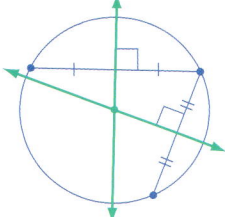

Communicate Your Understanding

C1 Describe how to find the point that is equidistant from three given points by
   a) folding a plot of the given points
   b) constructing lines
   c) using analytic geometry

C2 Describe how you would determine the balance point for a flat circular object.

Practise

For help with question 1, see Example 1.

1. a) Find the coordinates of the midpoint, M, of AB.
   b) Find the slope of the chord AB.
   c) Verify that OM is perpendicular to AB.

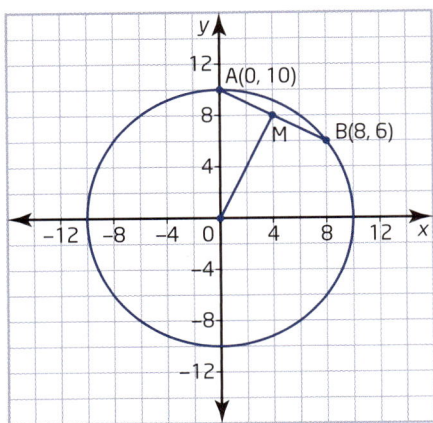

For help with questions 2 to 4, see Example 2.

2. a) Verify that the points P(−1, −2), Q(2, 7), and R(6, 5) are equidistant from the point C(2, 2).
   b) Draw the circle that passes through points P, Q, and R.

3. a) Verify that the points A(12, 6), B(4, 10), and C(0, 2) lie on a circle with its centre at D(6, 4).
   b) Determine the length of the radius of the circle.
   c) Plot points A, B, and C on grid paper, and draw the circle that passes through the points. Use your drawing to check your answers to parts a) and b).

4. a) Verify that the points E(−5, 0), F(−2, 3), and G(6, −11) lie on a circle with its centre at H(2, −4).
   b) Determine the length of the radius of the circle.

Connect and Apply

5. Verify that the centre of this circle lies on the right bisector of the chord PQ.

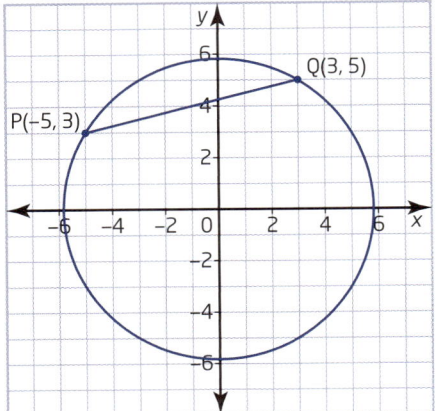

6. a) Explain how you know that the origin is the centre of the circle defined by the equation $x^2 + y^2 = 45$.
   b) Verify that the points R(−3, 6) and S(−6, −3) lie on the circle.
   c) Verify that the line through the origin and the midpoint of the chord RS is perpendicular to the chord.

7. A machinist needs to drill a hole in the centre of a circular part. Describe how the machinist could mark the correct location for this hole.

8. a) You have 3.0 m of edging to put around a flower bed. Find the maximum area you can enclose if the shape of the flower bed is an equilateral triangle.
   b) Find the maximum area you can enclose if the flower bed is square.
   c) Find the maximum area you can enclose if the flower bed is circular.
   d) What property of circles makes them a useful shape for the base of storage tanks and some types of buildings?

9. Find the centre of the circle that passes through the points A(−7, 4), B(−4, 5), and C(0, 3).

10. **Use Technology** Use geometry software to answer question 9. Outline your method.

11. Three friends live in Sudbury, Toronto, and Windsor. They are planning to go camping together and want to find a park that is approximately the same distance from each of their homes. Describe how the friends could fold an Ontario roadmap to help them find a suitable campground.

12. On a town map, the coordinates of three schools are J(8, 13), K(10, 7), and L(14, 15). The town is planning to build a new swimming pool that is the same distance from all three schools. Determine the coordinates for the pool.

13. Draw a circle with centre O. Add any chord PQ, with midpoint M. What can you conclude about △OMP and △OMQ? Explain your reasoning.

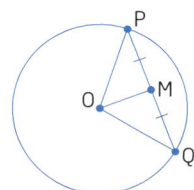

14. Draw any circle. Draw a diameter of the circle and label its endpoints J and K. Let L be any other point on the circumference of the circle. Use angle sums in triangles to show that △JKL is a right triangle.

15. **Use Technology** Use geometry software to answer question 14. Outline your method.

Extend

16. To find a good location for a community hospital, planners could find the smallest circle that encloses all the homes on a map of the community.

    a) What is the advantage of a location at the centre of the smallest enclosing circle?

    b) What other factors might prevent the centre from being the best location for the hospital?

    c) Using grid paper or geometry software, plot 15 points to represent neighbourhoods. Try to find the smallest circle that encloses these points. Describe the method that you used. Mark where you would place the hospital for the neighbourhoods that the dots represent. Explain why you chose this location.

17. A pilot filed a flight plan that listed a cruising speed of 160 km/h with enough fuel on board for 3.5 h of flying. After 2 h, the aircraft passed over Lake Traverse. The aircraft was reported missing when it failed to reach its planned destination.

    a) Sketch a diagram showing the area where the plane may have crashed.

    b) How large is this area?

    c) Which part of the search area should be searched first? Explain your reasoning.

18. **Math Contest** Show how ∠ABC and ∠AOC in quadrilateral ABCD are related.

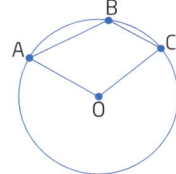

19. **Math Contest** Keshawn and Samantha are in a science class with 18 other students. The teacher randomly divides the class into 10 pairs of laboratory partners. The probability that Keshawn and Samantha are laboratory partners is

    A $\dfrac{1}{10}$

    B $\dfrac{1}{19}$

    C $\dfrac{1}{20}$

    D $\dfrac{1}{190}$

    E $\dfrac{1}{380}$

Chapter 3 Review

3.1 Investigate Properties of Triangles, pages 110–116

1. **a)** Define a median.
   b) List two additional properties of the medians of a triangle.
   c) Outline how you could use geometry software to show that the medians of all triangles have these properties.

2. **a)** Use congruent triangles to show how the lengths of the medians to the two equal sides of an isosceles triangle are related.
   b) Describe how you can use geometry software to demonstrate that this relationship applies for all isosceles triangles.

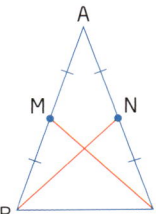

3. **a)** Draw a right triangle with the shorter sides aligned with the coordinate axes. Then, draw the right bisectors of all three sides.
   b) Show that the point of intersection of the right bisectors of the sides of any right triangle lies on the hypotenuse.
   c) Describe how you can use geometry software to answer part b).

3.2 Verify Properties of Triangles, pages 117–127

4. **a)** Verify that △DEF is a right triangle.

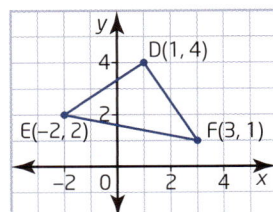

   b) Describe another method that you could use to answer part a).

5. **a)** Verify that the altitude from vertex J bisects side KL in the triangle with vertices J(−5, 4), K(1, 8), and L(−1, −2).
   b) Classify △JKL. Explain your reasoning.

3.3 Investigate Properties of Quadrilaterals, pages 128–136

6. List two properties of the diagonals of each geometric shape.
   a) square **b)** parallelogram **c)** kite

7. **a)** Show that the line segment joining the midpoints of opposite sides of any parallelogram bisects the area of the parallelogram.

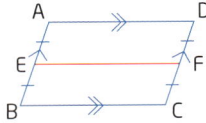

   b) Describe another way to answer part a).

3.4 Verify Properties of Quadrilaterals, pages 137–144

8. Verify that quadrilateral JKLM is a trapezoid.

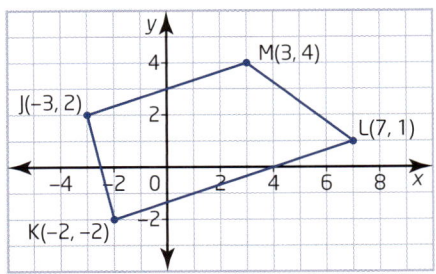

9. **a)** Classify the quadrilateral with vertices T(2, 4), U(8, 2), V(7, −1), and W(1, 1). Justify this classification.
   b) Verify a property of the diagonals of TUVW.

3.5 Properties of Circles, pages 145–151

10. a) Show that A(−12, −5) and B(12, 5) are endpoints of a diameter of the circle defined by $x^2 + y^2 = 169$.

  b) State the coordinates of another point, C, on the circle.

  c) Show that △ABC is a right triangle.

11. a) Verify that points P(5, 7) and Q(7, −5) lie on the circle with equation $x^2 + y^2 = 74$.

  b) Verify that the right bisector of the chord PQ passes through the centre of the circle.

12. Divers from scuba clubs in St. Catharines, Hamilton, and Oakville are working together to practise rescues in deep water. Describe how the clubs could find a practice site that is equidistant from the three towns.

Chapter Problem Wrap-Up

The golden ratio is also known as the divine proportion, the golden mean, and the golden section. Many people find that objects with proportions in the golden ratio are pleasing to the eye. For this reason, artists and architects sometimes use these proportions in their work.

a) Research the golden ratio at a library or on the Internet. Is the golden ratio a rational number? Explain.

b) Give an example of a regular geometric shape that involves the golden ratio. Describe how the golden ratio appears in this shape.

c) Give an example of a natural object that may contain the golden ratio. Explain why researchers disagree on whether the golden ratio occurs frequently in nature.

d) Some researchers argue that designers in ancient times used the golden ratio in buildings such as the Parthenon in Athens, Greece, and the Great Pyramid at Giza, Egypt. Do you think these claims are valid? Justify your answer.

e) Measure a textbook. Are any of the dimensions related by the golden ratio? Explain.

Go to www.mcgrawhill.ca/links/principles10 and follow the links to learn more about the golden ratio.

Chapter 3 Practice Test

1. Which of these triangles have at least two medians that are equal in length? Justify your choices.

   A 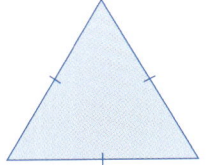   B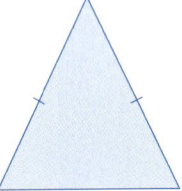

   C 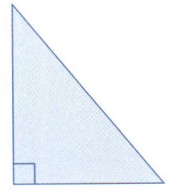   D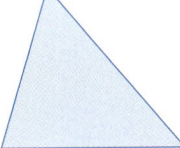

   E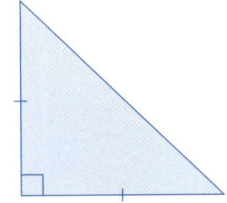

2. Which of the triangles in question 1 have a median that is also an altitude? Justify your choices.

3. Sketch an example of each of these types of quadrilateral. Show the diagonals on each sketch and indicate whether they are equal in length and whether they bisect each other.
   a) square
   b) rectangle
   c) parallelogram
   d) rhombus
   e) trapezoid
   f) quadrilateral with no equal sides

4. Show that two of the altitudes of an isosceles triangle are equal in length.

5. a) Verify that △ABC is isosceles.
   b) Verify that the centroid of △ABC lies at $(6, -1)$.

   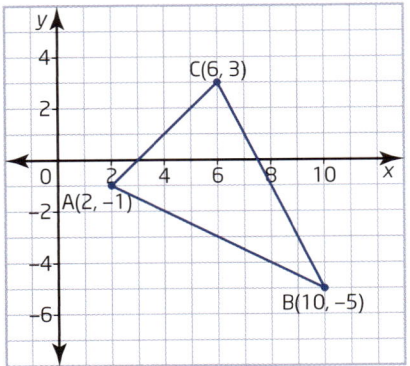

6. a) Show that the triangle with vertices $D(-2, 5)$, $E(-4, 1)$, and $F(2, 3)$ is a right triangle.
   b) Verify that the midpoint of the hypotenuse of △DEF is equidistant from all three vertices.

7. a) Use analytic geometry to verify that quadrilateral JKLM is a rhombus.
   b) Describe how to use geometry software to answer part a).

   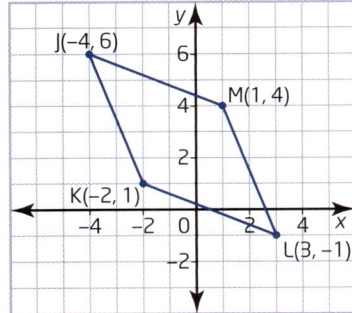

8. a) Find the midpoint of each side of the quadrilateral with vertices $P(-3, 8)$, $Q(1, 10)$, $R(5, 6)$, and $S(7, -4)$.
   b) Show that joining the midpoints of the adjacent sides of PQRS forms a parallelogram.

9. a) Verify that C(5, 2) is the centre of the circle that passes through points T(5, 15), U(17, −3), and V(−8, 2).

b) Find the radius of the circle.

10. Verify that quadrilateral ABCD is an isosceles trapezoid.

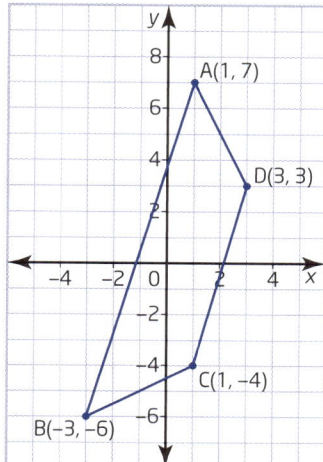

11. Describe how to use geometry software to answer question 10.

12. a) Verify that quadrilateral PQRS is a rhombus.

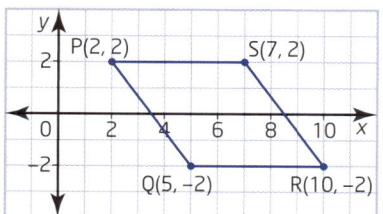

b) Verify that the diagonals of PQRS bisect each other.

c) Verify that the diagonals of PQRS meet at right angles.

13. A new hospital will serve the four small towns shown on the map. Where would you build the hospital? Justify this location.

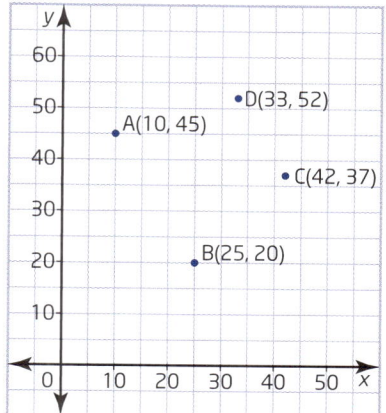

Achievement Check

14. The vertices of △EFG are E(−3, 5), F(0, −1), and G(6, 5).

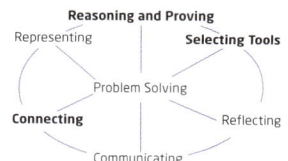

a) Find the coordinates of the point of intersection of the medians of △EFG.

b) Find the coordinates of the point of intersection of the right bisectors of the sides of △EFG.

c) Find the coordinates of the point of intersection of the altitudes of △EFG.

d) Verify that these three points of intersection are collinear.

Chapters 1 to 3 Review

Chapter 1 Linear Systems

1. Solve each linear system. For each system, explain why you chose the method that you used. Check each solution.
   a) $x + 2y = 3$
      $3x - y = 1$
   b) $x - y = -1$
      $2x + y = 4$
   c) $3x + 2y = 28$
      $5x - 3y = 15$
   d) $\frac{1}{2}x + y = 4$
      $x + \frac{1}{3}y = 2$

2. All 120 seats in a hall were filled for a concert. The tickets cost $10 for adults and $6 for students. The total proceeds were $980. How many adults attended the concert? How many students?

3. Two wind turbines generate a total of 57 kW of power. The larger turbine generates twice as much power as the smaller one. Find the power output of each turbine.

4. A contractor rented a sander and a polisher for 5 h for $50. For another job, she rented the sander for 4 h and the polisher for 8 h. The rental fees for that job totalled $56. Find the hourly rate charged for each tool.

5. Lou's class is selling T-shirts for a fundraiser. The supplier charges $750 for the initial design and set-up plus $5 for each imprinted T-shirt. The students sell the T-shirts for $15 each.
   a) How many T-shirts do the students need to sell to break even?
   b) How much profit will the students make if they sell 150 T-shirts?

6. For his coffee shop, Abdul wants to make a mocha-java blend that will sell for $18/kg. The mocha coffee beans sell for $20/kg, and the java coffee beans sell for $15/kg. How many kilograms of each kind of coffee bean should he use to make 50 kg of the mocha-java blend?

Chapter 2 Analytic Geometry

7. a) Determine the midpoint of each side of △ABC.
   b) Calculate the perimeter of △ABC.

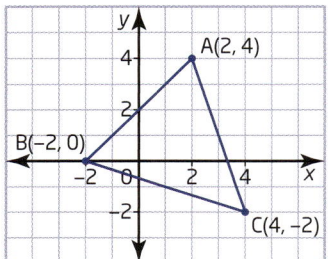

8. a) Plot the triangle with vertices D(6, 8), E(1, 8), and F(4, 2).
   b) Determine the equation of the right bisector of side DE.
   c) Determine the equation of the right bisector of side EF.
   d) Determine the coordinates of the point of intersection, M, of the right bisectors in parts a) and b).
   e) Show that point M is equidistant from vertices D, E, and F.

9. Classify the triangle with vertices G(−4, −1), H(2, −3), and I(4, 3). Explain your reasoning.

10. M and N are the midpoints of sides JK and KL. Show that MN is parallel to JL.

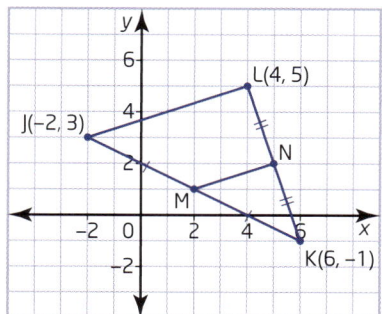

11. Find an equation for the circle that is centred at the origin and
    a) has a radius of 7
    b) has a radius of $\sqrt{10}$
    c) passes through the point $(-5, 12)$

12. On the plan for a new play area in a park, a paddling pool is represented by a circle with the equation $x^2 + y^2 = 16$. Dimensions on the plan are in metres. What will the perimeter of the pool be?

Chapter 3 Geometric Properties

13. a) Draw the triangle with vertices $P(-2, -2)$, $Q(2, 4)$, and $R(8, 0)$.
    b) Show algebraically that △PQR is a right triangle.
    c) Is △PQR also an isosceles triangle? Use algebraic reasoning to justify your answer.
    d) Determine the area of △PQR.

14. **Use Technology** Use *The Geometer's Sketchpad®* or *Cabri® Jr.* to verify your answers to question 12. Outline your method.

15. a) Plot the triangle with vertices $A(-1, 1)$, $B(3, 5)$, and $C(5, -1)$.
    b) What type of triangle does △ABC appear to be?
    c) Use analytic geometry to verify your answer in part a).
    d) Verify that the median from C to AB is also an altitude of the triangle.

16. Use analytic geometry to verify that $D(-1, 3)$, $E(2, 2)$, $F(3, -1)$, and $G(0, 0)$ are the vertices of a parallelogram.

17. JKLM is a trapezoid. P, Q, R, and S are the midpoints of the sides JK, KL, LM, and MJ, respectively. What type of quadrilateral is PQRS? Use analytic geometry to verify your answer.

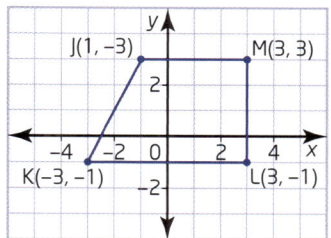

18. The vertices of rhombus TUVW are $T(-3, 2)$, $U(2, 2)$, $V(0, -2)$, and $W(5, -2)$.
    a) Use analytic geometry to show that the diagonals of TUVW are right bisectors of each other.
    b) Use *The Geometer's Sketchpad®* or *Cabri® Jr.* to verify the property in part a). Outline your method.

Tasks

Multiple Midpoints

Can you determine the coordinates of the vertices of a triangle given just the coordinates of the midpoints of its sides?

a) Start with the midpoints P(0, 0), Q(0, 4), and R(4, 0). Find the coordinates of the vertices of a △ABC that has P, Q, and R as the midpoints of its sides.

b) Next, find the vertex coordinates of a △DEF that has P(0, 0), Q(2, 4), and R(4, 0) as the midpoints of its sides.

c) Choose three midpoints yourself. Find the vertex coordinates of a △GHI that has these three points as the midpoints of its sides.

d) Describe the steps for finding the vertex coordinates of a △JKL that has P(0, 0), Q(k, m), and R(p, q) as the midpoints of its sides.

e) Is it always possible to find the vertices for such a triangle? Explain.

A Site for the New Hospital

A new hospital is being planned to serve three towns: Abbott, Banting, and Colton. On a map, the coordinates of the towns are A(10, 13), B(2, 9), and C(10, 1), respectively.

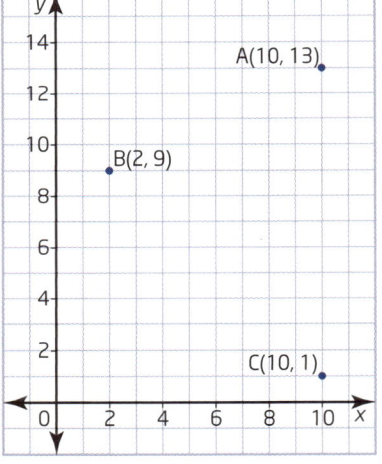

a) One proposal is to build the hospital at the point that is equidistant from the three towns.
- Use analytic methods to determine the coordinates of this point.
- Verify that this point is the same distance from each town.
- List some reasons why this point might not be the best site for the new hospital.

b) Prepare a letter to the area's planning council describing how to choose a good location. Use mathematical reasoning to justify the method you recommend.

c) Another proposal is to choose the location that has the shortest mean driving distance to the hospital for the residents of the three towns. Colton has twice the population of either Abbott or Banting. Therefore, the location for the hospital should be equidistant from Abbott and Banting, but half as far away from Colton. Use *The Geometer's Sketchpad*® to find the coordinates of this location. (Note: Analytic geometry can be used to find a "weighted" centre. However, the algebra for this method is quite challenging.)

Pythagoras Park

The mathematics department of a university is sponsoring a competition to design a new city park. The park will be constructed on a rectangular lot beside the department's offices. The lot is 250 m by 400 m.

To encourage applications of mathematics to landscaping, the rules for the competition require that all designs include at least five of the following geometric shapes:
- Triangles: equilateral, isosceles, right, scalene
- Quadrilaterals: square, rectangle, parallelogram, rhombus, trapezoid, kite
- Circle, semicircle

The designs must also have at least five of the following features:
- median
- altitude
- angle bisector
- right bisector
- centroid
- orthocentre
- incentre
- circumcentre
- parallel lines
- perpendicular lines
- diagonal
- chord

Form a design team with two of your classmates to enter the competition. Using grid paper, prepare a fully labelled scale diagram of your design. Write a description of the features of your design. The scale diagram and written description should include the location of any gardens, trees, walkways, lights, benches, fountains, gazebos, picnic areas, playgrounds, or other features.

CHAPTER 4

Quadratic Relations

This chapter introduces methods for analysing non-linear relations that can be characterized by an arch-shaped curve. This curve is seen in nature, art, and architecture. This type of non-linear relation is analysed by engineers to design bridges, by physicists to track the path of projectiles, and by analysts to maximize profit or predict trends in the consumer market.

Quadratic Relations of the Form $y = ax^2 + bx + c$

- Collect data that can be represented as a quadratic relation, graph the data, and draw a curve of best fit.
- Determine that a quadratic relation of the form $y = ax^2 + bx + c$ ($a \neq 0$) can be graphically represented as a parabola, and that the table of values yields a constant second difference.
- Identify the effect on the graph of $y = x^2$ of transformations by considering separately each parameter a, h, and k.
- Explain the roles of a, h, and k in $y = a(x - h)^2 + k$, and identify the vertex and the equation of the axis of symmetry.
- Sketch the graph of $y = a(x - h)^2 + k$ by applying transformations to the graph of $y = x^2$.
- Determine the equation, in the form $y = a(x - h)^2 + k$, of a given graph of a parabola.
- Identify the key features of a graph of a parabola, and use the appropriate terminology to describe them.
- Compare the features of the graph of $y = x^2$ and the graph of $y = 2^x$, and determine the meaning of a negative exponent and of zero as an exponent.

Vocabulary

non-linear relation
curve of best fit
quadratic relation
parabola
vertex
axis of symmetry
finite differences
zero

Chapter Problem

A city opened a new landfill site in 2000. The table shows the amount of garbage added to the landfill in each year from 2000 to 2007.

How can you model the relationship between the year and the total amount of garbage in the landfill?

Year	Garbage Added (1000s of tonnes)
2000	200
2001	230
2002	258
2003	287
2004	317
2005	347
2006	376
2007	406

Get Ready

Scatter Plots

An experiment measured how high a ball bounced after being dropped from six different heights.

Drop Height (m)	1.0	1.5	2.0	2.5	3.0	3.5
Bounce Height (m)	0.3	0.5	0.7	0.8	0.9	1.1

The independent variable is the drop height because it is being controlled in the experiment. So, the bounce height is the dependent variable.

The scatter plot shows that the relationship between the two variables is approximately linear.

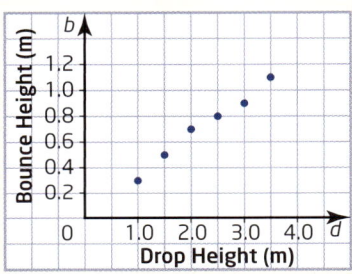
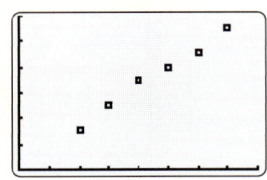

Making Connections

Refer to the Technology Appendix for help with creating a scatter plot on a TI-83 Plus or TI-84 Plus graphing calculator.

If the trend in the scatter plot continues, the bounce height of a ball that is dropped from 4.0 m will be approximately 1.2 m.

1. The table shows the height of a tomato plant during the first 2 weeks after it germinated.

Time (days)	1	2	3	4	5	6	7
Height (cm)	0.4	1.2	2.5	3.4	4.3	5.2	6.5
Time (days)	8	9	10	11	12	13	14
Height (cm)	7.5	8.5	9.3	10.3	11.2	12.4	13.4

a) Identify the independent variable and the dependent variable.

b) Make a scatter plot of the data.

c) Describe the relationship between the variables.

d) Predict the height of the plant after 17 days.

2. The table shows the heights and neck circumferences of 12 students.

Height (cm)	157	168	162	151	157	170
Neck Circumference (cm)	32	40	36	31	34	42
Height (cm)	167	159	168	171	176	154
Neck Circumference (cm)	38	38	38	40	40	32

a) Identify the independent variable and the dependent variable.

b) Make a scatter plot of the data.

c) Describe the relationship between the variables.

d) Predict the neck circumference for a 180-cm-tall student.

Translations and Reflections

Translations and reflections are two types of transformations that move one geometric figure onto another.

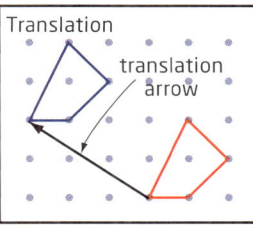
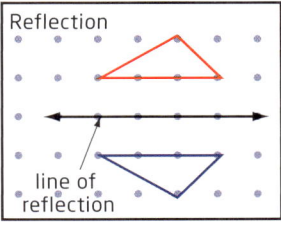

3. Describe the translation of the red figure to the blue figure.

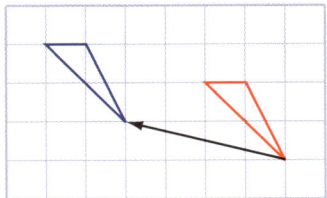

4. Copy the diagram. Show the location of the line of reflection.

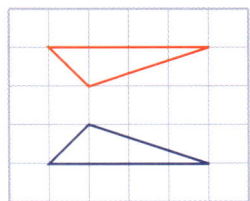

Operations With Powers

A power is a product of identical factors and consists of a base and an exponent.

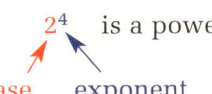

2^4 is a power.

base   exponent

The exponent laws can be used to simplify expressions involving powers with the same base.

Operation	Exponent Rule	Example
multiplication	$x^a \times x^b = x^{a+b}$	$3^2 \times 3^3 = 3^{2+3} = 3^5$
division	$x^a \div x^b = x^{a-b}$	$3^5 \div 3^2 = 3^{5-2} = 3^3$
powers	$(x^a)^b = x^{a \times b}$	$(3^2)^4 = 3^{2 \times 4} = 3^8$

5. Use the exponent laws to write each as a single power.

a) $2^3 \times 2^4$

b) $(-1)^2 \times (-1)^5$

c) $\left(\dfrac{1}{2}\right)^2 \times \left(\dfrac{1}{2}\right)^3$

d) $5^8 \div 5^3$

e) $(-3)^7 \div (-3)^4$

f) $(4^2)^5$

6. Use the exponent laws to write each as a single power.

a) $2^3 \times 2^4 \div 2^5$

b) $(-3)^9 \div (-3)^5 \times (-3)^2$

c) $(5^2)^4 \div 5^3$

d) $4^7 \times 4^3 \div (4^2)^4$

4.1 Investigate Non-Linear Relations

non-linear relation
- a relationship between two variables that does not follow a straight line when graphed

Most relations that you have studied in mathematics have been linear. However, many **non-linear relations** also exist in real life. For example, the area of a shape is measured in square units, so the graph of area versus length is non-linear. Similarly, when a rocket is launched, it follows an arch-like path.

Investigate

  **Tools**
- ruler
- grid paper

How can you use a scatter plot to model non-linear data?

A: Relate Thumb Length and Palm Area

Work in small groups.

1. Measure the length of your thumb.

2. Measure the length and width of your palm. Calculate the approximate area of your palm.

3. Record the thumb length and palm area data for each group member.

4. Identify the independent and dependent variables.

5. Make a scatter plot of the data.

6. Describe the relationship between thumb length and palm area.

7. Draw a **curve of best fit**.

curve of best fit
- a smooth curve drawn to approximate the general path or trend in a scatter plot

8. **Reflect** Why is a curve of best fit used for these data instead of a line of best fit?

9. Use your model to predict the area of a person's palm when that person's thumb is 8.1 cm long.

B: Relate Distance and Roll Time

Work in small groups.

1. Build a ramp using two textbooks as a support.

2. Place a can 30 cm from the bottom of the ramp.

3. Release the can and time how long it takes the can to roll to the bottom. You may wish to practise starting the stopwatch at the exact moment the can is released.

Tools
- board at least 1.2 m in length
- 2 textbooks
- 1 can of soup (or other object that rolls)
- metre stick or measuring tape
- stopwatch
- grid paper

4. Repeat by releasing the can from 40 cm, 50 cm, and so on.

5. Record all your data in a table. Choose your variables.

6. Identify the independent and dependent variables. Explain your choices.

7. Make a scatter plot of the results.

8. Describe the relationship between distance and roll time.

9. Draw a curve of best fit.

10. **Reflect** Why is a curve of best fit used for these data instead of a line of best fit?

11. Use your model to predict the time it would take for a can to roll down a longer ramp with the same slope from a distance of 160 cm.

Key Concepts

- The independent variable is the one that you control before the trial begins. The dependent variable is the one that you measure during the trial. It is affected by a change in the independent variable.

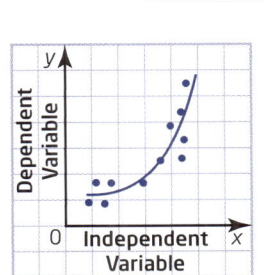

- Look at the pattern of the points in a scatter plot when deciding if the relation is linear or non-linear. The points in a non-linear relation will not lie along a line, but will form a graph that is curved.

Communicate Your Understanding

C1 State whether each line or curve of best fit is a good model for the data. Justify your answer.

a)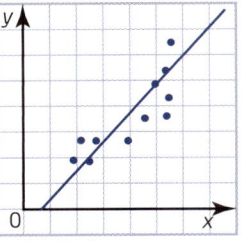

b)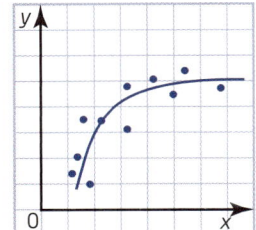

c)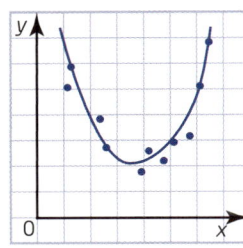

C2 The scatter plot shows the relationship between time, in 5-year intervals, and the population of a town. Explain why time was used as the independent variable.

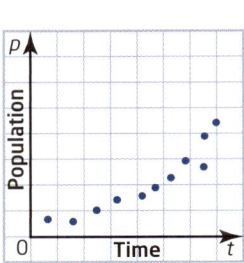

Practise

1. Which scatter plot(s) could be modelled using a curve instead of a line of best fit? Explain.

a)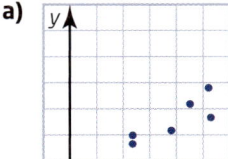

b)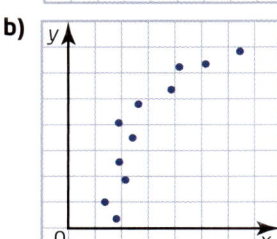

2. The scatter plot and curve of best fit show the relationship between the diameter of rain-collection barrels and the volume of water collected.

Is this relation linear or non-linear? Justify your answer.

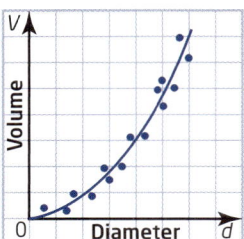

3. An altimeter is attached to a model rocket before it is launched. The table shows the recorded data from the rocket's flight.

Time (s)	1	2	3	4	5	6	7
Height (m)	230	310	350	360	350	300	220

a) Make a scatter plot of the data.
b) Describe the relation.
c) Draw a curve of best fit.
d) Use your model to predict the height of the rocket after 8 s.

4. The table shows the average fuel economy of a car at a test track.

Speed (km/h)	Fuel Economy (L/100 km)
10	14.26
20	12.85
40	10.65
60	10.10
70	10.24
80	10.84
100	12.14
120	15.64
130	16.88
150	22.50

a) Make a scatter plot of the data.
b) Describe the relation.
c) Draw a curve of best fit.
d) Use your model to predict the fuel economy at 200 km/h.
e) This car does not get very good fuel economy. How would a graph of a car with better fuel economy look? Why?

Did You Know?

New vehicles have an EnerGuide label that shows the city and highway fuel-consumption ratings and an estimated annual fuel cost for that vehicle. The fuel-consumption ratings are provided by vehicle manufacturers and are based on standardized testing procedures and driving cycles performed under controlled conditions.

5. The table shows the data for a bouncing ball.

Bounce Number	1	2	3	4	5	6	7
Rebound Height (cm)	270	180	120	80	53	45	25

a) Make a scatter plot of the data.
b) Describe the relation.
c) Draw a curve of best fit.
d) How would the relationship change for a ball that was bouncier?

6. **Chapter Problem** A city opened a new landfill site in 2000. The table shows how much garbage was added to the landfill in each year from 2000 to 2007.

Year	Garbage Added (1000s of tonnes)
2000	200
2001	230
2002	258
2003	287
2004	317
2005	347
2006	376
2007	406

a) Determine the total mass of garbage in the landfill at the end of each year.
b) Make a scatter plot of the total mass of garbage versus the year. Draw a curve of best fit.
c) What problems do you predict if growth continues at its current rate?

7. A rectangle has a width of x centimetres, and its length is double its width.
a) Create a table comparing the length and area of a rectangle for widths up to 8 cm.
b) Make a scatter plot of the data.
c) Draw a curve of best fit.
d) Explain why the graph of this relation is non-linear.

4.2 Quadratic Relations

The Galleria, in BCE Place in Toronto, has many arches. These curved structures are used to span a space while supporting weight. Just as a linear relation can be modelled with a linear equation, some non-linear relations, such as the shape of an arch, can be modelled using non-linear equations.

Tools
- grid paper

Investigate A

How can you compare relations of the form $y = ax^2 + bx + c$?

1. Make a table of values for each relation, using integer values of x from -3 to $+3$.

   a) $y = x^2$
   b) $y = 2x^2$
   c) $y = x^2 + 2x + 3$
   d) $y = -x^2$
   e) $y = -0.5x^2 + 3$

2. Graph all the relations in step 1 on the same set of axes. Plot each set of ordered pairs and draw a smooth curve through the points.

3. **Reflect** Describe the graphs you created in as many ways as you can. What is similar about the graphs? What is different?

quadratic relation
- a relation whose equation is in the form $y = ax^2 + bx + c$, where a, b, and c are real numbers and $a \neq 0$

parabola
- the graph of a quadratic relation, which is U-shaped and symmetrical

vertex
- the point on a parabola where the curve changes direction
- the maximum point if the parabola opens down
- the minimum point if the parabola opens up

axis of symmetry
- the line that divides a figure into two congruent parts

The relation described by $y = ax^2 + bx + c$ is called a **quadratic relation**. The graph of a quadratic relation is called a **parabola**. A parabola has a minimum point or a maximum point called the **vertex**. It is also symmetrical about a vertical line drawn through the vertex, called the **axis of symmetry**.

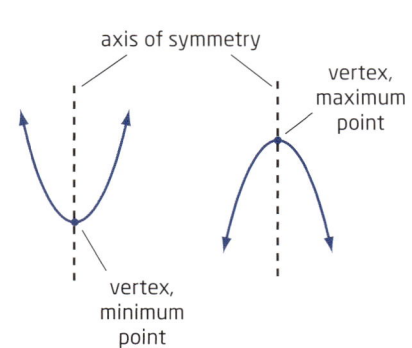

Investigate B

How can you use finite differences to determine if a relation is linear or quadratic?

1. Copy and complete the table for each linear relation. Calculate the *y*-values. Then, calculate the first differences by subtracting consecutive *y*-values.

   a) $y = 2x - 5$

x	y	First Differences
-2	-9	
-1	-7	-7 - (-9) = 2
0		
1		
2		

   b) $y = -6x + 2$

x	y	First Differences
-2	14	
-1	8	8 - 14 = -6
0		
1		
2		

finite differences
- differences found from the *y*-values in tables with evenly spaced *x*-values
- first differences are the differences between consecutive *y*-values, second differences are the differences between consecutive first differences, and so on

2. What is true about the first differences for a linear relation?

3. Copy and complete the table for each quadratic relation. Calculate the *y*-values and first differences. Then, calculate the second differences by subtracting successive first differences.

   a) $y = x^2 - 4$

x	y	First Differences	Second Differences
-2	0		
-1	-3	-3 - 0 = -3	
0	-4	-4 - (-3) = -1	-1 - (-3) = 2
1			
2			

   b) $y = 2x^2 + 3x - 1$

x	y	First Differences	Second Differences
-2	1		
-1	-2		
0			
1			
2			

4. a) What is true about the first differences for a quadratic relation?
   b) What is true about the second differences for a quadratic relation?

5. **Reflect** Write a rule for using finite differences to determine whether a relation is linear or quadratic.

Example Galleria Arches

Each arch in the BCE Place Galleria can be approximated by the relation $y = -0.55x^2 + 26$, where y is the height, in metres, above the floor and x is the width, in metres, from the centre of the hallway.

a) Graph the quadratic relation.

b) Describe the shape of the arch.

c) How tall and wide is the arch?

Solution

a) Method 1: Use Pencil and Paper

Use a table of values to help you sketch the graph.

x	y
−6	6.2
−4	17.2
−2	23.8
0	26.0
2	23.8
4	17.2
6	6.2

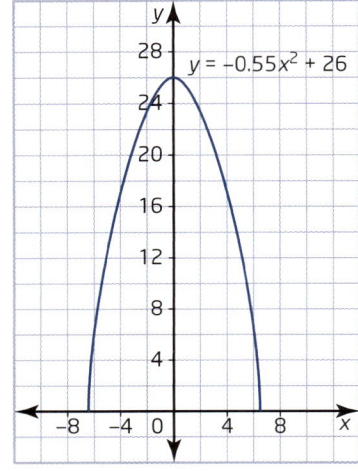

Method 2: Use a Graphing Calculator

Enter the equation using Y= .

Press WINDOW and enter the settings shown.

Then, press GRAPH.

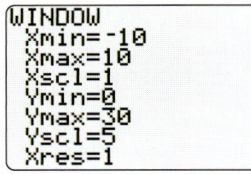 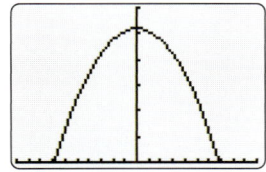

b) You can see that the shape of the arch is parabolic. The parabola is symmetrical about a vertical line, the y-axis. The graph has a maximum point.

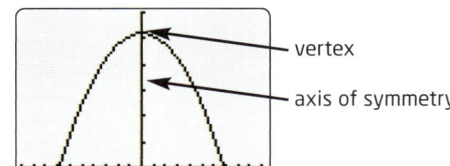

c) You can read the maximum y-value from the pencil-and-paper graph or use the TRACE feature on the graphing calculator.

Since the maximum value of y is 26, the height of each arch is 26 m.

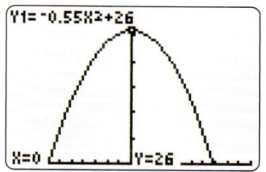

> I can see that the maximum occurs when $x = 0$. From the equation, when $x = 0$, $y = 26$.

The x-axis represents the floor of the hallway. The width of each arch is the difference between the two x-intercepts. From the pencil-and-paper graph, the x-intercepts appear to be about 7 and -7. Use the TRACE feature on the graphing calculator to find that the curve crosses the x-axis at about -6.9 and $+6.9$.

$6.9 - (-6.9) = 13.8$

The width of each arch is about 13.8 m.

Technology Tip

You can get a better approximation of the x-intercepts by zooming in.
- Position the cursor near one of the x-intercepts.
- Press ZOOM, select **2:Zoom In**, and then press ENTER.
- Press TRACE and reposition the cursor.

The accuracy of the approximation improves each time you repeat these steps.

Key Concepts

- The relation defined by $y = ax^2 + bx + c$ is a quadratic relation.

- The graph of a quadratic relation is called a parabola.

- The vertex of a parabola is either the minimum point or the maximum point on the graph.

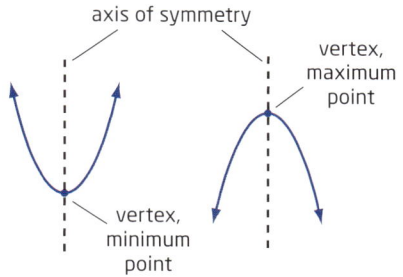

- A parabola is symmetric about a vertical line that passes through the vertex. This line is the axis of symmetry.

- If a relation is quadratic, the second differences are constant, but the first differences are not.

Communicate Your Understanding

C1 El-Noor used the following incorrect technique to determine that the relation is not quadratic. Explain the flaw in his reasoning.

x	y	First Differences	Second Differences
−3	13		
		−10	
−2	3		2
		−8	
0	−5		10
		2	
1	−3		4
		6	
2	3		18
		24	
4	27		

C2 In Section 4.1, Investigate Part A, you found that the relationship between thumb length and palm area is non-linear. Is the relation quadratic? Explain.

Practise

For help with questions 1 and 2, see the Example.

1. The table shows the path of a ball, where x is the horizontal distance, in metres, and h is the height, in metres, above the ground.

x	h
0	1
1	8
2	13
3	16
4	17
5	16
6	13
7	8
8	1

   a) Sketch a graph of the quadratic relation.
   b) Describe the flight path of the ball. Identify the axis of symmetry and the vertex.
   c) What is the maximum height that the ball reached?
   d) Verify that $h = -x^2 + 8x + 1$ can be used to model the flight path of the ball.

2. The underside of a bridge is an arch that can be approximated by the relation $y = -0.1x^2 + 10$, where y is the height, in metres, above the ground and x is the width, in metres, from the centre of the bridge.

   a) Graph the quadratic relation.
   b) Describe the shape of the arch.
   c) How tall and wide is the arch?

3. Use finite differences to determine whether each relation is linear, quadratic, or neither.

   a)
x	y
0	4
1	5
2	6
3	7
4	8

   b)
x	y
0	3
1	4
2	7
3	12
4	19

   c)
x	y
1	0
3	1
5	8
7	27
9	64

   d)
x	y
-2	6
1	0
4	12
7	42
10	90

Connect and Apply

4. This section has photographs of parabolic arches in architecture, furniture, bridge design, and nature. Find five more examples of parabolic arches. Some possible sources are the Internet, personal surroundings, or print-based material. Explain how you determined that your examples are parabolic.

5. The parabolic shape of the Humber River Pedestrian Bridge in Toronto can be approximated by the equation $h = -\frac{1}{144}x^2 + \frac{5}{6}x$, where x is the horizontal distance, in metres, from one end and h is the height, in metres, above the water.

   a) Graph the quadratic relation with or without technology.
   b) What is the height of the bridge 12 m horizontally from one end?
   c) How wide is the bridge at its base?
   d) What is the maximum height of the bridge? At what horizontal distance does it reach that height?
   e) Identify the axis of symmetry of the bridge.

6. **Use Technology** A ball is thrown upward at an initial velocity of 15 m/s, from a height of 1.5 m. The height, h, in metres, of the ball above the ground after t seconds can be found using the relation $h = -4.9t^2 + 15t + 1.5$.

   a) Graph this relation using a graphing calculator.

   b) Describe the relationship between time and height.

   c) Repeat parts a) and b) for a ball thrown upward on the Moon, with height defined by the relation $h = -0.81t^2 + 15t + 1.5$.

   d) Repeat parts a) and b) for a ball thrown upward on Jupiter, with height defined by the relation $h = -11.55t^2 + 15t + 1.5$.

   e) Compare the results from the three locations.

7. **Chapter Problem** A city opened a new landfill site in 2000. In Section 4.1, question 6, you created a table of values showing the total mass of garbage in the landfill for each year from 2000 to 2007. Use your table and finite differences to determine if the relationship more closely models a linear or a quadratic relation. Justify your decision.

8. Percé Rock is located at the eastern tip of Quebec's Gaspé Peninsula. Make a table of values of at least seven points, so that the x-values are equally spaced. Use finite differences to determine how close the arch is to a parabola.

■ **Achievement Check**

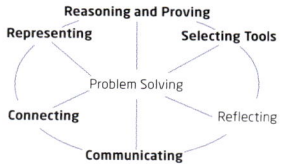

9. The path of a rocket fired at a Canada Day fireworks display is given by $h = -4.9t^2 + 19.6t + 0.4$, where h is the height, in metres, of the rocket above the ground and t is the time, in seconds.

   a) Make a table of values for $t = 0$ to $t = 4$.

   b) Make a table of first and second differences. What conclusion can you make?

   c) Draw a graph of the path of the rocket using the table of values from part a) or graphing technology. Describe the path of the rocket.

   d) How high above the ground was the rocket when it was set off? Explain your answer.

Extend

10. The flow rate of water through a garden hose depends on the water pressure and the diameter of the hose opening. At a normal water pressure of 345 kPa, the flow rate can be calculated using the formula $r = 2d^2$, where d is the diameter, in centimetres, of the hose opening and r is the flow rate, in litres per second. How long would it take to fill a 200-L barrel using a hose with a 0.3-cm-diameter opening?

11. The sum of the first n natural numbers is a quadratic relation. Determine that relation and verify it for the first six natural numbers.

4.3 Investigate Transformations of Quadratics

When police investigate car accidents, they often measure the length of a tire skid mark to determine the speed of the car before braking. Such calculations involve quadratic relations. On dry pavement, the length of a skid mark, l, is related to the speed of the car, s, before braking by the relation $l = 0.04s^2$.

Investigate

How do transformations of the graph of $y = x^2$ affect the equation?

A: Compare the Graphs of $y = x^2$ and $y = x^2 + k$

 **Tools**
- TI-83 Plus or TI-84 Plus graphing calculator
- grid paper

1. First, clear any graphed equations.
   - Press [Y=] and use the [CLEAR] key to remove any equations.
   - Make sure **Plot1**, **Plot2**, and **Plot3** are not highlighted. If they are, use the [▶], [◀], [▲], and [▼] keys to move to each and press [ENTER].

2. Use a standard window.
   - Press [ZOOM] and select **6:ZStandard**.
   - You can view the window settings by pressing [WINDOW].

   ```
   WINDOW
   Xmin=-10
   Xmax=10
   Xscl=1
   Ymin=-10
   Ymax=10
   Yscl=1
   Xres=1
   ```

3. Graph the equation $y = x^2$ as **Y1**.
   - Press [Y=]. Beside **Y1=**, press [X,T,θ,n] [x^2].
   - Press [GRAPH] to view the parabola.

4. Enter $y = x^2 + 2$ as **Y2** and $y = x^2 - 4$ as **Y3**. Press [GRAPH].

5. a) Sketch all three graphs on the same set of axes. Label each parabola with its equation.

b) Describe the transformations.

c) Without using a graphing calculator, sketch the graph of $y = x^2 - 8$.

6. Reflect Describe how the value of k in $y = x^2 + k$ changes the graph of $y = x^2$.

B: Compare the Graphs of $y = x^2$ and $y = ax^2$

1. a) Clear the equations from **Y2=** and **Y3=**, but keep $y = x^2$ in **Y1**.

b) Graph the equations $y = 2x^2$ and $y = 3x^2$.

2. a) Sketch all three graphs on the same set of axes. Label each parabola with its equation.

b) Describe the transformations.

3. Without using a graphing calculator, sketch the graph of $y = 4x^2$.

4. Repeat steps 1 and 2 for the equations $y = \frac{1}{2}x^2$ and $y = \frac{1}{4}x^2$.

5. Without using a graphing calculator, sketch the graph of $y = \frac{1}{3}x^2$.

6. Repeat steps 1 and 2 for the equations $y = -2x^2$ and $y = -0.5x^2$.

7. Without using a graphing calculator, sketch the graph of $y = -3x^2$.

8. Reflect Describe how the value of a in $y = ax^2$ changes the graph of $y = x^2$.

C: Compare the Graphs of $y = x^2$ and $y = (x - h)^2$

1. a) Clear all equations except $y = x^2$.

b) Graph the equations $y = (x - 2)^2$ and $y = (x - 5)^2$.

2. a) Sketch all three graphs on the same set of axes. Label each parabola with its equation.

b) Describe the transformations.

3. Without using a graphing calculator, sketch the graph of $y = (x - 3)^2$.

4. Repeat steps 1 and 2 using the equations $y = (x + 2)^2$ and $y = (x + 5)^2$.

5. Without using a graphing calculator, sketch the graph of $y = (x + 3)^2$.

6. Reflect Describe how the value of h in $y = (x - h)^2$ changes the graph of $y = x^2$.

Technology Tip

A table of values can help you sketch the graph of an equation entered using [Y=]. You can specify how a table of values is set up.

- Press [2nd] [TBLSET] to display the **TABLE SETUP** screen. Make sure both **Indpnt** and **Depend** are set to **Auto**. Enter the desired starting x-value (**TblStart**) and x increment (**ΔTbl**). For example, try **TblStart=−10** and **ΔTbl=1**.

- Press [2nd] [TABLE] to view the table of values.

Example Falling Stone

A stone is dropped from the top of a 50-m cliff above a river. Its height, y, in metres, above the water can be estimated using the relation $y = -4.9x^2 + 50$, where x is the time, in seconds.

a) Graph the relation.

b) Find the intercepts. What do they represent?

c) How would the equation change if the stone were dropped from a 75-m cliff instead of a 50-m cliff?

d) For what values of x is each equation valid?

Solution

a) Use a graphing calculator with the window settings shown.

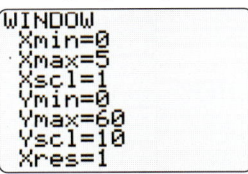
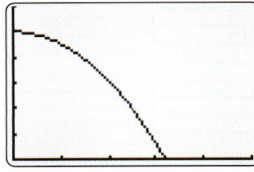

Since height and time cannot be negative, this graph shows only part of a parabola.

b) For the y-intercept, let $x = 0$.
$y = -4.9(0)^2 + 50$
$ = 50$

I can see that the y-intercept is 50 from the graph.

The y-intercept is 50. This represents the height from which the stone was dropped, 50 m above the water.

zero
- a value of x for which a relation has a value of 0
- corresponds to an x-intercept of the graph of the relation

To find the x-intercept, or **zero**, of the relation use the Zero operation on a graphing calculator.
- Press [2nd][CALC] to display the **CALCULATE** menu, and select **2:zero**.
- Move the cursor to the left of the x-intercept and press [ENTER].
- Move the cursor to the right of the x-intercept and press [ENTER].
- Press [ENTER] again.

The x-intercept is approximately 3.19.
This represents the time when the stone hits the water, 3.19 s.

c) The constant term would be 75 instead of 50. The equation would change to $y = -4.9x^2 + 75$.

d) The original equation $y = -4.9x^2 + 50$ is valid for $0 \leq x \leq 3.19$ (approximately).

Graph the new equation and use the Zero operation. You will need to change the WINDOW settings to be able to see the whole graph.

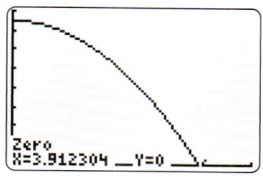

The new equation $y = -4.9x^2 + 75$ is valid for $0 \leq x \leq 3.91$ (approximately).

Key Concepts

- To graph $y = x^2 + k$, translate the graph of $y = x^2$ vertically k units.
  - If $k > 0$, then the graph is translated k units upward.
  - If $k < 0$, then the graph is translated k units downward.

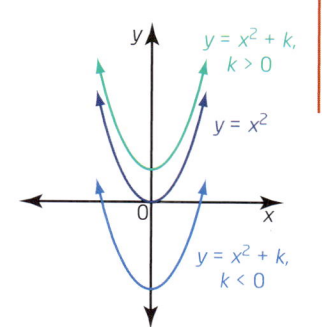

- To graph $y = ax^2$, stretch or compress the graph of $y = x^2$ vertically by a factor of a.
  - If $a < 0$, the parabola is reflected in the x-axis.
  - If $a > 1$ or $a < -1$, then the graph is stretched vertically (narrows).
  - If $-1 < a < 0$ or $0 < a < 1$, then the graph is compressed vertically (widens).

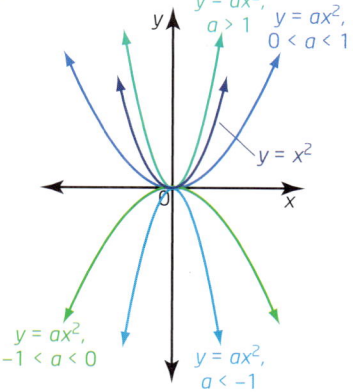

- To graph $y = (x - h)^2$, translate the graph of $y = x^2$ horizontally h units.
  - If $h > 0$, then the graph is translated h units to the right.
  - If $h < 0$, then the graph is translated h units to the left.

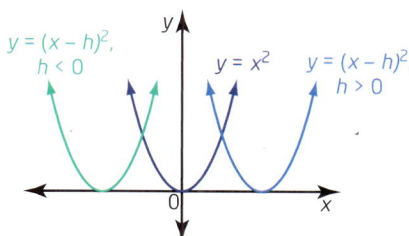

Communicate Your Understanding

C1 How do the graphs of $y = 2x^2$ and $y = -2x^2$ compare? Explain the similarities and the differences.

C2 Match each graph with the appropriate equation. Explain your reasoning.
   a) $y = x^2 + 2$
   b) $y = -\dfrac{1}{3}x^2$
   c) $y = x^2$
   d) $y = (x - 2)^2$

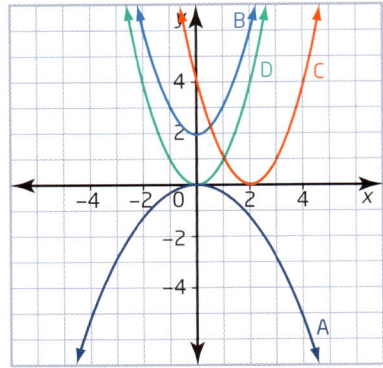

Practise

For help with questions 1 to 4, see the Investigate.

1. Sketch graphs of these three quadratic relations on the same set of axes.
   a) $y = -3x^2$
   b) $y = \dfrac{1}{4}x^2$
   c) $y = -\dfrac{1}{4}x^2$

2. Sketch graphs of these three quadratic relations on the same set of axes.
   a) $y = (x - 9)^2$
   b) $y = (x + 2)^2$
   c) $y = (x - 5)^2$

3. Sketch graphs of these three quadratic relations on the same set of axes.
   a) $y = x^2 + 8$
   b) $y = x^2 - 5$
   c) $y = x^2 - 10$

4. Sketch the graph of each parabola. Label at least three points on the parabola. Describe the transformation from the graph of $y = x^2$.
   a) $y = 4x^2$
   b) $y = \dfrac{2}{3}x^2$
   c) $y = x^2 - 5$
   d) $y = (x - 8)^2$
   e) $y = -\dfrac{1}{2}x^2$
   f) $y = (x + 3)^2$
   g) $y = x^2 + 0.5$
   h) $y = -x^2 + 2$

5. a) Make tables of values for $y = x^2$, $y = 2x^2$, $y = x^2 + 1$, and $y = (x - 3)^2$.
   b) Compare the y-values for $y = x^2$ and $y = 2x^2$.
   c) Compare the y-values for $y = x^2$ and $y = x^2 + 1$.
   d) Compare the y-values for $y = x^2$ and $y = (x - 3)^2$.

Connect and Apply

6. Write an equation for the quadratic relation that results from each transformation.
   a) The graph of $y = x^2$ is translated 6 units upward.
   b) The graph of $y = x^2$ is translated 4 units downward.

7. Write an equation for the quadratic relation that results from each transformation.
   a) The graph of $y = x^2$ is translated 7 units to the left.
   b) The graph of $y = x^2$ is translated 5 units to the right.
   c) The graph of $y = x^2$ is translated 8 units to the left.
   d) The graph of $y = x^2$ is translated 3 units to the right.

8. Write an equation for the quadratic relation that results from each transformation.

  a) The graph of $y = x^2$ is stretched vertically by a factor of 8.

  b) The graph of $y = x^2$ is compressed vertically by a factor of $\frac{1}{5}$.

For help with question 9, see the Example.

9. The grass in the backyard of a house is a square with side length 10 m. A square patio is placed in the centre. If the side length, in metres, of the patio is x, then the area of grass remaining is given by the relation $A = -x^2 + 100$.

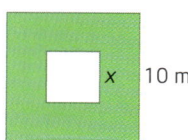

  a) Graph the relation.

  b) Find the intercepts. What do they represent?

  c) How does the equation change if the grass in the backyard of a house is a square with side length 12 m?

  d) For what values of x is each equation valid?

10. The relation $l = 0.04s^2$ can be used to calculate the length, l, in metres, of the skid mark for a car travelling at a speed, s, in kilometres per hour, on dry pavement before braking.

  a) What is the length of the skid mark for a car travelling at 50 km/h? 100 km/h?

  b) How do the results in part a) compare?

  c) For what values of s is this model valid?

  d) How would the skid marks and the equation change if the pavement were wet?

Did You Know?

A Technical Collision Investigator or Reconstructionist is a specially trained police officer who investigates serious traffic accidents. These officers collect and interpret evidence to determine the cause of the collision and if any charges should be laid.

11. The first three diagrams in a pattern are shown. Each square has a side length of 1 unit.

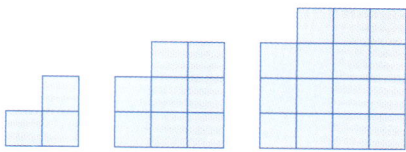

  a) Make a table comparing base length and area. Use finite differences to determine whether the relation is linear, quadratic, or neither.

  b) Determine an equation for the relationship between the base length and the area.

  c) Describe the transformation from the graph of $y = x^2$.

Extend

12. The transformations to graph $y = ax^2$ and $y = x^2 + k$ both follow what is indicated by the operation, but in $y = (x - h)^2$, the transformation is opposite to what the operation seems to indicate.

  a) Explain why this might be so.

  b) Describe the transformation you would use to graph $y = (2x)^2$.

13. A parabola $y = ax^2 + k$ passes through the points $(-1, 3)$ and $(3, -13)$. Find the values of a and k.

14. Compare the graphs of $y = (x - 2)^2$ and $y = (2 - x)^2$. Explain any similarities and differences.

15. Math Contest

  a) Identify the similarities and differences in the graphs of $y = (x - 2)^2 + 5$ and $x = (y - 2)^2 + 5$.

  b) Solve the second equation for y.

4.4 Graph $y = a(x - h)^2 + k$

The world's most important industry competition for fireworks manufacturers is L'International des Feux Loto-Québec. This event, also known as the Montréal Fireworks Festival, is held each summer in Montréal. The fireworks are synchronized to music that is also broadcast over a local radio station. Competing countries are judged on the synchronization, choice of music, and quality and originality of the visual display.

Paths of projectiles, such as rockets, balls, and fireworks, are often modelled using quadratic relations.

Investigate

Tools
- TI-83 Plus or TI-84 Plus graphing calculator
- grid paper

Technology Tip
Turn off all stat plots by pressing (2nd) (Y=) for [STAT PLOT], selecting **4:PlotsOff**, and then pressing (ENTER).

How do the graphs of $y = a(x - h)^2 + k$ and $y = x^2$ compare?

1. First, clear any graphed equations, and ensure all stat plots are turned off.

2. Use a standard window.
   - Press (ZOOM) and select **6:ZStandard**.
   - View the window settings by pressing (WINDOW).

3. Graph the equations $y = x^2$, $y = 2x^2 - 5$, and $y = -x^2 + 2$.

4. a) Sketch all three graphs on the same set of axes.
   b) Label the coordinates of the vertex and a second point on each parabola.
   c) Describe the transformations.
   d) Without using a graphing calculator, sketch the graph of $y = -2x^2 + 1$.

5. a) Clear all equations except $y = x^2$.
   b) Graph the equation $y = (x - 2)^2 + 1$.

180 MHR • Chapter 4

6. **a)** Sketch the two graphs on the same set of axes.

   b) Label the coordinates of the vertex and a second point on each parabola.

   c) Draw the axis of symmetry for each parabola. Label each axis of symmetry with its equation.

   d) Describe the transformations.

7. Without using a graphing calculator, sketch the graph of $y = (x - 1)^2 + 3$.

8. **a)** Repeat steps 5 and 6 for the equation $y = (x + 5)^2 - 4$.

   b) Without using a graphing calculator, sketch the graph of $y = (x + 4)^2 + 2$.

9. **a)** Repeat steps 5 and 6 for the equation $y = 2(x - 1)^2 - 5$.

   b) Without using a graphing calculator, sketch the graph of $y = -0.5(x + 2)^2 + 3$.

10. **Reflect** Write a summary of how to sketch a graph of a quadratic relation of the form $y = a(x - h)^2 + k$. Include a description of how to determine the coordinates of the vertex, the equation of the axis of symmetry, the values that x may take, and the values that y may take.

You can find the following from a quadratic relation of the form $y = a(x - h)^2 + k$:

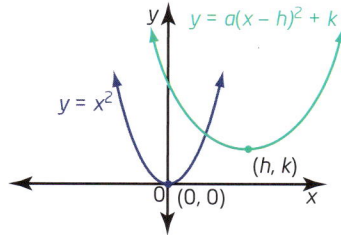

- The vertex of the parabola is (h, k), representing a horizontal translation of h units and a vertical translation of k units relative to the graph of $y = x^2$.
- The axis of symmetry of the parabola is the vertical line through the vertex with equation $x = h$.
- a indicates the vertical stretch or compression factor relative to the graph of $y = x^2$.
  - If $a > 0$, the parabola opens upward, and the vertex is the minimum point on the graph.
  - If $a < 0$, the parabola opens downward, and the vertex is the maximum point on the graph.

Example 1 Sketch the Graph of $y = a(x - h)^2 + k$

a) Describe the properties of the parabola with equation $y = 2(x - 4)^2 - 3$.

b) Sketch a graph of the parabola and label it fully.

c) Describe the set of values that x may take.

d) Describe the set of values that y may take.

Solution

a) Compare $y = 2(x - 4)^2 - 3$ with $y = a(x - h)^2 - k$.

Since $a = 2$, the graph of $y = 2(x - 4)^2 - 3$ will be stretched by a factor of 2 compared to the graph of $y = x^2$.

The parabola will open upward, since a is positive.

The vertex is (h, k), or $(4, -3)$, and it is a minimum point.

The equation of the axis of symmetry is $x = 4$.

b)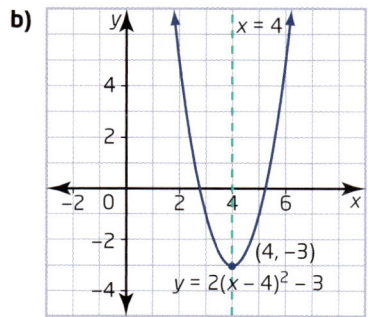

c) The graph shows that x may be any real number.

d) The graph shows that y may be any real number greater than or equal to -3, or $y \geq -3$.

Example 2 Write an Equation for a Graph

Determine an equation for the parabola shown.

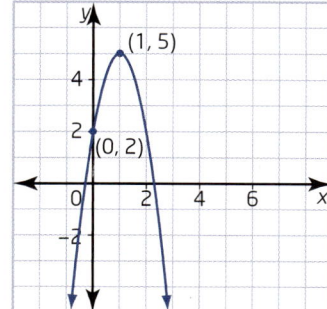

Solution

The vertex is (1, 5), so $h = 1$ and $k = 5$.
The parabola opens downward, so a is negative.

Substitute the values for h and k into the equation $y = a(x − h)^2 + k$.

$y = a(x − 1)^2 + 5$

The parabola passes through the point (0, 2). Substitute $x = 0$ and $y = 2$ and solve for a.

$2 = a(0 − 1)^2 + 5$
$2 = a(−1)^2 + 5$
$2 = a + 5$
$a = −3$

An equation for the parabola is $y = −3(x − 1)^2 + 5$.

Example 3 Fireworks

At a fireworks display, a firework is launched from a height of 2 m above the ground and reaches a maximum height of 40 m at a horizontal distance of 10 m.

a) Determine an equation to model the flight path of the firework.

b) The firework continues to travel an additional 1 m horizontally, after it reaches its maximum height, before it explodes. What is its height when it explodes?

c) At what other horizontal distance is the firework at the same height as in part b)?

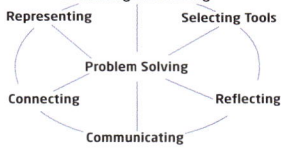

Solution

a) Sketch a graph of the situation.

The launch height of 2 m above the ground represents the point (0, 2).

The maximum height is 40 m at a horizontal distance of 10 m, so the vertex is (10, 40).
Substitute $h = 10$ and $k = 40$ into the equation $y = a(x − h)^2 + k$.

$y = a(x − 10)^2 + 40$

Substitute $x = 0$ and $y = 2$ and solve for a.

$2 = a(0 − 10)^2 + 40$
$2 = a(−10)^2 + 40$
$2 = 100a + 40$
$−38 = 100a$
$a = −\dfrac{38}{100}$
$a = −0.38$

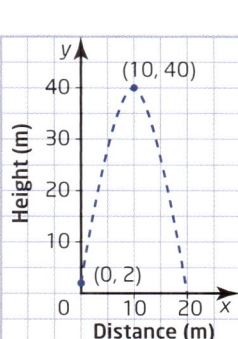

An equation that models the flight path of the firework is
$y = -0.38(x - 10)^2 + 40$, where x is the horizontal distance travelled, in metres, after the firework is launched and y is the height, in metres, above the ground.

b) The firework travels an additional 1 m horizontally after its maximum height of 40 m at $x = 10$, so $x = 11$. Substitute $x = 11$ into $y = -0.38(x - 10)^2 + 40$.

$y = -0.38(11 - 10)^2 + 40$
$ = -0.38(1)^2 + 40$
$ = 39.62$

The firework exploded at a height of 39.62 m.

c) Due to the symmetric property of a parabola, the firework is at the same height 1 m before the maximum point, or at a horizontal distance of 9 m.

Key Concepts

Property	$y = a(x - h)^2 + k$	$y = 2(x - 3)^2 - 1$	$y = -\frac{3}{4}(x + 1)^2 + 3$
Vertex	(h, k)	$(3, -1)$	$(-1, 3)$
Axis of symmetry	$x = h$	$x = 3$	$x = -1$
Stretch or compression factor relative to $y = x^2$	a	2	$-\frac{3}{4}$
Direction of opening	If $a > 0$, the parabola opens upward. The vertex is a minimum point. If $a < 0$, the parabola opens downward. The vertex is a maximum point.	Upward. $(3, -1)$ is a minimum point.	Downward. $(-1, 3)$ is a maximum point.
Graph	Parabola		
Values x may take	Any real number. Also depends on the situation.	Set of real numbers.	Set of real numbers.
Values y may take	If $a > 0$, then $y \geq k$. If $a < 0$, then $y \leq k$. Also depends on the situation.	$y \geq -1$	$y \leq 3$

Communicate Your Understanding

C1 Why is the vertical line through the vertex called the axis of symmetry? Illustrate with an example.

C2 When describing the transformation from $y = x^2$ to $y = 2x^2$, you say that it has been stretched vertically by a factor of 2, instead of compressed horizontally. Explain why vertical stretches are used in descriptions.

C3 Which equation is correct for the graph shown? Explain your reasoning.

A $y = (x + 2)^2 - 3$

B $y = \dfrac{1}{3}(x + 2)^2 - 3$

C $y = \dfrac{1}{2}(x + 2)^2 - 3$

D $y = -2(x + 2)^2 - 3$

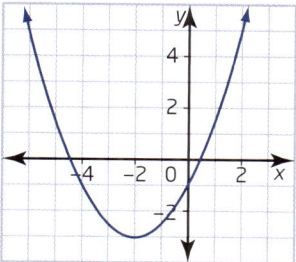

Practise

For help with questions 1 and 2, see Example 1.

1. Copy and complete the table for each parabola. Replace the heading for the second column with the equation for the parabola.

Property	$y = a(x - h)^2 + k$
Vertex	
Axis of symmetry	
Stretch or compression factor relative to $y = x^2$	
Direction of opening	
Values x may take	
Values y may take	

a) $y = (x - 4)^2$

b) $y = (x - 2)^2 - 4$

c) $y = (x + 3)^2 - 2$

d) $y = \dfrac{1}{2}(x + 1)^2 + 5$

e) $y = (x - 7)^2 - 3$

f) $y = -(x - 1)^2 + 7$

g) $y = 2(x - 4)^2 - 5$

h) $y = -3(x + 4)^2 - 2$

2. Sketch each parabola in question 1.

For help with questions 3 to 7, see Example 2.

3. Write an equation for the parabola with vertex at (2, 3), opening upward, and with no vertical stretch.

4. Write an equation for the parabola with vertex at (−3, 0), opening downward, and with a vertical stretch of factor 2.

5. Write an equation for the parabola with vertex at (4, −1), opening upward, and with a vertical compression of factor 0.3.

6. Write an equation for each parabola.

a)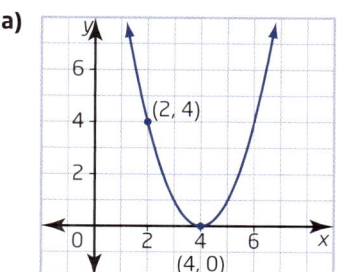

b)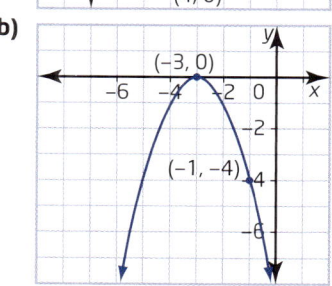

7. Write an equation for each parabola.

a)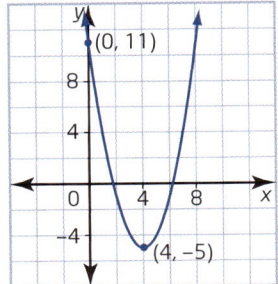

b)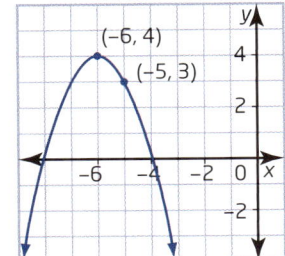

c)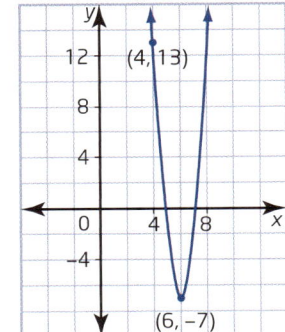

Connect and Apply

8. The graph of $y = x^2$ is stretched vertically by a factor of 3 and then translated 2 units to the left and 1 unit down. Sketch the parabola and write its equation.

9. The graph of $y = x^2$ is reflected in the x-axis, compressed vertically by a factor of $\frac{1}{2}$, and then translated 2 units upward. Sketch the parabola and write its equation.

10. a) Find an equation for the parabola with vertex (1, 4) that passes through the point (3, 8).

b) Find an equation for the parabola with vertex $(-2, 5)$ and y-intercept 1.

11. A stadium roof has a cross section in the shape of a parabolic arch with equation $y = -\frac{1}{45}x^2 + 20$. Which graph represents the arch? Justify your reasoning.

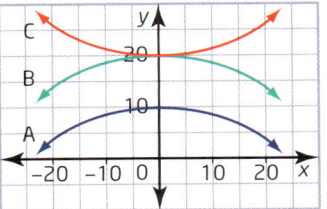

For help with questions 12 and 13, see Example 3.

12. The path of a soccer ball is modelled by the relation $h = -\frac{1}{16}(d - 28)^2 + 49$, where d is the horizontal distance, in metres, after it was kicked, and h is the height, in metres, above the ground.

a) Sketch the path of the soccer ball.

b) What is the maximum height of the ball?

c) What is the horizontal distance when this occurs?

d) What is the height of the ball at a horizontal distance of 20 m?

e) Find another horizontal distance where the height is the same as in part d).

13. A baseball is batted at a height of 1 m above the ground and reaches a maximum height of 33 m at a horizontal distance of 4 m.
    a) Determine an equation to model the path of the baseball.
    b) What is the height of the baseball once it has travelled a horizontal distance of 6 m?
    c) At what other horizontal distance is the baseball at the same height as in part b)?

14. The flight path of a firework is modelled by the relation $h = -5(t - 5)^2 + 127$, where h is the height, in metres, of the firework above the ground and t is the time, in seconds, since the firework was fired.
    a) What is the maximum height reached by the firework? How many seconds after it was fired does the firework reach this height?
    b) How high was the firework above the ground when it was fired?

15. Parabolic mirrors are used in telescopes to help magnify the image. The cross section of a parabolic mirror is shown.

    a) Sketch a graph to represent the cross section of the mirror, placing the vertex at (0, −0.24).
    b) Write an equation to represent the cross section of the mirror. Describe the values of x for which your equation is valid.
    c) Move the mirror to a different location on the same set of axes. Write a different equation to represent the cross section of the mirror. Describe the values of x for which your equation is valid.

    Did You Know?

    The Olympic Torch is lit by placing it in a parabolic mirror that concentrates rays of sunlight.

16. **Chapter Problem** Use Technology A city opened a new landfill site in 2000. In Section 4.1, question 6, you created a table of values showing the total mass of garbage in the landfill for each year from 2000 to 2007.
    a) Use a graphing calculator to create a scatter plot of the data and draw a curve of best fit.
       • With the scatter plot displayed, press (STAT), cursor over to display the **CALC** menu, and select **5:QuadReg**.
       • Press (VARS), and cursor over to display the **Y-VARS** menu. Select **1:Function** and then select **1:Y1**.
       • Press (ENTER) to get the **QuadReg** screen, and press (GRAPH).
    b) Use the Minimum operation of a graphing calculator to find the coordinates of the vertex.
       • Adjust the window settings so you can view the vertex of the parabola.
       • Press (2nd)[CALC] to display the **CALCULATE** menu, and select **3:minimum**.
       • Move the cursor to the left of the vertex and press (ENTER).
       • Move the cursor to the right of the vertex and press (ENTER).
       • Press (ENTER) again.
    c) Sketch the graph of the curve of best fit. Label the coordinates of the vertex and one other point on your sketch. Use these points to determine an equation for the curve of best fit in the form $y = a(x - h)^2 + k$.
    d) Describe the set of values that x may take and the set of values that y may take.

    Making Connections

    Refer to the Technology Appendix for help with creating a scatter plot on a TI-83 Plus or TI-84 Plus graphing calculator.

17. The cables of a suspension bridge form parabolas. If the minimum point of the centre cable is placed at the origin, determine an equation for each parabola. Describe the values of x for which each equation is valid.

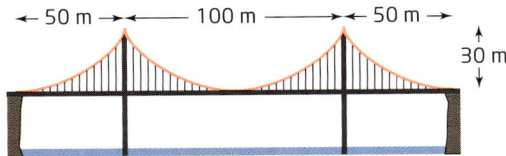

Achievement Check

18. The graph shows the path of a rocket fired from the deck of a barge in Lake Ontario at a Canada Day fireworks display. It is a parabola, where h is the height, in metres, of the rocket above the water and t is the time, in seconds.

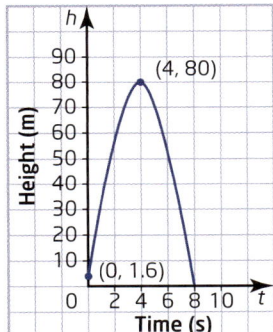

a) What is the maximum height reached by the rocket? Justify your answer.

b) When did the rocket reach its maximum height? Justify your answer.

c) How high was the rocket above the water when it was set off? Explain your answer.

d) Find an equation to describe the flight of the rocket.

e) After how long did the rocket fall into the water? Explain your answer.

Extend

19. A parabola has equation $y = 2(x - 4)^2 - 1$. Write an equation for the parabola after each set of transformations.

a) a reflection in the x-axis

b) a translation of 4 units to the left

c) a reflection in the x-axis, followed by a translation of 3 units upward

d) a reflection in the y-axis

20. a) In Chapter 2, you developed the equation of a circle centred at the origin. What is the equation of each circle?
- radius 5, centred at (0, 3)
- radius 7, centred at (6, 1)
- radius 8, centred at (−3, 5)
- radius r, centred at (h, k)

b) What do the equation of a circle and the equation of a parabola have in common?

21. Math Contest A locus is a set of points that satisfy a specific condition. For example, a circle is a set of points that are equidistant from a fixed point (the centre). Find an equation for the locus of points that is equidistant from the point (3, 2) and the line $y = -5$.

22. Math Contest Given that $a + b = 21$ and $\dfrac{1}{a} + \dfrac{1}{b} = \dfrac{7}{18}$, the value of ab is

A 18
B 36
C 54
D 72
E 90

4.5 Quadratic Relations of the Form $y = a(x - r)(x - s)$

The Dufferin Gate at the west end of the Canadian National Exhibition in Toronto is a parabolic arch. The arch is approximately 20 m high and approximately 22 m wide. In this section, you will model the arch using an equation of the form $y = a(x - r)(x - s)$.

Investigate

Tools
- grid paper

How does the equation $y = a(x - r)(x - s)$ relate to its graph?

1. Create a table of values for the equation $y = 2(x - 5)(x + 3)$. Use integer values of x from -6 to 6.

2. Use finite differences to show that this is a quadratic relation.

3. Graph the relation.

4. Identify the x-intercepts. How do they relate to the equation?

5. Identify the coordinates of the vertex. How could you use the x-intercepts to find the coordinates of the vertex?

6. **Reflect** Summarize your findings. Describe how to determine the x-intercepts and vertex of $y = a(x - r)(x - s)$.

7. **a)** Use your method to analyse the graph of
$$y = -\frac{1}{2}(x + 2)(x - 6).$$
   b) Sketch the graph of $y = -\frac{1}{2}(x + 2)(x - 6)$.

Making Connections

You will learn how to convert between the forms $y = ax^2 + bx + c$ and $y = a(x - r)(x - s)$ in Chapter 5.

A relation of the form $y = a(x - r)(x - s)$ is quadratic. The x-intercepts, or zeros, are r and s.

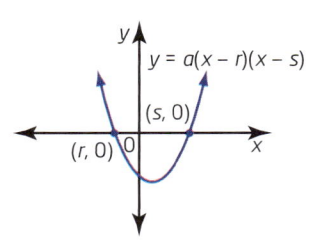

Example 1 Graph of $y = a(x - r)(x - s)$

Describe the graph of the quadratic relation $y = 2(x + 1)(x - 7)$. Sketch the graph and label the x-intercepts, vertex, and axis of symmetry.

Solution

Compare $y = 2(x + 1)(x - 7)$ with $y = a(x - r)(x - s)$.

The x-intercepts are -1 and 7.

Due to the symmetric property of a parabola, the x-coordinate of the vertex is on the axis of symmetry, which passes through the midpoint of the line segment connecting the x-intercepts.

$$x = \frac{-1 + 7}{2}$$
$$= 3$$

To find the y-coordinate of the vertex, substitute $x = 3$ into the equation.
$$y = 2(x + 1)(x - 7)$$
$$= 2(3 + 1)(3 - 7)$$
$$= 2(4)(-4)$$
$$= -32$$

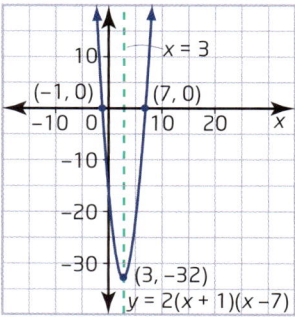

The vertex is $(3, -32)$.

The axis of symmetry has equation $x = 3$.

Example 2 Dufferin Gate

The Dufferin Gate is a parabolic arch that is approximately 20 m tall and approximately 22 m wide.

a) Sketch a graph of the arch with the left base located on the x-axis 4 units to the left of the y-axis. Label the x-intercepts and vertex.

b) Determine an equation to model the arch.

Solution

a) The x-intercepts are -4 and 18, so the x-coordinate of the vertex is $\frac{-4 + 18}{2}$, or 7.
The maximum height is 20 m, so the vertex is $(7, 20)$.

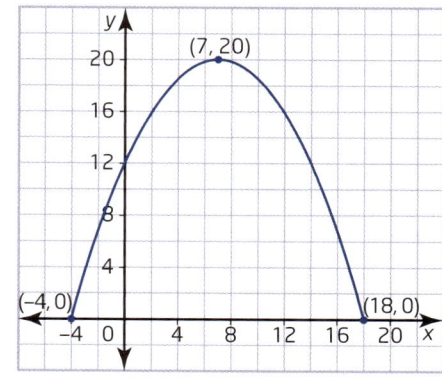

b) Use the x-intercepts to determine that the equation has the form
$y = a(x + 4)(x - 18)$.

Substitute the coordinates of the vertex and solve for a.

$20 = a(7 + 4)(7 - 18)$
$20 = a(11)(-11)$
$20 = -121a$
$a = -\dfrac{20}{121}$

An equation representing the shape of the arch is
$y = -\dfrac{20}{121}(x + 4)(x - 18)$, where y is the height, in metres, and x is the horizontal distance, in metres.

Key Concepts

- A relation of the form $y = a(x - r)(x - s)$ is quadratic.
- The x-intercepts, or zeros, are r and s.
- The x-coordinate of the vertex is on the axis of symmetry, which passes through the midpoint of the line connecting the x-intercepts.

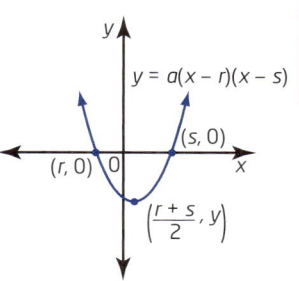

Communicate Your Understanding

C1 With the help of an example, describe a process that you can use to find the vertex of a parabola with equation of the form $y = a(x - r)(x - s)$.

C2 Which is the correct graph of the quadratic relation $y = 0.5(x - 3)(x + 1)$? Explain how you know.

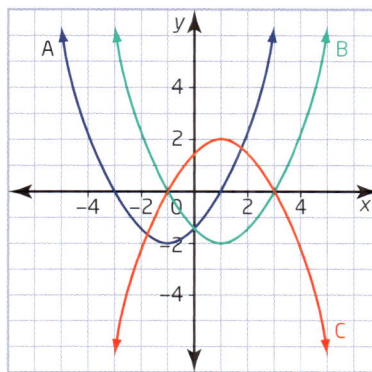

Practise

For help with questions 1 to 4, see Example 1.

1. Sketch graphs of all three relations on the same set of axes. Label the x-intercepts, vertex, and axis of symmetry for each parabola. Then, describe the similarities and differences between the graphs.

   a) $y = (x + 3)(x - 1)$
   b) $y = 2(x + 3)(x - 1)$
   c) $y = -2(x + 3)(x - 1)$

2. Sketch graphs of all three relations on the same set of axes. Label the x-intercepts, vertex, and axis of symmetry for each parabola. Then, describe the similarities and differences between the graphs.

   a) $y = (x - 4)(x - 8)$
   b) $y = \frac{1}{2}(x - 4)(x - 8)$
   c) $y = \frac{1}{4}(x - 4)(x - 8)$

3. Sketch each parabola. Label the x-intercepts and vertex.

   a) $y = (x - 6)(x - 2)$
   b) $y = -(x + 3)(x + 7)$
   c) $y = 2(x - 3)(x + 2)$
   d) $y = -2(x - 4)(x + 2)$

4. Sketch each parabola. Label the x-intercepts and vertex.

   a) $y = 3x(x + 2)$
   b) $y = \left(x + \frac{1}{2}\right)\left(x - \frac{7}{4}\right)$
   c) $y = -0.2(x - 4)(x + 10)$
   d) $y = \frac{2}{3}(x - 6)(x + 9)$
   e) $y = (x + 3.5)(x - 3.5)$
   f) $y = -\frac{1}{3}(x - 0.5)(x - 0.1)$

For help with question 5, see Example 2.

5. Determine an equation in the form $y = a(x - r)(x - s)$ to represent each parabola. Consider the vertex and x-intercepts.

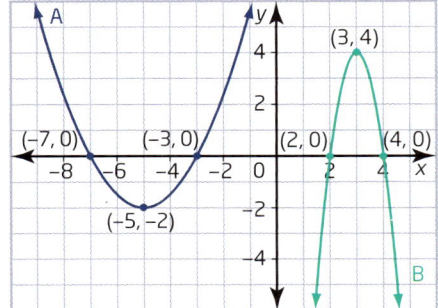

Connect and Apply

6. You investigated the graphs of $y = (x - h)^2$ in Section 4.3. Consider the quadratic relation $y = (x - 5)^2$.

   a) Write the coordinates of the vertex of the parabola.
   b) How many x-intercepts does the parabola have?
   c) Rewrite the equation in the form $y = a(x - r)(x - s)$.

7. A parabola has equation $y = (x + 2)^2$.

   a) Write its x-intercepts.
   b) Determine the coordinates of its vertex.

8. The predicted flight path of a toy rocket is defined by the relation $h = -2(d - 3)(d - 15)$, where d is the horizontal distance, in metres, from a safety wall, and h is the height, in metres, above the ground.

   a) Sketch a graph of the path of the rocket.
   b) How far from the wall is the rocket when it lands on the ground?
   c) What is the maximum height of the rocket, and how far, horizontally, is it from the wall at that moment?

9. Investigate the list of quadratic relations and make a conjecture relating the x-intercepts and the coordinates of the vertex. Test your conjecture with another example.
$y = (x + 1)(x - 1)$
$y = (x - 4)(x + 4)$
$y = -(x + 7)(x - 7)$
$y = 2(x + 6)(x - 6)$
$y = -\frac{1}{2}(x - 5)(x + 5)$

10. A soccer ball is kicked from a point 23 m to the left of the halfway line and lands at a point 17 m to the right of the halfway line. It reaches a maximum height of 10 m during its parabolic flight.
  a) Sketch a graph to show the flight of the soccer ball if the halfway line passes through the origin.
  b) Determine an equation to represent the path of the soccer ball.

11. The Ambassador Bridge is a suspension bridge that crosses the Detroit River and connects Windsor, Ontario, to Detroit, Michigan. The two towers that support the centre span of cables rise 118 m above the river and are 564 m apart. The cable reaches its lowest point approximately 46 m above the river.
  a) Sketch a graph to show the curve of the cable if the origin is centred under the lowest point of the cable at the river's surface.
  b) Determine an equation to represent the curve of the cables in the form $y = a(x - r)(x - s)$, if possible. If not, explain why.

12. An architect designed the cross section of a museum using the quadratic relations
$y = -\frac{1}{2}(x - 2)(x + 10)$, $y = -(x + 4)(x - 4)$,
and $y = -1.5(x - 2)(x - 10)$, where y is the height, in metres, of the building, and x is the horizontal distance, in metres, from the middle of the building.
  a) Sketch a graph of the cross section of the museum.
  b) How wide is the entire museum?
  c) How tall is each section of the museum?

13. The revenue, R, from concert ticket sales at a local venue is calculated as (number of tickets sold) × (price of ticket). The current price of a ticket is $20, and the venue typically sells 100 tickets. For each $1 increase in ticket price, 10 fewer tickets are sold. So, the revenue can be modelled using the equation $R = (100 - 10x)(20 + x)$, where x represents the number of $1 increases.
  a) Rewrite the equation in the form $R = a(x - r)(x - s)$.
  b) Sketch a graph of the relation.
  c) What does the R-intercept represent? What do the x-intercepts represent?
  d) What does a negative value of x represent?
  e) What price maximizes the revenue?

Extend

14. **Use Technology** Use a graphing calculator to graph each relation. Describe and justify how the shape of the graph relates to the number of factors.
  a) $y = (x - 2)(x - 5)(x - 7)$
  b) $y = 2(x + 6)(x + 3)(x - 1)(x - 9)$
  c) $y = -x(x + 2)(x - 4)(x - 6)(x - 9)$

15. A point lies 2 units above the x-axis on the axis of symmetry of the parabola with equation $y = (x + 4)(x - 6)$. How far is it from this point to the point on the curve where $x = 5$?

4.6 Negative and Zero Exponents

Archaeologists use radioactivity to determine the age of an artifact. For organic remains, such as bone, cloth, and wood, the typical method used is carbon-14 dating. This method focuses on the decay of carbon-14, which begins when an organism dies. Since this decay occurs at a constant, known rate, scientists can measure the amount of carbon-14 remaining and use a formula to determine the age of the sample. However, carbon-14 dating is only reliable for dating artifacts up to about 50 000 years old.

The decay of radioactive elements can be modelled mathematically, but not with a quadratic relation—scientists use a different non-linear model called an exponential relation.

Investigate

How can you determine the meaning of negative and zero exponents?

A: Compare $y = x^2$ and $y = 2^x$

Compare the quadratic relation $y = x^2$ to the exponential relation $y = 2^x$.

Tools
- TI-83 Plus or TI-84 Plus graphing calculator

1. Enter the window settings by pressing (WINDOW) and changing the values to match those shown. Enter the equation $y = x^2$ as **Y1** and the equation $y = 2^x$ as **Y2**. Press (GRAPH).

   ```
   WINDOW
   Xmin=-10
   Xmax=10
   Xscl=1
   Ymin=-2
   Ymax=50
   Yscl=5
   Xres=1
   ```

2. How is the graph of $y = 2^x$ similar to the graph of $y = x^2$? How is it different?

Technology Tip
You can change a decimal to a fraction.
- Enter the decimal value.
- Press (MATH), select 1:▶Frac, and then press (ENTER).

3. Press (2nd) [TABLE] to see a table of values for each relation. Compare the results for integer values of x from -3 to 3. Identify which relation grows faster over various intervals of x.

4. Make a table of values for $y = 2^x$, using integer values of x from -3 to 3. Express y-values in fraction form in lowest terms.

5. Compare the values of 2^3 and 2^{-3}, 2^2 and 2^{-2}, and 2^1 and 2^{-1}. What do you notice?

6. What is the value of 2^0?

7. Reflect How does the exponential relation $y = 2^x$ help you understand the meaning of negative and zero exponents?

B: Use Patterns

Tools
- grid paper

1. a) Copy and complete the list of decreasing powers of 2.

$2^5 = 32$
$2^4 = 16$
$2^3 = \blacksquare$
$2^2 = \blacksquare$
$2^1 = \blacksquare$

b) As you move down the list, by what fraction would you multiply each power to get the next result?

c) Extend the list. Use the pattern to determine the value of each power of 2.

$2^0 = \blacksquare$
$2^{-1} = \blacksquare$
$2^{-2} = \blacksquare$
$2^{-3} = \blacksquare$
$2^{-4} = \blacksquare$
$2^{-5} = \blacksquare$

2. a) Use your results to make a table of values for the relation $y = 2^x$, using integer values of x from -5 to 5.

b) Plot the ordered pairs.

c) Describe the graph. Will it cross the x-axis? If so, at what value? If not, why not?

d) Draw a curve of best fit.

3. Repeat steps 1 and 2 for powers of 3.

4. Reflect If a is any non-zero base, summarize your findings by describing how to evaluate the following.

a) a^0

b) a^{-1}

c) a^{-2}

d) a^{-3}

C: Use Exponent Laws

1. **a)** Copy and complete the table by simplifying each expression twice. First, expand and divide, and then use the exponent law for division.

Expression	Expand and Divide	Exponent Law
$\dfrac{3^2}{3^5}$	$\dfrac{3 \times 3}{3 \times 3 \times 3 \times 3 \times 3} = \dfrac{1}{3^3}$	$\dfrac{3^2}{3^5} = 3^{2-5}$ $= 3^{-3}$
$\dfrac{4^1}{4^3}$		
$\dfrac{2^4}{2^7}$		
$\dfrac{(-5)^2}{(-5)^3}$		
$\dfrac{(-2)^3}{(-2)^5}$		

b) How do the two results in each row compare? Does the sign of the base make a difference?

2. **a)** Copy and complete the table by simplifying each expression twice. First, expand and divide, and then use the exponent law for division.

Expression	Expand and Divide	Exponent Law
$\dfrac{3^5}{3^5}$	$\dfrac{3 \times 3 \times 3 \times 3 \times 3}{3 \times 3 \times 3 \times 3 \times 3} = 1$	$\dfrac{3^5}{3^5} = 3^{5-5}$ $= 3^0$
$\dfrac{5^2}{5^2}$		
$\dfrac{4^3}{4^3}$		
$\dfrac{(-3)^4}{(-3)^4}$		
$\dfrac{(-2)^2}{(-2)^2}$		

b) How do the two results in each row compare? Does the sign of the base make a difference?

3. **Reflect**

   a) Write a rule for a base raised to a negative exponent.

   b) Write a rule for a base raised to the exponent 0.

4. If a is any non-zero base, use your rules to evaluate each power.

   a) a^0

   b) a^{-1}

   c) a^{-2}

   d) a^{-3}

When a base is raised to a negative exponent, it is equal to the reciprocal of the base raised to the positive of the exponent. For example,

$$2^{-3} = \frac{1}{2^3}$$
$$= \frac{1}{8}$$

When a base is raised to an exponent of 0, the result is 1. For example, $2^0 = 1$.

Example 1 Negative and Zero Exponents

Evaluate.

a) 4^{-1} b) 8^0 c) $(-2)^{-3}$ d) $\left(\dfrac{2}{3}\right)^{-2}$ e) 0^{-2}

Solution

a) $4^{-1} = \dfrac{1}{4^1}$
$= \dfrac{1}{4}$

b) $8^0 = 1$

c) $(-2)^{-3} = \dfrac{1}{(-2)^3}$
$= \dfrac{1}{(-2)(-2)(-2)}$
$= -\dfrac{1}{8}$

d) $\left(\dfrac{2}{3}\right)^{-2} = \dfrac{1}{\left(\dfrac{2}{3}\right)^2}$
$= \dfrac{1}{\left(\dfrac{2}{3}\right)\left(\dfrac{2}{3}\right)}$
$= \dfrac{1}{\dfrac{4}{9}}$
$= 1 \times \dfrac{9}{4}$
$= \dfrac{9}{4}$

e) 0^{-2} is undefined because it has denominator 0 when written as $\dfrac{1}{0^2}$.

Example 2 Radioactive Decay

Carbon-14 is a radioactive element that decays to $\frac{1}{2}$, or 2^{-1}, of its original amount after every 5700 years. Determine the remaining mass of 10 g of carbon-14 after

a) 11 400 years
b) 28 500 years

> **Did You Know?**
>
> The time it takes for a radioactive element to decay to half its original amount is called its *half-life*. The half-life of carbon-14 is 5700 years.

Solution

a) For each 5700 years, the original amount decreases by a factor of $\frac{1}{2}$, or 2^{-1}.

Find how many 5700-year periods of time are in 11 400 years.
11 400 years $= 2 \times 5700$ years

$$\left(\frac{1}{2}\right)^2 \times 10 = \left(\frac{1}{2}\right)\left(\frac{1}{2}\right) \times 10$$
$$= \frac{1}{4} \times 10$$
$$= 2.5$$

or

$$(2^{-1})^2 \times 10 = 2^{-1 \times 2} \times 10$$
$$= 2^{-2} \times 10$$
$$= \frac{1}{2^2} \times 10$$
$$= \frac{1}{4} \times 10$$
$$= 2.5$$

> Multiplying by $\frac{1}{2}$ or 2^{-1} is the same as dividing by 2. So, I can also find the answer by dividing by 2, twice.
>
> $10 \div 2 \div 2 = 5 \div 2$
> $= 2.5$

The remaining mass after 11 400 years is 2.5 g.

b) 28 500 years $= 4 \times 5700$ years

$$(2^{-1})^4 \times 10 = 2^{-4} \times 10$$
$$= \frac{1}{2^4} \times 10$$
$$= \frac{1}{16} \times 10$$
$$= 0.625$$

The remaining mass after 28 500 years is 0.625 g.

Key Concepts

- When a non-zero base is raised to a negative exponent, the result is the reciprocal of the base raised to the positive of the exponent.
  For example, $2^{-3} = \frac{1}{2^3}$.

- When a non-zero number is raised to the exponent 0, the result is 1. For example,
  $$1 = \frac{100}{100} = \frac{10^2}{10^2} = 10^{2-2} = 10^0$$

Communicate Your Understanding

C1 Explain why 2^{-3} is not a negative number.

C2 Explain why 5^0 has a value of 1.

C3 Explain why it is often better not to rely on a calculator to evaluate powers with a fractional base, such as $\left(\dfrac{7}{2}\right)^{-2}$.

Practise

For help with questions 1 to 3, see Example 1.

1. Rewrite each power with a positive exponent.
   a) 3^{-2}
   b) 5^{-1}
   c) 10^{-4}
   d) 7^{-3}
   e) $(-2)^{-4}$
   f) $(-7)^{-1}$

2. Evaluate.
   a) 6^{-2}
   b) 9^0
   c) 7^{-1}
   d) 10^{-3}
   e) $(-9)^{-1}$
   f) $(-12)^{-2}$
   g) $(-3)^0$
   h) -89^0

3. Evaluate.
   a) $\left(\dfrac{1}{3}\right)^{-2}$
   b) 0^{-5}
   c) $\left(-\dfrac{1}{4}\right)^{-1}$
   d) $\left(\dfrac{5}{6}\right)^{-2}$
   e) $\left(-\dfrac{3}{8}\right)^{-4}$
   f) $\left(\dfrac{9}{4}\right)^{-3}$

Connect and Apply

4. Evaluate using pencil and paper. Check your results using a calculator.
   a) $6^0 + 6^{-2}$
   b) $8 - 8^{-1}$
   c) $(4 + 3)^0$
   d) $4^0 + 3^0$

For help with questions 5 and 6, see Example 2.

5. Iodine-123 is a radioactive element used in medical imaging. It decays to $\dfrac{1}{2}$, or 2^{-1}, of its original mass after 13 h. After 26 h, it decays to $\dfrac{1}{4}$, or 2^{-2}, of its original mass.
   a) What fraction remains after 52 h?
   b) What fraction remains after 78 h?
   c) Write each fraction as a power of 2 with a negative exponent.

6. Uranium-238 is a radioactive element found in rocks and many types of soils. Uranium-238 decays to $\dfrac{1}{2}$, or 2^{-1}, of its original amount after every 4.5 billion years. Determine the remaining mass of 0.5 kg of uranium-238 after
   a) 9 billion years
   b) 22.5 billion years

7. Radium-226 is a radioactive element that is used in a form of radiation treatment for various types of cancer. Radium-226 decays to $\dfrac{1}{16}$ of its mass in 6400 years.
   a) Write the fraction $\dfrac{1}{16}$ as a power of 2.
   b) What is the remaining mass of 8 mg of radium-226 after 6400 years?

8. Determine the value of x that makes each statement true.
   a) $x^{-3} = \dfrac{1}{27}$
   b) $x^{-1} = \dfrac{4}{5}$
   c) $2^x = \dfrac{1}{4}$
   d) $\left(\dfrac{2}{5}\right)^x = \dfrac{125}{8}$

9. Use a pattern, similar to that in Investigate, Part B, to verify that $(-4)^{-2} = \dfrac{1}{(-4)^2}$.

10. Refer to question 9. Make up your own patterning example to illustrate the meaning of the exponents 0 and -3.

11. The number of bees in a hive is 1000 on June 1 and doubles every month. This can be expressed as $N = 1000 \times 2^t$, where N represents the number of bees and t represents time, in months.
    a) Find the number of bees after 2, 3, 4, and 5 months.
    b) What does $t = 0$ represent in this situation?
    c) Is it possible for t to be -1? What does this mean?
    d) When were there 125 bees? Explain.

12. The intensity of light energy under water decreases rapidly. Many factors affect how quickly the intensity decreases. The light energy under water can be calculated using an exponential relation. For example,
    Ocean: $I = 325 \times (1.024)^{-d}$
    Lake Erie: $I = 401 \times (1.222)^{-d}$
    In these relations, d is the depth, in metres, and I is the light energy, in langleys.

    a) Why is a negative exponent used in the formulas?
    b) Sketch a graph of each relation.
    c) In which body of water does the intensity decrease more quickly? Explain why.

Did You Know?

The colours in light are absorbed at different rates, with the red end of the spectrum going first. As the diver descends, everything ends up as shades of blue.

Achievement Check

13. Mitosis is a process of cell reproduction in which one cell divides into two identical cells. A bacterium called *E. coli* often causes serious food poisoning. It can reproduce itself in 15 min.

    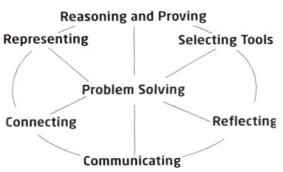

    a) Starting with one bacterium, make a table with time in $\frac{1}{4}$-h blocks and the corresponding number of *E. coli* bacteria up to 2 h of bacteria growth.
    b) Make a scatter plot from the table of data.
    c) What conclusions can you make from examining the table and scatter plot?
    d) About how long will it take before there are 10 000 bacteria?

Extend

14. Chris walks halfway along a 100-m track in 1 min, then half of the remaining distance in the next minute, then half of the remaining distance in the third minute, and so on.
    a) How far has Chris walked after 10 min?
    b) Will Chris get to the end of the track? Explain. Include a table of values and a graph to support your explanation.
    c) Write an equation to model this situation.

Did You Know?

The ancient Greek philosopher Zeno (450 BCE) argued that a number of truths about space and time were false. One of Zeno's paradoxes is that an object can never reach its target since the object must first cover an infinite number of finite distances, and this takes an infinite amount of time. For example, in question 15, Chris covers half of the remaining distance in each minute, so in theory he will never reach the end of the track.

15. When a patient takes a certain drug, $\frac{1}{10}$ of the drug that remains in his or her system is used per hour. A patient is given a 500-mg dose of a drug.

   a) Write an equation relating time and the remaining mass of the drug.

   b) After how many hours will less than 1% of the original mass remain?

16. Use Technology The popularity of fads and fashions often decays exponentially. One example is ticket sales for a popular movie. The table shows the total money spent per weekend on tickets in the United States and Canada for the movie *The Da Vinci Code*.

Weekend in 2006	Ticket Sales ($millions)
May 19–May 21	77.1
May 26–May 28	34.0
June 2–June 4	18.6
June 9–June 11	10.4
June 16–June 18	5.3
June 23–June 25	4.1
June 30–July 2	2.3

   a) Use a graphing calculator to create a scatter plot of the data.

   b) Draw a quadratic curve of best fit.
   - Press STAT, cursor over to display the **CALC** menu, and select **5:QuadReg**.
   - Press VARS, and cursor over to display the **Y-VARS** menu. Select **1:Function** and then select **1:Y1**.
   - Press ENTER to get the **QuadReg** screen, and press GRAPH.

   c) Draw an exponential curve of best fit.
   - Press STAT, cursor over to display the **CALC** menu, and select **0:ExpReg**.
   - Press VARS, and cursor over to display the **Y-VARS** menu. Select **1:Function** and then select **2:Y2**.
   - Press ENTER to get the **ExpReg** screen, and press GRAPH.

   d) Examine the two curves. Which curve of best fit best models the data?

17. Use Technology The table shows the atmospheric pressure compared to the altitude in a particular location.

Altitude (km)	Pressure (millibars)
0	1013.3
1	898.8
2	795.0
3	701.3
4	616.5
5	540.5
6	472.2
7	411.1
8	356.5
9	307.9
10	265.0

   a) Make a scatter plot of the data using a graphing calculator.

   b) Use the ExpReg operation to determine an exponential curve of best fit.

   c) Explain why an exponential model is better than a quadratic one.

18. Sketch the graphs of $y = x^2 + 1$ and $y = \frac{2^x - 2^{-x}}{2}$. Compare the values of y over various intervals.

19. Math Contest Solve each equation for x.

   a) $3^x = \frac{1}{81}$

   b) $4(2^{3x}) = \frac{1}{16}$

20. Math Contest The integers $-3, -2, -1, 0, 1, 2,$ and 3 are substituted into the expression $a^b + c^d + e^f + g$.

   a) What is the greatest possible value of the expression?

   b) What is the least possible value of the expression?

Chapter 4 Review

4.1 Investigate Non-Linear Relations, pages 164–167

1. Which scatter plot(s) could be modelled using a curve instead of a line of best fit? Explain.

a) 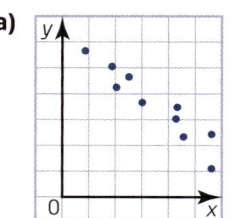   b)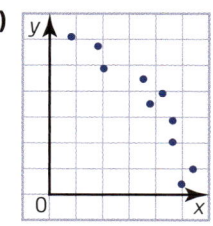

2. A scientist tested the strength of wood beams by securing beams of various lengths and placing a 500-kg mass at the end of each beam. The table shows the mean deflections, in centimetres.

Length (m)	Deflection (cm)
1.0	0.33
1.5	1.48
2.0	2.51
2.5	4.22
3.0	6.11
3.5	8.17
4.0	10.52
4.5	12.98
5.0	16.72

a) Make a scatter plot of the data. Draw a curve of best fit.

b) Describe the relationship between the length of the beam and the deflection.

c) Use your curve of best fit to predict the deflection of a 6.0-m-long beam.

4.2 Quadratic Relations, pages 168–173

3. Use finite differences to determine whether each relation is linear, quadratic, or neither.

a)
x	y
1	11
2	18
3	27
4	38
5	51

b)
x	y
−2	−10
−1	−2
0	0
1	2
2	10

c)
x	y
−2	−9
−1	−6
0	−3
1	0
2	3

4. The flight of an aircraft from Toronto to Montréal can be modelled by the relation $h = -2.5t^2 + 200t$, where t is the time, in minutes, and h is the height, in metres.

a) Graph the relation.

b) How long does it take to fly from Toronto to Montréal?

c) What is the maximum height of the aircraft? At what time does the aircraft reach this height?

4.3 Investigate Transformations of Quadratics, pages 174–179, and
4.4 Graph $y = a(x - h)^2 + k$, pages 180–188

5. Sketch the graph of each parabola. Describe the transformation from the graph of $y = x^2$.

a) $y = x^2 - 6$

b) $y = -0.5x^2$

c) $y = (x - 2)^2$

d) $y = -2x^2$

6. Copy and complete the table for each parabola. Replace the heading for the second column with the equation for the parabola. Then, sketch each parabola.

Property	$y = a(x - h)^2 + k$
Vertex	
Axis of symmetry	
Stretch or compression factor relative to $y = x^2$	
Direction of opening	
Values x may take	
Values y may take	

a) $y = (x - 1)^2 - 4$

b) $y = 2(x + 3)^2 + 1$

c) $y = \dfrac{1}{4}(x - 5)^2 + 1$

d) $y = -(x + 2)^2 + 6$

4.5 Quadratic Relations of the Form $y = a(x - r)(x - s)$, pages 189–193

7. Sketch a graph of each quadratic. Label the x-intercepts and the vertex.
   a) $y = -(x + 5)(x - 7)$
   b) $y = 2(x - 3)(x + 1)$

8. The path of a football can be modelled by the equation $h = -0.0625d(d - 56)$, where h represents the height, in metres, of the football above the ground and d represents the horizontal distance, in metres, of the football from the player.
   a) Sketch a graph of this relation.
   b) At what horizontal distance does the football land?
   c) At what horizontal distance does the football reach its maximum height? What is its maximum height?

4.6 Negative and Zero Exponents, pages 194–201

9. Evaluate.
   a) 7^{-2}
   b) 13^0
   c) 10^{-5}
   d) $(-34)^0$
   e) $(-6)^{-1}$
   f) $(-7)^{-2}$
   g) 6^0
   h) $\left(-\dfrac{2}{5}\right)^{-3}$

10. Joan won a multi-million dollar lottery. She decides to give $1 000 000 of her winnings to charity. Her plan is to give $\dfrac{1}{2}$, or 2^{-1}, to charity in January, and then give half of the remaining amount in February, half again in March, and so on.
    a) What fraction remains after 6 months?
    b) What fraction remains after 12 months?
    c) Write each fraction as a power of 2 with a negative exponent.
    d) What amount is remaining at the end of the year?

Chapter Problem Wrap-Up

In Section 4.1, question 6, Section 4.2, question 7, and Section 4.4, question 16, you used data from a landfill site to make a scatter plot, draw a curve of best fit, test for a quadratic relation, and determine an equation.

a) Identify the values of x for which your model is accurate.
b) Use your model to predict the total mass of garbage in the landfill in 2020. Comment on the accuracy of your prediction.
c) Analyse how the equation and the graph would change if this city instituted a mandatory recycling program.
d) A statistical analyst suggested that you could use an exponential model of the form $y = 200 \times b^x$, where x represents the number of years after 2000. What evidence could justify using this model? Determine an appropriate value of b.

Chapter 4 Practice Test

1. Sketch a graph of each parabola. Label the coordinates of the vertex and the equation of the axis of symmetry.
   a) $y = x^2 - 6$
   b) $y = 2(x - 5)^2$
   c) $y = -\dfrac{1}{3}(x + 3)^2 + 4$

2. Sketch a graph of each relation. Label the x-intercepts and the vertex.
   a) $y = (x - 6)(x + 2)$
   b) $y = -4(x - 1)(x - 9)$

3. Determine an equation to represent each parabola.
   a)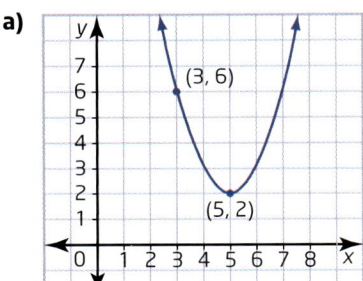
   b)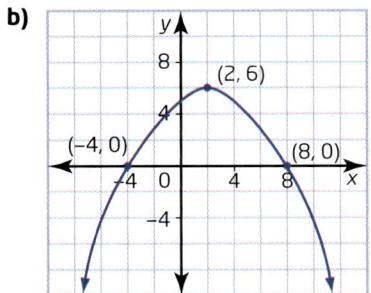

4. Evaluate.
   a) 4^0
   b) 5^{-1}
   c) $(-3)^{-3}$
   d) $\left(\dfrac{3}{4}\right)^{-2}$

5. The table shows the length of a spring under a specific load.

Load (kg)	Length (cm)
0	12.0
1	12.6
2	13.8
3	15.6
4	18.0
5	21.0
6	24.6

   a) Use finite differences to determine whether this is a quadratic relation.
   b) Make a scatter plot of the data. Draw a curve of best fit.
   c) Use your curve of best fit to predict the length of the spring under a load of 8 kg.

6. Board-feet are used to measure the total length, in feet, of boards that are 1 inch thick and 1 foot wide that can be cut from a tree to make lumber. You can use the equation $l = 0.011a^2 - 0.68a + 13.31$ to estimate the number of board-feet available in a certain type of tree, where l is the number of board-feet and a is the age, in years, of the tree.
   a) What is the approximate number of board-feet available to be cut from a 40-year-old tree?
   b) What is the approximate number of board-feet available to be cut from a 75-year-old tree?
   c) Why does the number of board-feet increase in a quadratic manner as a tree ages?
   d) Who would be interested in knowing this type of information? Explain.

7. The St. Louis Gateway Arch in St. Louis, Missouri, was built in 1965 and was designed as a catenary, which is a curve that approximates a parabola. The arch is 192 m wide and 192 m tall.

   a) Sketch a graph of the arch that is symmetrical about the y-axis.
   b) Label the x-intercepts and the vertex.
   c) Determine an equation to model the arch.

8. When a car is travelling at a given speed, there is a minimum turn radius it can safely make. A particular car's minimum radius can be calculated by $r = 0.6s^2$, where s is the speed, in kilometres per hour, and r is the turning radius, in metres. If the car uses tires with better grip, how does this affect the equation? Justify your response.

9. The maximum viewing distance on a clear day is related to how high you are above the surface of Earth. This relationship can be approximated by the formula $h = \dfrac{3}{40}d^2$, where d is the maximum distance, in kilometres, and h is your height, in metres, above the ground.
   a) How high do you need to be in order to see a distance of 25 km?
   b) How would the formula change if you were standing on a 20-m cliff?

10. A volleyball's height, h, in metres, above the ground after t seconds is modelled by the relation $h = -4.9t^2 + 5t + 2$.
    a) Graph the relation.
    b) What is the h-intercept? What does it represent?
    c) How long will it take the volleyball to hit the ground? What feature on the graph models this? Explain your answer.

11. An ant colony has 5000 ants on July 1 and doubles every year. This can be expressed as $N = 5000 \times 2^t$, where N represents the number of ants and t represents time, in years.
    a) Find the number of ants after 2, 3, 4, and 5 years.
    b) What does $t = 0$ represent in this situation? What does $t = -2$ represent?
    c) When were there 625 ants? Explain.

12. **Use Technology** The approximate cost of operating a certain car at a constant speed is given by the formula $C = 0.006(s - 50)^2 + 20$, for $10 \le s \le 130$, where s is the speed, in kilometres per hour, and C is the cost, in cents per kilometre. Use a graphing calculator to compare the operating costs, at different speeds, to those of a second vehicle with formula $C = 0.008(s - 55)^2 + 15$.

■ **Achievement Check**

13. a) Graph the following relations by developing a table of values and plotting points. Then, find the first and second differences.
    $y = x^2 - 4x$
    $y = x^2 - 4x + 5$
    $y = x^2 - 4x - 2$
    b) Examine each graph and use its properties to write an equation in the form $y = (x - h)^2 + k$.
    c) What conclusions can you make about the relation $y = x^2 - 4x + c$ for different values of c?

CHAPTER 5

Quadratic Expressions

Quadratic Relations of the Form $y = ax^2 + bx + c$

- Expand and simplify second-degree polynomial expressions, using a variety of tools and strategies.
- Factor polynomial expressions involving common factors, trinomials, and differences of squares, using a variety of tools and strategies.

Vocabulary
perfect square trinomial
difference of squares
quadratic expression

Polynomial expressions are used to model many situations. For example, the expression $2x + 5$ could represent the length of a basketball court or the number of seats in a theatre. Then, the expression $2x^2 + 11x + 15$ might represent the area of the basketball court or the revenue from theatre ticket sales.

In this chapter, you will learn how to multiply and factor polynomial expressions. In particular, you will develop skills for working with second-degree polynomials, or quadratic expressions.

Chapter Problem

A pedestal for trophies is to be made from three layers, each in the shape of a square-based prism with the same height. The pedestal can be made in any size, depending on the height, x, in centimetres.

How can you find the surface area of the pedestal?

Get Ready

Classify Polynomials

You can classify a **polynomial** by its number of terms or its degree.

The **degree of a polynomial** is the greatest degree of any of its terms.
The degree of a term is the sum of the exponents on its variables.

$2abc$ is a **monomial**, because it has one term.
The sum of the exponents is $1 + 1 + 1$, or 3. $2abc$ is a third-degree polynomial.

$7x^2 + x$ is a **binomial**, because it has two terms.
The greatest power is 2 from the term $7x^2$. $7x^2 + x$ is a second-degree polynomial.

$7k^2m + 15k^3m^2 - 6km^2$ is a **trinomial**, because it has three terms.
The greatest exponent sum is $3 + 2$, or 5, from the term $15k^3m^2$.
$7k^2m + 15k^3m^2 - 6km^2$ is a fifth-degree polynomial.

1. Classify each polynomial by its number of terms.

   a) $-3y$
   b) $5 + 6a^3$
   c) $6x^2 + x - 1$
   d) $8a^4b^4 - 6a^3b^2 + 2ab^2$
   e) $5d^3e - 7e$
   f) $19m + 8n - 3p$

2. State the degree of each polynomial.

   a) $9 + 5y^5 - 4y^2 + y$
   b) $8a^3b^2 + 9a^2b - 6a^4b^2$
   c) $10x^7y^2 - 3x^3y^3 + 5x^4y^4$
   d) $6abc - 5a^2bc^2 - 7abc^2$

Add and Subtract Polynomials

To add polynomials, remove the brackets and then collect **like terms**.

$$(2x^2 + 3x - 5) + (7x^2 - 6x - 2)$$
$$= 2x^2 + 3x - 5 + 7x^2 - 6x - 2$$
$$= 2x^2 + 7x^2 + 3x - 6x - 5 - 2$$
$$= 9x^2 - 3x - 7$$

To subtract polynomials, add the opposite polynomial.

$$(4a^2 + 5ab - 9b^2) - (7a^2 - 6ab + 2b^2)$$
$$= (4a^2 + 5ab - 9b^2) + (-7a^2 + 6ab - 2b^2)$$
$$= 4a^2 + 5ab - 9b^2 - 7a^2 + 6ab - 2b^2$$
$$= 4a^2 - 7a^2 + 5ab + 6ab - 9b^2 - 2b^2$$
$$= -3a^2 + 11ab - 11b^2$$

3. Simplify.

   a) $(5x + 7) + (2x - 11)$
   b) $(3b - 8) - (6b - 7)$
   c) $(5x^2 + 6x + 8) + (2x^2 + 5x - 9)$
   d) $(9y^3 - 7y^2 + 6) - (3y^3 - 5y^2 + 8)$
   e) $(7a^2 + 3a - 4) + (8a^2 - 2a - 15)$
   f) $(2c^2 - 3c + 1) - (-c^2 - 3c - 5)$

4. Simplify.

   a) $(7x^2 + 3xy - 2y^2) + (8x^2 - xy - y^2)$
   b) $(4g^2 + gh - 7h^2) - (g^2 - 2gh + 3h^2)$
   c) $(5ab^2 + 7a - b) + (3ab^2 - 5a + 6b)$
   d) $(3cd^2 + 2c + 9d) - (2cd^2 + 2c - d)$
   e) $(2x + 8) - (6x - 7) + (5x - 1)$
   f) $(5a^2 - b) + (6b - 2a^2) - (b^2 + 7a^2)$

The Product of a Monomial and a Polynomial

The **distributive property** allows you to expand algebraic expressions. When distributing, multiply the monomial by each term in the polynomial.

$2(x + 3)$
$= 2(x) + 2(3)$
$= 2x + 6$

The area is $2x + 6$.

$2x(x + 1)$
$= 2x(x) + 2x(1)$
$= 2x^2 + 2x$

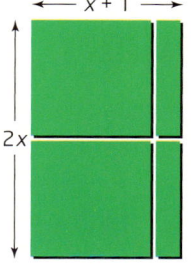

The area is $2x^2 + 2x$.

$-a(3a + 5)$
$= -a(3a) + (-a)(5)$
$= -3a^2 + (-5a)$
$= -3a^2 - 5a$

5. Use algebra tiles to model each product.

The dimensions of algebra tiles: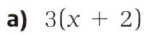

a) $3(x + 2)$
b) $4(x + 2)$
c) $x(x + 3)$
d) $4x(x + 4)$

6. Expand using the distributive property.

a) $7m(3m + 8)$ b) $-4(c + 9)$
c) $5a^2(6a^2 - 8a)$ d) $2(d^2 - 2d + 1)$

7. A rectangular prism has the dimensions shown.

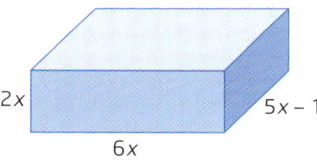

a) Find a simplified expression for the volume.
b) Find a simplified expression for the surface area.

Factors

The **factors** of 12 are 1, 2, 3, 4, 6, and 12. To find the **greatest common factor** (GCF) of 12 and 18, express each number as the product of its prime factors.

$12 = ⓶ × 2 × ③$
$18 = ⓶ × ③ × 3$

Since both 12 and 18 have factors of 2 and 3, their GCF is $2 × 3$, or 6.

8. Write the factors of each number.
a) 10   b) 24   c) 16   d) 32

9. Write each number as the product of its prime factors.
a) 8   b) 14   c) 28   d) 30

10. Find the GCF of each pair of numbers.
a) 6 and 9   b) 25 and 15
c) 24 and 16   d) 20 and 28
e) 36 and 15   f) 32 and 40

Get Ready • MHR **209**

5.1 Multiply Polynomials

A rectangular garden measures 3 m by 5 m. If each dimension is increased by the same amount to expand the garden, how can you model the area of the new garden using a polynomial?

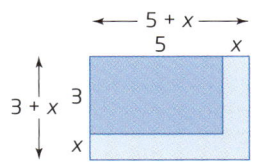

Investigate A

How can you model the multiplication of polynomials?

Method 1: Use Algebra Tiles

Tools
- algebra tiles

1. To show the product $(2x)(3x)$, use algebra tiles to model $2x$ and $3x$ as the dimensions of a rectangle. Then, fill in the rectangle with tiles to find an expression for the area. An x^2-tile has been placed to begin the process. How many x^2-tiles are needed to fill in the rectangle? What is the area of the rectangle? What is the product $(2x)(3x)$?

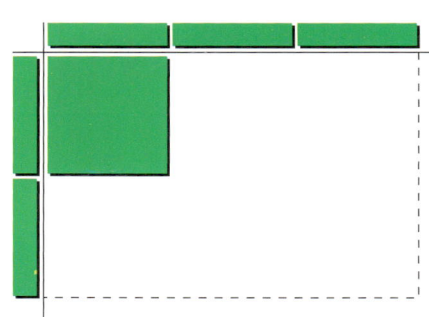

2. To show the product $(2x)(3x + 3)$, use algebra tiles to model $2x$ and $3x + 3$ as the dimensions of a rectangle.

   a) Use two x-tiles to form one dimension along the left side. Use three x-tiles and three unit tiles to form the other dimension along the top. Complete the area of the rectangle.

   b) How many x^2-tiles and x-tiles are needed? What is the resulting product?

3. Use algebra tiles to model the product $(3x)(2x + 1)$. What is the resulting product?

4. Use the same process to model the product of two binomials. What is each resulting product?

   a) $(x + 1)(x + 2)$ **b)** $(x + 2)(x + 4)$
   c) $(x + 3)(2x + 1)$ **d)** $(2x + 3)(x + 1)$

5. Reflect Consider your results from step 4.

   a) Describe how you can use algebra tiles to multiply two binomials.

   b) How are the terms in the resulting products related to the terms of the two binomials? Write a general rule for multiplying two binomials.

6. Use your rule to find each product.

   a) $(x + 3)(x + 8)$ **b)** $(2x + 5)(x + 4)$
   c) $(4x + 7)(3x + 1)$

Method 2: Use *The Geometer's Sketchpad*®

For this activity, you will use unit tiles, x-tiles (horizontal and vertical), and x^2-tiles.

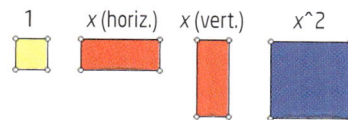

Tools
- computer with *The Geometer's Sketchpad*®
- Algebra Tiles.gsp

1. To show the product $(2x)(3x)$, use virtual algebra tiles to model $2x$ and $3x$ as the dimensions of a rectangle. Then, fill in the rectangle with tiles to find an expression for the area.

   • Click and hold the **Custom Tool** icon. Select **x (vertical)** and place two tiles along the vertical line, as shown.
   • Repeat for **x (horizontal)**, placing three tiles along the horizontal line, as shown.
   • Repeat for **x^2** (x^2-tile) to complete the area of the rectangle.

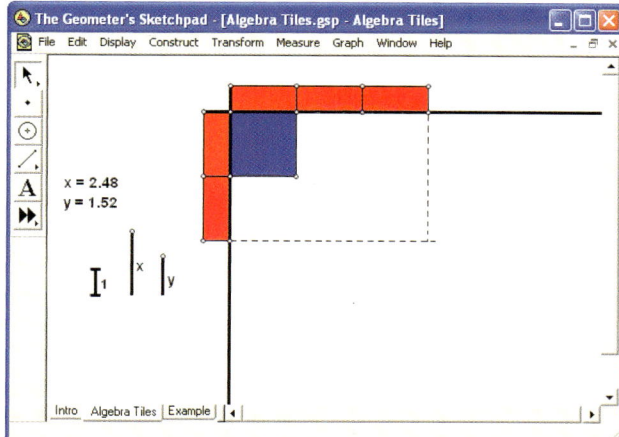

How many x^2-tiles are needed? What is the area of the rectangle? What is the product $(2x)(3x)$?

2. Model the product $2x(3x + 3)$ using virtual algebra tiles.
   a) Place two **x (vertical)** tiles along the vertical line. Place three **x (horizontal)** tiles and three unit tiles along the horizontal line.
   b) Complete the area of the rectangle.
   c) How many x^2-tiles and x-tiles are needed? What is the resulting product?

3. Use virtual algebra tiles to illustrate the product $3x(2x + 1)$. What is the resulting product?

4. Use the same process to model the product of two binomials. What is each resulting product?
   a) $(x + 1)(x + 2)$
   b) $(x + 2)(x + 4)$
   c) $(x + 3)(2x + 1)$
   d) $(2x + 3)(x + 1)$

5. **Reflect** Consider your results from step 4.
   a) Describe how you can use virtual algebra tiles to multiply two binomials.
   b) How are the terms in the resulting products related to the terms of the two binomials? Write a general rule for multiplying two binomials.

6. Use your rule to find each binomial product.
   a) $(x + 3)(x + 8)$
   b) $(2x + 5)(x + 4)$
   c) $(4x + 7)(3x + 1)$

Investigate B

Tools
- TI-89 calculator

How can you relate the distributive property to polynomial multiplication?

Turn on the TI-89 calculator. If necessary, press the HOME key to display the computer algebra system (CAS) Home screen.

1. Clear the calculator's memory.
   - Press 2nd [F6] to display the **Clean Up** menu.
   - Select **2:NewProb**.
   - Press ENTER.

2. Expand $2x(3x - 5)$.
   - Press F2.
   - Select **3:expand(**.
   - Type $(2x)(3x - 5)$.
   - Press) ENTER.

   What expression results?

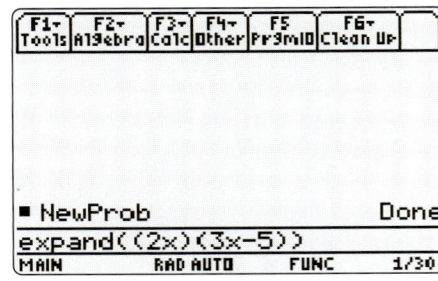

3. Apply the distributive property. Multiply 2x by each term in the binomial (3x − 5).
   - Type (2x)(3x) + (2x)(−5).
   - Press ENTER.

   What expression results?

   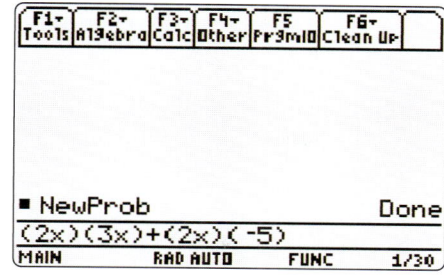

4. Compare your answers for steps 2 and 3. Describe the process the calculator used to expand the expression $2x(3x - 5)$.

5. Use a CAS to expand each expression.
   a) $2x(5x^2 - 3x + 1)$
   b) $-3x^2(2x^2 + 5x - 3)$
   c) $3xy(2x^2y - 4xy^2)$
   d) $ax(bx - cy + d)$

   Technology Tip
   To enter exponents, use the ^ key. For example, to enter x^2, press X ^ 2.

6. Use a CAS to apply the distributive property to expand each expression in step 5. Verify that the answers are the same.

7. Use a CAS to expand the product of two binomials. What is each resulting product?
   a) $(x + 1)(x + 2)$
   b) $(x + 2)(x + 4)$
   c) $(x + 3)(2x + 1)$
   d) $(2x + 3)(x + 1)$

   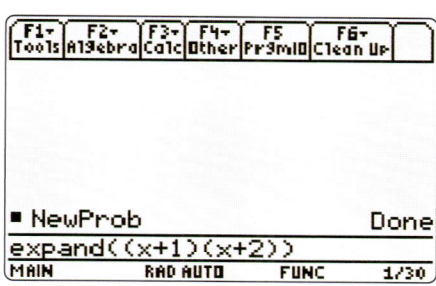

   Technology Tip
   To enter an expression containing variables multiplied together, you must use the × key. For example, to enter xy, press X × Y.

8. Use a CAS to apply the distributive property to expand each expression in step 7. Multiply each term of the first binomial by the second binomial. Verify that the answers are the same.

9. **Reflect** Consider your results from steps 7 and 8. How are the terms in the resulting products related to the terms of the two binomials? Write a general rule for multiplying two binomials.

Example 1 Model a Binomial Product

Model the binomial product $(x + 2)(2x + 3)$.

Solution

Method 1: Use Algebra Tiles

Use algebra tiles to create a rectangle with width $x + 2$ and length $2x + 3$.

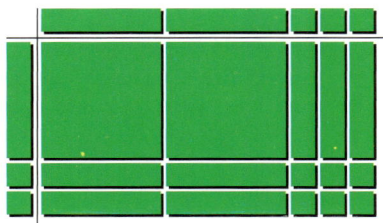

There are two x^2-tiles, seven x-tiles, and six unit tiles.

The area of the rectangle is $2x^2 + 7x + 6$.
$(x + 2)(2x + 3) = 2x^2 + 7x + 6$

Method 2: Use a Diagram

Draw a vertical segment of any length and label it $x + 2$ units. Divide the segment into a section x units long and a section 2 units long.

Perpendicular to the top of the vertical segment, draw a horizontal segment, $2x + 3$ units long, divided into a section $2x$ units long and a section 3 units long.

Complete the rectangle by drawing sides opposite $x + 2$ and $2x + 3$. Then, draw horizontal and vertical dashed segments from the section marks to the opposite sides, as shown. Find the areas of the four sections that make up the whole rectangle.

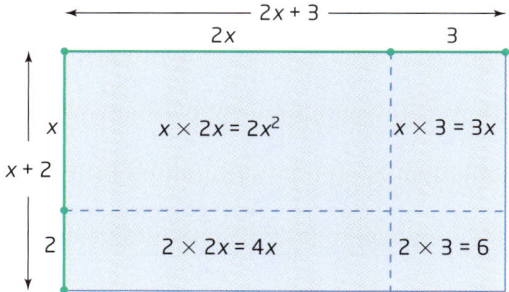

The binomial product $(x + 2)(2x + 3)$ equals the sum of the four areas.
$(x + 2)(2x + 3) = 2x^2 + 3x + 4x + 6$
$ = 2x^2 + 7x + 6$

Example 2 Use the Distributive Property

Find each binomial product.
a) $(x + 2)(x + 5)$
b) $(x - 2)(x + 4)$
c) $(3x + 7)(x - 5)$

Solution

a) To multiply two binomials, use the distributive property. Then, simplify by collecting like terms.

$$(x + 2)(x + 5)$$
$$= x(x + 5) + 2(x + 5)$$
$$= x(x) + x(5) + 2(x) + 2(5)$$
$$= x^2 + 5x + 2x + 10$$
$$= x^2 + 7x + 10$$

b) $(x - 2)(x + 4)$
$$= x(x + 4) - 2(x + 4)$$
$$= x^2 + 4x - 2x - 8$$
$$= x^2 + 2x - 8$$

c) Apply the distributive property mentally. Perform the multiplications indicated by the upper arrows and then the lower arrows. Then, simplify by collecting like terms.

$$(3x + 7)(x - 5)$$
$$= 3x^2 - 15x + 7x - 35$$
$$= 3x^2 - 8x - 35$$

You can find the product of two binomials by multiplying each term in the first binomial by each term in the second binomial. If necessary, simplify by collecting like terms.

$$(a + b)(c + d) = ac + ad + bc + bd$$

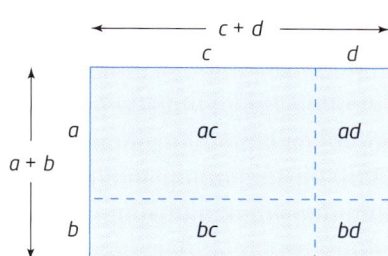

Example 3 Expand and Simplify

Expand and simplify.

a) $-2(4x - 5)(7x - 6)$

b) $2(x + 7)(x - 3) - (4x + 3)(2x - 1)$

Solution

a) First, find the product of the binomials. Then, multiply by -2.

$$-2(4x - 5)(7x - 6)$$
$$= -2(28x^2 - 24x - 35x + 30)$$
$$= -2(28x^2 - 59x + 30)$$
$$= -56x^2 + 118x - 60$$

b)
$$2(x + 7)(x - 3) - (4x + 3)(2x - 1)$$
$$= 2(x^2 - 3x + 7x - 21) - (8x^2 - 4x + 6x - 3)$$
$$= 2(x^2 + 4x - 21) - (8x^2 + 2x - 3)$$
$$= 2(x^2 + 4x - 21) - 1(8x^2 + 2x - 3)$$
$$= 2x^2 + 8x - 42 - 8x^2 - 2x + 3$$
$$= -6x^2 + 6x - 39$$

> Multiplying a polynomial by –1 produces the opposite polynomial:
> $(-1)(8x^2 + 2x - 3)$
> $= -8x^2 - 2x + 3$

Literacy Connections
Expand, find the product, and multiply all mean the same thing.

Key Concepts

- You can model a binomial product as the area of a rectangle with the binomials as the dimensions.

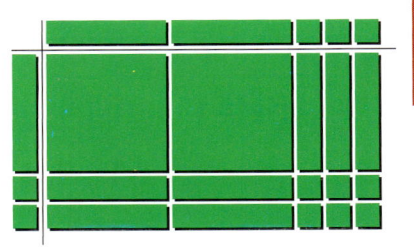

The area of the rectangle is $2x^2 + 7x + 6$.
$(x + 2)(2x + 3) = 2x^2 + 7x + 6$

- You can find the product of two binomials by multiplying each term in one binomial by each term in the other binomial. If necessary, simplify by collecting like terms.

$$(x + 2)(2x + 3)$$
$$= 2x^2 + 3x + 4x + 6$$
$$= 2x^2 + 7x + 6$$

Communicate Your Understanding

C1 Explain how the algebra tiles illustrate the product $(x + 1)(3x + 2)$.

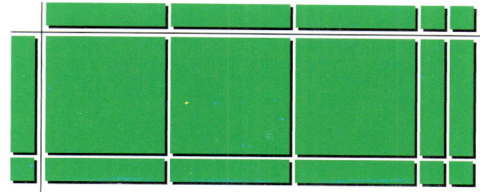

C2 Jason expands and simplifies $(x + 3)(x + 7)$ in his head. He adds 3 and 7 to get $10x$, and multiplies 3 and 7 to get 21. His final answer is $x^2 + 10x + 21$.

  a) Explain Jason's logic.

  b) Would Jason's method work when expanding $(2x + 3)(5x + 6)$? If yes, explain why. If no, how should he adapt his method?

  c) Would this method work for negative constant terms? Explain.

C3 Describe the steps you would use to expand $(3x + 5)(2x - 9)$.

C4 Rolly uses an acronym to help him remember how to expand two binomials. It is called the FOIL method, for *First*, *Outside*, *Inside*, *Last*. What does this mean?

Practise

For help with questions 1 and 2, see Example 1.

1. What binomial product does each model illustrate?

  a)

  b)

  c)   **d)**

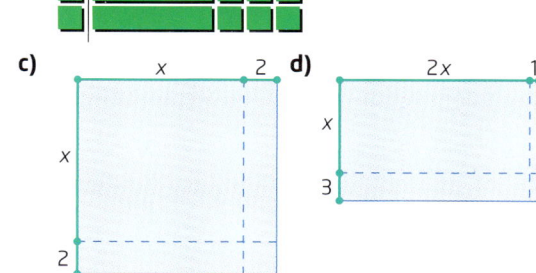

2. Model each binomial product using algebra tiles, virtual algebra tiles, or a diagram.

  a) $(2x + 1)(x + 1)$ **b)** $(x + 4)(x + 2)$
  c) $(x + 1)(x + 5)$ **d)** $(2x + 1)(3x + 2)$

For help with questions 3 to 6, see Example 2.

3. Use the distributive property to find each binomial product.

  a) $(x + 3)(x + 5)$ **b)** $(x + 3)(x + 4)$
  c) $(y + 2)(y + 4)$ **d)** $(r + 4)(r + 2)$
  e) $(n + 7)(n + 1)$ **f)** $(p + 9)(p + 9)$
  g) $(w + 7)(w + 8)$ **h)** $(d + 3)(d + 11)$

4. Use the distributive property to find each binomial product.

  a) $(k - 3)(k - 5)$ **b)** $(y - 3)(y - 4)$
  c) $(x - 2)(x - 4)$ **d)** $(q - 4)(q - 2)$
  e) $(j - 7)(j - 1)$ **f)** $(p - 9)(p - 3)$
  g) $(z - 7x)(z - 8x)$ **h)** $(b - 3c)(b - 11c)$

5. Use the distributive property to find each binomial product.
   a) $(x + 3)(x - 5)$
   b) $(y + 3)(y - 4)$
   c) $(c - 2)(c + 4)$
   d) $(w - 4)(w + 2)$
   e) $(m + 7)(m - 1)$
   f) $(y - 9)(y + 3)$
   g) $(x + 7y)(x - 8y)$
   h) $(a + 6b)(a - 10b)$

6. Find each binomial product.
   a) $(2x + 3)(x + 4)$
   b) $(y - 3)(5y - 7)$
   c) $(6c - 1)(3c + 5)$
   d) $(7w - 2)(2w + 1)$
   e) $(5m + 6)(5m - 6)$
   f) $(9y - 2)(2y + 2)$
   g) $(7d + 5c)(8d - 6c)$
   h) $(6q + 5r)(7q - 12r)$

For help with questions 7 and 8, see Example 3.

7. Expand and simplify.
   a) $3(x - 5)(x + 6)$
   b) $-2(x - 7)(x - 9)$
   c) $-(y + 2)(y - 8)$
   d) $2(k + 3)(k + 7)$
   e) $m(m - 3n)(m - 5n)$
   f) $2a(3a + 4b)(6a + 7b)$

8. Expand and simplify.
   a) $(x + 4)(x + 6) + (x - 1)(x + 7)$
   b) $(2x + 5)(3x - 7) + 2(4x + 9)(2x - 11)$
   c) $3(6x - 2)(6x - 1) - (2x - 3)(5x + 6)$
   d) $-(x - 2)(x - 3) + 2(3x + 5)(x + 4)$
   e) $(x + 4)^2 - (x - 4)^2$
   f) $-5(3x - 1)(5x - 2) + 6(6x + 3)(5x - 2)$

Connect and Apply

9. The predicted flight path of a firework is defined by the relation $h = -2(d - 3)(d - 15)$, where d is the horizontal distance, in metres, from a safety wall, and h is the height, in metres.
   a) Expand and simplify the relation.
   b) Verify that the relation from part a) is equivalent to the original relation. Use both relations to determine the height of the firework if d represents 10 m.

10. A square garden has side length x. One dimension is increased by 6 m and the other is increased by 3 m.

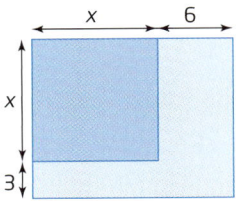

   a) Write an algebraic expression for the area of the original garden.
   b) Write an algebraic expression for the area of the new garden.
   c) Expand and simplify your area expression from part b).
   d) Find an expression that represents the increase in area.
   e) If x represents 12 m, find the increase in area.

11. a) For each situation, begin with a square field, measuring x metres by x metres. Then, draw a diagram of the new field, write an algebraic expression for its area, and expand and simplify your area expression.
   i) The length of one side is increased by 10 m.
   ii) The length of one side is doubled.
   iii) The length is increased by 5 m and the width is increased by 6 m.
   b) **Use Technology** Use a CAS to verify your answers to part a).

12. A parabola has equation $y = (x + 3)(x - 1)$.
   a) Find the x-intercepts of $y = (x + 3)(x - 1)$.
   b) Expand and simplify the equation.
   c) Graph the result from part b). Verify that the x-intercepts are the same.

Making Connections

In Chapter 4, you worked with quadratic relations of the form $y = (x - r)(x - s)$.

13. A rectangular prism has width w centimetres, length 2 cm more than its width, and height 2 cm.
    a) Draw a diagram of the prism.
    b) Express the volume as a product.
    c) Expand and simplify the volume expression.

14. A cube has side length x. Each dimension is increased by y.
    a) Draw a diagram of the cube.
    b) Write an algebraic expression for the surface area of the original cube.
    c) Write an algebraic expression for the surface area of the new cube.
    d) Write an algebraic expression for the difference in surface area. Expand and simplify.
    e) Write an algebraic expression for the difference in volume. Expand and simplify.

15. A scuba diver is drifting in a current of 0.3 m/s. If she swims with the current at an additional speed of v metres per second, the distance, d, in metres, that she travels before running out of air can be modelled by the relation $d = 3000(v + 0.3)(1.0 - v)$.
    a) Expand this relation.
    b) If she swims at 0.2 m/s, how far can she swim before running out of air?
    c) **Use Technology** Use a graphing calculator or computer software to investigate what swimming speed would result in the maximum distance before running out of air.

16. Write an algebraic expression for the area of each figure. Expand and simplify. Then, find the area in another way to verify your result.

    a) b)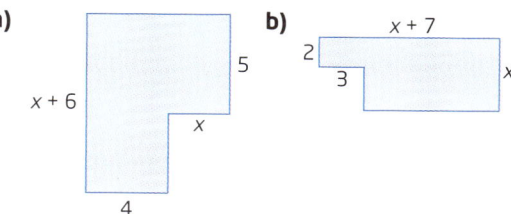

Extend

17. The number of hot dogs, n, sold by Wayne's Wiener World on a given day is modelled by $n = 500 - 100p$, where p is the price, in dollars.
    a) Solve this equation for p.
    b) The revenue generated by hot dog sales is $R = np$. Substitute your expression for p from part a), and expand to obtain an expression for the daily hot dog revenue.
    c) **Use Technology** Use a CAS to verify your answer to part b).

18. Determine an algebraic expression for the number of shaded small squares in the nth diagram. Test your expression for two more diagrams.

    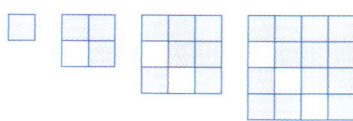

19. Pose and solve a problem in which the dimensions of a rectangular object are written as binomials.

20. **Math Contest** When a positive integer n is divided by 24, the remainder is 18. When n is divided by 8 the remainder is
    A 0   **B** 1   **C** 2   **D** 4   **E** 6

5.2 Special Products

The patterns in tile floors, brick patios, and quilts often repeat. Some quilts are made from square pattern blocks of material that are stitched together. The square pattern block shown starts with a square that is enlarged with the addition of rectangles to each of its dimensions until the desired square dimensions are reached. If the side length of the square pattern block is represented by $x + 3$, what is an expression for its area?

Investigate

How can you use patterns to find special products?

A: Squaring Binomials

Method 1: Use Pencil and Paper

1. Use algebra tiles or a diagram to square the binomial.
   $(x + 3)^2 = (x + 3)(x + 3)$

2. Expand and simplify.

   a) $(x + 3)^2$ b) $(x + 2)^2$ c) $(x - 6)^2$

   d) $(x - 4)^2$ e) $(2x + 5)^2$ f) $(3x - 1)^2$

   g) $(2x - 5y)^2$ h) $(4x + 7y)^2$

3. Consider each simplified expansion from step 2.

   a) How is the first term in each trinomial related to the first term in each binomial?

   b) How is the last term in each trinomial related to the last term in each binomial?

   c) How is the middle term in each trinomial related to the terms in the binomial?

4. **Reflect** Write a rule for expanding and simplifying $(a + b)^2$ or $(a - b)^2$.

5. Use your rule to square each binomial.

   a) $(5x + 3y)^2$ b) $(7c - 4d)^2$

Tools
Optional
- algebra tiles

Method 2: Use a Computer Algebra System (CAS)

- TI-89 calculator

1. Clear the calculator's memory by selecting **2:NewProb** from the **Clean Up** menu.

2. Use the **Expand** function on each square of a binomial. Record the results.
   a) $(x + 1)^2$
   b) $(x + 2)^2$
   c) $(x + 3)^2$
   d) $(x + 4)^2$
   e) $(x + 5)^2$

3. Compare the individual terms of the expansion to the binomial. Describe any patterns you notice, including any for the signs of the terms in the trinomial.

4. Use a CAS to expand each square of a binomial. Record the results.
   a) $(2x + 2)^2$
   b) $(2x + 3)^2$
   c) $(2x - 4)^2$
   d) $(2x - 5)^2$

5. Compare the individual terms of the expansion to the binomial. Describe any patterns you notice. How has your description of patterns changed compared to step 3?

6. Use a CAS to expand each square of a binomial. Record the results.
   a) $(3a + 2)^2$
   b) $(5m - 3)^2$
   c) $(4 + 2b)^2$
   d) $(7 - 3z)^2$
   e) $(2x + 3y)^2$

7. Compare the individual terms of the expansion to the binomial. Have the patterns you described in step 5 changed?

8. **Reflect** Write a rule for expanding each square of a binomial.
   a) $(a + b)^2$
   b) $(a - b)^2$

B: Product of a Sum and a Difference of Two Terms

Method 1: Use Pencil and Paper

1. Expand and simplify.
   a) $(x + 3)(x - 3)$
   b) $(2y + 5)(2y - 5)$
   c) $(x - 4)(x + 4)$
   d) $(3k - 7)(3k + 7)$

2. How are the two binomials in each multiplication in step 1 alike? How are they different?

3. Consider each simplified expansion from step 1.
   a) How is the first term related to the first terms of the two binomials?
   b) How is the last term related to the last terms of the two binomials?
   c) Explain why there are only two terms in the simplified expansion.

4. **Reflect** Write a rule for expanding and simplifying $(a + b)(a - b)$. Does your rule apply to $(a - b)(a + b)$? Explain.

5. Use your rule to find the product of each sum and difference of two terms.
   a) $(2x + 3y)(2x - 3y)$
   b) $(5m + 7)(5m - 7)$

Tools
- TI-89 calculator

Method 2: Use a CAS

1. Clear the calculator's memory by selecting **2:NewProb** from the **Clean Up** menu.

2. Use the **Expand** function on each binomial product. Record the results.
   a) $(x + 2)(x - 2)$
   b) $(x - 3)(x + 3)$
   c) $(2x - 1)(2x + 1)$
   d) $(3x + 4)(3x - 4)$
   e) $(2x + 3y)(2x - 3y)$
   f) $(3m - 4n)(3m + 4n)$

3. How are the two binomials in each multiplication in step 2 alike? How are they different?

4. Consider each expansion from step 2.
   a) How is the first term related to the first terms of the two binomials?
   b) How is the last term related to the last terms of the two binomials?
   c) Explain why there are only two terms in the simplified expansion.

5. **Reflect** Write a rule for expanding and simplifying $(a + b)(a - b)$. Does your rule apply to $(a - b)(a + b)$? Explain.

While you can always use the distributive property to find the product of two binomials, some pairs of binomials result in special products that follow specific patterns.

Squaring Binomials

You can visualize squaring a binomial using algebra tiles or a diagram. Surrounding the x^2 region, there are *two* regions of $3x$, which combine to give $6x$, and a region defined by 3×3, or 9, giving $x^2 + 6x + 9$.

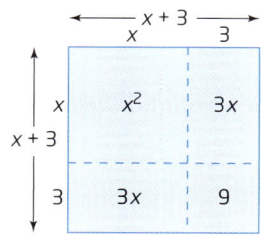

$(x + 3)^2 = (x + 3)(x + 3)$
$ = x^2 + 3x + 3x + 3^2$
$ = x^2 + 2(3x) + 9$
$ = x^2 + 6x + 9$

Alternatively, you can use the patterns for squaring a binomial. Square the first term, find twice the product of the terms, and square the last term. The middle term is added when you square a sum and subtracted when you square a difference.

$(a + b)^2 = a^2 + 2ab + b^2$ or $(a - b)^2 = a^2 - 2ab + b^2$

The resulting products are called **perfect square trinomials**.

Product of a Sum and a Difference

When you multiply the sum and the difference of two terms, there are only two terms in the simplified expansion. There is no middle term because the other two products have a sum of zero.

$(x + 3)(x - 3) = x^2 - 3x + 3x - 3^2$
$ = x^2 - 9$

To find the product of the sum and the difference of two terms, use the pattern. Find the product of the first terms and the product of the second terms.

$(a + b)(a - b) = a^2 - b^2$

The resulting product, $a^2 - b^2$, is called a **difference of squares**.

> I can change the order of the binomial factors and get the same result.
> $(a - b)(a + b) = a^2 - b^2$
> This happens because I can multiply two numbers or expressions in either order.

perfect square trinomial
- a trinomial of the form $a^2 + 2ab + b^2$ or $a^2 - 2ab + b^2$ that is the result of squaring a binomial

Literacy Connections

When you change the operation between the two terms of a binomial, the two forms are called conjugates. $x + 3$ and $x - 3$ are conjugates.

difference of squares
- an expression of the form $a^2 - b^2$ that involves the subtraction of two squares

Example 1 Apply Special Product Patterns

Expand and simplify.

a) $(x + 4)^2$ **b)** $(k - 5)^2$ **c)** $(3y + 7x)^2$
d) $(q - 11)(q + 11)$ **e)** $(4m + 3n)(4m - 3n)$

Solution

a) $(a + b)^2 = a^2 + 2ab + b^2$ Use the appropriate pattern
$(x + 4)^2 = (x)^2 + 2(x)(4) + (4)^2$ for squaring a binomial.
$= x^2 + 8x + 16$

b) $(a - b)^2 = a^2 - 2ab + b^2$ Use the appropriate pattern
$(k - 5)^2 = (k)^2 - 2(k)(5) + (5)^2$ for squaring a binomial.
$= k^2 - 10k + 25$

c) $(a + b)^2 = a^2 + 2ab + b^2$ Use the appropriate pattern
$(3y + 7x)^2 = (3y)^2 + 2(3y)(7x) + (7x)^2$ for squaring a binomial.
$= 9y^2 + 42xy + 49x^2$

d) $(a - b)(a + b) = a^2 - b^2$ Use the pattern for the product
$(q - 11)(q + 11) = (q)^2 - (11)^2$ of a sum and a difference.
$= q^2 - 121$

e) $(a + b)(a - b) = a^2 - b^2$ Use the pattern for the product
$(4m + 3n)(4m - 3n) = (4m)^2 - (3n)^2$ of a sum and a difference.
$= 16m^2 - 9n^2$

Example 2 Helicopter Pad

The radius of a circular helicopter landing pad is increased by 3 m.
a) Find a simplified expression for the area of the new circle.
b) Find a simplified expression for the increase in area.

Solution

a) Area of the original circle $= \pi r^2$

Area of the larger circle $= \pi(r + 3)^2$
$= \pi[(r)^2 + 2(r)(3) + (3)^2]$
$= \pi(r^2 + 6r + 9)$
$= \pi r^2 + 6\pi r + 9\pi$

> I can use the appropriate pattern for squaring a binomial.

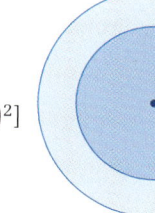

b) Increase in area $=$ (area of larger circle) $-$ (area of original circle)
$= (\pi r^2 + 6\pi r + 9\pi) - (\pi r^2)$
$= 6\pi r + 9\pi$

Key Concepts

- When squaring a binomial, you add the two equal middle terms after expansion.
  $(a + b)^2 = a^2 + 2ab + b^2$ and $(a - b)^2 = a^2 - 2ab + b^2$
- When you multiply the sum and the difference of two terms, the two middle terms are opposites, so they add to zero.
  $(a + b)(a - b) = a^2 - b^2$

Communicate Your Understanding

C1 Explain when the middle term is positive and when it is negative when you are squaring a binomial.

C2 Describe the steps you would use to expand and simplify each product.
  a) $(x - 2)^2$ **b)** $(x - 2)(x + 2)$

Practise

1. Draw a diagram to illustrate each product.
  a) $(x + 5)^2$
  b) $(x + 6)^2$
  c) $(x + a)^2$
  d) $(ax + b)^2$

For help with questions 2 to 6, see Example 1.

2. Expand and simplify.
  a) $(x + 5)^2$ **b)** $(y + 4)^2$ **c)** $(w + 6)^2$
  d) $(k + 7)^2$ **e)** $(m + 11)^2$ **f)** $(c + 10)^2$
  g) $(g + 9)^2$ **h)** $(x + 20)^2$

3. Expand and simplify.
  a) $(x - 5)^2$ **b)** $(z - 3)^2$ **c)** $(x - 9)^2$
  d) $(c - 1)^2$ **e)** $(v - 12)^2$ **f)** $(b - 100)^2$
  g) $(n - 2)^2$ **h)** $(m - 6)^2$

4. Expand and simplify.
  a) $(x + 3y)^2$ **b)** $(2x - y)^2$ **c)** $(5c + 2d)^2$
  d) $(3a - 4b)^2$ **e)** $(9k + 2m)^2$ **f)** $(4u - 5v)^2$

5. Expand and simplify.
  a) $(v + 1)(v - 1)$ **b)** $(a - 1)(a + 1)$
  c) $(y + 5)(y - 5)$ **d)** $(x - 7)(x + 7)$
  e) $(e - 9)(e + 9)$ **f)** $(z + 6)(z - 6)$
  g) $(x + 12)(x - 12)$ **h)** $(y - 3)(y + 3)$

6. Expand and simplify.
  a) $(w - v)(w + v)$ **b)** $(3m - n)(3m + n)$
  c) $(y + 6x)(y - 6x)$ **d)** $(3x + 4y)(3x - 4y)$
  e) $(7g - 3h)(7g + 3h)$
  f) $(9x - 8y)(9x + 8y)$

Connect and Apply

7. Expand and simplify. Verify your answers using one of three methods:
  - Check that substituting $x = 2$ into the original expression and the simplified expansion yields the same answer.
  - Check that graphing both the original expression and the simplified expansion using a graphing calculator yields only one graph.
  - Check that using a CAS to expand the original expression yields the same answer.

  a) $(x + 4)(x - 4)$ **b)** $(x - 8)^2$
  c) $(x + 8)^2$ **d)** $(x - 10)(x + 10)$
  e) $(x + 11)(x - 11)$ **f)** $(x + 12)^2$
  g) $(x - 7)^2$ **h)** $(x - 30)(x + 30)$

For help with questions 8 and 9, see Example 2.

8. The radius, r, of a circle has been increased by k. Both r and k are measured in the same units. Write a formula for the area of the new circle. Expand and simplify.

9. Each dimension of a square playground is increased by 5 m.
  a) Draw a diagram of the situation.
  b) Find a simplified algebraic expression for the area of the new playground.
  c) Find a simplified algebraic expression for the increase in area.

10. A parabola has equation $y = (x + 2)^2$.

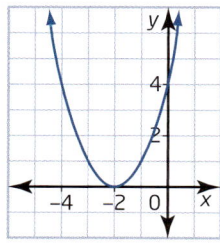

  a) Identify the coordinates of the vertex.
  b) Expand and simplify the equation.
  c) Verify that the coordinates of the vertex satisfy the equation from part b).

11. A square has side length $3x$. One dimension is increased by $2y$ and the other is decreased by $2y$.
  a) Find an algebraic expression for the area of the resulting rectangle. Expand.
  b) Find an algebraic expression for the change in area. Expand.
  c) Calculate the area of the rectangle and change in area if x represents 8 cm and y represents 5 cm.

12. Use two methods to determine an algebraic expression to represent the area of the figure. Verify that they are equivalent expressions.

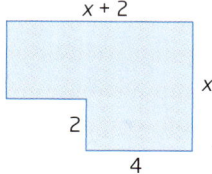

13. Chapter Problem A pedestal for trophies is to be made from three layers, each in the shape of a square-based prism. All three layers are the same height, x, in centimetres, but each base length is 3 cm less than that of the layer immediately below.

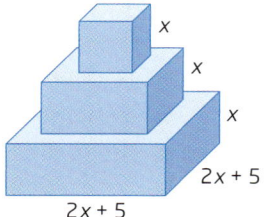

  a) Write algebraic expressions for the side and top surface areas of each prism used to make the pedestal.
  b) Write an algebraic expression for the exposed top surface area of the bottom layer of the pedestal. Expand and simplify.
  c) Write an algebraic expression for the exposed top surface area of the middle layer of the pedestal. Expand and simplify.

14. An interesting way to multiply 19×21 is
$$(20 - 1)(20 + 1)$$
$$= 20^2 - 1$$
$$= 400 - 1$$
$$= 399$$

Use this method to calculate each product.
  a) 31×29
  b) 59×61
  c) 99×101
  d) 71×69

15. Explain how to adapt the method in question 14 to multiply 32×28. Then, use your method to multiply each product.
  a) 76×84
  b) 35×25
  c) 104×96
  d) 77×83

16. A stone is dropped from a height of 10 m. Its height as it falls can be approximated by the relation $h = -5t^2 + 10$, where t is the time, in seconds, and h is the height, in metres.

   a) A delay of 3 s would cause the graph to shift 3 units to the right. Sketch a graph of this relation and of the relation after a 3-s delay.

   b) Rewrite the relation to represent a delay of 3 s.

   c) Expand the new relation and simplify.

17. Instead of film, a digital camera has an image sensor that converts light into electrical charges. The image sensor in most digital cameras is a charge coupled device (CCD). The CCD for an 8-megapixel digital camera measures 3264 pixels by 2448 pixels. A new model of CCD increases each dimension by x pixels.

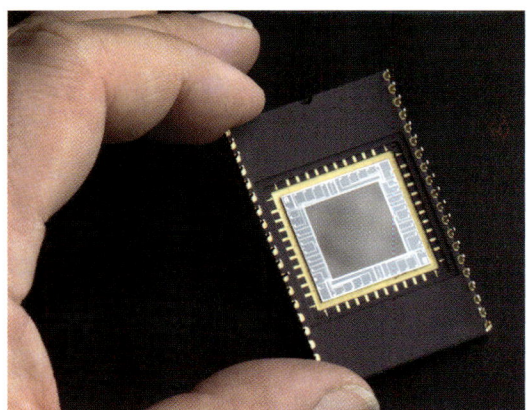

   a) Write an expression for the number of pixels in the new CCD, and expand.

   b) If x represents 1000 pixels, what is the resolution of the new CCD, in megapixels?

Literacy Connections

Mega is a prefix in the SI system of units for 10^6, or 1 000 000. For example, 1 megapixel equals one million pixels.

■ **Achievement Check**

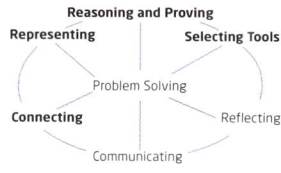

18. a) Use algebra tiles or a diagram to expand $(a + b)^2$.

   b) Use a diagram to expand $(a + b + c)^2$.

   c) The length and width of a rectangle are represented by $x + 2$ and $9 - 4x$. If x must be an integer, what are the possible values for the area of the rectangle?

Extend

19. Expand and simplify. Use a CAS to verify your answers.

   a) $(x - 2)^4$

   b) $(2x + 3)(x - 5)(4x + 7)$

   c) $(2x^2 + 5x + 3)^2$

   d) $(5x - 2)^3$

20. The kinetic energy, E, in joules, of a moving object is given by the formula $E = \frac{1}{2}mv^2$, where m is the mass, in kilograms, of the object, and v is its speed, in metres per second.

   a) Find an algebraic expression for the difference in kinetic energy of two objects with a difference in speed of 5 m/s.

   b) Find an algebraic expression for the difference in kinetic energy of two objects with a difference in speed of x metres per second.

   c) Expand each expression and simplify.

21. The sum of the cubes of the first n natural numbers can be found using the formula
$$1^3 + 2^3 + 3^3 + \ldots + n^3 = \frac{n^2(n + 1)^2}{4}.$$

   a) Verify that this is true for the first five natural numbers.

   b) Show that the right side of the formula can also be expressed in the form $\left[\dfrac{n(n + 1)}{2}\right]^2$.

5.3 Common Factors

During a performance at a sea-life park, a dolphin jumps out of the water. Its height, h, in metres, above the water after t seconds can be approximated by the relation $h = 10x - 5x^2$. This relation can also be written as $h = 5x(2 - x)$, because the terms in the polynomial $10x - 5x^2$ have a common factor of $5x$.

Investigate A

Tools
- algebra tiles

How can you use a model to find factors of a polynomial?

1. To factor $2x + 4$, use algebra tiles to create a rectangular area whose length and width represent the factors of the polynomial.

   a) Arrange two x-tiles and four unit tiles to form a rectangle with area $2x + 4$. Then, place tiles along the left side and top to find the length and width of the rectangle. One dimension has been done for you.

   b) Write an equation for the area as a product of the length and width.

2. Repeat step 1 for $6x + 18$. How many different rectangles can you find?

3. Use algebra tiles to find the factors of $x^2 + 2x$. Express the area as a product of the length and width.

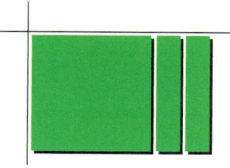

4. Use algebra tiles to factor $2x^2 + 4x$. How many different rectangles can you find? Write an area statement for each one.

5. Use algebra tiles to factor each expression, if possible. If it is not possible, explain why.

   a) $3x + 3$ b) $4x + 10$ c) $x^2 + 4x$
   d) $2x^2 + 6x$ e) $2x + 5$ f) $4x^2 + 10x$

6. **Reflect** Explain how you can express a polynomial as a product of factors.

Investigate B

How can you use the greatest common factor (GCF) to factor a polynomial?

Method 1: Use Pencil and Paper

1. Find the GCF for each set of numbers by first expressing each number as a product of prime factors.

   a) 12 and 8   b) 15 and 25
   c) 4, 10, and 6   d) 6, 18, and 24

2. a) Find the GCF of 12 and 9.

   b) Write each number as a product of two factors, where the first factor is the GCF. What operation did you use to obtain the second factor?

3. Find the GCF of each pair of terms.

   a) 7^3 and 7^2 b) 5^6 and 5^4
   c) x^2 and x d) x^3 and x^4

4. a) Find the GCF of x^6 and x^4.

   b) Write each term as a product of two factors, where the first factor is the GCF. What operation did you use to obtain the second factor?

5. Find the GCF of the polynomial $2x^2 + 4x$ by first expressing each term as a product.
   $2x^2 = 2 \times x \times x$
   $4x = 2 \times 2 \times x$
   Multiply the common factors to calculate the GCF.

   a) What is the GCF of $2x^2 + 4x$?

   b) Rewrite the polynomial as the sum of products. Express each term as a product of two factors, where the first factor is the GCF. Use division to determine the second factor of each term.

   c) Write the polynomial as a product of two factors, where the first factor is the GCF. What polynomial is the second factor?

   d) Verify your factors from part c) by expanding.

6. Repeat step 5 for each polynomial.

   a) $3x^2 + 6x$ b) $2x^2 + 8x$
   c) $4y + 10y^2$ d) $7y^3 + 14y^2$

7. **Reflect** Explain how to factor a polynomial using the GCF.

Tools
- TI-89 calculator

Method 2: Use a Computer Algebra System (CAS)

1. Clear the calculator's memory by selecting **2:NewProb** from the **Clean Up** menu.

2. Factor each expression. Press F2. Select **2:factor(**. Type the expression, and then press) ENTER. Record the results.
   a) $2x + 2$
   b) $2x + 4$
   c) $2x + 6$
   d) $2x + 8$
   e) $2x + 10$

3. Consider the pairs of factors from step 2. How are they the same? How are they different? Provide a reason for your answers.

4. Use a CAS to factor each polynomial. Record the results.
   a) $3x^2 + 6x + 9$
   b) $3x^2 + 12x + 15$

5. a) Look at the coefficients of the terms of each polynomial in step 4. What is the GCF?
   b) Look at the terms in the second factor from step 4. Since the first factor is the GCF of the polynomial, what operation provides the coefficients of the terms in the second factor?

6. a) Use a CAS to factor $6x^2 + 9x + 24$. Record the result.
   b) What is the GCF of the polynomial $6x^2 + 9x + 24$?
   c) Use a CAS to divide the GCF into each term of $6x^2 + 9x + 24$, as shown. Does the result match the second factor from part a)?

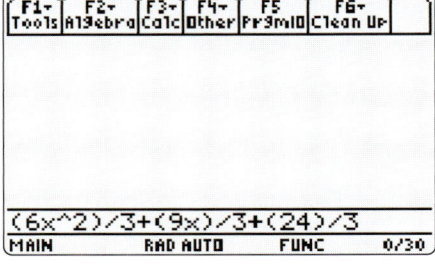

7. Use a CAS to factor each polynomial. Record the results.
   a) $2x^2 + 4x$
   b) $2x^2 + 8x$

8. a) Look at the coefficients of the terms of each polynomial in step 7. What is the GCF? Look at the variable parts. What is the GCF?
   b) The first factor of each result from step 7 is the GCF of the polynomial. How is it related to your answers for part a)?
   c) Look at the terms in the second factor from step 7. Since the first factor is the GCF of the polynomial, what operation provides the terms in the second factor?

9. a) Use a CAS to factor $6x^2 + 15x$. Record the result.
   b) What is the GCF of the polynomial $6x^2 + 15x$?
   c) Use a CAS to divide the GCF into each term of $6x^2 + 15x$. Does the result match the second factor from part a)?

10. **Reflect** Explain how to factor a polynomial using the GCF.

A polynomial is factored when it is written as a product of two or more polynomials. Factoring a polynomial is the reverse process of expanding. To factor a polynomial:
- Find the GCF of the terms.
- Write the GCF as the first factor outside a set of brackets.
- Divide each term by the GCF, writing the result inside the brackets.

Example 1 Use a Model

Use algebra tiles to factor $x^2 + 3x$.

Solution

The polynomial $x^2 + 3x$ can be represented by a rectangle with area $x^2 + 3x$. The width of the rectangle is x and the length is $x + 3$. The dimensions of the rectangle are the factors of the polynomial.

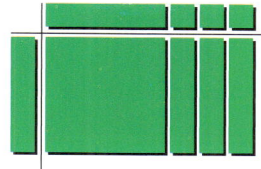

$x^2 + 3x = x(x + 3)$

Example 2 Monomial Common Factor

Factor fully, if possible.

a) $6x + 3$
b) $8x^2 - 7x$
c) $25k^6 + 15k^4$
d) $21c^4d^3 - 28c^2d^5 + 7cd^3$
e) $5x^5y^3 + 7w^5z^2$

Solution

a) The GCF of the coefficients, 6 and 3, is 3.
   There is no GCF of the variable parts.
   Therefore, the GCF of the polynomial is 3.
   Divide each term by 3.
   $$6x + 3 = 3\left(\frac{6x}{3} + \frac{3}{3}\right)$$
   $$= 3(2x + 1)$$

b) There is no common factor of the coefficients.
   The GCF of the variable parts, x^2 and x, is x.
   Therefore, the GCF of the polynomial is x.
   Divide each term by x.
   $$8x^2 - 7x = x\left(\frac{8x^2}{x} - \frac{7x}{x}\right)$$
   $$= x(8x - 7)$$

c) The GCF of the coefficients, 25 and 15, is 5.
The GCF of the variable parts, k^6 and k^4, is k^4.
Therefore, the GCF of the polynomial is $5k^4$.
Divide each term by $5k^4$.

$$25k^6 + 15k^4 = 5k^4\left(\frac{25k^6}{5k^4} + \frac{15k^4}{5k^4}\right)$$

$$= 5k^4(5k^2 + 3)$$

Apply the exponent laws.

When I compare the exponents, the GCF of the variable parts is the variable with the least exponent.

d) The GCF of the coefficients, 21, −28, and 7, is 7.
The GCF of the variable parts, c^4d^3, c^2d^5 and cd^3, is cd^3.
Therefore, the GCF of the polynomial is $7cd^3$.
Divide each term by $7cd^3$ mentally.
$21c^4d^3 - 28c^2d^5 + 7cd^3 = 7cd^3(3c^3 - 4cd^2 + 1)$

I can check my answer by expanding.

$7cd^3(3c^3 - 4cd^2 + 1)$
$= 21c^4d^3 - 28c^2d^5 + 7cd^3$

e) Since the GCF of the terms of the polynomial $5x^5y^3 + 7w^5z^2$ is 1, it is not factorable.

Example 3 Binomial Common Factor

Factor.
a) $3x(y + 1) + 7z(y + 1)$
b) $2x(x - 3) - 5(x - 3)$

Solution

a) Think of $(y + 1)$ as one factor.
The GCF is the binomial $(y + 1)$.
Divide each term by $(y + 1)$ mentally.
$3x(y + 1) + 7z(y + 1)$
$= (y + 1)(3x + 7z)$

Write the GCF first. Collect the $(3x + 7z)$ in the second set of brackets.

b) Think of $(x - 3)$ as one factor.
The GCF is the binomial $(x - 3)$.
Divide each term by $(x - 3)$ mentally.
$2x(x - 3) - 5(x - 3)$
$= (x - 3)(2x - 5)$

Often there is no common factor for all the terms in a polynomial, but some of the terms have a common factor. A process of factoring by grouping can sometimes be used with these polynomials. This process involves factoring groups of terms first, instead of factoring the entire polynomial.

Example 4 Factor by Grouping

Factor.

a) $ax + ay + 2x + 2y$

b) $9x^2 + 15x + 3x + 5$

Solution

a) Group terms with a common factor. Factor the GCF from each grouping. Then, remove the binomial common factor.

$$ax + ay + 2x + 2y$$
$$= (ax + ay) + (2x + 2y)$$
$$= a(x + y) + 2(x + y)$$
$$= (x + y)(a + 2)$$

or

$$ax + ay + 2x + 2y$$
$$= (ax + 2x) + (ay + 2y)$$
$$= x(a + 2) + y(a + 2)$$
$$= (a + 2)(x + y)$$

b)
$$9x^2 + 15x + 3x + 5$$
$$= (9x^2 + 15x) + (3x + 5)$$
$$= 3x(3x + 5) + 1(3x + 5)$$
$$= (3x + 5)(3x + 1)$$

or

$$9x^2 + 15x + 3x + 5$$
$$= (9x^2 + 3x) + (15x + 5)$$
$$= 3x(3x + 1) + 5(3x + 1)$$
$$= (3x + 1)(3x + 5)$$

Key Concepts

- Factoring a polynomial is the opposite of expanding a polynomial.

  ⎯⎯ **Factoring** ⟶
  $x^2 + 3x = x(x + 3)$
  ⟵ **Expanding** ⎯⎯

- To find the GCF of a polynomial, find the GCF of the coefficients, and then find the GCF of the variable parts.

- To factor a polynomial, remove the GCF as the first factor, and then divide each term by the GCF to obtain the second factor.
  $8x^2y^3 - 12x^4y = 4x^2y(2y^2 - 3x^2)$

- For polynomials with more than one variable, the GCF of the variable parts is the product of the common bases with the least exponent.
  The GCF of $2x^3y^4z^2 + 4x^2y^2z^3$ is $2x^2y^2z^2$.

- A common factor is not necessarily a monomial.
  $a(x + 2) + b(x + 2)$ has a binomial common factor of $(x + 2)$.

- To factor by grouping, factor groups of two terms with a common factor to produce a binomial common factor.
  $bx + 3x + by + 3y = (bx + 3x) + (by + 3y)$
  $ = x(b + 3) + y(b + 3)$
  $ = (b + 3)(x + y)$

Communicate Your Understanding

C1 Explain how the diagram illustrates the factoring of a polynomial.

C2 Each of the following is an example of a common error when factoring. Describe each error and make the appropriate correction.

a) $35x^2 - 5x = 5x(7x - 0)$
b) $4y^3 + 7y^2 = 4y^2(y + 7)$
c) $16k^3m^2 - 8k^2m = 4k^2m(4km - 2)$
d) $9a^3b^5 + 6a^2b^4 = 3ab(3a^2b^4 + 2ab^3)$

C3 Describe how you would factor each polynomial.

a) $3c(d - 5) - 8(d - 5)$
b) $10x^2 - 14xy - 15x + 21y$

Practise

1. Find the GCF of each pair of terms.
  a) $2x$ and $3x$
  b) $6ab$ and $-8ac$
  c) x^2 and x^3
  d) k^4 and k^7
  e) $3m^2$ and $5m$
  f) $-12y^2$ and $-15y^4$

For help with question 2, see Example 1.

2. Use algebra tiles or a diagram to illustrate the factoring of each polynomial.
  a) $x^2 + 5x$
  b) $3x^2 + 6x$
  c) $6x^2 + 4x$

For help with questions 3 and 4, see Example 2.

3. Factor fully, if possible.
  a) $15w + 25z$
  b) $3a - 11b$
  c) $17ca - 8cd$
  d) $9y - 8y^3$
  e) $12b^4 + 18b^2$
  f) $4g^2 - 8g + 6$
  g) $7h + 3m - 5k$
  h) $2n^5 + 12n^4 - 6n^3$

4. Factor fully, if possible.
  a) $14x^2y + 16xy^3$
  b) $10k^3m^2 - 6k^2m^2$
  c) $8s^2y + 11t^3$
  d) $66c^4de^2 - 22c^2de^2$
  e) $7gh + 2mn - 13pq$
  f) $5fg^2 - 25fg + 20f^2g$
  g) $27r^2s^2 - 18r^3s^2 - 36rs^3$
  h) $4n^2p^3 + 10n^4p^2 - 12n^3p^2$

For help with question 5, see Example 3.

5. Factor, if possible.
  a) $3x(x + 8) + 5(x + 8)$
  b) $a(b + 1) + 9c(b + 1)$
  c) $2y(x - 5) + 4(x + 5)$
  d) $4s(r + u) - t(r + u)$

For help with question 6, see Example 4.

6. Factor by grouping.
  a) $mx + my + 2x + 2y$
  b) $x^2 + 3x + 2x + 6$
  c) $ay^2 + 3ay + 4y + 12$
  d) $6x^2 + 9x - 2x - 3$
  e) $16v^2 - 12v - 12v + 9$

Connect and Apply

7. a) Write a polynomial with two terms that has a GCF of 6.
  b) Write a polynomial with three terms that has a GCF of x.
  c) Write a polynomial with two terms that has a GCF of $5y^2$.
  d) Write a polynomial with three terms that has a GCF of $2a^2b^3$.

8. The formula for the perimeter of a rectangle is $P = 2l + 2w$.

   a) Write the formula in factored form.

   b) If l represents 15 cm and w represents 9 cm, find the perimeter using both the original and the factored forms. What do you notice? Explain why this is so.

9. The formula for the surface area of a cylinder is $SA = 2\pi r^2 + 2\pi rh$.

   a) Write the formula in factored form.

   b) If r represents 3 cm and h represents 8 cm, find the surface area using both the original and the factored forms. What do you notice? Explain why this is so.

10. A rectangle has area given by the expression $6x^2 + 9x$. The length and width can be found by factoring the expression. Find all possible expressions for the length and width.

11. Binomial factors can differ by a factor of -1. An example is $7 - y$ and $y - 7$, since $7 - y$ can be rewritten as $-1(y - 7)$. Use this fact to factor each expression.

    a) $5x(7 - y) + 4(y - 7)$

    b) $5y(x - 1) + 2(1 - x)$

12. **Chapter Problem**

    The base length of each square-based prism in the pedestal design is 3 cm less than that of the layer immediately below.

    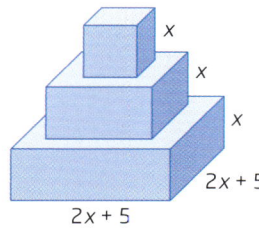

    a) Write an algebraic expression for the total of the top surface areas of the three prisms used to make the pedestal.

    b) Expand and simplify.

    c) Factor the resulting expression from part b).

13. Write an expression, in fully factored form, for each of the shaded regions.

    a)

    b)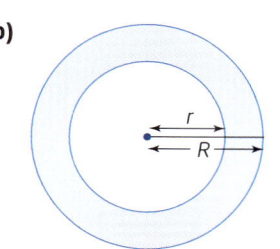

Extend

14. Factor the quadratic relation $y = 2x^2 - 3x$ to find the x-intercepts.

15. Factor each polynomial using a fraction as one of the common factors. Explain how this can simplify the operations when the values of the variables are known.

    a) $\frac{1}{2}x^2 + \frac{3}{2}y^2$

    b) $\frac{2}{3}a^3 - \frac{1}{3}ab$

    c) $\frac{1}{6}k^4m^2 - \frac{1}{2}km^3 + \frac{1}{3}k^2m^2$

16. **Math Contest** If $3a + 8b = 12$, then what is the value of $15a + 40b$?

    A 36

    B 48

    C 60

    D 84

    E 180

17. **Math Contest** Show that the sum of the squares of any five consecutive integers is divisible by 5.

5.4 Factor Quadratic Expressions of the Form $x^2 + bx + c$

quadratic expression
- a second-degree polynomial
- $4x^2 + 20$ and $x^2 + 7x + 10$ are quadratic expressions

Tools
- algebra tiles

A water garden combines a pond with aquatic plants and often ornamental fish, such as koi, to add visual appeal to the landscape. The area of a rectangular water garden can be represented by the **quadratic expression** $x^2 + 5x + 6$. To find the length and the width of the rectangle, you can write the trinomial as the product of two binomials.

Investigate A

How can you use a model to factor quadratic expressions of the form $x^2 + bx + c$?

1. To factor $x^2 + 5x + 6$, use algebra tiles to create a rectangular area whose length and width represent the factors of the trinomial.

   a) Arrange one x^2-tile, five x-tiles, and six unit tiles to form a rectangle with area $x^2 + 5x + 6$. Place tiles along the left side and top to find the length and width of the rectangle. One dimension has been done for you.

   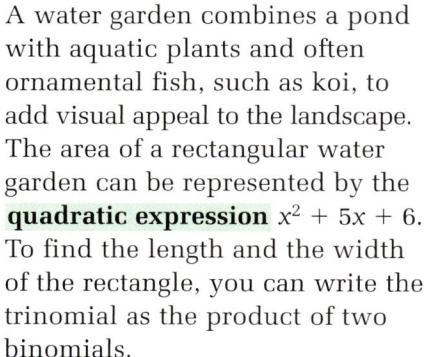

   b) Write the equation for the trinomial as a product of the binomial dimensions.

2. Repeat step 1 for each trinomial.

   a) $x^2 + 6x + 5$ b) $x^2 + 3x + 2$
   c) $x^2 + 4x + 3$ d) $x^2 + 6x + 8$

3. Each trinomial in steps 1 and 2 is of the form $x^2 + bx + c$. What do you notice about b and c and the binomial factors for each trinomial? Describe the relationship.

4. Test your conclusions from step 3 on each trinomial. Use algebra tiles to check your answer.

   a) $x^2 + 7x + 6$ b) $x^2 + 8x + 12$

5. **Reflect** Describe a process for finding the factors of a quadratic expression of the form $x^2 + bx + c$.

Investigate B

How can you use patterns to factor quadratic expressions of the form $x^2 + bx + c$?

A: Positive Values of b and c

1. Expand and simplify each product. Try to apply the distributive property mentally.
   a) $(x + 4)(x + 3)$
   b) $(x + 1)(x + 5)$
   c) $(x + 7)(x + 8)$

2. The result of expanding each binomial product of the form $(x + r)(x + s)$ in step 1 is a trinomial of the form $x^2 + bx + c$. Describe how you calculated b and c using the values of r and s.

3. Use the patterns from step 2 to reverse the process. Write each trinomial of the form $x^2 + bx + c$ as a binomial product of the form $(x + r)(x + s)$.
   a) $x^2 + 6x + 8$
   b) $x^2 + 7x + 10$
   c) $x^2 + 9x + 20$
   d) $x^2 + 10x + 21$

4. **Reflect** Describe a process for factoring quadratic expressions of the form $x^2 + bx + c$.

B: Negative Values of b and/or c

1. Expand and simplify each product. Try to apply the distributive property mentally.
   a) $(x - 3)(x - 2)$
   b) $(x - 1)(x - 5)$
   c) $(x - 1)(x + 5)$
   d) $(x + 3)(x - 8)$

2. The result of expanding each binomial product of the form $(x + r)(x + s)$ in step 1 is a trinomial of the form $x^2 + bx + c$.
   a) Describe how you determined the signs of the values of b and c when both values of r and s were negative.
   b) Describe how you determined the signs of the values of b and c when only one of the values of r and s was negative.

3. Use your process to factor each trinomial.
   a) $x^2 - 7x + 10$
   b) $x^2 + 4x - 5$
   c) $x^2 - 4x - 5$
   d) $x^2 - 3x - 10$

4. **Reflect** How does your process for factoring quadratic expressions of the form $x^2 + bx + c$ change when the values of b and/or c are negative?

By finding the dimensions of a rectangle whose area is a quadratic expression, you are reversing the process of expanding two binomials that you learned in Section 5.1. This process is called factoring.

Area is $x^2 + bx + c$.

Another way to factor a quadratic expression of the form $x^2 + bx + c$ is to study the patterns from multiplying two binomials.

$$(x + r)(x + s) = x^2 + sx + rx + rs$$
$$= x^2 + rx + sx + rs$$
$$= x^2 + (r + s)x + rs$$

Therefore, $x^2 + bx + c = (x + r)(x + s)$, where $r + s = b$ and $r \times s = c$.

In general, you will factor *over the integers*, meaning that the values of r and s are integers only.

Many quadratic expressions, such as $x^2 + 3x + 5$, cannot be factored over the integers. No two integers have a product of 5 and a sum of 3.

Example 1 Factor Quadratic Expressions

Factor, if possible.

a) $x^2 + 7x + 12$
b) $x^2 + 4x + 6$
c) $x^2 - 29x + 28$
d) $x^2 + 3x - 18$
e) $x^2 - 4x - 21$

Solution

a) For $x^2 + 7x + 12$, $b = 7$ and $c = 12$. Use a table to find two integers whose product is 12 and whose sum is 7. In order to have a positive product and a positive sum, both numbers must be positive.

Factors of 12	Product	Sum
1, 12	12	13
2, 6	12	8
3, 4	12	7

Therefore, r is 3 and s is 4.
$x^2 + 7x + 12 = (x + 3)(x + 4)$

b) For $x^2 + 4x + 6$, $b = 4$ and $c = 6$.

Since no two integers have a product of 6 and sum of 4, $x^2 + 4x + 6$ cannot be factored over the integers.

Factors of 6	Product	Sum
1, 6	6	7
2, 3	6	5

I need to find two positive integers whose product is 6 and whose sum is 4.

c) For $x^2 - 29x + 28$, $b = -29$ and $c = 28$.

Factors of 28	Product	Sum
−1, −28	28	−29
−2, −14	28	−16
−4, −7	28	−11

I need to find two integers whose product is 28 and whose sum is −29. To have a positive product and a negative sum, both numbers must be negative.

Therefore, r is −1 and s is −28.
$x^2 - 29x + 28 = (x - 1)(x - 28)$

d) For $x^2 + 3x - 18$, $b = 3$ and $c = -18$.

Factors of −18	Product	Sum
1, −18	−18	−17
−1, 18	−18	17
2, −9	−18	−7
−2, 9	−18	7
3, −6	−18	−3
−3, 6	−18	3

I need to find two integers whose product is −18 and whose sum is 3. To have a negative product and a positive sum, one number must be negative and the other positive.

Therefore, r is −3 and s is 6.
$x^2 + 3x - 18 = (x + 6)(x - 3)$

e) For $x^2 - 4x - 21$, $b = -4$ and $c = -21$.

Factors of −21	Product	Sum
1, −21	−21	−20
−1, 21	−21	20
3, −7	−21	−4
−3, 7	−21	4

I need to find two integers whose product is −21 and whose sum is −4. To have a negative product and a negative sum, one number must be negative and the other positive.

Therefore, r is 3 and s is −7.
$x^2 - 4x - 21 = (x + 3)(x - 7)$

Example 2 Dimensions of a Water Garden

a) Determine binomials that represent the dimensions of the rectangular water garden.
b) Determine the dimensions if x represents 1 m.

Area is $x^2 + 5x + 6$.

Solution

a) Factor the quadratic expression for the area. Find two integers whose product is 6 and whose sum is 5. The integers are 2 and 3.
$x^2 + 5x + 6 = (x + 2)(x + 3)$
The dimensions can be represented by $x + 2$ and $x + 3$.

b) Substitute $x = 1$ into $x + 2$ and $x + 3$.
$1 + 2 = 3$
$1 + 3 = 4$
The water garden has dimensions of 3 m by 4 m.

Key Concepts

- To factor a quadratic expression of the form $x^2 + bx + c$, first find two integers whose product is c and whose sum is b.
  - For $x^2 + 12x + 27$, find two integers whose product is 27 and whose sum is 12. The integers are 3 and 9.
  - Express the quadratic expression as a product,
  $x^2 + bx + c = (x + r)(x + s)$.
  $x^2 + 12x + 27 = (x + 3)(x + 9)$

- Not all quadratic expressions of the form $x^2 + bx + c$ can be factored over the integers.

Communicate Your Understanding

C1 Describe how to use algebra tiles to factor $x^2 + 8x + 7$.

C2 Explain the steps you would use to factor $y^2 - 6y - 40$.

C3 Explain why $k^2 + 5k - 9$ cannot be factored over the integers.

Practise

1. Illustrate the factoring of each trinomial using algebra tiles or a diagram.
  a) $x^2 + 4x + 3$ **b)** $x^2 + 7x + 10$
  c) $x^2 + 6x + 8$ **d)** $x^2 + 4x + 4$

2. Find two integers with the given product and sum.
  a) product = 45, sum = 14
  b) product = 6, sum = −5
  c) product = −10, sum = 3
  d) product = −20, sum = −8

For help with questions 3 to 5, see Example 1.

3. Factor, if possible.
  a) $x^2 + 7x + 10$ **b)** $j^2 + 12j + 27$
  c) $k^2 + 5k + 4$ **d)** $p^2 + 9p + 12$
  e) $w^2 + 11w + 25$ **f)** $d^2 + 10d + 24$

4. Factor, if possible.
  a) $m^2 - 7m + 10$ **b)** $x^2 - 5x + 7$
  c) $y^2 - 5y + 4$ **d)** $r^2 - 16r + 64$
  e) $w^2 - 9w + 24$ **f)** $q^2 - 10q + 9$

5. Factor, if possible.

   a) $a^2 - 3a - 10$
   b) $s^2 + 3s - 10$
   c) $d^2 - 8d - 9$
   d) $f^2 + 7f - 6$
   e) $g^2 - 5g - 14$
   f) $r^2 + 2r - 6$
   g) $x^2 + x - 42$
   h) $b^2 - 2b - 4$

Connect and Apply

For help with question 6, see Example 2.

6. Determine binomials that represent the length and width of each rectangle. Then, determine the dimensions of the rectangle if x represents 15 cm.

   a) Area is $x^2 + 18x + 80$.
   b) Area is $x^2 - 15x + 50$.

7. Factor completely by first removing the greatest common factor (GCF).

   a) $3x^2 + 12x + 9$
   b) $2d^2 - 22d + 56$
   c) $5z^2 + 40z + 60$
   d) $4s^2 - 8s - 32$
   e) $bx^2 + 10bx - 24b$
   f) $x^3 + 18x^2 + 72x$

8. Determine two values of b so that each expression can be factored.

   a) $x^2 + bx + 12$
   b) $x^2 - bx + 4$
   c) $x^2 - bx - 8$
   d) $x^2 + bx - 10$

9. Determine two values of c so that each expression can be factored.

   a) $x^2 + 6x + c$
   b) $x^2 - x + c$
   c) $x^2 - 8x - c$
   d) $x^2 + 2x - c$

10. Expand each pair of binomials. Compare the answers.

   a) $(x + 1)(x + 3)$ and $(x + y)(x + 3y)$
   b) $(x + 4)(x - 6)$ and $(x + 4y)(x - 6y)$
   c) $(x - 2)(x + 9)$ and $(x - 2y)(x + 9y)$
   d) $(x - 6)(x - 9)$ and $(x - 6y)(x - 9y)$

11. Factor. How does the additional variable change your thinking?

   a) $a^2 + 11ab + 24b^2$
   b) $k^2 - 11km + 18m^2$
   c) $c^2 + 4cd - 21d^2$
   d) $x^2 - 6xy - 16y^2$

12. a) Make up an example of a quadratic expression that cannot be factored.

   b) Explain why it cannot be factored.

13. A parabola has equation $y = x^2 - 4x - 12$.

   a) Factor the right side of the equation.
   b) Identify the x-intercepts of the parabola.
   c) Find the equation of the axis of symmetry, find the vertex, and draw the graph.

14. The height of a ball thrown from the top of a building can be approximated by the formula $h = -5t^2 + 15t + 20$, where t is the time, in seconds, and h is the height, in metres.

   a) Write the formula in factored form. Hint: Remove the GCF first.
   b) How can you use the factors to find when the ball lands on the ground?

Extend

15. a) Explain how $x^4 + 9x^2 + 20$ and $x^2 + 9x + 20$ are alike. How are they different?

   b) Factor $x^4 + 9x^2 + 20$.

16. Refer to question 15. Factor.

   a) $x^4 + 11x^2 + 30$
   b) $x^4 - 7x^2y^2 + 12y^2$
   c) $x^6 - 3x^3 - 54$
   d) $3(x - 5)^2 + 27(x - 5) - 66$

17. Math Contest

   a) Expand $(x + 2)^3$.
   b) Factor $x^3 + 9x^2 + 27x + 27$.
   c) Factor $8a^3 + 60a^2b + 150ab^2 + 125b^3$.

5.5 Factor Quadratic Expressions of the Form $ax^2 + bx + c$

The Ontario Summer Games are held every two years in even-numbered years to provide sports competition for youth between the ages of 11 and 22. At the Games, approximately 2500 athletes from across the province compete in 19 sports.

Beach volleyball is one of the sports on the Games program. It is played by two teams of two players on a sand court with area given by $3x^2 + 10x + 3$. Algebraic expressions for the dimensions of the court can be found by factoring the trinomial expression.

Investigate

Tools
- algebra tiles

How can you use a model to factor quadratic expressions of the form $ax^2 + bx + c$?

1. Use algebra tiles to form a rectangle to model the product $(2x + 1)(x + 2)$.

2. Arrange the algebra tiles representing the trinomial $2x^2 + 5x + 3$ to form a rectangle. Identify the binomials that represent the length and width of the rectangle.

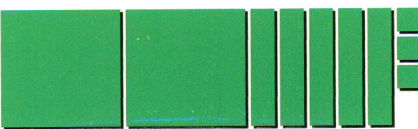

3. Repeat step 2 for each trinomial.
   a) $3x^2 + 5x + 2$ b) $4x^2 + 8x + 3$

4. Each trinomial represents the area of a rectangle. Draw diagrams and identify the binomials that represent the length and width of the rectangle.
   a) $2x^2 + 5x + 2$ b) $5x^2 + 8x + 3$

5. **Reflect** Describe how to use algebra tiles to factor a quadratic trinomial of the form $ax^2 + bx + c$.

6. **Reflect** Can you see a way to factor trinomials of the form $ax^2 + bx + c$ without using algebra tiles? If so, describe it.

When you expand two binomials, you add the two middle terms.

$(2x + 3)(3x + 4) = 6x^2 + 8x + 9x + 12$
$ = 6x^2 + 17x + 12$

Notice the following patterns.
$8 + 9 = 17$ and $8 \times 9 = 6 \times 12$

You can use these patterns and the method of factoring by grouping to factor trinomials of the form $ax^2 + bx + c$. Work in reverse by replacing the middle term with two terms whose integer coefficients have a product of $a \times c$ and a sum of b.

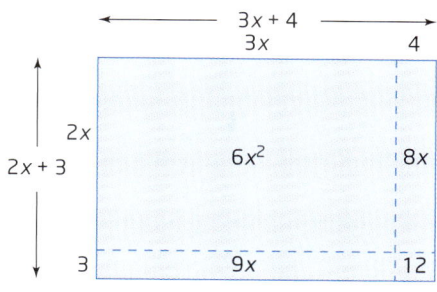

Example 1 Break up the Middle Term

Factor, if possible.

a) $3x^2 + 8x + 4$
b) $3x^2 + 2x + 4$
c) $6x^2 - 5x + 1$

Solution

a) For $3x^2 + 8x + 4$, $a = 3$, $b = 8$, and $c = 4$.
Use a table to find two integers whose product is 3×4, or 12, and whose sum is 8. In order to have a positive product and a positive sum, both integers must be positive.

Factors of 12	Product	Sum
1, 12	12	13
2, 6	12	8
3, 4	12	7

Since the integers 2 and 6 satisfy this product and sum, break up $8x$ into $2x + 6x$. Then, factor by grouping.
$3x^2 + 8x + 4$
$= 3x^2 + 2x + 6x + 4$
$= (3x^2 + 2x) + (6x + 4)$
$= x(3x + 2) + 2(3x + 2)$
$= (3x + 2)(x + 2)$

> **Literacy Connections**
>
> Since *break up* and *decompose* mean the same thing, the method of breaking up the middle term is sometimes referred to as the decomposition method.

b) For $3x^2 + 2x + 4$, $a = 3$, $b = 2$, and $c = 4$.
Since there is no pair of integers that satisfy these conditions, $3x^2 + 2x + 4$ is not factorable over the integers.

Factors of 12	Product	Sum
1, 12	12	13
2, 6	12	8
3, 4	12	7

> I need to find two integers whose product is 3×4, or 12, and whose sum is 2. Since the product and the sum are positive, I need two positive integers.

c) For $6x^2 - 5x + 1$, $a = 6$, $b = -5$, and $c = 1$.
Since the integers -2 and -3 satisfy this product and sum, break up $-5x$ into $-2x - 3x$. Then, factor by grouping.

$6x^2 - 5x + 1$
$= 6x^2 - 2x - 3x + 1$
$= (6x^2 - 2x) + (-3x + 1)$
$= 2x(3x - 1) - 1(3x - 1)$
$= (3x - 1)(2x - 1)$

Factors of 6	Product	Sum
-1, -6	6	-7
-2, -3	6	-5

> I need to find two integers whose product is 6×1, or 6, and whose sum is -5. Since the product is positive and the sum is negative, I need two negative integers.

Example 2 Trinomials With Two Variables

Factor $10x^2 - 3xy - 4y^2$.

Solution

For $10x^2 - 3xy - 4y^2$, $a = 10$, $b = -3$, and $c = -4$.

> I need to find two integers whose product is $10 \times (-4)$, or -40, and whose sum is -3. The integers 5 and -8 work.

Factors of –40	Product	Sum
1, –40	–40	–39
2, –20	–40	–18
4, –10	–40	–6
5, –8	–40	–3
–1, 40	–40	39
–2, 20	–40	18
–4, 10	–40	6
–5, 8	–40	3

$10x^2 - 3xy - 4y^2$
$= 10x^2 + 5xy - 8xy - 4y^2$
$= (10x^2 + 5xy) + (-8xy - 4y^2)$
$= 5x(2x + y) - 4y(2x + y)$
$= (2x + y)(5x - 4y)$

Break up $-3xy$ into $5xy - 8xy$.
Factor by grouping.

Example 3 Remove a Common Factor

Factor $16x^2 + 26x - 12$.

Solution

First, remove the greatest common factor (GCF), and then proceed as before.

The GCF of the polynomial $16x^2 + 26x - 12$ is 2.
$16x^2 + 26x - 12$
$= 2(8x^2 + 13x - 6)$

Factors of –48	Product	Sum
–1, 48	–48	47
–2, 24	–48	22
–3, 16	**–48**	**13**
–4, 12	–48	8
–6, 8	–48	2
1, –48	–48	–47
2, –24	–48	–22
3, –16	–48	–13
4, –12	–48	–8
6, –8	–48	–2

> To factor $8x^2 + 13x - 6$, I need to find two integers whose product is $8 \times (-6)$, or –48, and whose sum is 13. The integers –3 and 16 work.

$16x^2 + 26x - 12 = 2(8x^2 + 13x - 6)$
$\qquad\qquad\qquad\quad = 2(8x^2 - 3x + 16x - 6)$ **Break up $13x$ into $-3x + 16x$.**
$\qquad\qquad\qquad\quad = 2[(8x^2 - 3x) + (16x - 6)]$ **Factor by grouping.**
$\qquad\qquad\qquad\quad = 2[x(8x - 3) + 2(8x - 3)]$
$\qquad\qquad\qquad\quad = 2[(8x - 3)(x + 2)]$
$\qquad\qquad\qquad\quad = 2(8x - 3)(x + 2)$

Key Concepts

- Always look for a common factor first when factoring a trinomial.
- To factor $ax^2 + bx + c$, find two integers whose product is $a \times c$ and whose sum is b. Then, break up the middle term and factor by grouping.
- Not all quadratic expressions of the form $ax^2 + bx + c$ can be factored over the integers.

Communicate Your Understanding

C1 When you use algebra tiles to factor a trinomial, why do you need to be able to form a rectangle with the tiles?

C2 When factored, $2x^2 + 9x + 9$ can be written as $(2x + 3)(x + 3)$. Can it also be written as $(x + 3)(2x + 3)$? Justify your answer using words and a diagram.

C3 Describe how you would factor $5x^2 + 18x + 9$.

Practise

1. Use algebra tiles or a diagram to factor each trinomial.
   a) $2x^2 + 5x + 3$
   b) $3x^2 + 7x + 4$
   c) $6x^2 + 5x + 1$
   d) $6x^2 + 11x + 4$

For help with questions 2 to 4, see Example 1.

2. Factor, if possible.
   a) $2x^2 + 7x + 5$
   b) $6y^2 + 19y + 8$
   c) $4k^2 + 15k + 9$
   d) $3m^2 + 10m + 8$
   e) $10w^2 + 15w + 3$
   f) $12q^2 + 17q + 6$

3. Factor, if possible.
   a) $4x^2 - 11x + 6$
   b) $5n^2 - 11n + 6$
   c) $6c^2 - 3c + 1$
   d) $6a^2 - 7a + 1$
   e) $9b^2 - 24b + 7$
   f) $15k^2 - 19k + 6$

4. Factor, if possible.
   a) $3y^2 + 4y - 7$
   b) $2m^2 + 3m - 9$
   c) $8k^2 - 6k - 5$
   d) $12y^2 + y - 1$
   e) $9x^2 - 15x - 4$
   f) $5h^2 - 14h - 3$

For help with question 5, see Example 2.

5. Factor.
   a) $3x^2 + 7xy + 2y^2$
   b) $6m^2 + 13mn + 2n^2$
   c) $2p^2 - 11pq + 5q^2$
   d) $6c^2 - 7cd - 10d^2$
   e) $9x^2 - 9xy - 4y^2$
   f) $6d^2 + de - 2e^2$

For help with question 6, see Example 3.

6. Factor.
   a) $8k^2 - 16k + 6$
   b) $9p^2 + 15p - 6$
   c) $6m^2 - 14m - 12$
   d) $10x^2 + 15x - 10$
   e) $10r^2 - 22r + 4$
   f) $8y^2 - 22y + 12$

Connect and Apply

7. Factor. Then, substitute $x = 2$ into both forms. Are the results the same? Explain.
   a) $4x^2 + 12x + 5$
   b) $7x^2 - 23x + 6$
   c) $15x^2 - 2x - 8$
   d) $8x^2 + 14x - 4$
   e) $6x^2 - 19x + 15$
   f) $5x^2 + 18x + 9$

8. Find two values of n so that each trinomial can be factored over the integers.
   a) $x^2 + nx + 16$
   b) $3y^2 + ny + 25$
   c) $6a^2 + nab + 7b^2$

9. Find two values of k so that each trinomial can be factored over the integers.
   a) $36m^2 + 8m + k$
   b) $18y^2 - 42y + k$
   c) $kp^2 - 72pq + 16q^2$

10. Describe the steps in determining whether you can factor $ax^2 + bx + c$ over the integers.

11. Explain why it is easier to factor $ax^2 + bx + c$ if a and c are prime numbers.

12. A rectangle has area defined by $6x^2 + 13x - 8$.

    Area is $6x^2 - 13x - 8$.

    a) Factor to find algebraic expressions for the length and width of the rectangle.
    b) If x represents 10 cm, determine the perimeter and area of the rectangle.

13. The height, h, in metres, of a toy rocket at any time, t, in seconds, during its flight can be estimated using the formula $h = -5t^2 + 23t + 10$. Write the formula in factored form and determine when the rocket will fall to the ground.

14. **Use Technology** The range, r, in kilometres, of an airplane with full tanks at a power setting of p revolutions per minute (RPM) can be modelled by the relation $r = -0.0008p^2 + 3.2p - 2400$.

    a) Use a computer algebra system to factor the trinomial.
    b) Describe the set of values that p may take for this model.
    c) Determine what value of p results in the maximum range.

15. The total revenue from sales of ski jackets is modelled by the expression $720 + 4x - 2x^2$. Revenue is also calculated as the product of the number of jackets sold and the price per jacket. Determine expressions for the number sold and the price per jacket. Hint: As the price increases, the number sold decreases.

Achievement Check

16. a) Factor $5x^2 + 11x + 2$.
    b) Write a quadratic trinomial that cannot be factored over the integers. Explain how you know.
    c) The area of a square is $81 - 72x + 16x^2$. If x must be a positive integer, what is the least possible measure for the perimeter of the square?

Extend

17. Factor.
    a) $5x^4 + 18x^2 + 9$
    b) $7x^4 - 13x^2y^2 + 6y^4$
    c) $6x^6 + 13x^3y^3 - 8y^6$
    d) $10m^6 - 7m^3n^2 - 12n^4$

18. Factor.
    a) $2(x + a)^2 + 3(x + a) + 1$
    b) $2(x - b)^2 + 5(x - b) + 2$

19. a) A shape has area defined by $A = 8x^2 + 10x - 7$. Identify the shape(s).
    b) A solid has volume defined by $V = 4x^3 - 12x^2y + 9xy^2$. Identify the type of solid.

5.6 Factor a Perfect Square Trinomial and a Difference of Squares

One of the sponsors for the school yearbook has asked that the area of the art in their advertisement be increased by the same amount on all sides. The expression for the area of the enlarged art is given by $4x^2 + 12x + 9$, which is a perfect square trinomial.

In Section 5.2, you learned that some polynomial products can be expanded using special patterns. Similarly, you can factor polynomials that are perfect square trinomials or differences of squares using special patterns.

Investigate A

How can you use patterns to factor a difference of squares?

Method 1: Use Pencil and Paper

1. Expand and simplify or use the pattern for the product of the sum and the difference of two terms from Section 5.2.
   - **a)** $(x + 1)(x - 1)$
   - **b)** $(y + 2)(y - 2)$
   - **c)** $(3c - 10)(3c + 10)$
   - **d)** $(2m - 4)(2m + 4)$

2. How are the two binomials being multiplied in step 1 alike? How are they different?

3. Consider each simplified expansion from step 1.
   - **a)** How is the first term related to the first terms of the two binomials?
   - **b)** How is the last term related to the last terms of the two binomials?

4. **Reflect** Each resulting product in step 1 is a difference of squares. Explain how you can identify a difference of squares.

5. Confirm that each polynomial is a difference of squares. Then, use the reverse process to factor each. Check by expanding and simplifying.

   a) $x^2 - 25$ **b)** $y^2 - 36$
   c) $16k^2 - 49$ **d)** $25n^2 - 144$

6. Reflect Write a rule for factoring a difference of squares.

7. Use your rule to factor $100y^2 - 49x^2$. Check by expanding and simplifying.

Method 2: Use a Computer Algebra System (CAS)

- TI-89 calculator

1. Clear the calculator's memory by selecting **2:NewProb** from the **Clean Up** menu.

2. Use the **Factor** function on each polynomial. Record the results.

   a) $x^2 - 81$
   b) $y^2 - 64$
   c) $25d^2 - 36$
   d) $16k^2 - 121$
   e) $144b^2 - 25k^2$
   f) $4n^2 - 49p^2$

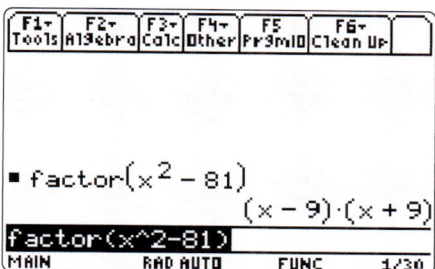

3. Reflect Each polynomial in step 2 is a difference of squares. Explain how you can identify a difference of squares.

4. Consider each pair of binomial factors from step 2.
   a) How are they alike? How are they different?
   b) How are the first terms of the factors related to the first term of the polynomial?
   c) How are the last terms of the factors related to the last term of the polynomial?

5. Reflect Write a rule for factoring a difference of squares.

Investigate B

How can you use patterns to factor a perfect square trinomial?

Method 1: Use Pencil and Paper

1. Expand and simplify or use the pattern for squaring a binomial from Section 5.2.

   a) $(x + 3)^2$ **b)** $(y - 5)^2$ **c)** $(k + 7)^2$
   d) $(2h + 3)^2$ **e)** $(3b - 5)^2$

2. Consider each simplified expansion from step 1.
   a) How is the first term in each trinomial related to the first term in each binomial?
   b) How is the last term in each trinomial related to the last term in each binomial?
   c) How is the middle term in each trinomial related to the terms in the binomial?

3. **Reflect** Each resulting product in step 1 is a perfect square trinomial. Explain how you can identify a perfect square trinomial.

4. Confirm that each polynomial is a perfect square trinomial. Then, use the reverse process to factor each. Check by expanding and simplifying.
   a) $x^2 + 12x + 36$ b) $y^2 - 6y + 9$
   c) $4k^2 + 20k + 25$ d) $9k^2 - 24k + 16$

5. **Reflect** Write a rule for factoring perfect square trinomials.

6. Test your rule by factoring $x^2 + 14x + 49$. Check by expanding and simplifying.

Method 2: Use a CAS

- TI-89 calculator

1. Clear the calculator's memory by selecting **2:NewProb** from the **Clean Up** menu.

2. Use the **Factor** function on each polynomial. Record the results.
   a) $x^2 + 8x + 16$ b) $y^2 - 10y + 25$
   c) $4k^2 - 20k + 25$ d) $9k^2 + 24k + 16$
   e) $25t^2 + 30t + 9$ f) $16z^2 - 8z + 1$

3. Consider each resulting square of a binomial from step 2.
   a) How is the first term of the binomial related to the first term of the trinomial?
   b) How is the last term of the binomial related to the last term of the trinomial?
   c) How are the terms of the binomial related to the middle term of the trinomial?

4. **Reflect** Each polynomial in step 2 is a perfect square trinomial. Explain how you can identify a perfect square trinomial.

5. **Reflect** Write a rule for factoring perfect square trinomials.

In Section 5.2, you saw that $(a + b)(a - b) = a^2 - b^2$. You can factor a difference of squares as $a^2 - b^2 = (a + b)(a - b)$.

You also saw that $(a + b)^2 = a^2 + 2ab + b^2$ and $(a - b)^2 = a^2 - 2ab + b^2$. You can factor a perfect square trinomial as $a^2 + 2ab + b^2 = (a + b)^2$ or $a^2 - 2ab + b^2 = (a - b)^2$.

Example 1 Difference of Squares

Factor.

a) $x^2 - 100$ b) $98a^2 - 450b^2$

Solution

a) $a^2 - b^2 = (a + b)(a - b)$ Use the pattern for a difference of squares.
   $x^2 - 100 = (x)^2 - 10^2$
   $= (x + 10)(x - 10)$

b) $98a^2 - 450b^2 = 2(49a^2 - 225b^2)$ Remove the greatest common factor.
   $= 2[(7a)^2 - (15b)^2]$
   $= 2(7a + 15b)(7a - 15b)$ Factor the difference of squares.

Example 2 Perfect Square Trinomials

Verify that each trinomial is a perfect square. Then, factor.

a) $x^2 + 6x + 9$
b) $x^2 - 12x + 36$

Solution

a) Since $x^2 = (x)^2$ and $9 = 3^2$, the first and last terms are perfect squares. Since $6x = 2(x)(3)$, the middle term is twice the product of the square roots of the first and last terms.
Therefore, $x^2 + 6x + 9$ is a perfect square trinomial.
   $a^2 + 2ab + b^2 = (a + b)^2$ Use the appropriate perfect
   $x^2 + 6x + 9 = (x)^2 + 2(x)(3) + 3^2$ square trinomial pattern.
   $= (x + 3)^2$

b) Since $x^2 = (x)^2$ and $36 = 6^2$, the first and last terms are perfect squares.
Twice the product of these square roots is $2(x)(6) = 12x$.
Therefore, $x^2 - 12x + 36$ is a perfect square trinomial.
   $a^2 - 2ab + b^2 = (a - b)^2$ Use the appropriate perfect
   $x^2 - 12x + 36 = (x)^2 - 2(x)(6) + 6^2$ square trinomial pattern.
   $= (x - 6)^2$

The middle term of the trinomial is $-12x$, so a difference has been squared.

Example 3 More Complex Perfect Square Trinomials

Verify that each trinomial is a perfect square. Then, factor.
a) $4x^2 + 28x + 49$
b) $25k^2 - 60km + 36m^2$

Solution

a) Since $4x^2 = (2x)^2$ and $49 = 7^2$, the first and last terms are perfect squares.
Since $28x = 2(2x)(7)$, the middle term is twice the product of the square roots of the first and last terms.
Therefore, $4x^2 + 28x + 49$ is a perfect square trinomial.
$$4x^2 + 28x + 49 = (2x)^2 + 2(2x)(7) + 7^2$$
$$= (2x + 7)^2$$

b) Since $25k^2 = (5k)^2$ and $36m^2 = (6m)^2$, the first and last terms are perfect squares.
Twice the product of these square roots is $2(5k)(6m) = 60km$.
Therefore, $25k^2 - 60km + 36m^2$ is a perfect square trinomial.
$$25k^2 - 60km + 36m^2 = (5k)^2 - 2(5k)(6m) + (6m)^2$$
$$= (5k - 6m)^2$$

> The middle term of the trinomial is $-60km$, so a difference has been squared.

Example 4 Area of a Region

a) Find an algebraic expression for the area of the shaded region.
b) Write the area expression in factored form.

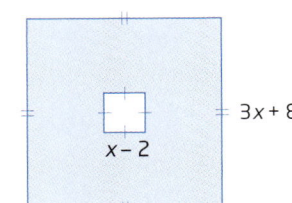

Solution

a) The area of the shaded region is the difference in the areas of the two squares.
Area $= (3x + 8)^2 - (x - 2)^2$

b) Method 1: Expand, Then Factor
$$(3x + 8)^2 - (x - 2)^2$$
$$= 9x^2 + 48x + 64 - (x^2 - 4x + 4)$$
$$= 9x^2 + 48x + 64 - x^2 + 4x - 4$$
$$= 8x^2 + 52x + 60$$
$$= 4(2x^2 + 13x + 15)$$
$$= 4(2x^2 + 10x + 3x + 15)$$
$$= 4[(2x^2 + 10x) + (3x + 15)]$$
$$= 4[2x(x + 5) + 3(x + 5)]$$
$$= 4[(x + 5)(2x + 3)]$$
$$= 4(x + 5)(2x + 3)$$

Method 2: Factor as a Difference of Squares

This is a difference of squares, $a^2 - b^2$, with $a = (3x + 8)$ and $b = (x - 2)$.

$(3x + 8)^2 - (x - 2)^2$
$= [(3x + 8) + (x - 2)][(3x + 8) - (x - 2)]$
$= (3x + 8 + x - 2)(3x + 8 - x + 2)$
$= (4x + 6)(2x + 10)$
$= 2(2x + 3)[2(x + 5)]$
$= 4(2x + 3)(x + 5)$

Key Concepts

- Always look for a common factor first when factoring a trinomial.
- You can factor a difference of squares as $a^2 - b^2 = (a + b)(a - b)$.
- You can factor a perfect square trinomial as
  $a^2 + 2ab + b^2 = (a + b)^2$ or $a^2 - 2ab + b^2 = (a - b)^2$.

Communicate Your Understanding

C1 Use words and diagrams to explain why $x^2 + 9$ cannot be factored over the integers.

C2 When her classmate showed Barbara the first step in Example 3b), $25k^2 - 60km + 36m^2 = (5k)^2 - 2(5k)(6m) + (6m)^2$, Barbara asked, "Where did the 2 come from?" Answer Barbara's question.

Practise

For help with questions 1 and 2, see Example 1.

1. Factor.
- **a)** $x^2 - 16$
- **b)** $y^2 - 100$
- **c)** $9k^2 - 36$
- **d)** $4a^2 - 121$
- **e)** $36w^2 - 49$
- **f)** $144p^2 - 1$
- **g)** $16n^2 - 25$
- **h)** $100g^2 - 81$

2. Factor.
- **a)** $m^2 - 49n^2$
- **b)** $h^2 - 25d^2$
- **c)** $100 - 9c^2$
- **d)** $169a^2 - 49b^2$
- **e)** $25x^2 - 36y^2$
- **f)** $16c^2 - 9d^2$
- **g)** $162 - 8s^2$
- **h)** $75h^2 - 27g^2$

For help with question 3, see Example 2.

3. Verify that each trinomial is a perfect square. Then, factor.
- **a)** $x^2 + 12x + 36$
- **b)** $k^2 + 18k + 81$
- **c)** $y^2 - 6y + 9$
- **d)** $m^2 - 14m + 49$
- **e)** $x^2 + 20x + 100$
- **f)** $64 - 16r + r^2$

For help with question 4, see Example 3.

4. Verify that each trinomial is a perfect square. Then, factor.
- **a)** $4c^2 + 12c + 9$
- **b)** $16k^2 - 8k + 1$
- **c)** $25x^2 + 70x + 49$
- **d)** $9y^2 - 30y + 25$
- **e)** $100c^2 - 180c + 81$
- **f)** $25 + 80y + 64y^2$

Connect and Apply

5. Each of the following is not factorable over the integers. Why not?
   a) $9x^2 - 16y$
   b) $36a^2 + 107a + 81$
   c) $10w^2 - 70wz + 49z^2$
   d) $25n^2 + 36m^2$

6. Factor fully, if possible.
   a) $4x^2 + 28xy + 49y^2$
   b) $9k^2 - 24km + 16m^2$
   c) $25p^2 + 60pq + 144q^2$
   d) $9y^2 - 7x^2$
   e) $2a^2 - 28ab + 98b^2$
   f) $196n^2 - 144m^2$
   g) $25x^2 + 70xy + 14y^2$
   h) $100f^2 - 120fg + 36g^2$
   i) $400p^3 - 900pq^2$

For help with question 7, see Example 4.

7. a) Find an algebraic expression for the area of the shaded region.
   b) Write the area expression in factored form.

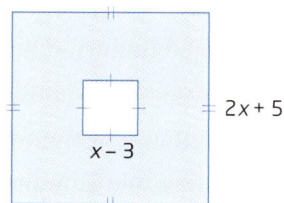

8. Determine all values of b so that each trinomial is a perfect square.
   a) $y^2 + by + 121$
   b) $4x^2 + bx + 25$
   c) $9n^2 + bnp + 49p^2$
   d) $w^2 + 10w + b$
   e) $81m^2 - 90m + b$
   f) $16x^2 - 88xy + b^2y^2$

9. Determine two values of k so that each trinomial can be factored as a difference of squares.
   a) $m^2 - kn^2$
   b) $kx^2 - 9$
   c) $49c^2 - k$

10. Factor, if possible.
    a) $9a^2b^2 - 24abcd + 16c^2d^2$
    b) $225 - (x + 5)^2$
    c) $(3c + 2)^2 - (3c - 2)^2$
    d) $4x^2 + 26x + 9$

11. The area of an unknown shape is represented by $9x^2 + 30x + 25$. If x must be an integer, what shape(s) could this figure be?

12. A box is in the shape of a rectangular prism. Its volume is given as $x^3 - 2x^2 + x$.
    a) Determine algebraic expressions for the dimensions.
    b) Describe the faces of the box.

13. **Chapter Problem** In Section 5.3, question 12, you found an algebraic expression for the total of the top surface areas of the three prisms used to make the pedestal.
    a) Write algebraic expressions for the exposed top surface areas of the middle and bottom layers of the pedestal.
    b) Factor each expression from part a).
    c) Compare the expressions for the exposed surface areas when x represents 5 cm.

14. The radius of a circle has been decreased by a certain amount. Its area is now given as $\pi r^2 - 14\pi r + 49\pi$, where r was the original radius, in centimetres.
    a) What was the decrease in radius?
    b) What was the decrease in area?

15. Is $x^2 - 1$ the same as $(x - 1)^2$? Explain using words and/or diagrams.

16. A parabola has equation $y = x^2 - 4x + 4$. Rewrite the equation in factored form to find the coordinates of the vertex.

17. Factor to evaluate each difference.
   a) $15^2 - 11^2$
   b) $37^2 - 27^2$
   c) $98^2 - 97^2$
   d) $28^2 - 22^2$

18. The first three diagrams in a pattern are shown.

 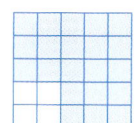 

   a) Use a table to develop a formula to represent the number of shaded small squares in the nth diagram.
   b) Write your formula in factored form.
   c) Calculate the number of shaded small squares in the 10th diagram using both versions of your formula.
   d) Which version is easier to use? Why?

Extend

19. A three-dimensional figure has volume given as $4\pi x^3 + 20\pi x^2 + 25\pi x$. What shape(s) could this figure be, and what are its dimensions?

20. Factor.
   a) $(x - 4)^2 - 16$
   b) $(x + 1)^2 + 2(x + 1) + 1$
   c) $25x^4 - 9y^4$
   d) $k^4 - 8k^2 + 16$
   e) $a^6 + 20a^3 + 100$
   f) $\dfrac{y^4}{81} - \dfrac{x^4}{625}$

21. Find all values of k so that each trinomial can be factored as a perfect square over the integers.
   a) $81x^4 + kx^2 + 16$
   b) $4y^4 + ky^2z^2 + 25z^4$

22. Use Technology
   a) Use a CAS to factor each expression:
   $x^2 - 1$
   $x^3 - 1$
   $x^4 - 1$
   $x^5 - 1$
   b) Look for a pattern in the factors. Which factored form does not appear to follow the pattern? Use a CAS to expand the last two factors of this factored form. Note what happens.
   c) Use your pattern to predict the result of factoring $x^6 - 1$ into two factors. Check your prediction using a CAS. If necessary, expand factors.

23. Math Contest
   a) Show that $x^3 - 8 = (x - 2)(x^2 + 2x + 4)$.
   b) Factor $m^3 - 64$.
   c) Factor $27y^3 - 125z^6$.

24. Math Contest
   a) Show that
   $a^3 + 1000 = (a + 10)(a^2 - 10a + 100)$.
   b) Factor $k^6 + 216e^3$.
   c) Factor $343q^{12} + 729r^{24}$.

25. Math Contest
   a) Expand $(a + b)^4$.
   b) Factor.
   $81x^4 - 216x^3y + 216x^2y^2 - 96xy^3 + 16y^4$

26. Math Contest If $a^2 + b^2 = 15$ and $ab = 3$, then the value of $(a - b)^2$ is
   A 21
   B 18
   C 12
   D 9
   E 3

Chapter 5 Review

5.1 Multiply Polynomials, pages 210–219

1. Use the distributive property to find each binomial product.
   a) $(x + 5)(x + 8)$
   b) $(x - 1)(x - 4)$
   c) $(x + 3y)(x - 6y)$
   d) $(5a - 6b)(2a + 9b)$

2. Expand and simplify.
   a) $-(k + 2)(k - 7)$
   b) $w(w - 7v)(w - 3v)$
   c) $7x(7x + 3y)(3x + 9y)$
   d) $(y + 1)(y + 8) + (y - 8)(y + 1)$
   e) $-4(2x - 6)(4x - 5) + 3(11x + 7)(11x - 4)$

3. Write an algebraic expression to represent the area of the figure. Expand and simplify.

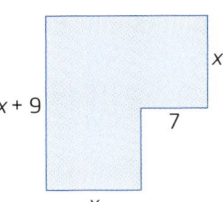

5.2 Special Products, pages 220–227

4. Draw a diagram to illustrate each product.
   a) $(x + 4)^2$
   b) $(a + 2)^2$

5. Expand and simplify.
   a) $(x + 6)^2$
   b) $(k + 8)^2$
   c) $(p + 7)^2$
   d) $(r - 2)^2$
   e) $(e - 9)^2$
   f) $(q - 20)^2$

6. Expand and simplify.
   a) $(b + 6)(b - 6)$
   b) $(a - 7)(a + 7)$
   c) $(y + 12)(y - 12)$
   d) $(x - 15)(x + 15)$
   e) $(e - 10)(e + 10)$
   f) $(x + 6)(x - 6)$

7. Expand and simplify.
   a) $(y + 4x)^2$
   b) $(7m - n)^2$
   c) $(2c + 9d)^2$
   d) $-2(5x + 7y)(5x - 7y)$
   e) $(3a - 8c)(3a + 8c)$
   f) $-(5x - 8y)(5x + 8y)$

5.3 Common Factors, pages 228–235

8. Use algebra tiles or a diagram to illustrate the factoring of each polynomial.
   a) $x^2 + 9x$
   b) $3x^2 + x$

9. Factor.
   a) $12y + 24z$
   b) $11xy - 9xz$
   c) $c^2 + 3c$
   d) $4k - 8k^3$

10. Factor by grouping.
    a) $4m^2 + 12m + 3m + 9$
    b) $9k^2 - 6k + 6k - 4$
    c) $8x^2 + 16x - 5x - 10$
    d) $16x^2 - 12xy - 12xy + 9y^2$

11. Factor, if possible.
    a) $8m^2 - 16m + 4$
    b) $18c^3 + 24c^2 - 8c + 6$
    c) $15m^2 - 22mn + 66mn^2$
    d) $ax^2z - az^2 + axz$

12. A rectangle has area given by the expression $10x^2 + 5x$. The length and width can be found by factoring the expression. Find all possible expressions for the length and width.

5.4 Factor Quadratic Expressions of the Form $x^2 + bx + c$, pages 236–241

13. Illustrate the factoring of each trinomial using algebra tiles or a diagram.
    a) $x^2 + 9x + 14$
    b) $x^2 + 11x + 18$
    c) $x^2 + 4x + 4$

14. Factor.
    a) $c^2 - 17c + 72$
    b) $x^2 - 8x + 15$
    c) $z^2 - 14z + 33$
    d) $x^2 + 3x - 10$
    e) $x^2 + 8x - 9$
    f) $x^2 - 2x - 8$

15. A parabola has equation $y = x^2 - 3x - 18$.
    a) Factor the right side of the equation.
    b) Identify the x-intercepts of the parabola.
    c) Find the equation of the axis of symmetry, find the vertex, and draw the graph.

5.5 Factor Quadratic Expressions of the Form $ax^2 + bx + c$, pages 242–249

16. Factor. Use a diagram, if needed.
    a) $2x^2 + 7x + 6$
    b) $6y^2 + 29y + 9$
    c) $6a^2 - 23a + 15$
    d) $4b^2 - 5b + 1$
    e) $12m^2 + 20m - 8$
    f) $14k^2 - 31k - 10$

17. Factor, if possible.
    a) $8x^2 + 2xy - 15y^2$
    b) $5c^2 - 4cd + 9d^2$
    c) $12m^2 + 13mn + 3n^2$
    d) $2w^2 - 9wx - 8x^2$
    e) $24x^2 + 6xy - 9y^2$
    f) $9g^2 + 4g - 10$

18. A rectangle has area defined by $8x^2 + 2x - 15$.

    Area is $8x^2 + 2x - 15$.

    a) Factor to find algebraic expressions for the length and width of the rectangle.
    b) If x represents 12 cm, determine the perimeter and the area of the rectangle.

5.6 Factor a Perfect Square Trinomial and a Difference of Squares, pages 248–255

19. Factor.
    a) $x^2 - 49$
    b) $y^2 - 121$
    c) $4k^2 - 9$
    d) $16 - 144a^2$
    e) $9w^2 - 25x^2$
    f) $1 - 81p^2$

20. Verify that each trinomial is a perfect square. Then, factor.
    a) $x^2 + 14x + 49$
    b) $k^2 + 8k + 16$
    c) $y^2 - 10y + 25$
    d) $25y^2 - 70y + 49$
    e) $36c^2 - 108c + 81$
    f) $121 + 176y + 64y^2$

21. Determine all values of k so that each trinomial is a perfect square.
    a) $25y^2 + ky + 144$
    b) $9x^2 - 42x + k$

22. Factor, if possible.
    a) $9w^2x^2 - 24wxyz + 16y^2z^2$
    b) $625 - (y - 5)^2$
    c) $144a^4 - 499b^4$
    d) $25x^2 + 30x + 4$

Chapter Problem Wrap-Up

In Section 5.2, question 13, you wrote algebraic expressions for the exposed top surface areas of the middle and bottom layers of the pedestal. In Section 5.6, question 13, you factored algebraic expressions for the exposed top surface areas of the middle and bottom layers of the pedestal.

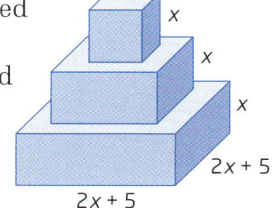

a) Consider your resulting expressions from Section 5.2. Factor these expressions.
b) Were the results the same as those from Section 5.6? Explain.
c) Calculate the total volume of wood that will be used in building the pedestal, if x represents 5 cm and if x represents 10 cm. Compare the results.
d) When you doubled the value of x in part c), did the volumes double? Why or why not?

Chapter 5 Practice Test

1. What binomial product does each diagram illustrate?

   a)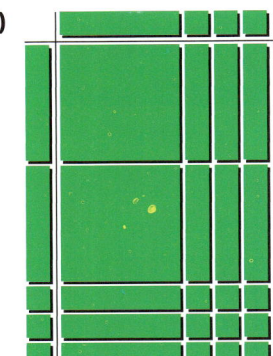

   b)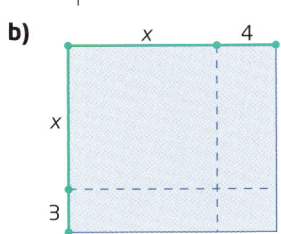

2. Simplify.
   a) $4x^2(3x - 5y + 8z)$
   b) $3m(6m^2 - 5m + 4) - (4m^3 - 8m^2 + 9)$

3. Expand and simplify.
   a) $(y + 5)(y + 9)$
   b) $(4x - 7)(3x + 2)$
   c) $(6k + 1)(6k - 1)$
   d) $(w - 8)^2$
   e) $(4c + 5d)^2$
   f) $2(x - 4)(x - 7) - 5(8x - 9)(8x + 9)$

4. The minimum stopping distance, after a delay of 1 s, for a particular car is modelled by the formula $d = 0.006(s + 1)^2$, where d represents the stopping distance, in metres, and s represents the initial speed, in kilometres per hour.
   a) Expand and simplify the formula.
   b) Compare the results in both versions of the formula for an initial speed of 60 km/h.

5. Factor.
   a) $9d^2e^2 + 6d^3e$
   b) $15p^2qr^3 - 25p^3q^2r + 5pqr$
   c) $5(x + 6) - 2(x + 6)$
   d) $16x^2 + 8x - 6x - 3$

6. a) Find an algebraic expression for the surface area of the square-based prism.

   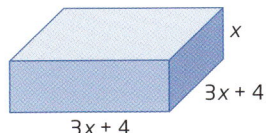

   b) Expand and simplify your expression from part a).
   c) Factor the resulting expression from part b).

7. Factor.
   a) $x^2 + 11x + 24$
   b) $y^2 - 15y + 56$
   c) $n^2 - n - 90$
   d) $x^2 - 14x + 49$
   e) $h^2 - 100$
   f) $d^2 + 16d + 64$

8. Factor.
   a) $3k^2 + 12km - 36m^2$
   b) $8y^2 + 19y + 6$
   c) $9w^2 - 24w + 7$
   d) $25a^2 + 60a + 36$
   e) $121w^2 - 144$
   f) $10x^2 - 7xy - 6y^2$

9. Explain how to determine whether or not you can factor $9x^2 - 10x + 18$ over the integers.

10. The area of a rectangle is given as $x^2 + 13x - 30$.
    a) Determine polynomials that represent the length and width of the rectangle.
    b) What is the smallest integer value of x for which this area expression makes sense?

11. Determine all values of k so that each trinomial is a perfect square.
   a) $36x^2 + kx + 121$
   b) $49d^2 - 56d + k$
   c) $25x^2 - 60xy + ky^2$
   d) $ka^2 + 30ab + 9b^2$

12. a) Write an algebraic expression for the area of the shaded region.

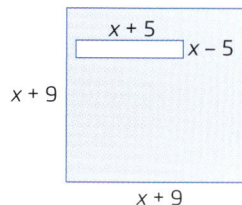

   b) Write the area expression in factored form.
   c) Substitute $x = 7$ into both forms. Are the results the same? Why?

13. A parabola has equation $y = 2(x + 6)^2 - 2$.
   a) Expand and simplify to write the equation in the form $y = ax^2 + bx + c$.
   b) Factor your equation from part a).
   c) Do the three equations represent the same parabola? Justify your response.

14. The volume of a rectangular prism is given as $9x^3 - 30x^2 + 25x$.
   a) Determine algebraic expressions for the dimensions.
   b) Describe the faces of the prism.

15. Determine two values of k so that each trinomial can be factored as a difference of squares.
   a) $km^2 - 25$
   b) $16d^2 - k$
   c) $a^2 - kb^2$

16. Factor to evaluate each difference.
   a) $34^2 - 31^2$
   b) $127^2 - 126^2$
   c) $52^2 - 48^2$

17. The first three diagrams in a pattern are shown.

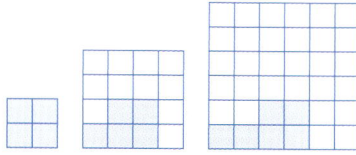

   a) Write a formula for the total number of small squares in the nth diagram.
   b) Write a formula for the number of shaded small squares in the nth diagram.
   c) Write a formula for the number of unshaded small squares in the nth diagram.
   d) Write your formula from part c) in factored form.
   e) Show that both forms of the formula give the same results for the 15th diagram.

■ **Achievement Check**

18. a) Find all values of b so that $x^2 + bx + 10$ can be factored over the integers.
   b) Find all values of b so that $4y^2 + by + 5$ can be factored over the integers.
   c) Write an algebraic expression for the shaded area. Then, write the expression in factored form.

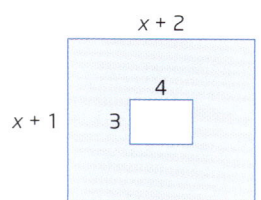

CHAPTER 6

Quadratic Equations

Quadratic Relations of the Form $y = ax^2 + bx + c$

- Express $y = ax^2 + bx + c$ in the form $y = a(x - h)^2 + k$ by completing the square in situations involving no fractions, using a variety of tools.
- Sketch or graph a quadratic relation whose equation is given in the form $y = ax^2 + bx + c$, using a variety of methods.
- Determine the zeros and the maximum or minimum value of a quadratic relation from its graph or from its defining equation.
- Solve quadratic equations that have real roots, using a variety of methods.
- Determine, through investigation, and describe the connection between the factors of a quadratic expression and the x-intercepts of the graph of the corresponding quadratic relation, expressed in the form $y = a(x - r)(x - s)$.
- Interpret real and non-real roots of quadratic equations, through investigation using graphing technology, and relate the roots to the x-intercepts of the corresponding relations.
- Explore the algebraic development of the quadratic formula.
- Solve problems arising from a realistic situation represented by a graph or an equation of a quadratic relation, with and without the use of technology.

Many real-world situations can be modelled using quadratic relations. Related problems can be solved using quadratic equations. For example, designs in architecture and engineering use parabolic arches. Because of constant gravity, the flight path of a ball, a rocket, or a skateboarder is a parabola. In business, quadratic models are used to solve problems of maximizing revenue or minimizing the cost of production.

In this chapter, you will relate quadratic equations to the graph of a quadratic relation and solve problems by modelling with quadratic equations.

Vocabulary

completing the square
quadratic equation
root
quadratic formula

Chapter Problem

Skateboard half-pipe ramps typically have a semicircular cross section. A manufacturer decides to build a half-pipe with a parabolic cross section.

In this chapter, you will solve related quadratic equations to find the dimensions of the new half-pipe.

Get Ready

Graph Quadratic Relations of the Form $y = a(x - h)^2 + k$

The graph of a **quadratic relation** of the form $y = a(x - h)^2 + k$ is a **parabola** with **vertex** at (h, k). The vertex is a minimum point when $a > 0$ and a maximum point when $a < 0$.

The **axis of symmetry** of the parabola has equation $x = h$.

Substitute $x = 0$ to find the y-intercept.

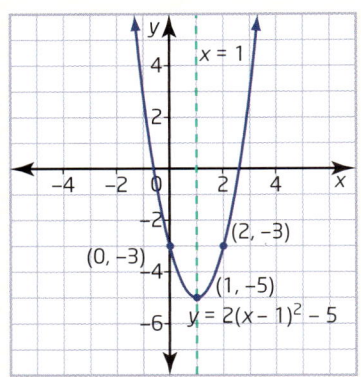

First, I plot the vertex and draw the axis of symmetry. Then, I determine one point on the curve, for example, the y-intercept, and plot that point. Next, I use symmetry to plot a second point. Finally, I draw a parabola through the points.

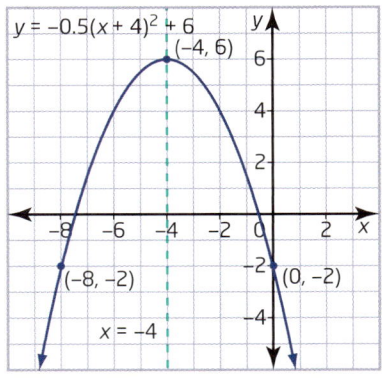

1. Sketch each parabola. Label the vertex, the axis of symmetry, and the y-intercept. Use a graphing calculator to check your answers.
   a) $y = (x - 4)^2 - 1$
   b) $y = 2(x + 3)^2 - 3$
   c) $y = -(x + 2)^2 + 5$
   d) $y = 3(x - 2)^2 + 2$

2. Sketch each parabola. Label the vertex, the axis of symmetry, and the y-intercept. Use a graphing calculator to check your answers.
   a) $y = -0.5(x + 1)^2 + 2$
   b) $y = -2(x - 3)^2 + 10$
   c) $y = \dfrac{1}{2}(x - 3)^2 - 7$
   d) $y = -\dfrac{3}{4}(x + 1)^2 + 6$

Square Roots

Since $81 = 9 \times 9$ and $81 = (-9) \times (-9)$, the square roots of 81 are $+9$ and -9.

Using mathematics notation, this can be written as $\pm\sqrt{81} = \pm 9$.

Literacy Connections

The symbol $\pm$ means *positive or negative*.

$\pm\sqrt{81}$ is read as *plus or minus the square root of 81*.

3. Find the square roots of each number, where possible. If necessary, round to the nearest tenth.
   a) 100
   b) 36
   c) 75
   d) -9

4. Use the order of operations to evaluate each expression.
   a) $\pm\sqrt{25 - 16}$
   b) $\pm\sqrt{3^2 + 4^2}$
   c) $\pm\sqrt{6^2 - 11}$
   d) $\pm\sqrt{8^2 - 3(5)}$

Factor Quadratic Expressions

When factoring a **quadratic expression**, first check for any common factor or special patterns.

Quadratic Expression	$x^2 + bx + c$	$a^2 - b^2$	$a^2 + 2ab + b^2$ $a^2 - 2ab + b^2$	$ax^2 + bx + c$
Factoring Technique	Find two integers, r and s, with a product of c and a sum of b. Then, write $x^2 + bx + c$ as $(x + r)(x + s)$.	Use the **difference of squares** pattern. $a^2 - b^2$ $= (a - b)(a + b)$	Use a **perfect square trinomial** pattern. $a^2 + 2ab + b^2 = (a + b)^2$ or $a^2 - 2ab + b^2 = (a - b)^2$	Find two integers with a product of $a \times c$ and sum of b. Then, break up the middle term and factor by grouping.
Example	For $x^2 + 11x + 18$, $b = 11$ and $c = 18$. The two integers are 9 and 2. $x^2 + 11x + 18$ $= (x + 9)(x + 2)$	$100x^2 - 9$ $= (10x)^2 - 3^2$ $= (10x - 3)(10 + 3)$	$x^2 + 6x + 9$ $= x^2 + 2(x)(3) + 3^2$ $= (x + 3)^2$ $25x^2 - 40x + 16$ $= (5x)^2 - 2(5x)(4) + 4^2$ $= (5x - 4)^2$	For $6x^2 - 11x - 7$, $a \times c = -42$ and $b = -11$. The two integers are 3 and -14. $6x^2 - 11x - 7$ $= 6x^2 + 3x - 14x - 7$ $= (6x^2 + 3x) - (14x + 7)$ $= 3x(2x + 1) - 7(2x + 1)$ $= (2x + 1)(3x - 7)$

5. Factor.

   a) $2x^2 + 10x + 12$
   b) $x^2 + 16x + 28$
   c) $x^2 - 16x + 63$
   d) $4x^2 - 36$
   e) $81x^2 - 49$
   f) $3x^2 - 6x - 24$
   g) $16x^2 - 8x + 1$
   h) $12x^2 + 19x + 4$

6. Factor.

   a) $x^2 - 4x - 32$
   b) $2x^2 + 12x + 18$
   c) $64x^2 - 1$
   d) $144x^2 - 312x + 169$
   e) $49x^2 + 70x + 25$
   f) $2x^2 - 9x - 5$
   g) $9x^2 - 18x + 8$
   h) $6x^2 + 21x + 9$

Translate From Words to Algebra

Sentence	Algebraic Expression
One number is double another.	The first number is x. The second number is $2x$.
The length is 6 cm more than the width.	The width is w. The length is $w + 6$.
The regular price of $5 is reduced by 25¢ an unknown number of times.	The number of price reductions is n. The new price, in cents, is $500 - 25n$.

7. Translate using algebraic expressions. Use one variable to represent the unknowns in each sentence.

   a) A number is half another number.
   b) The area of the garden is tripled.
   c) The regular price of $12 is reduced by $1 an unknown number of times.
   d) A number is the sum of the squares of two consecutive numbers.
   e) The length is three less than double the width.

8. Write an equation to represent each sentence, using two variables.

   a) The sum of two numbers is 100.
   b) The perimeter of the rectangle is 50 cm.
   c) Find the perimeter when the length is triple the width.
   d) The product of two numbers is equal to the square of double the smaller number.
   e) A triangle with a perimeter of 12 cm has one side measuring 3 cm.

6.1 Maxima and Minima

How can the owner of a snowboard rental business use mathematics to maximize sales or minimize cost? What dimensions of a rectangular field provide the greatest area? Questions like these are answered by finding the maximum or minimum point of a quadratic relation, which occurs at the vertex.

If a relation is of the form $y = a(x - h)^2 + k$, then the vertex is (h, k). However, if a relation is of the form $y = ax^2 + bx + c$, the coordinates of the vertex are not so obvious. In this section, you will learn how to express $y = ax^2 + bx + c$ in the form $y = a(x - h)^2 + k$.

Investigate

How can you model the process of creating a perfect square?

Tools
- algebra tiles
- graphing calculator

1. Consider the quadratic expression $x^2 + 6x + 9$.
   a) Show that the expression is a perfect square using algebra tiles.
   b) Factor the expression as a perfect square.

2. Repeat step 1 using the quadratic expression $x^2 + 4x + 4$.

3. Consider the quadratic expression $x^2 + 6x + 5$.
   a) Describe how algebra tiles have been used to create a perfect square using the *first two terms*.
   b) Explain how the relation $y = x^2 + 6x + 5$ relates to $y = (x + 3)^2 - 4$.
   c) Use a graphing calculator to compare the graphs of $y = x^2 + 6x + 5$ and $y = (x + 3)^2 - 4$.

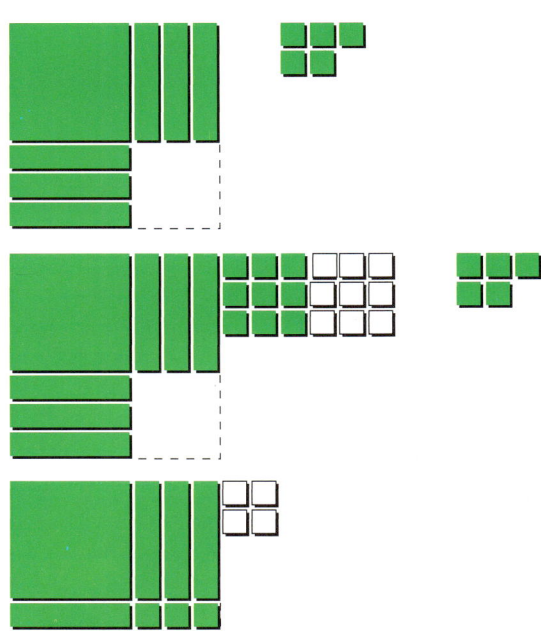

4. Consider the quadratic expression $x^2 + 4x + 3$.

   a) As in step 3, use algebra tiles or a diagram to create a perfect square using the first two terms.
   b) Explain how the relation $y = x^2 + 4x + 3$ relates to $y = (x + 2)^2 - 1$.
   c) Use a graphing calculator to compare the graphs of $y = x^2 + 4x + 3$ and $y = (x + 2)^2 - 1$.

5. **Reflect** Illustrate and explain how to use algebra tiles to rewrite the quadratic relation $y = x^2 + 2x + 7$ in the form $y = (x - h)^2 + k$.

The process of **completing the square** involves changing the first two terms of a quadratic relation of the form $y = ax^2 + bx + c$ into a perfect square while maintaining the balance of the original relation.

completing the square
- a process for expressing $y = ax^2 + bx + c$ in the form $y = a(x - h)^2 + k$

Example 1 Complete the Square

a) Rewrite $y = x^2 + 8x + 5$ in the form $y = a(x - h)^2 + k$.
b) Write the coordinates of the vertex of the parabola.
c) Sketch a graph of the relation. Label the vertex, the axis of symmetry, and two other points.

Solution

a) Method 1: Use Algebra Tiles

Create a perfect square using the first two terms in the quadratic expression $x^2 + 8x + 5$.

Arrange one x^2-tile and eight x-tiles so that the side lengths are equal. Place the five unit tiles to the side.

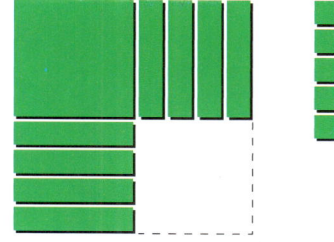

To complete the perfect square, you need to add 16 unit tiles.
In order to preserve the original quadratic expression, you must also add 16 negative unit tiles.

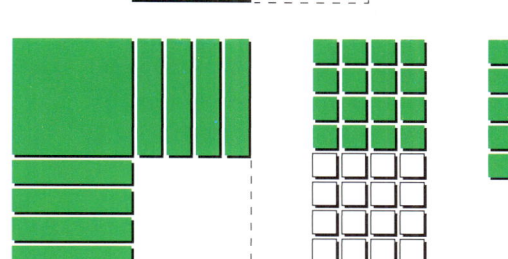

Complete the square and collect the unit tiles. Remove zero pairs.

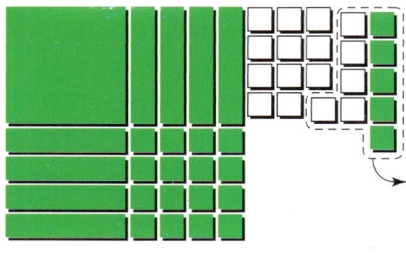

$x^2 + 8x + 5 = (x + 4)^2 - 11$

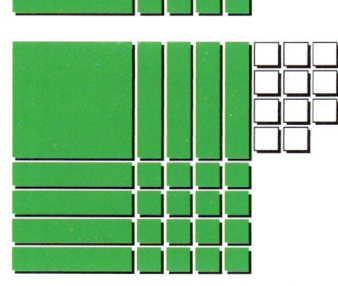

The relation $y = x^2 + 8x + 5$ in the form $y = a(x - h)^2 + k$ is $y = (x + 4)^2 - 11$.

Method 2: Use Algebraic Symbols

Rewrite the relation in the form $y = a(x - h)^2 + k$ by completing the square.

$y = x^2 + 8x + 5$
$= (x^2 + 8x) + 5$ **Group the first two terms.**
$= (x^2 + 8x + 4^2 - 4^2) + 5$ **To make a perfect square trinomial inside the brackets, add the square of half of 8, or 4^2. To balance the equation, also subtract 4^2.**
$= (x^2 + 8x + 4^2) - 4^2 + 5$ **Take -4^2 outside the brackets.**
$= (x + 4)^2 - 16 + 5$ **Factor the perfect square trinomial and simplify.**
$= (x + 4)^2 - 11$

The relation $y = x^2 + 8x + 5$ in the form $y = a(x - h)^2 + k$ is $y = (x + 4)^2 - 11$.

b) The vertex is (h, k), or $(-4, -11)$.

c) The equation of the axis of symmetry is $x = -4$.

To find another point on the graph, let x take any value.
Let $x = 0$.
$y = 0^2 + 8(0) + 5$
$ = 5$

Therefore, $(0, 5)$ is a point on the parabola.

Due to symmetry, another point is the *partner* to this, $(-8, 5)$.

Plot the three points and complete the sketch.

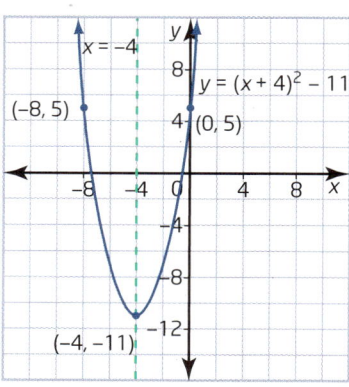

> Looking at the x-coordinate of this point, I know that it is located 4 units to the right of the axis of symmetry. So, its partner is located 4 units to the left of the axis of symmetry and has the same y-coordinate.

Example 2 Find a Maximum or a Minimum

Find the maximum or minimum point of the parabola with equation $y = 2x^2 + 12x + 11$.

Solution

Method 1: Complete the Square

When the coefficient of the x^2-term is not 1, the first step is to factor the coefficient of x^2 from the first two terms. Then, complete the square within the brackets.

$y = 2x^2 + 12x + 11$
$ = 2(x^2 + 6x) + 11$ Factor 2 from the first two terms to make the coefficient of the x^2-term 1.
$ = 2(x^2 + 6x + 3^2 - 3^2) + 11$ To make a perfect square trinomial inside the brackets, add the square of half of 6, or 3^2. Subtract the same value to balance the equation.
$ = 2(x^2 + 6x + 3^2) - 2(3^2) + 11$ Take -3^2 outside of the brackets by multiplying by 2.
$ = 2(x + 3)^2 - 18 + 11$ Factor the perfect square trinomial and simplify.
$ = 2(x + 3)^2 - 7$

The equation $y = 2(x + 3)^2 - 7$ is of the form $y = a(x - h)^2 + k$. The vertex is $(-3, -7)$. It is a minimum point, since a is positive.

Method 2: Use a Graphing Calculator

Enter the equation using `Y=`.
Press `ZOOM` and select **6:ZStandard**.

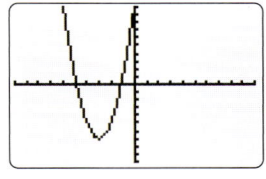

You can see that the parabola has a minimum. This is because the coefficient of x^2 is positive.

Use the Minimum operation of a graphing calculator to find the coordinates of the vertex.
- Press `2nd` [CALC] to display the **CALCULATE** menu, and select **3:minimum**.
- Move the cursor to the left of the vertex and press `ENTER`.
- Move the cursor to the right of the vertex and press `ENTER`.
- Move the cursor close to the vertex and press `ENTER`.

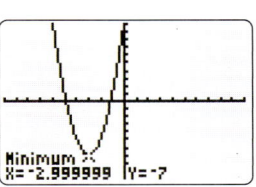

The calculator will give you the approximate ordered pair that best represents the minimum point of the graph.

The minimum point is $(-3, -7)$.

Technology Tip

The TI-83 Plus or TI-84 Plus graphing calculator displays cursor coordinates as eight-character numbers, which may include a negative sign. When **Float** is selected in the **MODE** settings, X and Y are displayed with a maximum accuracy of eight digits. Since the Minimum and Maximum operations are only calculated to an accuracy of 1×10^{-5} or 0.000 01, the result displayed on the graphing calculator screen may not be accurate to all eight displayed digits.

Example 3 Path of a Ball

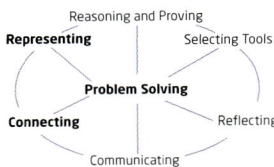

The path of a ball is modelled by the equation $y = -x^2 + 2x + 3$, where x is the horizontal distance, in metres, from a fence and y is the height, in metres, above the ground.

a) What is the maximum height of the ball, and at what horizontal distance does it occur?

b) Sketch a graph to represent the path of the ball.

Solution

a)
$$y = -x^2 + 2x + 3$$
$$= -1(x^2 - 2x) + 3$$ Factor –1 from the first two terms.

$$= -1(x^2 - 2x + (-1)^2 - (-1)^2) + 3$$ To complete the square inside the brackets, add the square of half of –2, or $(-1)^2$. Subtract the same value to balance the equation.

$$= -1(x^2 - 2x + (-1)^2) - (-1)(-1)^2 + 3$$ Take $-(-1)^2$ outside the brackets by multiplying by –1.

$$= -1(x - 1)^2 + 1 + 3$$ Factor the perfect square trinomial and simplify.

$$= -(x - 1)^2 + 4$$

The equation $y = -(x - 1)^2 + 4$ is of the form $y = a(x - h)^2 + k$. The vertex is (1, 4). It is a maximum point since a is negative.

The maximum height of the ball is 4 m after it has been thrown a horizontal distance of 1 m.

b) The vertex is (1, 4).
When $x = 0$, $y = 3$.
By symmetry, the partner point to (0, 3) is (2, 3).

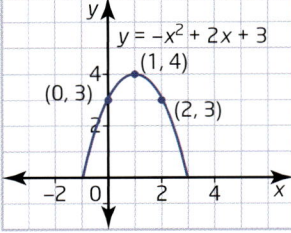

I can use these three points to graph the path of the ball. The parabola will not go below the x-axis because the height of the ball is always positive.

Example 4 Maximize Revenue

Alex runs a snowboard rental business that charges $12 per snowboard and averages 36 rentals per day. She discovers that for each $0.50 decrease in price, her business rents out two additional snowboards per day. At what price can Alex maximize her revenue?

Solution

Let R represent the total revenue, in dollars.
Let x represent the number of $0.50 decreases in price.

Then, the price, in dollars, can be calculated as $12 - 0.5x$ and the number of rentals can be calculated as $36 + 2x$.

Revenue is the product of the price and the number rented.
$R = (12 - 0.5x)(36 + 2x)$

To find the maximum revenue, expand the quadratic relation, and then complete the square.

$$\begin{aligned} R &= (12 - 0.5x)(36 + 2x) \\ &= 432 + 6x - x^2 \\ &= -x^2 + 6x + 432 \\ &= -1(x^2 - 6x) + 432 \\ &= -1(x^2 - 6x + (-3)^2 - (-3)^2) + 432 \\ &= -1(x^2 - 6x + (-3)^2) - (-1)(-3)^2 + 432 \\ &= -1(x - 3)^2 + 9 + 432 \\ &= -(x - 3)^2 + 441 \end{aligned}$$

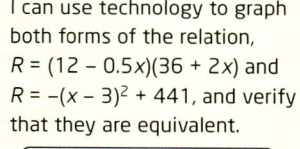

I can use technology to graph both forms of the relation, $R = (12 - 0.5x)(36 + 2x)$ and $R = -(x - 3)^2 + 441$, and verify that they are equivalent.

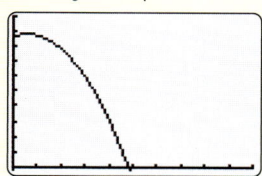

The relation reaches a maximum value of 441 when $x = 3$.

There should be three price reductions of $0.50 to maximize the revenue.
$12 - 0.5(3) = 10.50$

A price of $10.50 maximizes Alex's revenue.

Key Concepts

- You can rewrite a quadratic relation of the form $y = ax^2 + bx + c$ in the form $y = a(x - h)^2 + k$ by completing the square.

- For a quadratic relation in the form $y = a(x - h)^2 + k$, the vertex, (h, k), represents the maximum or minimum point of the parabola. The vertex is a minimum point when $a > 0$ and a maximum point when $a < 0$.

- Completing the square allows you to find the maximum or minimum point of a quadratic relation of the form $y = ax^2 + bx + c$ algebraically.

- You can use a graphing calculator to find the maximum or minimum point by using the Maximum or Minimum operation on the graph of the quadratic relation.

Communicate Your Understanding

C1 Describe the steps needed to complete the square for each relation.

a) $y = x^2 + 10x + 15$

b) $y = -2x^2 - 4x - 5$

C2 Identify the vertex of each relation in question C1. How do you know whether it is a maximum or a minimum point?

C3 Explain how to graph an equation of the form $y = a(x - h)^2 + k$.

Practise

For help with questions 1 to 6, see Example 1.

1. Use algebra tiles to rewrite each relation in the form $y = a(x - h)^2 + k$ by completing the square.

   a) $y = x^2 + 2x + 5$
   b) $y = x^2 + 4x + 7$
   c) $y = x^2 + 6x + 3$

2. Determine the value of c that makes each expression a perfect square.

   a) $x^2 + 6x + c$ b) $x^2 + 14x + c$
   c) $x^2 - 12x + c$ d) $x^2 - 10x + c$
   e) $x^2 + 2x + c$ f) $x^2 - 80x + c$

3. Rewrite each relation in the form $y = a(x - h)^2 + k$ by completing the square.

   a) $y = x^2 + 6x - 1$
   b) $y = x^2 + 2x + 7$
   c) $y = x^2 + 10x + 20$
   d) $y = x^2 + 2x - 1$
   e) $y = x^2 - 6x - 4$
   f) $y = x^2 - 8x - 2$
   g) $y = x^2 - 12x + 8$

4. Find the vertex of each quadratic relation by completing the square.

   a) $y = x^2 + 6x + 2$
   b) $y = x^2 + 12x + 30$
   c) $y = x^2 - 8x + 13$
   d) $y = x^2 - 6x + 17$

5. Match each graph with the appropriate equation.

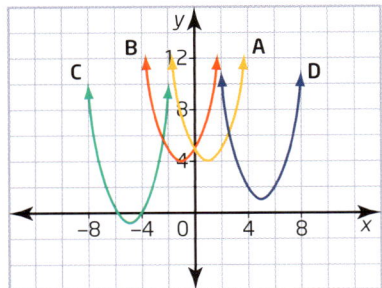

   a) $y = (x - 5)^2 + 1$
   b) $y = (x - 1)^2 + 4$
   c) $y = (x + 1)^2 + 4$
   d) $y = (x + 5)^2 - 1$

6. Find the vertex of each parabola. Sketch the graph, labelling the vertex, the axis of symmetry, and two other points.

   a) $y = x^2 + 10x + 20$
   b) $y = x^2 - 16x + 60$

For help with questions 7 to 9, see Example 2.

7. Rewrite each relation in the form $y = a(x - h)^2 + k$ by completing the square.

   a) $y = -x^2 + 80x - 100$
   b) $y = -x^2 - 6x + 4$
   c) $y = 3x^2 + 90x + 50$
   d) $y = 2x^2 - 16x + 15$
   e) $y = -7x^2 + 14x - 3$

8. Find the maximum or minimum point of each parabola by completing the square.
   a) $y = -x^2 - 10x - 9$
   b) $y = -x^2 + 14x - 50$
   c) $y = 2x^2 + 120x + 75$
   d) $y = 3x^2 - 24x + 10$
   e) $y = -5x^2 - 200x - 120$

9. **Use Technology** Use a graphing calculator to find the maximum or minimum point of each parabola, rounded to the nearest tenth.
   a) $y = x^2 + 6x - 1$
   b) $y = 0.2x^2 - 1.5x + 6.3$
   c) $y = -1.6x^2 + 4.3x - 5.2$
   d) $y = \frac{1}{2}x^2 - \frac{1}{8}x + \frac{1}{2}$
   e) $y = -57x^2 + 91x - 13$
   f) $y = 144x^2 + 25x + 14$

For help with questions 10 and 11, see Example 3.

10. Find the vertex of each parabola. Sketch the graph, and label the vertex and two other points.
    a) $y = -x^2 - 2x - 6$
    b) $y = 4x^2 + 24x + 41$
    c) $y = 5x^2 - 30x + 41$
    d) $y = -3x^2 + 12x - 13$
    e) $y = 2x^2 + 8x + 3$

11. Find the vertex of each parabola. Sketch the graph, and label the vertex and two other points.
    a) $y = -2x^2 - 3x + 7$
    b) $y = 3x^2 - 9x + 11$
    c) $y = -x^2 + 8x - 10$
    d) $y = 4x^2 - 16x + 11$
    e) $y = -5x^2 - 30x - 48$

Connect and Apply

12. The path of a ball is modelled by the equation $y = -x^2 + 4x + 1$, where x is the horizontal distance, in metres, travelled and y is the height, in metres, of the ball above the ground. What is the maximum height of the ball, and at what horizontal distance does it occur?

13. **Use Technology** A football is kicked at an angle of 30° to the ground, at an initial speed of 20 m/s, from a height of 1 m. Two quadratic relations can be used to model the height, in metres, above the ground:

    With respect to time, t, in seconds, the height is given by $h = -4.9t^2 + 10t + 1$.

    With respect to the horizontal distance, x, in metres, the height is given by $h = -0.0163x^2 + 0.5774x + 1$.

    Use a graphing calculator to verify that the maximum height is the same with both models.

    At what time and horizontal distance does the maximum height occur?

Did You Know?

Galileo was a mathematics professor at the University of Pisa, in Italy. At the beginning of the 17th century, he discovered the connection between quadratic equations and acceleration.

14. A diver dives from the 3-m board at a swimming pool. Her height, y, in metres, above the water in terms of her horizontal distance, x, in metres, from the end of the board is given by $y = -x^2 + 2x + 3$. What is the diver's maximum height?

15. The cost, in dollars, of operating a machine per day is given by the formula $C = 2t^2 - 84t + 1025$, where t is the time, in hours, the machine operates. What is the minimum cost of running the machine? For how many hours must the machine run to reach this minimum cost?

For help with question 16, see Example 4.

16. An artisan can sell 120 garden ornaments per week at $4 per ornament. For each $0.50 decrease in price, he can sell 20 more ornaments.

   a) Determine algebraic expressions for the price of a garden ornament and the number of ornaments sold.

   b) Write an equation for the revenue using your expressions from part a).

   c) Use your equation from part b) to find what price the artisan should charge to maximize revenue.

   d) Use Technology Graph both forms of the relation from parts b) and c) to verify that they are equivalent.

17. Find the maximum or minimum point of each parabola by completing the square.

   a) $y = 1.5x^2 + 6x - 7$
   b) $y = -0.1x^2 - 2x + 1$
   c) $y = 0.3x^2 + 3x$
   d) $y = -1.25x^2 + 5x$
   e) $y = 0.5x^2 - 6x + 12$
   f) $y = -0.02x^2 - 0.6x - 9$

18. Chapter Problem A manufacturer decides to build a half-pipe with a parabolic cross section modelled by the relation $y = 0.2x^2 - 1.6x + 4.2$, where x is the horizontal distance, in metres, from the platform, and y is the height, in metres, above the ground.

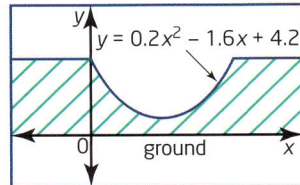

Complete the square to find the depth of the half-pipe.

19. Find the two missing values (b, c, and/or h) in each equation.

   a) $x^2 + 8x + c = (x + h)^2$
   b) $x^2 + bx + 36 = (x + h)^2$
   c) $x^2 + bx + c = (x - 5)^2 + 2$

20. The drag on a small aircraft is made up of induced drag from the wings as they produce lift and parasitic drag from the airframe. Over a limited speed range, the drag, d, in newtons, produced by a speed, v, in kilometres per hour, can be modelled by the quadratic relation $d = 0.15v^2 - 9v + 195$. Determine the speed that results in minimum drag.

21. Fred fires a toy spring from the top of a metre stick toward a cardboard box 4 m away and 1 m tall. The spring follows a path modelled by the relation $y = -x^2 + 10x - 21$. The ceiling of the room is 3.5 m above the point at which the spring is launched. Can the spring hit the box without hitting the ceiling first?

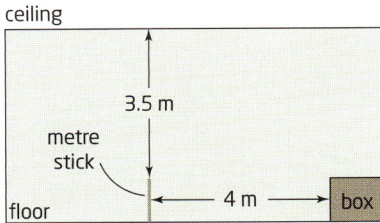

22. Use Technology Studies show that employees on an assembly line become more efficient as their level of training goes up. In one company, the number of products, P, produced per day, at a level of training of t hours, follows the quadratic model $P = -0.375t^2 + 10.25t - 8$, for $0 \leq t \leq 18$. Use a graphing calculator to determine what level of training will give the maximum productivity, rounded to the nearest tenth.

23. A pipe cleaner is 20 cm long. It is bent into a rectangle. Use a quadratic model to determine the dimensions that give the maximum area.

24. A field is bounded on one side by a river. The field is to be enclosed on three sides by a fence, to create a rectangular enclosure. The total length of fence to be used is 200 m. Use a quadratic model to determine the dimensions of the enclosure of maximum area.

Extend

25. **Use Technology** A projectile is propelled upward at various angles from the ground (known as angles of elevation), with initial velocity of 10 m/s. Use graphing technology to compare the maximum heights of the projectiles with the angles of elevation shown in the table.

Angle of Elevation	Equation
20°	$h = -4.9t^2 + 3.42t$
30°	$h = -4.9t^2 + 5.00t$
40°	$h = -4.9t^2 + 6.43t$
50°	$h = -4.9t^2 + 7.66t$
60°	$h = -4.9t^2 + 8.66t$
70°	$h = -4.9t^2 + 9.40t$

26. A parabola has a y-intercept of 5 and contains the points (3, 1) and (−1, 15). What are the coordinates of the vertex?

27. Verify that the x-coordinate of the vertex of a parabola of the form $y = ax^2 + bx + c$ is $-\dfrac{b}{2a}$.

28. **Math Contest** The maximum area for an equilateral triangle inscribed in a circle of radius R is $\dfrac{3\sqrt{3}}{4}R^2$. Determine the side length of the triangle.

29. **Math Contest** Two names from four friends, Jane, Farhad, Sonia, and Mehta, are drawn from a hat for two tickets to a concert. What is the probability that Jane and Farhad go to the concert together?

A $\dfrac{2}{3}$ B $\dfrac{1}{2}$

C $\dfrac{1}{4}$ D $\dfrac{1}{6}$

E $\dfrac{1}{12}$

30. **Math Contest** In 1920, the young nephew of American mathematician Edward Kasner coined the word *googol* to mean a really big number.
1 googol = 10^{100}
1000^{1000} is equivalent to

A 1000 googols B 3000 googols
C 30 googols D googol^{30}
E googol^{googol}

> **Did You Know?**
>
> The founders of the Internet search engine Google intended to use googol as their name. However, investors misspelled the name on a cheque.

6.2 Solve Quadratic Equations

The flight path of a toy rocket, a ball, or any projectile can be predicted using a quadratic model. This model can also be used to determine when and where a projectile will land. For example, the path of a stone thrown into a ravine is modelled by the quadratic relation $y = -x^2 + 5x + 84$, where x is the distance, in metres, it travels horizontally and y is the height, in metres, above the river at the bottom of the ravine. You can solve for x using a variety of methods, including factoring a **quadratic equation**.

quadratic equation
- an equation in the form $ax^2 + bx + c = 0$, where a, b, and c are real numbers and $a \neq 0$

Investigate

How can factoring help you solve a quadratic equation?

1. If the product of two numbers is zero, what must be true about one or both of the numbers?

2. If $a \times b = 0$, what must be true about the value of a or the value of b or both?

3. How do steps 1 and 2 relate to solving the equation $(x - 3)(x + 5) = 0$?

4. **a)** Solve the equation $(x - 3)(x + 5) = 0$.
   b) Explain why your solutions cause the left side of the equation to equal zero.

5. Use your method to solve each equation.
   a) $(x + 2)(x + 9) = 0$ **b)** $(2x + 5)(3x - 4) = 0$

6. **a)** How is the equation $x^2 + 6x + 8 = 0$ different from those in steps 3 to 5? Describe the extra steps needed to solve the equation.
   b) Solve the equation.

7. **Reflect** Describe how you can use factoring to solve a quadratic equation.

Example 1 Solve by Factoring

Solve for x. Check your answers by substitution.
a) $x^2 + 9x + 14 = 0$
b) $2x^2 + 5x = 0$
c) $6x^2 - x = 15$

> **Literacy Connections**
>
> To solve an equation means to find the values of the variable that make the statement true. This is also called finding the roots of the equation.

Solution

a) $x^2 + 9x + 14 = 0$
$(x + 7)(x + 2) = 0$ Factor the left side.
$x + 7 = 0$ or $x + 2 = 0$ One factor or the other must
$x = -7$ or $x = -2$ equal zero.

Check.
For $x = -7$:
$\text{L.S.} = x^2 + 9x + 14$ $\text{R.S.} = 0$
$= (-7)^2 + 9(-7) + 14$
$= 49 - 63 + 14$
$= 0$
$\text{L.S.} = \text{R.S.}$

For $x = -2$:
$\text{L.S.} = x^2 + 9x + 14$ $\text{R.S.} = 0$
$= (-2)^2 + 9(-2) + 14$
$= 4 - 18 + 14$
$= 0$
$\text{L.S.} = \text{R.S.}$

The solutions, or **roots**, are -7 and -2.

b) $2x^2 + 5x = 0$
$x(2x + 5) = 0$ Remove the common factor.
$x = 0$ or $2x + 5 = 0$ One factor or the other must
$2x = -5$ equal zero.
$x = -\dfrac{5}{2}$

The roots are 0 and $-\dfrac{5}{2}$. The check of these roots is left to the reader.

> **root (of an equation)**
> - the value of the variable that makes an equation true
> - the same as the solution of an equation

c)
$6x^2 - x = 15$
$6x^2 - x - 15 = 0$ Write in the form $ax^2 + bx + c = 0$.
$6x^2 - 10x + 9x - 15 = 0$ To factor the left side, break up the
$2x(3x - 5) + 3(3x - 5) = 0$ middle term and factor by grouping.
$(3x - 5)(2x + 3) = 0$
$3x - 5 = 0$ or $2x + 3 = 0$ One factor or the other must
$3x = 5$ or $2x = -3$ equal zero.
$x = \dfrac{5}{3}$ or $x = -\dfrac{3}{2}$

> To factor $6x^2 - x - 15$, I must find two integers whose product is $6 \times (-15)$, or -90, and whose sum is -1. The integers -10 and 9 work.

Check.

For $x = \dfrac{5}{3}$:

L.S. $= 6x^2 - x$ **R.S.** $= 15$
$= 6\left(\dfrac{5}{3}\right)^2 - \dfrac{5}{3}$
$= 6\left(\dfrac{25}{9}\right) - \dfrac{5}{3}$
$= \dfrac{50}{3} - \dfrac{5}{3}$
$= 15$

L.S. = R.S.

For $x = -\dfrac{3}{2}$:

L.S. $= 6x^2 - x$ **R.S.** $= 15$
$= 6\left(-\dfrac{3}{2}\right)^2 - \left(-\dfrac{3}{2}\right)$
$= 6\left(\dfrac{9}{4}\right) + \dfrac{3}{2}$
$= \dfrac{27}{2} + \dfrac{3}{2}$
$= 15$

L.S. = R.S.

The roots are $\dfrac{5}{3}$ and $-\dfrac{3}{2}$.

Example 2 Path of a Stone

The path of a stone thrown into a ravine is modelled by the quadratic relation $y = -x^2 + 5x + 84$, where x represents the distance, in metres, travelled horizontally and y represents the height, in metres, above the surface of the river at the bottom of the ravine. How far does the stone travel horizontally before it hits the water?

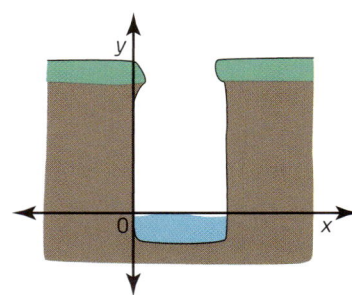

Solution

When the stone hits the water, its height is 0 m. So, let $y = 0$.

$-x^2 + 5x + 84 = 0$

$\dfrac{-x^2}{-1} + \dfrac{5x}{-1} + \dfrac{84}{-1} = \dfrac{0}{-1}$ Divide both sides of the equation by -1.

$x^2 - 5x - 84 = 0$
$(x + 7)(x - 12) = 0$ Factor the left side.
$x + 7 = 0$ or $x - 12 = 0$ One factor or the other must equal zero.
$x = -7$ or $x = 12$

Since x represents a distance, it cannot be negative. So, reject the root -7.
Check $x = 12$.

L.S. $= -x^2 + 5x + 84$ **R.S.** $= 0$
$= -(12)^2 + 5(12) + 84$
$= -144 + 60 + 84$
$= 0$

L.S. = R.S.

The stone travelled 12 m horizontally before it hit the water.

Example 3 Dimensions of a Rectangle

A rectangle has dimensions $3x + 1$ and $2x - 5$. Its area is 1150 cm². What are its dimensions?

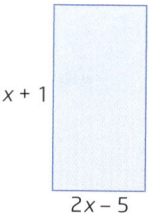

Solution

Method 1: Use Pencil and Paper

Substitute the area and expressions for the dimensions into the formula $A = l \times w$.

$$1150 = (3x + 1)(2x - 5)$$
$$1150 = 6x^2 - 13x - 5 \quad \text{Expand and simplify the right side.}$$
$$6x^2 - 13x - 1155 = 0 \quad \text{Write in the form } ax^2 + bx + c = 0.$$
$$6x^2 - 90x + 77x - 1155 = 0 \quad \text{Factor the left side.}$$
$$6x(x - 15) + 77(x - 15) = 0$$
$$(x - 15)(6x + 77) = 0$$
$$x - 15 = 0 \quad \text{or} \quad 6x + 77 = 0 \quad \text{One factor or the other must equal zero.}$$
$$x = 15 \quad \text{or} \quad x = -\frac{77}{6}$$

Since the dimensions cannot be negative, reject the solution $-\frac{77}{6}$.

Check $x = 15$.
Find the dimensions of the rectangle.

$3x + 1$ $2x - 5$
$= 3(15) + 1$ $= 2(15) - 5$
$= 46$ $= 25$

Check that these dimensions give an area of 1150 cm².
$46 \times 25 = 1150$
Therefore, the dimensions of the rectangle are 46 cm by 25 cm.

Method 2: Use a Computer Algebra System (CAS)

In the Home screen, use the **Expand** function with the area equation $(3x + 1)(2x - 5) = 1150$.

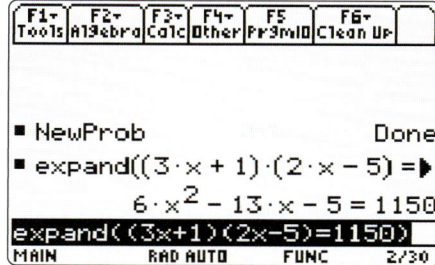

Express the equation in the form $ax^2 + bx + c = 0$.
Use the up cursor key to highlight the expanded form. Press ◆ ↑ for [COPY]. Cursor down to the command line. Press ◆ ESC for [PASTE]. Put brackets around the equation and subtract 1150. Press ENTER.

COPY and PASTE the new form of the equation into the command line. Cursor to the beginning of the equation. Press F2. Select **2:factor(**. At the end of the command line, press) ENTER.

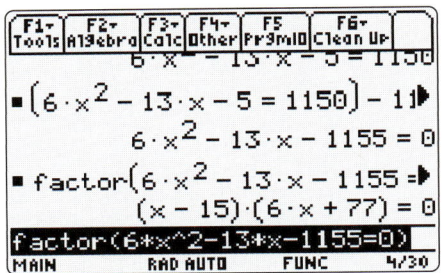

Note the two factors. The second factor results in a negative solution, and is rejected. Therefore, $x = 15$ is the solution.

To check the solution, type the original equation, followed by the *such that* symbol, | , and then $x = 15$. Press ENTER.

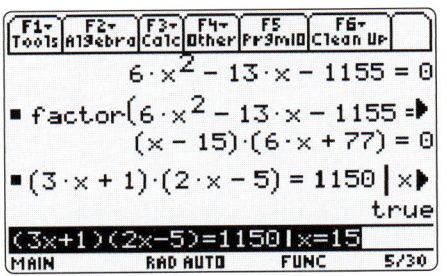

Note that the CAS returns a value of *true*.

Next, calculate the dimensions of the rectangle.
Type $3x + 1 \mid x = 15$ and press ENTER.
Type $2x - 5 \mid x = 15$ and press ENTER.

Check that these dimensions give an area of 1150 cm².
$46 \times 25 = 1150$
Therefore, the dimensions of the rectangle are 46 cm by 25 cm.

Key Concepts

- If two factors have a product of zero, then one or both of the factors must equal zero.
- A quadratic equation has degree two and has a single unknown. For example, $x^2 + 2x - 3 = 0$ is a quadratic equation.
- Some quadratic equations can be solved by factoring.
- To solve a quadratic equation by factoring, first write the equation in the form $ax^2 + bx + c = 0$, and then factor the left side. Next, set each factor equal to zero, and solve for the unknown.

    For example,
    $$x^2 + 2x = 3$$
    $$x^2 + 2x - 3 = 0$$
    $$(x + 3)(x - 1) = 0$$
    $$x + 3 = 0 \quad \text{or} \quad x - 1 = 0$$
    $$x = -3 \quad \text{or} \quad x = 1$$

- The solutions to a quadratic equation are also known as the roots of the equation.

Communicate Your Understanding

C1 When you are factoring to solve a quadratic equation such as $x^2 + 2x - 3 = 0$, the right side needs to be equal to zero. Why?

C2 Describe how you would solve each quadratic equation by factoring.
   a) $3x^2 + 12x + 9 = 0$
   b) $2x^2 - 11x = -15$

Practise

For help with questions 1 to 5, see Example 1.

1. Solve.
   a) $(x + 5)(x + 2) = 0$
   b) $(x - 3)(x + 4) = 0$
   c) $(x - 1)(x - 7) = 0$
   d) $x(x + 9) = 0$
   e) $(2x + 3)(x - 5) = 0$
   f) $(2x - 1)(3x + 4) = 0$
   g) $(3x - 5)(4x - 3) = 0$

2. Solve and check.
   a) $x^2 + 8x + 12 = 0$
   b) $h^2 + 9h + 18 = 0$
   c) $m^2 + 3m = 0$
   d) $w^2 - 18w + 56 = 0$
   e) $x^2 - 2x = 0$
   f) $c^2 - 17c + 30 = 0$
   g) $n^2 + 9n - 22 = 0$
   h) $y^2 - 11y = 0$

3. Solve.
   a) $3x^2 + 28x + 9 = 0$
   b) $4k^2 + 19k + 15 = 0$
   c) $8y^2 - 22y + 15 = 0$
   d) $16b^2 - 1 = 0$
   e) $10m^2 + 30m = 0$
   f) $4x^2 - 12x + 9 = 0$

4. Solve.
   a) $x^2 + 5x = -4$
   b) $8c + 15 = -c^2$
   c) $k^2 = 13k - 12$
   d) $b^2 + 1 = -2b$
   e) $m^2 = 300 - 20m$
   f) $y^2 = 7y$

5. Solve.
   a) $2m^2 = -7m - 6$
   b) $9x^2 = x + 8$
   c) $4y^2 - 12y = -9$
   d) $-5 = 2p - 16p^2$
   e) $12m^2 = 10 - 37m$
   f) $3w^2 + 22w = -7$

For help with questions 6 and 7, see Example 2.

6. Solve.
   a) $-x^2 - 10x - 16 = 0$
   b) $3t^2 + 24t + 45 = 0$
   c) $6d^2 + 15d = -9$
   d) $-10g^2 + 32g = 6$

Connect and Apply

7. A basketball is tossed from the top of a 3-m wall. The path of the basketball is defined by the relation $y = -x^2 + 2x + 3$, where x represents the horizontal distance travelled, in metres, and y represents the height, in metres, above the ground. How far has the basketball travelled horizontally when it lands on the ground?

For help with question 8, see Example 3.

8. A rectangle has dimensions $x + 10$ and $2x - 3$. Determine the value of x that gives an area of 54 cm².

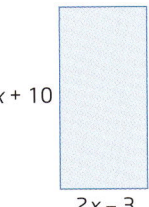

9. Write a quadratic equation in factored form for each situation.
   a) The roots of the equation are 5 and 4.
   b) The roots of the equation are -2 and 3.

10. a) Write a quadratic equation in the form $ax^2 + bx + c = 0$ with roots of 6 and -7.
    b) What would happen to the roots if you multiplied both sides of the equation in part a) by 3? Explain.

11. Write a quadratic equation with roots of $\frac{2}{3}$ and $-\frac{4}{5}$ in the form $ax^2 + bx + c = 0$, where a, b, and c are integers.

12. a) Create an example of a quadratic equation that can be factored and solved with integer solutions.
    b) Create an example of a quadratic equation that can be factored and solved with non-integer solutions.

13. Create an example of a quadratic equation that cannot be solved by factoring. Explain why it cannot be factored.

14. The hypotenuse of a right triangle measures 29 cm. One leg is 1 cm shorter than the other. What are the lengths of the legs?

15. For the equation $3n^2 = 15n$, Chris suggested dividing both sides by $3n$, leaving $n = 5$. Are there any other values that satisfy this equation? What is wrong with Chris's method? What is a more appropriate method?

16. The sum of the first n even natural numbers can be found using the formula $S = n(n + 1)$.

a) Verify the formula for $n = 1$ and $n = 2$.

b) What is the sum of the first five even natural numbers?

c) The sum of the first n even natural numbers is 306. What is the value of n?

17. At the Mini Market, as the price of milk drops, sales increase. On an average day, a 4-L bag of milk costs $3.90, and the store sells an average of 120 bags. For each $0.10 reduction in price of a 4-L bag, sales increase by 20 bags per day. The price and value of sales can be modelled as follows, where n is the number of $0.10 price reductions.

Price, in dollars: $3.90 - 0.10n$
Number of bags: $120 + 20n$

The total revenue is the product of the price and the number of bags sold. Find how many price reductions will result in revenue of $700.

? Did You Know?

According to the Canadian Dairy Information Centre, in 2005 the per capita consumption of fluid milk in Canada was 84.00 L. Fluid milk includes 3.25%, 2%, 1%, skim, chocolate, and buttermilk.

For the same year, Finland had the greatest per capita retail milk consumption, 116.99 L, while China had the least, 2.55 L.

Achievement Check

18. The length of the base of a rectangular prism is 2 m greater than the width, and the height of the prism is 15 m.

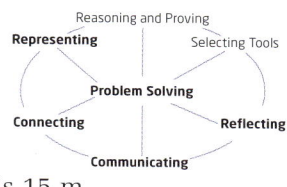

a) Write an algebraic expression for the volume of the rectangular prism. Express the relation in the form $y = a(x - h)^2 + k$.

b) If the volume of the prism is 2145 m³, write an equation to model the situation.

c) Solve the equation by factoring. What are the dimensions of the base of the rectangular prism?

d) Make up a similar problem. Trade with a partner and solve each other's problem.

Extend

19. The length of a rectangular plot of land is 7 m greater than its width. The diagonal is 8 m greater than the width of the plot of land. What are the dimensions of the plot of land?

20. Ralph is opening a BMX bike repair shop. His accountant models his profit, P, with the equation $P = 1125(t - 1)^2 - 4500$, where t is the number of years of operation. During the first 5 years of operation, when is Ralph's shop predicted to make a loss? a profit?

21. a) Solve the equation $y^2 + 3y + 2 = 0$. How is the equation $y^2 + 3yx + 2x^2 = 0$ related?

b) Solve for y in terms of x.

i) $y^2 + 3yx + 2x^2 = 0$

ii) $5y^2 - 6yx - 8x^2 = 0$

iii) $\dfrac{1}{9}y^2 - \dfrac{1}{3}yx + \dfrac{1}{4}x^2 = 0$

6.3 Graph Quadratics Using the *x*-Intercepts

In Chapter 4, you graphed quadratic relations of the form $y = a(x - r)(x - s)$ by using the *x*-intercepts. In this section, you will use *x*-intercepts to graph parabolas with equations of the form $y = ax^2 + bx + c$. With these skills, you will be able to calculate, for example, the width of an arch or the time it takes for a projectile to land on the ground.

Investigate A

How can you use factoring to graph a quadratic relation?

Tools
- grid paper

1. Compare the information you can get from quadratic relations of the form $y = ax^2 + bx + c$, $y = (ax + b)(cx + d)$, and $y = a(x - h)^2 + k$. Which form is easiest to use for finding the vertex? the *x*-intercepts? the *y*-intercept?

2. Consider the quadratic relation $y = (x - 2)(x + 4)$.
   a) Explain how you would find the *x*-intercepts. Find and plot the *x*-intercepts.
   b) How can you find the *x*-coordinate of the vertex? Explain why this method is appropriate.
   c) Find the *x*-coordinate of the vertex. Then, calculate the *y*-coordinate.
   d) Plot the vertex and sketch the graph of the quadratic relation.

3. For each relation, find the *x*-intercepts, the equation of the axis of symmetry, and the coordinates of the vertex. Use the information to sketch the graph.
   a) $y = (x + 5)(x + 1)$ b) $y = 2(2x - 1)(2x + 3)$

4. How would you find the *x*-intercepts and graph the following quadratic relations?
   a) $y = x^2 + 3x - 10$ b) $y = 6x^2 - 17x + 5$

5. **Reflect** Summarize your findings about how to use factoring to graph a quadratic relation of the form $y = ax^2 + bx + c$.

Investigate B

How are the *x*-intercepts of a quadratic relation related to the roots of the corresponding quadratic equation?

Tools
- TI-83 Plus or TI-84 Plus graphing calculator

1. **a)** Graph the relation $y = x^2 - 3x - 4$ as **Y1**. Press ZOOM and select **6:ZStandard**.

   b) Find the **zeros** of the relation.
   - Press 2nd [CALC] to display the **CALCULATE** menu, and select **2:zero**.
   - Move the cursor to the left of one *x*-intercept and press ENTER.
   - Move the cursor to the right of the *x*-intercept and press ENTER.
   - Move the cursor closer to the *x*-intercept and press ENTER.

   The calculator will give you the approximate ordered pair that best represents the location of the *x*-intercept. Repeat for the other *x*-intercept.

   c) What is the *y*-coordinate of each zero?

2. For the quadratic relation $y = x^2 - 3x - 4$, the corresponding quadratic equation is $x^2 - 3x - 4 = 0$.

   a) For which points on the graph of $y = x^2 - 3x - 4$ are the *x*-coordinates roots of $x^2 - 3x - 4 = 0$? Explain.

   b) How can you use these points to write the factors of the corresponding quadratic equation?

   c) Graph the factors as **Y2** and **Y3**. Explain why the graphs of the lines pass through the *x*-intercepts of the graph of the quadratic relation.

   d) Graph the product of the factors as **Y4**. Does a fourth graph appear in the window? What conclusion can you make?

3. Use the graphs to connect the values of factors to the quadratic relation.

   a) Find the values of the factors at $x = 1$. Verify that their product lies on the quadratic.
   - Press 2nd [CALC], select **1:value**, type 1, and press ENTER.
   - Use the up and down cursor keys to move from one graph to another.

   b) Use the procedure in part a) to examine the values of the factors at the *x*-intercepts, $x = -1$ and $x = 4$. Do both factors have a value of 0 at the *x*-intercepts? Explain.

4. Will a constant factor affect the graph of the quadratic relation?

   a) Graph $y = 2(x + 1)(x - 4)$ as **Y5**. Use the window settings shown.

   b) How is this graph different from that of $y = (x + 1)(x - 4)$? How is it similar?

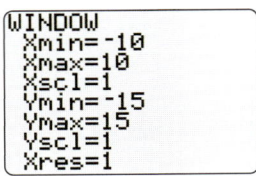

5. **Reflect** Explain how the x-intercepts, or zeros, of a quadratic relation are related to the corresponding quadratic equation.

Many quadratic relations of the form $y = ax^2 + bx + c$ can be factored to find the x-intercepts. By the definition of the x-intercepts, $y = 0$. For any product to equal zero, one or both of the factors must equal zero. For this reason, the x-intercepts are also known as the zeros of the quadratic relation.

For example, for the relation $y = (x - 2)(x + 5)$, the zeros occur when $y = 0$. If $(x - 2)(x + 5) = 0$, then either $x - 2 = 0$ or $x + 5 = 0$.

You can solve for x. Either $x = 2$ or $x = -5$.

Example 1 Use Factoring to Graph a Quadratic Relation

Find the x-intercepts and the coordinates of the vertex. Then, sketch each parabola.

a) $y = x^2 + 8x + 7$

b) $y = 2x^2 - x - 6$

c) $y = -x^2 + 6x - 9$

Solution

a) To find the x-intercepts, factor and solve the corresponding quadratic equation by letting $y = 0$.

$y = x^2 + 8x + 7$
$0 = x^2 + 8x + 7$
$0 = (x + 1)(x + 7)$
$x + 1 = 0$ or $x + 7 = 0$
    $x = -1$ or $x = -7$

The x-intercepts are -1 and -7.

Due to the symmetric property of a parabola, the x-coordinate of the vertex is on the axis of symmetry that passes through the midpoint of the line segment connecting the x-intercepts.

$x = \dfrac{-1 + (-7)}{2}$

$ = -4$

To find the y-coordinate of the vertex, substitute $x = -4$ into the equation of the parabola.

$y = x^2 + 8x + 7$
$ = (-4)^2 + 8(-4) + 7$
$ = 16 - 32 + 7$
$ = -9$

The coordinates of the vertex are $(-4, -9)$.

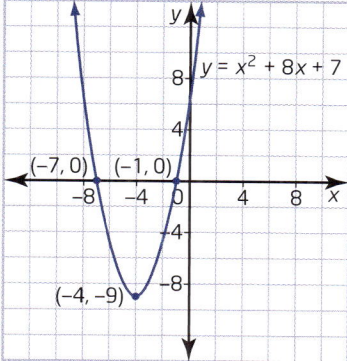

b) Factor and solve the corresponding quadratic equation.

$y = 2x^2 - x - 6$
$0 = 2x^2 - x - 6$
$0 = 2x^2 + 3x - 4x - 6$
$0 = x(2x + 3) - 2(2x + 3)$
$0 = (2x + 3)(x - 2)$
$2x + 3 = 0 \quad\quad \text{or} \quad\quad x - 2 = 0$
$x = -\dfrac{3}{2} \quad\quad \text{or} \quad\quad x = 2$

To factor $2x^2 - x - 6$, I need to find two integers whose product is $2 \times (-6)$, or -12, and whose sum is -1. These integers are 3 and -4.

The x-intercepts are $-\dfrac{3}{2}$ and 2.

Now, find the x-coordinate of the vertex.

$x = \dfrac{-\dfrac{3}{2} + 2}{2}$
$ = \dfrac{\dfrac{1}{2}}{2}$
$ = \dfrac{1}{4}$

Then, use its value to find the y-coordinate.

$y = 2x^2 - x - 6$
$ = 2\left(\dfrac{1}{4}\right)^2 - \dfrac{1}{4} - 6$
$ = \dfrac{2}{16} - \dfrac{1}{4} - 6$
$ = \dfrac{1}{8} - \dfrac{2}{8} - \dfrac{48}{8}$
$ = -\dfrac{49}{8}$

The coordinates of the vertex are $\left(\dfrac{1}{4}, -\dfrac{49}{8}\right)$.

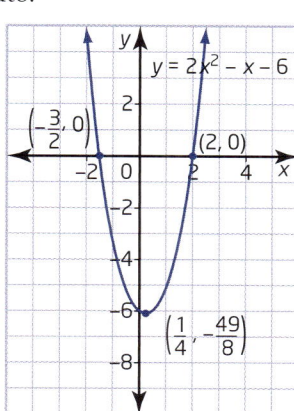

6.3 Graph Quadratics Using the x-Intercepts • MHR **285**

c) Factor and solve the corresponding quadratic equation.

$y = -x^2 + 6x - 9$
$0 = -x^2 + 6x - 9$
$0 = -(x^2 - 6x + 9)$
$0 = -(x - 3)^2$

After I factor out −1, the expression inside the brackets is a perfect square trinomial.

There is a single x-intercept at $x = 3$. Because of symmetry, all points except the vertex have a partner. Since this point has no partner, it is the vertex. Therefore, the coordinates of the vertex are (3, 0).

Find two more points on the parabola.

Let $x = 0$. Then $y = -9$.

I can choose any value for x, but x = 0 is easy to calculate.

The partner point to (0, −9) is (6, −9).

Plot the three points and complete the sketch.

I know that the axis of symmetry is a vertical line passing through the vertex. So, by comparing the x-coordinates of (0, −9) and the vertex (3, 0), I know that (0, −9) is located 3 units to the left of the axis of symmetry. Then, its partner is located 3 units to the right of the axis of symmetry and has the same y-coordinate.

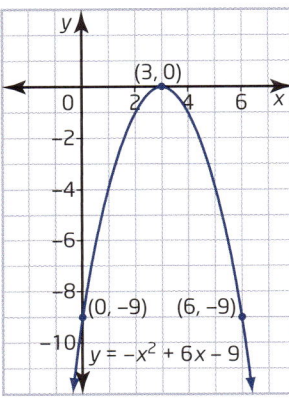

In Example 1, you looked at parabolas with two x-intercepts or one x-intercept. You will investigate parabolas with no x-intercepts in Section 6.4.

Example 2 Find an Equation From a Graph

Write an equation in the form $y = ax^2 + bx + c$ for the parabola shown.

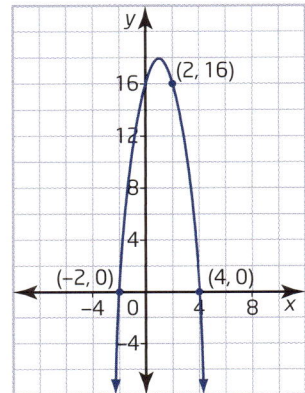

Solution

Since the x-intercepts are -2 and 4, the equation has the form
$y = a(x + 2)(x - 4)$.

To find a, substitute $(x, y) = (2, 16)$.
$16 = a(2 + 2)(2 - 4)$
$16 = -8a$
$-2 = a$
$y = -2(x + 2)(x - 4)$
$ = -2(x^2 - 2x - 8)$
$ = -2x^2 + 4x + 16$

Example 3 Design an Arch

To commemorate the 100th anniversary of the Newtonville Fair, an entrance arch will be built. The design engineer uses the equation $h = -d^2 + 16$ to model the arch, where h is the height, in metres, above the ground and d is the horizontal distance, in metres, from the centre of the arch.

a) How wide and how tall is the arch?

b) For what values of d is the relation valid? Explain.

c) If a width of 2.5 m is needed per line-up at the entrance, how many line-ups can there be?

Solution

a) $h = -d^2 + 16$
$0 = -(d^2 - 16)$
$0 = -(d - 4)(d + 4)$

The expression inside the brackets is a difference of squares.

The d-intercepts are 4 and -4, which are symmetric about the h-axis.

The arch is 8 m wide at its base.

At $d = 0$, $h = 16$. The arch is 16 m tall at the centre.

b) The relation is valid for $-4 \leq d \leq 4$. Negative values of d represent distances on the opposite side of the axis of symmetry of those on the positive side.

c) $8 \div 2.5 = 3.2$

The entrance arch could accommodate three line-ups.

Key Concepts

- The x-intercepts of some quadratic relations in the form $y = ax^2 + bx + c$ can be found by factoring.
- A quadratic relation can be graphed by using its x-intercepts.

  For example, to find the x-intercepts of the quadratic relation $y = x^2 - 2x - 3$, factor and solve the corresponding quadratic equation by letting $y = 0$.
  $$x^2 - 2x - 3 = 0$$
  $$(x - 3)(x + 1) = 0$$
  $$x - 3 = 0 \quad \text{or} \quad x + 1 = 0$$
  $$x = 3 \quad \text{or} \quad x = -1$$
  Since the roots of $x^2 - 2x - 3 = 0$ are 3 and -1, the x-intercepts of $y = x^2 - 2x - 3$ are 3 and -1.

- The x-intercepts, or zeros, of a quadratic relation $y = ax^2 + bx + c$ are the solutions to $ax^2 + bx + c = 0$.
- The x-coordinate of the vertex is on the axis of symmetry, which passes through the midpoint of the line segment connecting the x-intercepts. Substitute this value into the quadratic relation to find the y-coordinate of the vertex.
- When the x-intercepts and one other point are known, the information can be substituted into $y = a(x - r)(x - s)$ to find an equation representing the relation.

Communicate Your Understanding

C1 Describe the steps involved in finding the x-intercepts of the parabola with equation $y = x^2 - 3x - 70$.

C2 Explain why you can find the x-coordinate of the vertex of a quadratic relation by using the midpoint of the line segment connecting the x-intercepts.

Practise

For help with questions 1 to 5, see Example 1.

1. Find the x-intercepts.
   a) $y = x^2 + 5x + 6$
   b) $y = x^2 - 11x + 28$
   c) $y = x^2 + 9x$
   d) $y = x^2 + 5x - 24$
   e) $y = x^2 - 2x - 8$
   f) $y = x^2 + 9x - 36$

2. Find the x-intercepts.
   a) $y = 4x^2 + 20x + 9$
   b) $y = 8x^2 - 6x$
   c) $y = 6x^2 - 11x - 7$
   d) $y = 5x^2 + 6x - 8$
   e) $y = 3x^2 - 13x + 4$
   f) $y = 4x^2 - 20x + 25$

3. Find the x-intercepts and the vertex of each parabola. Then, sketch its graph.
   a) $y = x^2 + 9x + 14$
   b) $y = x^2 - 6x + 8$
   c) $y = -x^2 - 4x + 5$
   d) $y = -x^2 - 5x$

4. Find the x-intercepts and the vertex of each parabola. Then, sketch its graph.
   a) $y = x^2 - 9$
   b) $y = -x^2 + 10x - 9$
   c) $y = x^2 - 12x + 36$
   d) $y = 16 - x^2$

5. Find the zeros and the vertex of each parabola. Then, sketch its graph. Check your results with a graphing calculator.
   a) $y = 2x^2 + 15x + 7$
   b) $y = 12x^2 - 16x + 5$
   c) $y = -8x^2 - 13x + 6$
   d) $y = 8x^2 + 17x + 9$
   e) $y = 16x^2 - 24x + 9$
   f) $y = -4x^2 - 18x - 8$

For help with questions 6 and 7, see Example 2.

6. Write an equation, in the form $y = ax^2 + bx + c$, to represent each parabola.

   a)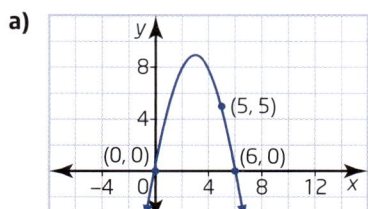

   b)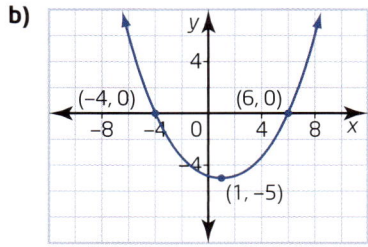

7. Write an equation, in the form $y = ax^2 + bx + c$, to represent each parabola.

   a)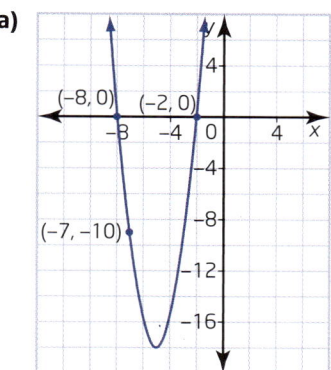

   b)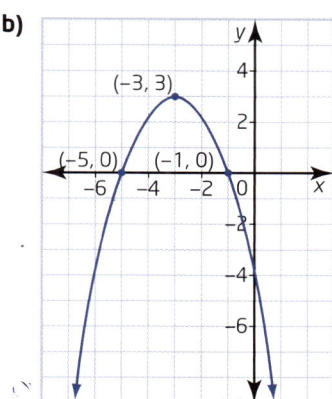

   c)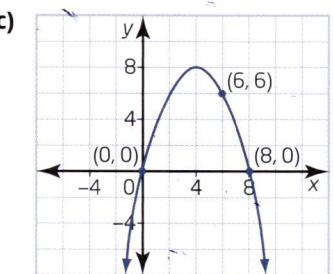

   d)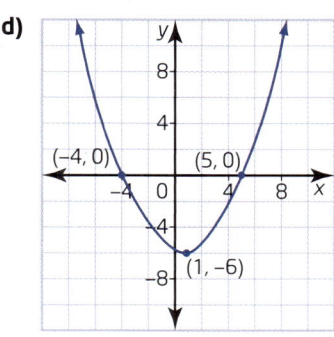

Connect and Apply

For help with question 8, see Example 3.

8. The parabolic cross section of a metal garage is modelled by the relation $h = -d^2 + 4$, where h is the height, in metres, above the ground and d is the horizontal distance, in metres, from the centre of the garage.
   a) How wide and how tall is the garage?
   b) Sketch a graph to represent the cross section.
   c) For what values of d is the relation valid? Explain.

9. The path of a toy rocket is defined by the relation $y = -3x^2 + 11x + 4$, where x is the horizontal distance, in metres, travelled and y is the height, in metres, above the ground.
   a) Determine the zeros of the relation.
   b) For what values of x is the relation valid?
   c) How far has the rocket travelled horizontally when it lands on the ground?
   d) What is the maximum height of the rocket above the ground, to the nearest hundredth of a metre?

10. A parabolic arch supports a bridge. The arch is 200 m wide at its base and 4 m tall in the middle.
    a) Show this information on a graph by placing the vertex on the y-axis so that the x-axis represents the base of the arch.
    b) How high is a point on the arch that is 20 m horizontally from one end?

11. A parabola has vertex $(-3, 7)$, and one x-intercept is -11. Find the other x-intercept and the y-intercept.

12. The path of a kicked ball can be defined by the equation $h = -\frac{1}{35}d^2 + \frac{16}{35}d + \frac{36}{35}$, where h is its height, in metres, above the ground and d is the horizontal distance, in metres.
    a) Find the d-intercepts.
    b) Sketch a graph of this relation.
    c) For what values of d is this relation valid? Explain.
    d) At what height was the ball kicked?
    e) How far had the ball travelled when it landed on the ground?

13. The paved surface of a road has a parabolic cross section, so that rainwater flows off the surface to the edges. The cross section of the road can be modelled as $d = -\frac{1}{125}w^2 + \frac{2}{25}w$, where d is the depth, in metres, of the road relative to the gravel base, and w is the width, in metres, from one curb.
    a) Sketch a graph of this relation.
    b) For what values of w is this relation valid? Explain.
    c) How wide is the road?
    d) How high does the road rise from the gravel base?

14. Explain what must be true for a parabola to have only one x-intercept.

15. Find the value(s) of n so that each quadratic relation has only one zero. Then, sketch its graph.
    a) $y = x^2 + nx + 25$
    b) $y = -x^2 + nx - 9$
    c) $y = 16x^2 - 8x + n$

16. In a science competition, two teams of students each design a machine to catapult a marble horizontally as far as possible, from a height of 3 m. The following equations represent the paths of the marbles for the teams, where x is the horizontal distance, in metres, and y is the height, in metres, above the ground.

The Marble Heads: $y = -x^2 + 2x + 3$
The XY Team: $y = -2x^2 + x + 3$

a) Which team's marble travels farther? How much farther?

b) At what horizontal distance are both marbles at the same height?

c) Which team's marble flies higher?

Extend

17. The cross section of the roof of an airplane hangar is parabolic. Its profile can be defined by the equation $y = -\dfrac{1}{100}x^2 + 50$, where y is the height, in metres, above the ground and x is the width, in metres, from the centre of the building. A Bombardier Canadair CRJ-700 jet airplane has a wingspan of 23.24 m.

a) How many CRJ-700s can fit side by side inside the hangar?

b) If you assume that the wings are 2 m above the floor of the hangar, does your answer in part a) change?

18. a) The parabolas shown do not have any x-intercepts. Use your knowledge of transformations to create an example of an equation that could be represented by each parabola.

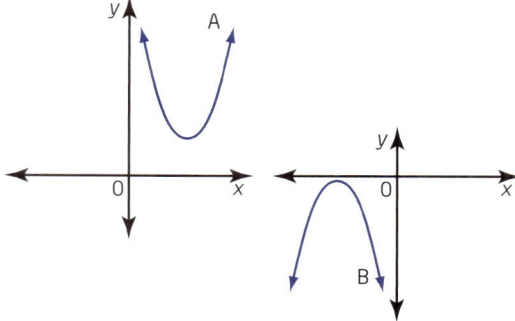

b) Explain how you know that the equations for these parabolas cannot be factored.

19. A parabola has equation $y = 4x^2 + x + c$. One x-intercept is -3. What is the value of c?

20. Sketch the graph of $y = x^2 + 4$. Are there any x-intercepts? Use this information to explain why $a^2 + b^2$ cannot be factored.

21. Math Contest Solve for x.

a) $3^{2x} - 12(3^x) + 27 = 0$

b) $2^{2x} - 3(2^{x+3}) + 128 = 0$

22. Math Contest

a) In a family of three children, determine the probability that there are exactly two boys.

b) John is one of three children. What is the probability that there are exactly two boys in John's family?

c) Explain the similarities or differences in your answers to parts a) and b).

6.4 The Quadratic Formula

Quadratic equations that can be factored are fairly simple to solve. But what about quadratics that cannot be factored? The Greek mathematicians Euclid (300 BCE) and Pythagoras (500 BCE) both derived geometric solutions to a quadratic equation. A general solution for quadratic equations, using numbers, was derived in about 700 AD by the Hindu mathematician Brahmagupta. The general formula used today was derived in about 1100 AD by another Hindu mathematician, Bhaskara. He was also the first to recognize that any positive number has two square roots, one positive and one negative.

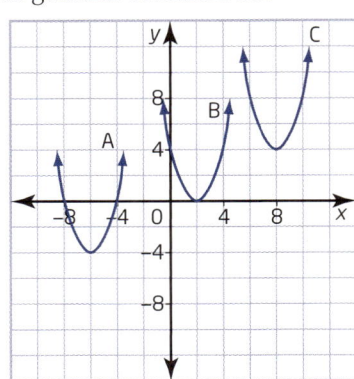

For each parabola shown, how many real roots does the related quadratic equation have?

Investigate A

Tools
- grid paper

How can you use the process of completing the square to solve quadratic equations?

1. Graph the relation $y = x^2 - 9$. How many x-intercepts are there?

2. a) Solve the equation $x^2 - 9 = 0$ by isolating x^2 first.
   b) How many roots are there?
   c) How do the roots relate to the graph in step 1?

3. a) Graph the relation $y = (x + 2)^2 - 9$. How many x-intercepts are there?
   b) Solve the equation $(x + 2)^2 - 9 = 0$ by isolating the perfect square, $(x + 2)^2$, then taking the square root of both sides, and finally solving for x. Remember that there are two square roots.
   c) How many roots are there? How do the roots relate to the graph in part a)?

4. a) Solve the equation $x^2 + 10x + 16 = 0$ by first completing the square.
   b) Describe the steps you used to solve for x.

5. **Reflect** Would the method you used to solve the quadratic equation in step 4 work for any quadratic equation? Explain.

6. Use your method to solve each quadratic equation.
   a) $3x^2 + 30x + 48 = 0$
   b) $5x^2 - 20x - 52 = 0$

Investigate B

How can you use completing the square to derive a formula for solving quadratic equations?

By completing the square, you can develop a formula that can be used to solve any quadratic equation. Copy the calculations in the table. Describe the steps in the example and how they relate to the development of the **quadratic formula**.

Example	Quadratic Formula
$2x^2 + 5x + 1 = 0$	$ax^2 + bx + c = 0$
$x^2 + \frac{5}{2}x + \frac{1}{2} = 0$	$x^2 + \frac{b}{a}x + \frac{c}{a} = 0$
$\left(x^2 + \frac{5}{2}x + \left(\frac{5}{4}\right)^2 - \left(\frac{5}{4}\right)^2\right) + \frac{1}{2} = 0$	$\left(x^2 + \frac{b}{a}x + \left(\frac{b}{2a}\right)^2 - \left(\frac{b}{2a}\right)^2\right) + \frac{c}{a} = 0$
$\left(x^2 + \frac{5}{2}x + \left(\frac{5}{4}\right)^2\right) - \left(\frac{5}{4}\right)^2 + \frac{1}{2} = 0$	$\left(x^2 + \frac{b}{a}x + \left(\frac{b}{2a}\right)^2\right) - \left(\frac{b}{2a}\right)^2 + \frac{c}{a} = 0$
$\left(x + \frac{5}{4}\right)^2 - \frac{25}{16} + \frac{1}{2} = 0$	$\left(x + \frac{b}{2a}\right)^2 - \frac{b^2}{4a^2} + \frac{c}{a} = 0$
$\left(x + \frac{5}{4}\right)^2 - \frac{25}{16} + \frac{8}{16} = 0$	$\left(x + \frac{b}{2a}\right)^2 - \frac{b^2}{4a^2} + \frac{4ac}{4a^2} = 0$
$\left(x + \frac{5}{4}\right)^2 - \frac{17}{16} = 0$	$\left(x + \frac{b}{2a}\right)^2 - \frac{b^2 - 4ac}{4a^2} = 0$
$\left(x + \frac{5}{4}\right)^2 = \frac{17}{16}$	$\left(x + \frac{b}{2a}\right)^2 = \frac{b^2 - 4ac}{4a^2}$
$x + \frac{5}{4} = \pm\sqrt{\frac{17}{16}}$	$x + \frac{b}{2a} = \pm\sqrt{\frac{b^2 - 4ac}{4a^2}}$
$x + \frac{5}{4} = \pm\frac{\sqrt{17}}{4}$	$x + \frac{b}{2a} = \pm\frac{\sqrt{b^2 - 4ac}}{2a}$
$x = -\frac{5}{4} \pm \frac{\sqrt{17}}{4}$	$x = -\frac{b}{2a} \pm \frac{\sqrt{b^2 - 4ac}}{2a}$
$x = \frac{-5 \pm \sqrt{17}}{4}$	$x = \frac{-b \pm \sqrt{b^2 - 4ac}}{2a}$

quadratic formula
- a formula for determining the roots of a quadratic equation of the form $ax^2 + bx + c = 0$, $a \neq 0$
- $x = \frac{-b \pm \sqrt{b^2 - 4ac}}{2a}$

Example 1 Real Roots

Use the quadratic formula to solve each quadratic equation. Where necessary, round to the nearest hundredth.
Verify graphically using technology.

a) $2x^2 + 9x + 6 = 0$

b) $4x^2 - 12x = -9$

Solution

a) For $2x^2 + 9x + 6 = 0$, $a = 2$, $b = 9$, and $c = 6$.

$$x = \frac{-b \pm \sqrt{b^2 - 4ac}}{2a}$$

$$= \frac{-9 \pm \sqrt{9^2 - 4(2)(6)}}{2(2)}$$

$$= \frac{-9 \pm \sqrt{81 - 48}}{4}$$

$$= \frac{-9 \pm \sqrt{33}}{4}$$

The exact roots are $\dfrac{-9 + \sqrt{33}}{4}$ and $\dfrac{-9 - \sqrt{33}}{4}$.

You can also express the answers as approximate roots.

$$x = \frac{-9 + \sqrt{33}}{4} \quad \text{or} \quad x = \frac{-9 - \sqrt{33}}{4}$$
$$\doteq -0.81 \qquad\qquad\qquad \doteq -3.69$$

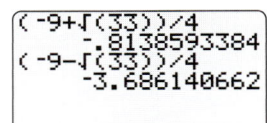

The approximate roots are -0.81 and -3.69, to the nearest hundredth.

Use the Zero operation of a graphing calculator to verify that the roots are the zeros of the related quadratic relation $y = 2x^2 + 9x + 6$.

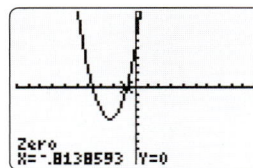 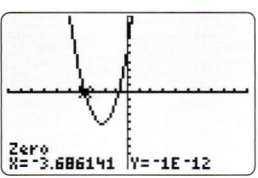

Technology Tip

When a graphing calculator displays a result such as $-1E-12$, it represents a number in scientific notation.

$-1E-12 = -1 \times 10^{-12}$

b) First, write $4x^2 - 12x = -9$ in the form $ax^2 + bx + c = 0$.
$4x^2 - 12x + 9 = 0$
For $4x^2 - 12x + 9 = 0$, $a = 4$, $b = -12$, and $c = 9$.

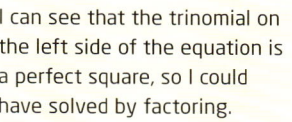
I can see that the trinomial on the left side of the equation is a perfect square, so I could have solved by factoring.

$$x = \frac{-b \pm \sqrt{b^2 - 4ac}}{2a}$$

$$= \frac{-(-12) \pm \sqrt{(-12)^2 - 4(4)(9)}}{2(4)}$$

$$= \frac{12 \pm \sqrt{144 - 144}}{8}$$

$$= \frac{12 \pm \sqrt{0}}{8}$$

$$= \frac{12}{8}$$

$$= \frac{3}{2}$$

The root is $\frac{3}{2}$ or 1.5.

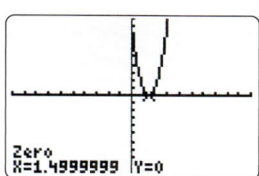

When the x-intercepts are known, you can find the x-coordinate of the vertex by finding the midpoint of the line segment connecting the x-intercepts.

Use the two x-intercepts from the quadratic formula.

$$x = \frac{\frac{-b + \sqrt{b^2 - 4ac}}{2a} + \frac{-b - \sqrt{b^2 - 4ac}}{2a}}{2}$$

$$= \frac{\frac{-b + \sqrt{b^2 - 4ac} - b - \sqrt{b^2 - 4ac}}{2a}}{2}$$

$$= \frac{\frac{-2b}{2a}}{2}$$

$$= \frac{-2b}{4a}$$

$$= -\frac{b}{2a}$$

The square root expressions have a zero sum.
$\sqrt{b^2 - 4ac} - \sqrt{b^2 - 4ac} = 0$

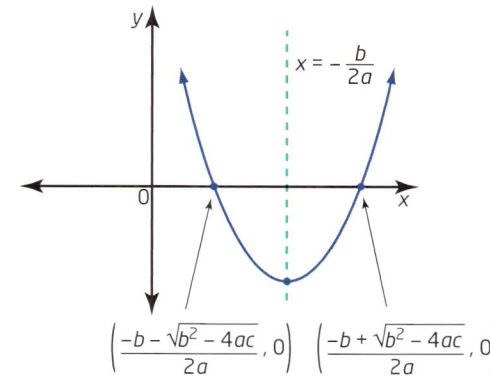

The x-coordinate of the vertex is $-\frac{b}{2a}$.

This also gives the equation of the axis of symmetry, $x = -\frac{b}{2a}$.

Example 2 Use the Quadratic Formula to Sketch a Parabola

Find the x-intercepts, the vertex, and the equation of the axis of symmetry of the quadratic relation $y = -5x^2 + 8x - 3$. Sketch the parabola.

Solution

To find the x-intercepts, let $y = 0$ and use the quadratic formula to solve the quadratic equation.

For $-5x^2 + 8x - 3 = 0$, $a = -5$, $b = 8$, and $c = -3$.

$$\begin{aligned} x &= \frac{-b \pm \sqrt{b^2 - 4ac}}{2a} \\ &= \frac{-8 \pm \sqrt{8^2 - 4(-5)(-3)}}{2(-5)} \\ &= \frac{-8 \pm \sqrt{64 - 60}}{-10} \\ &= \frac{-8 \pm \sqrt{4}}{-10} \\ &= \frac{-8 \pm 2}{-10} \end{aligned}$$

Therefore,

$$x = \frac{-8 - 2}{-10} \quad \text{or} \quad x = \frac{-8 + 2}{-10}$$

$$= 1 \qquad\qquad\qquad = \frac{3}{5} \text{ or } 0.6$$

The x-intercepts are 0.6 and 1.

To find the x-coordinate of the vertex, use $x = -\dfrac{b}{2a}$.

$$\begin{aligned} x &= -\frac{8}{2(-5)} \\ &= -\frac{8}{-10} \\ &= \frac{4}{5} \text{ or } 0.8 \end{aligned}$$

> I can check this one mentally. The x-coordinate of the midpoint of the line segment connecting the x-intercepts, 0.6 and 1, is 0.8.

Substitute $x = 0.8$ into $y = -5x^2 + 8x - 3$ to find the y-coordinate of the vertex.

$$\begin{aligned} y &= -5(0.8)^2 + 8(0.8) - 3 \\ &= -3.2 + 6.4 - 3 \\ &= 0.2 \end{aligned}$$

The coordinates of the vertex are (0.8, 0.2). The axis of symmetry has equation $x = 0.8$.

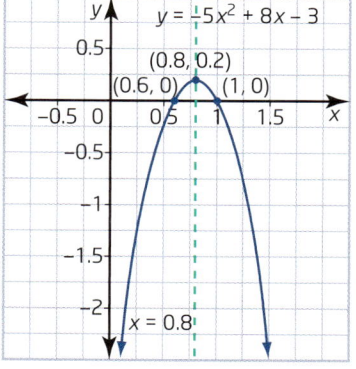

Example 3 Connect a Parabola and No Real Roots

A parabola has equation $y = (x - 2)^2 + 3$.
- **a)** State the coordinates of the vertex, the equation of the axis of symmetry, and the direction of opening.
- **b)** Determine the x-intercepts. Verify using the quadratic formula.
- **c)** Sketch the parabola.

Solution

a) The vertex is (2, 3). The equation of the axis of symmetry is $x = 2$. The parabola opens upward, since a is positive.

b) Since the vertex of the parabola is above the x-axis and it opens upward, it has no x-intercepts. This can be verified using the quadratic formula after expanding and simplifying the original equation.

$$y = (x - 2)^2 + 3$$
$$= x^2 - 4x + 4 + 3$$
$$= x^2 - 4x + 7$$

Let $y = 0$ and use the quadratic formula with $a = 1$, $b = -4$, and $c = 7$.

$$x = \frac{-b \pm \sqrt{b^2 - 4ac}}{2a}$$

$$= \frac{-(-4) \pm \sqrt{(-4)^2 - 4(1)(7)}}{2(1)}$$

$$= \frac{4 \pm \sqrt{16 - 28}}{2}$$

$$= \frac{4 \pm \sqrt{-12}}{2}$$

Since the square root of a negative number is not a real number, there are no real roots.

Therefore, the parabola has no x-intercepts.

c) Let $x = 0$. A second point on the curve is (0, 7).

> Looking at the x-coordinate of this point, I know that it is located 2 units to the left of the axis of symmetry. So, its partner is located 2 units to the right of the axis of symmetry and has the same y-coordinate.

Then, due to symmetry, the partner point on the parabola is (4, 7).

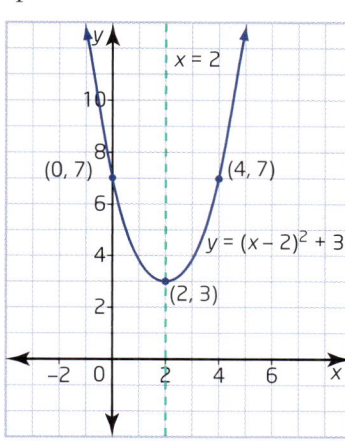

Example 4 Path of a Basketball

The path of a basketball after it is thrown from a height of 1.5 m above the ground is given by the equation
$h = -0.25d^2 + 2d + 1.5$,
where h is the height, in metres, and d is the horizontal distance, in metres.

a) How far has the ball travelled horizontally, to the nearest tenth of a metre, when it lands on the ground?

b) Find the horizontal distance when the basketball is at a height of 4.5 m above the ground.

Solution

a) When the basketball lands on the ground, the height is 0 m. Let $h = 0$.
For $-0.25d^2 + 2d + 1.5 = 0$, $a = -0.25$, $b = 2$, and $c = 1.5$.

$$d = \frac{-b \pm \sqrt{b^2 - 4ac}}{2a}$$

$$= \frac{-2 \pm \sqrt{2^2 - 4(-0.25)(1.5)}}{2(-0.25)}$$

$$= \frac{-2 \pm \sqrt{4 + 1.5}}{-0.5}$$

$$= \frac{-2 \pm \sqrt{5.5}}{-0.5}$$

So, $d \doteq -0.7$ or $d \doteq 8.7$.

Since d represents distance, it must be positive.
The basketball has travelled a horizontal distance of about 8.7 m when it lands on the ground.

b) Let $h = 4.5$.
$$-0.25d^2 + 2d + 1.5 = 4.5$$
$$-0.25d^2 + 2d - 3 = 0$$

> I need to express the equation in the form $ax^2 + bx + c = 0$.

For $-0.25d^2 + 2d - 3 = 0$, $a = -0.25$, $b = 2$, and $c = -3$.

$$d = \frac{-b \pm \sqrt{b^2 - 4ac}}{2a}$$
$$= \frac{-2 \pm \sqrt{2^2 - 4(-0.25)(-3)}}{2(-0.25)}$$
$$= \frac{-2 \pm \sqrt{4 - 3}}{-0.5}$$
$$= \frac{-2 \pm \sqrt{1}}{-0.5}$$
$$= \frac{-2 \pm 1}{-0.5}$$

```
(-2+1)/-0.5
              2
(-2-1)/-0.5
              6
```

So, $d = 2$ or $d = 6$.

The basketball will be at a height of 4.5 m twice along its parabolic path: on the way up at a horizontal distance of 2 m and on the way down at a horizontal distance of 6 m.

Key Concepts

- A quadratic equation of the form $ax^2 + bx + c = 0$, $a \neq 0$, can be solved for x using the quadratic formula $x = \dfrac{-b \pm \sqrt{b^2 - 4ac}}{2a}$.

- The x-coordinate of the vertex of a parabola is $-\dfrac{b}{2a}$, and the equation of the axis of symmetry is $x = -\dfrac{b}{2a}$.

Solving Quadratic Equations: $ax^2 + bx + c = 0$

Method	When It Can Be Used	Comments
graphing	always	The solutions will not always be exact: this is best used only when an approximate answer is needed.
factoring	sometimes	Use when $c = 0$ or when factors are easily found.
completing the square	always	This is best used for equations of the form $x^2 + bx + c = 0$, where b is an even number.
quadratic formula	always	This method always gives exact solutions, but in some cases the other methods are easier to use.
computer algebra system (CAS)	always	Use the solve (or factor) function of the CAS.

Communicate Your Understanding

C1 Jan calculated the x-intercepts of a quadratic relation as $x = \dfrac{-2 \pm \sqrt{5}}{8}$.

a) What are the individual x-intercepts?

b) Describe how to use the x-intercepts to find the equation of the axis of symmetry.

C2 After using the quadratic formula, explain how you would know if a quadratic equation has

a) two real roots

b) one real root

c) no real roots

Practise

For help with questions 1 and 2, see Example 1.

1. Use the quadratic formula to solve each equation. Express answers as exact roots.

    a) $7x^2 + 24x + 9 = 0$
    b) $2x^2 + 4x - 7 = 0$
    c) $4x^2 - 12x + 9 = 0$
    d) $2x^2 - 7x = -4$
    e) $3x^2 + 5x = 1$
    f) $16x^2 + 24x = -9$

2. **Use Technology** Use the quadratic formula to solve. Express your answers as exact roots and as approximate roots, rounded to the nearest hundredth. Verify graphically with technology.

    a) $3x^2 + 14x + 5 = 0$
    b) $8x^2 + 12x + 1 = 0$
    c) $4x^2 - 7x - 1 = 0$
    d) $10x^2 - 45x - 7 = 0$
    e) $-5x^2 + 16x - 2 = 0$
    f) $-6x^2 + 17x + 5 = 0$

For help with questions 3 to 5, see Examples 2 and 3.

3. Find the x-intercepts, the vertex, and the equation of the axis of symmetry of each quadratic relation. Then, sketch the parabola.

    a) $y = 5x^2 - 14x - 3$
    b) $y = 2x^2 - 5x - 12$
    c) $y = x^2 + 10x + 25$
    d) $y = 9x^2 - 24x + 16$
    e) $y = x^2 - 2x + 3$
    f) $y = -x^2 - 3x - 3$

4. For each quadratic relation, state the coordinates of the vertex and the direction of opening. Then, determine how many x-intercepts the relation has.

    a) $y = (x - 3)^2 + 2$
    b) $y = -(x - 2)^2 + 4$
    c) $y = 2(x + 4)^2 - 5$
    d) $y = -2(x + 3)^2 - 1$
    e) $y = (x - 5)^2$

5. Verify the number of x-intercepts for each relation in question 4 by using the quadratic formula to find the x-intercepts.

Connect and Apply

For help with question 6, see Example 4.

6. The path of a soccer ball after it is kicked from a height of 0.5 m above the ground is given by the equation $h = -0.1d^2 + d + 0.5$, where h is the height, in metres, above the ground and d is the horizontal distance, in metres.

    a) How far has the soccer ball travelled horizontally, to the nearest tenth of a metre, when it lands on the ground?

    b) Find the horizontal distance when the soccer ball is at a height of 2.6 m above the ground.

7. A ball is thrown upward at an initial velocity of 8.4 m/s, from a height of 1.5 m above the ground. The height of the ball, in metres, above the ground, after t seconds, is modelled by the equation $h = -4.9t^2 + 8.4t + 1.5$.

    a) After how many seconds does the ball land on the ground? Round your answer to the nearest tenth of a second.

    b) What is the maximum height, to the nearest metre, that the ball reaches?

8. Write an equation of a parabola, in the form $y = a(x - h)^2 + k$, satisfying each description. Then, write each relation in the form $y = ax^2 + bx + c$. Use graphing technology or the quadratic formula to verify that your equation satisfies the description.

    a) two x-intercepts

    b) one x-intercept

    c) no x-intercept

9. Solve. Round answers to the nearest hundredth, where necessary.

    a) $7x^2 - 12x = 9$

    b) $4x^2 = 12 - 13x$

    c) $4x^2 = 2.8x + 4.8$

    d) $x(3x - 8) = -1$

    e) $(x - 3)^2 = -2(x + 3)$

    f) $(x + 3)^2 = (2x + 5)(2x - 5)$

10. The shape of the Humber River pedestrian bridge in Toronto can be modelled by the equation $y = -0.0044x^2 + 21.3$. All measurements are in metres. Determine the length of the bridge and the maximum height above the ground, to the nearest tenth of a metre.

11. A toy rocket is launched from a 3-m platform, at 8.1 m/s. The height of the rocket is modelled by the equation $h = -4.9t^2 + 8.1t + 3$, where h is the height, in metres, above the ground and t is the time, in seconds.

    a) After how many seconds will the rocket rise to a height of 6 m above the ground? Round your answer to the nearest hundredth.

    b) When does the rocket fall again to a height of 6 m above the ground?

    c) Use your answers from parts a) and b) to determine when the rocket reached its maximum height above the ground.

12. **Chapter Problem** The platforms on the ends of the half-pipe are at the same height.

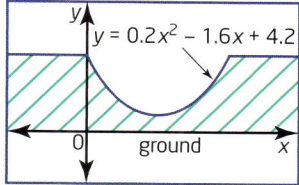

    a) How wide is the half-pipe?

    b) How far would a skater have travelled horizontally after a drop of 2 m? Round to the nearest hundredth of a metre.

13. A shopping mall entrance contains a parabolic arch, modelled by the equation $h = -0.5(d - 8)^2 + 32$, where h is the height, in metres, above the floor and d is the distance, in metres, from one end of the arch. How wide is the arch at its base?

14. The fuel flowing to the engine of a small aircraft can be modelled by a quadratic equation over a limited range of speeds using the relation $f = 0.0048v^2 - 0.96v + 64$, where f represents the flow of fuel, in litres per hour, and v represents speed, in kilometres per hour.
    a) Show that this quadratic relation has no v-intercepts.
    b) Determine the speed that minimizes fuel flow.

Achievement Check

15. The parks department is planning a new flower bed outside city hall. It will be rectangular with dimensions 9 m by 6 m. The flower bed will be surrounded by a path of constant width with the same area as the flower bed. Calculate the perimeter of the outside of the path.

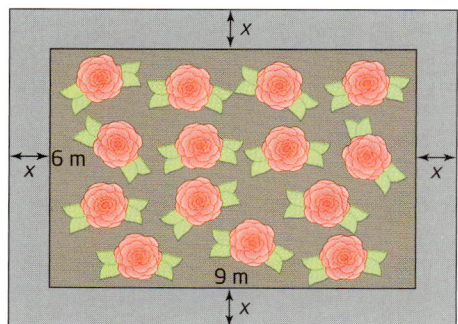

   a) Set up a quadratic equation to model the question.
   b) Use the quadratic formula to solve the problem.
   c) **Use Technology** Check your solution using a CAS or a graphing calculator.

Extend

16. Find a quadratic equation with each pair of roots.
    a) $x = \dfrac{14 \pm \sqrt{140}}{4}$
    b) $x = \dfrac{-11 \pm \sqrt{145}}{6}$

17. Points are drawn on a circle.

    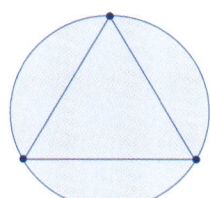

    a) If there are three points, how many line segments can be drawn joining any two points?
    b) What if there are four points? five points? six points?
    c) If there are n points, how many line segments can be drawn joining any two points?
    d) How many points are needed in order to have at least 1000 line segments?

18. When $b^2 - 4ac = 0$, there is only one real root. Give an example showing why this is so.

19. **Math Contest** Find the points of intersection of $x^2 + y^2 = 16$ and $y = x^2 - 9$, and sketch a graph.

20. **Math Contest** What are the different possibilities for the number of points of intersection for a circle and a parabola? For each case, give an equation for the circle and for the parabola.

21. **Math Contest** Show that the roots of $x = 1 + \dfrac{1}{x}$ are negative reciprocals. The positive root of $x = 1 + \dfrac{1}{x}$ is called the *golden ratio*.

22. Math Contest A continued fraction is a fraction of the form $a + \cfrac{1}{b + \cfrac{1}{c + \cfrac{1}{d + \cdots}}}$.

a) Evaluate the continued fraction
$2 + \cfrac{1}{3 + \cfrac{1}{4 + \cfrac{1}{5}}}$.

b) Evaluate the infinite continued fraction $1 + \cfrac{1}{1 + \cfrac{1}{1 + \cfrac{1}{1 + \cdots}}}$.

23. Math Contest In 1202, Leonardo of Pisa (1175–1250), better known as Fibonacci, published a book called *Liber Abaci*. In it, he showed a sequence of numbers now called the Fibonacci sequence: 1, 1, 2, 3, 5, 8, 13, 21, ….

a) Find the next three terms and a formation rule for this sequence.

b) Examine the ratios of successive terms of the Fibonacci sequence $\dfrac{(n+1)\text{th term}}{n\text{th term}}$. Conjecture a possible value for the ratio $\dfrac{1000\text{th term}}{999\text{th term}}$.

24. Math Contest Solve the system of equations.
$a - b + c = 0$
$a - c + d = 1$
$a + 2b + 2d = 0$
$b - d = 3$

Making Connections

A mind map can provide a mental picture of how many of the concepts you have learned about quadratics in Chapters 4, 5, and 6 are connected. One is started here. Make a larger version for yourself. Complete the shaded parts and add any other details that help you.

Quadratic Relations

A $y = ax^2 + bx + c$
 $a > 0$ means
 $a < 0$ means
 c is the

B $y = a(x - h)^2 + k$
 a means the same as in form **A**
 (h, k) is the

C $y = a(x - r)(x - s)$
 a means the same as in form **A**
 r and s are the

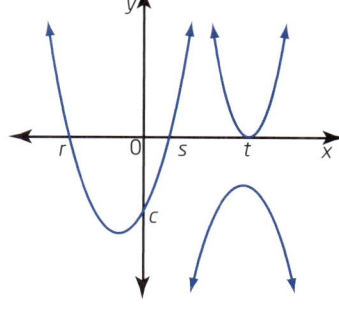

x-intercepts ↔ zeros ↔ roots

Quadratic Equations

$ax^2 + bx + c = 0$

If the quadratic expression factors:
- $a(x - r)(x - s) = 0$
 2 zeros are at
- $a(x - t)^2 = 0$ perfect square
 1 zero at t
- $a(x - p)(x + p) = 0$ difference of squares
 roots are
 axis of symmetry is

If no easy factors are found:
- complete the square to get form **B**
- use the quadratic formula
 if no real roots exist, then parabola

6.5 Solve Problems Using Quadratic Equations

In this chapter, you have learned a variety of methods for solving quadratic equations: graphing, factoring, completing the square, and the quadratic formula. You have applied these skills to solve problems related to situations that can be modelled by quadratic relations, such as paths of projectiles, shapes of parabolic structures, measurement problems involving area, and maximizing revenue.

Learning to use the most appropriate method in a given situation is an important step in becoming a good problem solver.

Example 1 Model the Path of a Toy Rocket

The formula $h = -\frac{1}{2}gt^2 + v_0 t + h_0$ can be used to model the height of a projectile, where g is acceleration due to gravity, which is 9.8 m/s² on Earth, v_0 is the initial vertical velocity, in metres per second, and h_0 is the initial height, in metres.

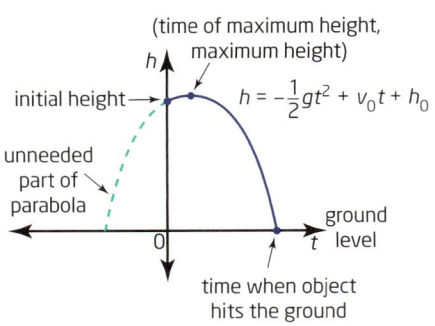

a) Create a model for the height of a toy rocket launched upward at 60 m/s from the top of a 3-m platform.

b) How long would the rocket take to fall to Earth, rounded to the nearest hundredth of a second?

c) What is the maximum height of the rocket, rounded to the nearest metre?

d) Over what time interval is the height of the toy rocket greater than 150 m? Round to the nearest hundredth of a second.

Solution

a) Use the formula $h = -\frac{1}{2}gt^2 + v_0 t + h_0$ with $g = 9.8$, $v_0 = 60$, and $h_0 = 3$.

$$h = -\frac{1}{2}(9.8)t^2 + 60t + 3$$

$$= -4.9t^2 + 60t + 3$$

b) Method 1: Use Pencil and Paper

Let $h = 0$ and apply the quadratic formula.
For $-4.9t^2 + 60t + 3 = 0$, $a = -4.9$, $b = 60$, and $c = 3$.

$$t = \frac{-b \pm \sqrt{b^2 - 4ac}}{2a}$$

$$= \frac{-60 \pm \sqrt{60^2 - 4(-4.9)(3)}}{2(-4.9)}$$

$$= \frac{-60 \pm \sqrt{3600 + 58.8}}{-9.8}$$

$$= \frac{-60 \pm \sqrt{3658.8}}{-9.8}$$

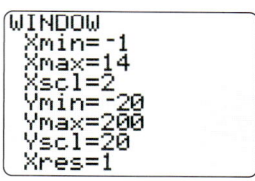

So, $t \doteq -0.05$ or $t \doteq 12.29$.
Since t represents the time after the rocket was launched, $t > 0$.
Therefore, reject the root $t = -0.05$.
It would take about 12.29 s for the rocket to fall to Earth.

Method 2: Use a Graphing Calculator

Graph the relation $h = -4.9t^2 + 60t + 3$ using the window settings shown.

Then, use the Zero operation of the graphing calculator to find the t-intercept farthest to the right.

It would take about 12.29 s for the rocket to fall to Earth.

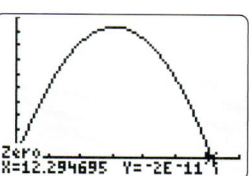

c) Method 1: Use Pencil and Paper

The t-coordinate of the vertex can be found using $t = -\dfrac{b}{2a}$.

$$t = -\frac{60}{2(-4.9)}$$

$$\doteq 6.12$$

Substitute 6.12 for t into $h = -4.9t^2 + 60t + 3$.
$h = -4.9(6.12)^2 + 60(6.12) + 3$
$\doteq 187$
The rocket reached a maximum height of about 187 m.

Method 2: Use a Graphing Calculator
Use the Maximum operation of a graphing calculator to find the coordinates of the vertex.
The rocket reached a maximum height of about 187 m.

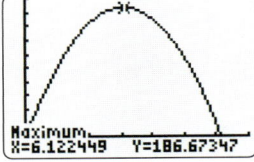

d) Method 1: Use Pencil and Paper
Let $h = 150$ and then express the equation in the form $ax^2 + bx + c = 0$.
$-4.9t^2 + 60t + 3 = 150$
$-4.9t^2 + 60t - 147 = 0$
Use the quadratic formula with $a = -4.9$, $b = 60$, and $c = -147$.

$$t = \frac{-b \pm \sqrt{b^2 - 4ac}}{2a}$$

$$= \frac{-60 \pm \sqrt{60^2 - 4(-4.9)(-147)}}{2(-4.9)}$$

$$= \frac{-60 \pm \sqrt{3600 - 2881.2}}{-9.8}$$

$$= \frac{-60 \pm \sqrt{718.8}}{-9.8}$$

So, $t \doteq 3.39$ or $t \doteq 8.86$.
Therefore, the height of the toy rocket is greater than 150 m from about 3.39 s to 8.86 s.

Method 2: Use a Graphing Calculator
Let $h = 150$. Graph both the original relation $h = -4.9x^2 + 60x + 3$ and $h = 150$. Use the Intersect operation of a graphing calculator to find the t-coordinates of the points of intersection.

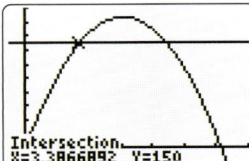 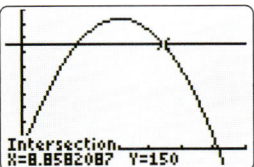

Therefore, the height of the toy rocket is greater than 150 m from about 3.39 s to 8.86 s.

Example 2 Width of a Path

A rectangular park measures 100 m by 60 m. A path of constant width is to be paved around the perimeter. The mayor wants to be sure that the path does not reduce the area of grass by more than 10%. What is the maximum allowable width of the path, rounded to the nearest tenth of a metre?

Solution

Let x represent the width of the path.
Write and solve an equation to find x.
The dimensions of the park inside the path are $100 - 2x$ by $60 - 2x$.
The original area is 100×60, or 6000 m².
The minimum new area is $90\% \times 6000$, or 5400 m².

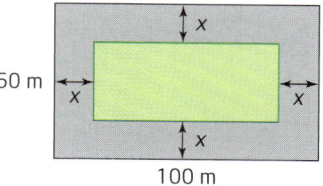

$$(100 - 2x)(60 - 2x) = 5400$$
$$6000 - 200x - 120x + 4x^2 = 5400 \quad \text{Expand the left side.}$$
$$4x^2 - 320x + 6000 = 5400 \quad \text{Simplify.}$$
$$4x^2 - 320x + 600 = 0 \quad \text{Write in the form } ax^2 + bx + c = 0.$$
$$x^2 - 80x + 150 = 0 \quad \text{Divide both sides by 4 to simplify.}$$

Use the quadratic formula with $a = 1$, $b = -80$, and $c = 150$.

$$x = \frac{-b \pm \sqrt{b^2 - 4ac}}{2a}$$

$$= \frac{-(-80) \pm \sqrt{(-80)^2 - 4(1)(150)}}{2(1)}$$

$$= \frac{80 \pm \sqrt{6400 - 600}}{2}$$

$$= \frac{80 \pm \sqrt{5800}}{2}$$

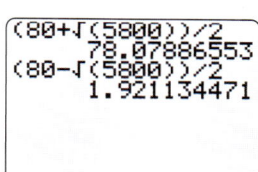

So, $x \doteq 78.1$ or $x \doteq 1.9$.
It appears that there are two possible widths for the path, 78.1 m and 1.9 m.

Check.
If the width of the path is 78.1 m, then the dimensions of the grass are $100 - 2(78.1)$ by $60 - 2(78.1)$, or -56.2 m by -96.2 m. This is not possible because the dimensions must be positive.

If the width of the path is 1.9 m, then the dimensions of the grass are $100 - 2(1.9)$ by $60 - 2(1.9)$, or 96.2 m by 56.2 m.

The area of grass is 96.2×56.2, or 5406.44 m², which is greater than 5400 m². Therefore, the path should be no wider than 1.9 m.

Example 3 Consecutive Numbers

The product of two consecutive even numbers is 5624. What are the numbers?

Solution

Consecutive even numbers differ by two.
Let x represent one even number and $x + 2$ represent the other.
Write and solve an equation to find x.

$$\begin{aligned} x(x + 2) &= 5624 \quad &&\text{Expand the left side.} \\ x^2 + 2x &= 5624 \quad &&\text{Simplify.} \\ x^2 + 2x - 5624 &= 0 \quad &&\text{Write in the form } ax^2 + bx + c = 0. \\ (x - 74)(x + 76) &= 0 \quad &&\text{Factor the left side.} \end{aligned}$$

$x - 74 = 0 \quad$ or $\quad x + 76 = 0$
$\quad x = 74 \quad$ or $\quad x = -76$

Verify that each value of x solves the problem.
If $x = 74$, then the next consecutive even number is 76.
$74 \times 76 = 5624$
If $x = -76$, then the next consecutive even number is -74.
$(-76) \times (-74) = 5624$

The numbers are 74 and 76 or -76 and -74.

Example 4 Right Triangle

One leg of a right triangle is 1 cm longer than the other leg. The length of the hypotenuse is 9 cm greater than that of the shorter leg. Find the lengths of the three sides.

Solution

Let x represent the length of the shorter leg. The length of the longer leg is $x + 1$ and the length of the hypotenuse is $x + 9$.

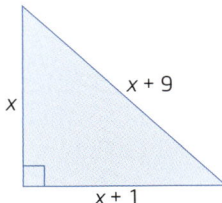

Use the Pythagorean theorem.
$$\begin{aligned} x^2 + (x + 1)^2 &= (x + 9)^2 \\ x^2 + x^2 + 2x + 1 &= x^2 + 18x + 81 \\ 2x^2 + 2x + 1 &= x^2 + 18x + 81 \\ x^2 - 16x - 80 &= 0 \\ (x - 20)(x + 4) &= 0 \end{aligned}$$

$x - 20 = 0 \quad$ or $\quad x + 4 = 0$
$\quad x = 20 \quad$ or $\quad x = -4$

Since the length cannot be negative, reject the root $x = -4$.

Check $x = 20$.
Find the side lengths of the triangle.
Shorter leg: 20   Longer leg: Hypotenuse:
                    $x + 1$ $x + 9$
                    $= 20 + 1$ $= 20 + 9$
                    $= 21$ $= 29$

Verify that this is a right triangle.
$20^2 + 21^2$
$= 400 + 441$
$= 841$
$= 29^2$

Therefore, the three sides of the right triangle have lengths 20 cm, 21 cm, and 29 cm.

Example 5 Path of a Soccer Ball

Matt uses a digital video recorder to record Paul's kick of a soccer ball. He then chooses an origin and a scale, and makes measurements of the height of the soccer ball at several horizontal distances from the television screen during playback.

Horizontal Distance (m)	2.5	5.0	7.5	10.0	12.5	15.0
Height (m)	3.25	4.80	5.75	6.10	5.85	5.00

a) Use technology to determine an equation for the quadratic relation.

b) Where does the soccer ball hit the ground? Round to the nearest tenth of a metre.

Solution

a) Method 1: Use a Graphing Calculator

Clear all lists by pressing (2nd) [MEM], selecting **4:ClrAllLists**, and pressing (ENTER).
Enter the horizontal distance values in list **L1** and the height values in list **L2**.
Set up the scatter plot using the settings shown.
Press (ZOOM) and select **9:ZoomStat**.

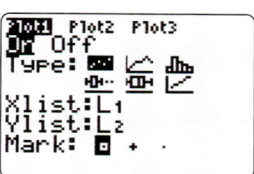

Determine the equation of the curve of best fit.
- Press (STAT), cursor over to display the **CALC** menu, and select **5:QuadReg**.
- Press (2nd) [L1] (,) (2nd) [L2] (,). Press (VARS), cursor over to display the **Y-VARS** menu, select **1:Function**, and then select **1:Y1**.

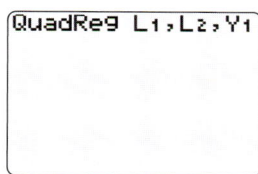

- Press ENTER to get the QuadReg screen.

The equation is $y = -0.48x^2 + 0.98x + 1.1$.

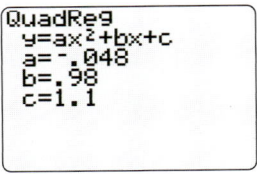

Method 2: Use a Spreadsheet

Enter the horizontal distance values in the first column and the height values in the second column. Select the data, and click the chart wizard. For chart type, select scatter. Enter a title and the labels for the axes.

Right-click on one of the data points, and add a trend line to the graph. Select a polynomial regression, of order 2, and the option to display the equation on the graph.

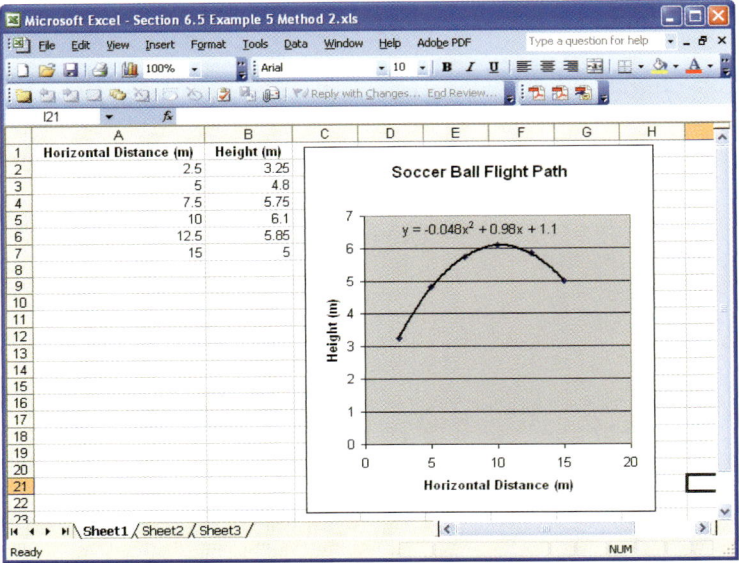

b) Method 1: Use a Graphing Calculator

Use the window settings shown.
Press GRAPH.
Use the Zero operation to find the x-intercept farthest to the right. The soccer ball hits the ground about 21.5 m from where it was kicked.

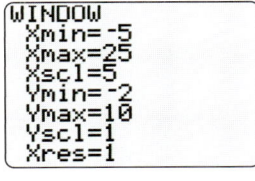
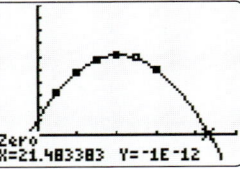

Method 2: Use a Spreadsheet

Extrapolate the curve until it crosses the horizontal axis. If necessary, adjust the axis parameters to make the graph easier to read. Estimate the value of x where this occurs. The soccer ball hits the ground about 21.5 m from where it was kicked.

Key Concepts

- The solution to some problems can be determined by multiplying two linear expressions together, resulting in a quadratic expression.
- Gravitational pull causes projectiles to have a height-time relationship that is quadratic, modelled by $h = -\frac{1}{2}gt^2 + v_0 t + h_0$, where g is the acceleration due to gravity, which is 9.8 m/s² on Earth, v_0 is the initial vertical velocity, in metres per second, and h_0 is the initial height, in metres, above the ground.
- Length-area relationships are quadratic since area is a length times a length, measured in square units.
- Follow these steps when determining an algebraic solution:
  - Define your variables.
  - Write an equation to model the situation.
  - Simplify the equation, if necessary.
  - Solve the equation using an appropriate method.
  - Consider the allowable values of the unknown. Reject a solution if necessary, providing an appropriate reason.
  - Provide a concluding statement, answering the original question.

Communicate Your Understanding

C1 In Example 4, a quadratic model is used to solve the problem. Explain why a quadratic equation occurs.

C2 Multiplying two linear expressions together results in a quadratic expression. Explain why.

C3 Fahad's solutions to a quadratic model involving the dimensions of a triangle were 4.5 cm and −3.8 cm. What should his next step be? Explain.

Practise

For help with questions 1 and 2, see Example 1.

1. a) Create a quadratic model for the height of a toy rocket launched upward at 45 m/s from a 2-m platform.

   b) How long would the rocket take to fall to Earth, rounded to the nearest hundredth of a second?

2. A firework is launched upward at an initial velocity of 49 m/s, from a height of 1.5 m above the ground. The height of the firework, in metres, after t seconds, is modelled by the equation $h = -4.9t^2 + 49t + 1.5$.

   a) What is the maximum height of the firework above the ground?

   b) Over what time interval is the height of the firework greater than 100 m above the ground? Round to the nearest hundredth of a second.

For help with question 3, see Example 2.

3. The length of a rectangle is 16 cm greater than its width. The area is 35 m². Find the dimensions of the rectangle, to the nearest hundredth of a metre.

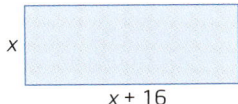

For help with questions 4 and 5, see Example 3.

4. The product of two consecutive numbers is 3306. What are the numbers?

5. Determine two consecutive odd integers whose product is 323.

For help with question 6, see Example 4.

6. The length of one leg of a right triangle is 7 cm more than that of the other leg. The length of the hypotenuse is 3 cm more than double that of the shorter leg. Find the lengths of each of the three sides.

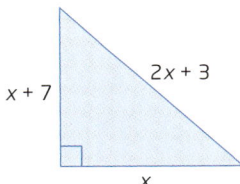

For help with question 7, see Example 5.

7. **Use Technology** Measurements from the flight path of a tennis ball are recorded.

Horizontal Distance (m)	6	8	10	12	14
Height (m)	4.4	4.9	5.0	4.7	4.0

a) Use a graphing calculator or a spreadsheet to create a scatter plot of the data and add a curve of best fit.

b) Determine the equation of the quadratic relation.

Connect and Apply

8. A cylindrical can with height 12 cm has capacity 600 mL. What is its radius, to the nearest millimetre? [Remember that 1 mL = 1 cm³.]

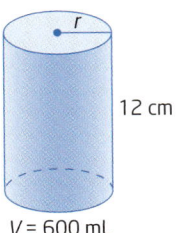

9. The area of a triangle is 20 cm², and the altitude is 4 cm greater than the base. Find the length of the base, to the nearest millimetre.

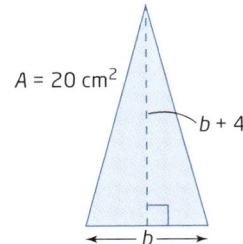

10. The sum of the squares of two consecutive integers is 365. Find the integers.

11. A rectangle has perimeter 23 cm. Its area is 33 cm². Determine the dimensions of the rectangle. Include a diagram in your solution.

12. A rectangular construction site is enclosed on three sides using 1200 m of fencing. The remaining side is formed by an existing wall. What dimensions enclose 180 000 m² of land?

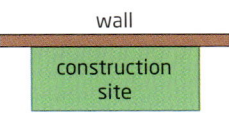

13. The three sides of a right triangle are consecutive even integers. What is the length of each side?

14. A ladder is 6 m long. If the height of the top of the ladder must be no greater than 10 times the distance from the base to the wall, how high up a wall can the top of the ladder be placed? Include a diagram in your solution. Round to the nearest millimetre.

15. A science experiment involves launching a small rocket. The following measurements are taken:
    Initial height: 0.61 m
    Initial vertical velocity: 36.85 m/s
    a) Create a quadratic model for the height, in metres, of the rocket after a given number of seconds.
    b) Verify the following results of the experiment:
       Total time in the air: 7.54 s
       Maximum height: 69.89 m
    c) Sketch a graph of this relation and label the key information as in Example 1 of this section.

16. The acceleration due to gravity on Earth is 9.8 m/s^2. A ball is thrown upward at an initial velocity of 15 m/s from a height of 1 m above the ground. Round answers to the nearest tenth.
    a) Write an equation for the height of the ball.
    b) What is the height of the ball after 1 s?
    c) After how many seconds does the ball land?
    d) What is the maximum height of the ball? When does this occur?
    e) Repeat parts a) to d) for a ball thrown on the Moon, where $g = 1.62$ m/s^2.
    f) Repeat parts a) to d) for a ball thrown on Jupiter, where $g = 23.1$ m/s^2.

17. Sherri sells photos of athletes to baseball, basketball, and hockey fans after their games. Her regular price is $10 per photograph, and she usually sells about 30 photographs. Sherri finds that, for each reduction in price of $0.50, she can sell an additional two photographs.
    a) Total sales revenue is the product of the number of units sold and the price. Make an algebraic model to represent Sherri's total sales revenue.
    b) At what price will Sherri's revenue be $150?
    c) At what price will her maximum revenue occur?
    d) At what price will her revenue be $0?
    e) Graph the relationship between revenue and the number of price reductions. Which features on the graph represent the solutions to parts b), c), and d)?

18. A rectangular picture frame measures 20 cm by 30 cm. A new frame is to be made by increasing each side length by the same amount. The resulting enclosed area is to be 1064 cm^2. Find the dimensions of the new picture frame. Include a diagram in your solution.

19. A rectangular garden measures 15 m by 24 m. A larger garden is to be made by increasing each side length by the same amount. The resulting area is to be 1.5 times the original area. Find the dimensions of the new garden, to the nearest tenth of a metre. Include a diagram in your solution.

20. The length of a rectangular field is 2 m greater than three times its width. The area of the field is 1496 m^2. What are the dimensions of the field?

21. An open-topped box is to be made from a rectangular piece of tin measuring 50 cm by 40 cm by cutting squares of equal size from each corner. The base area is to be 875 cm².

   a) Draw a diagram representing the information.
   b) What is the side length of the squares being removed?
   c) What is the volume of the box?

22. A photograph measures 21 cm by 15 cm. A strip of constant width is to be cut from each side of the photo, so the area is reduced to 216 cm². Find the width of the cut. Include a diagram in your solution.

23. A photograph measures 20 cm by 16 cm. A strip of constant width is to be cut off the top and one side of the photo, so the area is reduced to 60% of the area of the original photo. Find the width of the cut. Include a diagram in your solution.

24. A rectangular field measures 15 m by 20 m. A rectangular area is to be fenced in by reducing each dimension by the same amount. The fenced-in area will be $\frac{1}{2}$ the original area. What will the dimensions of the fenced-in area be? Include a diagram in your solution.

25. A rotating liquid surface takes on the shape of a parabolic mirror. This is the principle behind the 6 m in diameter reflecting telescope at the University of British Columbia, which uses mercury as a reflecting surface. The vertex is 23 cm below the edges. Find an equation to model the parabolic cross section of the mirror. Note: The mirror must always point straight up for the principle to work.

 Go to www.mcgrawhill.ca/links/principles10 and follow the links to learn more about liquid mirror telescopes.

26. **Use Technology** An automotive magazine tested the stopping distance required by a particular car, starting from various speeds. The data are shown in the table.

Speed (km/h)	Stopping Distance (m)
30	3.6
40	6.2
50	10.0
60	14.1
70	19.6
80	27.8
90	36.5
100	49.3

   a) Use technology to create a scatter plot of the data and add a curve of best fit.
   b) Determine the equation of the quadratic relation.
   c) Extrapolate to determine the stopping distance for a speed of 110 km/h.
   d) Determine what approximate speed results in stopping distances of 30 m, 65 m, and 200 m.
   e) Comment on the validity of extrapolation for this model.

Extend

27. Determine the number of points of intersection of each pair of parabolas. Justify your answer.

   a) $y = x^2 + 2x + 7$
      $y = x^2 - 4x - 1$
   b) $y = 3x^2 - 12x + 16$
      $y = -2x^2 - 4x + 3$
   c) $y = x^2 - 6x + 10$
      $y = 5x^2 - 30x + 46$

28. **Use Technology** Wind chill is the temperature that the air feels like at a given wind speed. The chart shows the wind chill, in degrees Celsius, for various air temperatures and wind speeds.

		Air Temperature (°C)					
		20	15	10	5	0	−5
Wind Speed (km/h)	10	17	12	7	2	−3	−8
	20	14	9	4	−1	−6	−11
	30	11	6	1	−4	−9	−14
	40	9	4	−1	−6	−11	−16
	50	8	3	−2	−7	−12	−17
	60	7	2	−3	−8	−13	−18

a) Use a graphing calculator to create a quadratic model for wind chill at a given wind speed, for an air temperature of 5°C.

b) Use a graphing calculator to create a quadratic model for wind chill at a given air temperature, for a wind speed of 60 km/h.

c) How accurate are your wind-chill models for 5°C at 60 km/h? Explain any differences in the results.

29. Explain why the quadratic model for the height of a projectile changes if the initial speed is measured in a diagonal direction instead of vertically.

30. In the TV show *Junkyard Wars*, a trebuchet was used to catapult a pumpkin from a height of 4 m for a total horizontal distance of 24 m. It reached a maximum height of 14 m. At what horizontal distances was the height of the pumpkin 10 m, to the nearest metre?

31. **Math Contest** The French mathematician Jacques Binet (1786−1856) developed a formula for the terms in the Fibonacci sequence:

$$f_n = \frac{(1+\sqrt{5})^n - (1-\sqrt{5})^n}{2^n \sqrt{5}}$$

Verify that Binet's formula gives the correct values for the first five terms of the Fibonacci sequence.

Making Connections

Parabolic Flight

The Falcon 20 aircraft of the National Research Council is a modified commercial jet that can create conditions similar to zero gravity by performing parabolic manoeuvres. During parabolic flight, the aircraft climbs into a steep arc and then descends. The aircraft is in free fall for 15 s to 20 s, which creates the zero-gravity conditions. During this time, Canadian space science researchers can conduct experiments.

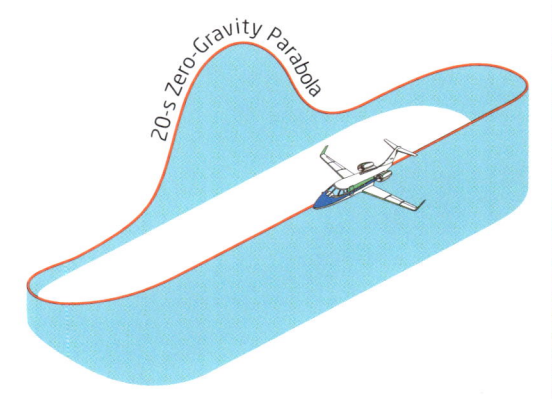

Chapter 6 Review

6.1 Maxima and Minima, pages 264–273

1. Rewrite each relation in the form $y = a(x - h)^2 + k$ by completing the square. Use algebra tiles or a diagram to support your solution.
   a) $y = x^2 + 8x - 7$
   b) $y = x^2 + 2x + 7$
   c) $y = x^2 + 4x + 6$
   d) $y = x^2 + 6x - 3$

2. Find the vertex of each parabola. Sketch the graph, labelling the vertex, the axis of symmetry, and two other points.
   a) $y = x^2 + 12x + 30$
   b) $y = x^2 - 14x + 50$
   c) $y = -x^2 + 6x - 7$
   d) $y = 5x^2 - 40x + 76$

3. **Use Technology** Use a graphing calculator to find the maximum or minimum point of each parabola, rounded to the nearest tenth.
   a) $y = 2.1x^2 - 2.5x + 8.0$
   b) $y = -338x^2 + 127x - 212$
   c) $y = \frac{1}{5}x^2 - \frac{2}{25}x + \frac{3}{5}$

6.2 Solve Quadratic Equations, pages 274–281

4. Solve by factoring. Check your solutions.
   a) $x^2 + 10x + 21 = 0$
   b) $m^2 + 8m - 20 = 0$
   c) $6y^2 + 21y + 9 = 0$
   d) $5n^2 + 13n - 6 = 0$

5. Solve.
   a) $y^2 = 8y + 9$
   b) $x^2 - 8x = -7$
   c) $3m^2 = -10m - 7$
   d) $30x - 25x^2 = 9$
   e) $8k^2 = -5 + 14k$
   f) $3x^2 + 2 = -5x$

6. The length of the hypotenuse of a right triangle is 1 cm more than triple that of the shorter leg. The length of the longer leg is 1 cm less than triple that of the shorter leg. Find the lengths of the three sides of the triangle.

6.3 Graph Quadratics Using the x-Intercepts, pages 282–291

7. Find the x-intercepts and the vertex of each quadratic relation. Then, sketch its graph.
   a) $y = x^2 + 8x + 12$
   b) $y = x^2 - 4x - 5$
   c) $y = -x^2 - 6x + 27$
   d) $y = 3x^2 + 10x + 8$
   e) $y = -x^2 - 3x$
   f) $y = x^2 - 4$

8. If two different quadratic relations have the same zeros, will they necessarily have the same axis of symmetry? Will they have the same vertex? Explain your reasoning.

9. Find the value(s) of k so that each parabola has only one x-intercept.
   a) $y = x^2 + kx + 100$
   b) $y = -4x^2 + 28x + k$

6.4 The Quadratic Formula, pages 292–303

10. Use the quadratic formula to solve each equation. Express your answers as exact roots.
    a) $-3x^2 - 2x + 5 = 0$
    b) $9x^2 - 8x - 3 = 0$
    c) $5x^2 + 7x + 1 = 0$
    d) $25x^2 + 90x + 81 = 0$

11. If a baseball is batted at an angle of 35° to the ground, the distance the ball travels can be estimated using the equation $d = 0.0034s^2 + 0.004s - 0.3$, where s is the bat speed, in kilometres per hour, and d is the distance flown, in metres. At what speed does the batter need to hit the ball in order to have a home run where the ball flies 125 m? Round to the nearest tenth.

6.5 Solve Problems Using Quadratic Equations, pages 304–315

12. A diver bounces off a 3-m springboard at an initial upward speed of 4 m/s.

  a) Create a quadratic model for the height of the diver above the water.

  b) After how many seconds does the diver enter the water? Round to the nearest hundredth of a second.

  c) Over what time interval is the height of the diver greater than 3.5 m above the water? Round to the nearest hundredth of a second.

13. A rectangular garden measures 5 m by 7 m. Both dimensions are to be extended by the same amount so that the area of the garden is doubled. By how much should the dimensions increase, to the nearest tenth of a metre?

14. The Sticker Warehouse sells rolls of stickers for $4.00 each. The average customer buys six rolls of stickers. The owner finds that, for every $0.25 decrease in price, the average customer buys an additional roll.

  a) Total sales revenue is the product of the number of units sold and the price. Make an algebraic model to represent The Sticker Warehouse's total revenue per customer.

  b) With how many price reductions will the revenue per customer be $30?

  c) What is the maximum predicted sales revenue per customer? With how many price reductions will this occur?

Chapter Problem Wrap-Up

In Section 6.1, question 18, and Section 6.4, question 12, you explored the dimensions of a parabolic skateboard half-pipe ramp defined by the equation $y = 0.2x^2 - 1.6x + 4.2$, where x is the horizontal distance, in metres, from the platform, and y is the height, in metres, above the ground.

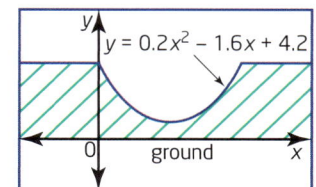

a) The company's standard model of a half-pipe ramp with a semicircular cross section is modelled by the equation $x^2 + y^2 = 16$, where x and y are the horizontal and vertical distances, in metres, respectively, from the centre of the semicircle. Write a one-paragraph report comparing the two half-pipe ramps.

b) The company is considering a deluxe ramp that includes two inverted quarter circles at the top of the standard model of a half-pipe ramp, as shown. The radius of the quarter circles is half the radius of the half-pipe. Add to your report any advantages or disadvantages that you see in this new design.

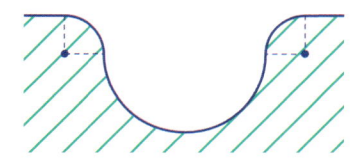

Chapter 6 Practice Test

1. Graph each parabola by completing the square. Label the vertex, the axis of symmetry, and two other points.
   a) $y = x^2 + 6x + 4$
   b) $y = -x^2 + 8x - 3$
   c) $y = 3x^2 + 24x + 10$

2. Solve each quadratic equation by factoring.
   a) $x^2 - 5x + 4 = 0$
   b) $9y^2 - 1 = 0$
   c) $x^2 = 3x + 10$
   d) $9b^2 - 12b + 4 = 0$
   e) $3x^2 + 13x = 10$
   f) $6m^2 + 30m = 0$
   g) $5x^2 = 10x$
   h) $4d + 1 = -4d^2$

3. Explain the process for finding the vertex of a quadratic relation using factoring. Include an example in your explanation.

4. Find the x-intercepts, axis of symmetry, and vertex of each parabola. Then, graph the relation, labelling it fully.
   a) $y = x^2 + 2x - 35$
   b) $y = -x^2 - x + 20$
   c) $y = -3x^2 - 6x$
   d) $y = x^2 - 10x + 25$

5. Use the quadratic formula to solve, if possible. Express your answers as exact roots.
   a) $4x^2 - 11x - 3 = 0$
   b) $x^2 + 5x = 7$
   c) $9x^2 = 30x - 25$
   d) $7k^2 - 9k + 3 = 0$
   e) $4s^2 - 9s = -3$
   f) $3t^2 - 7 = t$

6. Use an appropriate method to find the roots of each equation.
   a) $3x^2 + 12x + 6 = 0$
   b) $x^2 - 8x + 3 = 0$
   c) $4m^2 - 10 = 0$
   d) $-5x^2 + 10x = 5$
   e) $(k - 5)^2 = 16$
   f) $\dfrac{x^2}{2} + x + \dfrac{1}{2} = 0$
   g) $2(m - 1)^2 = (m + 2)(m + 1)$
   h) $(5x + 2)(3x - 1) = 4x^2 + 5$

7. Compare the axis of symmetry of $y = 3x^2 + 18x - 17$ to that of $y = 3x^2 + 18x + 1$. Explain your findings.

8. The path of a firework is modelled using the equation $h = -5d^2 + 20d + 1$, where h is the height, in metres, above the ground and d is the horizontal distance, in metres. What is the maximum height of the firework?

9. A parabola is defined by the equation $y = -2(x + 1)^2 + 18$.
   a) Without solving, explain how you can tell how many x-intercepts there are.
   b) Given the current form of the equation, what is the easiest way to find the x-intercepts?
   c) How far apart are the x-intercepts?

10. Write a quadratic equation in the form $ax^2 + bx + c = 0$ for each situation, where a, b, and c are integers.
    a) The roots of the equation are 5 and -3.
    b) The roots of the equation are $\dfrac{1}{2}$ and $\dfrac{3}{5}$.

11. An equipment storage shed has a parabolic cross section modelled by the relation $h = -d^2 + 4d$, where h is the height, in metres, and d is the horizontal distance, in metres, from one edge of the shed.
    a) How wide and how tall is the shed?
    b) Sketch the graph.
    c) For what values of d is the relation valid? Explain.

12. The cost, in dollars, of operating a machine per day is given by the formula $C = 3t^2 - 96t + 1014$, where t is the time the machine operates, in hours. What is the minimum cost of running the machine? For how many hours must the machine run to reach this minimum cost?

13. A triangle has base $2x + 1$ and height $6x - 3$. What value of x would give an area of 240 m²? Round to the nearest hundredth.

14. The relation $d = 0.0052s^2 + 0.13s$ models the stopping distance, d, in metres, of a car travelling at a speed of s, in kilometres per hour, when the driver brakes hard. At what speed was a car travelling if its stopping distance is 20 m? Round to the nearest tenth.

15. Van dives off a 4-m springboard. His height, h, in metres, above the surface of the water is defined by the relation $h = -d^2 + 3d + 4$, where d is his horizontal distance, in metres, from the end of the board.
    a) Determine the zeros of the relation.
    b) Sketch a graph of the relation.
    c) For what values of d is the relation valid?
    d) What is Van's horizontal distance from the board when he enters the water?
    e) What is Van's maximum height above the water?

16. In a volleyball match, Jenny serves the volleyball at 14 m/s, from a height of 2.5 m above the court. The height of the ball in flight can be estimated using the equation $h = -4.9t^2 + 14t + 2.5$, where h is the height, in metres, and t is the time, in seconds, after she serves the ball.
    a) What is the maximum height of the volleyball above the court? When does this occur? Round answers to the nearest tenth.
    b) If a player on the other team contacts the ball at a height of 0.5 m above the court, how long does it take for the ball to reach her? Round to the nearest second.

17. The hypotenuse of a right triangle has length 17 cm. The sum of the lengths of the legs is 23 cm. What are their lengths?

18. An open-topped box is to be constructed from a square piece of cardboard by removing a square with side length 8 cm from each corner and folding up the edges. The resulting box is to have a volume of 512 cm³. Find the dimensions of the original piece of cardboard.

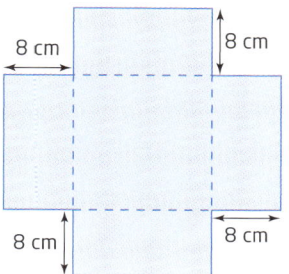

Achievement Check

19. a) Solve the quadratic equation $x^2 - 2x - 15 = 0$ by factoring and by graphing. Use the graph to find the minimum value of the quadratic relation $y = x^2 - 2x - 15$.
    b) Solve the quadratic equation $x^2 + 2x - 15 = 0$ by completing the square and by using a computer algebra system.
    c) For what value of b will the quadratic equation $9x^2 + bx + 25 = 0$ have one root? What is the value of the root?
    d) For what values of b will the quadratic equation $x^2 + bx + 10 = 0$ have no real roots?

Chapters 4 to 6 Review

Chapter 4 Quadratic Relations

1. Use finite differences to determine whether each relation is linear, quadratic, or neither.

   a)
x	y
-2	9
-1	7
0	5
1	3
2	1

   b)
x	y
-2	-3
-1	3
0	5
1	3
2	-3

2. Sketch the graph of each quadratic relation. Describe the transformation from the graph of $y = x^2$.
   a) $y = x^2 + 2$
   b) $y = (x + 3)^2$
   c) $y = -\dfrac{1}{4}x^2$

3. Dianne dove from the 10-m diving board. Her height h, in metres, above the water when she is x metres away from the end of the board is given by $h = -(x - 1)^2 + 11$.
   a) Sketch a graph of her dive.
   b) What was her maximum height above the water?
   c) What horizontal distance had she travelled when she entered the water? Answer to the nearest tenth of a metre.

4. Determine an equation to represent the parabola in the form $y = a(x - r)(x - s)$.

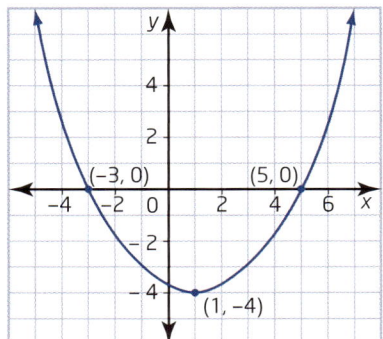

5. Evaluate.
   a) 2^{-4}
   b) $(-3)^{-2}$
   c) 25^0
   d) 8^{-1}
   e) $(-1)^{12}$
   f) $\left(\dfrac{3}{4}\right)^{-3}$

6. Cobalt-60 is a radioactive element that is used to sterilize medical equipment. Cobalt-60 decays to $\dfrac{1}{2}$, or 2^{-1}, of its original amount after every 5.2 years. Determine the remaining mass of 20 g of cobalt-60 after
   a) 20.8 years
   b) 36.4 years

Chapter 5 Quadratic Expressions

7. Write an algebraic expression to represent the area of the figure. Expand and simplify.

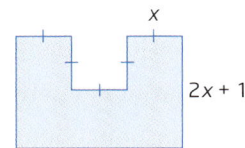

8. Expand and simplify.
   a) $(n + 3)(n - 3)$
   b) $(h + 5)^2$
   c) $(d - 4)(d - 2)$
   d) $(m + 3)(m + 7)$
   e) $(3t - 5)(3t + 5)$
   f) $(x - 7)^2$

9. Expand and simplify.
   a) $x(3x + 1)(2x - 5)$
   b) $(2k + 3)^2 - (k + 2)(k - 2)$
   c) $5(y - 4)(3y + 1) + (3y - 4)^2$
   d) $3(2a + 3b)(3a - 2b)$

10. The area of a rectangle is given by the expression $8x^2 + 4x$. Draw diagrams to show the possible rectangles, labelling the length and width of each.

11. Factor, if possible.
    a) $y^2 + 12y + 27$
    b) $x^2 + 2x - 3$
    c) $n^2 + 22n + 21$
    d) $p^2 - 8p + 15$
    e) $x^2 + 2x - 15$
    f) $k^2 - 5k + 24$

12. Factor.
    a) $p^2 + 12p + 36$
    b) $9d^2 - 6d + 1$
    c) $x^2 - 49$
    d) $4a^2 - 20a + 25$
    e) $8t^2 - 18$
    f) $a^2 - 4b^2$

13. Find the value of k so that each trinomial can be factored over the integers.
    a) $m^2 + km + 10$
    b) $9a^2 - ka + 4$

14. The area of a circle is given by the expression $\pi(4x^2 + 36x + 81)$. What expression represents the diameter of this circle?

Chapter 6 Quadratic Equations

15. Complete the square to rewrite each relation in the form $y = a(x - h)^2 + k$. Then, sketch a graph of each parabola, labelling the vertex, the axis of symmetry, and two other points.
    a) $y = x^2 + 6x - 16$
    b) $y = x^2 - 8x + 7$
    c) $y = x^2 + 4x + 10$
    d) $y = -x^2 + 6x - 8$
    e) $y = 2x^2 + 8x + 5$
    f) $y = -2x^2 - 12x - 7$

16. Solve by factoring. Check your solutions.
    a) $x^2 - 14x + 24 = 0$
    b) $n^2 + 4n - 21 = 0$
    c) $m^2 - 16 = 0$
    d) $2y^2 + 5y + 2 = 0$
    e) $7t^2 = 70t - 175$

17. Find the x-intercepts and the vertex of each parabola. Then, sketch its graph.
    a) $y = x^2 - 3x + 2$
    b) $y = x^2 - 16$
    c) $y = 2x^2 - 5x - 12$
    d) $y = -x^2 - 7x - 12$
    e) $y = -3x^2 + 6x$

18. A quadratic relation has roots 0 and -6 and a maximum at $(-3, 4)$. Determine the equation of the relation.

19. Find the exact roots of each equation.
    a) $x^2 - 6x + 1 = 0$
    b) $3x^2 - 5x + 1 = 0$
    c) $3.2x^2 - 5.6x - 7.1 = 0$
    d) $2x^2 + 5x = 9$
    e) $3x^2 - 8x = -3$

20. The perimeter of a rectangle is 8 m and its area is 2 m². Find the length and width of the rectangle to the nearest tenth of a metre.

21. A ferry operator takes tourists to an island. The operator carries an average of 500 people per day for a round-trip fare of $20. The operator estimates that for each $1 increase in fare, 20 fewer people will take the trip. What fare will maximize the number of people taking the ferry?

Tasks

Cari Sports Centre

Some of the costs of running Cari Sports Centre decrease as the number of people using the facility increases. Other costs, such as the salaries of staff needed to serve the additional people, grow.

As part of a budget review, city council would like to improve the profit from the Cari Sports Centre. City council surveys people using the centre and develops a formula by examining
- the price of admission to the centre
- the number of tickets sold
- the constant daily expenses in running the centre

The centre manager, Emily, was given the formula that related the number of admission tickets, the price of a ticket, and the daily profit. Unfortunately, Emily lost the paper on which the formula was written, but she had already calculated the following data list.

Ticket Price ($)	Daily Profit ($)
8	56
10	200
12	296
14	344

a) Copy the table and find the first and second differences. What can you conclude about the formula?

b) Make a scatter plot of the data. Draw a curve of best fit. What ticket price will give the greatest daily profit?

c) What are the constant daily expenses?

d) What range of admission prices will ensure that the daily profit is at least $326?

York Leisure Centre

A formula based on admission revenue and maintenance costs is used to determine the daily profit at the York Leisure Centre. The formula expresses the daily profit, y, in dollars, in relation to the price of admission, x, in dollars.

$y = -4x^2 + 100x - 500$

a) Graph this relation. Find the coordinates of the vertex and the equation of the axis of symmetry.

b) Write the relation in the form $y = a(x - h)^2 + k$.

c) What information does the solution of the equation $0 = -4x^2 + 100x - 500$ give about the York Leisure Centre's daily profit situation?

d) If each person entering the York Leisure Centre spends an average of $2.50 at the coffee shop, how is the rule for daily profit affected? What price should be charged for an admission ticket in this case? Justify your answer.

Abbey Leisure Centre

Abbey Leisure Centre currently has 300 members. The centre's management board wants to expand the facilities. The board has decided to raise the cost of annual membership from the current price of $400. A survey has found that for each $20 increase in the annual fee, 10 members will not renew their membership.

Prepare a report for the board of Abbey Leisure Centre, advising them of the cost of annual membership that will maximize the revenue.

CHAPTER 7
Trigonometry of Right Triangles

Consider the riders on the Drop Zone ride. How high in the air do you think they are? Did you know that you could calculate this height by examining the shadows cast on the ground? All you need is a metre stick and a little understanding of the geometry of triangles.

In ancient times, astronomers studied the motion of the stars and planets and wondered about how far away they were and how fast they were travelling. Eventually, techniques were discovered that allowed them to determine such measures right here on Earth! The branch of mathematics they invented to do this is called trigonometry.

Trigonometry

- Verify, through investigation, the properties of similar triangles.
- Describe and compare the concepts of similarity and congruence.
- Solve problems involving similar triangles in realistic situations.
- Determine, through investigation, the relationship between the ratio of two sides in a right triangle and the ratio of the two corresponding sides in a similar right triangle, and define the sine, cosine, and tangent ratios.
- Determine the measures of the sides and angles in right triangles, using the primary trigonometric ratios and the Pythagorean theorem.
- Solve problems involving the measures of sides and angles in right triangles in real-life applications, using the primary trigonometric ratios and the Pythagorean theorem.

Vocabulary
congruent figures
similar figures
isometry
scale factor, k
slope angle
tangent of an angle
primary trigonometric ratios
angle of depression
angle of elevation

Chapter Problem

Welcome to the Great North American Trigonometry Race! As one of several competing teams, you are equipped with a map and a number of clues. Each clue requires you to combine your knowledge of trigonometry and geography to find a new destination. See you at the finish line. Good luck!

Get Ready

Angle Properties

When two lines intersect, the **opposite angles** are equal.

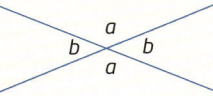

The angles opposite the equal sides of an isosceles triangle are equal.

Supplementary angles sum to 180°.

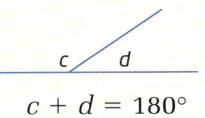

$c + d = 180°$

Complementary angles sum to 90°.

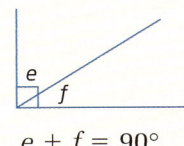

$e + f = 90°$

The sum of the interior angles in a triangle is 180°.

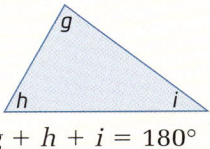

$g + h + i = 180°$

When a transversal crosses parallel lines, many pairs of angles are related.

alternate angles are equal

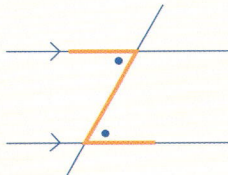

corresponding angles are equal

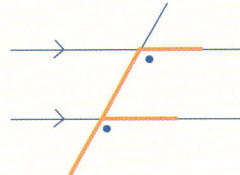

co-interior angles are supplementary

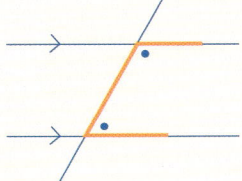

1. Find each unknown angle.

   a)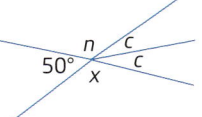

   b)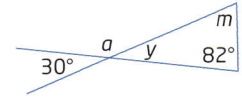

   c)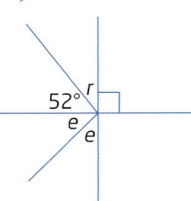

   d)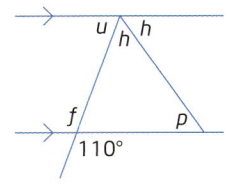

   e)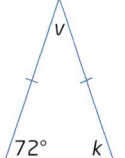

2. Prove that each interior angle of an equilateral triangle measures 60°.

3. Prove that for any right triangle, the two acute angles are complementary.

   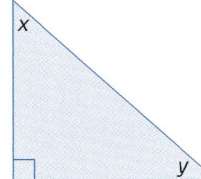

4. The exterior angle theorem states that the exterior angle of a triangle is equal to the sum of the two opposite interior angles.

   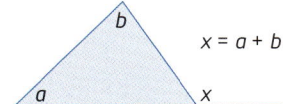

   $x = a + b$

   Prove the exterior angle theorem.

326 MHR • Chapter 7

Pythagorean Theorem

The three side lengths of a right triangle are related by the equation $c^2 = a^2 + b^2$.

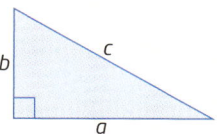

How far up the wall will the ladder reach?

Substitute the known values into the Pythagorean theorem.

$$c^2 = a^2 + b^2$$
$$6.0^2 = 1.4^2 + b^2$$
$$36 = 1.96 + b^2$$
$$36 - 1.96 = b^2$$
$$34.04 = b^2$$
$$\sqrt{34.04} = \sqrt{b^2}$$
$$5.83 \doteq b$$

I have to substitute carefully in the Pythagorean theorem. The square of the length of the hypotenuse usually appears alone on one side of the equation.

Subtract 1.96 from both sides of the equation.

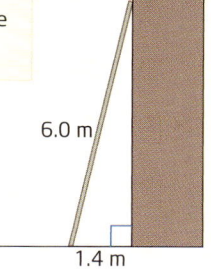

The ladder will reach approximately 5.8 m up the wall.

5. Find the unknown side length in each triangle. Round your answers to the nearest tenth of a unit.

6. Find the unknown side length in each triangle. Round your answers to the nearest tenth of a unit.

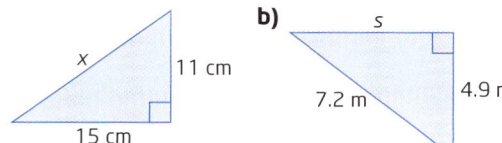
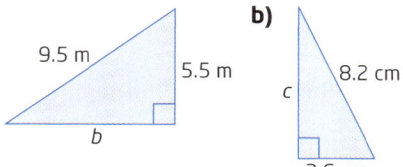

Slope

The slope of a line or line segment is the ratio of its rise to its run. The letter m is often used to indicate slope.

The slope of the ramp can be found by calculating this ratio.

$$m = \frac{\text{rise}}{\text{run}}$$
$$= \frac{40}{80}$$
$$= \frac{1}{2} \text{ or } 0.5$$

Slope can be expressed as a fraction in lowest terms or as a decimal.

7. Find the slope of each ramp.

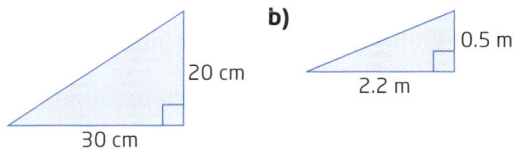

8. For safety reasons, a ramp should have a slope of not more than $\frac{1}{12}$. Determine whether each ramp is safe.

Equivalent Ratios

A ratio compares two quantities with the same units. For example, the photograph of a flea has been magnified 30 times.

The ratio 1:30 describes the relationship between the actual size and the image size of the flea. You can write this as a fraction:

$\dfrac{1}{30}$ ← actual size
     ← image size

The image length of the flea is 45 mm. Using equivalent ratios, you can find the actual length, L, of the flea.

$$\dfrac{\text{actual}}{\text{image}} = \dfrac{1}{30}$$

$$\dfrac{L}{45} = \dfrac{1}{30}$$

$$L = 45\left(\dfrac{1}{30}\right) \quad \textbf{Multiply both sides by 45.}$$

$$L = 1.5$$

The actual length of the flea is 1.5 mm.

---

9. Solve each proportion.

   a) $\dfrac{x}{6} = \dfrac{1}{2}$

   b) $\dfrac{3}{y} = \dfrac{2}{3}$

   c) $\dfrac{a}{2} = \dfrac{2}{a}$

   d) $\dfrac{x+2}{2} = \dfrac{4}{x}$

10. Pick two parts of your choice on the flea. Measure their image lengths. Use equivalent ratios to find their actual lengths.

11. **Chapter Problem** Before looking at your first clue and beginning the race, you need to understand how to read distances on your map. Look at the scale in the bottom right corner.

   a) Write a ratio to describe the relationship between map distance and actual distance.

   b) Measure the map distances for the following. Then, find the actual distances, to the nearest 100 km.
      • Moosonee to Ottawa
      • Toronto to Miami

   c) Pick two other points on the map. Determine how far apart they are.

Transformations

The diagrams illustrate the images produced when a shape is transformed in different ways.

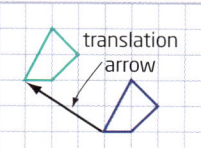 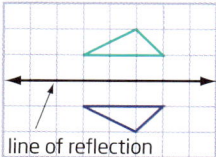 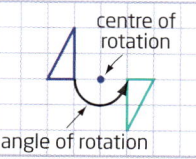 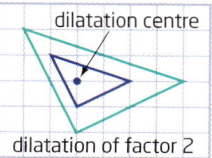

A **translation** is a slide along a fixed distance and direction.

A **reflection** is a flip across a mirror line, or line of reflection.

A **rotation** is a turn about a centre point, or centre of rotation.

A **dilatation** is an enlargement or reduction by a fixed factor, measured from a centre point.

12. Identify the type of transformation in each case.

    a)

    b)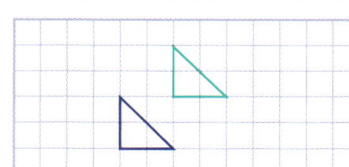

    c)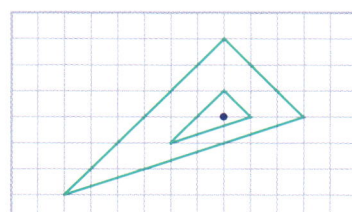

    d)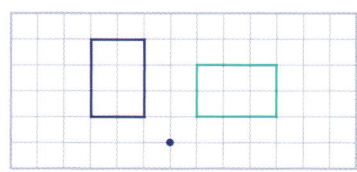

13. Draw a right triangle and label its vertices. Draw a triangle that is
    a) a rotated image of the original
    b) a dilated image of the original
    c) a reflected image of the original
    d) a translated image of the original

14. Draw an acute triangle and label its vertices. Draw a triangle that is
    a) a rotated image of the original
    b) a dilated image of the original
    c) a reflected image of the original
    d) a translated image of the original

7.1 Investigate Properties of Similar Triangles

Geometric shapes are often used in construction and design. Not only are certain shapes naturally pleasing to the eye, but they are also often useful for their structural properties.

Consider the shed shown. What geometric shapes can you recognize? Identify at least one pair of

- **congruent figures**
- **similar figures**

congruent figures
- identical shapes
- same size

similar figures
- identical shapes
- different sizes

Tools
- copy of shed drawing
- ruler
- protractor

Optional
- tracing paper

Investigate

How can I recognize similar and congruent figures?

Look at the front face of the shed.

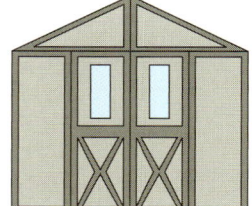

1. a) What pairs of congruent figures can you find?

   b) Copy two or three pairs of congruent figures from the drawing of the shed. Label the vertices of each figure. What special properties do the corresponding sides and angles have?

2. **Reflect** Summarize the properties of congruent triangles.

3. a) What pairs of similar, but not congruent, figures can you find?

   b) Make copies of two or three pairs of similar figures from the drawing of the shed. Label the vertices of each figure. What special properties do the corresponding sides and angles have?

4. **Reflect**

   a) What is true about the corresponding angles in two congruent figures? in two similar figures?

   b) What is true about the corresponding side lengths in two congruent figures? in two similar figures?

   c) Copy and complete the table to summarize your answers to parts a) and b).

	Corresponding Angles Are ...	Corresponding Side Lengths Are ...
Congruent Figures		
Similar Figures		

Example 1 Use Angles to Show That Two Triangles Are Similar

Identify a pair of similar triangles and explain why they are similar. Support each statement with a reason.

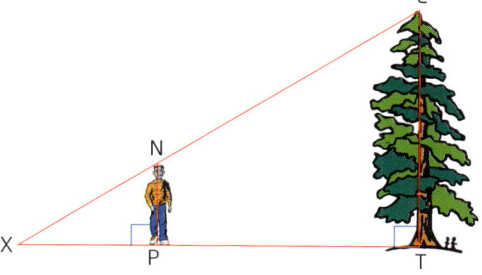

Literacy Connections

In △ABC, the interior angle at vertex B can be called ∠ABC, ∠CBA, or ∠B. In the first two cases, the middle letter corresponds to the vertex of the angle.

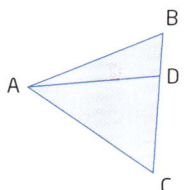

The three-letter system is useful to describe the three interior angles at vertex A: ∠BAD, ∠DAC, and ∠BAC. Referring simply to ∠A can lead to confusion.

Solution

There are two overlapping similar triangles: △XPN and △XTE. The diagram shows them separated:

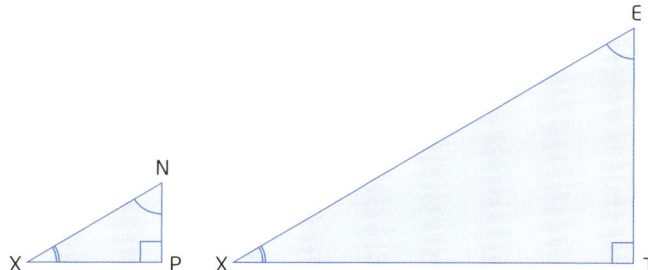

You can show that these two triangles are similar by identifying three pairs of equal angles.

You can see three pairs of equal angles.

Statement	Reason
∠XPN = ∠XTE	Both are 90°.
∠PXN = ∠TXE	These are the same angle.
∠XNP = ∠XET	The sum of the angles in any triangle is 180°.
△XPN ~ △XTE	All three pairs of angles are equal.

The third pair of angles in any two triangles is equal if the other two pairs are equal. So, it is only necessary to have two pairs of equal corresponding angles to show that two triangles are similar.

Literacy Connections

The symbol ~ means "is similar to." When you write a similarity statement, the order of the vertices must correctly identify pairs of equal angles and pairs of corresponding sides. In Example 1, △XPN ~ △XTE is correct because the vertices correctly indicate pairs of equal angles and pairs of corresponding sides.

7.1 Investigate Properties of Similar Triangles • MHR 331

Example 2 Use Sides to Show That Two Triangles Are Similar

Are the two triangles in the diagram similar? Explain your reasoning.

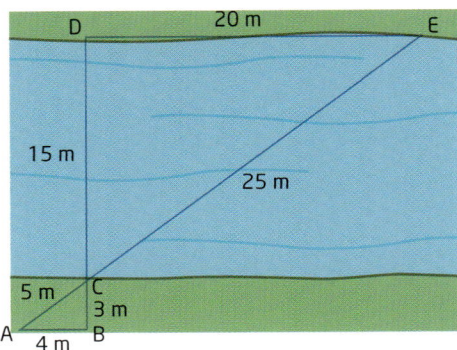

Solution

You can show that two triangles are similar by showing that three pairs of corresponding sides are proportional.

The two triangles are △EDC and △ABC.

$$\frac{ED}{AB} = \frac{20}{4} \qquad \frac{CE}{CA} = \frac{25}{5} \qquad \frac{DC}{BC} = \frac{15}{3}$$

$$= \frac{5}{1} \qquad\qquad = \frac{5}{1} \qquad\qquad = \frac{5}{1}$$

The three pairs of corresponding sides are all in the ratio 5:1. Therefore, △EDC ~ △ABC.

Since the triangles in Example 2 are similar, their corresponding angles are equal. That is, ∠CAB = ∠CED, ∠CBA = ∠CDE, and ∠ACB = ∠ECD.

Key Concepts

- Congruent figures have the same size and shape. Similar figures have the same shape, but different sizes.

- Similar triangles have the following properties:
  - Corresponding angles are equal:
    ∠A = ∠T
    ∠B = ∠U
    ∠C = ∠V
  - Ratios of corresponding sides are equal:
    $\frac{AB}{TU} = \frac{BC}{UV} = \frac{CA}{VT}$, or, in ratio notation, AB:TU = BC:UV = CA:VT

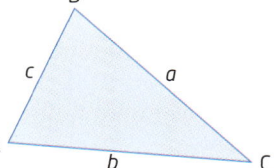

Communicate Your Understanding

C1 a) Explain the difference between similar figures and congruent figures.

b) Draw an example for each.

C2 a) How are the angles of similar figures related?

b) How are the side lengths of similar figures related?

c) How do these relationships differ from those involving congruent figures?

C3 Describe two ways that you can show that two triangles are similar.

C4 Why is it only necessary to show that two pairs of corresponding angles are equal in order to show that two triangles are similar?

Practise

For help with questions 1 to 6, see the Investigate.

1. Look in the room around you. Identify at least two sets of

   a) congruent figures

   b) similar figures

2. Identify at least two examples outside the classroom of where you see

   a) congruent figures

   b) similar figures

3. a) Copy the diagram.

   b) Draw each of the following:
   - a figure congruent to the one in part a)
   - a smaller figure that is similar to the one in part a)
   - a larger figure that is similar to the one in part a)

   c) Verify the accuracy of your sketches by measuring angles and side lengths.

4. For each situation, identify whether you would use similar figures, congruent figures, or neither. Justify your answers.

   a) a tile pattern on a floor

   b) a team's logo for the chest and shoulder patches of their jerseys

   c) a door frame and a window frame for the front of a house

   d) a three-dimensional model of a skyscraper building

5. Name the similar triangles in each case. Write the letters so that equal angles appear in corresponding order.

a)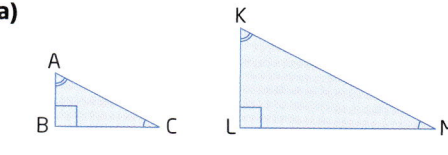

b)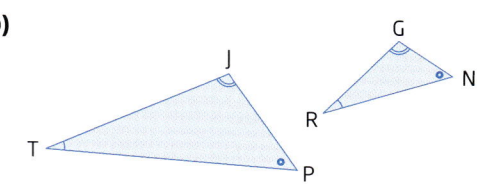

c)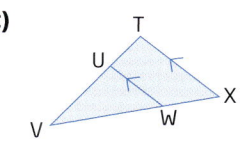

d)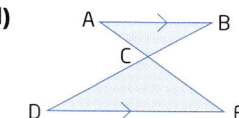

6. For each pair of similar triangles in question 5, write the equivalent ratios of side lengths.

For help with questions 7 to 9, see Examples 1 and 2.

7. Name a pair of similar triangles in each diagram and explain why they are similar.

   a)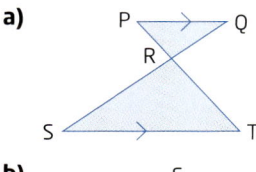

   b)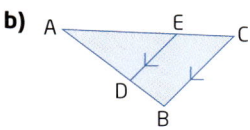

   c)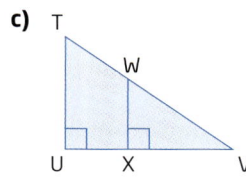

8. Name a pair of similar triangles in each diagram and explain why they are similar.

   a)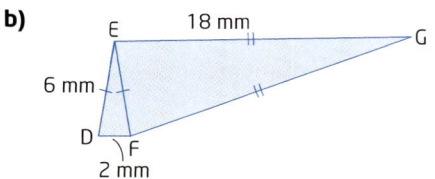

   b)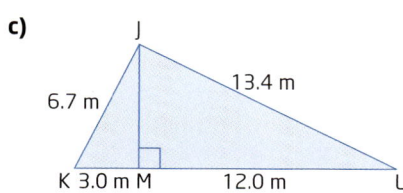

   c)

9. For each pair of similar triangles in questions 7 and 8, list all the pairs of corresponding angles and corresponding sides.

Connect and Apply

Carefully copy or trace the diagram of the truss bridge. Use it to answer questions 10 to 12.

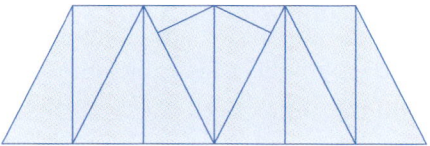

10. Identify an example of each of the following. Use different colours and/or additional sketches to illustrate your answers.
    a) a pair of congruent triangles
    b) a pair of congruent rectangles
    c) a pair of congruent parallelograms
    d) a pair of similar triangles
    e) a set of three similar triangles

11. Identify a pair of congruent triangles that are related by a
    a) translation
    b) reflection
    c) rotation

12. a) Describe the combination of transformations that relates one pair of congruent triangles.
    b) Describe a different combination of transformations that relates another pair of congruent triangles.

13. a) Draw a right triangle.
    b) Draw a right triangle that is
       • congruent to the one you drew
       • similar to the one you drew
       • neither congruent nor similar to the one you drew

14. Are all equilateral triangles similar? Justify your answer.

15. Are all isosceles triangles similar? Justify your answer.

Extend

16. Congruent figures occur in music composition. This is a two-bar lead-in that was commonly used in the early days of rock 'n' roll music:

Carefully copy the music into your notebook. Then, use line segments to join the centres of the note heads (the round part) so they form two congruent triangles. What kind of transformation relates the two triangles?

17. A type of bass grows so that it retains its shape. Its length, height, and width all remain in the same proportion for its first few years of life. The average length, l, and height, h, of a baby bass are shown. The average width, w, of this type of bass is about half its height. If the bass triples in length each month for the first 3 months of life, find the dimensions of this bass after

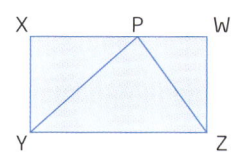

a) 1 month   **b)** 2 months

18. Refer to question 17. The density of this type of bass is about 10% greater than that of water, which is 1 g/cm³. Use the relationship density $= \dfrac{\text{mass}}{\text{volume}}$ to estimate the mass of this bass after 3 months. To estimate the volume of the bass, find the volume of a rectangular prism with the same width, length, and height as the bass.

19. Math Contest XYZW is a rectangle, with YZ = 10 cm, YP = 8 cm, and ZP = 6 cm. Determine the area of XYZW.

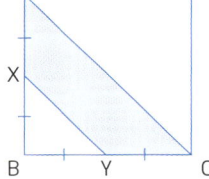

20. Math Contest ABCD is a square. X is the midpoint of AB and Y is the midpoint of BC. What percent of the square is shaded?

A 37.5%   **B** 25%
C 18.75%   **D** $33\dfrac{1}{3}$%   **E** 30.75%

Making Connections

The triangle is the strongest polygon structurally. The only way you can change its shape is to change the length of one or more of its sides. A square, by contrast, can be deformed into a rhombus under a heavy load.

It is this property that makes the triangle so popular in designs such as truss bridges.

The Quebec Bridge, shown here, which spans the St. Lawrence River, is the longest cantilever truss bridge in the world.

Go to www.mcgrawhill.ca/links/principles10 and follow the links to learn more about the Quebec Bridge and its fascinating history.

Use Technology

Create Designs With Similar and Congruent Figures Using Dynamic Geometry Software

Investigate

How can you use dynamic geometry software to create and use similar and congruent figures?

A: Create and Transform Congruent and Similar Figures

Method 1: Use *The Geometer's Sketchpad*®

 **Tools**
- computer with *The Geometer's Sketchpad*®

1. **a)** Open *The Geometer's Sketchpad*® and begin a new sketch.
   b) Construct a triangle.
   - Plot three points.
   - Select all of the points.
   - From the **Construct** menu, choose **Segments**. A triangle will appear.
   - Select the points. From the **Construct** menu, choose **Triangle Interior**. You can change the colour by right clicking on the interior that appears and choosing a colour.
   c) Measure the side lengths, all at once.
   - Select the three sides.
   - From the **Measure** menu, choose **Length**.
   d) Measure the angles, one at a time.
   - Select three vertices, taking careful note of the order. The middle vertex you select is where the angle will be measured.
   - From the **Measure** menu, choose **Angle**.
   - Repeat for the other two angles.
   e) Measure the area.
   - Select the triangle interior.
   - From the **Measure** menu, choose **Area**.
   You can click and drag the measures to place them wherever you like.
   f) Click and drag one or more of the vertex points. Notice that the measures change dynamically as you change the triangle.

2. Return to page 1 of your sketch by clicking on the **1** at the bottom left of the sketch. Create an image triangle using a translation.
   a) Select all parts of the triangle, including the
   - vertices
   - line segments
   - interior

Technology Tip

To avoid having to create a new triangle for each part of this activity, attach three more pages to your sketch with the same triangle on each page.
- From the **File** menu, choose **Document Options**.
- Click on **Add Page**, choose **Duplicate**, and then choose **1**.
- Repeat these steps to add two more pages.

336 MHR • Chapter 7

b) From the **Transform** menu, choose **Translate**. A dialogue box will appear.

c) Experiment with different translations. Explain the difference between **Polar** and **Rectangular** translations.

d) Is the resulting triangle similar to the original, congruent to the original, or neither? Verify by measuring.

e) What happens to the area of the triangle after the translation? Explain.

f) Click and drag one or more of the vertices of either triangle and describe what happens.

3. Go to page 2 of your sketch. Create an image triangle using a reflection.

a) Draw a line segment near the triangle.

b) From the **Transform** menu, choose **Mark Mirror**.

c) Select all parts of the triangle. From the **Transform** menu, choose **Reflect**. Explain what happens.

d) Is the resulting triangle similar to the original, congruent to the original, or neither? Verify by measuring.

e) What happens to the area of the triangle after the reflection? Explain.

f) Click and drag one or more vertices of either triangle and describe what happens.

g) Click and drag either vertex of the mirror line and describe what happens.

4. Go to page 3 of your sketch. Create an image triangle using a rotation.

a) Construct a point near the triangle.

b) From the **Transform** menu, choose **Mark Center**.

c) Select all parts of the triangle. From the **Transform** menu, choose **Rotate**. A dialogue box will appear. Enter an angle of your choice. Click on **Rotate** and explain what happens.

d) Is the resulting triangle similar to the original, congruent to the original, or neither? Verify using measurements.

e) What happens to the area of the triangle after the rotation? Explain.

f) Click and drag one or more vertices of either triangle and describe what happens.

g) Click and drag the centre of rotation and describe what happens.

h) Create another image triangle by rotating in the opposite direction by changing the sign of the angle when the **Rotate** dialogue box appears.

Technology Tip

To select multiple objects that are close together, follow these steps.
- Place the cursor above and to one side of all the objects you want to select.
- Click and drag to a point below and to the other side of the objects. A dashed box will appear.
- Release the mouse button. Any objects within the box will be selected.

Literacy Connections

The Geometer's Sketchpad® and Cabri® Jr. use the term "dilation" instead of "dilatation." The two words mean the same thing.

 **Tools**
- TI-83 Plus or TI-84 Plus graphing calculator

5. Go to page 4 of your sketch. Create an image triangle using a dilatation.

a) Construct a point near the triangle.

b) From the **Transform** menu, choose **Mark Center**.

c) Select all parts of the triangle. From the **Transform** menu, choose **Dilate**. A dialogue box will appear. Dilate by a fixed ratio of your choice by entering values into the numerator and denominator fields. Click **Dilate** and explain what happens.

d) Is the resulting triangle similar to the original, congruent to the original, or neither? Verify using measurements.

e) What happens to the area of the triangle after the dilatation? How is the new area related to the ratio you chose in part c)?

f) Click and drag one or more vertices of either triangle and describe what happens.

g) Create new triangles using dilatations. Experiment with different values in the numerator and denominator of the **Dilate** dialogue box. Describe what happens when
- numerator < denominator
- numerator > denominator
- numerator = denominator

How is this ratio related to the ratio of corresponding side lengths of the original and image triangles?

Method 2: Use a Graphing Calculator

1. a) Press APPS and choose **Cabri Jr**. If the axes are not visible, choose the **F5** menu. Choose **Hide/Show**, and then **Axes**. Move the cursor to the origin. Press ALPHA, and move the origin until the first quadrant occupies most of the screen, as shown.

b) Construct a triangle.
- Choose **Triangle** from the **F2** menu. Draw a triangle as shown.

c) Measure the side lengths of the triangle.
- Choose **Measure** from the **F5** menu. Then, choose **D. & Length**.
- Move the cursor to one of the sides of the triangle until it flashes. Press ENTER. Move the measurement to a suitable location, and press ENTER again.
- Repeat this procedure to measure the lengths of the other two sides.

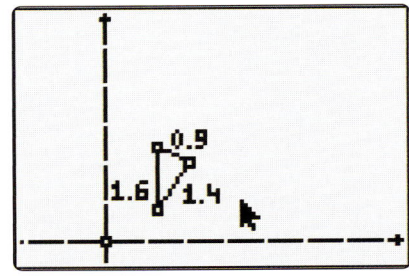

d) Measure the angles, one at a time.
- Choose **Measure** from the **F5** menu. Then, choose **Angle**.
- Move the cursor to one of the vertices of the triangle. Press (ENTER). Move to the next vertex. Press (ENTER). This is the middle vertex for the angle being measured. Move to the third vertex. Press (ENTER). Move the measurement to a convenient location, and press (ENTER).
- Repeat this procedure to measure the two remaining angles.

e) Measure the area.
- Choose **Measure** from the **F5** menu. Then, choose **Area**.
- Move the cursor to one of the sides of the triangle until it flashes. Press (ENTER). Move the area measurement to a convenient location, and press (ENTER).

f) Move the cursor to one of the vertices of the triangle. Press (ALPHA). Drag the vertex. Note how the measurements change.

g) Save your sketch.
- Choose **Save As …** from the **F1** menu. Enter a suitable name. Press (ENTER).

2. Create an image triangle using a translation.

a) Choose **Segment** from the **F2** menu. Draw a line segment, as shown. This segment indicates the direction and length of the translation.

b) From the **F4** menu, choose **Translation**. Move the cursor to one of the sides of the triangle until it flashes. Press (ENTER). Move the cursor to the line segment that defines the translation. Press (ENTER). The translated triangle will appear.

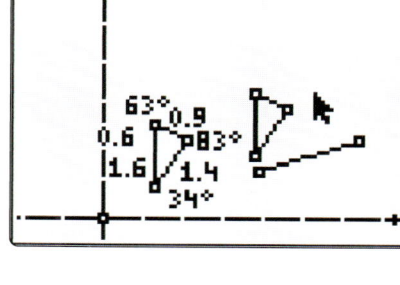

c) Is the resulting triangle similar to the original, congruent to the original, or neither? Verify using measurements.

d) What happens to the area of the triangle after the translation? Explain.

e) Select and drag one or more of the vertex points of the original triangle and describe what happens.

3. Create an image triangle using a reflection.

a) Open the file that you saved in step 1 g). When you are asked whether you want to save the changes, choose **No**.

b) Choose **Segment** from the **F2** menu. Draw a line segment, as shown. This segment serves as the mirror line.

c) From the **F4** menu, choose **Reflection**. Move the cursor to one of the sides of the triangle until it flashes. Press (ENTER). Move the cursor to the mirror line. Press (ENTER). The reflected triangle will appear.

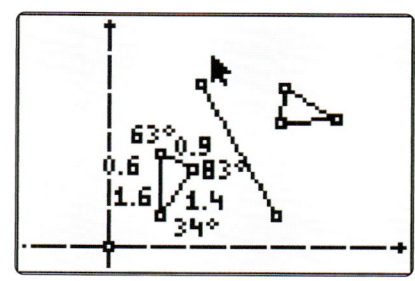

d) Is the resulting triangle similar to the original, congruent to the original, or neither? Verify using measurements.

e) What happens to the area of the triangle after the reflection? Explain.

f) Select and drag one or more vertices of the original triangle and describe what happens.

g) Select and drag either endpoint of the mirror line and describe what happens.

4. Create an image triangle using a rotation.

   a) Open the file that you saved in step 1 g). When you are asked whether you want to save the changes, choose **No**.

   b) Choose the **Point** tool from the **F2** menu. Draw a point near the origin to serve as the centre of rotation. Draw three points to define the angle of rotation.

   c) From the **F4** menu, choose **Rotation**. Move the cursor to one of the sides of the triangle until it flashes. Press (ENTER). Move the cursor to the point that defines the centre of rotation. Press (ENTER). Select the three points that define the angle of rotation. Press (ENTER). The rotated triangle will appear.

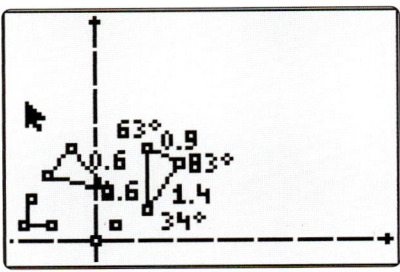

   d) Is the resulting triangle similar to the original, congruent to the original, or neither? Verify using measurements.

   e) What happens to the area of the triangle after the rotation? Explain.

   f) Select and drag one or more vertices of the original triangle and describe what happens.

   g) Select and drag the centre of rotation and describe what happens.

   h) Select and drag one of the ends of the angle of rotation, and describe what happens.

5. Create an image triangle using a dilatation.

   a) Open the file that you saved in step 1 g). When you are asked whether you want to save the changes, choose **No**.

   b) Choose the **Point** tool from the **F2** menu. Draw a point near the origin to serve as the centre of dilatation. Choose the **Alpha-Num** tool from the **F5** menu. Move to a convenient location to place the dilatation factor. Press (ENTER) and then (ALPHA). Use a dilatation factor of 3. Press (ENTER).

c) From the **F4** menu, choose **Dilation**. Move the cursor to one of the sides of the triangle until it flashes. Press ENTER. Move the cursor to the point that defines the centre of dilatation. Press ENTER. Move the cursor to the dilatation factor. Press ENTER. The dilated triangle will appear.

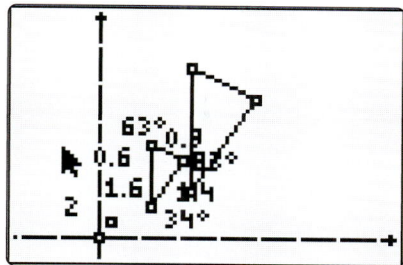

d) Is the resulting triangle similar to the original, congruent to the original, or neither? Verify using measurements.

e) What happens to the area of the triangle after the dilatation? How is the new area related to the dilatation factor in part b)?

f) Select and drag one or more vertices of the original triangle and describe what happens.

g) Select and drag the centre of dilatation and describe what happens.

h) Start with a new triangle, and use a different dilatation factor. Try a factor between 0 and 1.

B: Create a Design

1. Choose an object that you would like to design, such as a building, a bridge, or a vehicle.

2. Create your design, using the following guidelines.
   - Include at least two sets of congruent shapes.
   - Include at least two sets of similar shapes.
   - Use at least three different types of transformations.

   a) Find the ratio that relates corresponding sides for each pair of similar shapes.

   b) Find the ratio of areas for each pair of similar shapes, and identify how this value in each case is related to the ratio in part a).

3. **Reflect**

   a) Describe the processes you used to create similar and congruent objects in your design.

   b) Explain how you can prove that two objects are either similar or congruent.

   c) Which types of transformations are **isometries**? Which are not? Explain your reasoning.

isometry
- a transformation that preserves size and shape

7.2 Use Similar Triangles to Solve Problems

The geometry of similar figures is a powerful area of mathematics. Similar triangles can be used to measure the heights of objects that are difficult to get to, such as trees, tall buildings, and cliffs. They can also be used to measure distances across rivers and even galaxies!

The students in the photo are using a metre stick and shadows to measure the height of the tree. How can they do this? What role do similar triangles play in this type of problem?

Investigate

How can you apply the properties of similar triangles to solve problems?

Tools
- ruler
- metre stick

Suppose you have a metre stick and it is sunny outside. Your task is to plan a problem solving strategy so that you can determine the height of an inaccessible object, such as a tree, a building, or a cliff.

1. Look at the illustration. Discuss with a partner, or in a small group, how the students could find the height of the tree.

2. Draw a diagram that relates to this problem. Explain how similar triangles are involved.

3. Create some numbers to represent reasonable measures to solve this problem and solve it. Does your answer seem reasonable? Explain.

4. **Reflect** Trade strategies with another pair or group. Compare strategies. Do you think they will work? Make any improvements you like to your own strategy. Later you will apply your method to solve a real measurement problem.

The **scale factor, *k*** , is a useful quantity when working with similar triangles such as the ones shown.

The value of *k* relating corresponding sides in these two triangles is 3, because if you multiply each side length in △ABC by 3, you obtain the corresponding side length in △PQR.

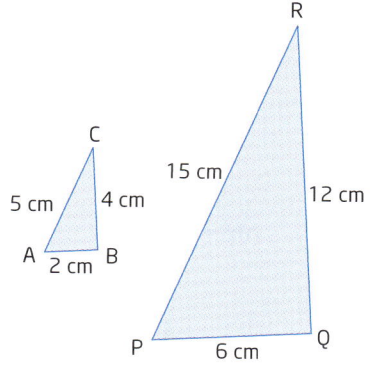

scale factor, *k*
- factor that relates corresponding side lengths of two similar triangles

△ABC Side Lengths (cm)	Multiply by *k*	△PQR Side Lengths (cm)
AB = 2	2 × 3 = 6	PQ = 6
BC = 4	4 × 3 = 12	QR = 12
CA = 5	5 × 3 = 15	RP = 15

You can apply the scale factor to find an unknown side length in one triangle if you know the corresponding side length in a similar triangle.

Example 1 Solve for an Unknown Side

To determine the width of a river, Naomi finds a willow tree and a maple tree that are directly across from each other on opposite shores. Using a third tree on the shoreline, Naomi plants two stakes, A and B, and measures the distances shown.

Find the width of the river using the information that Naomi found.

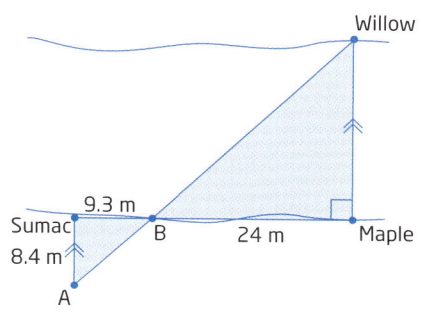

Solution

You can find two similar triangles and then use the scale factor to find the width.

Step 1: Show that △ABS is similar to △WBM.

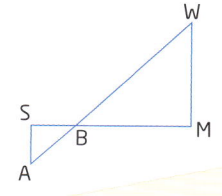

Statement	**Reason**
∠ABS = ∠WBM	These are opposite angles.
∠BSA = ∠BMW	These are both 90°, because AS is parallel to WM.
△ABS ~ △WBM	Two pairs of corresponding angles are equal.

If two pairs of corresponding angles are equal, I know that the angles in the third pair are also equal.

7.2 Use Similar Triangles to Solve Problems • MHR 343

Step 2: Find the scale factor.

In △ABS and △WBM, BS and BM are corresponding sides. Their ratio gives the scale factor, k:

$$k = \frac{BM}{BS}$$

$$= \frac{24}{9.3}$$

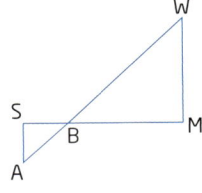

Each side in the larger triangle is $\frac{24}{9.3}$ times as long as its corresponding side in the smaller triangle. Leave the scale factor in this form for more accuracy in later calculations.

Step 3: Find the width of the river.

In △ABS and △WBM, AS and WM are corresponding sides. Use the scale factor to find WM.

$$\frac{WM}{AS} = k$$

$$\frac{WM}{8.4} = \frac{24}{9.3}$$

$$WM = \frac{24}{9.3}(8.4) \quad \text{\textbf{Multiply both sides by 8.4.}}$$

$$\doteq 21.667$$

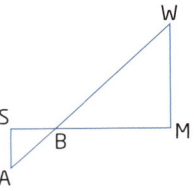

21.677 m is too precise an answer based on the measurements given. One of the measures, BM, is only accurate to the nearest metre. So, it is reasonable to round the answer to the nearest metre.

Therefore, the width of the river is approximately 22 m.

Example 2 Areas of Similar Figures

a) What is the relationship between the areas in each pair of similar figures?

i) [triangles with sides 3, 4, 5 and 6, 8, 10]

ii) [rectangles 2 × 3 and 8 × 12]

b) Find the scale factor, k, for each pair of figures.

c) Compare your answers to parts a) and b).

Solution

a) Find the areas of the figures.

i) Smaller Triangle

$A = \dfrac{1}{2}bh$

$= \dfrac{1}{2}(3)(4)$

$= 6$

The area of the smaller triangle is 6 square units.

Larger Triangle

$A = \dfrac{1}{2}bh$

$= \dfrac{1}{2}(6)(8)$

$= 24$

The area of the larger triangle is 24 square units.

The area of the larger triangle is 4 times the area of the smaller triangle.

ii) Smaller Rectangle

$A = l \times w$

$= 2 \times 3$

$= 6$

The area of the smaller rectangle is 6 square units.

Larger Rectangle

$A = l \times w$

$= 8 \times 12$

$= 96$

The area of the larger rectangle is 96 square units.

The area of the larger rectangle is 16 times the area of the smaller rectangle.

b) i) Since each side length of the larger triangle is 2 times the length of the corresponding side of the smaller triangle, the scale factor is $k = 2$.

ii) Since each side length of the larger rectangle is 4 times the length of the corresponding side of the smaller rectangle, the scale factor is $k = 4$.

c) In both cases, the ratio of the area of the larger figure to the area of the smaller figure is equal to the square of the scale factor, k.

This relationship holds for all similar figures: the ratio of the areas of two similar figures is equal to the square of the scale factor.

Another way to write this is $A_{\triangle PQR} = k^2(A_{\triangle ABC})$. You can use this to solve for an unknown area.

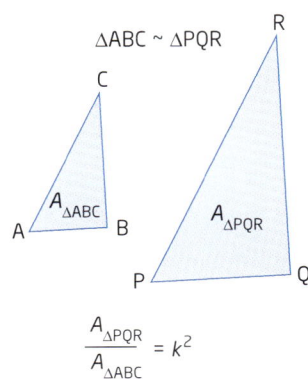

$\triangle ABC \sim \triangle PQR$

$\dfrac{A_{\triangle PQR}}{A_{\triangle ABC}} = k^2$

Example 3 Solve for an Unknown Area

The shaded area is to be an industrial zone.

Find the area of the industrial zone. Assume that King and Queen are parallel and that all streets and the track are straight.

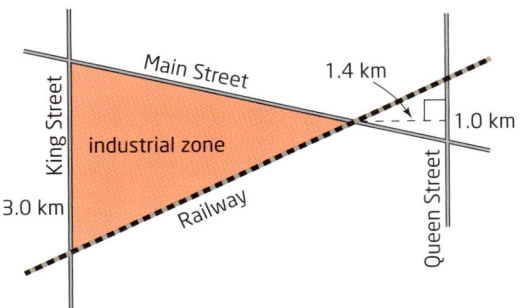

Solution

Identify two similar triangles. Find the scale factor and use it to find the area of the larger triangle.

I'll make a simplified diagram.

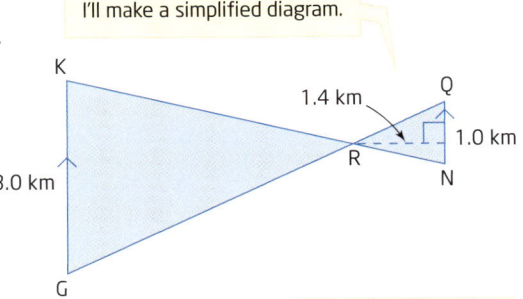

Statement	Reason
$\angle KRG = \angle NRQ$	Opposite angles are equal.
$\angle RKG = \angle RNQ$	Alternate angles are equal.
$\triangle KRG \sim \triangle NRQ$	Corresponding angles are equal.

If two pairs of corresponding angles are equal, I know that the angles in the third pair are equal, too.

The scale factor is equal to the ratio of corresponding sides:

$$k = \frac{KG}{NQ}$$
$$= \frac{3.0}{1.0}$$
$$= 3$$

Find the area of the smaller triangle using the given information.

$A_{\triangle NRQ} = \frac{1}{2}bh$ **Apply the formula for the area of a triangle.**

$\phantom{A_{\triangle NRQ}} = \frac{1}{2}(1.0)(1.4)$

$\phantom{A_{\triangle NRQ}} = 0.7$

The area of the smaller triangle is 0.7 km². Use this and the scale factor, $k = 3$, to find the area of the larger similar triangle.

$A_{\triangle KRG} = k^2(A_{\triangle NRQ})$
$\phantom{A_{\triangle KRG}} = 3^2(0.7)$
$\phantom{A_{\triangle KRG}} = 9(0.7)$
$\phantom{A_{\triangle KRG}} = 6.3$

The area of the industrial zone is 6.3 km².

Key Concepts

- The scale factor, k, relates the lengths of corresponding sides of similar figures. For example, in △ABC and △PQR,

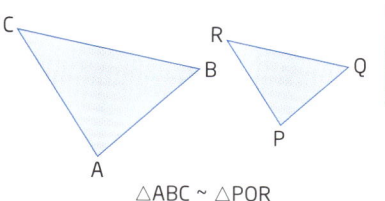

△ABC ~ △PQR

$$\frac{AB}{PQ} = \frac{BC}{QR} = \frac{CA}{RP} = k$$

These relationships can also be written as follows:
AB = k(PQ)   BC = k(QR)   CA = k(RP)

- The square of the scale factor relates the areas of two similar figures:

$$\frac{A_{\triangle ABC}}{A_{\triangle PQR}} = k^2$$

This relationship can also be written as $A_{\triangle ABC} = k^2(A_{\triangle PQR})$.

Communicate Your Understanding

C1 **a)** Explain how the scale factor relates two similar triangles.

b) Explain how you can use the scale factor to find an unknown side length.

C2 **a)** How are the areas of two similar figures related?

b) Explain using words and diagrams how you can find the area of a triangle using the area of a similar triangle and the scale factor.

C3 Explain how you can use a metre stick and shadows to measure the height of an inaccessible object, such as a flagpole or a tree.

Practise

1. A right triangle has side lengths 3 cm, 4 cm, and 5 cm.
   a) Draw the triangle.
   b) A similar triangle has hypotenuse 30 cm long. What is the scale factor?
   c) What are the lengths of the legs?

2. Refer to question 1.
   a) Find the area of each triangle.
   b) How are these areas related?
   c) How do the areas help to confirm that the triangles are similar?

3. a) Draw a triangle.
   b) Draw a similar triangle using a scale factor of 2.
   c) Repeat part b) using a scale factor of 4.

4. Refer to question 3.
   a) Measure, as accurately as possible, the base and height of the first triangle. Use this information to find the area of the triangle. Round your answer to the nearest tenth.
   b) Use your answer from part a) and the scale factors to calculate the areas of the two larger triangles.
   c) Measure the base and height of each larger triangle and use them to calculate their areas. Compare these results with those obtained in part b). Are they the same? If they are not the same, describe what factors might explain why not.

For help with questions 5 to 7, see Example 1.

5. a) Show why △PQR is similar to △STR.
   b) Find the lengths *x* and *y*.

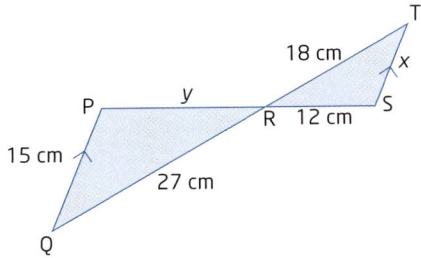

6. The triangles in each pair are similar. Find the unknown side lengths.

a)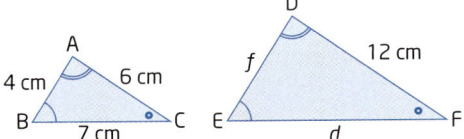

b)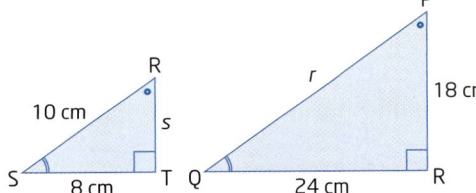

c)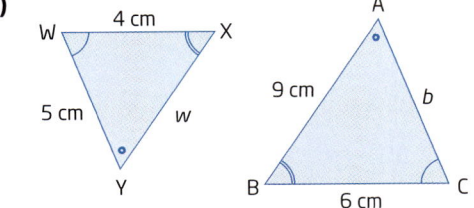

d)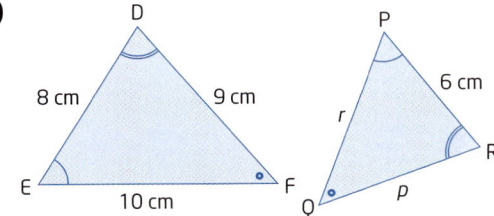

e)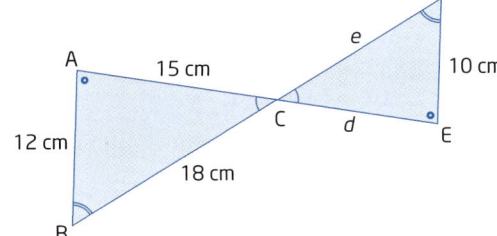

7. Find the length of *x* in each.

a)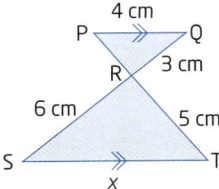

b)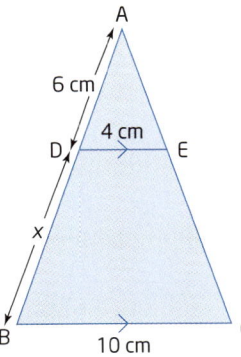

For help with question 8, see Examples 2 and 3.

8. a) △PQR ~ △STU. Find the area of △PQR.

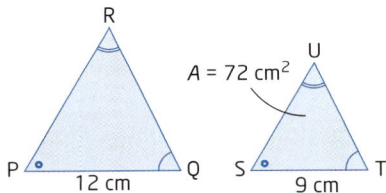

b) △ABC ~ △DEF. Find the area of △ABC.

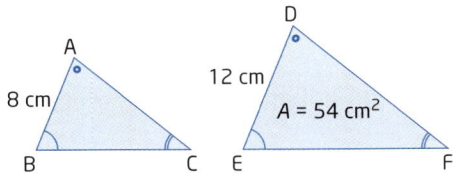

c) △GHI ~ △KLM. Find the area of △KLM.

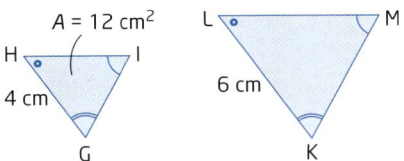

d) △STU ~ △XYZ. Find the area of △STU.

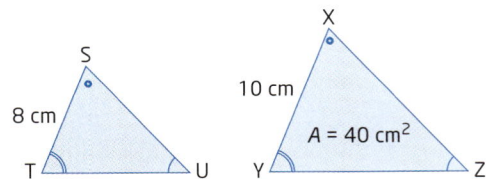

Connect and Apply

9. To measure the height of a tree, Cynthia has her little brother, BR, stand so that the tip of his shadow coincides with the tip of the tree's shadow, at point C.

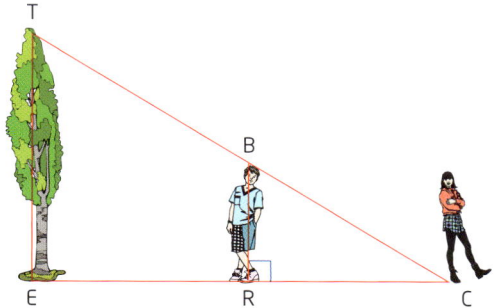

Cynthia's brother, who is 1.2 m tall, is 4.2 m from Cynthia, who is standing at C, and 6.5 m from the base of the tree. Find the height of the tree, TE.

10. Find the width of the canyon.

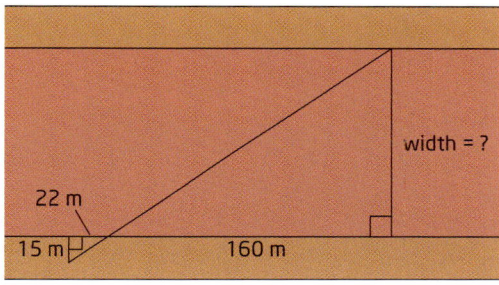

11. Use the dimensions of the surveyors' triangles to find the width of the river, to the nearest metre.

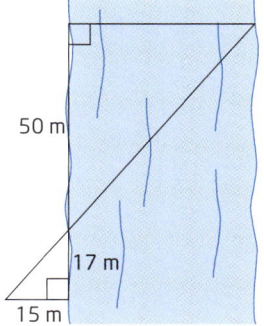

12. Melanie is designing a crest for her hockey team, the Trigazoids. Her prototype consists of four congruent equilateral triangles.

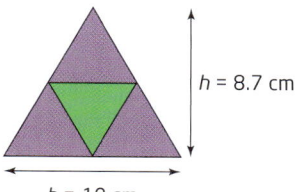

a) What is the total area of this crest?
b) What is the area of
   • the green section?
   • the purple sections?
c) What is the area of a giant similar crest with base 30 cm?
d) What is the height of a similar crest with area 500 cm^2?

13. The front of each brick in the fireplace measures 10 cm by 20 cm.

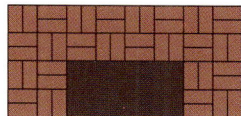

a) How many similar rectangles of different sizes can you find? Sketch a diagram to illustrate them. Label their dimensions (length and width).
b) What is the area of the front of one brick?
c) Find the area of the entire fireplace, including the opening.
d) Find the area of the opening.
e) Find the area of the fireplace, excluding the opening.

14. Find the length and width of the pond. The following measures are known:
AB = 14 m
BC = 11 m
Assume that XY is a line of symmetry for the pond.

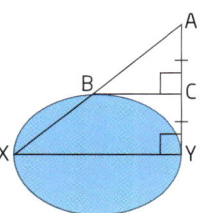

7.2 Use Similar Triangles to Solve Problems • MHR 349

15. Determine the height of a tall tree, a flagpole, or the side of a building in your schoolyard using similar triangles. Explain your method using words and diagrams.

16. While looking through a cylindrical tube, Rita moves to a point where the height of a picture just fits within her field of view, as shown.

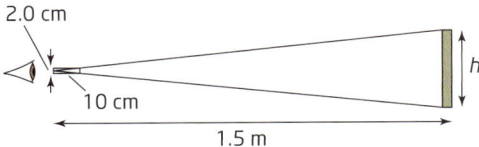

Rita is standing 1.5 m from the picture. The length and diameter of the viewing tube are as shown. Find the height of the picture.

17. Use algebraic and geometric reasoning to show how the areas of two similar right triangles are related by the square of the scale factor, k^2.

18. a) Sketch several pairs of similar acute triangles with different scale factors, k.
   b) Find the areas of the triangles in each pair.
   c) Find the ratio of the areas of the triangles in each pair. How is this ratio related to the scale factor, k?

19. The areas of two similar triangles are 72 cm² and 162 cm². What is the ratio of the lengths of their corresponding sides?

20. △ABC and △DEF are similar. The ratio of their corresponding sides is 3:5. What is the ratio of their perimeters? Explain.

21. Use similar triangles to measure the height of the building in which you live. Write a brief report on how you solved this problem. Include diagrams. Discuss how accurate you think your answer is. Suggest ways to improve your method to get a more accurate height.

22. Chapter Problem The first leg of your race will begin on the southern shore of James Bay, at Moosonee. From there you will travel to Regina, then to Churchill, located on the eastern shore of Hudson Bay. Take note of your journey. The triangle formed by these three locations is similar to the triangle formed by Pittsburgh, Repulse Bay (located near the Arctic Circle), and your next destination. Identify the similar triangles and determine your next destination. *Hint: Move quickly, and you will be glad that you beat the rest of the flock!*

Achievement Check

23. Teschia is making a scale drawing to help her redesign her flower garden.

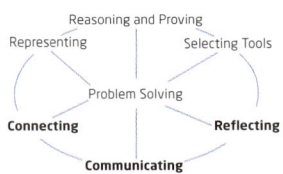

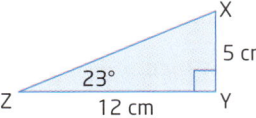

a) Calculate the length of ZX and the measure of ∠ZXY.

b) If the hypotenuse of the actual flower garden measures 6.5 m, what is the perimeter of the actual garden?

c) What is the scale factor of Teschia's drawing?

d) What is the ratio of the area of the flower garden to the area of the scale drawing?

Extend

24. Carol is building a staircase from the floor of her barn to the loft, which is 3.6 m above the floor. She is using steps that are each 30 cm high and 40 cm deep.

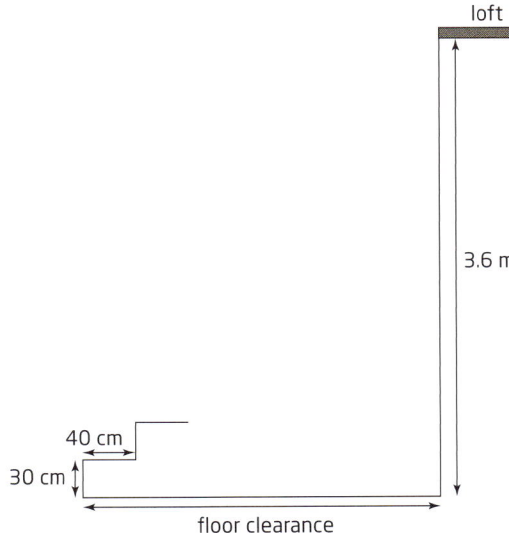

a) How much floor clearance will Carol need in order to fit the staircase?

b) How many steps will be required?

25. The scale on a map is 1 cm represents 5 km. A provincial park has an area of 6 cm² on the map. What is the actual area of the park, to the nearest square kilometre?

26. Krista used her Global Positioning System (GPS) device to obtain information on the distance and direction from Niagara Falls to London, England, and to Miami, Florida. She drew a triangle, and calculated the angles in the triangle from the GPS data. She noticed that the sum of the angles was not 180°, as expected.

a) Why did this occur?

b) Would you expect the sum to be more or less than 180°? Explain.

27. Math Contest A naturalist's study in Northern Ontario finds that 25% of the area is water and 60% of the remaining area is forest. The rest, 12 000 ha, is rock. How large is the study area, in hectares?

A 36 000 ha

B 40 000 ha

C 68 000 ha

D 80 000 ha

E 100 000 ha

28. Math Contest In △ABC, AB = 24 cm and BC = 10 cm. BD is perpendicular to AC. Find the ratio of the shaded area to the unshaded area.

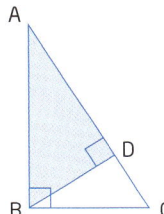

29. Math Contest Express the length of the hypotenuse of a right triangle in terms of its area, A, and it perimeter, P.

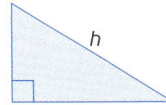

30. Math Contest Two neighbouring houses are located at A and B, near a straight section of a rural road, RD. The electric company plans to place a pole, P, at the roadside and connect wires from the pole to the two houses. How far from point R should the pole be located so that the minimum length of wire is needed?

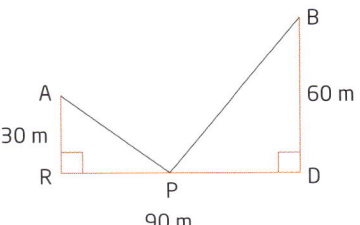

7.3 The Tangent Ratio

Cory is installing wheelchair ramps at a high school. Not all locations require the same vertical climb, so he will need to adjust the length of the ramp in each case. In general, a wheelchair ramp should have a slope of not more than $\frac{1}{12}$.

How can Cory ensure that all ramps have the same slope? How is the slope related to the angle the ramp makes with the floor?

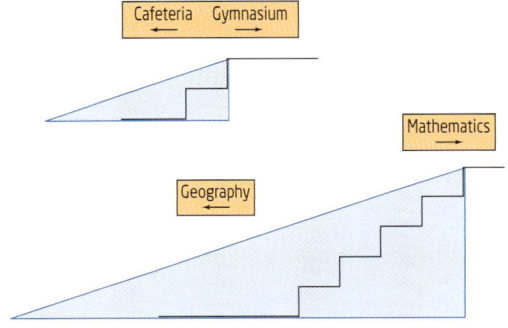

Investigate

Tools
- grid paper
- protractor
- ruler

slope angle
- angle opposite the rise and adjacent to the run

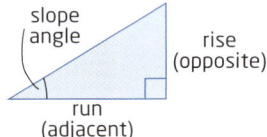

What is the tangent ratio and how is it related to slope?

Method 1: Use Pencil and Paper

1. Draw three similar right triangles on grid paper for each **slope angle**. Each triangle represents a different ramp.
   - 10°
   - 25°
   - 60°

2. **a)** Measure the rise and run of each triangle, and use these to calculate the slope. Record your results in a table like this one.

Triangle	Slope Angle	Rise	Run	Slope (to three decimal places)

   b) What do you notice about the slope of the ramp for similar right triangles?

352 MHR • Chapter 7

3. The slope in your table in step 2 is called the **tangent** of the slope angle.

   a) Draw three more similar ramps with a different slope angle than those in step 1. Measure the rise, run, and slope of these ramps and record your results in your table. Explain what you notice.

   b) Add a column to your table labelled **Tangent** and use a calculator to calculate the tangent ratio of the slope angle. What do you notice?

4. How can you find the tangent of the other acute angle in the triangle? Rotate each original triangle 90° counterclockwise and repeat the investigation.

5. **Reflect**

   a) What is the tangent ratio of an angle? What is it the same as?

   b) How does the tangent of an angle change when you change the size of the triangle but keep the angle the same?

Method 2: Use *The Geometer's Sketchpad*®

1. Open *The Geometer's Sketchpad*® and begin a new sketch.

2. Construct a small ramp.
   - Construct a short horizontal line segment.
   - Select the segment and the right endpoint.
   - From the **Construct** menu, choose **Perpendicular Line**.
   - From the **Construct** menu, choose **Point on Perpendicular Line**.
   - Select the perpendicular line. From the **Display** menu, choose **Hide Perpendicular Line**.
   - Construct segments to complete the right triangle.

3. a) Set the precision of the measurements to thousandths. From the **Edit** menu, choose **Preferences**. Set the **Precision** to **thousandths** for **Angle**, **Distance**, and **Other**.

   b) Measure the rise and run of the ramp, and use these to calculate the slope.
   - Select the vertical and horizontal segments. From the **Measure** menu, choose **Length**.
   - From the **Measure** menu, choose **Calculate**. A calculator will appear.
   - Select the rise measure.
   - Click on ÷.
   - Select the run measure.
   - Click **OK**.

   c) A ratio measure will appear. What does this ratio represent?

   d) Right click on the measure and choose **Label Measurement** to rename the measure to correspond to your answer to part c).

tangent of an angle

- the ratio of the side opposite an angle to the side adjacent to the angle

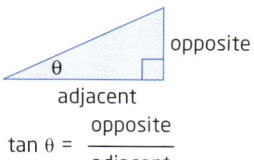

$$\tan \theta = \frac{\text{opposite}}{\text{adjacent}}$$

Literacy Connections

The short form for tangent is tan. The Greek letter θ, pronounced "theta," is often used to represent angles.

Tools

- computer with *The Geometer's Sketchpad*®

Technology Tip

- Holding the **Shift** key as you draw a segment keeps it horizontal or vertical.
- From the **Display** menu, use the **Hide** command, or press **Ctrl + H**, to tidy up your sketch.

4. Measure the angle the ramp makes with the floor.
   - Select the three points in order so that you select the point where the ramp meets the floor second.
   - From the **Measure** menu, choose **Angle**.

   Label this measure the **slope angle**.

5. **a)** Click and drag each vertex of the triangle. Explain what happens in each case.

   b) Does the triangle remain a right triangle? Explain why or why not.

   c) Return the triangle to the way you had it at the end of step 3.

6. **a)** Record how the measures change as you change the triangle. To make a table in *The Geometer's Sketchpad*®:
   - Select the measurements in the following order: slope angle, rise, run, slope.
   - From the **Graph** menu, choose **Tabulate**.
   - Right click on the table and choose **Add Table Data**.
   - Choose **Add 10 Entries As Values Change**.

   Click and drag the vertex above the right angle to change the slope angle. Ten sets of measurements will be recorded in your table.

   b) Discover what happens to the slope if you change the size of the triangle but keep the slope angle. Make a new table, as in part a). Click on and drag the vertex at the right angle to make similar triangles with the same slope angle. Record your results in your new table. Describe what happens to each of the following measures:
   - rise
   - run
   - slope
   - slope angle

7. Repeat step 6 for a different slope angle. Does the slope of the ramp change if the angle remains the same? Explain.

8. The slope in your table in steps 6 and 7 is called the **tangent** of the slope angle.

   You can use *The Geometer's Sketchpad*® to calculate the tangent of an angle.
   - From the **Measure** menu, choose **Calculate**.
   - Click on the **Functions** key. From the menu of functions, click on **tan**.
   - Select the angle measure of the ramp.
   - Click **OK**.

   Calculate the tangents of several slope angles and compare them to the slope of the ramp. What do you notice?

> **Technology Tip**
>
> In step 3, you created a dynamic calculation that automatically updated itself when you changed your sketch.

9. How can you find the tangent of the other acute angle in the triangle? Rotate your original triangle 90° counterclockwise and repeat the investigation.

10. **Reflect**

   a) What is the tangent ratio of an angle? What is it the same as?

   b) How does the tangent of an angle change when you change the size of the triangle but keep the angle the same?

Method 3: Use a Graphing Calculator

Tools

- TI-83 Plus or TI-84 Plus graphing calculator

1. Press APPS and choose **Cabri Jr**. If the axes are not visible, choose the **F5** menu. Choose **Hide/Show**, and then **Axes**. Move the cursor to the origin. Press ALPHA and move the origin until the first quadrant occupies most of the screen, as shown.

2. Construct a small ramp.
   - Choose the **Segment** tool from the **F2** menu. Draw a horizontal line segment, as shown.
   - Choose **Perp.** from the **F3** menu.
   - Move the cursor to the right endpoint of the segment. Press ENTER. Move the cursor to the segment until it flashes. Press ENTER. A line perpendicular to the segment appears, through the right endpoint.
   - Choose **Point** from the **F2** menu, and then **Point on**. Move the cursor to a point on the perpendicular line, and press ENTER.
   - Choose **Hide/Show** from the **F5** menu. Then, choose **Object**. Move the cursor to the perpendicular line until it flashes. Press ENTER. The line is hidden.
   - Construct segments to complete the right triangle.

3. a) Measure the rise and run of the ramp, and use these to calculate the slope.
   - Choose **Measure** from the **F5** menu. Then, choose **D. & Length**.
   - Move the cursor to the run until it flashes. Press ENTER. Move the measurement to a suitable location, and press ENTER again.
   - Repeat this procedure to measure the rise.
   - Choose **Calculate** from the **F5** menu. Move the cursor to the rise measurement, and press ENTER. Move the cursor to the run measurement. Press ENTER. Then, press ÷. Move the calculation to a convenient location, and press ENTER.

   b) What does this ratio represent?

4. Measure the angle the ramp makes with the floor.
   - Choose **Measure** from the **F5** menu. Then, choose **Angle**.
   - Move the cursor to the top vertex of the triangle. Press ENTER. Move to the left vertex. Press ENTER. Move to the third vertex. Press ENTER. Move the measurement to a convenient location, and press ENTER.

   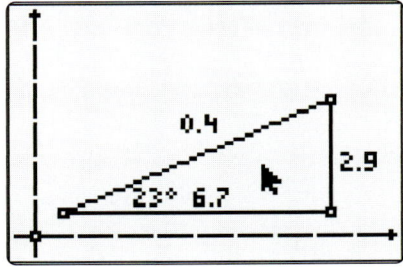

   Call this the **slope angle**.

5. **a)** Move the cursor to one of the vertices of the triangle. Press ALPHA. Drag the vertex of the triangle. Explain what happens. Try dragging the other vertices, one at a time. Explain what happens.

   b) Does the triangle remain a right triangle? Explain why or why not.

   c) Return the triangle to the way you had it at the end of step 4.

6. **a)** Select and drag the vertex above the right angle to change the slope angle. Record the measures in a table like this one.

Slope Angle	Rise	Run	Slope (to three decimal places)

   b) Discover what happens to the slope if you change the size of the triangle but keep the slope angle the same. Select and drag the left vertex of the triangle. Record your results in the table from part a). Describe what happens to each of the following measures:
   - rise
   - run
   - slope
   - slope angle

7. Repeat step 6 for a different slope angle. Does the slope of the ramp change if the angle remains the same? Explain.

8. The slope in your table in steps 6 and 7 is called the **tangent** of the slope angle. Calculate the tangent of several slope angles and compare it to the slope of the ramp. What do you notice?

9. How can you find the tangent of the other acute angle in the triangle? Rotate your original triangle 90° counterclockwise and repeat the investigation.

10. **Reflect**
    a) What is the tangent ratio of an angle? What is it the same as?
    b) How does the tangent of an angle change when you change the size of the triangle but keep the angle the same?

In the Investigate, you saw that the tangent of an acute angle in a right triangle is constant if the angle stays the same, even if the size of the triangle changes. This is because of the properties of similar triangles. Since the ratios of corresponding sides of similar triangles are equal, and the tangent is a ratio of sides, the tangents of the angles of similar triangles are equal. For example, in similar triangles △ABC and △DEF,

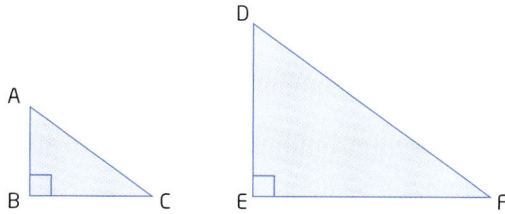

$$\tan C = \frac{\text{opposite}}{\text{adjacent}} \quad \text{and} \quad \tan F = \frac{\text{opposite}}{\text{adjacent}}$$

$$= \frac{AB}{BC} \qquad\qquad\qquad = \frac{DE}{EF}$$

By similar triangles,

$$\frac{AB}{DE} = \frac{BC}{EF}$$

$$\frac{AB}{BC} = \frac{DE}{EF} \quad \text{Divide both sides by BC and multiply both sides by DE.}$$

So, tan C = tan F.

Example 1 Find the Tangent Ratio From Given Sides

Find tan θ for each triangle, expressed as a fraction and as a decimal correct to four decimal places.

a) 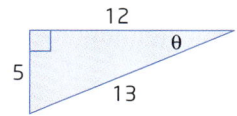 b) 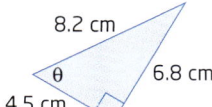 c)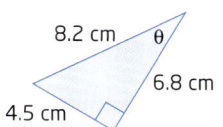

Solution

a) Identify the opposite and adjacent sides relative to the angle θ.

$$\tan \theta = \frac{\text{opposite}}{\text{adjacent}}$$

$$= \frac{5}{12}$$

$$\doteq 0.4167$$

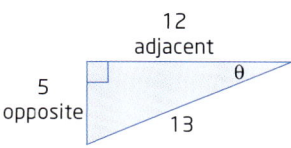

Literacy Connections

Expressions involving tangent mean "the tangent of." For example, tan A means "the tangent of angle A." Similarly, tan 25° means "the tangent of 25°."

b) Identify the opposite and adjacent sides.

$$\tan \theta = \frac{\text{opposite}}{\text{adjacent}}$$

$$= \frac{6.8}{4.5}$$

$$\doteq 1.5111$$

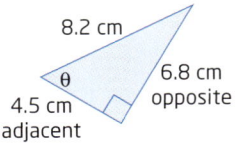

c) When you go from one acute angle to the other in a right triangle, the opposite and adjacent sides relative to the angle become reversed.

$$\tan \theta = \frac{\text{opposite}}{\text{adjacent}}$$

$$= \frac{4.5}{6.8}$$

$$\doteq 0.6618$$

> This is the same triangle as in part b), but I am calculating the tangent of the other acute angle.

Example 2 Find the Tangent of an Angle

Evaluate each of the following with a calculator. Record your answer rounded to four decimal places.

a) tan 25°

b) tan 60°

Solution

Use a scientific or graphing calculator.

a) tan 25° $\doteq$ 0.4663

b) tan 60° $\doteq$ 1.7321

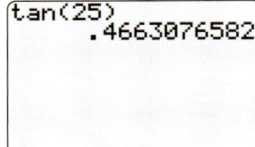

Technology Tip

Not all scientific calculators work the same way. With some, you press

With others, you press

On a graphing calculator, press

TAN 25) =

Make sure your calculator is in degree mode.

Calculators have an inverse function that allows you to apply the tangent ratio in reverse. If you know the ratio $\frac{\text{opposite}}{\text{adjacent}}$, you can find the angle whose tangent this ratio represents.

Example 3 Find an Angle Using the Tangent Ratio

Fiona is building a skateboarding ramp. She wants the ramp to rise 1 m in a horizontal distance of 2 m. At what acute angles should she cut the wood, rounded to the nearest degree?

Solution

Sketch and label a diagram of the ramp.

Find ∠A.

tan A = $\dfrac{\text{opposite}}{\text{adjacent}}$

$= \dfrac{2}{1}$

$= 2$

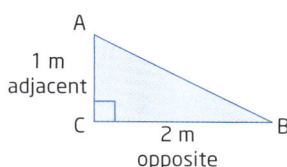

To find ∠A, calculate the inverse tangent of 2.
∠A = $\tan^{-1}(2)$
$\doteq 63.43$

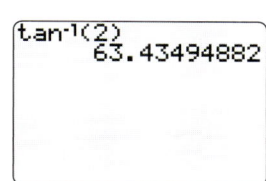

One of the acute angles is about 63°.

Find ∠B.

Method 1: Apply the Tangent Ratio

tan B = $\dfrac{\text{opposite}}{\text{adjacent}}$

$= \dfrac{1}{2}$

$= 0.5$

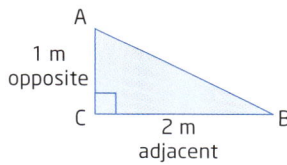

Apply the inverse tangent operation.
∠B = $\tan^{-1}(0.5)$
$\doteq 26.56$

The other acute angle is about 27°.

Method 2: Use Geometric Reasoning

The sum of three interior angles in any triangle is 180°.

∠A + ∠B + ∠C = 180°
63° + ∠B + 90° = 180°
         ∠B = 180° − (63° + 90°)
             = 180° − 153°
             = 27°

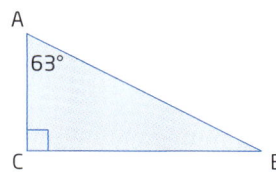

The other acute angle is about 27°.

Fiona should cut the wood using acute angles of approximately 63° and 27°.

Note that Method 1 will give a more accurate measure for the angle, since only given information is being used.

Literacy Connections

Tangent and **inverse tangent** are opposite operations, like addition and subtraction. For example,

tan 60° $\doteq$ 1.7321

$\tan^{-1}(1.7321) \doteq 60°$

The second statement is read as "the inverse tangent of 1.7321 is approximately equal to 60 degrees."

Technology Tip

With some scientific calculators, you press
[2nd] [TAN⁻¹] 0.5 [=]

With others, you press
0.5 [2nd] [TAN⁻¹]

The tangent ratio relates two sides of a right triangle and an angle. If you know an angle and the length of one of the legs of the triangle, you can find the length of the other leg.

Example 4 Find a Side Length Using the Tangent Ratio

Find the length, x, in the diagram, rounded to the nearest tenth of a centimetre.

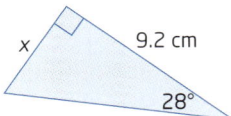

Solution

Write the tangent ratio for the given angle in terms of the side lengths.

$$\tan 28° = \frac{\text{opposite}}{\text{adjacent}}$$

$$\tan 28° = \frac{x}{9.2}$$

$9.2(\tan 28°) = x$ **Multiply both sides by 9.2.**

$4.891 \doteq x$ 9.2 [×] 28 [TAN] [=] or 9.2 [×] [TAN] 28 [=]

The length of side x is about 4.9 cm.

Example 5 Solve a Multi-Step Problem Using the Tangent Ratio

A radio transmitter is to be supported with a guy wire, as shown. The wire is to form a 65° angle with the ground and reach 30 m up the transmitter.

The wire can be ordered in whole-number lengths of metres. How much wire should be ordered?

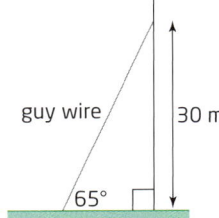

Solution

Use the tangent ratio of the given angle to find the distance, d, from the tower that the guy wire should be secured.

Then, apply the Pythagorean theorem to find the length, w, of wire needed.

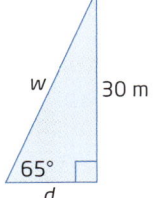

$$\tan 65° = \frac{\text{opposite}}{\text{adjacent}}$$

$$\tan 65° = \frac{30}{d}$$

$d(\tan 65°) = 30$ **Multiply both sides by d.**

$d = \dfrac{30}{\tan 65°}$ **Divide both sides by tan 65°.**

Apply the Pythagorean theorem to find the length of wire needed.

$w^2 = d^2 + 30^2$

$w^2 = \left(\dfrac{30}{\tan 65°}\right)^2 + 900$

$w = \sqrt{\left(\dfrac{30}{\tan 65°}\right)^2 + 900}$

$w \doteq 33.101$

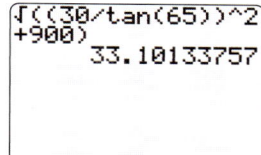

The length of guy wire needed is about 33.1 m. It can only be ordered in whole-number lengths. 33 m is too short, so round up to the next metre. At least 34 m of guy wire should be ordered.

Key Concepts

- The ratio of the opposite side to the adjacent side of an angle in a right triangle is called the tangent of that angle.

  $\tan \theta = \dfrac{\text{opposite}}{\text{adjacent}}$

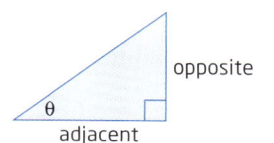

- You can use a scientific or graphing calculator to
  - express the tangent of an angle as a decimal
  - find one of the acute angles when both leg lengths are known in a right triangle
  - find a side length if one acute angle and one leg of a right triangle are known

Communicate Your Understanding

C1 Explain how the tangent of the slope angle is related to the slope of a ramp.

C2 a) Explain how you can identify the opposite and adjacent sides of a right triangle.

b) Explain how these can change in a given triangle. Use a diagram to support your explanation.

C3 a) Explain what each calculator function does:
- tangent
- inverse tangent

b) When would you use each function?

c) How are these functions related to each other?

Practise

For help with questions 1 and 2, see Example 1.

1. Find the tangent of the angle indicated, to four decimal places.

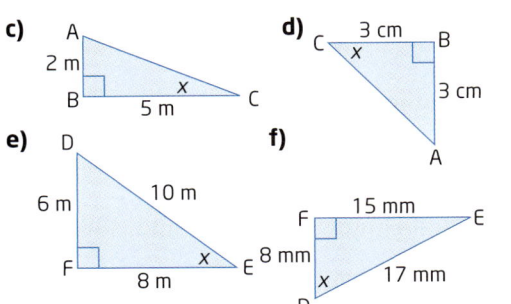

2. Refer to question 1. Find the tangent of the other acute angle, to four decimal places.

For help with question 3, see Example 2.

3. Evaluate with a calculator. Record your answer to four decimal places.
   a) tan 65°   b) tan 15°
   c) tan 62°   d) tan 5°
   e) tan 30.7° f) tan 82.4°
   g) tan 20.5° h) tan 45°

For help with questions 4 to 8, see Example 3.

4. Find the measure of each angle, to the nearest degree.
   a) tan θ = 1.5   b) tan A = $\frac{3}{4}$
   c) tan B = 0.6000   d) tan W = $\frac{4}{5}$
   e) tan C = 0.8333   f) tan θ = $\frac{6}{7}$
   g) tan X = 3.0250   h) tan θ = $\frac{15}{9}$

5. Find the measures of both acute angles in each triangle, to the nearest degree.

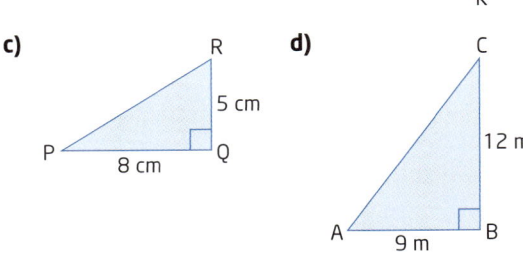

6. Find the length of the unknown side, to the nearest tenth.

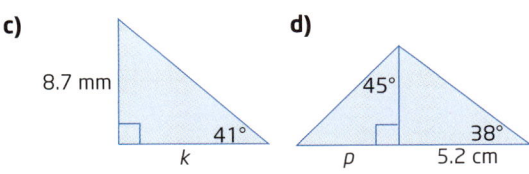

7. Find the length of x, to the nearest tenth of a metre.

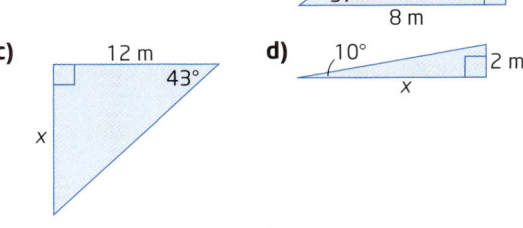

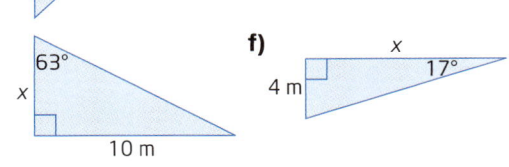

8. Find the length of *x*, to the nearest tenth of a metre.

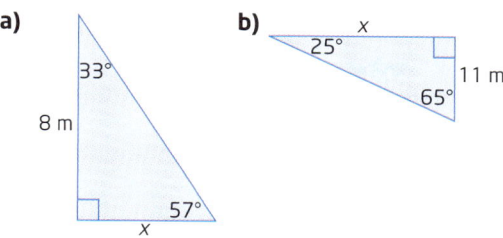

Connect and Apply

9. To measure the width of a river, Kirstyn uses a large rock, an oak tree, and an elm tree, which are positioned as shown.

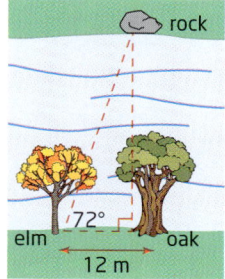

Show how Kirstyn can use the tangent ratio to find the width of the river, to the nearest metre.

10. A surveyor is positioned at a traffic intersection, viewing a marker on the other side of the street. The marker is 18 m from the intersection. The surveyor cannot measure the width directly because there is too much traffic. Find the width of James Street, to the nearest tenth of a metre.

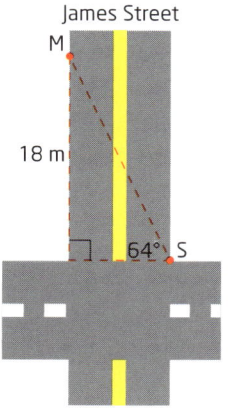

11. Rocco and Biff are two koalas sitting at the top of two eucalyptus trees, which are located 10 m apart, as shown. Rocco's tree is exactly half as tall as Biff's tree. From Rocco's point of view, the angle separating Biff and the base of his tree is 70°.

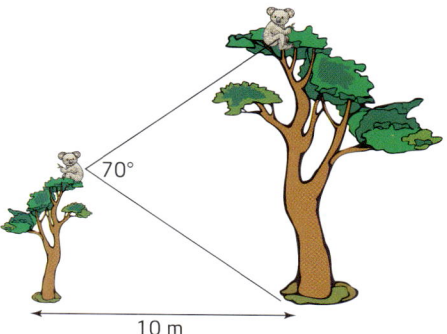

How high off the ground is each koala?

12. Police are responding to a distress call:

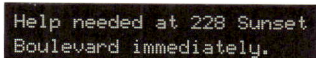

Police headquarters and the trouble site are shown.

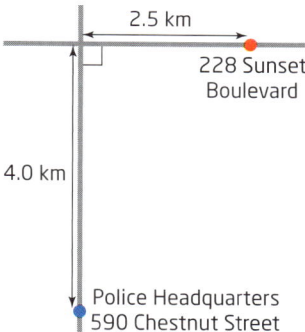

Squad cars and a helicopter are both immediately dispatched to the site from headquarters.

a) At what angle to Chestnut Street should the helicopter travel?

b) Assuming that the squad cars can travel at an average speed of 60 km/h and the helicopter can travel twice as fast, how much longer will it take for the squad cars to reach the site than the helicopter?

c) Describe any assumptions you make in your solutions.

13. The diagram shows the roof of a house. How wide is the house, to the nearest metre?

    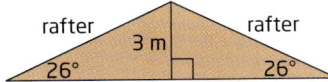

14. Petra walked diagonally across a rectangular schoolyard measuring 45 m by 65 m. To the nearest degree, at what angle with respect to the shorter side did she walk?

15. Comfortable stairs have a slope of $\frac{3}{4}$.

    What angle do the stairs make with the horizontal, to the nearest degree?

16. Find the length of x, then the length of y, to the nearest tenth of a metre.

    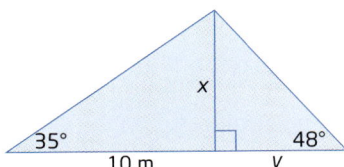

17. Find the length of x, to the nearest tenth of a centimetre, then the measure of ∠y, to the nearest degree.

    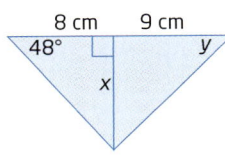

18. To measure the height of a building, Chico notes that its shadow is 8.5 m long. He also finds that a line joining the top of the building to the tip of the shadow forms a 65° angle with the flat ground.

    a) Draw a diagram to illustrate this situation.

    b) Find the height of the building, to the nearest tenth of a metre.

19. a) Find the tangent of several angles with values between 1° and 44°. Organize your results in a table like this one.

Angle, θ	tan θ

    b) What is the value of tan 45°?

    c) Add the tangents of several angles with values between 46° and 89° to your table.

    d) Add the tangents of several angles with values very close to, but not equal to, 90° to your table.

    e) Based on your findings, what conclusions can you make about the tangents of angles
    - less than 45°?
    - greater than 45° and less than 90°?
    - very close to, but not equal to, 90°?

    f) Use the definition of the tangent ratio and geometric reasoning to justify your conclusions. Include diagrams in your explanation.

20. a) Use a calculator to evaluate the following:
    - tan 0°
    - tan 90°

    b) Use the definition of the tangent ratio and geometric reasoning to explain your results. Include diagrams in your explanation.

21. At hockey practice, Lars has the puck in front of the net, as shown.

    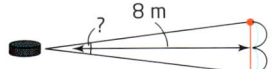

    He is exactly 8 m away from the middle of the net, which is 2 m wide. Within what angle must Lars fire his shot in order to get it in the net, to the nearest degree?

22. Refer to question 21.

    a) Does Lars have a better chance, a worse chance, or the same chance to score if he positions himself directly in front of one of the posts, as shown? Explain your reasoning and any assumptions you make.

    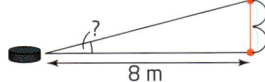

    b) Repeat part a) for the case in which Lars moves
    - directly closer to the net
    - directly farther from the net

Extend

23. a) Make a table of values for tan θ for values of θ between 0° and 90°.

b) Graph the relationship. Is the relationship linear or non-linear? Explain.

c) Describe the shape of the graph and any interesting features you can identify.

24. The angle θ at which a skier slides down a hill with a coefficient of friction, μ, at a constant speed, is given by tan θ = μ. Natalie is skiing on a hill with a reported coefficient of friction of 0.6. If Natalie skis down at a constant speed, what is the angle of the hill?

25. The tangent ratio is used to design the bank angle for a curved section of roadway.

Let θ be the bank angle required for a speed limit, v, in kilometres per hour, and a radius, r, in metres. The angle and the speed limit are related by the formula $\tan \theta = \dfrac{v^2}{9.8r}$. Find the bank angle required for a highway curve of radius 50 m that will carry traffic moving at 100 km/h.

Did You Know?

This same relation applies to banking a bicycle or motorcycle when going around a curve, and banking an aircraft in a turn.

26. For each graph,
   i) find the slope of the line
   ii) draw a triangle to find the tangent of the acute angle that the line makes with the x-axis
   iii) compare your answers to parts i) and ii)
   iv) find the acute angle in part ii)

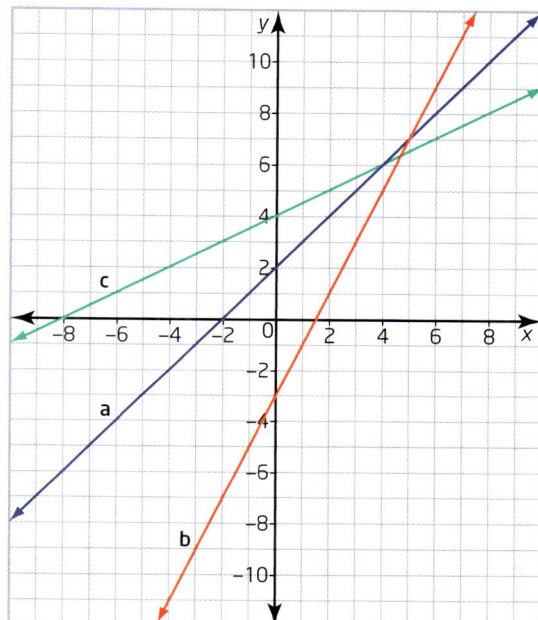

27. Math Contest How many numbers less than 10 000 contain at least one 5?

   A 5000
   B 6561
   C 3439
   D 625
   E 4944

28. Math Contest In the figure, PR = PQ and ∠RPS = 30°. IF PS = PT, what is the measure of △QST?

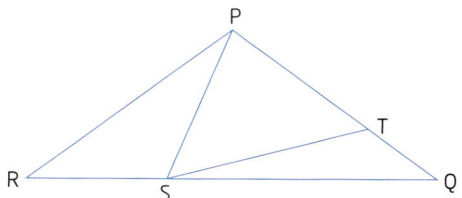

7.4 The Sine and Cosine Ratios

We depend on ships and aircraft to transport goods and people all over the world. If you were the captain of a ship or the pilot of an airplane, how could you make sure that you did not get lost in the middle of the ocean? In ancient times, this was a significant problem.

Today, navigational equipment such as Global Positioning System (GPS) devices makes it much easier to find your way around the planet. Even so, factors such as wind and water currents can sometimes complicate travel plans. How can trigonometry help when this happens?

Investigate

What are the sine and cosine ratios?

In the last section, you learned the tangent ratio. In this activity, you will investigate two other important ratios. In addition to the opposite and adjacent sides, these ratios involve the third side of a right triangle: the hypotenuse.

 Tools
- computer with *The Geometer's Sketchpad®*

OR
- TI-83 Plus or TI-84 Plus graphing calculator

OR
- grid paper
- protractor
- ruler

1. a) Draw a large right triangle △ABC.

b) Measure the length of the side opposite ∠A.

c) Measure the length of the hypotenuse.

d) Calculate the ratio $\dfrac{\text{opposite}}{\text{hypotenuse}}$.

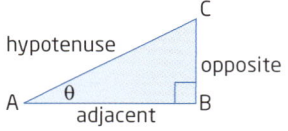

2. a) Create overlapping triangles by adding line segments parallel to one of the legs as shown.

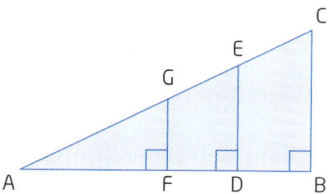

b) Explain why these triangles are similar to the first one.

c) Measure and calculate the following for each similar triangle:
- length of the opposite side
- length of the hypotenuse
- the ratio $\dfrac{\text{opposite}}{\text{hypotenuse}}$

d) Compare the $\dfrac{\text{opposite}}{\text{hypotenuse}}$ ratios for each triangle and describe what you notice.

3. a) Measure the length of the sides adjacent to ∠A for each triangle.

b) Calculate the ratio $\dfrac{\text{adjacent}}{\text{hypotenuse}}$ for each triangle. Describe what you notice.

4. a) Draw a new set of similar triangles, with a different value for ∠A.

b) Calculate and compare the ratio of $\dfrac{\text{opposite}}{\text{hypotenuse}}$ for each similar triangle.

c) Calculate and compare the ratio of $\dfrac{\text{adjacent}}{\text{hypotenuse}}$ for each similar triangle.

d) Repeat for another set of similar triangles.

The two ratios you have just explored are called the sine and cosine ratios. They are defined as

$$\text{sine } A = \dfrac{\text{opposite}}{\text{hypotenuse}} \quad \text{and} \quad \text{cosine } A = \dfrac{\text{adjacent}}{\text{hypotenuse}}$$

Together with the tangent ratio, they are the three **primary trigonometric ratios**.

5. Reflect Summarize what you have discovered about the three primary trigonometric ratios, using words and diagrams.

Technology Tip

To do step 2 using dynamic geometry software, follow these steps:
- Select the horizontal line segment. Construct a point on it.
- Select this segment and the new point, and construct a perpendicular line.
- Select the perpendicular line and the hypotenuse. Construct the point of intersection.
- Hide the perpendicular line. Construct a line segment connecting the two new points.

Literacy Connections

The short forms for sine and cosine are sin and cos.

primary trigonometric ratios
- sine, cosine, and tangent
- often abbreviated as sin, cos, and tan

Example 1 Find the Primary Trigonometric Ratios

Find the three primary trigonometric ratios for θ. Express the ratios as decimals, rounded to four decimal places.

a) 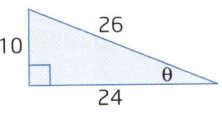   b)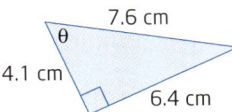

Solution

I need to identify the opposite, adjacent, and hypotenuse sides relative to the angle θ.

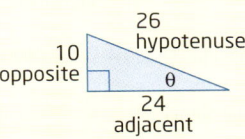

a) $\sin \theta = \dfrac{\text{opposite}}{\text{hypotenuse}}$ $\cos \theta = \dfrac{\text{adjacent}}{\text{hypotenuse}}$ $\tan \theta = \dfrac{\text{opposite}}{\text{adjacent}}$

$ = \dfrac{10}{26}$ $ = \dfrac{24}{26}$ $ = \dfrac{10}{24}$

$ = \dfrac{5}{13}$ $ = \dfrac{12}{13}$ $ = \dfrac{5}{12}$

$ \doteq 0.3846$ $ \doteq 0.9231$ $ \doteq 0.4167$

b)

7.6 cm hypotenuse
4.1 cm adjacent
6.4 cm opposite

$\sin \theta = \dfrac{\text{opposite}}{\text{hypotenuse}}$ $\cos \theta = \dfrac{\text{adjacent}}{\text{hypotenuse}}$ $\tan \theta = \dfrac{\text{opposite}}{\text{adjacent}}$

$ = \dfrac{6.4}{7.6}$ $ = \dfrac{4.1}{7.6}$ $ = \dfrac{6.4}{4.1}$

$ \doteq 0.8421$ $ \doteq 0.5395$ $ \doteq 1.5610$

Since sine, cosine, and tangent are ratios, they have no units.

Literacy Connections

A memory device (or mnemonic) for the three primary trigonometric ratios uses these short forms:

$S = \dfrac{O}{H}$ $C = \dfrac{A}{H}$ $T = \dfrac{O}{A}$

These short forms produce the nonsense phrase soh cah toa. This phrase may help you remember the formulas for the trigonometric ratios.

Making Connections

Trigonometric ratios are often expressed with three or four digits of accuracy. This is to ensure that angles are found with enough precision. Consider the difference in the following two calculations:

$\tan^{-1}(0.2) \doteq 11.310°$ $\tan^{-1}(0.3) \doteq 16.699°$

Compare the difference between these two angles:

$\tan^{-1}(0.2492) \doteq 13.993°$ $\tan^{-1}(0.2493) \doteq 13.998°$

In both cases, the tangents of the angles differ by one decimal place. But in the second case, the angles are much closer together. Possible discrepancies due to rounding are reduced by carrying more digits until the final step in a calculation.

Just as with the tangent ratio, you can find the sine and cosine of an angle using a scientific or graphing calculator.

Example 2 Find the Sine and Cosine of an Angle

Evaluate the following, to four decimal places.
a) $\sin 26°$
b) $\cos 75°$

Solution

Make sure that your calculator is in degree mode.
a) $\sin 26° \doteq 0.4384$
b) $\cos 75° \doteq 0.2588$

Example 3 Find an Angle Using the Sine and Cosine Ratios

a) Captain Jack is navigating his ship to Port Harbour, which is directly north of the ship's location. To compensate for an easterly current, he aims for a point on shore that is 5 km west of Port Harbour. Assuming that the point on shore is 20 km from his position now, at what bearing must Jack head his ship?

b) Captain Jack is in communication with a submarine that is cruising at a depth of 400 m below sea level. If Jack's radar tells him that the submarine is 500 m from Jack, due north of his ship, at what angle is the submarine located with respect to Captain Jack's ship, to the nearest degree?

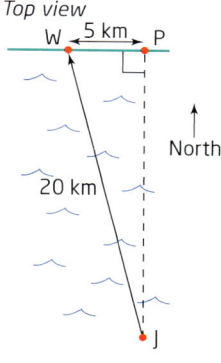

Literacy Connections

Bearing is a navigational term that describes a direction. It is expressed as an angle in terms of north, south, east, and/or west.

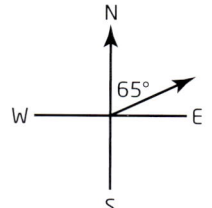

This bearing can be described as N65°E, which is read as "65 degrees east of north."

Solution

a) Captain Jack's ship, Port Harbour, and the western target form a right triangle.

For the unknown bearing angle, the opposite and hypotenuse sides are known.

Apply the sine ratio to find Jack's bearing.

$$\sin \theta = \frac{\text{opposite}}{\text{hypotenuse}}$$
$$= \frac{5}{20}$$
$$= 0.25$$

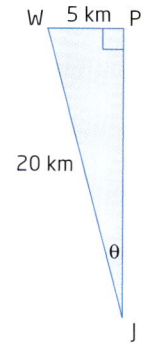

To find θ, calculate the inverse sine of 0.25.
$\theta = \sin^{-1}(0.25)$
$ \doteq 14.477°$

Jack must head his ship on a bearing of approximately N15°W.

b) Draw a diagram that shows the relative positions of Captain Jack's ship and the submarine. Captain Jack's ship, the submarine, and a line segment that points straight down from Captain Jack's ship form a right triangle.

Side view, facing west

For the unknown angle relating the submarine's position to Captain Jack, the adjacent and hypotenuse sides are known. Apply the cosine ratio to find this angle.

$$\cos \theta = \frac{\text{adjacent}}{\text{hypotenuse}}$$

$$\cos \theta = \frac{400}{500}$$

$$\theta = \cos^{-1}\left(\frac{400}{500}\right)$$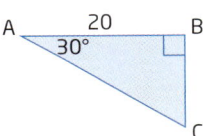

$$\doteq 36.870$$ or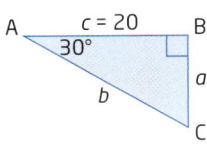

The submarine is approximately 37° north of Captain Jack's ship with respect to a line that points straight down to the bottom of the sea.

Example 4 Solve a Right Triangle

Solve △ABC. Round side lengths to the nearest unit and angles to the nearest degree.

Solution

Label the sides according to their corresponding angles.

Use the two known angles to find ∠C.
$$\angle A + \angle B + \angle C = 180°$$
$$30° + 90° + \angle C = 180°$$
$$120° + \angle C = 180°$$
$$\angle C = 180° - 120°$$
$$\angle C = 60°$$

Note that in a right triangle, the two acute angles are complementary. You can find ∠C by subtracting: 90° − 30° = 60°.

Literacy Connections

A triangle has six measures: three side lengths and three angle measures. To solve a triangle means to find all six of these values.

Literacy Connections

When naming parts of triangles, use capital letters to represent the angles and vertices and corresponding lowercase letters to represent opposite sides.

Use the cosine ratio to find side b.

$$\cos A = \frac{\text{adjacent}}{\text{hypotenuse}}$$

$$\cos A = \frac{c}{b}$$

$$\cos 30° = \frac{20}{b}$$

$b(\cos 30°) = 20$ **Multiply both sides by b.**

$$b = \frac{20}{\cos 30°}$$ **Divide both sides by cos 30°.**

$b \doteq 23.094$ 20 ÷ COS 30 = or 20 ÷ 30 COS =

Use the tangent ratio to find a.

$$\tan A = \frac{\text{opposite}}{\text{adjacent}}$$

$$\tan A = \frac{a}{c}$$

$$\tan 30° = \frac{a}{20}$$

$20(\tan 30°) = a$ **Multiply both sides by 20.**

$a \doteq 11.547$ 20 × TAN 30 = or 20 × 30 TAN =

The diagram shows the solved triangle.

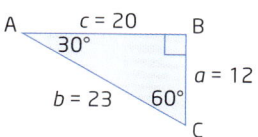

There is often more than one way to solve a right triangle. If you know the value of any side plus an additional side or angle, you can find the other measures. Notice, however, that some answers may be slightly different, due to rounding in the intermediate steps of a solution.

Key Concepts

- The three primary trigonometric ratios are sine, cosine, and tangent. They are defined as follows:

$$\sin \theta = \frac{\text{opposite}}{\text{hypotenuse}} \qquad \cos \theta = \frac{\text{adjacent}}{\text{hypotenuse}} \qquad \tan \theta = \frac{\text{opposite}}{\text{adjacent}}$$

- You can find any side length or angle measure of a right triangle if you know two pieces of information in addition to the right angle.

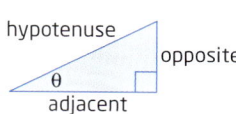

Communicate Your Understanding

C1 Explain why the primary trigonometric ratios depend only on a given angle and not the size of a right triangle.

C2 a) Create a problem for which you would need to apply the cosine function on your calculator. Solve the problem and explain each step.

b) Repeat part a) for the inverse sine function of your calculator.

C3 a) List the steps you would use to solve △PQR.

b) List a different set of steps to solve △PQR using another method.

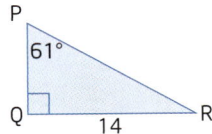

Practise

For help with questions 1 and 2, see Example 1.

1. Find sin θ, cos θ, and tan θ for each triangle, expressed as fractions in lowest terms.

a)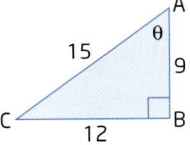

b)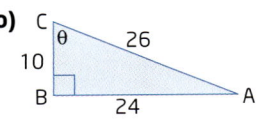

c)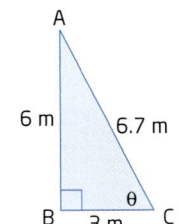

d)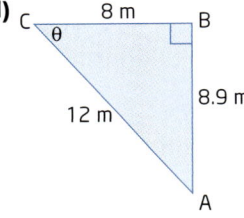

e), f)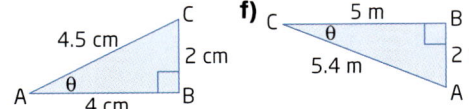

g), h)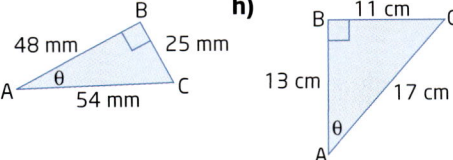

2. Find the three primary trigonometric ratios for ∠A, to four decimal places.

a)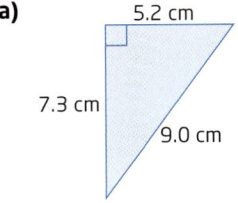

b)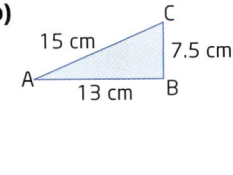

c)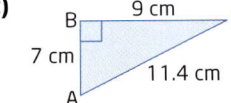

d)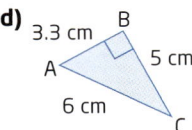

e)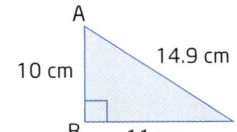

f)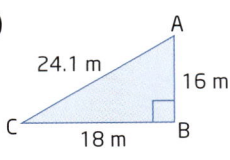

For help with questions 3 to 5, see Example 2.

3. Evaluate each of the following with a calculator, rounded to four decimal places.

a) sin 35°
b) sin 45°
c) sin 60°
d) sin 37°
e) sin 25°
f) sin 0°
g) sin 89°
h) sin 30°

4. Evaluate each of the following with a calculator, rounded to four decimal places.
   a) cos 80.2°
   b) cos 45°
   c) cos 30°
   d) cos 60°
   e) cos 89°
   f) cos 0°
   g) cos 5°
   h) cos 83°

5. Compare your results to questions 3 h) and 4 d). Use a diagram to help explain these results.

For help with questions 6 to 9, see Example 3.

6. Find the measure of each angle, to the nearest degree.
   a) $\sin \theta = 0.8933$
   b) $\sin \theta = 0.5032$
   c) $\sin P = \dfrac{1}{2}$
   d) $\sin S = \dfrac{2}{3}$
   e) $\sin \theta = \dfrac{3}{4}$
   f) $\sin A = 0.9511$
   g) $\sin \theta = 0.7123$
   h) $\sin \theta = \dfrac{2}{5}$
   i) $\sin X = 0.3035$
   j) $\sin \theta = 0.9976$
   k) $\sin V = \dfrac{1}{8}$
   l) $\sin \theta = 0$

7. Find the measure of each angle, to the nearest degree.
   a) $\cos \theta = 0.4481$
   b) $\cos A = 0.6329$
   c) $\cos C = \dfrac{5}{11}$
   d) $\cos \theta = 0.3432$
   e) $\cos Q = 0.8871$
   f) $\cos M = \dfrac{3}{14}$
   g) $\cos \theta = \dfrac{1}{6}$
   h) $\cos \theta = 0.6215$
   i) $\cos B = \dfrac{15}{16}$
   j) $\cos X = 0.0193$
   k) $\cos \theta = 0$
   l) $\cos J = \dfrac{1}{2}$

8. Calculate sin T in each triangle. Then, find ∠T, to the nearest degree.

a)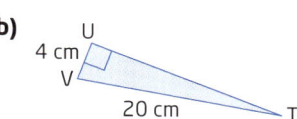

b) Triangle with U, V, T; UV = 4 cm, VT = 20 cm, right angle at V.

9. Calculate cos T in each triangle. Then, find ∠T, to the nearest degree.

a) Triangle R, S, T with S = 1 cm, RT via S; RS = 2 cm, ST = 1 cm, right angle at S.

b) Triangle V, T, U with VT = 10 m, TU = 3 m, right angle at U.

For help with questions 10 to 14, see Example 4.

10. Find the length of x, to the nearest tenth of a unit, by applying the sine ratio.

a) Triangle with hypotenuse 13 cm, angle 25°, side x.

b) Triangle with angle 66°, side 5.6 cm, side x.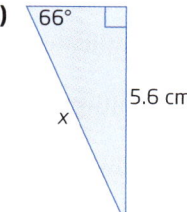

c) Triangle with 24 cm, 33°, side x.

d) Triangle with 65°, 32 cm, side x.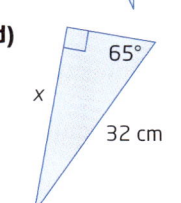

e) Triangle with 55 cm, 61°, side x.

f) Triangle with 12 cm, 50°, side x.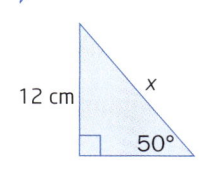

g) Triangle with 15 cm, 55°, side x.

h) Triangle with 18 cm, 41°, side x.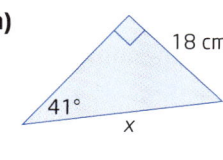

11. Find the length of *x*, to the nearest tenth of a unit, by applying the cosine ratio.

a)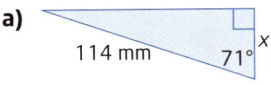

b)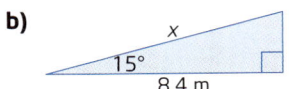

c) 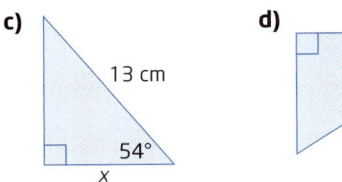   d)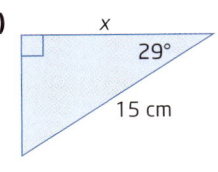

e) 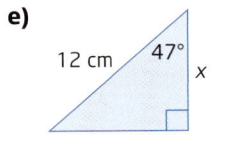   f)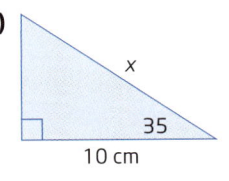

g) 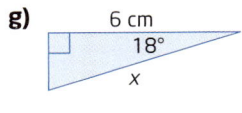   h)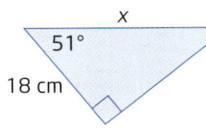

In questions 12 to 14, round side lengths to the nearest tenth of a unit and angles to the nearest degree.

12. Solve each triangle.

a)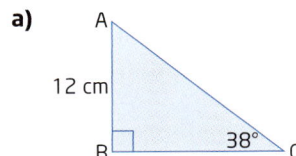

b)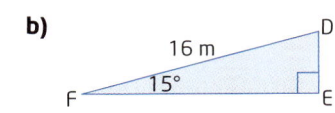

c)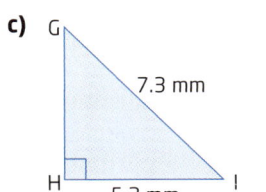

d)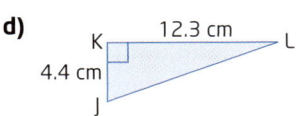

13. In △DEF,
DF = 6.0 km
∠E = 44°
∠F = 90°

a) Draw this triangle and label the given information.

b) Solve △DEF.

14. In △XYZ,
XY = 16 cm
YZ = 11 cm
∠Z = 90°

a) Draw this triangle and label the given information.

b) Solve △XYZ.

Connect and Apply

15. Dmitri has let out 40 m of his kite string, which makes an angle of 72° with the horizontal ground.

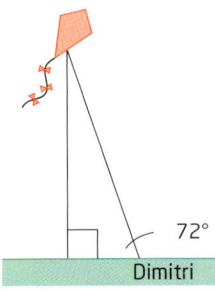

a) Find the height of the kite, to the nearest metre.

b) Suppose the Sun is shining directly above the kite. How far is the kite's shadow from Dmitri, to the nearest metre?

16. During take-off a plane must rise at least 20 m during its first 1.5 km of flight to successfully clear the runway.

a) At what minimum average angle must the plane climb for a safe take-off, to the nearest hundredth of a degree?

b) If the required rise is doubled to 40 m, does this double the climb angle? Explain.

17. In △PQR, ∠Q = 90° and PR = 20 cm. Find PQ, to the nearest tenth of a centimetre, if ∠R = 41°.

18. In △DEF, find ∠F, to the nearest degree, if DE = 15 cm, DF = 18 cm, and ∠E = 90°.

19. The towrope pulling a parasailor is 70 m long. A boat crew member estimates that the angle between the towrope and the water is about 30°. Find the height of the parasailor above the water.

20. △ABC is an isosceles triangle. The height of the triangle is 3 cm, and the two acute angles at its base are each 56°. How long are the two equal sides, to the nearest tenth of a centimetre?

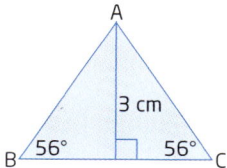

21. A tree is splintered by lightning 2 m up its trunk, so that the top part of the tree touches the ground. The angle the top of the tree forms with the ground is 70°. Before it was splintered, how tall was the tree, to the nearest tenth of a metre?

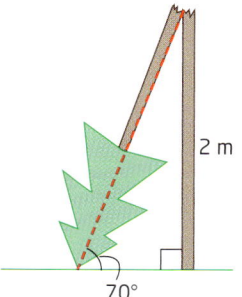

22. The side adjacent to the 74° angle in a right triangle is 6 cm long. How long is the hypotenuse, to the nearest tenth of a centimetre?

23. The hypotenuse of a right triangle is 10 m long. How long is the side adjacent to the 21° angle, to the nearest tenth of a metre?

24. A kite string is 35 m long. The angle the string makes with the ground is 50°. To the nearest metre, how far from the person holding the string is a person standing directly under the kite?

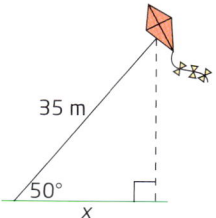

25. Find all the angles in △WXY, to the nearest degree.

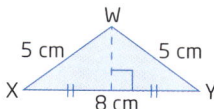

26. To get to school, Enzo can travel 1.2 km east on Rutherford Street and then south on Orchard Avenue to his school. Or, he can take a shortcut through the park, as shown. His shortcut takes him 20 min.

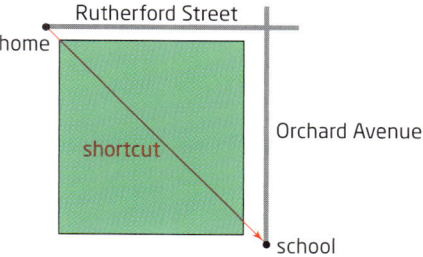

Enzo's walking speed is 6 km/h.

a) What angle does Enzo's shortcut make with Rutherford Street? Describe any assumptions you must make.

b) How much time does Enzo save by taking his shortcut? Explain your answer.

27. In Example 5, Section 7.3, this problem was solved. A radio transmitter is to be supported with a guy wire. The wire is to form a 65° angle with the ground and reach 30 m up the transmitter. The wire can be ordered in whole-number lengths of metres. How much wire should be ordered?

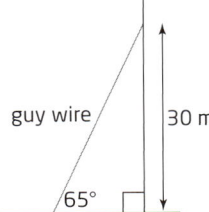

Solve this problem using a more efficient method.

28. How are the sines and cosines of the acute angles of a right triangle related? Plan and carry out an investigation to explore this. Write a brief report of your findings, using words, diagrams, and mathematical notation.

29. a) Is it possible for the sine or cosine of an angle to be greater than 1? Use geometric reasoning to explain your answer.

   b) Is it possible for the tangent of an angle to be greater than 1? Use geometric reasoning to explain your answer.

30. **Chapter Problem** A right triangle is formed by the following locations:
   - your current location (in the race)
   - the capital of the United States
   - your next destination

   The cosine of the angle at your current location is approximately 0.8. What city is your next destination, and how far do you have to travel to get there?

Achievement Check

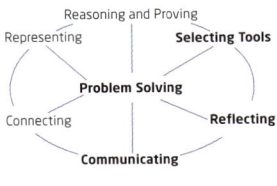

31. When it is leaning against a wall, the foot of a ladder is 2 m from the base of the wall. The angle between the ladder and the ground is 75°.

   a) How high up the wall does the ladder reach, to the nearest centimetre?

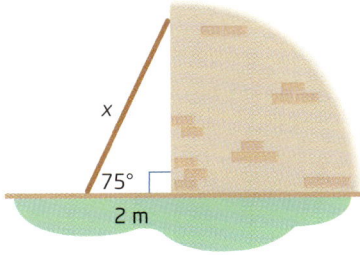

   b) How long is the ladder, to the nearest centimetre?

   c) If the ladder slips down the wall so that it makes an angle of 55° with the ground, does the end on the ground slip more than the end against the wall? Explain.

Extend

32. Find the length of x, then the length of y, to the nearest tenth of a centimetre.

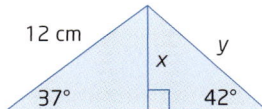

33. Find the length of x, to the nearest tenth of a metre, then the measure of y, to the nearest degree.

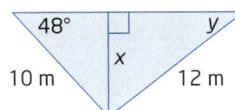

34. a) Use △ABC and △DEF. Copy and complete the table. Leave all ratios in fraction form.

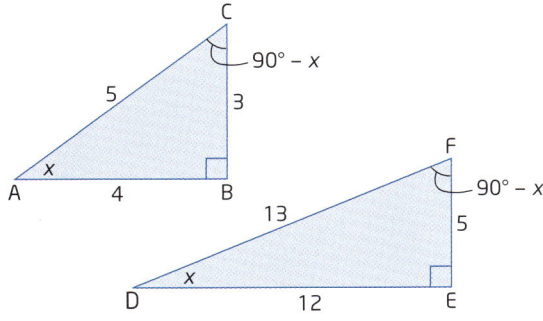

Triangle	△ABC	△DEF
tan x		
sin x		
cos x		
tan (90° − x)		
sin (90° − x)		
cos (90° − x)		

b) How is tan x related to tan (90° − x) in these two triangles?

c) How is sin x related to cos (90° − x) in these two triangles?

d) How is cos x related to sin (90° − x) in these two triangles?

e) Explain the relationships in parts b), c), and d).

35. Use geometric reasoning to show that $\sin \theta = \cos(90° - \theta)$ in all right triangles, if θ is one of the acute angles.

36. Use algebraic reasoning to show that $\tan \theta = \dfrac{\sin \theta}{\cos \theta}$.

37. a) Select three different values for an angle x between 0° and 90°. For each value of x, evaluate the expression $(\sin x)^2 + (\cos x)^2$.

b) Use your results from part a) to write a conjecture.

c) Verify your conjecture from part b) using geometric reasoning.

38. Pilots use a "wind triangle" to determine which way to aim the aircraft to overcome the effects of wind. For example, Seymour has an airplane that cruises at 200 km/h in still air. A stiff wind of 28 km/h is blowing from the west. Seymour wants to fly from A directly north to B.

a) Find the angle at which Seymour must aim the airplane.

b) How fast will he be flying relative to the ground?

39. Math Contest At the senior prom, four couples are seated randomly around a circular table. What is the probability that Dan sits beside his date Ranjit?

A $\dfrac{1}{4}$

B $\dfrac{1}{8}$

C $\dfrac{1}{2}$

D $\dfrac{2}{7}$

E $\dfrac{3}{8}$

40. Math Contest An equilateral triangle and a hexagon have equal perimeters. The area of the triangle is 2 m². What is the area of the hexagon?

41. Math Contest The lengths of the sides of a triangle are 20 cm, 21 cm, and 29 cm. The shortest distance from the longest side to the opposite vertex is

A $\dfrac{400}{9}$ cm

B $\dfrac{410}{29}$ cm

C $\dfrac{420}{29}$ cm

D $\dfrac{580}{21}$ cm

E $\dfrac{609}{20}$ cm

7.5 Solve Problems Involving Right Triangles

The primary trigonometric ratios are applied in many areas of study, including architecture, engineering, astronomy, medicine, and criminal detection. For example, have you ever seen a television show or movie in which forensic evidence is used to recreate the events of an accident or crime? How can scientists use a few tiny clues, such as bloodstains, to piece together what actually happened? How could trigonometry be useful?

Example 1 Angles of Depression and Elevation

Kim and Yuri live in apartment buildings that are 30 m apart, as shown. The **angle of depression** from Kim's balcony to where Yuri's building meets the ground is 40°. The **angle of elevation** from Kim's balcony to Yuri's balcony is 20°.

a) How high is Kim's balcony above the ground, to the nearest metre?
b) How high is Yuri's balcony above the ground, to the nearest metre?

angle of depression
- angle measured below the horizontal
- also called the **angle of declination**

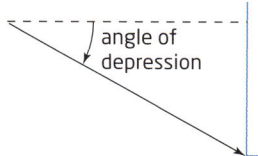

angle of elevation
- angle measured above the horizontal
- also called the **angle of inclination**

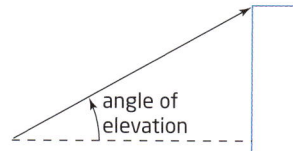

Solution

a) Simplify the problem by focusing on the lower right triangle.

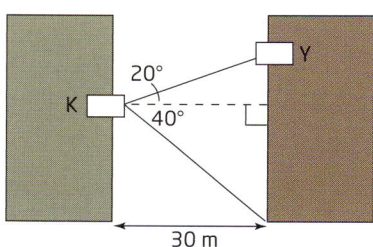

$$\tan 40° = \frac{\text{opposite}}{\text{adjacent}}$$

$$\tan 40° = \frac{k}{30}$$

$30 \tan 40° = k$ **Multiply both sides by 30.**
$25.17 \doteq k$

Kim's balcony is about 25 m above the ground.

378 MHR • Chapter 7

b) Focus on the upper right triangle.

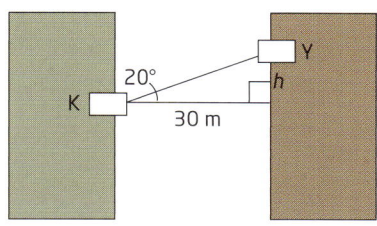

$$\tan 20° = \frac{\text{opposite}}{\text{adjacent}}$$

$$\tan 20° = \frac{h}{30}$$

$30 \tan 20° = h$ **Multiply both sides by 30.**

$10.92 \doteq h$

Yuri's balcony is about 11 m higher than Kim's. Add this to the height of Kim's balcony to find the height of Yuri's balcony, y.

$y = h + k$
$ = 25 + 11$
$ = 36$

Yuri's balcony is about 36 m above the ground.

Example 2 Solve a Three-Dimensional Problem

A theodolite is an instrument used by a surveyor to measure horizontal and vertical angles. Measurements are taken in order to find the height of a cliff on the other side of a river, as shown.

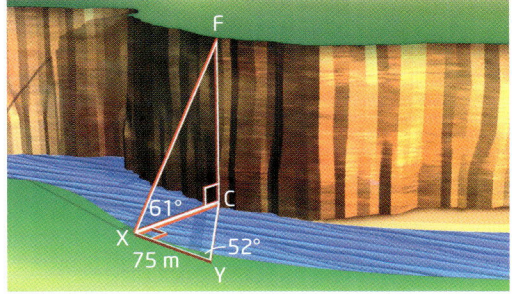

Find the height of the cliff, to the nearest metre.

Literacy Connections

In this situation, using a single letter to identify a side can lead to confusion. For example, side c could refer to the hypotenuse in △CXF or the 75-m side of △CYX. Use endpoints to distinguish line segments, FX and XY in this case, to avoid confusion.

Solution

Use △CYX to find the width of the river, CX. Then, use △CXF to find the height of the cliff, CF. Focus on △CYX first.

Top View

Apply the tangent ratio to find CX.

$$\tan \angle Y = \frac{CX}{XY}$$

$$\tan 52° = \frac{CX}{75}$$

$75 \tan 52° = CX$ **Multiply both sides by 75.**

$95.996 \doteq CX$

CX is shared by both triangles. Use it to find the height of the cliff.

Focus on △CXF.

Apply the tangent ratio to find CF.

$$\tan \angle X = \frac{CF}{CX}$$

$$\tan 61° = \frac{CF}{96}$$

$$96 \tan 61° = CF$$

$$173.2 \doteq CF$$

Multiply both sides by 96.

The cliff is about 173 m high.

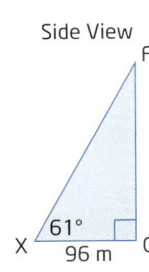

Side View

Key Concepts

- Angles of elevation and depression are measured above and below a horizontal line, respectively.
- The primary trigonometric ratios can be applied to solve two-dimensional and three-dimensional problems involving right triangles.
- Some complex problems involve working with more than one right triangle.

Communicate Your Understanding

C1 a) What is an angle of elevation?

b) How is it measured?

C2 a) What is an angle of depression?

b) How is it measured?

C3 a) What triangles can you identify in the diagram?

b) Describe the steps you would use to find the side length CD.

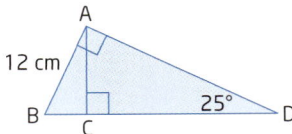

Practise

For help with questions 1 and 2, see Example 1.

1. A telephone pole is secured at its top with a guy wire, as shown. The guy wire makes an angle of 70° with the ground and is secured 5.6 m from the bottom of the pole. Find the height of the telephone pole.

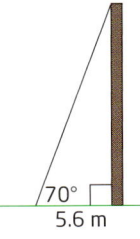

2. a) Find the length of the guy wire in question 1.

b) Use a different method to find the length of the guy wire in question 1.

For help with questions 3 to 7, see Example 2.

3. Refer to question 1. A second guy wire is to be added to support the pole. It is to be secured on the ground twice as far from the pole as the first wire, on the same side of the pole and attached to the top of the pole.
   a) Draw a diagram illustrating the telephone pole and both guy wires.
   b) Find the length of the second wire and the angle it will make with the ground.
   c) Find the angle formed between the two wires at the top of the pole.

4. Refer to question C3. Solve for side length CD. Record your answer to the nearest centimetre.

5. Jack and Sangita are facing each other on opposite sides of a 10-m flagpole. From Jack's point of view, the top of the flagpole is at an angle of elevation of 50°. From Sangita's it is 35°.

   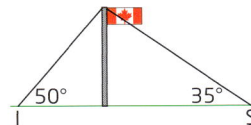

   How far apart are Jack and Sangita?

6. Alexa and Emma are looking up at their house from the backyard. From Alexa's point of view, the top of the house is at an angle of elevation of 40°. From Emma's point of view, directly closer to the house, it is 60°. The house is 15 m high. How far apart are the two girls?

7. At the bottom of a ski lift, there are two vertical poles: one 15 m tall and the other 8 m tall. The ground between the poles is level, and the bases of the poles are 6 m apart. The poles are connected by two straight wires.

   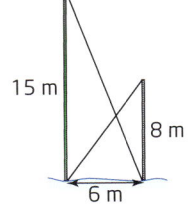

   a) What angle does each wire make with the ground?
   b) What is the length of each wire?

8. Refer to question 7.
   a) Use a different method to answer part b).
   b) At what height above the ground do the wires intersect, to the nearest tenth of a metre?

Connect and Apply

Use this information to answer questions 9 and 10.

Cheryl is golfing. She is 100 m from the hole, which is her target. Blocking her direct path is a line of trees, the midpoint of which is 30 m from her current position. She has two choices:

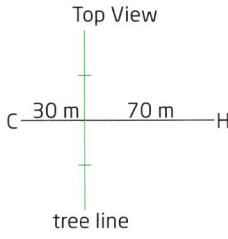

- Option 1: Aim directly for the hole, over the trees.
- Option 2: Go around the trees in two shots.

Cheryl's average distances using various clubs are shown in the table.

Club	Distance (m)
Lob wedge	25
Sand wedge	50
Pitching wedge	90
9-iron	100

9. Cheryl considers Option 1, to aim over the trees. The closest tree, which is in line with the hole, is about 30 m away, as shown. She estimates that the angle of inclination from her ball to the top of the tree is about 40°. She judges that the maximum height she can hit from this position is 20 m. Should she take this shot? Explain why or why not.

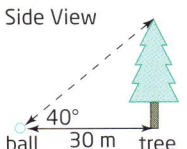

10. Cheryl considers Option 2, to go around the tree in two shots. In shot one, she will shoot to the end of the line of trees to position A. In shot two, she will aim for the hole.

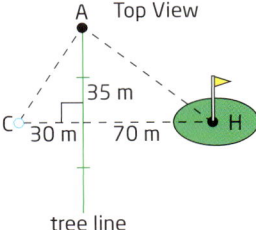

The tree line is 70 m long, and the line joining Cheryl's ball and the hole, CH, passes through the middle of the tree line, at a right angle.

a) At what angle from CH should Cheryl make her first shot, in order to land near A?

b) Which club should she choose for this shot? Explain.

c) Assume that Cheryl succeeds with her first shot and her golf ball lands at A. At what angle from the tree line must she aim for her second shot?

d) Which club should she choose for this shot? Explain.

11. Captain Jack is sitting in the crow's-nest of his ship, as shown.

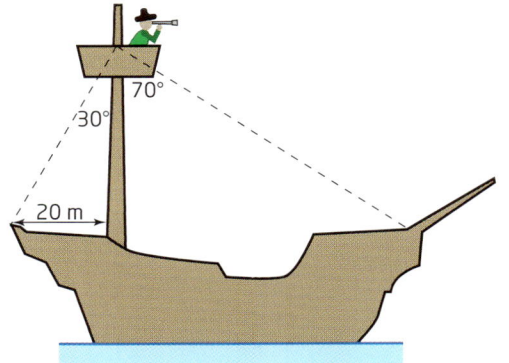

a) How high above the deck is Captain Jack?

b) What is the length of Captain Jack's ship?

c) How long is each wire holding up the crow's-nest?

12. Lucy Starstrider is trapped on Level 17 of a space station. The evil Dark Raider and his Clone Warriors, who are on Levels 18 and 16 across a deep trench, face her. Lucy's retreat path behind her has been blocked. Her only chance for escape is to try to jump directly across the trench. If she does not make it, she will fall to certain doom.

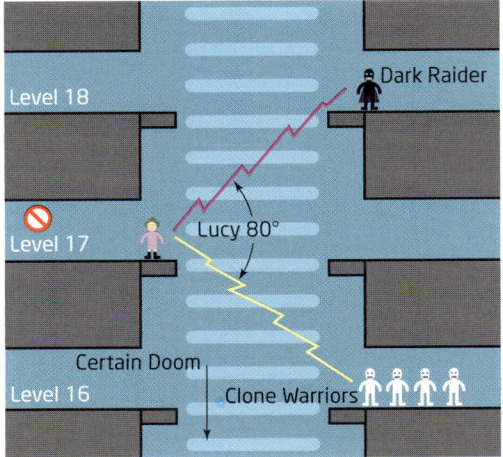

Lucy estimates that the lines of sight to her enemies are 80° apart, as shown. She also recalls, from the technical plans of the space station, that consecutive levels are 10 m apart, vertically. Using the Source of Power, Lucy can leap a horizontal distance of 12 m. Time is quickly running out! Will Lucy Starstrider escape the clutches of the evil ones, or will she perish? Justify your answer.

13. A scuba diver swam north at 1.5 m/s, across a current running from east to west at 2.0 m/s. She swam for 3 min and then surfaced.

a) Draw a diagram showing where the dive boat will pick her up relative to where she dove.

b) How far did she travel?

14. The observation deck at Peggy's Cove lighthouse, in Nova Scotia, is about 20 m above sea level. From the observation deck, the angle of depression of a boat on the water is 6°. How far is the boat from the lighthouse, to the nearest metre?

15. Theresa and Branko are competing in a series of outdoor challenges that will eventually lead them to a hidden treasure. Each clue they find helps them find a new clue. Theresa is at the top of a cliff that she knows to be 100 m high, looking down at three anchored floating bottles, as shown.

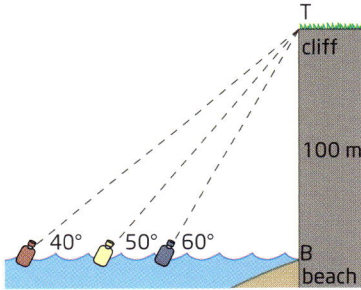

She reads the clue that she and Branko just found:

> From the top of the cliff, find the bottle whose angle of depression is 50°.

Branko is waiting on the beach below for instructions from Theresa.

a) What colour bottle should Theresa tell Branko to look for?

b) How far out should she tell him to swim?

16. Refer to Example 1. Yuri's balcony is four floors above Kim's. What floors do they live on? Explain any assumptions you must make.

17. An octahedron is formed by attaching eight congruent equilateral triangles, as shown.

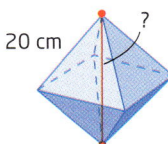 

net of octahedron

If the length along one of the edges is 20 cm, find the distance between opposite vertices.

18. Joanne and Sandy are hiking from Cedar Camp to Lookout Point along the hiking trail shown.

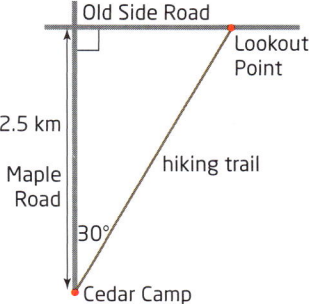

Cedar Camp is 2.5 km from Old Side Road along Maple Road, which runs flat. The hiking trail makes an angle of 30° with Maple Road and climbs at an average angle of elevation of 15°.

a) How far apart would Cedar Camp and Lookout Point appear, according to a normal map?

b) What distance do the hikers actually walk? Why are these answers different?

c) What is the difference in elevation between Lookout Point and Cedar Camp?

d) What is the average angle of elevation of the section of Old Side Road that is shown?

Making Connections

The octahedron is one of five Platonic solids, polyhedra that are formed by attaching congruent regular polygons.

The Platonic solids are named after Plato, a great Greek mathematician and teacher, who lived from 427 to 347 B.C.E.

Plato is famous for founding the world's first known university in Athens, Greece, called The Academy.

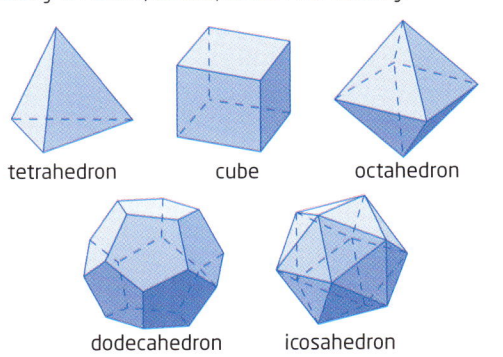

7.5 Solve Problems Involving Right Triangles • MHR 383

19. Ropes are used to pull a totem pole upright. Then, the ropes are anchored in the ground to hold the pole until the hole is filled. One of the ropes holding this totem pole is 18 m long and forms an angle of 48° with the ground.

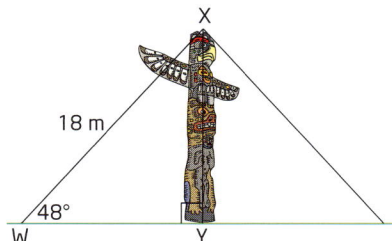

   a) Find the height of the totem pole, to the nearest metre.
   b) How far is the anchor point from the base of the totem pole, to the nearest metre?

20. Edmonton's CN Tower is a highrise office building. From a point 35 m from the base of the building and level with the base, the angle of elevation of the top is 72.5°. Find the height of Edmonton's CN Tower, to the nearest metre.

21. A coast guard patrol boat is 14.8 km east of the Brier Island lighthouse. A disabled yacht is 7.5 km south of the lighthouse.
   a) How far is the patrol boat from the yacht, to the nearest tenth of a kilometre?
   b) At what angle south of due west, to the nearest degree, should the patrol boat travel to reach the yacht?

22. The Capilano Suspension Bridge in North Vancouver is the world's highest footbridge of its kind. The bridge is 140 m long. From the ends of the bridge, the angles of depression of a point on the river under the bridge are 41° and 48°. How high is the bridge above the river, to the nearest metre?

23. The Great Pyramid of Cheops is a square-based pyramid with a height of 147 m and a base length of 230 m. Find the angle, to the nearest degree, that one of the edges of the pyramid makes with the base.

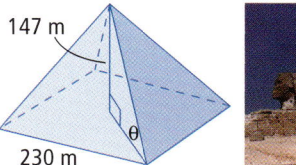 

24. **Chapter Problem** The city you are now in is next to a large river. Take a boat downstream to another city located at the river's end. From there you must fly to a town known as the Gateway to the Yukon. This town, your current location in the race, and Canada's capital form a right triangle. The tangent of the angle at the city you have just sailed to is 1.75. What is your final destination?

Extend

Use this information to answer questions 25 and 26.

Forensic scientists can recreate an accident or crime by examining bloodstains. A blood droplet starts out in the shape of a sphere. When it falls straight down to the floor, it usually forms a circle with the same diameter as the sphere.

However, when blood hits the floor at an angle, due to the force of a blow, the circle becomes elongated into a shape called an ellipse. The ellipse's width is the same as the sphere's diameter, but because of the force in the direction of motion, its length is greater than the sphere's diameter.

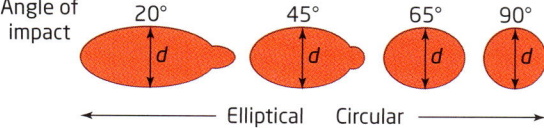

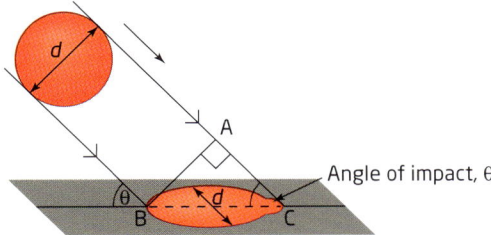

The angle of impact, θ, is the acute angle formed between the path of the blood drop and the floor.

25. Use geometric reasoning to show that the angle of impact can be found using the relationship $\sin\theta = \dfrac{d}{BC}$.

26. Three bloodstains from a victim are shown. The point of convergence, C, has been found by extrapolating the directions of these stains along the floor. The origin of the blow, O, is some height above C.

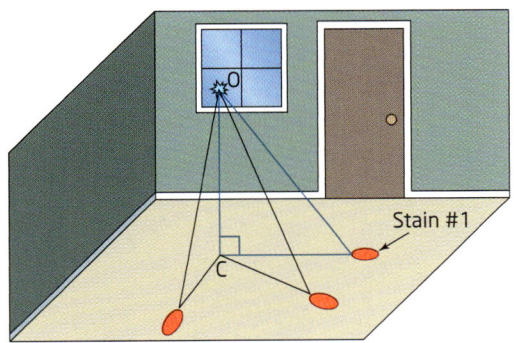

Forensic analysis of Stain #1 provides the following data.

```
Length of bloodstain: ...... 4.2 cm
Width of bloodstain: ....... 2.6 cm
Distance from point
of convergence ............. 2.1 m
```

Determine the height at which the blow struck the victim.

27. A sign shows that a hill has a grade of 9%. What angle does the hill make with the horizontal, to the nearest tenth of a degree?

28. An airplane is cruising at an altitude of 10 000 m. It is flying in a straight line away from Chandra, who is standing on the ground. If she sees the angle of elevation of the airplane change from 70° to 33° in 1 min, what is its cruising speed, to the nearest kilometre per hour?

29. A special type of aircraft is designed to fly at the very low height of 20 m. To measure such a small altitude, two spotlights are mounted on the aircraft:
- one on the nose, pointing straight down
- another mounted on the tail of the aircraft, 10 m away

Find the angle at which the second light needs to be set, with respect to the body of the aircraft, so that the beams will meet 20 m below the aircraft.

30. The angle of elevation to a building is 30°. From a point 20 m directly toward the building, the angle of elevation changes to 40°. Find the height of the building. Include a diagram with your solution.

31. Math Contest In a family of four children, what is the probability that there are at least two girls if the eldest child is a girl?

A $\dfrac{15}{16}$ B $\dfrac{7}{16}$ C $\dfrac{3}{4}$ D $\dfrac{7}{8}$ E $\dfrac{3}{8}$

32. In the diagram, △ABC is isosceles, with AB = AC, and △RST is equilateral. Express ∠x in terms of ∠y and ∠z.

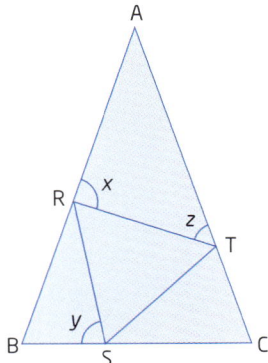

Chapter 7 Review

7.1 Investigate Properties of Similar Triangles, pages 330–335

1. **a)** Explain the difference between similar and congruent figures.
   b) Draw two triangles that are congruent.
   c) Draw two rectangles that are similar.
   d) Draw two pentagons that are similar.
   e) Draw two non-similar pentagons whose corresponding sides are in the same ratio.

2. Are all circles similar? Justify your reasoning.

3. Name the two similar triangles and explain why they are similar.

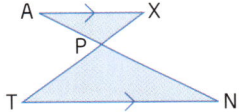

4. Name the two similar triangles and explain why they are similar.

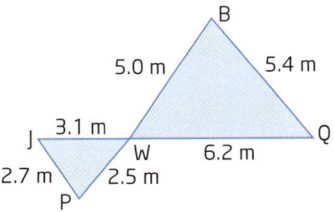

7.2 Use Similar Triangles to Solve Problems, pages 342–351

5. The pairs of triangles are similar. Find the unknown side lengths.

   a)

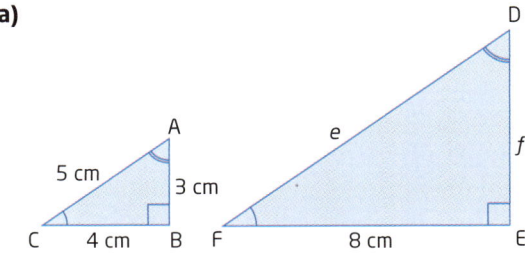

   b)

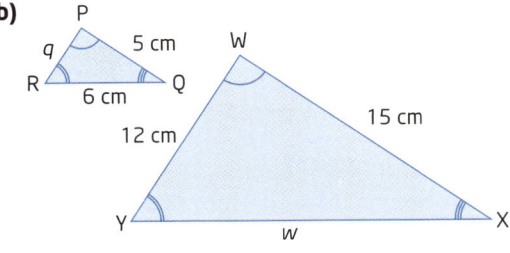

   c)

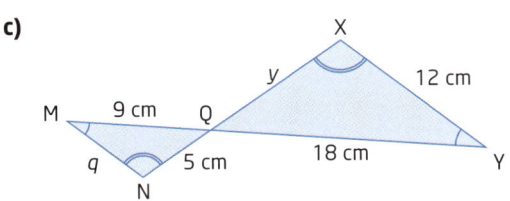

6. The tips of the shadows of a tree and of a metre stick meet at the point X.

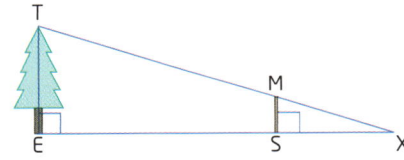

   The following measurements are taken:
   XS = 3.5 m
   ES = 6.5 m

   Use this information to find the height of the tree, to the nearest tenth of a metre.

7. Janke's garden is in the shape of a right isosceles triangle with base 3.4 m. If she enlarges her garden to a similar shape whose base is doubled, what will the area of her new garden be?

8. Sid wants to find the height of a tree without having to climb it, but it is a cloudy day, so he cannot use shadows. He takes a mirror from his pocket and places it on the ground 7.2 m from the base of the tree. He backs up until he can see the top of the tree in the mirror, a distance of 1.2 m from the mirror. If Sid's eyes are 1.5 m above the ground, what is the height of the tree?

7.3 The Tangent Ratio, pages 352–365

9. Find the measure of ∠A, to the nearest degree.

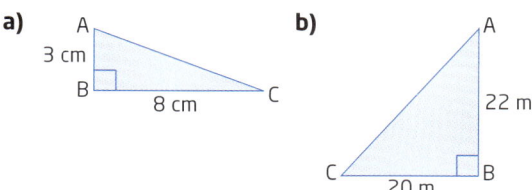

10. Find x, to the nearest tenth of a centimetre.

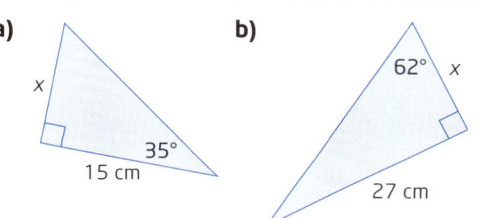

11. A jet climbs at a steady rate at an angle of inclination of 0.5° during take-off. What will its height be after a 2.2-km initial ascent at this angle?

12. Cory is building a ramp for his school theatre production. It must climb a height of 60 cm and have a slope angle of 10°.
   a) Draw a diagram and label the given information.
   b) What distance will the ramp run along the floor?
   c) What will the distance along the surface of the ramp be?

13. a) What are the following values?
   • tan 0°
   • tan 45°
   • tan 90°
   b) Use words and diagrams to explain these values.

14. To avoid damaging a vital organ, a surgeon will fire a laser at an angle to the patient's skin, to reach a cyst (an abnormal growth). The cyst is 8.2 cm directly below the skin, and the laser is positioned at a distance of 9.6 cm away in order to miss the vital organ, as shown.

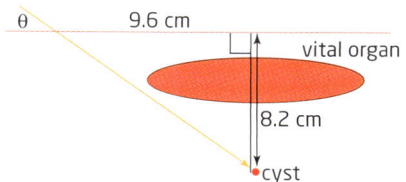

At what angle, θ, should the surgeon position the laser with respect to the skin's surface?

7.4 The Sine and Cosine Ratios, pages 366–377

15. Find the measure of both acute angles in each triangle, to the nearest degree.

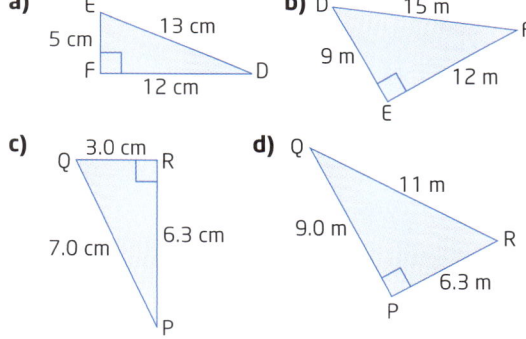

16. Find x, to the nearest tenth of a unit.

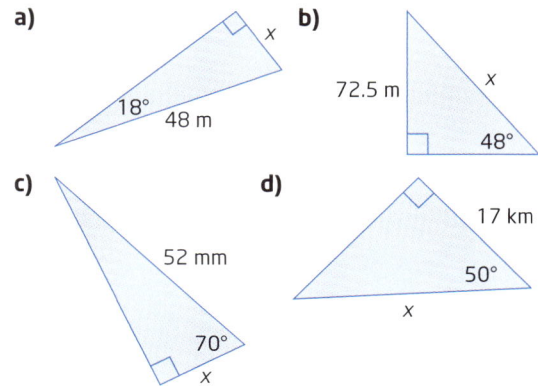

17. Solve △FGH.

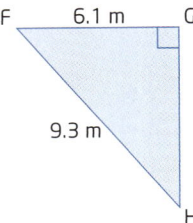

18. In △TUV,
UV = 7.4 km
∠U = 90°
∠T = 38°

a) Draw the triangle and label the given information.
b) Solve △TUV.

19. During a football game, Danny, the quarterback, has the football and is facing the other team's goal line. His receiver, Javier, is about 5.5 m to Danny's left, at an angle of 30°, as shown.

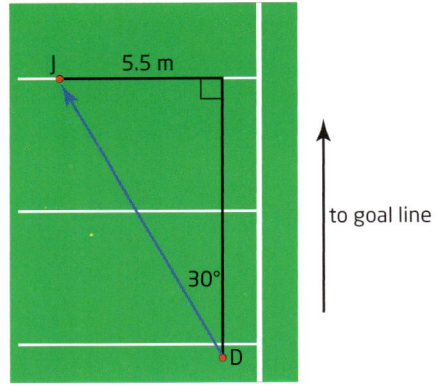

How far should Danny throw the ball to his receiver, to the nearest metre?

20. Rachel is heading due south in her sailboat toward a port. After travelling 12 km, she reaches shore 4 km west of her intended destination, due to the water's current. By what angle did the current push Rachel off course? Include a diagram in your solution and describe any assumptions you must make.

7.5 Solve Problems Involving Right Triangles, pages 378–385

21. Solve each triangle. Round each side length to the nearest tenth of a unit and each angle to the nearest degree.

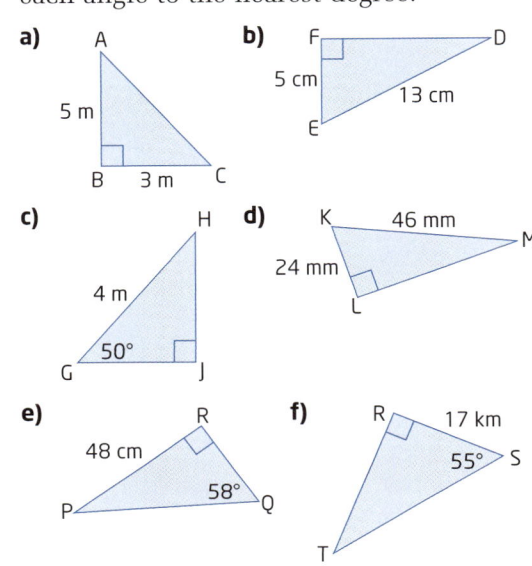

22. The maximum angle of climb for a certain light aircraft is 9°. A line of electric wires 20 m above the ground is located 120 m from the end of the runway. Will the aircraft clear the wires after take-off?

23. A stairway runs up the edge of the pyramid. From bottom to top the stairway is 92 m long.

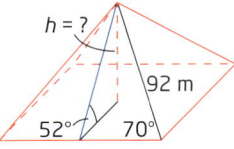

The stairway makes an angle of 70° to the base edge, as shown. A line from the middle of one of the base edges to the top of the pyramid makes an angle of elevation of 52° with respect to the flat ground. Find the height of the pyramid.

24. Kathe is 4 m from the base of a long wooden fence, under which her baseball has just rolled. Kathe estimates that the angle of elevation from where she is to the top of the fence is about 30°. Kathe thinks she can climb over a fence that is a maximum of 2 m high. Can she climb over the fence, or does she have to go around? Justify your reasoning.

25. When a road has a 10% gradient, it means that the road rises 10 m for every 100 m of horizontal distance travelled. What is the angle of inclination of the road, to the nearest degree?

26. If you were in a hot air balloon 500 m above the ground, at what angle of depression would you look at a point on the ground 800 m horizontally from the balloon?

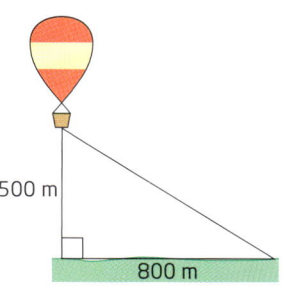

27. A flagpole casts a shadow 28 m long when the Sun's rays make an angle of 25° with the ground. How tall is the flagpole, to the nearest metre?

28. The world's longest escalator is in the subway system in St. Petersburg, Russia. The escalator is 330.7 m long and rises a vertical distance of 59.7 m. What is the angle of elevation of the top of the escalator when viewed from the bottom, to the nearest degree?

29. The world's longest covered bridge crosses the Saint John River in Hartland, New Brunswick. From two points, X and Y, 100 m apart on the same side of the river, the lines of sight to the far end of the bridge, Z, make angles of 85.6° and 79.8° with the river bank, as shown. What is the length of the bridge, b, to the nearest 10 m?

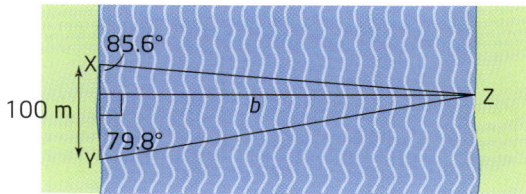

Chapter Problem Wrap-Up

Look back at your answers to question 22 in Section 7.2, question 30 in Section 7.4, and question 24 in Section 7.5. Describe your journey from the start to the finish line, including
- the names of all your destinations
- directions
- distances

Include a diagram to help you illustrate your description.

Chapter 7 Practice Test

1. Identify a pair of similar figures and a pair of congruent figures. Explain your choices.

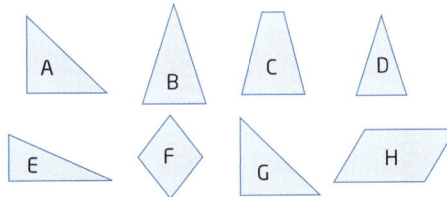

2. Are all rectangles similar? Justify your answer.

3. Are all squares similar? Justify your answer.

4. Evaluate the following, to four decimal places.
   a) tan 29°
   b) cos 78°
   c) sin 90°
   d) sin 45°
   e) cos 45°
   f) tan 85°

5. Solve for each angle, to the nearest degree.
   a) sin θ = 0.8872
   b) tan θ = 1.443
   c) cos C = 0.3561
   d) cos θ = 0.2147
   e) tan X = 5.3212
   f) sin P = 0.9111

6. Solve △PQR. Express lengths to the nearest tenth of a centimetre and angles to the nearest degree.

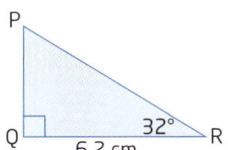

7. In △ABC,
   AB = 19 m
   BC = 27 m
   ∠B = 90°
   a) Draw this triangle and label the given information.
   b) Solve △ABC. Express lengths to the nearest metre and angles to the nearest degree.

8. Billy has lost track of time. He will get in trouble if he is late for dinner, but he will get in *more* trouble if he comes home with wet shoes. Racing home, Billy suddenly encounters a creek, as shown. Glancing at some nearby rocks, he estimates the distances indicated.

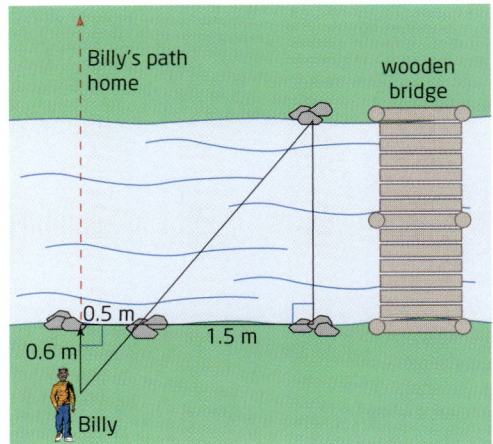

Billy can long jump about 2 m. Should he try to jump the creek, or take the long way home across the wooden bridge? Justify your reasoning.

9. Salma is at the top of a cliff looking down at Rico's boat. They both have Global Positioning System (GPS) devices and are communicating via cell phones. They determine that Rico's boat is 5.0 km from a point on the shore directly below Salma, and 6.0 km from Salma herself.
   a) Draw a diagram to represent this situation and label the given information.
   b) Find the angle of depression at which Salma is viewing Rico's boat.
   c) Find the height of the cliff.

10. From the top of the CN Tower, the angle of depression to the tip of the tower's shadow is 88°. The shadow is 19.5 m long. How tall is the CN Tower?

11. Theresa and Branko are competing in a series of outdoor challenges that will eventually lead them to a hidden treasure. Each clue they find helps them find a new clue. Theresa is getting ready to climb a steep cliff to find their next clue at the Lookout Point. She has two options:
- Option A: Climb straight up the cliff, and then jog over to Lookout Point.
- Option B: Climb directly to Lookout Point along the diagonal shown.

She is awaiting instructions from Branko, who is positioned directly facing Lookout Point at a distance of 30 m from the base of the cliff.

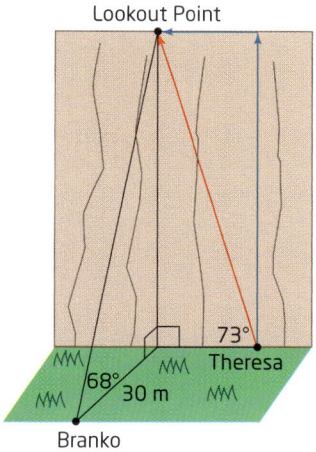

From Branko's point of view, Lookout Point is at an angle of elevation of 68°. He also observes that the diagonal path up the cliff makes a 73° angle with the ground. Branko knows that Theresa can climb at a speed of 1.0 m/s and jog at a speed of 5.0 m/s after a climb. It is a tight race and seconds count. Which option should Branko tell Theresa to take: A or B?

12. A cat, sitting in the top of a tree, spots a dog and a firefighter, both on the flat ground below. From the cat's point of view, the dog is 10 m south, at an angle of depression of 65°, and the firefighter is some distance east of the tree, at an angle of depression of 50°. How far is the firefighter from the dog?

■ **Achievement Check**

13. A vertical communications tower is supported by two cables on opposite sides of the tower, as shown in the diagram. One cable is attached to the top of the tower and the other is attached to the tower at a height of 60 m. Both cables are attached to the ground with fasteners.

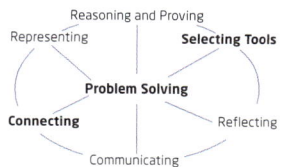

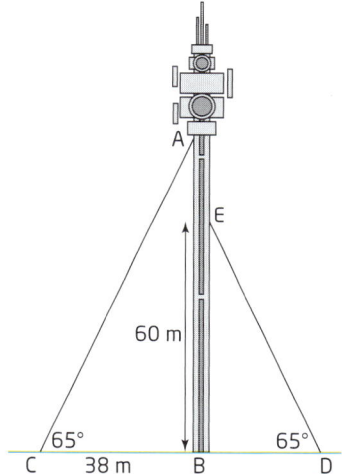

a) Verify that △ABC is similar to △EBD and list the corresponding sides and angles.

b) What is the height of the tower, to the nearest metre?

c) How long are the supporting cables, to the nearest metre?

d) How far apart are the cable fasteners, to the nearest metre?

Note: This is a simplified diagram. Normally it takes three or four cables to support a tower.

CHAPTER 8

Trigonometry of Acute Triangles

Trigonometry

- Explore the development of the sine law within acute triangles.
- Explore the development of the cosine law within acute triangles.
- Determine the measures of sides and angles in acute triangles, using the sine law and the cosine law.
- Solve problems involving the measures of sides and angles in acute triangles.

Vocabulary

sine law
cosine law

The word **trigonometry** comes from two Greek words that together mean "measurement of triangles." The first known evidence of trigonometry can be traced as far back as 4000 years to the civilizations of ancient Egypt and Babylon. Today, many of the same concepts are used to solve modern-day problems.

Triangles are special—any polygon can be split into two or more triangles. If you can solve triangles, you can solve many other shapes. In this chapter, you will expand your knowledge of trigonometry to include methods for solving acute triangles.

Chapter Problem

Welcome to Fowler's Aeronautical School! After successful completion of this course, you will be one step closer to becoming a licensed pilot. Expect your mathematical ability and bravery to be challenged. Good luck!

Get Ready

Primary Trigonometric Ratios

The **primary trigonometric ratios** for $\angle A$ in right $\triangle ABC$ are

$\sin A = \dfrac{\text{opposite}}{\text{hypotenuse}}$ $\cos A = \dfrac{\text{adjacent}}{\text{hypotenuse}}$ $\tan A = \dfrac{\text{opposite}}{\text{adjacent}}$

$= \dfrac{5}{13}$ $= \dfrac{12}{13}$ $= \dfrac{5}{12}$

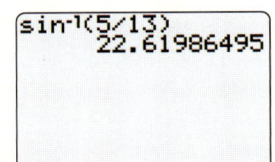

You can use the inverse trigonometric operations on a calculator to find angle measures. For example,

$\angle A = \sin^{-1}\left(\dfrac{5}{13}\right)$

$\doteq 23°$

1. **a)** Find the primary trigonometric ratios for $\angle X$ in $\triangle XYZ$.

   b) Find the measures of the acute angles in $\triangle XYZ$, to the nearest degree.

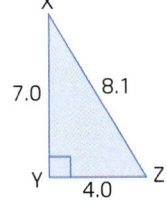

2. **a)** Apply the Pythagorean theorem to find side k. Then, find the primary trigonometric ratios for $\angle M$.

   b) Find the measures of the acute angles in $\triangle BKM$, to the nearest degree.

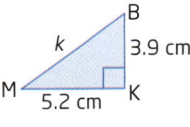

Solve Triangles

To solve a triangle means to find all the unknown side lengths and unknown angle measures.

You can apply the primary trigonometric ratios to find the missing side lengths in right $\triangle TUV$.

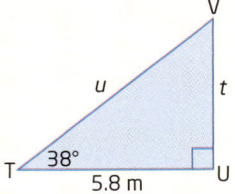

$\cos T = \dfrac{\text{adjacent}}{\text{hypotenuse}}$ $\tan T = \dfrac{\text{opposite}}{\text{adjacent}}$

$\cos 38° = \dfrac{5.8}{u}$ $\tan 38° = \dfrac{t}{5.8}$

$u = \dfrac{5.8}{\cos 38°}$ $5.8(\tan 38°) = t$

$u \doteq 7.4$ $4.5 \doteq t$

$\angle V = 180° - 38° - 90°$
$ = 52°$

Literacy Connections

When naming parts of triangles, use capital letters to represent the angles and vertices, and corresponding lowercase letters to represent opposite sides.

In $\triangle TUV$, u is 7.4 cm, t is 4.5 cm, and $\angle V$ is 52°.

3. Describe two other methods that you could use to find side t in $\triangle$TUV.

4. Solve $\triangle$RML. Round side lengths to the nearest tenth of a centimetre.

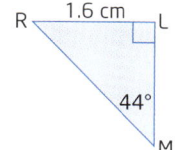

5. In $\triangle$PWF, $\angle$P = 90°, w is 4.8 km, and f is 5.3 km.

   a) Draw and label $\triangle$PWF.

   b) Solve $\triangle$PWF. Round side lengths to the nearest tenth of a kilometre and angle measures to the nearest degree.

Angles of Elevation and Depression

Angles of elevation and depression are measured above and below a horizontal line, respectively. For example, the angle of elevation from the top of one building to the top of a taller building is 20° and the angle of depression from the top of the shorter building to the base of the taller building is 35°.

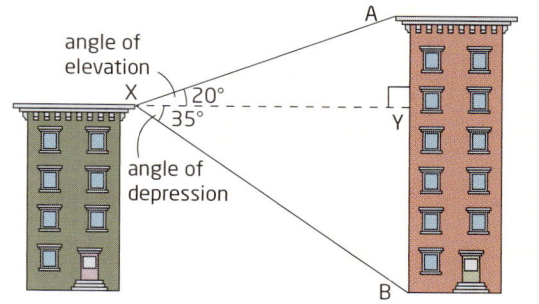

6. The two buildings in the diagram above are 25 m apart.

   a) Apply the tangent ratio to find BY, to the nearest tenth of a metre.

   b) Use trigonometry to find the height of the taller building, to the nearest tenth of a metre.

7. From the top of a vertical cliff that is 40 m high, a ship is spotted at an angle of depression of 25°. How far from the base of the cliff is the ship, to the nearest metre?

Rearranging Formulas

Formulas are equations that show how two or more variables are related. You can rearrange a formula to isolate any of the variables in the equation. For example, $y = mx + b$ can be rearranged to express x in terms of y, m, and b.

$y = mx + b$
$y - b = mx + b - b$ **Subtract b from both sides to isolate the term containing x.**
$y - b = mx$
$\dfrac{y - b}{m} = \dfrac{mx}{m}$ **Divide both sides by m to isolate x.**
$\dfrac{y - b}{m} = x$

8. Rearrange each formula to isolate the variable indicated.

   a) $y = mx + b$ for b

   b) $s = \dfrac{d}{t}$ for d

   c) $P = 4s$ for s

   d) $P = a + b + c$ for b

9. Rearrange each formula to isolate the term or variable indicated.

   a) $a(\sin B) = b(\sin A)$ for a

   b) $c^2 = a^2 + b^2$ for b^2

   c) $A = 6s^2$ for s

   d) $\dfrac{x}{\sin X} = \dfrac{y}{\sin Y}$ for y

8.1 The Sine Law

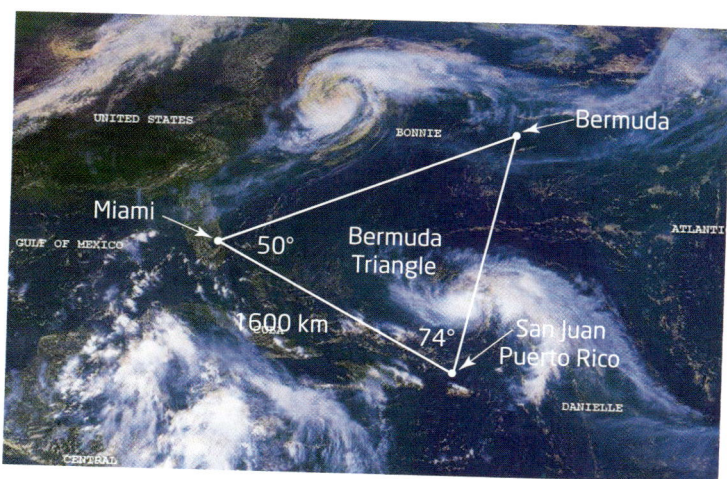

The Bermuda Triangle, in the north Atlantic Ocean, is the location of several unexplained plane and ship disappearances. Various theories have been suggested to explain this mysterious phenomenon, such as volatile weather patterns, magnetic compass variation, human error, and even alien abduction.

Suppose you took a cruise around the Bermuda Triangle. How could you determine its perimeter from the given information?

Investigate

Tools
- protractor and ruler

OR

- computer with The Geometer's Sketchpad®

Technology Tip
If you are using The Geometer's Sketchpad®, you can access the sine function from the **Functions** drop-down menu on the calculator.

Technology Tip
Instead of constructing new triangles to compare results, simply move one of the vertices of △ABC to examine other acute triangles. The calculated measures will change automatically.

How are the side lengths and sines of angles related in an acute triangle?

1. **a)** Draw an acute △ABC.
   b) Measure the side lengths and the angles.
   c) Calculate the sine of each angle.

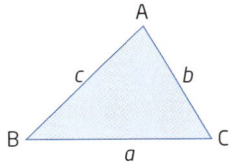

2. **a)** Calculate the ratios $\dfrac{a}{b}$, $\dfrac{\sin A}{\sin B}$, $\dfrac{a}{c}$, $\dfrac{\sin A}{\sin C}$, $\dfrac{b}{c}$, and $\dfrac{\sin B}{\sin C}$.
   b) Do you notice any relationships between the ratios? Explain.

3. **a)** Calculate each ratio.
   $$\dfrac{a}{\sin A} \qquad \dfrac{b}{\sin B} \qquad \dfrac{c}{\sin C}$$
   b) Compare these results and explain what you notice.

4. Repeat steps 1 to 3 for two different triangles. Are the results the same? Explain.

5. **Reflect** Summarize the relationship of the sides and sines of angles in an acute triangle.

The relationship you investigated is called the **sine law**. To show why the sine law holds true, draw an acute triangle and add an altitude, h, from one of the vertices.

The altitude splits △ABC into two smaller right triangles, △AXC and △BXC.

sine law
- the relationship between the sides and their opposite angles in any acute △ABC:
$$\frac{a}{\sin A} = \frac{b}{\sin B} = \frac{c}{\sin C}$$

Find an expression for h.

Focus on △AXC:

$$\sin A = \frac{h}{b}$$ **Multiply both sides by b.**

$$b(\sin A) = h$$

Focus on △BXC:

$$\sin B = \frac{h}{a}$$ **Multiply both sides by a.**

$$a(\sin B) = h$$

Set the two expressions for h equal.

$$b(\sin A) = a(\sin B)$$

$$\frac{b(\sin A)}{\sin A} = \frac{a(\sin B)}{\sin A}$$ **Divide both sides by sin A.**

$$b = \frac{a(\sin B)}{\sin A}$$

$$\frac{b}{\sin B} = \frac{a(\sin B)}{\sin A (\sin B)}$$ **Divide both sides by sin B.**

$$\frac{b}{\sin B} = \frac{a}{\sin A}$$

This process can be repeated using a different altitude.

Combining the results gives the sine law.

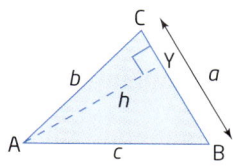

$$\frac{a}{\sin A} = \frac{b}{\sin B} = \frac{c}{\sin C}$$

Even though there are three parts to this equation, you only use two parts at a time. The choice of which two to use depends on what information is given.

You can apply the sine law to find an unknown side length of an acute triangle if you know two angles and one of the side lengths.

Example 1 Find a Side Length Using the Sine Law

A bicycle path forms a 66° angle with one lock of a canal. At a distance of 2.5 km along the bicycle path, the angle separating this lock from the next lock is 52°. How far apart are the two locks, to the nearest tenth of a kilometre?

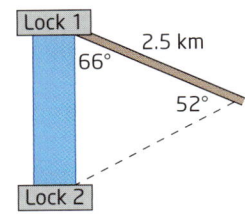

Solution

Draw a simplified diagram showing the given information.

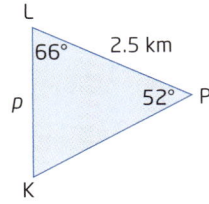

Before you can use the sine law to find length p, you need to find the measure of $\angle K$.

$\angle K = 180° - 66° - 52°$ **The sum of the interior angles in a triangle is 180°.**
$ = 62°$

Now, apply the sine law.

$$\frac{p}{\sin P} = \frac{k}{\sin K}$$

$$\frac{p}{\sin 52°} = \frac{2.5}{\sin 62°}$$ **Substitute the given information.**

$$\cancel{\sin 52°}\left(\frac{p}{\cancel{\sin 52°}}\right) = \sin 52° \left(\frac{2.5}{\sin 62°}\right)$$ **Multiply both sides by sin 52°.**

$$p = \sin 52° \left(\frac{2.5}{\sin 62°}\right)$$

$$p \doteq 2.2$$

```
sin(52)*2.5/sin(
62)
           2.231193448
```

The distance between the two locks is 2.2 km, to the nearest tenth of a kilometre.

You can also use the sine law to find an unknown angle if you know two sides and an angle opposite one of the known sides.

Sometimes the sine law appears in a different form. Recall the result obtained earlier for △ABC.

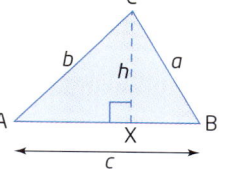

$b(\sin A) = a(\sin B)$

$\dfrac{\cancel{b}(\sin A)}{a\cancel{b}} = \dfrac{\cancel{a}(\sin B)}{\cancel{a}b}$ **Divide both sides by *ab*.**

$\dfrac{\sin A}{a} = \dfrac{\sin B}{b}$

Combining the results gives an alternative form of the sine law.

$$\dfrac{\sin A}{a} = \dfrac{\sin B}{b} = \dfrac{\sin C}{c}$$

Either form can be used to find a missing side or angle—this alternative form is a little easier to use when finding an unknown angle.

Literacy Connections

A proportion is a statement that says that two ratios are equal. For example,

$\dfrac{2}{3} = \dfrac{4}{6}$

The proportion still holds true if you invert the numerator and denominator of *both* ratios.

$\dfrac{3}{2} = \dfrac{6}{4}$

This is why either form of the sine law can be applied.

Example 2 Find an Angle Using the Sine Law

In acute △TUV, TU = 11.1 cm, UV = 5.8 cm, and ∠T = 31°. Find the measure of ∠V, to the nearest degree.

Solution

Draw a diagram and label the given information.

Apply the sine law.

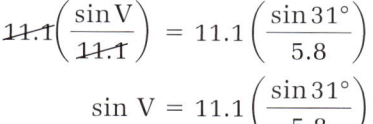

$\dfrac{\sin V}{v} = \dfrac{\sin T}{t}$

$\dfrac{\sin V}{11.1} = \dfrac{\sin 31°}{5.8}$ **Substitute the given information.**

$\cancel{11.1}\left(\dfrac{\sin V}{\cancel{11.1}}\right) = 11.1\left(\dfrac{\sin 31°}{5.8}\right)$ **Multiply both sides by 11.1.**

$\sin V = 11.1\left(\dfrac{\sin 31°}{5.8}\right)$

$\sin V = 0.9856\ldots$

∠V = $\sin^{-1}(0.9856\ldots)$ **Use the inverse sine operation.**

∠V ≐ 80°

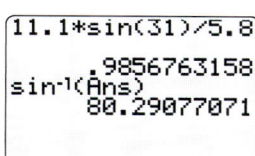

Technology Tip

Ans in the calculator display indicates the last answer. To use the last answer in a calculation, press [2nd] [(-)] for [ANS].

The measure of ∠V is about 80°.

Example 3 Perimeter of the Bermuda Triangle

Use the information given on the diagram to determine the perimeter of the Bermuda Triangle, to the nearest hundred kilometres.

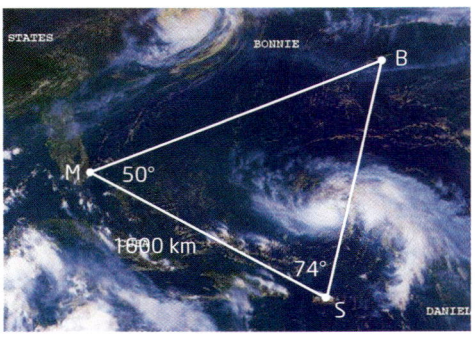

Solution

Draw a simplified diagram showing the given information.

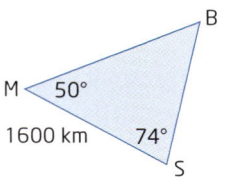

First, find $\angle B$.

$$\begin{aligned}\angle B &= 180° - 50° - 74° \\ &= 56°\end{aligned}$$

Now, apply the sine law twice to find sides m and s.

$$\frac{m}{\sin M} = \frac{b}{\sin B}$$

$$\frac{m}{\sin 50°} = \frac{1600}{\sin 56°}$$

$$m = \sin 50°\left(\frac{1600}{\sin 56°}\right)$$

$$m \doteq 1478$$

Method 1: Use Side b

$$\frac{s}{\sin S} = \frac{b}{\sin B}$$

$$\frac{s}{\sin 74°} = \frac{1600}{\sin 56°}$$

$$s = \sin 74°\left(\frac{1600}{\sin 56°}\right)$$

$$s \doteq 1855$$

Method 2: Use Side m

$$\frac{s}{\sin S} = \frac{m}{\sin M}$$

$$\frac{s}{\sin 74°} = \frac{1478}{\sin 50°}$$

$$s = \sin 74°\left(\frac{1478}{\sin 50°}\right)$$

$$s \doteq 1855$$

To find the perimeter, add the sides.

$$\begin{aligned}P &= b + m + s \\ &= 1600 + 1478 + 1855 \\ &= 4933\end{aligned}$$

Therefore, the perimeter of the Bermuda Triangle is approximately 4900 km.

Key Concepts

- In an acute △ABC, the sine law states that
$$\frac{a}{\sin A} = \frac{b}{\sin B} = \frac{c}{\sin C}$$

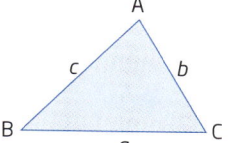

- The sine law can be used to find
  - an unknown side if two angles and a side are known
  - an unknown angle if two sides and the angle opposite one of the known sides are known

- The sine law can also be written in the form
$$\frac{\sin A}{a} = \frac{\sin B}{b} = \frac{\sin C}{c}$$

Communicate Your Understanding

C1 **a)** Why does the sine law have three parts to its equation?

   b) Do you use all three parts at once? How can you tell which parts to use?

C2 Which of the following triangles can be solved using the sine law? For those that can, explain how. For those that cannot, explain why not.

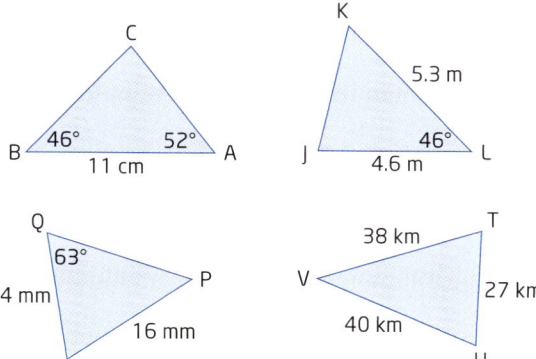

C3 How many pieces of information about a triangle's side lengths and angles are needed in order to solve it using the sine law? What possible combinations will work?

C4 There are two forms of the sine law, relating sides a and b and ∠A and ∠B:
$$\frac{a}{\sin A} = \frac{b}{\sin B} \quad \text{and} \quad \frac{\sin A}{a} = \frac{\sin B}{b}$$

Explain when it is easier to apply each form. Create examples to support your explanation.

Practise

For help with questions 1 and 2, see Example 1.

1. Find the length of the indicated side in each triangle, to the nearest unit.

   a) 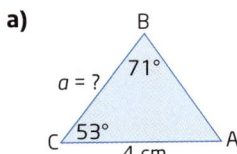   b)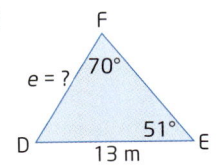

2. Find the length of the indicated side in each triangle, to the nearest tenth of a unit.

   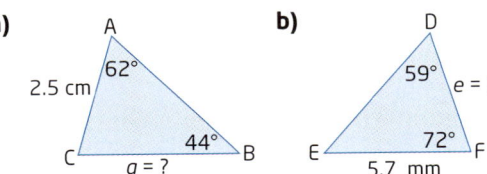

For help with questions 3 and 4, see Example 2.

3. Find the measure of the indicated angle in each triangle, to the nearest degree.

   a) 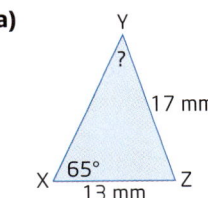   b)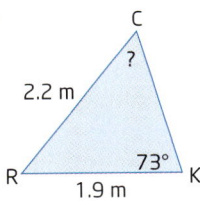

4. Draw a diagram and label the given information. Then, find the measure of the indicated angle in each triangle, to the nearest degree.

   a) In acute $\triangle$GHK, $\angle$G = 47°, h = 5 cm, and g = 4 cm. Find $\angle$H.

   b) In acute $\triangle$RST, $\angle$S = 72°, t = 1.5 m, and s = 1.8 m. Find $\angle$T.

For help with questions 5 to 7, see Example 3.

5. Solve each triangle. Round answers to the nearest unit, if necessary.

   a) 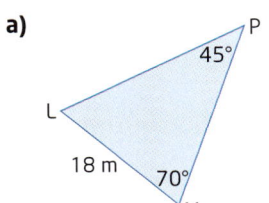   b)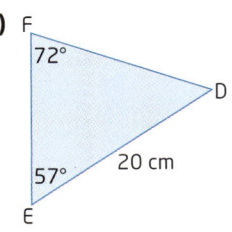

6. Solve each triangle. Round answers to the nearest unit, if necessary.

   a)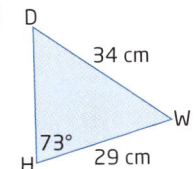

   b)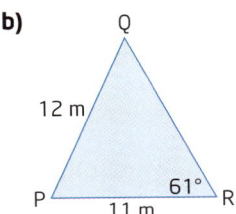

7. Draw a diagram and label the given information. Then, solve each triangle. Round answers to the nearest unit, if necessary.

   a) In acute $\triangle$AKR, k = 15 mm, r = 13 mm, and $\angle$K = 68°.

   b) In acute $\triangle$UJF, j = 23 km, $\angle$U = 57°, and $\angle$F = 48°.

8. **Use Technology** Check your answers to question 7 using dynamic geometry software.

Connect and Apply

9. A sign is supported by a pole and a cable, as shown. The cable is attached to the wall 2.2 m above the base of the pole.

   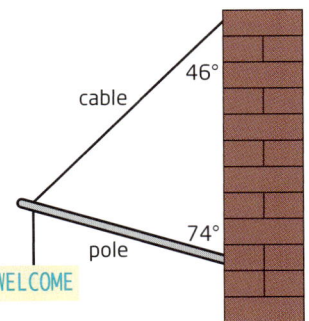

   a) Find the length of the pole, to the nearest tenth of a metre.

   b) Find the length of the cable, to the nearest tenth of a metre.

10. A small commercial plane and a jet airliner are 7.5 km from each other, at the same altitude. From an observation tower, the two aircraft are separated by an angle of 68°. If the jet airliner is 5.2 km from the observation tower, how far is the commercial plane from the observation tower, to the nearest tenth of a kilometre?

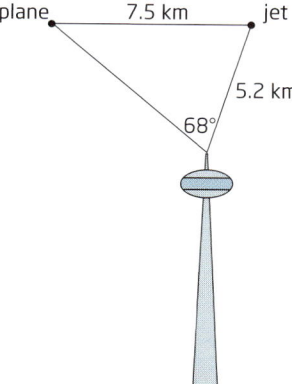

11. A telephone pole is supported by an 18-m guy wire that makes an angle of 50° with the horizontal ground. A 14-m guy wire is to be fastened on the other side of the pole for reinforcement. Both wires attach to the pole at its top. Round your answers to the nearest unit, if necessary.
    a) What angle should the second wire make with the ground?
    b) How tall is the pole?
    c) How far is the base of each wire from the base of the pole?
    d) Could you solve this problem without using the sine law? Explain.

12. A bridge across a valley is 150 m in length. The valley walls make angles of 60° and 54° with the bridge that spans it, as shown. How deep is the valley, to the nearest metre?

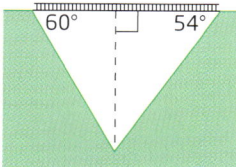

13. **Chapter Problem** You and your partner are observing an aircraft from two observation decks, located 5.0 km apart. From your point of view, the aircraft is at an angle of elevation of 70°. From your partner's point of view, the angle of elevation is 55°. Determine the altitude of the aircraft, to the nearest tenth of a kilometre.

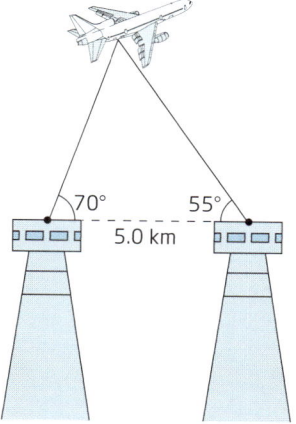

14. In isosceles △ABC, $c = 15$ cm, $a = 11$ cm, and ∠B = 68.5°. Can this triangle be solved using the sine law? If so, solve it and explain your reasoning. If not, explain why not.

15. To measure the height of a water tower, Kelly walks 0.15 km from the base of the tower along an inclined path to point P. From P, the top of the tower appears at an angle of elevation of 12°.

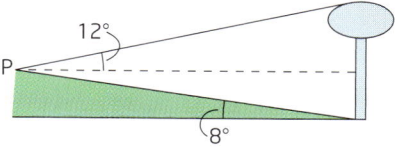

Find the height of the water tower, to the nearest metre.

16. You can find the area of a triangle if you know all three of its side lengths by applying Heron's formula,
    $A = \sqrt{s(s-a)(s-b)(s-c)}$, where a, b, and c are the side lengths, and
    $s = \frac{1}{2}(a+b+c)$.
    a) Use Heron's formula to find the area of the Bermuda Triangle.
    b) Check this result by estimating the height of the triangle and applying the formula for the area of a triangle, $A = \frac{bh}{2}$.

    Did You Know?
    Heron was a mathematician, engineer, and inventor born in Alexandria, Greece, during the first century. Among his accomplishments was the invention of the first steam engine, called an *aelopile*. The principle Heron used in the aelopile is similar to that used in today's jet engines.

17. Refer to question 16. Lan's garden is in the shape of an acute triangle. Two of the vertices have angles of 55° and 58°. The side joining these vertices is 6.2 m in length. What is the area of this garden, to the nearest tenth of a square metre?

18. a) Create a problem involving the sine law for which the answer is 15 m.
    b) Solve the problem.
    c) Trade with a partner and solve each other's problem. Check your solutions.

19. Does the sine law work if you replace sines with cosines or tangents? Investigate several triangles and explain whether there is such a relationship.

Extend

20. a) Show that the sine law simplifies to the sine ratio when one of the angles of a triangle is 90°.
    b) Would you use the sine law to solve right triangles? Explain.

21. Refer to question 16. Show that Heron's formula can also be written as follows:
    $A = \frac{1}{4}\sqrt{(a+b+c)(a+b-c)(b+c-a)(c+a-b)}$

22. **Math Contest** Frishta, Michelle, Daniel, and Vahpav each shoot two arrows at the target shown. Each ring has a different point value.

    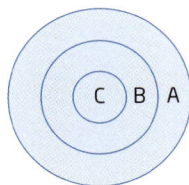

    - Frishta shoots one arrow in ring B and one in ring C. Her score is 17.
    - Michelle shoots one in ring A and one in ring B. Her score is 12.
    - Daniel shoots one in ring C and one in ring A. His score is 15.
    - Vahpav shoots two arrows into ring A.

    Vahpav's score is
    A 8
    B 10
    C 12
    D 18
    E 20

23. **Math Contest** When each of three different numbers is added to the average of the other two, the results are 105, 106, and 125. What is the average of the three original numbers?
    A 51
    B 55
    C 56
    D 57
    E 63

8.2 The Cosine Law

Sailing can be a lot of fun as long as you are careful to avoid hazardous situations, such as shallow water. Occasionally, when the ship's navigational instruments are out of order, a ship's captain can use trigonometry to find important distances and directions.

Suppose that as captain you know the measures of two sides and one angle in the acute triangle shown. Can you use the sine law to solve the triangle?

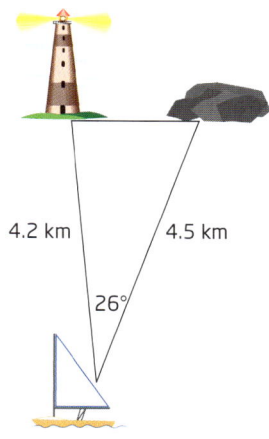

Tools
- protractor and ruler

OR

- computer with *The Geometer's Sketchpad*®

Technology Tip

If you are using *The Geometer's Sketchpad*®, calculate the square of a measure by clicking ^2 after it.

To calculate $2ab(\cos C)$, use the * key for multiplication and access the cosine function from the **Functions** drop-down menu on the calculator.

Investigate

How are the side lengths and cosines of angles related in an acute triangle?

1. **a)** Draw an acute $\triangle ABC$.
   b) Measure the side lengths a, b, and c.
   c) Measure $\angle C$.

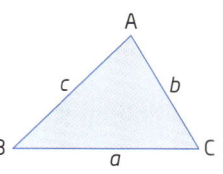

2. **a)** Calculate a^2, b^2, and c^2.
   b) For acute $\triangle ABC$, compare $a^2 + b^2$ and c^2. When would $a^2 + b^2 = c^2$? What is this relationship called?
   c) Calculate $2ab(\cos C)$.
   d) Describe any relationship you notice between $a^2 + b^2$, c^2, and $2ab(\cos C)$.
   e) Examine two or three other acute triangles to see if this relationship holds true.

3. Suppose $\angle C$ is 90°.

   a) What happens to the quantity $2ab(\cos C)$?

   b) What relationship applies to the three sides of the triangle when this happens?

4. **Reflect**

   a) Write an equation that relates the cosine of an angle and the three sides of an acute triangle.

   b) What happens to this relationship when the measure of one of the angles is 90°?

cosine law

- the relationship between the cosine of an angle and the lengths of the three sides in any acute $\triangle ABC$:
  $a^2 = b^2 + c^2 - 2bc(\cos A)$
  $b^2 = c^2 + a^2 - 2ca(\cos B)$
  $c^2 = a^2 + b^2 - 2ab(\cos C)$

The **cosine law** relates the cosine of an angle to the three side lengths of an acute triangle. To derive the cosine law, draw a triangle and add an altitude, h, from one of the vertices.

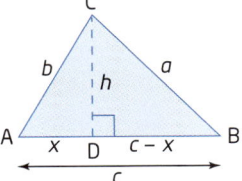

The altitude splits $\triangle ABC$ into two smaller right triangles, $\triangle ADC$ and $\triangle BDC$.

Let $AD = x$.
Then, $BD = c - x$.

Focus on $\triangle ADC$:
From the Pythagorean theorem, $b^2 = x^2 + h^2$.
Also, the cosine ratio gives
$\dfrac{x}{b} = \cos A$
$x = b(\cos A)$

Focus on $\triangle BDC$:
Write an equation using the Pythagorean theorem.
$\begin{aligned} a^2 &= h^2 + (c - x)^2 \\ &= h^2 + c^2 - 2cx + x^2 &&\text{Expand the binomial.} \\ &= x^2 + h^2 + c^2 - 2cx &&\text{Rearrange the terms.} \\ &= b^2 + c^2 - 2c[b(\cos A)] &&\text{Substitute } b^2 \text{ for } x^2 + h^2 \text{ and } b(\cos A) \text{ for } x. \\ &= b^2 + c^2 - 2cb(\cos A) \\ &= b^2 + c^2 - 2bc(\cos A) \end{aligned}$

This equation allows you to find the side length a if you know the side lengths b and c and the measure of $\angle A$.

You can derive similar equations for the other side lengths. Combining the results gives the three forms of the cosine law.
$a^2 = b^2 + c^2 - 2bc(\cos A)$
$b^2 = c^2 + a^2 - 2ca(\cos B)$
$c^2 = a^2 + b^2 - 2ab(\cos C)$

Example 1 Find a Side Length Using the Cosine Law

A boat is sailing north through a narrow strait. Through one particularly narrow section, a lighthouse marks the western shoreline, while a buoy indicates a rock hazard directly east of the lighthouse, as shown. What is the width of this section of the strait, to the nearest tenth of a kilometre?

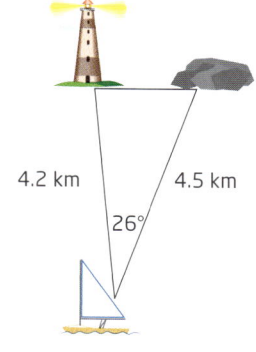

Did You Know?

The Clipper Round The World Yacht Race gives paying amateur crew members the chance to sail around the world. The race started in 1996 and takes place every 2 years.

It is the world's longest yacht race, at over 35 000 nautical miles, and takes the fleet of identical yachts 10 months to complete.

Solution

Draw a simplified diagram and label the given information. Choose variables for the vertices.

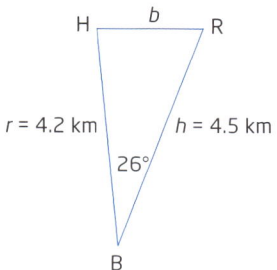

Since two sides and the contained angle are given, use the cosine law to find b.

$b^2 = r^2 + h^2 - 2rh(\cos B)$
$b^2 = 4.2^2 + 4.5^2 - 2(4.2)(4.5)(\cos 26°)$ **Substitute the given information.**
$b^2 = 3.9155...$
$b = \sqrt{3.9155...}$ **Take the square root of both sides.**
$b \doteq 2.0$

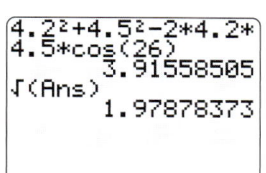

Literacy Connections

A contained angle is the interior angle that is formed at the vertex of two adjacent sides in a triangle.

The width of this section of the strait is approximately 2.0 km.

Example 2 Solve a Triangle

In acute △DEF, $d = 4.9$ cm, $f = 6.2$ cm, and $\angle E = 64°$. Solve △DEF. Round measures to the nearest degree or tenth of a centimetre, if necessary.

Solution

Draw a diagram and label the given information.

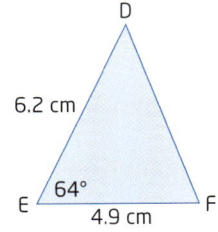

Since two sides and the contained angle are given, use the cosine law first to find side e.
$e^2 = d^2 + f^2 - 2df(\cos E)$
$e^2 = 4.9^2 + 6.2^2 - 2(4.9)(6.2)(\cos 64°)$
$e^2 = 35.814...$
$e = \sqrt{35.814...}$
$e \doteq 6.0$

Side e is about 6.0 cm.

> Since I do not know the length of the side opposite the given angle, ∠E, I cannot use the sine law.

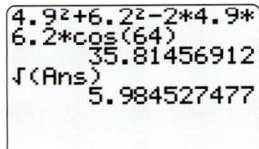

Use the sine law to find the measure of one of the other angles.

$\dfrac{\sin D}{d} = \dfrac{\sin E}{e}$

$\dfrac{\sin D}{4.9} = \dfrac{\sin 64°}{6.0}$

$\sin D = 4.9\left(\dfrac{\sin 64°}{6.0}\right)$

$\sin D = 0.7340...$
$\angle D = \sin^{-1}(0.7340...)$
$\angle D \doteq 47°$

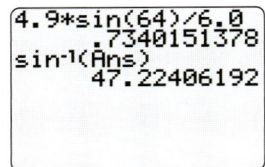

Determine the measure of the third angle.
$\angle F = 180° - 47° - 64°$
$ = 69°$

△DEF has been solved for all side lengths and angle measures.

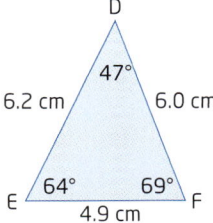

Key Concepts

- In an acute △ABC, the cosine law states that
  $a^2 = b^2 + c^2 - 2bc(\cos A)$
  $b^2 = c^2 + a^2 - 2ca(\cos B)$
  $c^2 = a^2 + b^2 - 2ab(\cos C)$

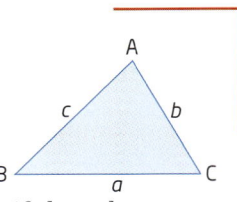

- The cosine law can be used to find a missing side if the other two sides and their contained angle are known.

Communicate Your Understanding

C1 a) What is meant by a contained angle in a triangle? Draw a diagram to illustrate your answer.

b) Why is this concept important when applying the cosine law?

C2 a) How are the cosine law and the Pythagorean theorem similar? How are they different?

b) Under what conditions can you apply
- the Pythagorean theorem?
- the cosine law?

C3 Describe the steps you would use to solve △PQR.

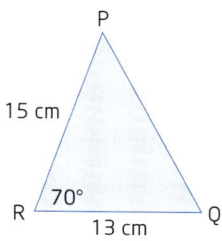

Practise

For help with questions 1 to 3, see Example 1.

1. Find the missing side length in each triangle, to the nearest unit.

a) 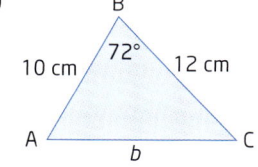   b)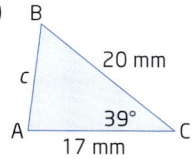

2. Find the missing side length in each triangle, to the nearest tenth of a unit.

a) 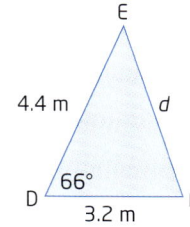   b)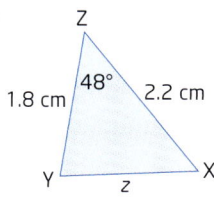

c)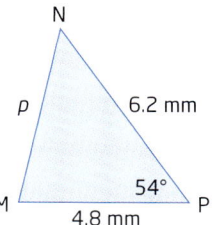

3. Sketch each triangle and use the given information to find the missing side length, to the nearest tenth of a unit.

a) In acute △TUV, $t = 1.8$ cm, $v = 1.4$ cm, and ∠U = 52°.

b) In acute △DEF, $e = 1.1$ km, $f = 1.6$ km, and ∠D = 74°.

For help with questions 4 and 5, see Example 2.

4. Solve each triangle. Round answers to the nearest unit, if necessary.

a) 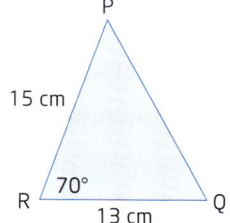   b)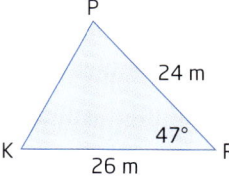

c)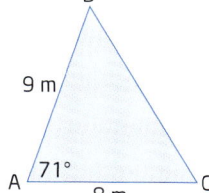

5. Draw a diagram and label the given information. Then, solve each triangle. Round answers to the nearest unit, if necessary.

   a) In acute △EFG, $e = 5$ cm, $f = 6$ cm, and ∠G = 63°.

   b) In acute △WXY, $w = 10$ m, $y = 11$ m, and ∠X = 80°.

6. **Use Technology** Check your answers to question 5 using dynamic geometry software.

Connect and Apply

7. Find the length of the bridge, to the nearest metre.

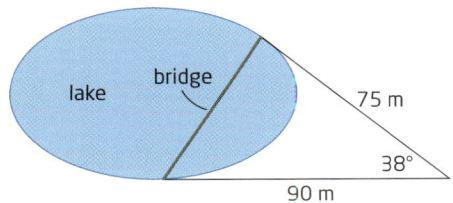

8. Chandra is riding in a hot-air balloon and spots her house and her school. She estimates how far away they are from her, and the angle separating their lines of sight, as shown.

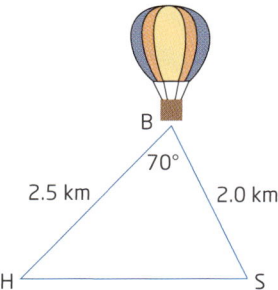

   Use Chandra's estimated measures.

   a) How far apart are Chandra's home and school, to the nearest tenth of a kilometre?

   b) Chandra's mom is watching her from home, and her friends are watching from school. At what angle of elevation does Chandra appear to each of them, to the nearest degree?

9. A drive belt wraps around three pulleys, as shown.

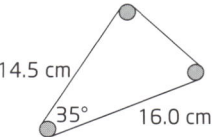

   Find the total length of the drive belt, to the nearest tenth of a centimetre. Ignore the curved sections.

10. Two ships leave port at the same time, travelling at the same speed of 10 knots. *Wavedancer* sails north, while *Ocean Princess* travels northeast.

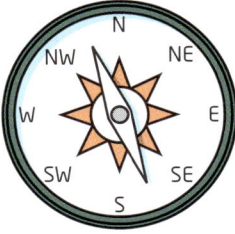

    a) How far apart are the two ships after 1 h?

    b) How far apart are they after 2 h?

    c) How do these answers change if *Wavedancer* travels twice as fast? Justify your answer.

Did You Know?

A "knot" is short for a "nautical mile per hour."

1 knot = 1.852 km/h

1 nautical mile is the distance between two points on the equator that are separated by $\frac{1}{60}$ of a degree, making the circumference of Earth 21 600 nautical miles.

11. Connor is building a toy model of a track-type bulldozer. Three sprockets for one of the tracks are to be assembled as shown.

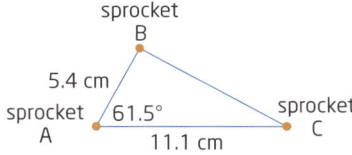

    a) How far should sprocket C be placed from sprocket B, to the nearest centimetre?

    b) Find the interior angles of the triangle formed by these sprockets, to the nearest tenth of a degree.

12. a) Create a problem involving the cosine law for which the answer is 24 cm.
   b) Solve the problem.
   c) Trade with a partner and solve each other's problem. Check your solutions.

13. The airport at Goderich, Ontario, has two runways with lengths 1525 m and 915 m. The beginnings of the runways meet at an angle of 37°. The other ends of the runways are called the thresholds.
   a) Draw a diagram and label the given information.
   b) How far apart are the thresholds of the runways, to the nearest metre?

14. Chapter Problem While cruising at a steady speed of 400 km/h, you identify a storm cloud straight ahead 45 km away. To avoid turbulence, you start climbing at an angle of elevation of 15°. If you maintain this speed and direction for 6 min, how far will you be from the storm cloud? Round to the nearest kilometre.

15. Show that the cosine law simplifies to the Pythagorean theorem when the contained angle between the two known sides is 90°.

Achievement Check

16. One of the tallest totem poles in the world is located in Alert Bay, British Columbia.

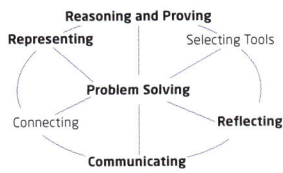

When the angle of elevation of the Sun is 62°, the totem pole casts a shadow of 30 m.
   a) Suppose the totem stood vertical—how tall would it be, to the nearest tenth of a metre?
   b) Suppose it was not quite vertical so that it made an angle of 89° with the ground. In this case, would your answer for its height be taller or shorter than your answer in part a)? Justify without calculations.
   c) Calculate the difference between these two heights.

Extend

17. Design and carry out an investigation to determine if the cosine law holds true for obtuse triangles. Write a brief report of your findings.

18. Lee is building a scale model of a water molecule for his science project. The molecule consists of one oxygen atom and two hydrogen atoms, chemically bonded as shown.

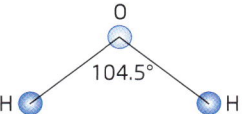

Lee models the bond for each hydrogen atom with the oxygen atom using a 10-cm straw.
   a) How far will the two hydrogen atoms be from each other, to the nearest tenth of a centimetre?
   b) What angles will a line joining the two hydrogen atoms make with the lines of their chemical bonds?

19. Refer to question 9. Suppose that the measured distances are taken between the centres of each pulley, and that the diameter of each pulley is 2.8 cm. Find a more accurate total length of the drive belt. State any assumptions you make.

20. Math Contest Sam and Nick are both members of the basketball team, along with 10 other players. When the team is seated on the bench, what is the probability that Sam and Nick do not sit beside each other?

   A $\dfrac{11}{12}$ **B** $\dfrac{1}{6}$

   C $\dfrac{3}{4}$ **D** $\dfrac{5}{6}$

   E $\dfrac{10}{11}$

21. Math Contest Show that for any ∠A, $(\sin A)^2 + (\cos A)^2 = 1$.

8.3 Find Angles Using the Cosine Law

You have learned when the sine law and cosine law can each be used to solve acute triangles.

What if you are given three side lengths in an acute triangle?

Runners in a 10-K race follow a triangular course. The three legs of the race, in order, are 3.8 km, 2.4 km, and 3.8 km. Can you apply the sine law or the cosine law to find the angle between the starting leg and the finishing leg?

Investigate

- protractor
- ruler

How can you solve an acute triangle if three side lengths are given?

1. **a)** Draw an acute scalene △ABC.
   b) Measure the side lengths a, b, and c.

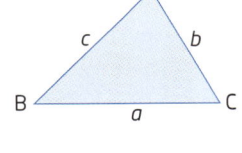

2. Can you use the lengths of the three sides with the sine law to find the measure of one of the angles in △ABC? Explain.

3. **a)** Can you use the lengths of the three sides with the cosine law to find the measure of one of the angles in △ABC? Explain.
   b) Does the choice of angle matter? Explain.

4. **a)** Solve for one of the unknown angles using a trigonometric law and algebraic manipulation.
   b) Check your answer with a protractor.

5. **Reflect** Explain which trigonometric law can be used to find an angle measure if three side lengths are known in an acute triangle. How would you solve the equation?

If you know any three measurements of an acute triangle, including at least one side length, you can find the remaining measurements using the sine law and the cosine law. The choice depends on which law allows you to relate the three given measurements to one unknown measurement.

Example 1 Find an Angle Using the Cosine Law

Three towns are connected by two roads, as shown.

A third road is planned that will directly connect Brookside and High Cliff, which are 16.5 km apart. Find the angle, to the nearest tenth of a degree, between the new road and the existing road from

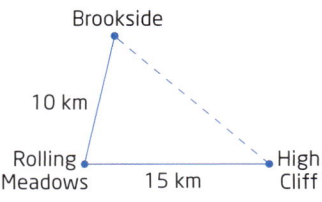

a) Rolling Meadows to Brookside
b) Rolling Meadows to High Cliff

Solution

Draw a simplified diagram and label it with the given information.

The new road will make unknown angles at B and H.

a) Use the cosine law to find ∠B.

Method 1: Substitute, Then Rearrange

$$b^2 = h^2 + r^2 - 2hr(\cos B)$$
$$15^2 = 10^2 + 16.5^2 - 2(10)(16.5)(\cos B)$$
$$225 = 100 + 272.25 - 330(\cos B) \quad \text{Simplify.}$$
$$225 = 372.25 - 330(\cos B)$$
$$225 - 372.25 = -330(\cos B) \quad \text{Isolate the term containing cos B.}$$
$$-147.25 = -330(\cos B)$$
$$\frac{-147.25}{-330} = \frac{-330(\cos B)}{-330} \quad \text{Divide both sides by }-330.$$
$$\frac{147.25}{330} = \cos B$$
$$\cos^{-1}\left(\frac{147.25}{330}\right) = \angle B \quad \text{Apply the inverse cosine to find }\angle B.$$
$$63.5° \doteq \angle B$$

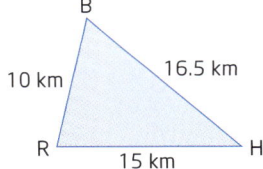

The new road will make an angle of approximately 63.5° with the existing road from Rolling Meadows to Brookside.

Method 2: Rearrange, Then Substitute

$$b^2 = h^2 + r^2 - 2hr(\cos B)$$

$$b^2 - h^2 - r^2 = -2hr(\cos B) \quad \text{Isolate the term containing cos B.}$$

$$\frac{b^2 - h^2 - r^2}{-2hr} = \frac{-2hr(\cos B)}{-2hr} \quad \text{Divide both sides by } -2hr.$$

$$\frac{b^2 - h^2 - r^2}{-2hr} = \cos B$$

$$\frac{15^2 - 10^2 - 16.5^2}{-2(10)(16.5)} = \cos B \quad \text{Substitute the known information.}$$

$$\frac{-147.25}{-330} = \cos B \quad \text{Simplify.}$$

$$\cos^{-1}\left(\frac{147.25}{330}\right) = \angle B \quad \text{Apply the inverse cosine to find } \angle B.$$

$$63.5 \doteq \angle B$$

The new road will make an angle of approximately 63.5° with the existing road from Rolling Meadows to Brookside.

Method 3: Rearrange, Then Substitute, Using a Computer Algebra System

Ensure that angle measurements are calculated in degrees.

Let $\angle B$ be represented by x.

In the Home screen, type the cosine law:
$b^2 = h^2 + r^2 - 2hr(\cos x)$

Subtract h^2 and r^2 to isolate the term with cos x.

Divide by the expression $-2hr$.

Technology Tip

To set the angle mode to degrees on a TI-89 calculator:
- Press MODE. Cursor down to the **Angle** mode setting.
- Press ▶, and select **2:DEGREE**.
- Press ENTER to save the settings.

Substitute the values for b, h, and r.
- Press (2nd) ((-)) for [ANS], followed by the *such that* symbol, (|).
- Type $b = 15$. Press (2nd) [MATH] to display the **MATH** menu, select **8:Test**, and then **8:and**.
- Type $h = 10$. Press (2nd) [MATH], select **8:Test**, and then **8:and**.
- Type $r = 16.5$ and press (ENTER).

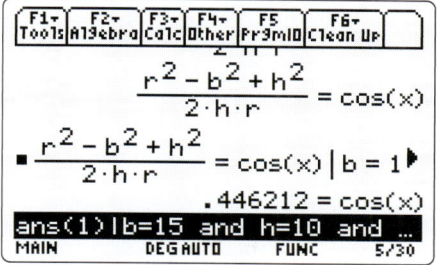

Find the angle.
- Press (♦) [COS^{-1}], and then (2nd) [ANS], followed by ( )).
- Press (ENTER).

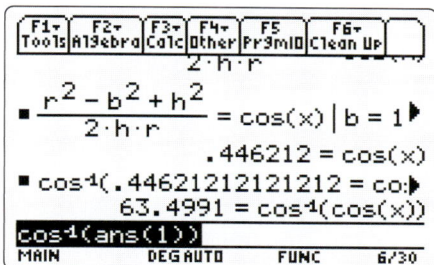

The new road will make an angle of approximately 63.5° with the existing road from Rolling Meadows to Brookside.

b) You could apply the cosine law a second time to find ∠H. However, now you have enough information to apply the sine law. The sine law requires fewer calculation steps.

$$\frac{\sin H}{h} = \frac{\sin B}{b}$$

$$\frac{\sin H}{10} = \frac{\sin 63.5°}{15}$$

$$\sin H = 10 \left(\frac{\sin 63.5°}{15} \right)$$

$$\sin H = 0.5966...$$
$$\angle H = \sin^{-1}(0.5966...)$$
$$\angle H \doteq 36.6°$$

The new road will make an angle of approximately 36.6° with the existing road from Rolling Meadows to High Cliff.

Example 2 Solve an Acute Triangle

Runners in a 10-K race follow a triangular course. The three legs of the race, in order, are 3.8 km, 2.4 km, and 3.8 km. Find the angle between the legs in each pair, to the nearest degree.

a) first and second
b) second and third
c) first and third

Solution

Draw a diagram and label it with the known information.

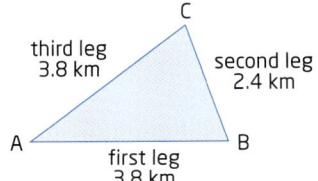

a) Since the measures of three sides are given, use the cosine law to find ∠B.

$$b^2 = a^2 + c^2 - 2ac(\cos B)$$

$$\cos B = \frac{b^2 - a^2 - c^2}{-2ac} \qquad \text{Rearrange to isolate cos B.}$$

$$\cos B = \frac{3.8^2 - 2.4^2 - 3.8^2}{-2(2.4)(3.8)} \qquad \text{Substitute known values.}$$

$$\cos B = \frac{-5.76}{-18.24} \qquad \text{Simplify.}$$

$$\angle B = \cos^{-1}\left(\frac{5.76}{18.24}\right) \qquad \text{Solve for ∠B.}$$

$$\angle B \doteq 72°$$

The angle between the first and second legs of the race is 72°.

b) **Method 1: Apply the Sine Law**

$$\frac{\sin C}{c} = \frac{\sin B}{b}$$

$$\frac{\sin C}{3.8} = \frac{\sin 72°}{3.8}$$

$$\sin C = 3.8\left(\frac{\sin 72°}{3.8}\right)$$

$$\sin C = \sin 72°$$

Therefore, ∠C = 72°.

The angle between the second and third legs of the race is 72°.

Method 2: Apply Geometric Reasoning
Since AC = AB, △ABC is isosceles. The two angles opposite the two equal sides of an isosceles triangle are equal. Since $c = b$, then ∠C = ∠B. Therefore, ∠C = 72°.
The angle between the second and third legs of the race is 72°.

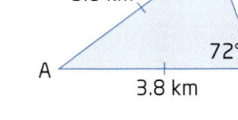

c) Use the two known angles to find ∠A.
$$\angle B = 180° - 72° - 72°$$
$$= 36°$$

The angle between the first and third legs of the race is 36°.

Key Concepts

- You can rearrange the cosine law to find an angle if you know three side lengths of an acute $\triangle ABC$.

  For example, to find the measure of $\angle B$, rearrange the appropriate form of the cosine law.

  $b^2 = a^2 + c^2 - 2ac(\cos B) \Rightarrow \cos B = \dfrac{b^2 - a^2 - c^2}{-2ac}$

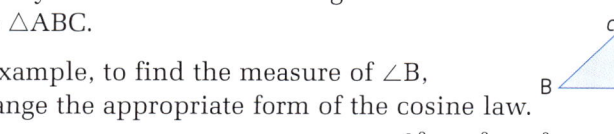

- Once you have found one angle, you can apply the sine law to find a second angle.

- When applying trigonometry to solve problems involving acute triangles, there is often more than one valid strategy.

Communicate Your Understanding

C1 When can you use the sine law to find an unknown angle in an acute triangle? When must you use the cosine law? Draw diagrams to support your answer.

C2 The following steps show how the cosine law can be rearranged to find $\angle A$. Copy the steps and write a short explanation beside each one.

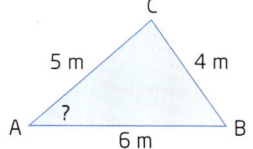

Steps	Explanation
$a^2 = b^2 + c^2 - 2bc(\cos A)$	Write the cosine law that includes $\angle A$.
$a^2 - b^2 - c^2 = -2bc(\cos A)$	
$\dfrac{a^2 - b^2 - c^2}{-2bc} = \dfrac{-2bc(\cos A)}{-2bc}$	
$\dfrac{a^2 - b^2 - c^2}{-2bc} = \cos A$	
$\dfrac{4^2 - 5^2 - 6^2}{-2(5)(6)} = \cos A$	
$\dfrac{-45}{-60} = \cos A$	
$\cos^{-1}\left(\dfrac{45}{60}\right) = \angle A$	
$41° \doteq \angle A$	

C3 **a)** Describe the steps you would take to solve $\triangle TUV$.

b) Describe a different set of steps that will also work.

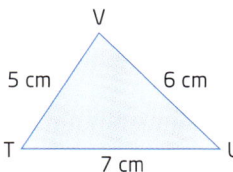

Practise

For help with questions 1 to 3, see Example 1.

1. Solve for the indicated angle, to the nearest degree.

   a)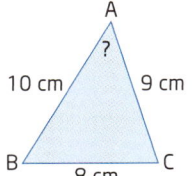

   b)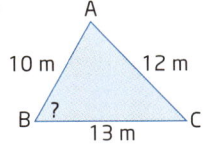

   c)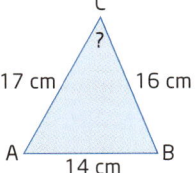

2. Solve for the indicated angle, to the nearest degree.

   a)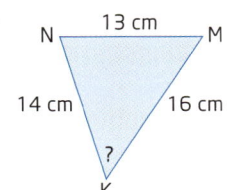

   b)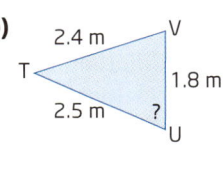

   c)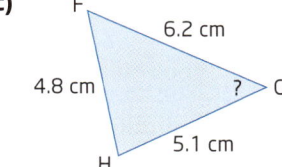

3. Sketch each triangle. Then, use the given information to find the indicated angle, to the nearest degree.

   a) In acute △ARD, $a = 170$ mm, $r = 190$ mm, and $d = 210$ mm. Find ∠D.

   b) In acute △HWN, $h = 1.4$ km, $w = 1.7$ km, and $n = 1.2$ km. Find ∠W.

For help with questions 4 to 6, see Example 2.

4. Consider △JVM.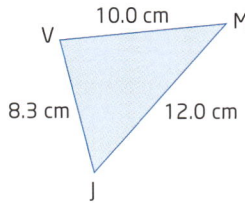

   a) Follow these steps in order to solve △JVM. Round answers to the nearest tenth of a degree.
      - Use the cosine law to find ∠J.
      - Use the cosine law to find ∠V.
      - Use the cosine law to find ∠M.

   b) Solve △JVM using a more efficient method.

   c) Compare your answers in parts a) and b). Explain why your method is more efficient.

5. Solve each triangle. Round answers to the nearest tenth of a degree.

   a)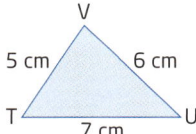

   b)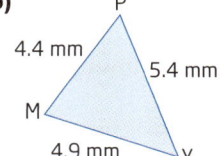

6. Sketch each triangle and label it with the given information. Then, solve the triangle. Round answers to the nearest tenth of a degree.

   a) In acute △NBG, $n = 15$ m, $b = 14$ m, and $g = 12$ m.

   b) In acute △DRT, $d = 5.0$ km, $r = 3.8$ km, and $t = 4.6$ km.

7. **Use Technology** Check your answers to question 6 using dynamic geometry software.

Connect and Apply

8. Ling is designing a garden for her backyard. It will consist of two congruent triangular flower beds on either side of a path, as shown.

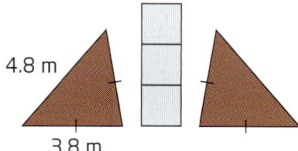

a) Find the interior angles of the flower beds, to the nearest degree.
b) Find the total area of the flower beds, to the nearest square metre.

9. A distress signal is received from a ship that is 21 km from one port and 17 km from another port. The eastern port is 24 km directly east of the western port. At what angle to the western shoreline should the ship head, in order to dock at the western port? Round to the nearest degree.

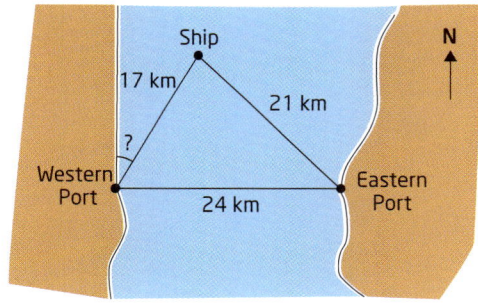

10. A leaning pole is braced at its midpoint, as shown. The pole is 8.2 m long, and the bracing beam is 6.0 m long. The foot of the beam is placed 5.0 m from the base of the pole. Determine, to the nearest degree,

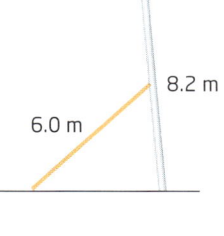

a) the angle the pole makes with the ground
b) the angle the beam makes with the ground
c) the angle the beam makes with the pole

11. Find the interior angles of the isosceles trapezoid, to the nearest tenth of a degree.

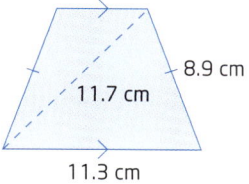

12. Create a problem involving the cosine law for which the answer is 72°.

13. **Chapter Problem** You and two of your team are to fly in a V-formation such that the distances between you are 80 m, 80 m, and 100 m. Find the angles that illustrate how the three aircraft should be arranged, to the nearest tenth of a degree. Is there more than one possible solution? Explain.

■ **Achievement Check**

14. Pinder, Dino, and Ursala all live on the edge of a park, as shown.

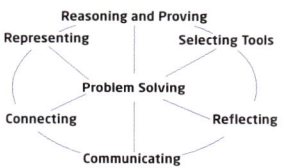

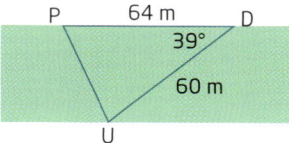

They agree to meet at one of their homes to study for a trigonometry test.

a) Is it possible to solve this triangle? Justify your response.
b) What tools will you use?
c) Whose home should they pick in order to minimize travel time? State any assumptions you make.

Extend

15. a) Acute △ABC is isosceles, with $b = c$. Show that $\cos A = 1 - \dfrac{a^2}{2b^2}$.
b) Solve △ABC, if the equal sides are 1.5 cm and the third side is 0.8 cm.

16. Draw an equilateral triangle and label its sides a. Mark one of the angles 60°. Use the cosine law to prove that $\cos 60° = \dfrac{1}{2}$.

Use Technology

Program a Graphing Calculator

You can use graphing calculators or computer software to perform the computational steps of the sine law or the cosine law. Once you have written these programs, all you need to do is enter the given information for your triangle, and let technology do the work!

■ Investigate

How can you program a graphing calculator to calculate an unknown measure in an acute triangle?

Tools
- TI-83 Plus or TI-84 Plus graphing calculator

Technology Tip
Before entering and testing your programs, make sure that the graphing calculator is in Degree mode.

A: The Sine Law

You can enter a graphing calculator program that will allow you to use the sine law to find an unknown angle measure.

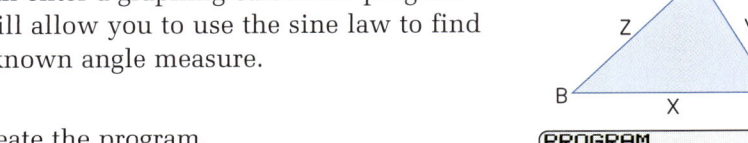

1. Create the program.
   - Press PRGM.
   - Cursor over to the **NEW** menu, and select **1:Create New**.
   - Type a name that makes sense to you, such as ANGLESL.
   - Press ENTER.

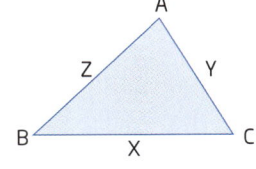

2. Enter the program.

   a) Clear the home screen.
      - Press PRGM.
      - From the **I/O** menu, select **8:ClrHome**.
      - Press ENTER.

   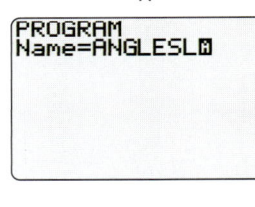

   b) Ask for the known angle, ∠A, and the two known sides, X and Y.
      - Press PRGM.
      - From the **I/O** menu, select **2:Prompt**.
      - Press ALPHA [A] , ALPHA [X] , ALPHA [Y].
      - Press ENTER.

   c) Calculate the unknown angle, ∠B.
      - Press 2nd [SIN⁻¹]. Type Y × sin A ÷ X, using the ALPHA key for variables and brackets as needed. Then, press) STO▶, and type B.
      - Press ENTER.

d) Display the answer.
- Press PRGM.
- From the **I/O** menu, select **3:Disp**.
- Type "ANGLE B:", using ALPHA [⊔] for a blank. Then, press , and type B.
- Press ENTER.

3. Test the program.

a) Press 2nd [QUIT] to return to the home screen.

b) Run the program.
- Press PRGM.
- From the **EXEC** menu, select the title of your program, for example, **ANGLESL**.
- Press ENTER twice.

You will be prompted for the known information of an acute triangle.

Enter the given information for △ABC and let the program calculate the measure of ∠B.

c) Verify the answer given by the program by using the sine law to calculate the value of ∠B.

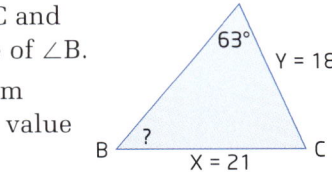

4. a) Create and enter a sine law program that will allow you to find a missing side, Y, if you are given a side, X, and the two angles corresponding to X and Y, ∠A and ∠B.

b) Test the program using the triangle shown. Check the result by manual calculation.

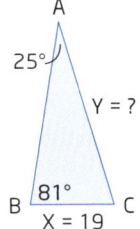

B: The Cosine Law

1. a) Create and enter the program shown.

b) What does this program do?

c) Test the program using △ABC. Verify the answer.

PROGRAM:SIDECL
:ClrHome
:Prompt X,Y,C
:√(X²+Y²-2XYcos(C))→Z
:Disp "SIDE Z:",Z

2. a) Create and enter a program that will allow you to find an unknown angle of an acute triangle if you are given three sides.

b) Test the program using the triangle shown. Verify the answer.

Use Technology

Program a TI-89 Calculator

The following instructions show how to program a TI-89 calculator. The same logic can be used for other programmable calculators or computer software.

■ Investigate

Tools
- TI-89 calculator

Technology Tip
Before entering and testing your programs, make sure that the calculator is set to DEGREE for Angle mode and APPROXIMATE for Exact/Approx mode.

How can you program a TI-89 calculator to calculate an unknown measure in an acute triangle?

A: The Sine Law

You can enter the following program to use the sine law to find an unknown angle measure.

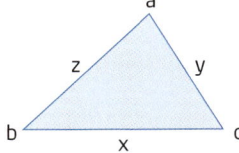

1. Create the program.
   - Press APPS, and select **Program Editor**.
   - Select **3:New…**.
   - Cursor down to the **Variable:** box. Type a name that makes sense to you, such as anglesl.
   - Press ENTER twice.

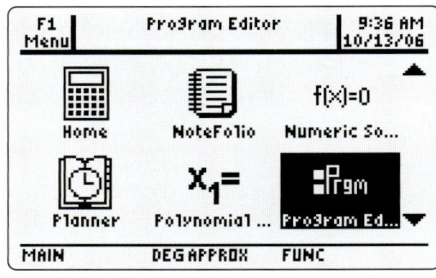

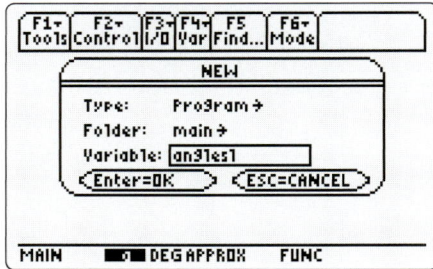

2. Enter the program.
   a) Ask for the known angle, ∠a, and the two known sides, x and y.
      - Cursor down to the blank line after Prgm.
      - Press F3 and select **5:Prompt**.
      - Press ALPHA [A] , X , Y .
      - Press ENTER.

b) Calculate the unknown angle, ∠b.
- Press ⬥[SIN⁻¹]. Type y × sin a ÷ x, using the ALPHA key and brackets as needed. Then, press) STO⬥, and type b.
- Press ENTER.

c) Display the answer.
- Press F3 and select **2:Disp**.
- Type "angle b=", using 2nd 1 for ["] and ALPHA [⎵] for a blank. Then, press , and type b.
- Press ENTER.

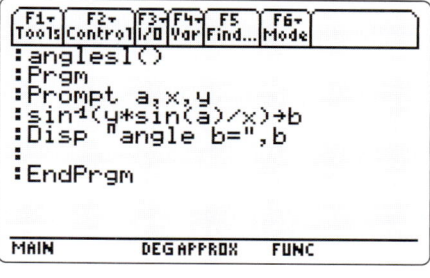

3. Test the program.
   a) Press HOME to return to the Home screen.
   b) Run the program.
      - Type anglesl().
      - Press ENTER.

      You will be prompted for the known information of an acute triangle.

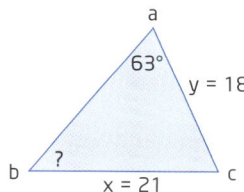

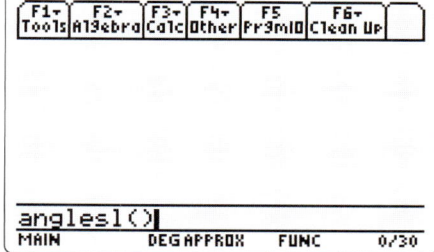

Enter the given information for the triangle shown and let the program calculate the measure of ∠b.

c) Verify the answer given by the program by using the sine law to calculate the value of ∠b.

4. a) Create and enter a sine law program that will allow you to find a missing side, y, if you are given a side, x, and the two angles corresponding to x and y, ∠a and ∠b.
   b) Test the program using the triangle shown. Check the result by manual calculation.

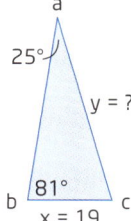

B: The Cosine Law

1. a) Create and enter the program shown.
   b) What does this program do?
   c) Test the program using the triangle shown. Verify the answer.

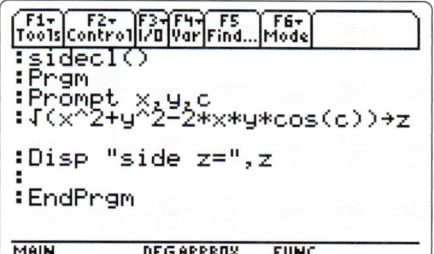

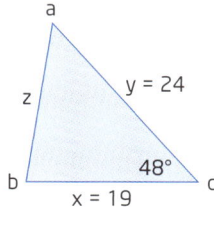

2. a) Create and enter a program that will allow you to find an unknown angle of an acute triangle if you are given three sides.
   b) Test the program using the triangle shown. Verify the answer.

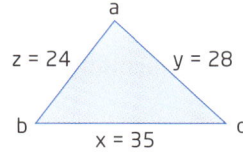

8.4 Solve Problems Using Trigonometry

Engineers, scientists, and architects apply a variety of mathematical tools, including trigonometry. When solving problems or creating designs, they must be able to efficiently combine algebraic and geometric reasoning. It is also important for them to be able to communicate their ideas to others effectively.

Example 1 Bridge Truss

A section of a bridge truss design is shown. Find the total length of the beams required to build the section, to the nearest tenth of a metre.

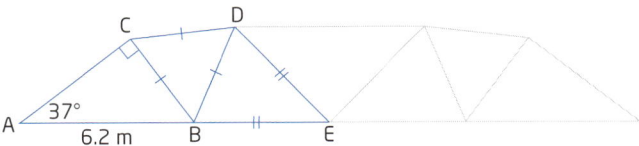

Solution

The section of the truss consists of three triangles. Solve for each side length using trigonometry and other mathematical tools.

Start with the triangle with the most given information, △ABC.

Notice that △ABC is a right triangle. First, use the sine ratio to find a. Then, use the cosine ratio to find b.

$$\frac{a}{c} = \sin A \qquad\qquad \frac{b}{c} = \cos A$$

$$\frac{a}{6.2} = \sin 37° \qquad\qquad \frac{b}{6.2} = \cos 37°$$

$$a = 6.2(\sin 37°) \qquad\qquad b = 6.2(\cos 37°)$$

$$a \doteq 3.7 \qquad\qquad\qquad b \doteq 5.0$$

I can use the Pythagorean theorem to check.

$c^2 = 3.7^2 + 5.0^2$
$c^2 = 38.44$
$c \doteq 6.2$

Label these lengths on the diagram.

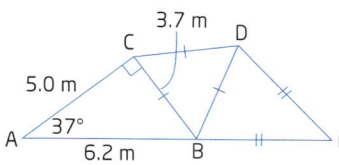

Focus on △BCD:

Notice that △BCD is an equilateral triangle. All sides have equal length. Therefore,
BC = CD = DB = 3.7 m

Focus on △BDE:

Notice that △BDE is an isosceles triangle. You can apply the sine law, but you need to find ∠EBD first. The three angles at point B are supplementary.

In △ABC, ∠CBA and ∠BAC are complementary because the third angle is 90°.

∠CBA = 90° − 37°
= 53°

Since △BCD is an equilateral triangle, the three interior angles are equal. Therefore,
∠CBD = 60°

Use the two known angles at B to find ∠DBE.
53° + 60° + ∠DBE = 180°
∠DBE = 180° − 53° − 60°
∠DBE = 67°

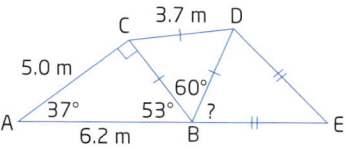

△BDE is isosceles with BE = DE. So, ∠EDB = ∠DBE = 67°.

Use this information to find ∠E.
∠E = 180° − 2(67°)
= 46°

Now use the sine law in △BDE to find the lengths of beams DE and BE.

$$\frac{b}{\sin B} = \frac{e}{\sin E}$$

$$\frac{b}{\sin 67°} = \frac{3.7}{\sin 46°}$$

$$b = \sin 67° \left(\frac{3.7}{\sin 46°}\right)$$

$$b \doteq 4.7$$

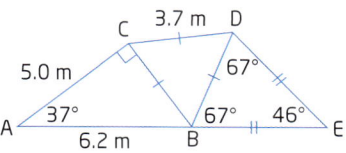

To find the total length of the beams required to build this section of the truss, add all the lengths.

Total length = 5.0 + 6.2 + 3(3.7) + 2(4.7)
= 31.7

The total length of the beams required is 31.7 m.

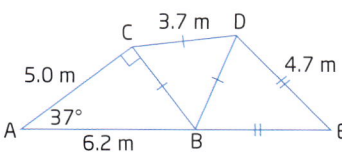

Example 2 Height of a Cliff

Find the height of the cliff shown, to the nearest metre.

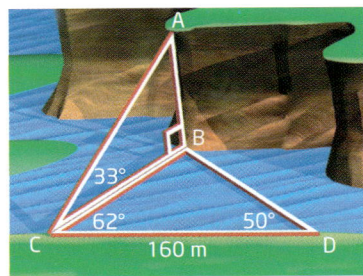

Literacy Connections

In complicated diagrams involving more than one triangle, using one letter to identify side lengths can be confusing. In this example, side *b* could mean side AC or side CD. In such cases, use the two endpoints of a line segment to identify it. Similarly, use three letters to identify angles, as needed.

Solution

There is not enough given information in △ABC to solve for the height directly. Use the given information in △BCD to solve for the width of the river, BC. Then, use this to find the height of the cliff.

Focus on △BCD:

Find the measure of ∠CBD.
∠CBD = 180° − 62° − 50°
    = 68°

Now, use the sine law to find the width of the river, BC.

$$\frac{BC}{\sin BDC} = \frac{CD}{\sin CBD}$$

$$\frac{BC}{\sin 50°} = \frac{160}{\sin 68°}$$

$$BC = \frac{160}{\sin 68°}(\sin 50°)$$

$$BC \doteq 132$$

The width of the river is about 132 m. Use this to find the height of the cliff, AB.

Focus on △ABC:

When working with right triangles, the sine law and cosine law still apply. However, it is easier to apply the primary trigonometric ratios in right triangles.

$$\tan ACB = \frac{AB}{BC}$$

$$\tan 33° = \frac{AB}{132}$$

$$132(\tan 33°) = AB$$

$$AB \doteq 86$$

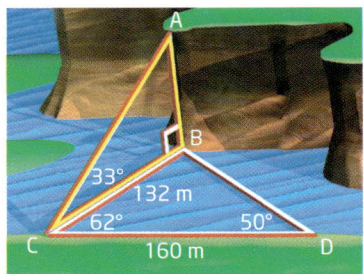

The height of the cliff is approximately 86 m.

Key Concepts

- When solving problems involving right triangles, you can apply the primary trigonometric ratios.
- When solving problems involving acute triangles, you can apply the sine law or the cosine law:
  - Use the sine law if you are given an angle and the opposite side, plus one other side or angle.
  - Use the cosine law if you are given two sides and the contained angle, or three sides.
- A number of problems involving trigonometry require multiple steps. Look for techniques and make connections to other branches of mathematics, such as geometry, in order to solve problems efficiently.

Communicate Your Understanding

C1 a) Do the sine law and the cosine law hold true in right triangles? Explain.

b) What other techniques can you use to solve right triangles?

C2 Explain how you can decide whether to apply the sine law or the cosine law in an acute triangle.

C3 a) Describe the steps you would take to find the length of x in the diagram shown.

b) Describe a different set of steps that will also work.

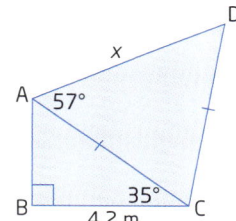

Practise

1. Determine whether the primary trigonometric ratios, the sine law, or the cosine law should be used first to solve each triangle.

a)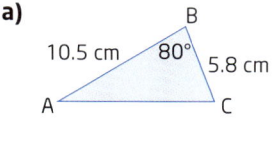

b)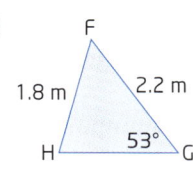

c)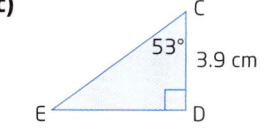

d)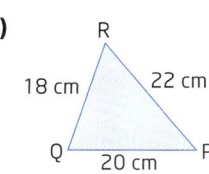

For help with questions 2 and 3, see Examples 1 and 2.

2. Refer to question C3.

  a) Use your method from part a) to find x, to the nearest tenth of a centimetre.

  b) Find x using another method. Compare your answers. Are they equal?

3. a) Find x, to the nearest tenth of a centimetre.

  b) Find x using a different method.

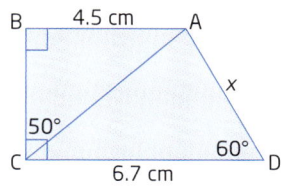

Connect and Apply

4. While flying at an altitude of 1.5 km, a plane measures angles of depression to opposite ends of a large crater, as shown. Find the width of the crater, to the nearest tenth of a kilometre.

   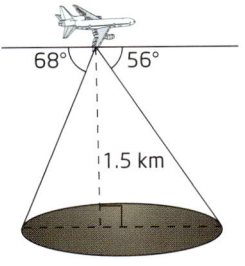

5. Earth is 149 600 000 km from the Sun. This distance is equal to 1 A.U. (astronomical unit). Mars is 1.5 A.U. from the Sun. One evening, Mars is seen from Earth to make an angle of 68° with the Sun.
   a) Draw a diagram and label the given information.
   b) How far apart are Earth and Mars at this point, in kilometres?
   c) Do you think the distance between Earth and Mars is always the same? Explain why or why not.

6. Lena is in a bicycle road race. In the first leg, she rides 12 km from Riverside to Danton. Then, she turns and rides 17 km to Humberville, making a 74° angle from the first leg. The final turn leads back to Riverside.
   a) What is the total length of the race, to the nearest kilometre?
   b) At what angles are the three towns situated with respect to each other? Round to the nearest degree.

7. Trevor, who is 1.5 m tall, is standing at a distance of 14 m from a building. From his point of view, the bottom and top of the building are separated by 36°, as shown. How tall is the building, to the nearest tenth of a metre?

   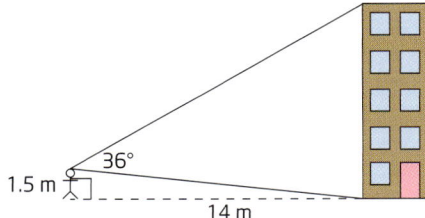

8. Rocco and Biff are two koala bears frolicking in a meadow. Suddenly, a tasty clump of eucalyptus falls to the ground, catching their attention. Biff glances at Rocco, who appears to be 15 m away, then over to the eucalyptus, which appears to be 18 m away. From Biff's point of view, Rocco and the eucalyptus are separated by an angle of 45°. Rocco's top running speed is 1.0 m/s, but Biff can run one and a half times as fast. Can Biff beat Rocco to the eucalyptus? State any assumptions you make.

9. Find the total length of materials required to build the bridge truss shown, to the nearest tenth of a metre.

   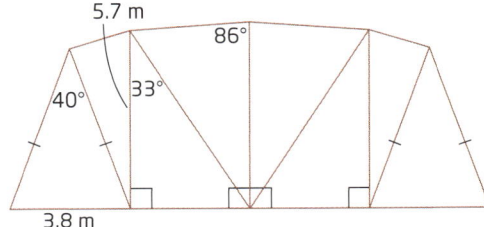

   Describe the steps in your solution and state any assumptions you make.

10. Lookout Point is accessible from two trails, both of which start from the same altitude and climb upward. Path p travels east to the point and climbs at an average angle of elevation of 20°. Path q travels northeast to the point at an average angle of elevation of 15°. Path p is 2.0 km long. Jack and Debbie parked at the base of path p. They hiked a round trip up path p to Lookout Point, then down path q, and then finally straight from the base of path q back to their truck. How far did they hike, to the nearest tenth of a kilometre? State any assumptions you make.

    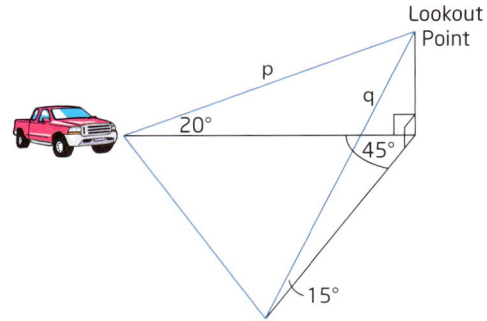

11. A tetrahedron has edges that are 10 cm in length. Find the height of this tetrahedron, to the nearest tenth of a centimetre.

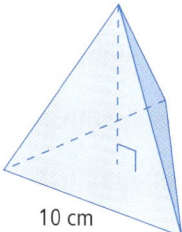

12. Doctors Jones and Hwang are astronomers observing the sun from opposite ends of Earth. The radius of Earth is 6400 km.

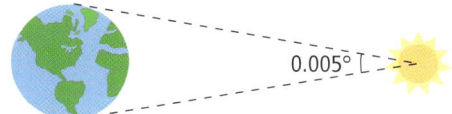

a) Use this information to verify the distance from Earth to the Sun, which was given in question 5. State any assumptions you make.

b) At approximately what times of day were these observations made by each astronomer? Explain your answer.

13. **Chapter Problem** Pilots must take wind into account when flying, or the wind will blow them off course and they will not reach the desired destination. Your aircraft cruises at a speed of 100 km/h. There is a strong wind blowing from N60°E at a speed of 90 km/h. You need to fly south to home base.

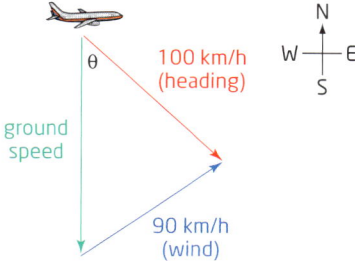

a) Find the direction, θ, you must aim the plane, to the nearest degree.

b) What will your speed be, over the ground? Round to the nearest unit.

Extend

14. Helen, Javier, and Raquel live in two identical apartment buildings, located 30 m apart. Javier lives two floors higher than Helen. Raquel lives four floors lower than Helen. There is a 36° angle of separation when Helen looks from her balcony to those of her two friends.

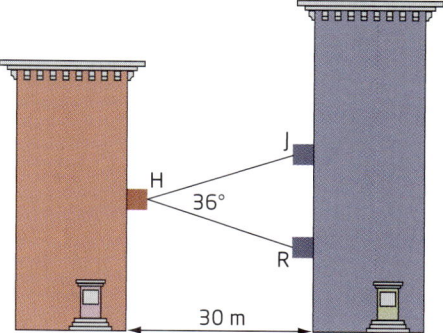

a) How far apart, vertically, do Javier and Raquel live? Round to the nearest tenth of a metre.

b) Explain how you solved this problem and discuss any assumptions you made.

15. A box is in the shape of a square-based prism. The height of the box is twice the width of the base.

a) Show that the longest thin rod that can be encased in the box has length $\sqrt{6}w$, where w is the width of the base.

b) Find the angles that such a rod would make with each edge of the box.

16. A ship travels 100 km at a bearing of N60°E and then turns and travels 80 km at a bearing of S20°E before reaching its destination. Suppose the ship travelled directly from its starting point to its destination, following a direct route. What distance and at what bearing would the ship travel? Round to the nearest unit.

17. Who uses trigonometry in their careers? Do some research to find out what types of careers require the use of trigonometry and why. Write a brief report of your findings.

Chapter 8 Review

8.1 The Sine Law, pages 396–404

1. Find the length of x, to the nearest centimetre.

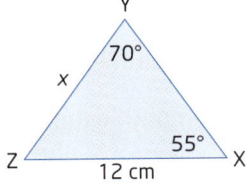

2. Find the measure of $\angle P$, to the nearest degree.

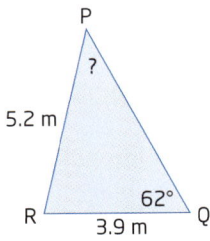

3. Solve each triangle. Round answers to the nearest unit, if necessary.

   a)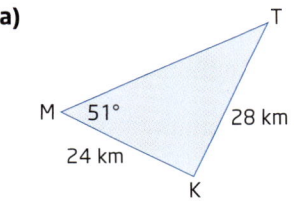

   b) In acute $\triangle NRC$, $\angle N = 47°$, $\angle R = 80°$, and $r = 27$ mm.

4. Three billiard balls are lying as shown.

   The white cue ball is 55 cm from the red ball and 62 cm from the black ball. The line segment from the red ball to the white ball and the line segment from the red ball to the black ball form an angle of 82°.

   a) How far apart are the red and black balls, to the nearest centimetre?

   b) Find the measures of the other angles in the triangle formed by these three billiard balls, to the nearest degree.

8.2 The Cosine Law, pages 405–411

5. Find the length of t, to the nearest metre.

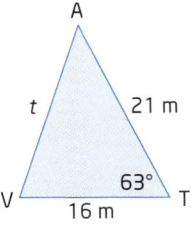

6. Solve each triangle. Round answers to the nearest unit, if necessary.

   a)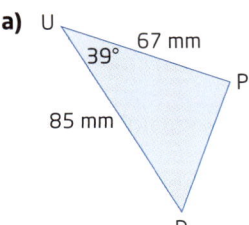

   b) In acute $\triangle EQW$, $\angle W = 77°$, $e = 11$ km, and $q = 14$ km.

7. Lucy's space shuttle is 35 km from her mother ship and 42 km from a space station. From Lucy's point of view, the mother ship and space station appear to be 49° apart, as shown.

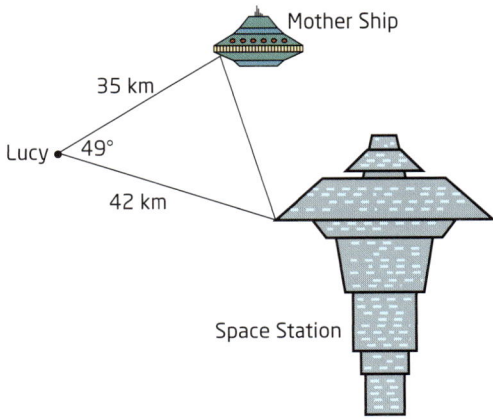

   a) How far apart are the mother ship and the space station, to the nearest kilometre?

   b) From the space station, by what angle do the shuttle and mother ship appear to be separated, to the nearest degree?

8.3 Find Angles Using the Cosine Law, pages 412–419

8. Find the measure of ∠B, to the nearest degree.

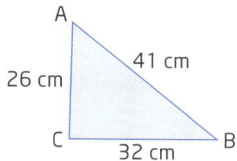

9. Solve each triangle. Round answers to the nearest tenth of a degree.

  a) In acute △VSF, $v = 2.9$ km, $s = 3.5$ km, and $f = 3.0$ km.

  b) In acute △SBZ, $s = 19$ m, $b = 21$ m, and $z = 13$ m.

10. While flying, a helicopter pilot spots a water tower that is 4.8 km away to the north. At the same time, she also sees a monument that is 5.6 km away to the south. The tower and the monument are separated by a distance of 7.0 km along the flat ground. Find the angles at which the pilot is viewing the water tower and the monument, to the nearest degree.

8.4 Solve Problems Using Trigonometry, pages 424–429

11. A person on the ground is directly between two helicopters that are flying toward each other at the same altitude. The first helicopter is 2.0 km away from the observer, at an angle of elevation of 30°, while the second helicopter is 3.5 km away. Round answers to the nearest tenth of a kilometre, if necessary.

  a) Draw a diagram and label the known information.

  b) How far apart are the helicopters?

  c) What is their altitude?

12. Percé Rock is located on the shore of the Gaspé Peninsula in Québec. The measurements shown were taken at low tide.

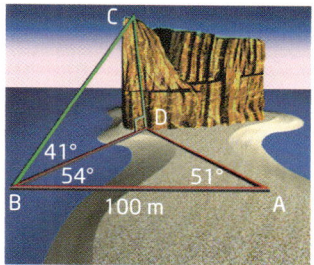

Find the height of Percé Rock, to the nearest metre.

Chapter Problem Wrap-Up

Congratulations! You have passed your first course at Fowler's Aeronautical School. Your last assignment is to create an aeronautical problem of your own involving trigonometry for next year's class. Once you have created the problem, solve it. Then, trade with a partner and solve each other's problem.

 If you are interested in finding the next steps you need to take in order to become a pilot, go to www.mcgrawhill.ca/links/principles10 and follow the links.

Chapter 8 Practice Test

1. Find the length of the indicated side, to the nearest centimetre.

   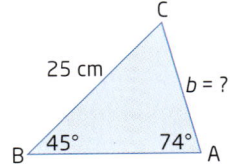

2. Find the length of the indicated side, to the nearest tenth of a metre.

   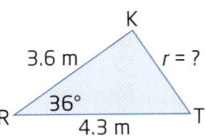

3. Find the measure of the indicated angle, to the nearest degree.

   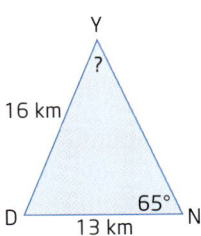

4. Find the measure of the indicated angle, to the nearest degree.

   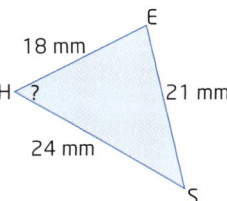

5. Two wires are supporting a tent pole, as shown.

   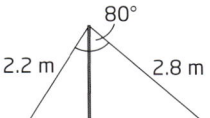

   a) How far apart are the wires fixed in the ground, to the nearest tenth of a metre?
   b) Find the angle each wire makes with the ground, to the nearest degree. State any assumptions you make.

6. Cheryl is trying to hit her golf ball between two trees. She estimates the distances shown.

   Within what angle must Cheryl make her shot, in order to pass between the trees? Round to the nearest tenth of a degree.

   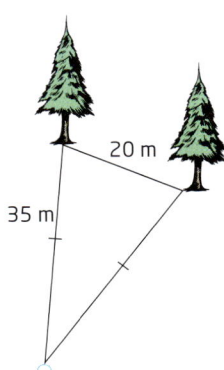

7. Solve △XYZ. Round the side length to the nearest tenth of a metre and the angle measures to the nearest degree.

   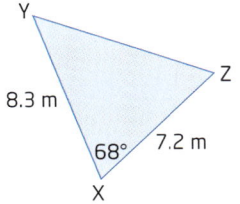

8. In acute △NTW, ∠N = 54°, n = 2.3 km, and w = 1.8 km.
   a) Sketch this triangle and label the given information.
   b) Solve this triangle. Round the side length to the nearest tenth of a metre and the angle measures to the nearest degree.

9. Students of Fowler's Aeronautical School have this crest on their pilot's cap. Find the total length of gold trim needed to make a crest, to the nearest tenth of a centimetre. State any assumptions you make.

   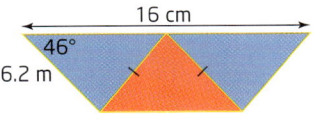

10. Use the measurements given to find the height of the Peace Tower in Ottawa, to the nearest metre.

    AB = 50 m
    ∠XAY = 43°
    ∠XAB = 60°
    ∠ABX = 82°

    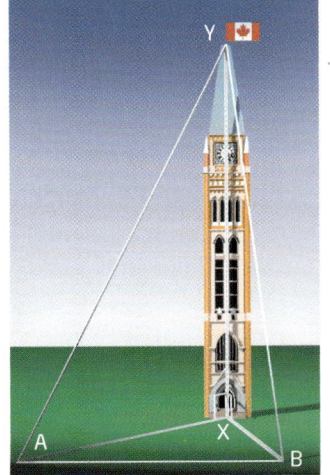

11. Tess was flying from Toronto to Hamilton at night. She noticed that her heading indicator was malfunctioning and decided to check her position. She called Hamilton Tower and St. Catharines Radio, knowing that the stations were 50 km apart. Hamilton reported that the position of her plane formed an angle of 65° with the line joining the two stations. St. Catharines reported that her position made an angle of 48°. How far was the plane from Hamilton, to the nearest kilometre?

12. Scuba divers count fin strokes to estimate the distance they have travelled under water. Felipe uses this method and a compass to swim 300 m north from the dive boat. He then turns right 120° and swims 400 m. How far from the boat is he, to the nearest metre? In what direction must Felipe swim to return to the boat?

13. While standing exactly halfway between two tall trees, Nikki spots a blue jay at the top of one tree and a cardinal at the top of the other, as shown.

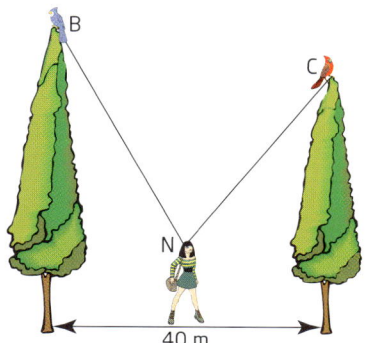

From Nikki's point of view, the angles of elevation to the blue jay and to the cardinal are 60° and 50°, respectively. The trees are 40 m apart.
   a) If Nikki is 1.5 m tall, find the height of each tree, to the nearest tenth of a metre.
   b) How far apart are the two birds, to the nearest tenth of a metre?

14. A fire station serves an area bordered by three highways that join the towns of West Port, Sackville, and Jonestown, as shown.

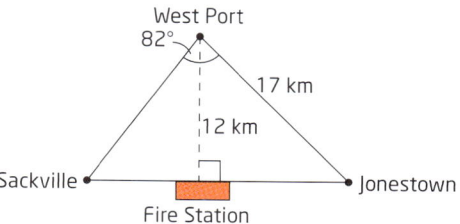

The fire station serves a total area of 126 km². Find the number of minutes it would take for a fire truck to drive the perimeter of this region, assuming an average speed of 80 km/h.

15. From his cockpit, the pilot of a flying plane observes a jet flying directly above an airport, as shown. From the plane, the angle of elevation to the jet is 14° and the angle of depression to the airport is 38°. Find the altitude of both aircraft, to the nearest kilometre.

Achievement Check

16. A small lake has three approximately straight shorelines so it forms a triangle, △LAK.
   a) List all of the possible measurements that could be determined for this lake.
   b) If you were a surveyor standing at point L, which of these measurements would you measure and which ones would you calculate? Justify your choice.
   c) Could you have made a different choice in part b)? Is this choice better than your previous one? Explain.

Chapters 7 and 8 Review

Chapter 7 Trigonometry of Right Triangles

1. Name the two similar triangles and explain why they are similar.

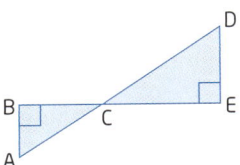

2. The two triangles are similar. Find the unknown side lengths.

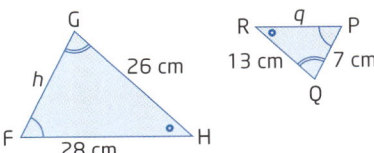

3. Find the measure of both acute angles in each triangle, to the nearest degree.

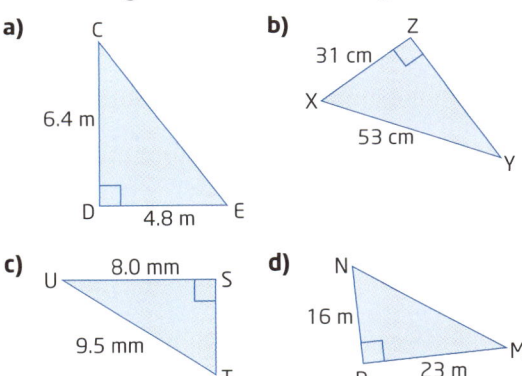

4. Find the length of x, to the nearest tenth of a unit.

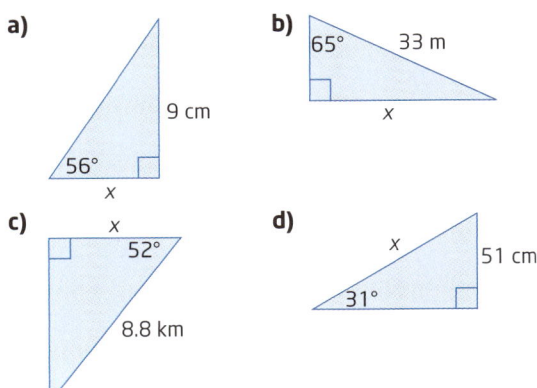

5. Solve each triangle. Round each side length to the nearest tenth of a unit and each angle to the nearest degree.

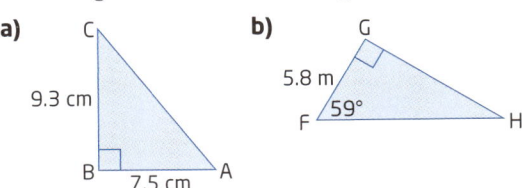

6. In a roof, a 1.5-m support is to be placed at point B, as shown. Find the length of the support to be placed at point A, to the nearest tenth of a metre.

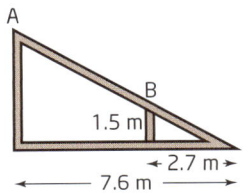

7. From a rock ledge, the angle of elevation to the top of a tree is 22°. The angle of depression to the base of the tree is 12°.

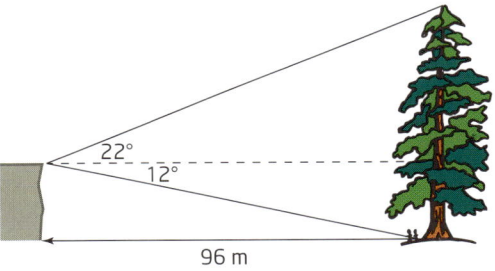

a) Find the height of the rock ledge, to the nearest metre.
b) Find the height of the tree, to the nearest metre.

Chapter 8 Trigonometry of Acute Triangles

8. Find the length of x, to the nearest centimetre.

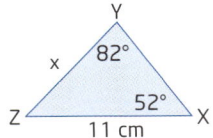

9. Find the length of c, to the nearest tenth of a metre.

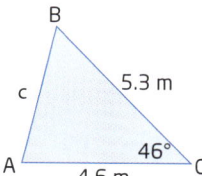

10. Find the measure of ∠P, to the nearest degree.

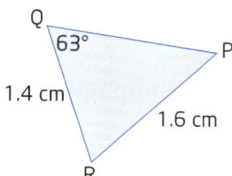

11. Find the measure of ∠E, to the nearest degree.

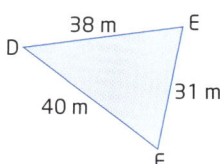

12. Solve each triangle. Round answers to the nearest unit, if necessary.

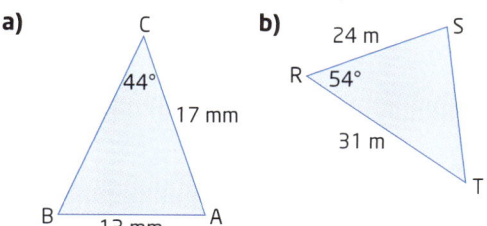

c) In acute △WXY, ∠X = 81°, ∠W = 32°, and w = 16 cm.

d) In acute △EFG, ∠E = 84°, f = 32 km, and g = 21 km.

13. Solve each triangle. Round answers to the nearest tenth of a degree.

a) In acute △ABC, a = 6.8 cm, b = 8.7 cm, and c = 9.6 cm.

b) In acute △TUV, t = 10.3 m, u = 11.4 m, and v = 12.5 m.

14. A ship is sighted at sea from two observation points on the coastline that are 60 km apart. The angle between the coastline and the ship at the first observation point is 43°. From the second observation point, the angle between the coastline and the ship is 55°. How far is the ship from the second observation point, to the nearest kilometre?

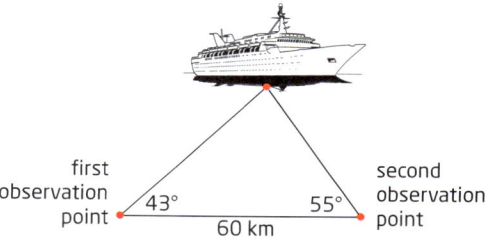

15. Find the length of the tunnel, to the nearest metre.

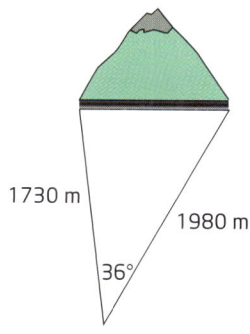

16. Find the height of the mountain, to the nearest metre.

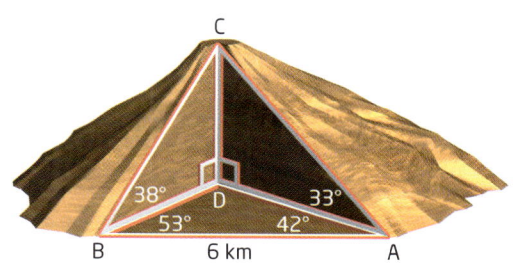

Tasks

Solar Lights

Solar-powered lighting is an attractive and popular way of providing illumination for paths and walkways. In the Queen's Gardens, two pathways meet at an angle of 60°, as shown.

Solar lights are placed 5 m apart on one of the paths at points A, B, and C. These lights have an illumination radius of 7 m.

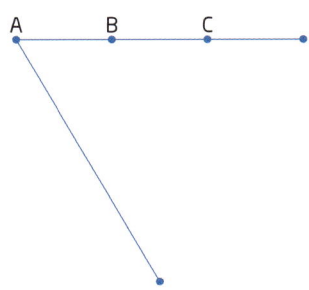

a) What length of the second path will be illuminated by light A, to the nearest metre?

b) What length of the second path will be illuminated by lights A and B, to the nearest metre?

c) What length of the second path will be illuminated by all three lights, to the nearest metre?

Lighting the Park

Julia works for the city parks department. She has been given the task of placing solar lights to illuminate the paths around the edges of a featured triangular flower bed.

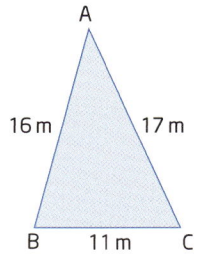

What is the least number of solar lights with an illumination radius of 7 m needed for the task? Where should Julia place them, to the nearest tenth of a metre? Justify your conclusions.

Trigonometry Using *The Geometer's Sketchpad*®

All trigonometry problems are based on solving triangles, given certain information. Three common situations involve solving a triangle given measures for side-angle-side, side-side-side, and angle-side-angle. These problems could be solved using the sine and cosine laws. *The Geometer's Sketchpad*® provides an alternative method of solving trigonometry problems with a high degree of precision.

The precision of measurements in *The Geometer's Sketchpad*® can be set to the nearest hundred thousandth of a unit, which is more accurate than most commonly available measuring devices. In addition, sides and angles can be drawn precisely using the **Transform** menu.

For example, to draw △ABC with ∠A = 23.5°, AB = 2.23 cm, and AC = 3.0 cm:

- Open a new sketch. Construct point A. Select point A. From the **Transform** menu, choose **Mark Center**.
- Select point A. From the **Transform** menu, choose **Translate…**. In the Translate dialogue box, choose **Polar**, and enter Fixed Distance 2.23 and Fixed Angle 0.0. Click on **Translate**. Label the new point B.
- Again, select point A. From the **Transform** menu, choose **Translate…**. In the Translate dialogue box, choose **Polar**, and enter Fixed Distance 3.0 and Fixed Angle 23.5. Click on **Translate**. Label the new point C.
- Join points A, B, and C.

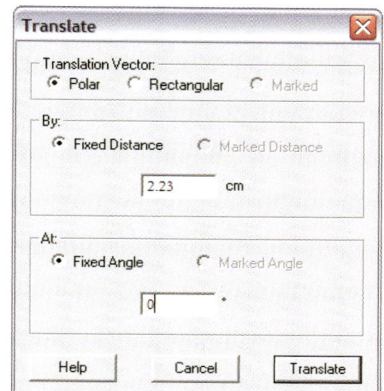

Then, to solve △ABC, use the **Measure** menu to find the measures of ∠B, ∠C, and side BC.

a) Use *The Geometer's Sketchpad*® to solve acute △DEF, where ∠E = 55.2°, ∠F = 63.0°, and EF = 3.2 cm.

b) Use *The Geometer's Sketchpad*® to solve acute △XYZ, where ∠X = 40.5°, XY = 1.45 cm, and XZ = 1.74 cm.

c) Use *The Geometer's Sketchpad*® to solve acute △GHI, where GH = 2.567 cm, HI = 2.869 cm, and GI = 3.473 cm.

d) Comment on the advantages and disadvantages of using *The Geometer's Sketchpad*® to solve these problems, compared to using the sine and cosine laws.

Course Review

Chapter 1 Linear Systems

1. Translate each sentence into an equation. Tell how you are assigning the two variables.
   a) The perimeter of a basketball court is 40 m.
   b) The average of two numbers is 15.
   c) The value of the quarters and loonies in a vending machine is $37.
   d) The total receipts from adult tickets at $20 each and student tickets at $12 each was $9250.

2. Use graphing to find the point of intersection of each pair of lines.
   a) $x - y = 4$
      $3x + 2y = 7$
   b) $y = \frac{1}{2}x - 4$
      $y = 2x - 1$
   c) $x + y - 4 = 0$
      $5x - y - 8 = 0$

3. Solve each linear system using the method of substitution.
   a) $x + 4y = 6$
      $2x - 3y = 1$
   b) $y = 6 - 3x$
      $y = 2x + 1$
   c) $5x - y = 4$
      $3x + y = 4$

4. Solve by elimination. Check each solution.
   a) $x + y = 55$
      $2x - y = -4$
   b) $2a + b = 5$
      $a - 2b = 10$
   c) $4k + 3h = 12$
      $4k - h = 4$
   d) $5a - 2b = 5$
      $3a + 2b = 19$

5. Explain why the following linear system has no solution.
   $y - 2x = 1$
   $y = 2x + 3$

6. Use a graphing calculator to find the point of intersection of each pair of lines. Round your answers to the nearest tenth.
   a) $y = x - 5$
      $x + 2y = 10$
   b) $2x + 5y + 20 = 0$
      $5x - 3y + 15 = 0$
   c) $y = 7x$
      $3y = 5x - 2$

7. Find the values of a and b in the diagram shown.

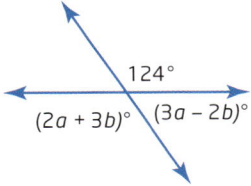

8. A boat took 5 h to travel 60 km up a river, against the current. The return trip took 3 h. Find the speed of the boat in still water and the speed of the current.

9. What volumes of 60% hydrochloric acid solution and 30% hydrochloric acid solution must be mixed to make 125 mL of 36% hydrochloric acid solution?

10. Solve the linear system.
    $$\frac{x-2}{3} + \frac{y+1}{5} = 2$$
    $$\frac{x+2}{7} - \frac{y+5}{3} = -2$$

Chapter 2 Analytic Geometry

11. Find the coordinates of the midpoint and the length of each line segment.

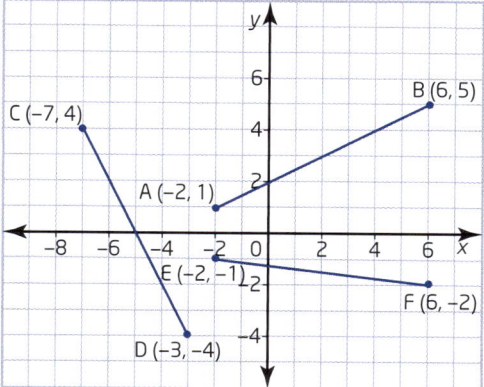

12. For △JKL, find an equation for
    a) the median from vertex J
    b) the median from vertex K
    c) the right bisector of side JL

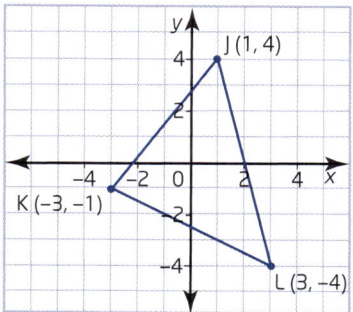

13. On a street map, the coordinates of the two fire stations in a town are A(10, 63) and B(87, 30). A neighbour reports smoke coming from the kitchen of a house at C(41, 18).
    a) Which fire station is closer to this house?
    b) Describe how to use geometry software to answer part a).

14. Use analytic geometry to classify the quadrilateral with vertices D(10, 0), E(2, 4), F(−8, −6), and G(6, −8). Explain your reasoning and show all your work.

15. a) Draw the triangle with vertices J(2, 10), K(6, −6), and L(14, 6).
    b) Calculate the coordinates of the midpoint, M, of side JK and the coordinates of the midpoint, N, of side JL.
    c) Show that MN is half the length of KL.
    d) Show that MN is parallel to KL.

16. Does the point P(−3, −2) lie on the right bisector of the line segment with endpoints Q(−2, 5) and R(4, 1)? Justify your answer.

17. a) Determine the type of quadrilateral that has vertices at A(4, 6), B(−4, −2), C(2, −5), and D(11, 4).
    b) Describe how to use geometry software to verify your answer to part a).

18. On a site plan for a new house, a water main runs along the edge of the property straight from point W(10, 34) to point M(2, 2). The water service will enter the house at point H(24, 22). The grid intervals on the plan represent 0.5 m.
    a) At what point on the water main should the connector to take water to the house be located? Explain your reasoning.
    b) What length of pipe will this connection require?

19. Find an equation for the circle centred at the origin and passing through the point
    a) J(0, 7)
    b) K(5, 6)
    c) $(8, \sqrt{3})$

20. Find the diameter and the area of the circle defined by $x^2 + y^2 = 64$.

21. You are designing a chute for loading grain into rail cars. The cars have a round hatch 60 cm in diameter. The chute will have a square cross section. Find the side length of the largest chute that will fit into the hatch. Round your answer to the nearest centimetre.

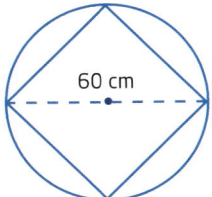

Chapter 3 Geometric Properties

22. a) What is the centroid of a triangle?
    b) Describe how to use analytic geometry to find the coordinates of the centroid of a triangle, given the coordinates of the vertices.
    c) Outline how to use geometry software to find the centroid of a triangle.

23. a) Show that each median of a triangle bisects the area of the triangle.
    b) Outline how to use geometry software to answer part a).

24. Verify that △ABC is isosceles.

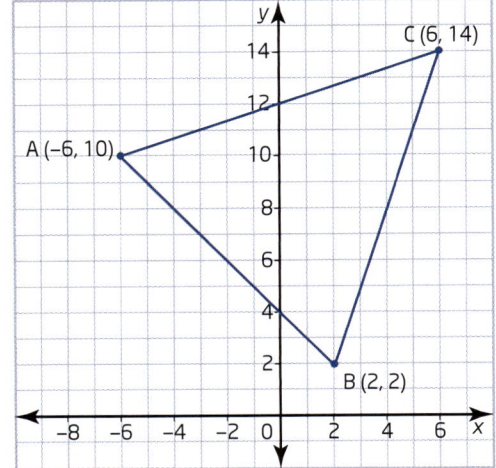

25. a) Verify that △DEF is a right triangle.

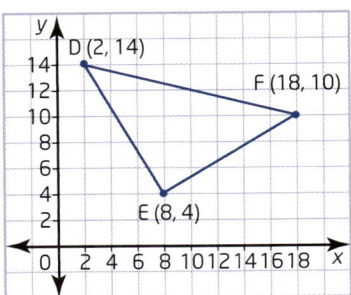

   b) Describe another way to use analytic geometry to answer part a).

26. a) Draw the triangle with vertices J(−4, −6), K(2, −4), and L(8, 10).
    b) Verify that the triangle formed by joining the midpoints of the sides of △JKL is similar to △JKL.

27. a) Find an equation for each of the right bisectors of the sides of △JKL.

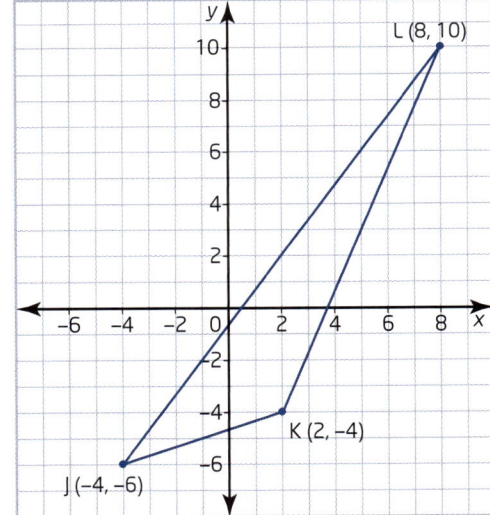

   b) Find the circumcentre of △PQR, the point of intersection of the right bisectors of the three sides.
   c) Show that the circumcentre of △PQR is equidistant from its vertices.

440 MHR • Course Review

28. List the types of quadrilaterals that have diagonals that
    a) are equal in length
    b) bisect each other
    c) meet at right angles

29. a) Show that a line segment that joins the midpoints of opposite sides of a parallelogram has the same length as the other two sides of the parallelogram.
    b) Outline how to use geometry software to answer part a).

30. a) Verify that the quadrilateral with vertices A(2, 7), B(−2, 2), C(4, −2), and D(8, 3) is a rectangle.
    b) Verify that the diagonals of ABCD are equal in length.
    c) Verify that the diagonals bisect each other.
    d) Verify that the diagonals are not perpendicular.

31. Determine the type of quadrilateral created by the points of intersection of the lines
    $x - y + 3 = 0$, $y = x - 2$, $y = -\frac{1}{2}x + 5$, and $x + 2y + 12 = 0$.

32. a) Verify that the points P(2, 5), Q(6, −1), and R(7, 4) all lie on a circle centred at C(4, 2).
    b) Verify that the centre of the circle lies on the right bisector of chord PQ.

33. Outline how to use geometry software to find the centre of a circle given the coordinates of three points on the circle.

Chapter 4 Quadratic Relations

34. Use finite differences to determine whether each relation is linear, quadratic, or neither.

a)
x	y
−2	−12
−1	−3
0	0
1	−3
2	−12
3	−36

b)
x	y
−2	−6
−1	−3
0	0
1	3
2	6
3	9

c)
x	y
−2	−12
−1	−7
0	−2
1	3
2	8
3	13

35. A basketball shot is taken from a horizontal distance of 5 m from the hoop. The height of the ball can be modelled by the relation $h = -7.3t^2 + 8.25t + 2.1$, where h is the height, in metres, and t is the time, in seconds, since the ball was released.
    a) From what height was the ball released?
    b) What was the maximum height reached by the ball?
    c) If the ball reached the hoop in 1 s, what was the height of the hoop?

36. Sketch each parabola. Label the coordinates of the vertex and the equation of the axis of symmetry.
    a) $y = x^2 - 3$
    b) $y = (x + 1)^2 - 1$
    c) $y = -2(x - 4)^2 - 3$
    d) $y = 0.5(x + 6)^2 + 3$

37. The height of lava ejected from the Stromboli volcano can be modelled by the relation $h = -5t(t - 11)$, where h is the height, in metres, of the lava above the crater and t is the time, in seconds, since it was ejected.

   a) Graph the relation.

   b) Find the maximum height reached by the lava, to the nearest metre.

   c) How long does the lava take to reach the maximum height?

   d) Is the length of time that the lava is in the air twice the answer from part c)? Explain why or why not.

38. Determine an equation to represent each parabola.

   a)

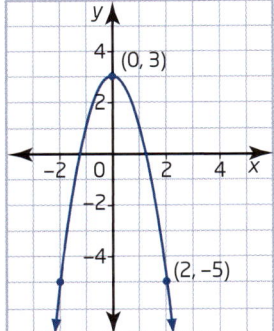

   b)

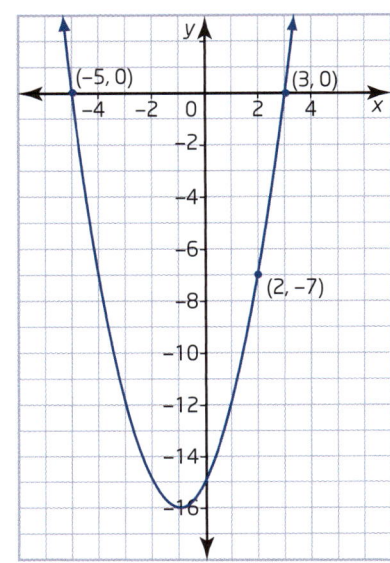

39. The vertex of a parabola is $(-2, -4)$. One x-intercept is 7. What is the other x-intercept?

40. Evaluate.

   a) 8^0

   b) 3^{-1}

   c) $(-2)^{-5}$

   d) $\left(\dfrac{2}{5}\right)^{-2}$

   e) $(-18)^0$

   f) $\left(\dfrac{4}{3}\right)^{-1}$

41. A piece of wood burns completely in 1 s at 600°C. The time it takes for the wood to burn is doubled for every 10°C drop in temperature and halved for every 10°C increase in temperature. Determine how long the piece of wood would take to burn at each temperature.

   a) 500°C

   b) 650°C

Chapter 5 Quadratic Expressions

42. Expand and simplify.

   a) $3(x - 4) + 5(x + 6)$

   b) $6(a + 3) - 2(a - 5)$

   c) $4(1 - 3k) - (2 - 4k)$

   d) $2t(3t - 4) + t(2t + 5)$

   e) $\dfrac{1}{2}(6 + 3p) - \dfrac{3}{4}(8 - 10p)$

   f) $3y(y^2 - y - 1) - y(2y^2 - 3y + 4)$

43. a) Write an algebraic expression to represent the surface area of the rectangular prism. Expand and simplify.

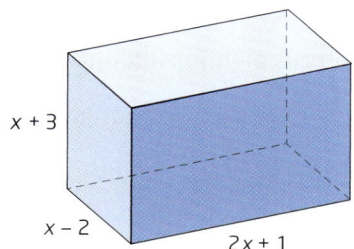

b) If x represents 5 cm, what is the surface area?

44. Expand and simplify.
   a) $(x + 4)^2$
   b) $(y - 4)(y + 4)$
   c) $(a - 5)^2$
   d) $(3t + 1)(3t - 1)$
   e) $(5a + 3b)(5a - 3b)$
   f) $2(3m + 1)^2$

45. Expand and simplify.
   a) $(m - 3)(m + 3) + (m - 4)^2$
   b) $3(2t + 1)^2 + 2(3t - 1)(3t + 1)$
   c) $2(3x + 2y)(3x - 2y) - 3(3x - y)^2$
   d) $(2y - 1)^2 + (y + 2)^2 - (1 - 2y)(1 + 2y)$
   e) $(4m + n)^2 + 2(m - 2n)^2$
   f) $5(2t - 5z)^2 + 3(4t - 3z)(4t + 3z)$

46. Factor.
   a) $5k - 35$
   b) $4h^2 - 20h$
   c) $2xy - 8xy^2$
   d) $x^2 - 25$
   e) $1 - 49m^2$
   f) $4a^2 - 16b^2$

47. The area of the rectangle is given by the expression $n^2 - 5n + 6$.

Area is $n^2 - 5n + 6$.

   a) Find expressions for the length and the width.
   b) If n represents 8 cm, determine the perimeter and the area of the rectangle.

48. Factor each trinomial, if possible.
   a) $x^2 - x - 12$
   b) $y^2 + 3y - 18$
   c) $m^2 + 11m + 24$
   d) $t^2 - 8t + 15$
   e) $x^2 + 3x + 4$
   f) $n^2 - 13n + 40$
   g) $w^2 - w - 30$
   h) $14 + 5m - m^2$

49. Factor, if possible.
   a) $x^2 + 10x + 25$
   b) $y^2 - 12y + 36$
   c) $m^2 + 6m + 16$
   d) $4x^2 + 12x + 9$
   e) $25r^2 - 20rs + 4s^2$
   f) $5x^2 - 20xy + 20y^2$

50. Write two different trinomials that have $x + 2$ as a factor.

51. Determine all values of p so that each trinomial is a perfect square.
   a) $x^2 + px + 16$
   b) $4x^2 - 12x + p$
   c) $px^2 + 40x + 16$

52. If m and n are integers, find values of m and n such that $m^2 - n^2 = 21$.

Chapter 6 Quadratic Equations

53. Rewrite each relation in the form $y = a(x - h)^2 + k$ by completing the square. Graph the relation and give the vertex and the equation of the axis of symmetry.
    a) $y = x^2 + 4x + 1$
    b) $y = -x^2 - 6x - 5$
    c) $y = 3 - 4x - x^2$

54. **Use Technology** Use a graphing calculator to find the maximum or minimum point of each parabola, rounded to the nearest tenth.
    a) $y = 2x^2 + 6x + 5$
    b) $y = -3x^2 + 2x + 1$
    c) $y = 0.8x^2 + 0.5x - 3.6$

55. Find the x-intercepts of each parabola.
    a) $y = x^2 + 2x - 3$
    b) $y = x^2 + 6x + 5$
    c) $y = x^2 - 4x + 4$
    d) $y = 4x^2 - 12x + 9$

56. Solve by factoring. Check your solutions.
    a) $x^2 + 3x - 28 = 0$
    b) $m^2 + 7m + 10 = 0$
    c) $2n^2 = 27 - 15n$
    d) $3k(k - 4) + k + 4(k + 1) = 0$

57. Write a quadratic equation with the given roots.
    a) $5, -2$
    b) $-\dfrac{3}{4}, -\dfrac{2}{3}$

58. Find the value of k so that each parabola has only one x-intercept.
    a) $kx^2 - 5x + 2 = 0$
    b) $x^2 + kx + 9 = 0$
    c) $25x^2 + 20x + k = 0$

59. The area of the rectangle is 36 cm². What are its dimensions?

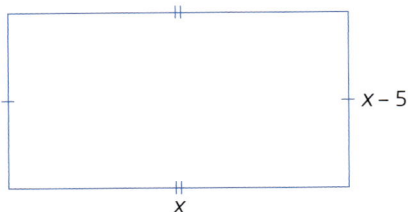

60. Use the quadratic formula to solve each equation. Express your answers as exact roots.
    a) $x^2 - x - 4 = 0$
    b) $7k^2 - 2k - 2 = 0$
    c) $2x^2 = 3 - 8x$
    d) $4h = 5 - 4h^2$
    e) $0 = -3a^2 + 4a + 1$

61. A store sells 90 ski jackets for $200 each. A survey indicates that for each $10 decrease in price, five more jackets will be sold.
    a) Find the number of jackets sold and the selling price when the total revenue is $17 600.
    b) What is the lowest price that will give revenues of at least $15 600? How many jackets would be sold at this price?

62. The hypotenuse of a right triangle measures 20 cm. The sum of the lengths of the legs is 28 cm. Find the length of each leg of the triangle.

63. A rectangular swimming pool measuring 10 m by 4 m is surrounded by a deck of uniform width. The total area of the pool and deck is 135 m². What is the width of the deck?

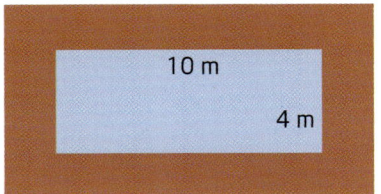

Chapter 7 Trigonometry of Right Triangles

64. Identify the two similar triangles and explain why they are similar.

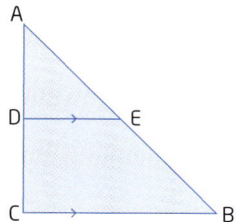

65. At noon, the shadow of a tree is 4.3 m long. At the same time, the shadow of a metre stick is 0.2 m long. What is the height of the tree?

66. Find the measure of ∠A, to the nearest degree.

a)

b)

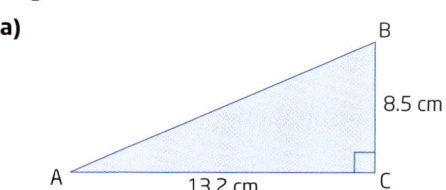

67. A road sign shows that a hill has a grade of 8%. What is the angle of inclination of the hill, to the nearest tenth of a degree?

68. Find x, to the nearest tenth of a unit.

a)

b)

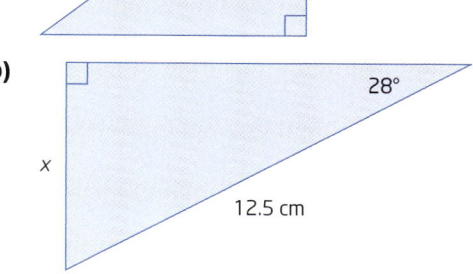

69. Solve each triangle. Round lengths to the nearest unit and angle measures to the nearest degree.

a)

b)

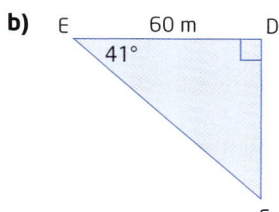

c)

d)

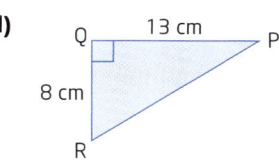

70. In △XYZ, ∠X = 90°, XY = 3.5 cm, and YZ = 4.8 cm. Solve △XYZ. Round lengths to the nearest tenth of a metre and angle measures to the nearest degree.

71. In △ABC, ∠C = 90°. If sin A = 0.5, what is the measure of ∠B?

72. A coast guard boat is 14.8 km east of a lighthouse. A disabled yacht is 7.5 km south of the lighthouse.
    a) How far is the coast guard boat from the yacht, to the nearest tenth of a kilometre?
    b) At what angle south of due west, to the nearest tenth of a degree, should the coast guard boat travel to reach the yacht?

73. The Confederation Bridge joins New Brunswick and Prince Edward Island. From a boat in the Northumberland Strait, the angle of elevation of the highest point on the bridge is 26.6°. When the boat is 100 m closer to the bridge, the angle of elevation is 71.7°. What is the height of the bridge, to the nearest tenth of a metre?

74. Find the length of x, to the nearest centimetre.

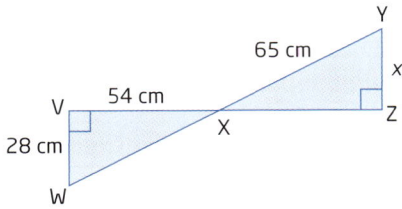

Chapter 8 Trigonometry of Acute Triangles

75. Find the measure of ∠A, to the nearest degree.

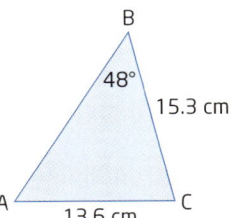

76. In △ABC, ∠B = 38.2°, ∠C = 65.6°, and b = 54 cm. Find c, to the nearest tenth of a centimetre.

77. Solve each triangle. Round answers to the nearest tenth, if necessary.
    a)
    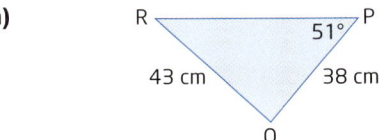

    b) In △JKL, ∠L = 32°, j = 20.5 cm, and ∠K = 75°.

78. The longer diagonal of a parallelogram measures 8.5 cm. This diagonal makes angles of 43° and 32° with the sides of the parallelogram, as shown. Find the length of each side of the parallelogram, to the nearest tenth of a centimetre.

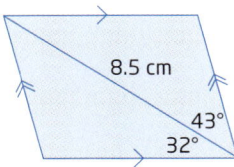

79. Find the unknown side length, to the nearest tenth of a metre.

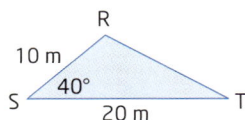

446 MHR • Course Review

80. Solve △KLM. Round answers to the nearest tenth of a degree.

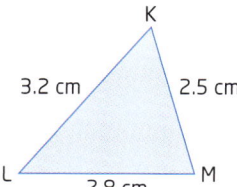

81. Determine the area of △RST, to the nearest square metre.

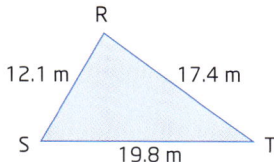

82. Determine the perimeter of isosceles △ABC, to the nearest tenth of a centimetre.

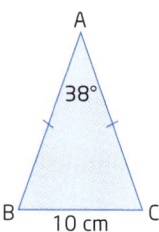

83. Find the length x in each, to the nearest tenth of a metre.

a)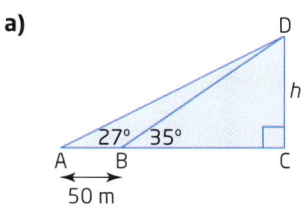

b)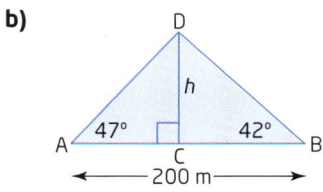

84. Two boats left the harbour at the same time. One travelled at 10 km/h on a bearing of N47°E. The other travelled at 8 km/h on a bearing of N79°E. How far apart were the boats after 45 min? Round the distance to the nearest tenth of a kilometre.

85. Solve the following triangles. Round lengths to the nearest tenth of a metre and angle measures to the nearest degree.
   a) In △DEF, ∠D = 58°, ∠E = 53°, and d = 8 cm.
   b) In △RST, ∠R = 73°, r = 8 m, and t = 6 m.
   c) In △ABC, ∠A = 68°, b = 5 cm, and c = 7 cm
   d) In △WXY, w = 11 m, x = 10 m, and y = 14 m

86. The three sides of a triangle measure 15 cm, 17 cm, and 18 cm. Find the measure of the largest angle, to the nearest degree.

Challenge Problems Appendix

1. Write an equation that forms a system of equations with $x + y = 4$, so that the system has
   a) no solution
   b) infinitely many solutions
   c) one solution

2. Sketch a graph to represent a system of two equations with one solution, so that the two lines have
   a) different x-intercepts and different y-intercepts
   b) the same x-intercepts but different y-intercepts
   c) different x-intercepts but the same y-intercept
   d) the same x-intercept and the same y-intercept

3. Find the point of intersection of each linear system.
   a) $2(x - 4) + y = 6$
      $3x - 2(y - 3) = 13$
   b) $2(x - 1) - 3(y - 3) = 0$
      $3(x + 2) - (y - 7) = 20$
   c) $2(3x - 1) - (y + 4) + 7 = 0$
      $4(1 - 2x) - 3(3 - y) + 12 = 0$
   d) $2(x - 1) - 4(2y + 1) = -1$
      $x + 3(3y + 2) = 2$

4. In the figure, the side of each small square represents 1 cm. Determine the area of the shaded part.

5. Solve the following linear system for x and y by letting $a = \dfrac{1}{x}$ and $b = \dfrac{1}{y}$.

   $\dfrac{1}{x} + \dfrac{3}{y} = \dfrac{3}{4}$

   $\dfrac{3}{x} - \dfrac{2}{y} = \dfrac{5}{12}$

6. Write a linear system in the form
   $Ax + By = C$
   $Dx + Ey = F$
   where A, B, C, D, E, and F are integers and the point of intersection is $(6, -5)$.

7. Each letter represents a different integer. The sums of the columns and two of the rows are shown. Find the two missing row sums.

A	B	A	B	36
A	C	A	C	34
B	B	B	C	?
D	E	F	A	?
37	40	41	32	

8. Greg drove from his home in Point Alexander to Belleville at an average speed of 75 km/h. From her home in Chalk River, Claire drove the 18 km to Point Alexander and continued on to Belleville at an average speed of 85 km/h. Greg and Claire left home at the same time.
   a) After what length of time did Claire pass Greg?
   b) How far were they from Point Alexander when Claire passed Greg?

9. Determine the next three numbers in each sequence.
   a) 6, 12, 11, 18, 17, …
   b) 2, 4, 6, 10, 16, 26, …
   c) 1, 2, 5, 10, 17, 26, …

10. The endpoints of AB are A(3, −4) and B(11, b). The midpoint of AB is M(n, 3). Find the values of b and n.

11. The base of an isosceles triangle lies on the x-axis. The coordinates of the midpoints of the equal sides of the triangle are (2, 3) and (−2, 3). What are the coordinates of the vertices of the triangle?

12. A quadrilateral has vertices P(−3, 1), Q(−1, −5), R(11, 1), and S(1, 3). Verify each property.
    a) PQRS is a trapezoid.
    b) The line segment joining the midpoints of the two non-parallel sides is parallel to the bases.
    c) The line segment from part b) is half as long as the sum of the lengths of the bases.

13. Copy the grid. Draw six circles in six of the small squares, so that none of the circles is in the same row, column, or diagonal.

14. Determine the area of the trapezoid with vertices A(−4, 3), B(−1, 4), C(10, 1), and D(−5, −4).

15. Find the area of quadrilateral ABCD.

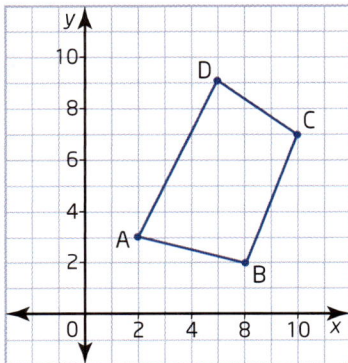

16. The first time Rohan and Mark raced 20 km on their bicycles, Mark was 2 km from the finish line when Rohan reached it. The next time they raced, Rohan agreed to start 2 km behind Mark. So, Rohan rode 22 km while Mark rode 20 km. If each person went at the same average speed as they did during their first race, who won the second race?

17. The area of the shaded region is 400 cm². Find the dimensions of the larger rectangle.

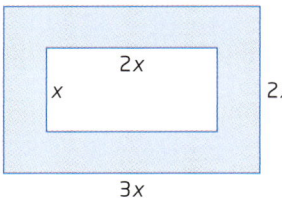

18. Use finite differences to determine whether the data follow a linear relation, a quadratic relation, or neither. For the linear data, find the equation of the line. For the quadratic data, use a graphing calculator to find the quadratic relation.

a)

x	y
−2	−8
−1	−5
0	−2
1	1
2	4
3	7
4	10

b)

x	y
−1	1
0	4
1	1
2	−8
3	−23
4	−44
5	−71

c)

x	y
−5	0
−4	−3
−3	−4
−2	−3
−1	0
0	5
1	12

d)

x	y
0	0
1	1
2	3
3	7
4	15
5	31
6	63

19. The path of a heavy object thrown into the air is modelled by the equation $h = -0.05d^2 + 0.3d + 0.8$, where h represents the height of the object above the ground and d represents the horizontal distance the object travels, both in metres.

a) From what height was the object thrown?

b) How far does the object travel horizontally before it hits the ground?

c) What was the maximum height of the object?

20. The side length of the square is $a + b + c$.

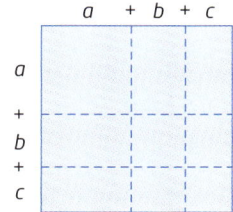

a) Write, expand, and simplify an expression for the area of the square.

b) Use your result from part a) to expand $(2x + 3y + 1)^2$.

21. Factor.
   a) $x^4 + 2x^2 + 1$
   b) $x^4 + x^2 - 6$
   c) $x^4 - 3x^2 - 10$
   d) $x^4 + 10x^2y + 9y^2$

22. A small shopping plaza has a U-shaped building with a rectangular parking lot in the middle, as shown. The floor area of the building is 896 m².

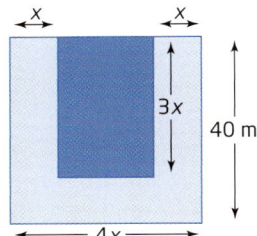

   a) Determine the length of x, in metres.
   b) If each parking space requires an area of 24 m², how many cars can park in this parking lot?

23. The number 12 is the first *abundant* number. It is the least whole number for which the sum of its factors, not including itself, is greater than itself.

   $1 + 2 + 3 + 4 + 6 = 16$

   Find the next three abundant numbers.

24. Factor.
   a) $2x^4 + 3x^2 + 1$
   b) $2x^4 + 5x^2 - 3$
   c) $3x^4 - x^2 - 4$
   d) $6x^4 - 13x^2 + 6$
   e) $2x^4 + 5x^2y + 2y^2$
   f) $3x^4 + 11x^2y - 4y^2$

25. The area of a square is represented by the expression $49 - 28a + 4a^2$, where a is a natural number. What are the possible values for the perimeter of the square?

26. Write and simplify the equation obtained when the given expression is substituted for x.
   a) $y = x^2 + 1$; $x = m - 1$
   b) $y = 2x^2 - 3$; $x = 2k + 1$
   c) $y = x^2 + 4x - 1$; $x = 3t - 1$
   d) $y = 3x^2 - 2x + 4$; $x = 3 - 2w$

27. The length, width, and height of a rectangular prism measure whole numbers of centimetres. Three faces of the prism have areas of 144 cm², 72 cm², and 32 cm². What are the dimensions of the prism?

28. Pam and Theo opened a coffee bar. The business lost $2100 in the first month and $1900 in the second month. As they hoped, the business continued to improve by $220/month for the first 2 years.
   a) Make a scatter plot showing their financial position at the end of each month.
   b) In which month did they start to make a profit?
   c) Find an equation to represent the relation between their profit and the number of months since they opened the coffee shop.

29. The cost of renting an ice rink includes an initial fee, plus an additional fee for each hour or part of an hour of use. The graph shows how cost is related to time. Up to and including 1 h costs $120, greater than 1 h and up to and including 2 h costs $200 and so on.

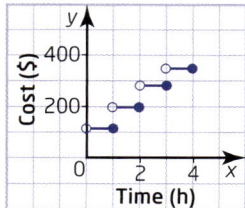

   a) Explain why open and closed dots are used on the graph.
   b) If you were charged $360, for how many hours did you rent the rink?
   c) If you want to rent the rink for 1.5 h, how much will it cost?

30. A photocopier was set to enlarge an original to 150% of its dimensions. A diagram of a rectangle was enlarged and then the image was enlarged again at the same setting. If the final rectangle measured 20.25 cm by 13.5 cm, what were the dimensions of the rectangle on the original diagram?

31. Find a and k so that the quadratic relation $y = ax^2 + k$ passes through each pair of points.
   a) $(-3, 11)$ and $(4, 18)$
   b) $(-1, -2)$ and $(3, -10)$
   c) $(2, 5)$ and $(1, -1)$
   d) $(2, 2)$ and $(-4, -4)$

32. Determine an equation for the parabola with the given vertex and passing through the given point.
   a) vertex $(-4, -5)$, passing through $(-2, -1)$
   b) vertex $(1, 6)$, passing through $(3, 2)$
   c) vertex $(-2, 3)$, passing through $(-1, 6)$

33. Find the values of a and k so that the given points lie on the parabola.
   a) $y = a(x - 1)^2 + k$; $(2, 6)$, $(3, 12)$
   b) $y = a(x + 3)^2 + k$; $(-5, -8)$, $(1, 20)$
   c) $y = a(x - 4)^2 + k$; $(1, -13)$, $(-1, -45)$

34. For the relation $y = -2x^2 + 8x + k$, what value(s) of k will result in
   a) one x-intercept?
   b) two x-intercepts?
   c) no x-intercepts?

35. Evaluate each expression. Write answers with positive exponents.
   a) $\dfrac{2^{-3} \times 2^{-4}}{2^{-2}}$
   b) $\dfrac{5^{-3} \times 5^{-1}}{5^2} \times \dfrac{5^{-1} \times 5^3}{5^{-2}}$
   c) $\dfrac{3^{-3} \times 27^{-1}}{9^{-1} \times 81^{-2}}$

36. Simplify each expression. Write answers with positive exponents.
   a) $3x^{-2} \times (3x^{-2})^{-2}$
   b) $\dfrac{5x^{-8} \times 3^{-2}x^3}{3x^{-4}} \times \dfrac{x^{-4}}{5x^{-2}}$
   c) $\dfrac{4x^2y^{-3} \times 2^{-2}x^{-4}y^{-2}}{8x^{-2}y^{-2}}$

37. A town is separated into two parts by a river that is crossed by a bridge at M. How many routes are there for a bus to get from A to B if the bus only travels north and east?

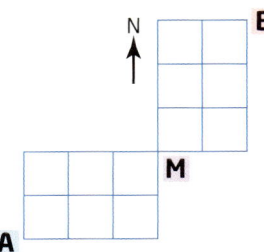

38. Consider the equation $x^2 + bx = 0$.
  a) For what value of b will the equation have two equal real roots?
  b) If the equation has two distinct real roots, what value must one of them have? How is the other root related to b?

39. a) Write a quadratic equation in the form $ax^2 + bx + c = 0$ whose roots are -2 and 3.
  b) Is it possible to write another quadratic equation with the same roots? Explain.

40. If -3 is one root of the equation $3x^2 + bx + 3 = 0$,
  a) what is the value of b?
  b) what is the other root?

41. The difference between the squares of two consecutive whole numbers is 63. What are the numbers?

42. The smallest rectangle shown is 3 m wide and 2 m tall. The next rectangle is 4 m wide and 3 m tall. The largest rectangle is 5 m wide and 4 m tall. Find the area of the shaded region.

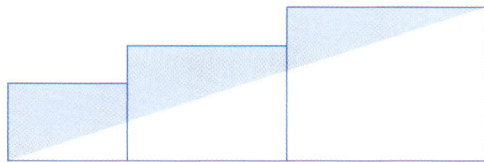

43. A cylinder has a height of 5 cm and a surface area of 100 cm². Find the radius of the cylinder, to the nearest tenth of a centimetre.

44. Describe the roots of the equation $ax^2 + bx + c = 0$ in each case. Explain your reasoning and give examples to support your answers.
  a) $b^2 - 4ac < 0$
  b) $b^2 - 4ac = 0$
  c) $b^2 - 4ac$ is a perfect square
  d) $b^2 - 4ac > 0$ but is not a perfect square

45. The areas of two similar triangles are 28 cm² and 112 cm². What is the ratio of the lengths of their corresponding sides?

46. The diagonals of a kite measure 10 cm and 12 cm. What is the area of the kite?

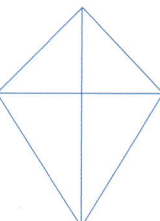

47. Find the length of x, to the nearest tenth of a metre, and the measure of $\angle A$, to the nearest degree.

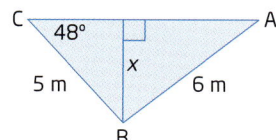

48. When a pendulum swings 40° from the vertical, its lower end moves 20 cm horizontally and 7.3 cm vertically. What is the length of the pendulum, to the nearest centimetre?

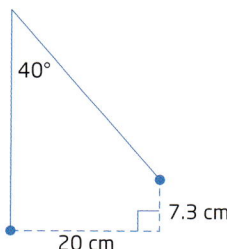

49. Solve $\triangle ABC$ with vertices A(2, 1), B(7, 4), and C(1, 5). Round each measure to the nearest tenth of a unit.

50. Try to solve a triangle with side lengths 3 cm, 8 cm, and 4 cm using the cosine law. What do you find? Explain why.

51. Solve the following system of equations.
$a + b + c = 9$
$ab + bc + ac = 26$
$abc = 24$

52. If x, y, and z are three different numbers whose sum is zero and whose product is two, what is the value of $x^3 + y^3 + z^3$?

53. Three identical rectangles are placed as shown to form a large rectangle that has an area of 1536 m².

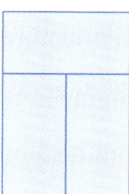

a) Find the area of a square that has the same perimeter as the large rectangle.

b) Two diagonals are drawn, as shown. Find the measure of ∠ABC, to the nearest degree.

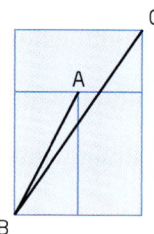

54. The area of a triangle is 24 cm². Its height is 2 cm more than its base. Determine the base and the height.

55. The vertices of a cube lie on a sphere of radius 5 cm. Find the volume of the cube, to the nearest tenth of a cubic centimetre.

56. The number 144 is a perfect square. The sum of the digits of 144 is 9, which is also a perfect square. How many other three-digit numbers have this property?

57. A rectangular floor is covered with identical square tiles. The floor is 40 tiles long and 30 tiles wide. If a straight line is drawn across the floor from corner to corner, how may tiles will it cross?

58. If $9x + 24 = A[x + B(x + C)]$ and A, B, and C are integers, find the values of A, B, and C.

Prerequisite Skills Appendix

Adding Polynomials

To add $2x + 5y - 4$, add the like terms.
$\phantom{\text{To add }}3x - 2y - 5$

$$\begin{array}{r} 2x + 5y - 4 \\ 3x - 2y - 5 \\ \hline 5x + 3y - 9 \end{array}$$

1. Add.

a) $\begin{array}{r} 3x + 2y + 5 \\ 4x + 3y + 7 \\ \hline \end{array}$

b) $\begin{array}{r} 3x - 4y - 5 \\ 6x - 2y - 7 \\ \hline \end{array}$

c) $\begin{array}{r} x^2 + 6x - 4 \\ 2x^2 - 4x + 8 \\ \hline \end{array}$

d) $\begin{array}{r} 3a^2 - a + 2 \\ 2a^2 + 4a - 1 \\ \hline \end{array}$

e) $\begin{array}{r} 2y^2 + y - 3 \\ 3y^2 - y + 2 \\ \hline \end{array}$

f) $\begin{array}{r} -6a + 2b + 4 \\ 4a - 3b - 7 \\ \hline \end{array}$

Angle Properties

To find the measure of x, recall that the sum of the interior angles of a triangle is 180°.
$x + 72° + 67° = 180°$
$x + 139° = 180°$
$x = 180° - 139°$
$x = 41°$

When a transversal intersects two parallel lines:

a) the alternate angles are equal

b) the corresponding angles are equal

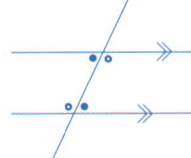
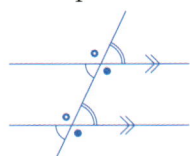

c) the co-interior angles are supplementary

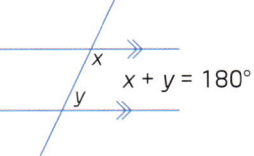

$x + y = 180°$

To find the measures of x, y, and z, use the fact that, since AC is parallel to EF, the alternate angles are equal.
$\angle BEF = \angle ABE$ (alternate angles)
$x = 54°$
$\angle BFE = \angle CBF$ (alternate angles)
$z = 73°$

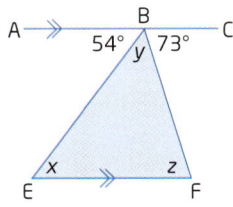

$$x + y + z = 180°$$
$$54° + y + 73° = 180°$$
$$y + 127° = 180°$$
$$y = 180° - 127°$$
$$y = 53°$$

1. Find the unknown angle measures.

a)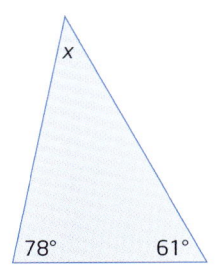

b)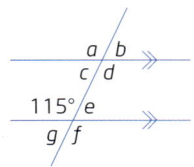

c)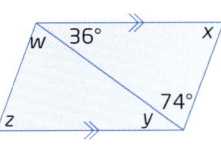

d)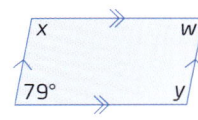

Common Factoring

To factor the expression $10y^2 + 8y$, determine the greatest common factor of both terms. Refer to greatest common factors in this appendix.

$10y^2 = 2 \times 5 \times y \times y$
$8y = 2 \times 2 \times 2 \times y$

The greatest common factor is $2y$.

The second factor is $\dfrac{10y^2}{2y} + \dfrac{8y}{2y}$ or $5y + 4$.

The factors of $10y^2 + 8y$ are $2y$ and $5y + 4$.
Therefore, $10y^2 + 8y = 2y(5y + 4)$.

1. State the missing factor.
  a) $6x + 8y = 2(\blacksquare)$
  b) $2x^2 - 5x = x(\blacksquare)$
  c) $4abc + 10ab = 2ab(\blacksquare)$
  d) $8a^3 - 12a^2 = 4a^2(\blacksquare)$
  e) $-5ab - 10c = -5(\blacksquare)$
  f) $-4x^2 + 8x = -4x(\blacksquare)$

2. Factor.
  a) $5y + 15$
  b) $24x - 16$
  c) $4ab + 6a$
  d) $3x^2 - 18x$
  e) $2x^2 + 4x - 6$
  f) $6x^3 - 3x^2 + 9x$
  g) $8ab^2 + 4ab + 12a^2b$
  h) $10y^3 - 10$

Congruent Triangles

Congruent triangles have the same shape and the same size. When two triangles are congruent, their corresponding angles and corresponding sides are equal.

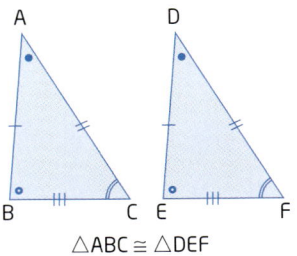

△ABC ≅ △DEF

△ABC is congruent to △DEF.

The following corresponding parts are equal.

∠A = ∠D   AB = DE
∠B = ∠E   AC = DF
∠C = ∠F   BC = EF

1. List the corresponding equal parts in each pair of congruent scalene triangles.

   a)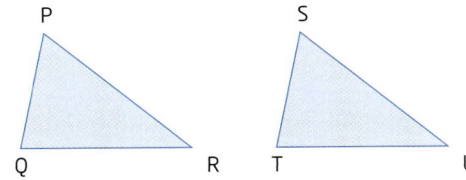

   b)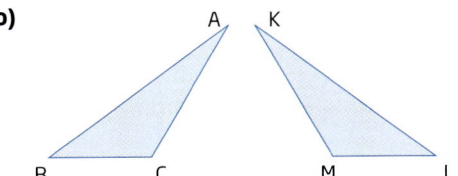

Evaluating Expressions

To evaluate the expression $4x^2 - 5y$ for $x = 2$ and $y = -3$, substitute 2 for x and -3 for y in the expression. Then, simplify using the order of operations.

$4x^2 - 3y = 4(2)^2 - 5(-3)$
$ = 4(4) - 5(-3)$
$ = 16 + 15$
$ = 31$

1. Evaluate for $x = 3$, $y = 2$, and $z = 1$.

   a) $3x + 4$
   b) $2x + 4y - 3z$
   c) $3(x + z)$
   d) $x^2 - y^2 + z^2$
   e) $3xy - yz + 2$
   f) $2y^2 + x$
   g) $3(4z + 3y)$
   h) $2z(x - 2y)$
   i) $3y^2 - 2x^2 + 3z^2$
   j) $x(z - 4y)$
   k) $(yz)^2$
   l) $4(x - y - z)$

460 MHR • Prerequisite Skills Appendix

2. Evaluate for $x = -2$, $y = 3$, and $z = -1$.
   a) $x + y - z$
   b) $4x + 3y$
   c) $5x + 3z - 4y$
   d) $3xyz - 6$
   e) $4yz - x$
   f) $xy + yz - xz$
   g) $x^2 + y^2 - z^2$
   h) $3(2z - x)$
   i) $(x + y)(y - z)$
   j) $(xyz)^3$
   k) $2z(4y - 3x)$
   l) $2z^2 - 3y^2 - 4x^2$

To complete the table of values for $y = x^2 - 5x$, substitute the given values for x in $x^2 - 5x$ and determine y.

$y = x^2 - 5x$

x	y
-2	
0	
2	

When $x = -2$, $y = (-2)^2 - 5(-2)$
$= 4 + 10$
$= 14$

When $x = 0$, $y = (0)^2 - 5(0)$
$= 0 - 0$
$= 0$

When $x = 2$, $y = (2)^2 - 5(2)$
$= 4 - 10$
$= -6$

$y = x^2 - 5x$

x	y
-2	14
0	0
2	-6

3. Copy and complete each table of values.

a) $y = x + 4$

x	y
2	
1	
0	
-1	
-2	

b) $y = 2x - 3$

x	y
2	
1	
0	
-1	
-2	

c) $y = -x + 5$

x	y
4	
2	
0	
-2	
-4	

d) $y = x^2 + 1$

x	y
2	
1	
0	
-1	
-2	

e) $y = x^2 + 2x$

x	y
2	
1	
0	
-1	
-2	

f) $y = x^2 - 2x + 4$

x	y
4	
2	
0	
-2	
-4	

Evaluating Radicals

Since $7 \times 7 = 49$, $\sqrt{49} = 7$.
Since $0.4 \times 0.4 = 0.16$, $\sqrt{0.16} = 0.4$.

1. Evaluate.
   a) $\sqrt{4}$
   b) $\sqrt{25}$
   c) $\sqrt{0.81}$
   d) $\sqrt{1.21}$
   e) $\sqrt{0.09}$
   f) $\sqrt{0.01}$
   g) $\sqrt{225}$
   h) $\sqrt{1.69}$

To evaluate $\sqrt{56}$, to the nearest tenth, use a calculator.

$\sqrt{56} \doteq 7.483\,314\,774$

so $\sqrt{56} = 7.5$, to the nearest tenth.

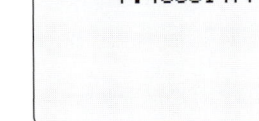

2. Evaluate, to the nearest tenth.
   a) $\sqrt{44}$
   b) $\sqrt{129}$
   c) $\sqrt{3422}$
   d) $\sqrt{20.5}$
   e) $\sqrt{89.4}$
   f) $\sqrt{747}$
   g) $\sqrt{65\,771}$
   h) $\sqrt{0.7}$

Expanding Expressions

To expand $3x(x - 4)$, use the distributive property.

$3x(x - 4) = 3x(x - 4)$
$ = 3x^2 - 12x$

1. Expand.
   a) $2(x + 3)$
   b) $3(x + y - 7)$
   c) $5(a - b + c)$
   d) $-2(5a - 4)$
   e) $-(2x - y)$
   f) $x(x + 6)$
   g) $2x(3x + 7)$
   h) $x(x^2 - x + 5)$
   i) $-3a(a^2 + 2a - 1)$

Exponent Rules

To multiply powers with the same base, add the exponents.
$x^2 \times x^3 = x^{2+3}$
$ = x^5$

To divide powers with the same base, subtract the exponents.
$x^5 \div x^2 = x^{5-2}$
$ = x^3$

To raise a power to a power, multiply the exponents.
$(x^2)^4 = x^{2 \times 4}$
$ = x^8$

1. Simplify, using the exponent rules. Express each answer in exponential form.

   a) $2^2 \times 2^5$
   b) $3^6 \times 3^4$
   c) $4^2 \times 4^3 \times 4^2$
   d) $5^3 \times 5^2 \times 5$
   e) $2^5 \div 2^3$
   f) $3^7 \div 3^4$
   g) $4^6 \div 4$
   h) $(2^3)^2$
   i) $(3^4)^3$
   j) $y^4 \times y^7$
   k) $z^3 \times z^3$
   l) $y^5 \div y^4$
   m) $z^8 \div z^2$
   n) $(x^3)^5$
   o) $(y^2)^8$
   p) $3x^4 \times 2x^3$
   q) $(-2y^3)(-4y^4)$
   r) $-10m^7 \div (-2m^3)$
   s) $(3y^3)^2$
   t) $(-2x^3)^3$

First Differences

First differences are calculated from tables of values in which the x-coordinates are evenly spaced. First differences are found by subtracting consecutive y-coordinates.

If the first differences are constant, the relation is linear. If the first differences are not constant, the relation is non-linear.

This relation is linear.

x	y	First Differences
1	3	
2	5	5 − 3 = 2
3	7	7 − 5 = 2
4	9	9 − 7 = 2

This relation is non-linear.

x	y	First Differences
1	1	
2	4	4 − 1 = 3
3	9	9 − 4 = 5
4	16	16 − 9 = 7

1. Use first differences to determine whether each relation is linear or non-linear.

   a)
x	y
1	5
2	8
3	11
4	14

   b)
x	y
1	7
2	5
3	3
4	1

   c)
x	y
1	2
2	5
3	10
4	17

   d)
x	y
1	2
2	6
3	10
4	14

Graphing Equations

To graph the line $x + y = 6$ using a table of values, choose suitable values for x.
Complete a table of values by finding the value of y for each value of x.

$x + y = 6$

x	y
5	1
3	3
1	5
−1	7

Plot the points on a grid and draw a line through the points.

1. Graph each equation using a table of values.

    a) $x + y = 4$
    b) $x - y = 2$
    c) $y = x + 2$
    d) $y = 2x + 1$

To graph $x + 2y = 6$ using the intercepts, find the points where the graph of $x + 2y = 6$ crosses the x- and y-axes.

To find the x-intercept, let $y = 0$.
$x + 2y = 6$
$x + 2(0) = 6$
$\quad\quad x = 6$
One point on the line is (6, 0).

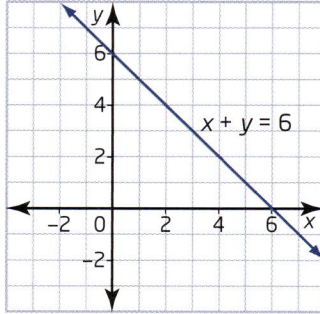

To find the y-intercept, let $x = 0$.
$x + 2y = 6$
$0 + 2y = 6$
$\quad\quad y = 3$
Another point on the line is (0, 3).

Plot the points on a grid.
Draw a line through the points.

2. Graph each equation using the intercepts.

    a) $x + y = 3$
    b) $x - y = 4$
    c) $4x + y = 8$
    d) $2x - 5y = 10$

To graph $y = x + 3$ using the slope and y-intercept, first find the point where the graph crosses the y-axis.

Since the y-intercept is 3, plot the point $(0, 3)$. The slope is 1. Use the slope to find another point on the line.

Draw the graph.

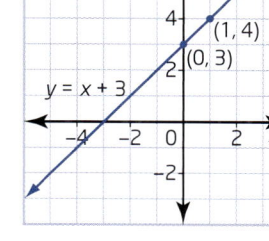

3. Graph each equation using the slope and y-intercept.

a) $y = x + 3$
b) $y = -x - 4$
c) $y = 2x + 3$
d) $y = 3x - 1$

To find the point of intersection of the lines $y = x - 3$ and $y = 5 - x$, graph the lines on the same set of axes.

The coordinates of the point of intersection are $(4, 1)$.

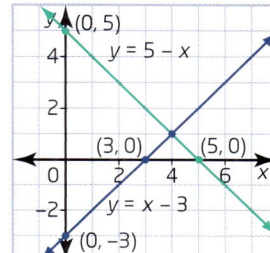

4. Graph each pair of lines and find the coordinates of the point of intersection.

a) $y = x - 4$ and $y = 8 - x$
b) $y = x + 3$ and $y = 7 - x$
c) $y = x - 6$ and $y = 2 - x$
d) $y = x + 5$ and $y = 3 - x$

Greatest Common Factors

To determine the greatest common factor (GCF) of $4c^2d$ and $6cd^3$, write each expression as a product. Then, write the factors that are common to both.

$4c^2d = 2 \times 2 \times c \times c \times d$

$6cd^3 = 2 \times 3 \times c \times d \times d \times d$

The GCF of $4c^2d$ and $6cd^3$ is $2 \times c \times d$ or $2cd$.

1. Determine the GCF of each pair.

a) $4x, 10x$
b) $12y, 8y$
c) $15z, 10z$
d) $30a, 20a$
e) $6x^2, 14x$
f) $14ab, 7abc$
g) $12x^3, 18x^2$
h) $9ab^2c, 7a^2bc$

2. Determine the GCF of each set.

a) $4ab, 2abc, 6a$
b) $3xyz, 9yz, 12xy$
c) $8x^3, 20x^2, 24x^4$
d) $15mn^2, 18m^2n, 12mn$
e) $10rt^3, 15r^2t^2, 20r^3t^4$
f) $9rs, 18ab, 27xy$

Prerequisite Skills Appendix • MHR 465

Lengths of Line Segments

The length of any line segment is a positive number. To find the length of the horizontal line segment joining (3, 5) and (−4, 5), subtract the lesser x-coordinate from the greater x-coordinate.

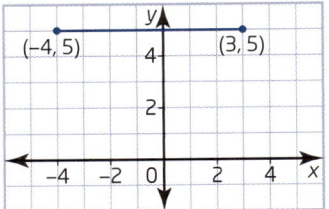

$3 - (-4) = 3 + 4$
$ = 7$

The length of the horizontal line segment joining (3, 5) and (−4, 5) is 7 units.

To find the length of the vertical line segment joining (2, −4) and (2, 7), subtract the y-coordinates.
$7 - (-4) = 7 + 4$
$ = 11$

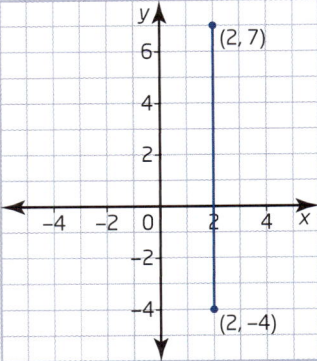

The length of the vertical line segment joining (2, −4) and (2, 7) is 11 units.

1. Find the length of the line segment joining each pair of points.
   a) (8, 7) and (2, 7)
   b) (5, 1) and (9, 1)
   c) (3, 8) and (3, 2)
   d) (5, 1) and (5, 9)
   e) (2, 4) and (−5, 4)
   f) (1, 7) and (1, −6)
   g) (−4, −3) and (−8, −3)
   h) (−2, 5) and (−2, −7)
   i) (6, 3) and (0, 3)
   j) (−6, −7) and (−6, 0)
   k) (−6, 4) and (8, 4)
   l) (−7, −9) and (−7, −3)

Like Terms

Like terms have exactly the same variables raised to exactly the same exponents. An expression is in simplest form when there are no like terms.
To simplify $x^2 + 5x - 7 - 2x + 4 + 3x^2$, collect like terms.
$x^2 + 5x - 7 - 2x + 4 + 3x^2 = x^2 + 3x^2 + 5x - 2x - 7 + 4$
$ = 4x^2 + 3x - 3$

1. Simplify by collecting like terms.
   a) $4x + 7x - 5x$
   b) $2y - 6 + 3y - 8$
   c) $2x + 3y - 2 + x - 4y - 5$
   d) $3a - 2b + 4c - 3b + a$
   e) $x^2 - 2x - 7x - 3 - 3x^2$
   f) $3 - t^2 + 8t - 7 - 6t - t$
   g) $3x + 2y - 5 - 3 + x + 7y$
   h) $3y^2 - 4y^2 - 11y + 3 - 7y$
   i) $15 - 4t - 5t - t^2 - t^2 - t$

Number Skills

To evaluate expressions, use the order of operations (BEDMAS).

$(-2)(-6) - 5(-3)^2$
$= 12 - 5(9)$
$= 12 - 45$
$= -33$

$$\frac{2}{3} + \frac{1}{2}\left(2\frac{3}{4} - 1\frac{1}{2}\right) = \frac{2}{3} + \frac{1}{2}\left(\frac{11}{4} - \frac{3}{2}\right)$$
$$= \frac{2}{3} + \frac{1}{2}\left(\frac{11}{4} - \frac{6}{4}\right)$$
$$= \frac{2}{3} + \frac{1}{2}\left(\frac{5}{4}\right)$$
$$= \frac{2}{3} + \frac{5}{8}$$
$$= \frac{16}{24} + \frac{15}{24}$$
$$= \frac{31}{24} \text{ or } 1\frac{7}{24}$$

1. Evaluate each expression.

a) $-3(5) + (-6)(-8)$

b) $(12)(11) - (-9)(7)$

c) $-10(3)(2) + (-12)(7)(-2)$

d) $\frac{3}{5} + 2\frac{2}{3}$

e) $8 - 2\left(\frac{7}{8} + 3\frac{3}{4}\right)$

f) $\left(\frac{3}{4}\right)^2\left(\frac{8}{3}\right)$

g) $\frac{5}{2} - \frac{4}{5}\left(\frac{3}{2}\right)^3$

h) $3.2\left(\frac{1}{2}\right) - 2.5\left(\frac{3}{5}\right) + 1.4\left(\frac{2}{7}\right)$

i) $0.3(5.5)^2 - (-6.7)(2.1)^3 + 4.2(-1.1)^5$

2. Order each set of fractions from least to greatest.

a) $\frac{5}{8}, \frac{2}{3}, \frac{3}{5}, \frac{7}{12}, \frac{1}{2}$

b) $3\frac{3}{4}, 3\frac{7}{8}, 3\frac{5}{9}, 3\frac{6}{7}$

3. Explain why the two expressions are not equal.

a) $\sqrt{9 + 16}, \sqrt{9} + \sqrt{16}$

b) $(x + y)^2, x^2 + y^2$

c) $\frac{2}{3} + \frac{5}{6}, \frac{7}{9}$

Percents

The table shows how equivalent fractions, percents, and decimals can be expressed.

Fraction	Percent	Decimal
$\frac{63}{100}$	63%	0.63
$\frac{8}{100} = \frac{2}{25}$	8%	0.08
$\frac{5}{1000} = \frac{1}{200}$	0.5%	0.005
$\frac{150}{100} = \frac{3}{2}$	150%	1.5

1. Copy and complete the following table. Express all fractions in lowest terms.

	Fraction	Percent	Decimal
a)	$\frac{75}{100}$		
b)	$\frac{1}{2}$		
c)	$8\frac{2}{5}$		
d)		34%	
e)		0.03%	
f)		5.6%	
g)			0.45
h)			0.03
i)			2.68

Polynomials

The degree of a polynomial in one variable is the greatest power of the variable in any term.

For the polynomial $3x^2 - 2x + 7$, the greatest power, 2, is contained in the term $3x^2$.

$3x^2 - 2x + 7$ is a second-degree polynomial.

1. State the degree of each polynomial.

a) $4x - 3$
b) x^3
c) $4 - 2y^2 - 5y$
d) $6m^2 - m^3 - 2$
e) $2x + 7 - 5x^4$
f) $2 - 4t^5 - 3t^3 + 9t$

Pythagorean Theorem

To find the length of d in the right triangle, to the nearest tenth of a unit, use the Pythagorean theorem. This states that, in a right triangle, the square of the length of the hypotenuse is equal to the sum of the squares of the lengths of the other two sides.

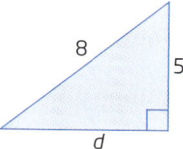

$d^2 + 5^2 = 8^2$
$d^2 + 25 = 64$
$\quad d^2 = 64 - 25$
$\quad d^2 = 39$
$\quad d = \sqrt{39}$
$\quad d \doteq 6.244\ 997\ 998$

The length of d is 6.2 units, to the nearest tenth of a unit.

1. In each right triangle, find the unknown side length, to the nearest tenth of a unit.

   a)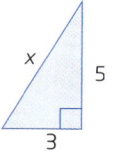

   b)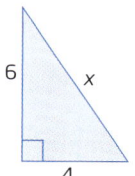

   c)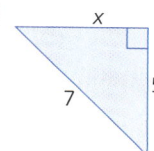

   d)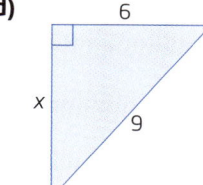

   e)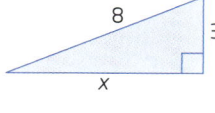

   f)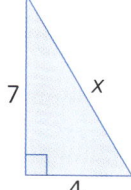

Simplifying Expressions

To simplify $3(x + 2) - (x - 4)$, remove brackets and collect like terms.

$3(x + 2) - (x - 4) = 3(x + 2) - 1(x - 4)$
$\qquad\qquad\qquad\quad = 3x + 6 - x + 4$
$\qquad\qquad\qquad\quad = 2x + 10$

1. Simplify.
   a) $5x + 2(x + 7)$
   b) $3(2a - 7) + 3a$
   c) $4(x - 3) - 2x$
   d) $-5(y - 3) + 6$
   e) $2(t + 4) + 3(t - 4)$
   f) $8(y - 3) - (y + 6)$
   g) $-4(z + 3) - 2(z - 2)$
   h) $7(2 - w) - (w - 3)$
   i) $6(x - 4) + 2(3 + x)$

2. Simplify.
   a) $(3x + 4y) + (2x + 3y)$
   b) $(4r - 3s) + (r + 4s)$
   c) $(3p + 5q) - (4p - q)$
   d) $2(x - 3y) + 3(6x - y)$
   e) $4(3a + 5b) - (7a - b)$
   f) $-4(c - 5d) + 3c - d$
   g) $4a - b + 3c - 2(a + b - c)$
   h) $3(x + y - 2z) + 7x - 5$
   i) $6x + 4(2x + 3y - z) + 5y$

Slope

To find the slope of the line passing through the points $(-2, 1)$ and $(3, 5)$, use the slope formula.

$m = \dfrac{y_2 - y_1}{x_2 - x_1}$

$= \dfrac{5 - 1}{3 - (-2)}$

$= \dfrac{4}{5}$

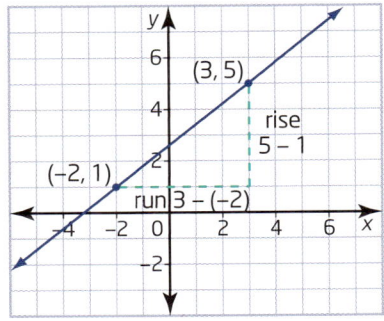

1. Find the slope of the line passing through each pair of points.
   a) $(0, 0)$ and $(2, 6)$
   b) $(0, 0)$ and $(4, 2)$
   c) $(1, 2)$ and $(3, 6)$
   d) $(2, 5)$ and $(3, 7)$
   e) $(3, 0)$ and $(0, 6)$
   f) $(-3, 5)$ and $(2, 6)$
   g) $(-4, 2)$ and $(5, 2)$
   h) $(-3, -4)$ and $(-1, -8)$
   i) $(5, -7)$ and $(3, -10)$

Parallel lines have the same slope. The slope of a line parallel to $y = 2x + 3$ is 2.
The product of the slopes of perpendicular lines is -1.
The slope of a line perpendicular to $y = 2x + 3$ is $-\dfrac{1}{2}$, since $2 \times -\dfrac{1}{2} = -1$.

2. State the slope of a line parallel to and a line perpendicular to each line.
   a) $y = 3x + 5$
   b) $y = -2x - 4$
   c) $y = -x + 7$
   d) $y = \dfrac{1}{4}x - 4$
   e) $y = -\dfrac{2}{3}x + 1$
   f) $y = \dfrac{4}{5}x - 6$

470 MHR • Prerequisite Skills Appendix

Solving Equations

To solve $2x - 3 = 11$, isolate the variable.

$$2x - 3 = 11$$

Add 3 to both sides: $\quad 2x - 3 + 3 = 11 + 3$

Simplify: $\quad 2x = 14$

Divide both sides by 2: $\quad \dfrac{2x}{2} = \dfrac{14}{2}$

Simplify: $\quad x = 7$

To check, substitute 7 for x in the original equation.

L.S. $= 2x - 3 \qquad$ **R.S.** $= 11$
$ = 2(7) - 3$
$ = 14 - 3$
$ = 11$

Since **L.S.** = **R.S.**, the solution is $x = 7$.

1. Solve and check.

a) $3x + 2 = 11$
b) $2x - 5 = 7$
c) $5x - 2 = -17$
d) $4x - 7 = 9$
e) $1 - 2x = 15$
f) $8 + 7x = -6$
g) $3x + 4 = 2x + 5$
h) $5x + 7 = 3x - 9$
i) $2x - 3 = 5x + 9$

To solve $3(x - 2) = 9$, expand to remove the brackets.

$$3(x - 2) = 9$$

Expand: $\quad 3x - 6 = 9$

Add 6 to both sides: $\quad 3x - 6 + 6 = 9 + 6$

Simplify: $\quad 3x = 15$

Divide both sides by 3: $\quad \dfrac{3x}{3} = \dfrac{15}{3}$

Simplify: $\quad x = 5$

To check, substitute 5 for x in the original equation.

L.S. $= 3(x - 2) \qquad$ **R.S.** $= 9$
$ = 3(5 - 2)$
$ = 3(3)$
$ = 9$

Since **L.S.** = **R.S.**, the solution is $x = 5$.

2. Solve and check.

a) $2(x + 4) = 10$
b) $4(x - 1) = 16$
c) $6(x - 5) + 7 = 1$
d) $5(x + 1) = -15$
e) $2(x - 3) = 3(x + 1)$
f) $5(x - 3) = 3(x + 7)$
g) $7(x + 2) - 3(x - 4) = 30$
h) $5(x - 2) + 3(x - 1) = 3$
i) $7(x + 6) - (x + 7) = -1$

To solve $\dfrac{x-1}{3} = \dfrac{2x-3}{5}$, eliminate fractions by multiplying by the lowest common denominator, 15.

$$\dfrac{x-1}{3} = \dfrac{2x-3}{5}$$

Multiply both sides by 15: $\quad 15 \times \dfrac{x-1}{3} = 15 \times \dfrac{2x-3}{5}$

Simplify: $\quad 5(x-1) = 3(2x-3)$

Expand: $\quad 5x - 5 = 6x - 9$

Add 5 to both sides: $\quad 5x - 5 + 5 = 6x - 9 + 5$

Simplify: $\quad 5x = 6x - 4$

Subtract 6x from both sides: $\quad 5x - 6x = 6x - 4 - 6x$

Simplify: $\quad -x = -4$

Divide both sides by –1: $\quad x = 4$

To check, substitute 4 for x in the original equation.

$$\text{L.S.} = \dfrac{x-1}{3} \qquad \text{R.S.} = \dfrac{2x-3}{5}$$
$$= \dfrac{4-1}{3} \qquad\qquad = \dfrac{2(4)-3}{5}$$
$$= \dfrac{3}{3} \qquad\qquad\quad = \dfrac{5}{5}$$
$$= 1 \qquad\qquad\qquad = 1$$

Since **L.S.** = **R.S.**, the solution is $x = 4$.

3. Solve and check.

a) $\dfrac{x}{3} + 1 = 4$

b) $\dfrac{x}{2} + \dfrac{1}{3} = \dfrac{5}{6}$

c) $\dfrac{x}{5} - \dfrac{1}{2} = \dfrac{3}{10}$

d) $\dfrac{x+3}{2} = x - 2$

e) $\dfrac{x-1}{2} = \dfrac{x+1}{3}$

f) $\dfrac{2x+1}{3} = \dfrac{x-6}{8}$

g) $\dfrac{x+4}{2} - \dfrac{x+10}{4} = -1$

h) $\dfrac{x+7}{5} - \dfrac{2x}{3} = 0$

i) $\dfrac{x+1}{8} + \dfrac{x+3}{5} = 3$

Solving Proportions

Proportions can be solved using the cross-product rule, which states that, if $\frac{a}{b} = \frac{c}{d}$, then $a \times d = b \times c$.

To solve $2:5 = 3:x$, first write the proportion in fraction form, $\frac{2}{5} = \frac{3}{x}$. Then, use the cross-product rule.

$\frac{2}{5} = \frac{3}{x}$

$2x = 5 \times 3$

$2x = 15$

$x = \frac{15}{2}$ or 7.5

1. Solve for x. Express each answer as a fraction in lowest terms.

    a) $\frac{x}{6} = \frac{2}{5}$ b) $\frac{4}{5} = \frac{x}{3}$

    c) $\frac{2}{x} = \frac{3}{7}$ d) $\frac{3}{2} = \frac{4}{x}$

    e) $x:4 = 5:6$ f) $8:x = 6:7$

    g) $4:9 = x:6$ h) $5:8 = 2:x$

2. Solve for x. Express each answer as a decimal. Round to the nearest hundredth, if necessary.

    a) $\frac{x}{3.4} = 4.5$ b) $\frac{2.6}{x} = 5.8$

    c) $3.2 = \frac{x}{4.3}$ d) $\frac{x}{1.5} = \frac{2.6}{3}$

    e) $\frac{0.8}{x} = \frac{4.2}{1.4}$ f) $\frac{3.8}{1.7} = \frac{2.8}{x}$

    g) $6.3:x = 7.5:8.3$ h) $1.4:0.5 = 2.9:x$

Subtracting Polynomials

To subtract
$$5x - 2y + 8$$
$$\underline{2x + 3y - 2}$$

add the opposite of the polynomial that is being subtracted. The opposite of $2x + 3y - 2$ is $-2x - 3y + 2$.

$$5x - 2y + 8$$
$$\underline{-2x - 3y + 2}$$
$$3x - 5y + 10$$

1. Subtract.

   a) $5x + 6y + 8$
      $\underline{3x + 2y + 5}$

   b) $7x - 5y - 8$
      $\underline{4x - 3y - 7}$

   c) $3x^2 - 6x - 4$
      $\underline{4x^2 + 2x + 5}$

   d) $5a^2 - a + 3$
      $\underline{2a^2 - 7a - 8}$

   e) $-4a + 3b + 1$
      $\underline{3a - 3b - 6}$

   f) $4y^2 + 2y - 3$
      $\underline{-3y^2 + 6y - 1}$

Transformations

To translate △ABC 5 units to the left and 4 units up, translate each vertex of the triangle 5 units to the left and 4 units up. Join the new points to form the translation image, △A′B′C′. △ABC and its translation image, △A′B′C′, are congruent, since corresponding side lengths and angles are equal.

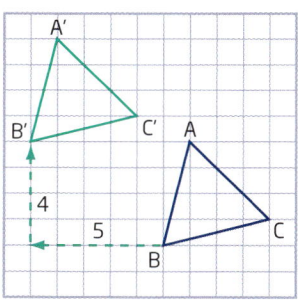

1. Draw each triangle on grid paper. Then, draw the translation image for the given translation.

   a)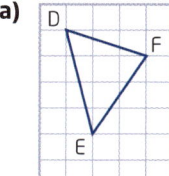
      3 right, 3 down

   b)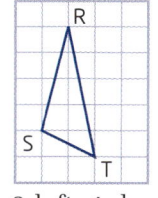
      2 left, 4 down

   c)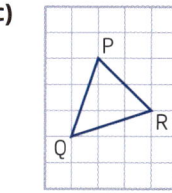
      2 right, 4 up

To reflect △DEF in the reflection line m, reflect each vertex of △DEF in the line. Each vertex of △DEF and its reflection image are the same perpendicular distance from the line m.

Join the new points to form the reflection image, △D′E′F′.

△DEF and its reflection image, △D′E′F′, are congruent, since corresponding side lengths and angles are equal.

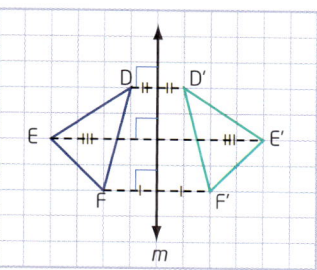

2. Draw each triangle on grid paper. Then, draw the reflection image in the given reflection line.

a)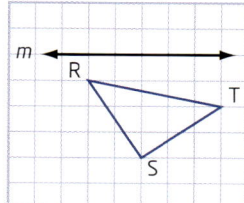

b)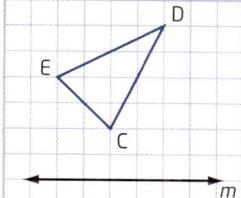

c)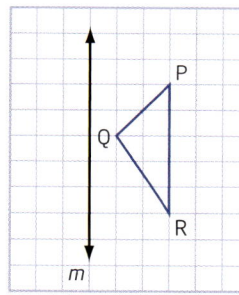

Technology Appendix

CONTENTS

The Geometer's Sketchpad® Geometry Software

	page
The Geometer's Sketchpad® Basics	477
Menu Bar	477
Creating a Sketch	477
Opening an Existing Sketch	477
Saving a Sketch	478
Closing a Sketch Without Exiting *The Geometer's Sketchpad*®	478
Exiting *The Geometer's Sketchpad*®	478
Setting Preferences	478
Selecting Points and Objects	479
Using a Coordinate System and Axes	479
Plotting Points	479
Graphing Relations	480
Constructing a Line Segment and a Point on the Segment	480
Animating a Point	481
Constructing a Line Through Two Points and Displaying the Equation	481
Finding a Point of Intersection	482
Hiding Objects	482
Constructing a Circle Using the Compass Tool	483
Constructing a Circle by Centre and Point or Centre and Radius	483
Constructing Parallel and Perpendicular Lines	483
Constructing Midpoints	484
Using the Measure Menu	484
Changing Labels of Measures	485
Using the On-Screen Calculator	485
Constructing the Right Bisector of a Line Segment	486
Constructing an Altitude of a Triangle	486
Constructing a Median of a Triangle	486
Constructing an Angle Bisector	487

TI-83 Plus and TI-84 Plus Graphing Calculators

	page
TI-83 Plus and TI-84 Plus Basics	488
Adjusting the Contrast	488
Setting the Format	488
Displaying a Decimal as a Fraction	489
Turning Stat Plots Off	489
Graphing Linear Relations	489
Setting Window Variables	489
Changing the Appearance of a Line	490
Setting Up a Table of Values	491
Using Zoom	491
Tracing a Graph	492
Using the Intersect Operation	492
Changing the Mode Settings	493
Entering Data Into Lists	493
Creating a Scatter Plot	494
Line of Best Fit: Linear Regression	494
Finding the Maximum or Minimum	495
Finding Zeros	496
Using the Value Operation	496
Curve of Best Fit: Quadratic Regression and Exponential Regression	497
Calculations Involving the Sine Law	497
Calculations Involving the Cosine Law	498

TI-89 Titanium Computer Algebra System

	page
TI-89 Titanium Computer Algebra System Basics	499
Changing the MODE Settings	499
Starting a New Problem	500
Operations on Equations	500
Copying and Pasting	500
Using the CLEAR key and the Backspace Key	501
Collecting Like Terms	501
Evaluating an Expression for a Given Value	502
Checking the Solution for an Equation	502
Using the Expand Operation	502
Using the Factor Operation	503

The Geometer's Sketchpad® Basics

Menu Bar

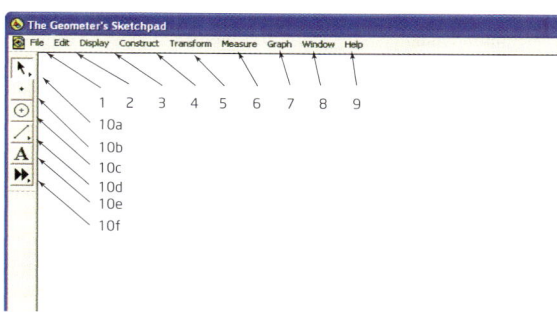

1. **File** menu—open/save/print sketches
2. **Edit** menu—undo/redo actions/set preferences
3. **Display** menu—control appearance of objects in sketch
4. **Construct** menu—construct new geometric objects based on objects in sketch
5. **Transform** menu—apply geometric transformations to selected objects
6. **Measure** menu—make various measurements on objects in sketch
7. **Graph** menu—create axes and plot measurements and points
8. **Window** menu—manipulate windows
9. **Help** menu—access the help system, an excellent reference guide
10. **Toolbox**—access tools for creating, marking, and transforming points, circles, and straight objects (segments, lines, and rays); also includes text and information tools

10a. **Selection Arrow Tool** (Arrow)—select and transform objects
10b. **Point Tool** (Dot)—draw points
10c. **Compass Tool** (Circle)—draw circles
10d. **Straightedge Tool**—draw line segments, rays, and lines
10e. **Text Tool** (Letter A)—label points and write text
10f. **Custom Tool** (Double Arrow)—create or use special "custom" tools

Creating a Sketch

- Under the **File** menu, choose **New Sketch** to start with a new work area.

Opening an Existing Sketch

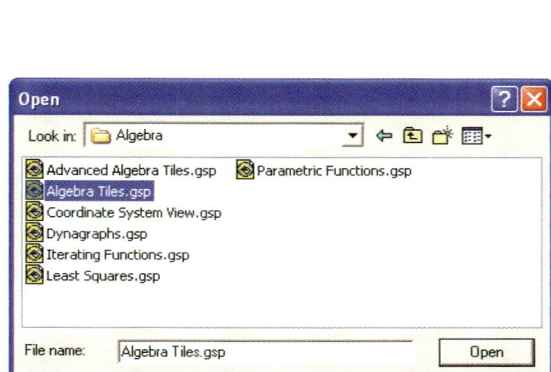

- Under the **File** menu, choose **Open**....
  The **Open** dialogue box will appear.
- Choose the sketch you wish to work on. Then, click on **Open**.

  OR

- Type in the name of the sketch in the **File name:** entry box. Then, click on **Open**.

Saving a Sketch

If you are saving for the first time in a new sketch:
- Under the **File** menu, choose **Save**. The **Save As** dialogue box will appear.
- You can save the sketch with the name assigned by *The Geometer's Sketchpad*®. Click on **Save**.

OR

- Press the Backspace or Delete key to clear the name.
- Type in whatever you wish to name the sketch file. Click on **Save**.

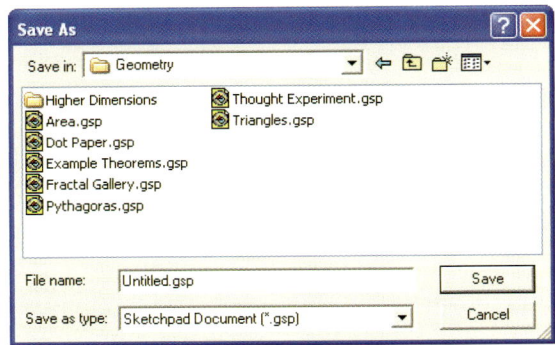

If you have already given your file a name:
- Choose **Save** from under the **File** menu.

Closing a Sketch Without Exiting *The Geometer's Sketchpad*®

- Under the **File** menu, choose **Close**.

Exiting *The Geometer's Sketchpad*®

- Under the **File** menu, choose **Exit**.

Setting Preferences

- From the **Edit** menu, choose **Preferences…**.
- Click on the **Units** tab.
- Set the units and precision for angles, distances, and calculated values such as slopes or ratios.

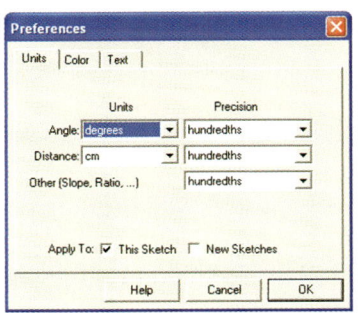

- Click on the **Text** tab.
- If you check the auto-label box **For All New Points**, then *The Geometer's Sketchpad*® will label points as you create them.
- If you check the auto-label box **As Objects Are Measured**, then *The Geometer's Sketchpad*® will label any measurements that you define.

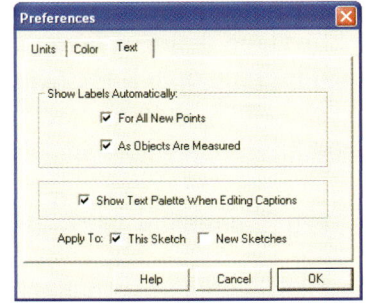

You can also choose whether the auto-labelling functions will apply only to the current sketch, or also to any new sketches that you create.

Be sure to click on **OK** to apply your preferences.

Selecting Points and Objects

- Choose the **Selection Arrow Tool**. The mouse cursor appears as an arrow.

To select a single point:
- Select the point by moving the cursor to the point and clicking on it.

The selected point will now appear as a darker point, similar to a *bull's-eye* ⊙.

To select an object such as a line segment or a circle:
- Move the cursor to a point on the object until it becomes a horizontal arrow.
- Click on the object. The object will change appearance to show it is selected.

To select a number of points or objects:
- Select each object in turn by moving the cursor to the object and clicking on it.

To deselect a point or an object:
- Move the cursor over it, and then click the left mouse button.
- To deselect all selected objects, click in an open area of the workspace.

Using a Coordinate System and Axes

- From the **Graph** menu, choose **Show Grid**.

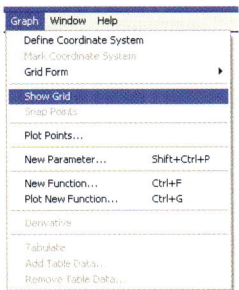
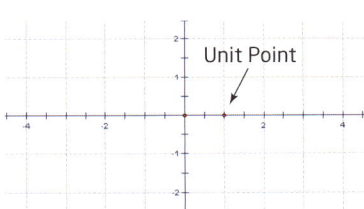

The default coordinate system has an origin point in the centre of your screen and a unit point at (1, 0). Drag the origin to relocate the coordinate system and drag the unit point to change the scale.

Plotting Points

- From the **Graph** menu, choose **Show Grid**.
- If you want points plotted exactly at grid intersections, also choose **Snap Points**.
- Choose the **Point Tool**.

If you have chosen **Snap Points,** a point will "snap" to the nearest grid intersection as you move the cursor over the grid.

- Click the left mouse button to plot the point.

Alternatively, you can plot points by typing in the desired coordinates.

- From the **Graph** menu, choose **Plot Points…**. A dialogue box will appear. Type the desired *x*- and *y*-coordinates in the boxes. Then, click on **Plot**.
- When you are finished plotting points, click on **Done**.

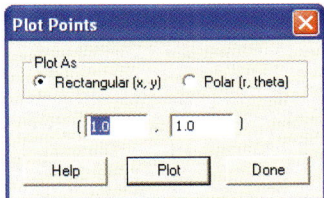

Graphing Relations

Consider the equations $y = 2x - 1$ and $y = -3x + 2$ as examples.

- From the **Graph** menu, choose **Show Grid**.
- From the **Graph** menu, choose **Plot New Function…**.

The calculator interface will appear. Enter the first equation:
$2 * x - 1$

- Click on **OK**. The graph of the first equation appears, along with the equation in function notation. You can move the equation next to the line.

Use the same procedure to graph the second equation.

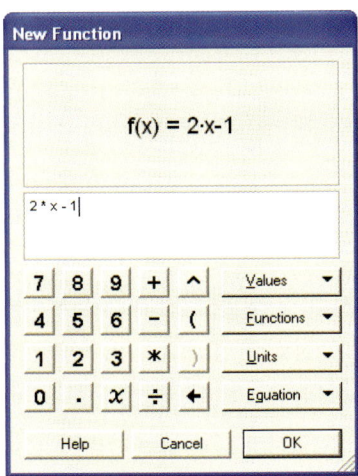

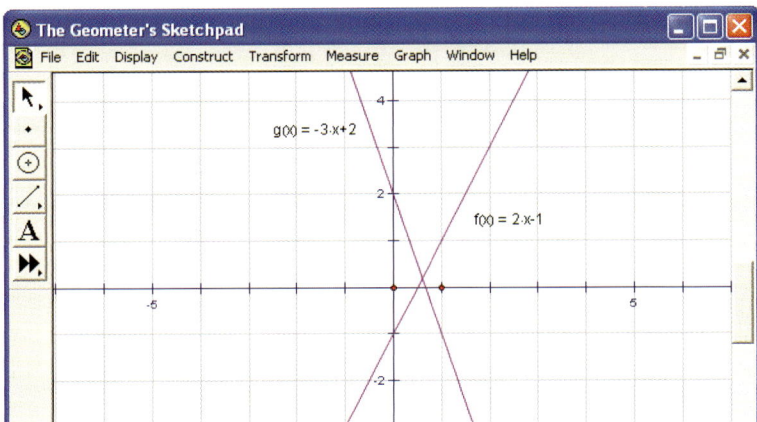

Constructing a Line Segment and a Point on the Segment

To draw a line segment:
- Use the **Point Tool**. Create two points in the workspace.
- Use the **Selection Arrow Tool** to select both points.
- From the **Construct** menu, choose **Segment**.

Your final screen will appear as shown, perhaps with different names for the points.

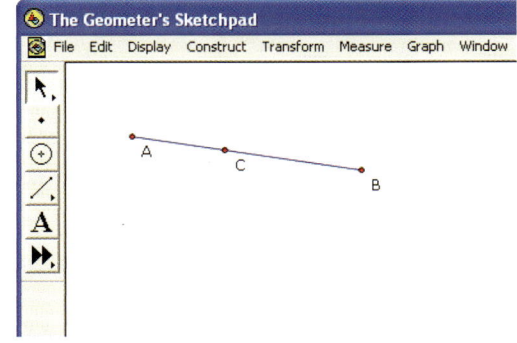

You can also use the **Straightedge Tool**. Choose this tool.

Move the cursor to the workspace. Then, click and hold the left mouse button. Drag the cursor to the desired location, and release the mouse button.

To draw a point on the line segment:
Use the **Point Tool**. Move the cursor over the line segment. The segment will change colour. Click the left mouse button. The point is plotted on the line segment. Try to drag the point. Notice that it cannot be moved off the line segment.

Animating a Point

To animate a point on a line segment:
- Use the **Selection Arrow Tool** to select the point on the line.
- From the **Display** menu, choose **Animate Point**.

Notice that the point moves back and forth on the line segment.

The **Motion Controller** also appears. Experiment with the controls to see what they do.

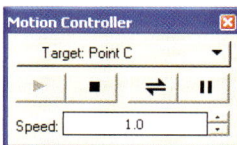

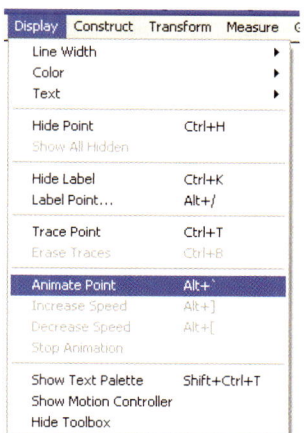

To stop the animation:
- From the **Display** menu, choose **Stop Animation**.

Constructing a Line Through Two Points and Displaying the Equation

- From the **Graph** menu, choose **Show Grid**.
- Use the **Point Tool**. Plot two points.
- Ensure that both points are selected. From the **Construct** menu, choose **Line**.
- Ensure that the line is selected. From the **Measure** menu, choose **Equation**.

You can move the equation next to the line.

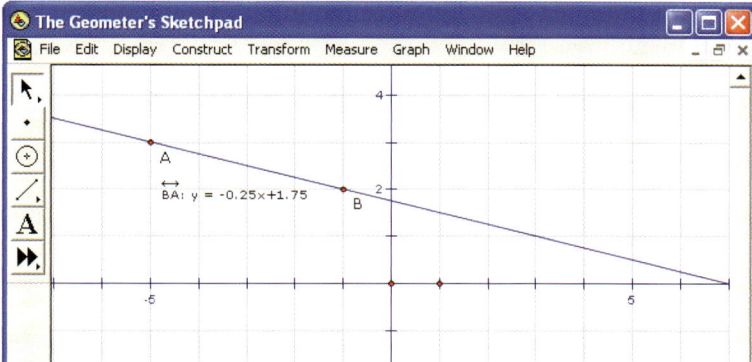

OR

- Click and hold the small arrowhead on the **Straightedge Tool**.
- Choose the **Line Tool**. The **Line Tool** has arrowheads at both ends.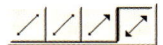
- Move the cursor to the workspace.
- Click and drag to draw the line. Release the mouse button when the line is in the desired location. Label the line with its equation.

Finding a Point of Intersection

Consider the equations $y = 2x - 1$ and $y = -3x + 2$ as examples.

- Turn on the grid, and plot the graphs of the two equations.
- Use the **Point Tool** to plot two points on each line, such that the intersection lies between the points.
- Select one pair of points on a line. From the **Construct** menu, choose **Segment**. Use the same procedure to construct a segment on the other line.
- Select the two segments. From the **Construct** menu, choose **Intersection**. The point of intersection will appear.
- Select the point of intersection. From the **Measure** menu, choose **Coordinates**.

The coordinates of the point of intersection will appear.

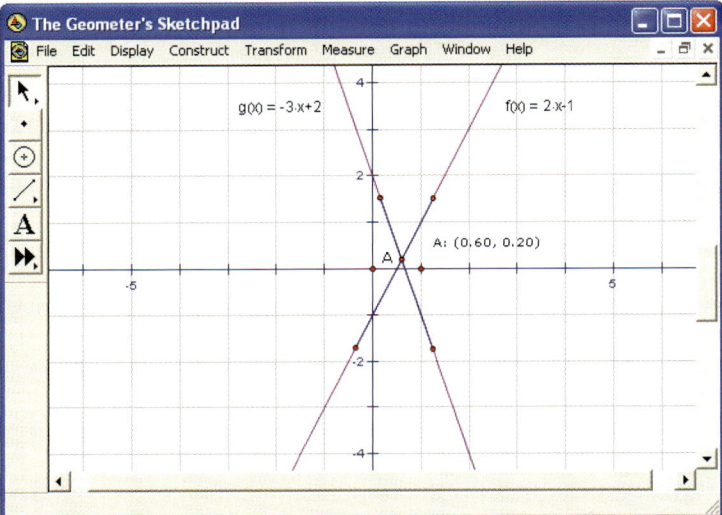

Hiding Objects

Open a new sketch. Draw several objects such as points and line segments.

To hide a point:
- Select the point.
- From the **Display** menu, choose **Hide Point**.

To hide an object:
- Select another point and a line segment.
- From the **Display** menu, choose **Hide Objects**.

Shortcut: You can hide any selected objects by holding down (CTRL), and typing **H**.
You can make hidden objects reappear by choosing **Show All Hidden** from the **Display** menu.

Constructing a Circle Using the Compass Tool

- Choose the **Compass Tool**.
- Move the cursor to the point where you want the centre of the circle.
- Click and hold the left mouse button. Drag the cursor to the desired radius.
- Release the mouse button.

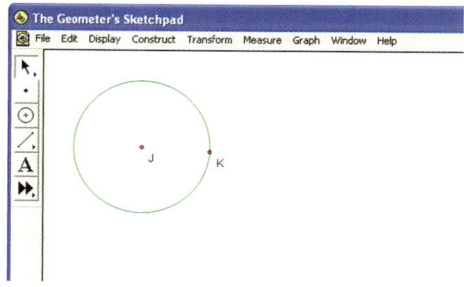

Constructing a Circle by Centre and Point or Centre and Radius

To construct a circle using **Center+Point**:
- Use the **Point Tool**. Plot a point for the centre of the desired circle. Plot another point to lie on the circumference.
- Select the centre and then the point on the circumference.
- From the **Construct** menu, choose **Circle by Center+Point**.

The circle will appear.

To construct a circle using **Center+Radius**:
- Plot a point for the centre.
- Draw a line segment whose length is the desired radius.
- Select the centre and then the segment.
- From the **Construct** menu, choose **Circle by Center+Radius**.

The circle will appear.

Constructing Parallel and Perpendicular Lines

To construct a line parallel to LM, passing through N:
- Select line segment LM (but not the endpoints) and point N.
- From the **Construct** menu, choose **Parallel Line**.

To construct a line perpendicular to LM, passing through N:
- Select line segment LM (but not the endpoints) and point N.
- From the **Construct menu**, choose **Perpendicular Line**.

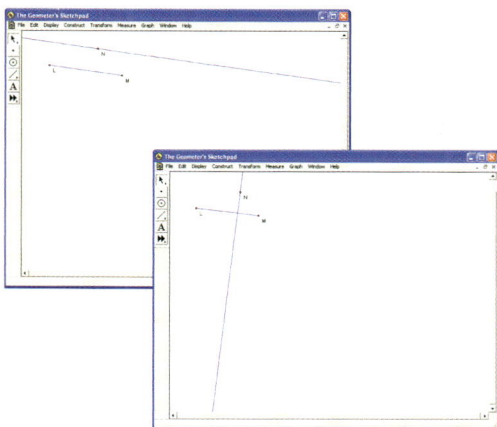

Constructing Midpoints

To construct the midpoint of line segment PQ:
- Select line segment PQ (but not the endpoints).
- From the **Construct** menu, choose **Midpoint**.

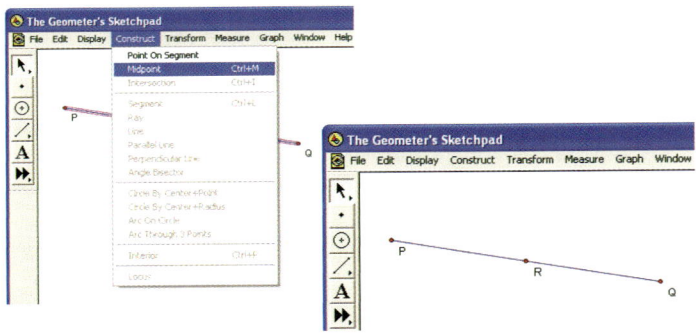

Using the Measure Menu

To measure the distance between two points:
- Ensure that nothing is selected.
- Select the two points.
- From the **Measure** menu, choose **Distance**.

The Geometer's Sketchpad® will display the distance between the points, using the units and accuracy selected in **Preferences...** under the **Edit** menu.

To measure the length of a line segment:
- Ensure that nothing is selected.
- Select the line segment (but not the endpoints).
- From the **Measure** menu, choose **Length**.

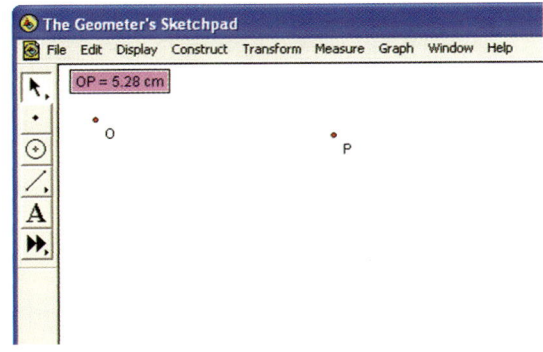

To measure an angle:
- Ensure that nothing is selected.
- Select the three points that define the angle so that the second point selected is the vertex of the angle. For this angle, select Q, then R, then S.
- From the **Measure** menu, choose **Angle**.

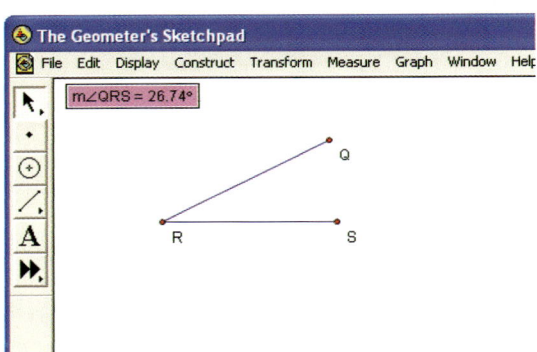

To calculate the ratio of two lengths:
- Select the two lengths to be compared.
- From the **Measure** menu, choose **Ratio**.

To measure the area of a triangle or other closed figure:
- Use the **Straightedge Tool** to draw a triangle.
- Select the points on the vertices of the triangle.
- From the **Construct** menu, choose **Triangle Interior**.
- Select the triangle interior.
- From the **Measure** menu, choose **Area**.

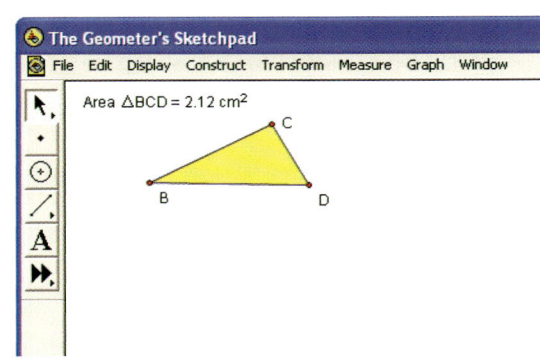

You can construct and measure the area of other closed figures in a similar manner.

To measure the slope of a line, ray, or line segment:
- Select the line, ray, or line segment.
- From the **Measure** menu, choose **Slope**.

Changing Labels of Measures

- Right click on the measure and choose **Label Measurement** (or **Label Distance Measurement** depending on the type of measure) from the drop-down menu.
- Type in the new label.
- Click on **OK**.

Using the On-Screen Calculator

You can use the on-screen calculator to do calculations involving measurements, constants, functions, or other mathematical operations.

To add two lengths:
- From the **Measure** menu, choose **Calculate**. The on-screen calculator will appear.
- On the workspace, select the first measure.
- On the keyboard, click on **+**.
- On the workspace, select the second measure.
- Click on **OK**.

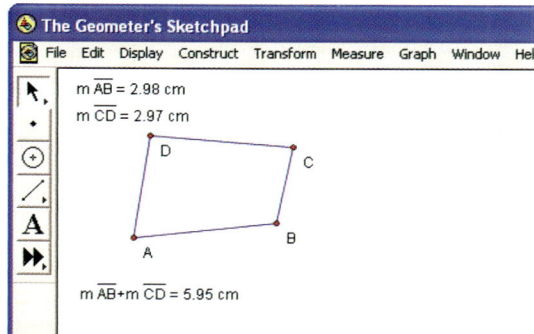

The sum of the measures will appear in the workspace.

OR

- Select the two measures. Then, choose **Calculate** from the **Measure** menu. This adds the measures to the drop-down list available by clicking on the **Values** button of the on-screen calculator.
- Click on the **Values** button. Select the first measure.
- Click on **+**.
- Click on the **Values** button. Select the second measure.
- Click on **OK**.

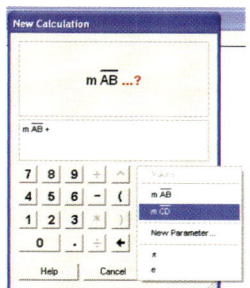

Technology Appendix • MHR 485

Constructing the Right Bisector of a Line Segment

The right bisector of a line segment is a line that intersects a line segment at its midpoint at a 90° angle.

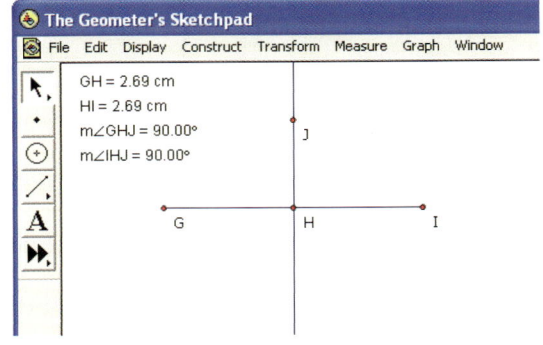

- Use the **Straightedge Tool** to draw a line segment.
- Select the line segment.
- From the **Construct** menu, choose **Midpoint**.
- Select the midpoint and the line segment.
- From the **Construct** menu, choose **Perpendicular Line**.

You can verify the construction:
- Draw a point on the perpendicular line.
- Measure the lengths of the two halves of the line segment.
- Measure the angles formed by the line segment and the perpendicular line.

Constructing an Altitude of a Triangle

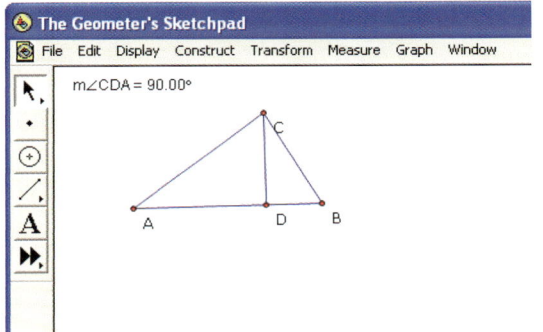

- Use the **Straightedge Tool** to construct a triangle, △ABC.
- Select one vertex, C, and the side opposite that vertex, AB.
- From the **Construct** menu, choose **Perpendicular Line**.
- Select the perpendicular line and the side BC.
- From the **Construct** menu, choose **Intersection**. Point D on side AB will appear.
- Select the perpendicular line, and choose **Hide Perpendicular Line** from the **Display** menu.
- Construct the line segment CD. CD is an altitude of △ABC.

You can check that CD is an altitude by measuring ∠CDA.

Constructing a Median of a Triangle

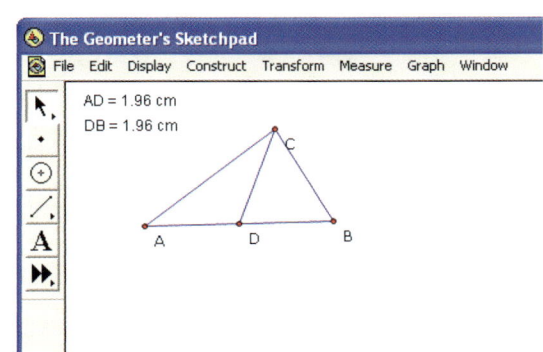

- Use the **Straightedge Tool** to construct a triangle, △ABC.
- Select side AB. From the **Construct** menu, choose **Midpoint**.
- Construct line segment CD.

To check that CD is a median:
- Measure the distances AD and DB.

Constructing an Angle Bisector

- Use the **Straightedge Tool** to construct line segments AB and AC to form ∠CAB.
- Select the points C, A, and B, in that order.
- From the **Construct** menu, choose **Angle Bisector**. The angle bisector will appear.

To verify that this is the angle bisector:
- Construct a point D on the angle bisector.
- Measure angles CAD and BAD.

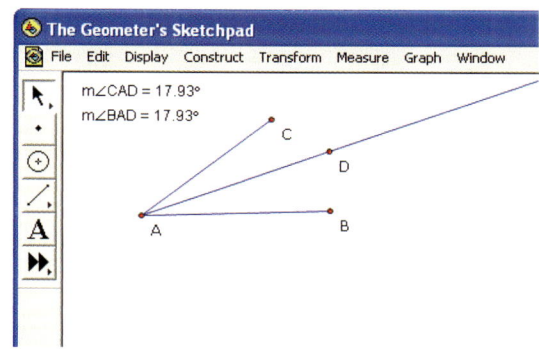

TI-83 PLUS AND TI-84 PLUS BASICS

The keys on the TI-83 Plus and TI-84 Plus are colour-coded to help you find the various functions.

- The white keys include the number keys, decimal point, and negative sign. When entering negative values, use the white (-) key, not the grey (−) key.
- The grey keys on the right side are the math operations.
- The grey keys across the top are used when graphing.
- The primary function of each key is printed on the key, in white.
- The secondary function of each key is printed in yellow and is activated by pressing the yellow (2nd) key. For example, to find the square root of a number, press (2nd) (x^2) for [$\sqrt{\ }$].
- The alpha function of each key is printed in green and is activated by pressing the green (ALPHA) key.

Adjusting the Contrast

If the calculator screen appears unclear, you can adjust the contrast.
- Press (2nd).

To increase the contrast,
- Press and hold (▲) until the desired level is reached.

To decrease the contrast,
- Press and hold (▼) until the desired level is reached.

If you want to change the contrast more slowly, you can repeatedly press (2nd) followed by (▲) or (2nd) followed by (▼).

Setting the Format

To define a graph's appearance:
- Press (2nd) (ZOOM) for [FORMAT] to see the choices available.

The **Default Settings**, shown here, have all the features on the left "turned on."

To use Grid Off/Grid On:
- Select [FORMAT] by pressing (2nd) (ZOOM). Cursor down and right to **GridOn**. Press (ENTER).
- Press (2nd) (MODE) for [QUIT].

Displaying a Decimal as a Fraction

- Key in a decimal, such as 0.375.
- Press MATH. Select **1:Frac**.
- Press ENTER.

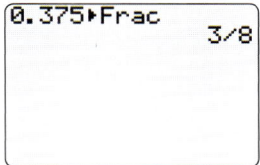

The decimal will be displayed as a fraction.

Turning Stat Plots Off

Before graphing a line, it is wise to ensure that all statistical plots are turned off, or you may see unwanted data on your graph.

- Press 2nd Y= to access the **STAT PLOTS** menu.
- Select **4:PlotsOff**.

Graphing Linear Relations

- Press Y=. Enter the equation.
- If there are any equations already present in the **Y=** editor, delete them using CLEAR.
- To display the graph, press GRAPH.

For example, enter $y = \frac{3}{5}x - 2$ by pressing

Y= (3 ÷ 5) X,T,θ,n − 2.
Press GRAPH.

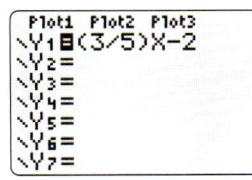 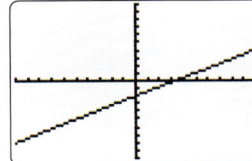

Setting Window Variables

The WINDOW key defines the appearance of the graph. The standard (default) window settings are shown.

To change the window settings:
- Press WINDOW. Enter the desired window settings.

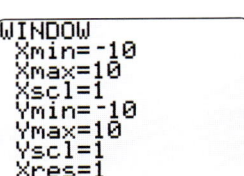

In the example shown,
- the minimum x-value is -47
- the maximum x-value is 47
- the scale of the x-axis is 10
- the minimum y-value is -31
- the maximum y-value is 31
- the scale of the y-axis is 10
- the resolution is 1, so equations are graphed at each horizontal pixel

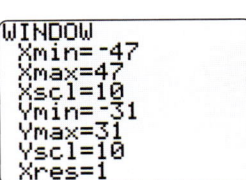

Changing the Appearance of a Line

The default graph style is a thin, solid line. The line style is displayed to the left of the equation. There are seven options for the appearance of a line.

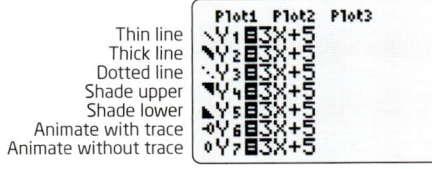

- Press [Y=] and clear any equations there from previous use of the calculator.
- Enter the relation $y = 3x + 5$ for **Y1**.
- Use the standard window settings.
- Press [GRAPH].

Note the thin, solid line style.

- Press [Y=]. Cursor left to the slanted line.
- Press [ENTER] repeatedly until the thick, solid line shows, as in **Y2** above.
- Press [GRAPH].

Note the thick, solid line.

- Press [Y=]. Cursor left to the slanted line.
- Press [ENTER] repeatedly until the thin dotted line shows, as in **Y3** above.
- Press [GRAPH].

Note the thin, dotted line.

- Press [Y=]. Cursor left to the slanted line.
- Press [ENTER] repeatedly until the solid triangle with hypotenuse down shows, as in **Y4** above.
- Press [GRAPH].

Note that the graph is shaded above the line.

- Press [Y=]. Cursor left to the slanted line.
- Press [ENTER] repeatedly until the solid triangle with hypotenuse up shows, as in **Y5** above.
- Press [GRAPH].

Note that the graph is shaded below the line.

- Press [Y=]. Cursor left to the slanted line.
- Press [ENTER] repeatedly until the circle with a tail shows, as in **Y6** above.
- Press [GRAPH].

Note the flying ball tracing the graph.

- Press [Y=]. Cursor left to the slanted line.
- Press [ENTER] repeatedly until the plain circle shows, as in **Y7** above.
- Press [GRAPH].

Note the flying ball that follows the graph, but does not leave a trace.

Setting Up a Table of Values

To set up a table of values, specifying a starting *x*-value and an *x*-increment:
- Press (Y=). Enter a relation, such as $2x + 1$.
- Press (2nd) (WINDOW) for [TBLSET].

Enter the desired starting *x*-value for **TblStart**, such as -3.

Enter the desired *x*-increment for **ΔTbl**, such as 1.

Ensure that **Indpnt** and **Depend** are both set to **Auto**.

- Press (2nd) (GRAPH) for [TABLE] to view the table.

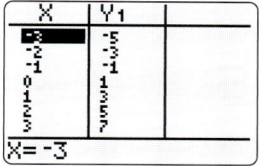

Using Zoom

The (ZOOM) key is used to change the area of the graph that is displayed in the graphing window.

To set the size of the area you want to zoom in on:
- Press (ZOOM). Select **1:Zbox**. The graph screen will be displayed, and the cursor will be flashing.
- If you cannot see the cursor, use the (▶), (◀), (▲), and (▼) keys to move the cursor until you see it.
- Move the cursor to an area on the edge of where you would like a closer view. Press (ENTER) to mark that point as a starting point.
- Press the (◀), (▶), (▲), and (▼) keys as needed to move the sides of the box to enclose the area you want to look at.
- Press (ENTER) when you are finished. The area will now appear larger.

To zoom in on an area without identifying a boxed-in area:
- Press (ZOOM). Select **2:Zoom In**.

To zoom out of an area:
- Press (ZOOM). Select **3:Zoom Out**.

To display the viewing area where the origin appears in the centre and the *x*- and *y*-axes intervals are equally spaced:
- Press (ZOOM). Select **4:ZDecimal**.

To reset the axes ranges on your calculator to the standard window:
- Press (ZOOM). Select **6:ZStandard**.

To display all data points in a **STAT PLOT**:
- Press (ZOOM). Select **9:ZoomStat**.

Technology Appendix • MHR 491

Tracing a Graph

- Enter a function using `Y=`.
- Press `TRACE`.
- Press `◄` and `►` to move along the graph.
- You can also input an *x*-value when you are in TRACE, to get exact *y*-values.

The *x*- and *y*-values are displayed at the bottom of the screen.

If you have more than one graph plotted, use the `▲` and `▼` keys to move the cursor to the graph you wish to trace.

You may want to turn off all STAT PLOTS before you trace a function:
- Press `2nd` `Y=` for [STAT PLOT]. Select **4:PlotsOff**.
- Press `ENTER`.

Using the Intersect Operation

The **intersect** operation will find the point at which two relations intersect.

For example, consider the lines $y = 3x - 2$ and $y = -x + 6$.

Turn off all STAT PLOTS.
- Press `Y=`. Clear any relations already present.

Enter the relations in **Y1** and **Y2**.
- Press `ZOOM`. Select **6:ZStandard**.
- Press `2nd` `TRACE` to access the **CALCULATE** menu. Select **5:intersect**.

If necessary, use the cursor keys to select the first relation.
- Press `ENTER`.

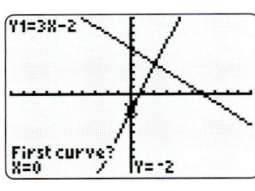

If necessary, use the cursor keys to select the second relation.
- Press `ENTER`.

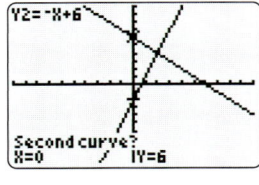

Use the cursor keys to position the cursor as close as possible to your guess for the point of intersection.
- Press `ENTER`.

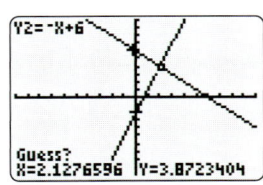

The coordinates of the point of intersection will be displayed.

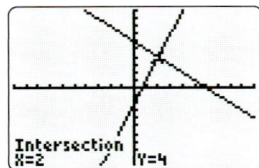

Changing the Mode Settings

The mode settings are used to control the way the calculator displays and interprets numbers and graphs.

- Press [MODE].

The first line controls the number display. Most of the time, you will use **Normal**. You can also select **Scientific** or **Engineering**.

The second line controls the number of decimal places that are displayed. If you choose **FLOAT**, the calculator will select the appropriate number. You can also choose the number of decimal places. For example, if you are working with money, you might want to have all numbers displayed with two decimal places.

The third line selects angle measures as **RADIAN** or **DEGREE**. You will normally use degree measure.

The bottom line lets you set the clock on a TI-84 Plus calculator. Note: The TI-83 Plus does not have a clock.

To change a setting:
- Use the cursor keys to navigate to the desired setting.
- Press [ENTER] to select the setting.

To leave the mode screen:
- Press [2nd] [MODE] for [QUIT].

Entering Data Into Lists

To enter data:
- Press [STAT]. The cursor will highlight the **EDIT** menu.
- Press **1** or [ENTER] to select **1:Edit…**.

This allows you to enter new data, or edit existing data, in lists **L1** to **L6**.

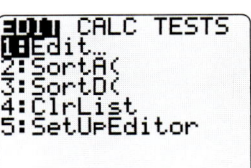

For example, press [STAT], select **1:Edit…**, and then enter six test scores in list **L1**.
- Use the cursor keys to move around the editor screen.
- Complete each data entry by pressing [ENTER].
- Press [2nd] [MODE] for [QUIT] to exit the list editor when the data are entered.

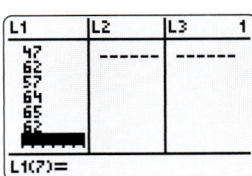

You may need to clear a list before you enter data into it. For example, to clear list **L1**:
- Press [STAT] and select **4:ClrList**.
- Press [2nd] **1** for [L1], and press [ENTER].

OR

To clear all lists:
- Press [2nd] [+] for [MEM] to display the **MEMORY** menu.
- Select **4:ClrAllLists**, and then press [ENTER].

Creating a Scatter Plot

To create a scatter plot:
- Enter the two data sets in lists **L1** and **L2**.
- Press 2nd Y= for [STAT PLOT].
- Press **1** or ENTER to select **1:Plot1…**.
- Press ENTER to select **On**.
- Cursor down, and then press ENTER to select the top left graphing option, a scatter plot.
- Cursor down and press 2nd **1** for [L1].
- Cursor down and press 2nd **2** for [L2].
- Cursor down and select a mark style by pressing ENTER.
- Press 2nd MODE for [QUIT] to exit the **STAT PLOTS** editor when you are finished.

To display the scatter plot:
- Press Y= and use the CLEAR key to remove any graphed equations.
- Press 2nd MODE for [QUIT] to exit the **Y=** editor.
- Press ZOOM and select **9:ZoomStat** to display the scatter plot.

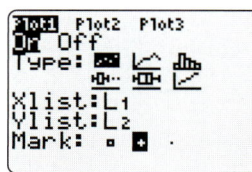 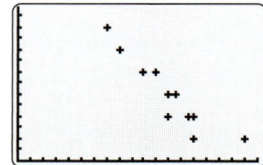

Line of Best Fit: Linear Regression

You can add the line of best fit to a scatter plot by using the **LinReg** function.

- Create a scatter plot.
- Press STAT. Cursor over to the **CALC** menu. Then, select **4:LinReg(ax+b)**.
- Press 2nd **1** for [L1], followed by ,.
- Press 2nd **2** for [L2], followed by ,.
- Press VARS. Cursor over to the **Y-VARS** menu. Select **1:FUNCTION**, and then press ENTER. Select **1:Y1** and press ENTER.
- Press ENTER to obtain the **LinReg** screen. The equation of the line is displayed.

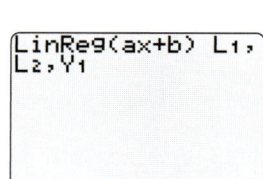

Note: If the diagnostic mode is turned on, you will see values for **r** and **r²** displayed on the **LinReg** screen. To turn the diagnostic mode off:
- Press 2nd **0** for [CATALOG].
- Scroll down to **DiagnosticOff**. Press ENTER to select this option.
- Press ENTER again to turn off the diagnostic mode.

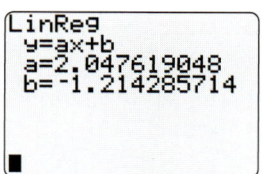

Press GRAPH to see the line of best fit overlaid on the scatter plot.

The linear regression equation is stored in the **Y=** editor. Press Y= to display the equation generated by the calculator.

You can use the line of best fit to estimate values.

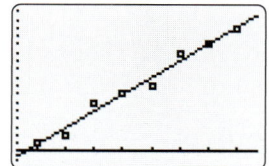

Turn STAT PLOTs off.
- Press GRAPH.
- Press TRACE.

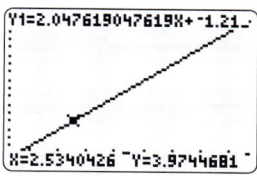

Use the cursor keys to move the cursor back and forth along the line of best fit to estimate values.

Finding the Maximum or Minimum

To find the maximum or minimum of a relation such as $y = x^2 - 4x + 3$:
- Press Y=. Enter the relation.
- Press ZOOM. Select **6:ZStandard**.
- Press TRACE. Use the cursor keys to find the minimum value for y.

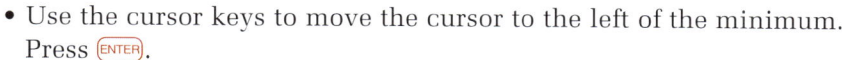
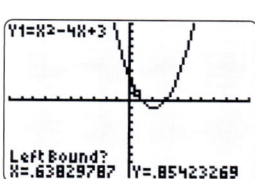

The TRACE method may not give an exact answer.

You can obtain a more accurate value for the maximum or minimum as follows:
- Press 2nd TRACE to access the **CALCULATE** menu. Select **3:minimum**.

- Use the cursor keys to move the cursor to the left of the minimum. Press ENTER.

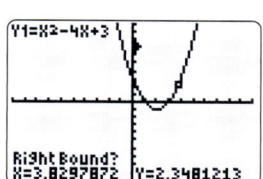

- Use the cursor keys to move the cursor to the right of the minimum. Press ENTER.

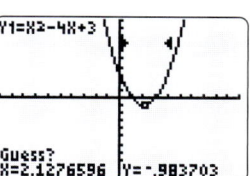

- Use the cursor keys to move the cursor close to your guess for the minimum. Press ENTER.

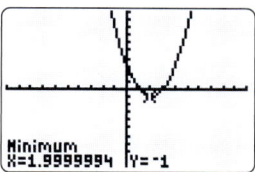

- The coordinates of the minimum are displayed.

If the graph has a maximum, rather than a minimum, select **4:maximum** from the **CALCULATE** menu.

Technology Appendix • MHR 495

Finding Zeros

To find the zeros of a relation such as $y = x^2 - x - 6$:
- Press (Y=). Enter the relation.
- Press (ZOOM). Select **6:ZStandard**.
- Press (2nd)(TRACE) to access the **CALCULATE** menu. Select **2:zero**.

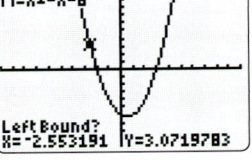

- Use the cursor keys to move the cursor to the left of the left zero.
- Press (ENTER).

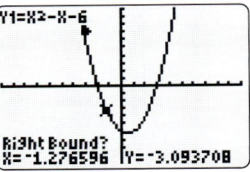

- Use the cursor keys to move the cursor to the right of the left zero.
- Press (ENTER).

- Use the cursor keys to move the cursor close to your guess for the left zero.
- Press (ENTER).

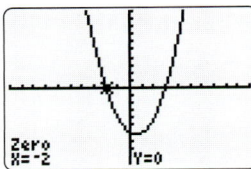

The coordinates of the zero are displayed.

Use a similar procedure to find the right zero.

Using the Value Operation

To find the corresponding y-value for any x-value for a relation such as $y = x^2 + x - 2$:
- Press (Y=). Enter the relation.
- Press (ZOOM). Select **6:ZStandard**.
- Press (2nd)(TRACE) to access the **CALCULATE** menu. Select **1:value**.
- Enter a value for x, such as $x = 3$.
- Press (ENTER).

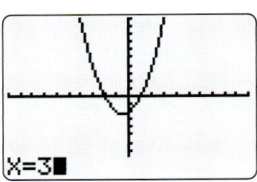

The corresponding y-value, $y = 10$, is displayed.

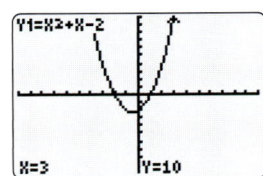

Curve of Best Fit: Quadratic Regression and Exponential Regression

You can add a curve of best fit to a scatter plot by using the QuadReg operation to try a quadratic fit, or the ExpReg operation to try an exponential fit.

Create a scatter plot using the data shown.

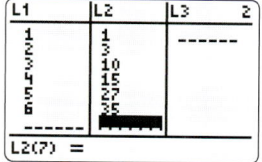 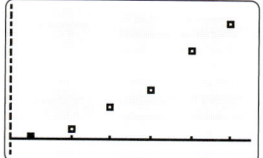

- Press **STAT**. Cursor over to the **CALC** menu. Then, select **5:QuadReg**.
- Press **2nd** **1** for L1, followed by **,**.
- Press **2nd** **2** for L2, followed by **,**.
- Press **VARS**. Cursor over to the **Y-VARS** menu. Select **1:Function**, and press **ENTER**. Select **1:Y1**.

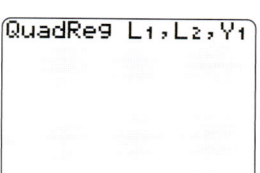

- Press **ENTER** to obtain the **QuadReg** screen. The equation of the quadratic curve is displayed.

Note: If the diagnostic mode is turned on, you will see values for **r** and **r²** displayed on the **QuadReg** screen. To turn the diagnostic mode off:
- Press **2nd** **0** for [CATALOG].
- Scroll down to **DiagnosticOff**. Press **ENTER** to select this option.
- Press **ENTER** again to turn off the diagnostic mode.

Press **GRAPH** to see the curve of best fit overlaid on the scatter plot.

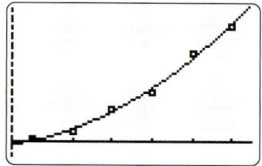

The quadratic regression equation is stored in the **Y=** editor.

- Press **Y=** to display the equation generated by the calculator.

If you want to fit an exponential curve, select **0:ExpReg** from the **STAT CALC** menu, rather than **5:QuadReg**.

Calculations Involving the Sine Law

For example, consider △ABC. Find the measure of ∠B and the length of side c.

Use the sine law to find the measure of ∠B:

$$\sin B = \frac{\sin 28°}{10} \times 12$$

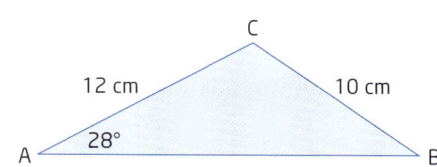

To solve for ∠B:
- Ensure that the **MODE** is set to **Degree**.
- Enter [SIN] 28 [)] [×] 12 [÷] 10 [ENTER].
- Press [2nd] [SIN]. This will access the [SIN⁻¹] function to calculate the angle.
- Press [2nd] [(-)] for [ANS]. This will insert the answer from the previous calculation.
- Press [)] and then [ENTER].

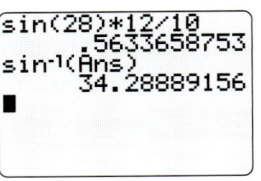

The measure of ∠B is about 34°.

Use the sine law to find the length of side c:

$$c = \frac{10 \sin 118°}{\sin 28°}$$

Solve for c:
- Press 10 [×] [SIN] 118 [)] [÷] [SIN] 28 [)] [ENTER].

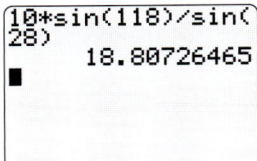

The length of side AB is about 18.8 cm.

Calculations Involving the Cosine Law

Consider △DEF. Find the length of EF and the measure of ∠E.

Use the cosine law to find d:
$$d^2 = e^2 + f^2 - 2ef \cos D$$
$$= 10^2 + 8^2 - 2 \times 10 \times 8 \times \cos 48°$$
$$d = \sqrt{10^2 + 8^2 - 2 \times 10 \times 8 \times \cos 48°}$$

To evaluate d:
- Press [2nd] [x^2] for [√].
- Press [(] 10 [x^2] [+] 8 [x^2] [−] 2 [×] 10 [×] 8 [×] [COS] 48 [)] [)].
- Press [ENTER].

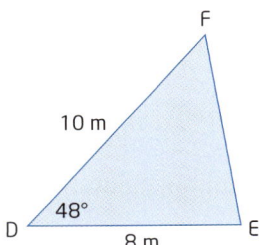

The length of EF is about 7.5 m.

Use the cosine law to find ∠E:
$$e^2 = d^2 + f^2 - 2df \cos E$$
$$10^2 = 7.5^2 + 8^2 - 2 \times 7.5 \times 8 \times \cos E$$
$$10^2 - 7.5^2 - 8^2 = -2 \times 7.5 \times 8 \times \cos E$$
$$\cos E = \frac{10^2 - 7.5^2 - 8^2}{-2 \times 7.5 \times 8}$$

To solve for ∠E:
- Press [(] 10 [x^2] [−] 7.5 [x^2] [−] 8 [x^2] [)] [÷] [(] [(-)] 2 [×] 7.5 [×] 8 [)].
- Press [ENTER].
- Press [2nd] [COS]. This will access the COS⁻¹ function to calculate the angle.
- Press [2nd] [(-)] for [ANS]. This will insert the answer from the previous calculation.
- Press [)] and then [ENTER].

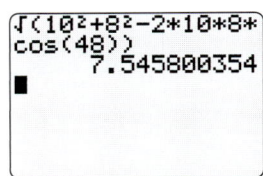

The measure of ∠E is about 80°.

TI-89 TITANIUM COMPUTER ALGEBRA SYSTEM BASICS

A Computer Algebra System, or CAS, is a program that contains tools for manipulation of symbolic expressions. It is sometimes called a symbolic manipulator. You can expand expressions, factor expressions, solve equations, check solutions, and perform many other operations with a CAS.

Keypad Tips: Use the 2ND key to access functions that are in **blue**. Use the ◆ key to access functions that are in **green**. Use the ALPHA key to access letters and other text characters. Use the (−) key to enter a negative, but use the − key for the subtraction operation.

Changing the Mode Settings

The mode settings are used to control the way the calculator displays and interprets numbers and other quantities.

- Press MODE.

The **Display Digits** line determines the number of decimal places that will be displayed. If you choose **FLOAT**, the calculator will select the appropriate number of decimal places. You can also choose the number of decimal places. For example, if you are working with money, you might want to have all numbers displayed with two decimal places.

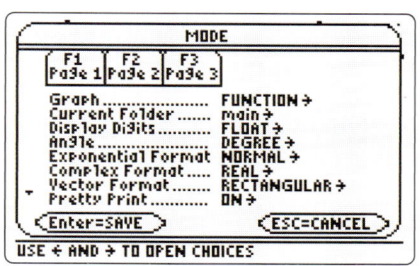

The **Angle** line selects the type of angle measure used by the calculator. You will normally use degree measure.

The remaining lines should be set as shown, unless you are instructed otherwise.

- To leave the mode screen, press ESC.

Starting a New Problem

Before you start using the calculator, it is wise to clear the memory. Otherwise, values that a previous user has entered may produce unexpected results.

- Press (2nd) (F1) to access the **F6** menu. This is known as the **Clean Up** menu.
- Select **2:NewProb**. Then, press (ENTER).

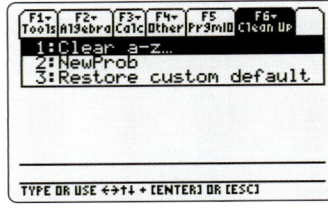
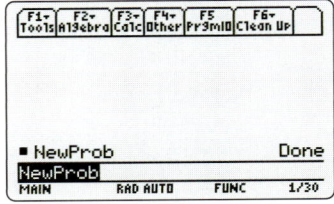

Operations on Equations

The syntax for CAS operations is somewhat different from that usually used in pencil and paper calculations.

For example, consider solving the equation $x + 2 = 5$. When using pencil and paper, you subtract 2 from both sides.

$x + 2 - 2 = 5 - 2$

When using a CAS, you place the entire equation in brackets, and then indicate the subtraction operation outside the brackets, as shown.

- Press (ENTER) to finish the operation.

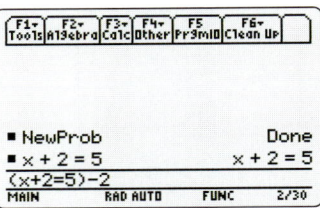
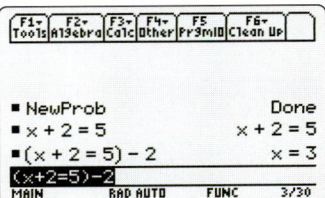

Copying and Pasting

You can copy a previous entry in the workspace and paste it into the command line. This is useful for several purposes, such as when solving an equation.

As an example, consider a step-by-step solution of the equation $2x + 3 = 7$, as shown.

- Enter the equation $2x + 3 = 7$.
- Subtract 3 from both sides.
- Press (ENTER).

For the next step, you want to divide the intermediate result by 2.

- Use the cursor key to move up to $2x = 4$.
- Press (♦) (↑) for [COPY].
- Move the cursor back to the command line.
- Press (♦) (ESC) for [PASTE].

Note that $2x = 4$ is pasted into the command line.

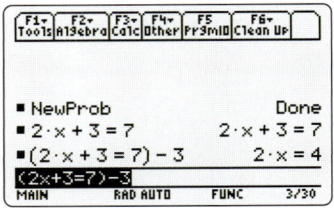
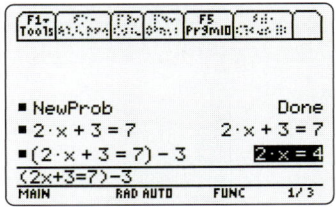
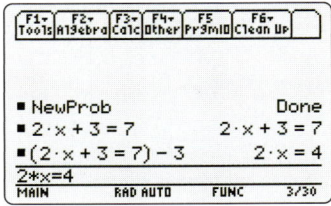

500 MHR • Technology Appendix

- Insert brackets around $2x = 4$, and divide by 2.
- Press ENTER.

The solution is $x = 2$.

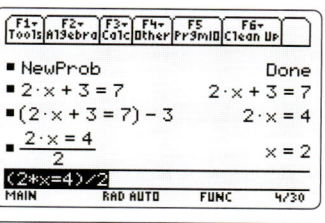

To check the solution:
- Use the cursor to move up to the original equation, $2x + 3 = 7$.
- Press ♦ ↑ for [COPY].
- Move the cursor back to the command line.
- Press ♦ ESC for [PASTE].
- Type | $x = 2$.
- Press ENTER.

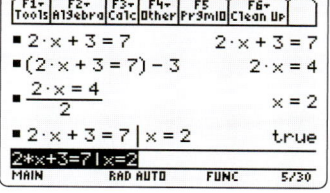

Note that the CAS returns a **true** message. This means that $x = 2$ is a solution.

For a simple equation such the one shown in this example, it may be just as fast to retype each time. However, COPY and PASTE can be very useful for more complicated expressions.

Note: The calculator remembers your entries even if they have "disappeared" off the top of the work space. You can cursor upward, and they will reappear. They will remain until you clear the memory or until you fill up all available memory.

Using the CLEAR Key and the Backspace Key

When the cursor is in the command line:
Pressing ←, the backspace key, will delete the character immediately to the left of the cursor. You can use it to correct typos.

Pressing CLEAR will delete the entire contents of the command line. You can use it to clear the command line.

When the cursor is in the work space, pressing either key will delete the line that the cursor is on.

Collecting Like Terms

A CAS can collect like terms in an algebraic expression.

Consider the expression $5x + 2y - 3x - 7y$.

- Type this expression into the calculator.
- Press ENTER.

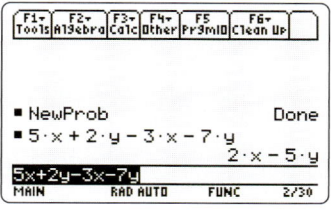

Note that the CAS has collected and combined like terms.

Tip: The variables x, y, z, and t have dedicated keys. Other variables can be accessed using ALPHA. When entering a term such as $5x$, you do not need to enter a multiplication operator between the 5 and the x. However, if you enter a term such as xy, the situation is different. If you do not enter a multiplication operator between the x and the y, the CAS considers this as a single variable named xy, not as the product of x and y. If you want the term to mean the product of x and y, you must enter a multiplication operator between the two letters.

Technology Appendix • MHR 501

Evaluating an Expression for a Given Value

You can evaluate an expression for a given value of the variable.

For example, consider the expression $5x + 2$.

To evaluate the expression for $x = 3$:
- Type $5x + 2$ ⎕ $x = 3$.
- Press ENTER.

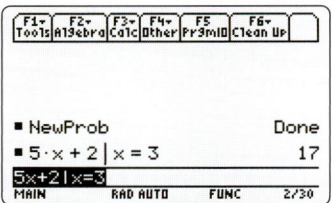

The calculator returns a value of 17.

Checking the Solution for an Equation

You can use a CAS to check whether a given value is the correct solution for an equation.

For example, consider the equation $2x + 1 = -3x - 4$. Check $x = 1$ and $x = -1$ as possible solutions.

Check $x = 1$:
- Type $2x + 1 = -3x - 4$ ⎕ $x = 1$.
- Press ENTER.

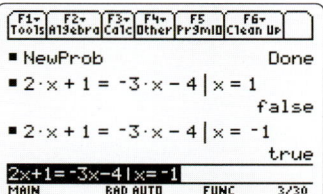

Note that the CAS returns a **false** message. This means that $x = 1$ is not a solution.

Check $x = -1$:
- Type $2x + 1 = -3x - 4$ ⎕ $x = -1$.
- Press ENTER.

Note that the CAS returns a **true** message. This means that $x = -1$ is a solution.

Using the Expand Operation

You can use a CAS to expand expressions.

For example, consider the expression $3(2x + 1)$.

- Press F2 and select **3:expand(**.
- Type in the expression and a closing bracket.
- Press ENTER.

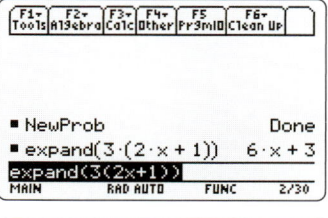

Note that the CAS has expanded the expression using the distributive property.

The CAS will expand any algebraic expression.

For example, try $(2x + 3)(5x - 1)$.

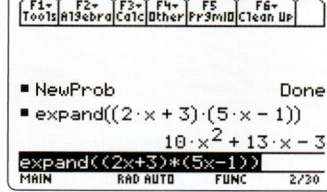

502 MHR • Technology Appendix

Using the Factor Operation

You can use a CAS to factor expressions.

For example, consider the expression $7x + 21$.

- Press `F2` and select **2:factor(**.
- Type in the expression and a closing bracket.
- Press `ENTER`.

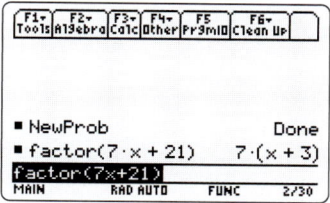

Note that the CAS has factored the expression by taking out a common factor.

The CAS will factor other algebraic expressions.

For example, try $6x^2 + 11x - 10$.

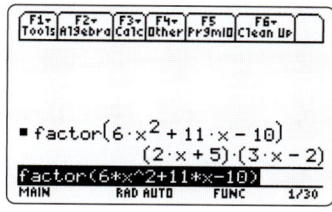

Answers

Chapter 1

Get Ready, pages 4–7

1. a) 6 b) -8 c) -11
   d) -4 e) 2 f) $-2\frac{5}{6}$

2. a) 0 b) 2 c) -4
   d) 12 e) 2 f) -3

3. a) $7x - 2y$ b) $7a - 11b$ c) $5x - 5y$

4. a) $-2x + 35y$ b) $-7x - 13y$ c) $-a + 16b - 4$

5. a) 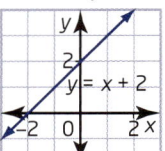 b)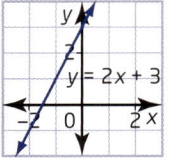

   c)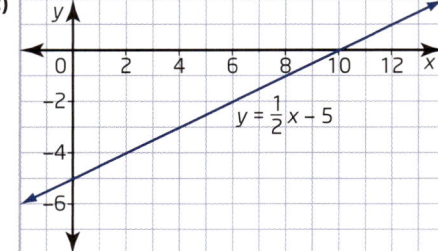

   d)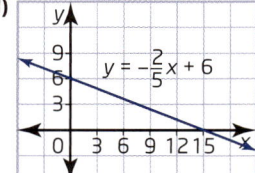

6. a) $y = x + 1$ b) $y = -2x + 3$
   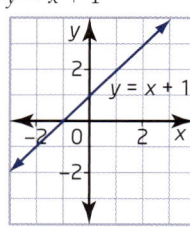 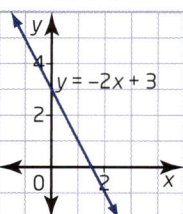

   c) $y = -x + 7$
   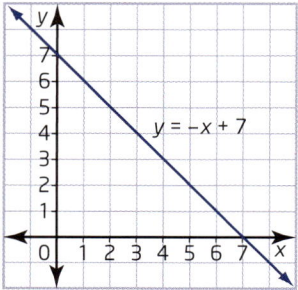

   d) $y = -\frac{5}{2}x - 1$
   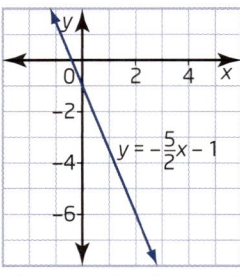

7. a) x-intercept 3, y-intercept 3
   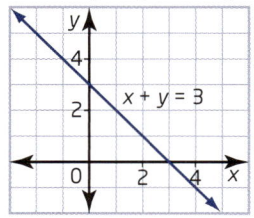

   b) x-intercept 3, y-intercept -5
   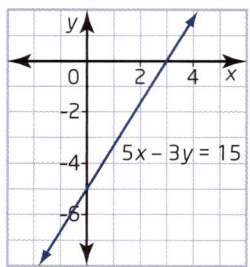

   c) x-intercept 3, y-intercept -7
   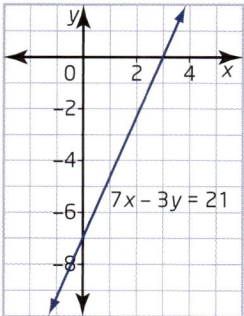

   d) x-intercept 4, y-intercept -2
   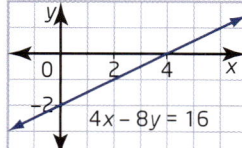

8. a)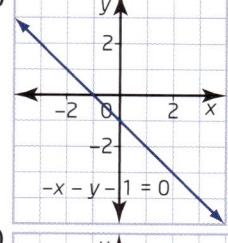

b)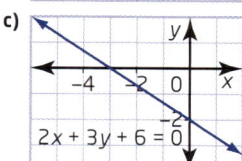

c) 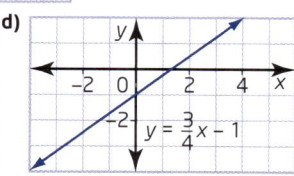 **d)**

9. a) 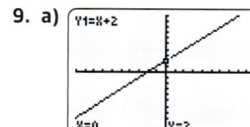 **b)**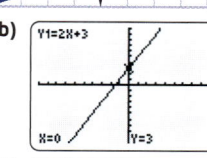

c) 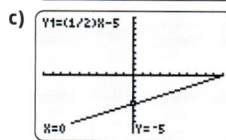 **d)**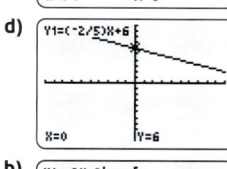

10. a) 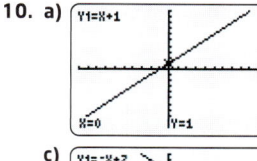 **b)**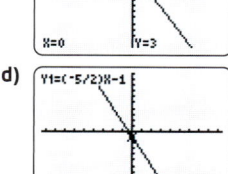

c) **d)**

11. a) 4.2 L **b)** 0.72 kg **c)** 44 g
12. a) $80 **b)** $34.80 **c)** $46.50 **d)** $562.50
13. a) 7 **b)** 2 **c)** -2
14. Answers will vary.
15. Answers will vary.

1.1 Connect English With Mathematics and Graphing Lines, pages 8–19

1. a) $2x - 7$ **b)** $\frac{1}{2}x + 4$ **c)** $(x - 6)y$ **d)** $x + \frac{2}{3}$
2. a) $2d$ **b)** $0.2n$ **c)** $2l$ **d)** $0.07p$
3. a) $\frac{1}{5}n - 17 = 41$ **b)** $5 - 2n = 7n + 3$
 c) $5n = 825$ **d)** $l + w = 96$

4. a) decreased **b)** subtracted
 c) minus **d)** less than
5. a) addition **b)** Answers will vary.
6. Answers may vary. For example: An expression is a combination of numbers, operations, and/or variables that can be evaluated. An equation equates two expressions.
7. C
8. a) $(2, 7)$ **b)** $(-3, -4)$ **c)** $(-20, -12)$ **d)** $(3, 7)$
9. a) $(2, 1)$ **b)** $(-2, -1)$ **c)** $(2, -3)$ **d)** $(2, 1)$
10. a) $(3, -2)$ **b)** $(-4.67, 8)$
 c) $(1.45, 4.73)$ **d)** $(-1.29, 7.86)$
 e) $(-1.49, 0.62)$ **f)** $(1.26, -4.75)$
11. a) $C = 150 + 20m$ **b)** $C = 100 + 30m$
 c) 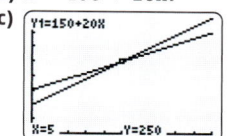 **d)** $(5, 250)$

 e) Answers may vary. For example: The point of intersection represents the number of months it will take for the costs to be the same at both clubs.
 f) Answers may vary. For example: You should join CanFit because it will be cheaper for 1 year.
12. a) $C = 10 + 3n$ **b)** $C = 7 + 4n$ **c)** $(3, 19)$
 d) Answers may vary. For example: The cost is the same at both stores when you rent three video games. The cost is $19.
13. a) $C = 15h$ **b)** $C = 150$ **c)** $(10, 150)$
 d) Jeff charges the same price for 10 h of work as Hesketh's Snow Removal charges for the season.
14. a) $C = 5000 + 75n$
 b) $C = 7500 + 50n$
 c) 100
 d) Limestone Hall is less expensive for fewer than 100 guests.
 e) Answers will vary. For example: convenience of location, parking availability, reputation for good food, attractiveness of the hall
15. a) $E = 80 + 1.50n$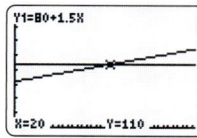
 b) $E = 110$
 c) 20 pairs of jeans

16. $500 was invested in the account paying 5%/year interest and $4500 was invested in the GIC paying 7.2%/year interest.
17. a) $C = 525 + 0.20d$
 b) $C = 500 + 0.30d$
 c)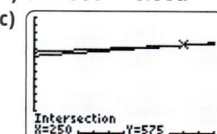

 d) The cost of $575 is the same when the Clarkes rent the car from either of the two companies and drive 250 km.

18. a) i) $E = 25\,000$ **ii)** $E = 40n$ **iii)** $E = 15\,000 + 25n$
b)

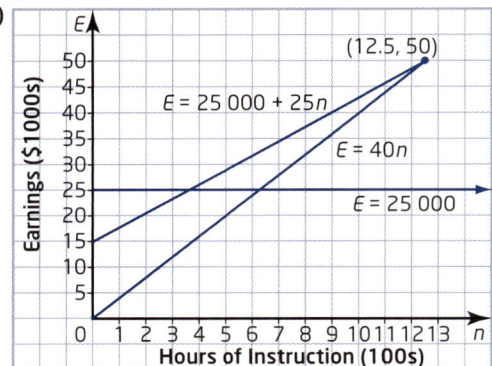

c) If Alain is going to give fewer than 400 h of instruction, then package (i) is best. For 400 h, packages (i) and (ii) pay the same amount, $25 000. For more than 400 h but fewer than 1000 h, package (ii) pays more. For 1000 h, packages (ii) and (iii) pay the same, $40 000. For more than 1000 h, package (iii) pays the most. It would not make sense for him to work more than 1250 h (25 h per week for 50 weeks), because that is the most he can work for packages (ii) and (iii). If he did work more than 1250 h, he would have to go with package (i), the flat rate of $25 000.

19. The three lines intersect at the same point.
20. Answers may vary. For example:
  a) No, because they represent the same line and intersect everywhere.
  b) No, because the lines are parallel and do not intersect.
  c) If two lines have the same slopes and y-intercepts, then there is an infinite number of solutions. If two lines have the same slope and different y-intercepts, then there is no solution. If two lines have different slopes, then there is one solution.
21. $(-2, -6)$ and $(2, -2)$. The second equation is not linear because it has an x^2-term.
22. a) 31   **b)** $2n + 1$
23. 28%
24. C

1.2 The Method of Substitution, pages 20–28
1. a) $x = 3$, $y = 5$ **b)** $x = 9$, $y = -1$
   c) $x = 1$, $y = 1$ **d)** $x = 4$, $y = -3$
2. a) equation 1: $x = -2y + 5$ **b)** equation 1: $y = -2x + 6$
   c) equation 2: $x = 3y - 2$ **d)** equation 1: $y = 3x - 5$
   e) either equation 1: $(y = 2x - 2)$ or equation 2: $(y = -4x + 16)$
3. No. $(3, -5)$ satisfies the first equation but not the second equation.
4. a) $x = \dfrac{2}{3}$, $y = \dfrac{7}{6}$ **b)** $x = 2$, $y = -1$
   c) $m = 1$, $n = 0$ **d)** $a = 8$, $b = -10$
   e) $x = 1$, $y = 2$
5. a) $\left(-\dfrac{4}{5}, -\dfrac{33}{5}\right)$ **b)** $\left(\dfrac{19}{2}, -\dfrac{31}{2}\right)$ **c)** $\left(\dfrac{1}{3}, \dfrac{2}{3}\right)$
   d) $(-1, -5)$ **e)** $(4, 1)$

6. Answers may vary. For example:
  a) Let S represent the number of hours that Samantha works. Let A represent the number of hours that Adriana works.
  b) $S = 2A$ **c)** $S + A = 39$
  d) Samantha worked 26 h and Adriana worked 13 h.
7. Answers may vary. For example:
  a) Let J represent the number of T-shirts bought by Jeff and S represent the number of T-shirts bought by Stephen. Then, $J + S = 15$.
  b) $S = 2J - 3$
  c) Jeff bought 6 T-shirts and Stephen bought 9 T-shirts.
  d) Jeff spent $53.94 and Stephen spent $80.91, before tax.
8. Answers may vary. For example:
  a) Let g represent the number of goals and a represent the number of assists. Then, $2g + a = 86$; $g = a - 17$.
  b) $g = 23$, $a = 40$
  c) Ugo scored 23 goals and made 40 assists.
9. Answers may vary. For example:
  a) Let C represent the cost of renting a hall and n be the cost of a meal. Then, $C = 500 + 15n$; $C = 350 + 18n$.
  b) 50 guests
10. 2.5 h
11. The companies charge the same for 200 km. It is better to rent from Joe's Garage for distances less than 200 km.
12. Answers may vary. For example: It is not easy to isolate either of the variables.
13. Answers may vary. For example: It is easy to isolate y in either equation. Both lines are simple to graph.
14. a) $(-1, 6)$, $(1, 2)$, $(2, 3)$
   b) Explanations may vary. For example: Yes, because the slope of the first line, m_1, and the slope of the third line, m_3, are negative reciprocals.
15. 6 wins
16. Answers may vary. For example:
  a) Let C represent the cost of renting a car and d represent the number of kilometres driven. Then, $C = 90$.
  b) $C = 40 + 0.25d$
  c) The costs are the same for driving a distance of 200 km.
  d) The mid-size car costs less for driving fewer than 200 km during a 1-day car rental.
  e) The full-size car is cheaper by $10.
18. 8750 adults
19. a) You get $-2 = 9$, which is impossible.
   b) Since the lines are parallel and distinct, the lines do not intersect. There is no solution.
20. a) $x = 5$, $y = 4$ **b)** $x = 0.5$, $y = -0.5$
21. $(-4, 5)$; $k = -5$
22. $\dfrac{n}{6}(n + 1)(n + 2)$
23. C

1.3 Investigate Equivalent Linear Relations and Equivalent Linear Systems, pages 29–33
1. A and C
2. C
3. Answers may vary. For example:
   a) $2y = 6x - 4$; $3y = 9x - 6$
   b) $x + 2y = 4$; $2x + 4y = 8$
   c) $5y = 3x + 10$; $10y = 6x + 20$
   d) $4x + 2y = 5$; $2x + y = 2.5$

506 MHR • Answers

4. Answers may vary. For example: $2l + 2w = 24$; $l + w = 12$

5. Answers may vary. For example: $0.05n + 0.10d = 0.70$; $5n + 10d = 70$

6. The systems are equivalent because equation ③ is equation ① divided by 3, and equation ④ is equation ② multiplied by 2.

7. a) Since both systems have the same solution, (2, 4), they are equivalent linear systems.

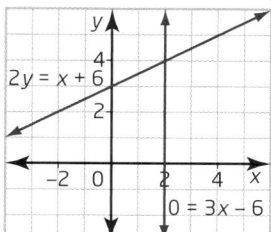

b) Add: equation ① + equation ②.
c) Subtract: equation ① − equation ②.

8. a) Equation ③ was obtained by multiplying both sides of equation ① by three and then subtracting $2x$ from both sides. Equation ④ was obtained by multiplying both sides of equation ② by three and then adding x to both sides. The linear system formed by equation ③ and equation ④ is an equivalent linear system to the linear system formed by equation ① and equation ② and has the same point of intersection.
b) You expect to see only two distinct lines intersecting at the point (3, 1).

9. Answers will vary.
10. 1729
11. B

1.4 The Method of Elimination, pages 34–41

1. a) $x = 1, y = 1$ **b)** $x = -2, y = -1$
  c) $x = 1, y = 2$ **d)** $x = -1, y = -3$
2. a) $x = -1, y = -3$ **b)** $x = 1, y = 5$
  c) $x = 2, y = 4$ **d)** $x = -1, y = 1$
3. a) $(-2, 2)$ **b)** $(-1, 3)$ **c)** $(3, 4)$ **d)** $(2, 0)$
4. a) $x = \frac{1}{4}, y = 1$ **b)** $x = 2, y = -5$
  c) $x = 6, y = 9$ **d)** $x = 1, y = 2$
5. a) $x = 3, y = 2$ **b)** $m = -1, n = 5$
  c) $a = 6, b = 2$ **d)** $h = -1, k = -2$
6. a) $(3, 4)$ **b)** $(-3, -4)$
  c) $\left(\frac{5}{2}, \frac{19}{4}\right)$ **d)** $\left(-\frac{1}{2}, 3\right)$
7. a) $x = -\frac{1}{2}, y = -\frac{2}{3}$ **b)** $x = 7, y = -2$
  c) $a = -2, b = -1$ **d)** $u = 8, v = 6$
8. a) 11 **b)** 17
9. a) 10 large bottles **b)** 27 small bottles
10. a) $x = \frac{29}{14}, y = -\frac{2}{7}$ **b)** $x = \frac{29}{14}, y = -\frac{2}{7}$
  c) Answers will vary.
11. Answers may vary. For example: Multiply the first equation by 4 and the second equation by 3, and then subtract the equations. Solve for y, substitute this value of y into the first equation, and then solve for x.

12. a) $x = -1, y = -5$ **b)** $a = 4.5, b = 6.5$
  c) $k = 5, n = -3$
13. Answers may vary. For example: Brent multiplied each equation by 10 to write equivalent equations without decimals. The equivalent equations, without decimals, are easier to solve. $x = -1, y = -3$
14. a) $x = 5, y = -1$ **b)** $a = 3, b = -4$
15. $4
16. a) $50/day **b)** $0.20/km
17. a) $C = 250 + 0.22d$ **b)** $C = 96 + 0.50d$
  c) If they drive 550 km, the cost of renting either car is $371.
  d) The daughter's suggestion is less expensive.
18. Answers may vary. For example: You get $0 = 18$, which is impossible. On a graph, the lines are parallel and distinct so there is no solution.
20. a) $m = -4, n = -2$ **b)** $a = 6, b = 7$
  c) $t = -4, w = 7$
21. $(x, y) = \left(\dfrac{ce - bf}{ae - bd}, \dfrac{cd - af}{bd - ae}\right)$, where $ae \neq bd$.
22. $(x, y, z) = (4, -5, 3)$

1.5 Solve Problems Using Linear Systems, pages 42–47

1. 24 crocus bulbs and 8 tulip bulbs
2. 10 Beta tapes and 7 VHS tapes
3. 30 cars and 14 vans
4. $2650 at 8%/year and $400 at 7.5%/year
5. Answers may vary. For example: The numbers are smaller and it is easier to isolate one variable in both equations.
6. a) Answers will vary. $(-23, -77)$
  b) $(-23, -77)$
7. average rowing speed 3.5 km/h, speed of current 1.5 km/h
8. wind speed 50 km/h, speed of plane 550 km/h
9. 15 L of 3% milk, 5 L of 15% cream
10. 6 L of 30% sulphuric acid solution, 4 L of 60% sulphuric acid solution
11. a) 10 months **b)** Kool Karate
  c) Karate Klub
12. 30 medium T-shirts
13. 240 g of granola with 30% nuts, 360 g of granola with 15% nuts
14. 100 g of metal alloy that is 25% copper, 400 g of metal alloy that is 50% copper
15. 32 fruit pies, 20 meat pies
16. $10 per meal, $50 per day for accommodation
17. best cruise speed 200 km/h, economy cruise speed 150 km/h
18. 200 km
19. 400 g of 18-karat gold, 200 g of 9-karat gold
20. 83.5%

Chapter 1 Review, pages 48–49

1. a) Let n represent the number of nickels and d represent the number of dimes. $0.05n + 0.10d = 2.50$
  b) Let M represent Maggie's age and J represent Janice's age. $M + 3 = 2J - 9$
  c) Let n represent the number. $2n - 9 = \frac{1}{2}n + 6$

Answers • MHR **507**

2. $(4, -3)$
3. **a)** $C = 1500 + 25n$ **b)** $C = 1000 + 30n$
   c) 100 guests
   d) Allison should choose La Casa if she invites more than 100 guests because it will cost less.
   e) She should choose Hastings Hall if she invites fewer than 100 guests because it will cost less.
4. **a)** $x = -4, y = 2$ **b)** $x = 6, y = -3$
   c) $x = -1, y = 4$ **d)** $x = 3.75, y = 0.5$
5. 41 chickens
6. Josie should choose the flat rate if she uses the Internet for more than 30 h per month.
7. 21 males, 14 females
8. B
9. **a)** $(2, -1)$ **b)** $(1, 1)$ **c)** $(-1, 1)$ **d)** $(2, 3)$
10. **a)** $x = 2, y = 3$ **b)** $x = 4, y = 11$
    c) $a = -1, b = 5$ **d)** $k = -0.5, h = 0.3$
11. Answers will vary.
12. **a)** $x = 5, y = 2$ **b)** $x = -0.1, y = -0.5$
    c) $x = -1, y = 2$ **d)** $x = 4, y = 5$
13. **a)** 10 km
    b) Choose company A for distances greater than 10 km.
14. $4200 at 5%/year, $5800 at 3.5%/year
15. average speed of the boat in still water 16 km/h, speed of the current 4 km/h
16. 200 kg of fertilizer with 30% nitrogen, 400 kg of fertilizer with 15% nitrogen
17. Fran earns $48 000; Winston earns $32 000.

Chapter 1 Practice Test, pages 50–51

1. **a)** Let m represent the number of men and w represent the number of women. $m + w = 20$; $m = w + 7$
   b) Let n represent the number. $7 + 2n = 3n$
2. Answers will vary.
3. **a)** $(7, -1)$ **b)** $x = 7, y = -1$
4. **a)** $x = 4, y = -5$ **b)** $a = 5, b = 0$
   c) $x = 1, y = -\frac{1}{3}$ **d)** $m = -6.4, n = -3.6$
5. **a)** The second equation is three times $y = \frac{2}{3}x - 3$, rearranged.
   b) Both linear systems have the same point of intersection, $(-3, -5)$.
   c) The first equation is twice $y = 2x + 1$, rearranged. The second equation is six times $y = \frac{2}{3}x - 3$, rearranged.
6. **a)** $x = 3, y = 5$ **b)** $x = \frac{5}{2}, y = -\frac{5}{3}$
   c) $k = 5, h = -2$ **d)** $p = -2.5, q = -8$
7. **a)** $x = 1, y = 3$ **b)** $x = -2, y = -7$
   c) $x = -2, y = 2$ **d)** $x = -1, y = -1$
8. Answers will vary.
9. $(0.2, 3.6), (1, 2), (1.8, 4.4)$
10. **a)** $G = \frac{1}{2}P$ **b)** $G + P = 48$
    c) Gregory works 16 h; Paul works 32 h.
11. Rolly answered 17 questions correctly.
12. length 33 m, width 15 m
13. adult $11.65, child $8.55

14. 11 nickels, 16 dimes
15. They charged $110 for 2 h of work.
16. **a)** $x = -2, y = -3$
    b) $c = 1.05, d = -2.1875$
    c) $x = 40, y = 5$
17. $20 000 at 5%/year, $30 000 at 10%/year
18. 320 L of 25% acid solution, 180 L of 50% acid solution
19. 400 km by bus, 1500 km by airplane

Chapter 2

Get Ready, pages 54–55

1. **a)** 4 **b)** 3 **c)** 24 **d)** 0.25
2. **a)** $y = x + 2$ **b)** $y = -3x + 5$
   c) $y = \frac{1}{2}x + \frac{7}{4}$ **d)** $y = \frac{1}{6}x + \frac{5}{3}$
3. **a)** $\frac{1}{2}$ **b)** $\frac{1}{2}$ **c)** $-\frac{2}{3}$ **d)** $-\frac{1}{4}$
4. **a)** $\frac{1}{2}$ **b)** $-\frac{1}{4}$ **c)** $-\frac{1}{2}$ **d)** $\frac{12}{73}$
5. **a)** $y = -2x + 4$ **b)** $y = \frac{2}{7}x - 14$
   c) $y = 4x - 21$ **d)** $y = -\frac{1}{2}x + 3$
6. **a)** $y = 2x - 1$ **b)** $y = \frac{3}{2}x + \frac{5}{2}$
   c) $y = \frac{1}{2}x + 3$ **d)** $y = -2x + 2$
7. **a)** 3 **b)** $-\frac{1}{6}$ **c)** $\frac{1}{4}$ **d)** $-\frac{4}{3}$
8. **a)** $y = -3x - 4$ **b)** $y = \frac{2}{3}x + \frac{5}{3}$
   c) $y = -\frac{3}{4}x - \frac{11}{4}$
9. **a)** 60° **b)** 2.5 cm
10. If P is any point on the right bisector of line segment AB and Q is the point of intersection of AB and the right bisector, then AQ = QB and ∠PQA = ∠PQB = 90°. Side PQ is common to △PQA and △PQB. Therefore, △PQA is congruent to △PQB (side-angle-side). PA and PB are corresponding sides, so PA = PB.

2.1 Midpoint of a Line Segment, pages 56–69

1. **a)** $(4, 6)$ **b)** $(1, 3)$
   c) $(2, 2)$ **d)** $\left(-\frac{1}{2}, -2\right)$
2. **a)** $(4, 8)$ **b)** $(0, -3)$
   c) $(-2, 2)$ **d)** $(-2, -5)$
3. **a)** $(1.9, 0.85)$ **b)** $(-0.4, -4.25)$
   c) $(1, 0)$ **d)** $\left(\frac{13}{16}, -\frac{3}{8}\right)$
4. **a)** $-\frac{5}{4}$ **b)** $\frac{12}{17}$
5. $(51.6, 40.9)$
6. $(-4, 3)$

7. Answers may vary.
   The Geometer's Sketchpad® example: Plot the endpoints, and construct the line segment between them. Construct the midpoint of this line segment. Then, select the midpoint and choose **Coordinates** from the **Measure** menu.
   Cabri® Jr. example: Choose **Point** from the **F2** menu to plot the endpoints. Choose **Coord. & Eq.** from the **F5** menu, and check the placement of the endpoints. Adjust the endpoints if necessary. Choose **Segment** from the **F2** menu, and construct the line segment between the endpoints. Choose **Midpoint** from the **F3** menu, and construct the midpoint. Then, choose **Coord. & Eq.** again to display the coordinates of the midpoint.

8. $y = \frac{1}{2}x + 2$

9. Answers may vary.
   The Geometer's Sketchpad® example: Plot the vertices of △ABC, and construct the midpoint, M, of side BC. Construct a line through AM. Select the line, and choose **Equation** from the **Measure** menu.
   Cabri® Jr. example: Choose **Point** from the **F2** menu, and plot the vertices of △ABC. Choose **Coord. & Eq.** from the **F5** menu, and check the placement of the vertices. Adjust the vertices if necessary. Choose **Segment** from the **F2** menu, and construct the line segment between vertices B and C. Select this line segment and choose **Midpoint** from the **F3** menu. Choose **Line** from the **F2** menu, and construct the line through the midpoint and vertex A. Then, choose **Coord. & Eq.** again to display the equation of the line.

10. a) $y = \frac{3}{13}x + \frac{6}{13}$ b) $y = 3x - 6$

11. Answers may vary.
    The Geometer's Sketchpad® example:
    a) Plot the vertices of △PQR. Construct the midpoint, S, of side QR. Construct a line through points P and S. Select the line, and choose **Equation** from the **Measure** menu.
    b) Construct the midpoint, T, of side PR, and the line though points Q and T. Select the line, and choose **Equation** from the **Measure** menu.
    Cabri® Jr. example:
    a) Choose **Point** from the **F2** menu, and plot the vertices of △PQR. Choose **Coord. & Eq.** from the **F5** menu, and check the placement of the vertices. Adjust the vertices if necessary. Choose **Segment** from the **F2** menu, and construct the line segment between vertices Q and R. Select this line segment, and choose **Midpoint** from the **F3** menu. Choose **Line** from the **F2** menu, and construct the line through the midpoint and vertex P. Then, choose **Coord. & Eq.** again to display the equation of the line.
    b) Use the method in part a) to construct the midpoint T of side PR and the line through points Q and T. Then, choose **Coord. & Eq.** from the **F5** menu to display the equation of the line.

12. $(2a, 1.5b)$; these coordinates are the mean of the x-coordinates of the endpoints and the mean of the y-coordinates of the endpoints.

13. a) $(2, -1)$
    b) Answers may vary. For example: Let the coordinates of the other endpoint be D(x, y). Solving the equation $\frac{x + 6}{2} = 4$ gives $x = 2$. Similarly, solving the equation $\frac{y + 5}{2} = 2$ gives $y = -1$.
       Alternative method: Since the run from C to M is -2, subtract 2 from the x-coordinate of M to find the x-coordinate of D. Since the rise from C to M is -3, subtract 3 from the y-coordinate of M to find the y-coordinate of D.
    c) Answers may vary. For example: Substitute the coordinates of points C and D into the midpoint formula to confirm that M is the midpoint of CD.

14. $(3, -4)$

15. a) $(-4, 0)$ or $(5, 6)$
    b) Answers may vary. For example: The centre of the circle could be either point D or point E.

16. $y = -x + 1$

17. a) Answers may vary. For example: Any point on the right bisector of a line segment is equidistant from the endpoints. Therefore, points on the right bisector of the line segment joining the two towns are possible locations for the relay tower.
    b) $y = \frac{4}{3}x - 5$

18. Answers may vary.
    The Geometer's Sketchpad® example: Plot the points A(2, 6) and B(10, 0). Construct the line segment AB and the midpoint of AB. Then, construct a perpendicular line through the midpoint. Select the perpendicular line, and choose **Equation** from the **Measure** menu.
    Cabri® Jr. example: Choose **Segment** from the **F2** menu, and plot the endpoints at points (2, 6) and (10, 0). Use **Coord. & Eq.** from the **F5** menu to check the placement of the endpoints, and adjust them if necessary. Select the line segment, and choose **Midpoint** from the **F3** menu. Choose **Perp.** from the **F3** menu, and construct the perpendicular line through the midpoint. Then, choose **Coord. & Eq.** again to display the equation of the line.

19. a)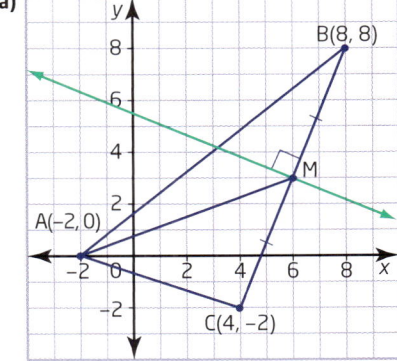

    b) $y = \frac{3}{8}x + \frac{3}{4}$ c) $y = -\frac{2}{5}x + \frac{27}{5}$

    d) Answers may vary. For example: Check that the slopes and y-intercepts on the drawing match those in the equations.

20. a), b), e)

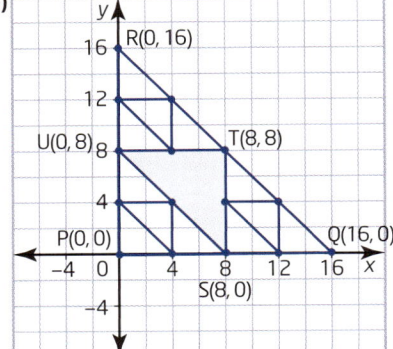

c) Answers may vary. For example: Since U is the midpoint of PR, RU = UP = $\frac{1}{2}$ PR. Since ST joins the midpoints of two sides of △PQR, ST = $\frac{1}{2}$ PR. Therefore, ST = RU = UP. Similarly, UT = PS = SQ and RT = TQ = US. Therefore, △RUT ≅ △UPS ≅ △STU ≅ △TSQ (side-side-side).

d) The area of △STU is $\frac{1}{4}$ the area of △PQR.

f) The area of one of the smallest triangles is $\frac{1}{4}$ the area of △STU and $\frac{1}{16}$ the area of △PQR.

21. b) Answers may vary. For example: Join the midpoints of the sides of an equilateral triangle to form four equilateral triangles inside the original triangle. Shade the centre triangle. For each of the other three triangles, repeat the process of joining the midpoints to form smaller similar triangles, and shade the centre triangle. The procedure works with any triangle. The area relationships are the same as shown in question 20 since the line segment joining the midpoints of two sides of any triangle is half the length of the third side.

c)

d) Answers may vary. For example: Sierpinski's triangle is a fractal since all of the smaller triangles in each step are similar to the original triangle.

22. 16
23. a) (5, 7) and (8, 13)
    b) Answers may vary. For example: For the first dividing point, add $\frac{1}{3}$ of the run to the x-coordinate of the first endpoint and add $\frac{1}{3}$ of the rise to the y-coordinate of the first endpoint. For the second dividing point, add $\frac{2}{3}$ of the run to the x-coordinate of the first endpoint and add $\frac{2}{3}$ of the rise to the y-coordinate of the first endpoint.

24. a) A(−1, −2), B(1, 6), C(3, 2)
    b) Substituting the coordinates of each pair of vertices should give the coordinates of one of the midpoints.
25. a) (4, 5, 3)
    b) M(x, y, z) = $\left(\frac{x_1 + x_2}{2}, \frac{y_1 + y_2}{2}, \frac{z_1 + z_2}{2}\right)$
26. Answers may vary. For example: All of the points equidistant from the first two towns lie on the right bisector of the line segment joining the two towns. Similarly, all of the points equidistant from the second and third towns lie on the right bisector of the line segment joining them. The point of intersection of these two right bisectors is the only location equidistant from all three towns.
27. a) Answers may vary. For example: Latitude and longitude are not linear coordinates since the distance between lines of longitude decreases as the distance from the equator increases. The midpoint formula is accurate only for Cartesian coordinates.
28. Explanations may vary.
    a) Sometimes true: Line segments can bisect each other without being equal in length.
    b) Never true: Parallel lines have no points in common.
    c) Always true: The midpoint is the only point that is both on the line segment and equidistant from the endpoints.
    d) Sometimes true: The midpoint of a line segment is equidistant from the endpoints, but so is every other point on the right bisector of the line segment.
29. c = 10, d = 7
30. D
31. C

2.2 Length of a Line Segment, pages 70–79

1. Estimates may vary. Calculated lengths:
   a) $\sqrt{5}$ b) $\sqrt{17}$ c) $\sqrt{68}$
2. a) $\sqrt{125}$ b) $\sqrt{90}$ c) $\sqrt{32}$ d) 10
3. a) 14.6   b) 21.3   c) $\sqrt{26}$
4. 5 km
5. a) The school at (0, 5) is closer to Jordan's house.
   b) Make a scale diagram and measure the distances with a ruler, or use geometry software to plot the points and measure the distances between them.
6. a) AB = AC = 10, BC = 16
   b) 36
   c) isosceles
7. a) Applying the length formula shows that DE = EF = DF = 2. Therefore, △DEF is equilateral.
   b) Answers may vary. For example: any enlargement of △DEF, such as (−2, 0), (2, 0), and (0, 2$\sqrt{3}$), or any translation, such as (0, 0), (2, 0) and (1, $\sqrt{3}$).
8. $\sqrt{\frac{41}{2}}$

9. Answers may vary.
The Geometer's Sketchpad® example: Plot the points J, K, and L. Construct line segment KL and its midpoint, M. Then, construct and measure line segment JM.
Cabri® Jr. example: Choose **Triangle** from the **F2** menu, and construct △JKL. Choose **Coord. & Eq.** from the **F5** menu, and display the coordinates of the vertices. Adjust the vertices if necessary. Choose **Midpoint** from the **F3** menu, and select side KL. Choose **Segment** from the **F2** menu, and construct the line segment from the midpoint to vertex J. Choose **Measure/D. & Length** from the **F5** menu, and select the median.

10. 36 square units

11. Answers may vary.
The Geometer's Sketchpad® example: Construct the triangle with vertices R, S, and T. Then, select and measure the interior of △RST.
Cabri® Jr. example: Choose **Triangle** from the **F2** menu, and construct △RST. Choose **Coord. & Eq.** from the **F5** menu, and display the coordinates of the points. Adjust the position of a vertex if its coordinates are not correct. Choose **Measure/Area** from the **F5** menu, and select △RST.

12. Applying the length formula shows that
$AC = CB = \sqrt{45} = \frac{1}{2} AB$.

13. a) $M\left(1, 2\frac{1}{2}\right)$
b) Both distances are $\sqrt{\frac{117}{4}}$, which is half of KL.

14. $53.55

15. a), b)

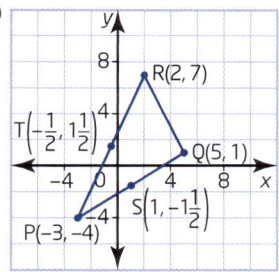

c) $ST = \frac{1}{2}\sqrt{45}$ and $QR = \sqrt{45}$
d) $m_{ST} = m_{QR} = -2$. Therefore, ST is parallel to QR.
e) Answers may vary. For example: Use the length formula to show that each side of △PST is exactly half the length of the corresponding side of △PQR.

16. Answers may vary.
The Geometer's Sketchpad® example:
a) Construct the triangle with vertices P, Q, and R.
b) Construct the midpoint of PQ and of PR. Then, display the coordinates of the midpoints.
c) Measure and compare the lengths of ST and QR.
d) Measure and compare the slopes of ST and QR.
e) Measure and compare either the side lengths or the angles of △PQR and △STU, where U is the midpoint of QR.

Cabri® Jr. example:
a) Choose **Triangle** from the **F2** menu, and construct △PQR. Choose **Coord. & Eq.** from the **F5** menu, and display the coordinates of the vertices. Adjust the vertices if necessary.
b) Choose **Midpoint** from the **F3** menu, and construct the midpoint of PQ and of PR. Choose **Coord. & Eq.** from the **F5** menu, and select the midpoints.
c) Choose **Measure/D. & Length** from the **F5** menu. Then, select ST and QR.
d) Choose **Measure/Slope** from the **F5** menu. Then, select ST and QR.
e) Use the **Measure** options in the **F5** menu to compare either the side lengths or the angles of △PQR and △STU, where U is the midpoint of QR.

17. a) Edmonton–Ottawa 2851 km; Montréal–Toronto 504 km; Edmonton–Toronto 2710 km
b) Answers may vary. For example: The flying distances are about 2840 km for Edmonton–Ottawa, 505 km for Montréal–Toronto, and 2705 km for Edmonton–Toronto. The telephone coordinate system gives distances that are close to the flying distances.

18. a) $(1, 0), (2, 0), \left(1\frac{1}{2}, -\frac{\sqrt{3}}{2}\right)$
b) Yes. Explanations may vary. For example: The sides inserted in each step are similar to two sides in the original triangle and the angle at each new point of the snowflake is equal to the angles in the original triangle.

20. a) 2
b) Yes. Explanations may vary. For example: The equation $5 = \sqrt{(2-x)^2 + (6-1)^2}$ simplifies to $(2-x)^2 = 0$, so $x = 2$.

21. a) Answers may vary. For example: For the simplest solutions, locate one endpoint at the origin. Substituting $x_1 = 0$ and $y_1 = 0$ into the length formula then shows that the sum of the squares of the x- and y-coordinates of the other endpoint equals the square of the required length. Example endpoints are **i)** (1, 1) **ii)** (2, 1) **iii)** (3, 2) **iv)** (5, 4)

22. a) $(5, 0), (0, 5), (-5, 0), (0, -5)$
b) $(7, 1), (2, 6), (-3, 1), (2, -4)$
c) $(5, -2), (-5, 8), (-15, -2), (-5, -12)$

23. $(-2, 11)$; 11.2 m

24. A

25. Answers may vary. For example: Substituting the Pythagorean relationship into the area formula for the large semicircle gives
$$\frac{1}{2}\pi a^2 = \frac{1}{2}\pi(b^2 + c^2)$$
$$= \frac{1}{2}\pi b^2 + \frac{1}{2}\pi c^2$$

2.3 Apply Slope, Midpoint, and Length Formulas, pages 80–91

1. $y = \frac{1}{2}x - \frac{1}{2}$

2. Answers may vary. For example: If the triangle has a right angle, the slopes of two of the sides are negative reciprocals of each other and the lengths of the sides are related by the Pythagorean theorem.

3. a)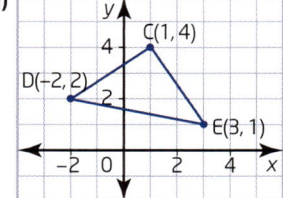

   b) $m_{CD} \times m_{CE} = -1$
4. $\sqrt{13}$
5. a) $m_{MN} = m_{QR} = 2$ b) $MN = 2\sqrt{5} = \frac{1}{2}QR$
6. Answers may vary. For example: Any point on the right bisector of a line segment is equidistant from the endpoints of the segment. Applying the length formula shows that $VT \neq UT$. Therefore, point T does not lie on the right bisector of UV.
7. a) $m_{OP} = m_{RQ} = \frac{5}{3}$ and $m_{PQ} = m_{OR} = \frac{1}{5}$. Therefore, opposite sides are parallel and OPQR is a parallelogram.
   b) Answers may vary. For example: Use geometry software to construct OPQR and measure the slope of each side. These slopes show that the opposite sides are parallel.
8. a) (3, 6) b) $\sqrt{37}$
9. Since $AB = AC = \sqrt{40}$, △ABC is isosceles.
10. $\frac{9}{\sqrt{5}}$
11. $\frac{4}{\sqrt{5}}$
12. $\frac{5\sqrt{1394}}{34}$
13. $\frac{30}{\sqrt{17}}$
14. $4\sqrt{5}$
15. Answers may vary.
    The Geometer's Sketchpad® example:
    a) Construct line segment AB and point R. Construct a perpendicular from point R to AB. Construct point D, the point of intersection of the perpendicular and AB. Display the coordinates of point D. Line segment RD represents the shortest route. Measure the length of RD, and multiply by 0.5 to find the length of the side road in kilometres.
    b) Construct △ABC. Measure the angles or compare the slopes of the sides to determine that ∠ACB is a right angle.
    c) Construct the midpoint, D, of side AB. Construct line segment CD. Measure and compare the lengths of AB and CD.
    Cabri® Jr. example:
    a) Choose **Segment** from the **F2** menu, and construct line segment AB. Choose **Coord. & Eq.** from the **F5** menu, and display the coordinates of the points. Adjust their positions if necessary. Choose **Point** from the **F2** menu, and construct point R. Choose **Perp.** from the **F3** menu, and construct the perpendicular from point R to AB. Choose **Coord. & Eq.** from the **F5** menu, and select point D, the point of intersection of the perpendicular and AB. Line segment RD represents the shortest route. Choose **Measure/D. & Length** from the **F5** menu, and select RD. Multiply the displayed length by 0.5 to find the length of the side road in kilometres.
    b) Choose **Triangle** from the **F2** menu, and construct △ABC. Choose **Coord. & Eq.** from the **F5** menu, and display the coordinates of the vertices. Adjust the vertices if necessary. Choose **Measure** from the **F5** menu. Then, choose **Angle** and measure the angles of △ABC, or choose **Slope** and measure the slopes of the three sides. Both sets of measurements show that ∠ACB is a right angle.
    c) Choose **Midpoint** from the **F3** menu, and select side AB. Choose **Segment** from the **F2** menu, and construct line segment CD. Choose **Measure/D. & Length** from the **F5** menu, and select AB and CD.
16. (6, 0). Methods may vary. For example: Find an equation for the line that is parallel to AB and passes through point C. Then, find an equation for the line that is parallel to BC and passes through point A. Vertex D is the point of intersection of these two lines. Alternative method: The run and rise from vertex B to vertex C are the same as those from vertex A to vertex D. Therefore, adding this run and rise to the coordinates of vertex A gives the coordinates of vertex D.
17. a) $y = -\frac{1}{2}x - 1$ b) $2\sqrt{5}$
18. a)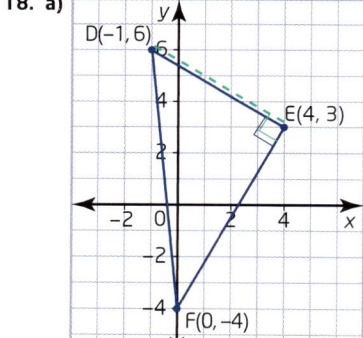

    b) $y = -\frac{4}{7}x + \frac{38}{7}$
19. Answers may vary.
    The Geometer's Sketchpad® example:
    a) Construct the triangle with vertices D, E, and F. Then, construct the perpendicular from D to EF.
    b) Select the perpendicular and choose **Equation** from the **Measure** menu.
    Cabri® Jr. example:
    a) Choose **Triangle** from the **F2** menu, and construct △DEF. Choose **Coord. & Eq.** from the **F5** menu, and display the coordinates of the vertices. Adjust the vertices if necessary. Choose **Perp.** from the **F3** menu, and construct the perpendicular from D to EF.

b) Choose **Coord. & Eq.** from the **F5** menu, and select the perpendicular.

20. a) Since $m_{PQ} = m_{RS} = \frac{4}{3}$ and $m_{PS} = m_{QR} = -\frac{3}{4}$, each pair of adjacent sides is perpendicular.
b) $PR = QS = 5\sqrt{5}$
c) The midpoint of both diagonals is $\left(\frac{1}{2}, 3\right)$.
d) The diagonals bisect each other.

21. a) $y = 2x - 8$ **b)** $\dfrac{26}{\sqrt{5}}$
c) 39 square units

22. Answers may vary.
The Geometer's Sketchpad® example:
a) Construct the triangle with vertices J, K, and L. Construct the perpendicular from L to JK. Construct point M, the point of intersection of the perpendicular and JK. Construct line segment LM. Measure the length of LM.
b) Select the perpendicular, and choose **Equation** from the **Measure** menu.
c) Select the interior of △JKL and choose **Area** from the **Measure** menu.
Cabri® Jr. example:
a) Choose **Triangle** from the **F2** menu, and construct △JKL. Choose **Coord. & Eq.** from the **F5** menu, and display the coordinates of the vertices. Adjust the vertices if necessary. Choose **Perp.** from the **F3** menu, and construct the perpendicular from L to JK. Choose **Measure/D. & Length** from the **F5** menu, and select the endpoints of the altitude.
b) Choose **Coord. & Eq.** from the **F5** menu, and select the perpendicular.
c) Choose **Measure/Area** from the **F5** menu, and select △JKL.

23. a) (10.8, 9.4) **b)** 85 m
24. a) (4.5, 6.5)
b) Answers may vary. For example: The shortest route might be blocked by fences or thick woods, or it might involve trespassing on private land.

25. a)

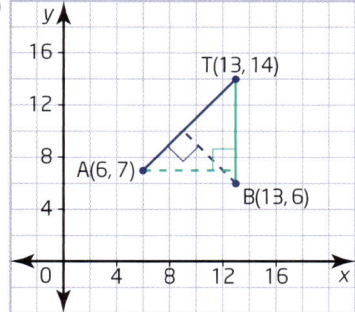

b) Connect the transformer to cottage B, and continue to cottage A.

26. Answers may vary.
The Geometer's Sketchpad® example:
a) Plot the points A, B, and T. Construct line segment AT and the perpendicular from AT to B. Construct point C where the perpendicular meets AT. Then, construct line segment BT and the perpendicular from BT to A. Construct point D where the perpendicular meets BT.
b) Measure the lengths of AT, BC, BT, and AD. Use these measurements to show that BT + AD is less than AT + BC.
Cabri® Jr. example:
a) Choose **Point** from the **F2** menu, and plot the points A, B, and T. Choose **Coord. & Eq.** from the **F5** menu, and display the coordinates of the points. Adjust the points if necessary. Choose **Segment** from the **F2** menu, and construct line segments AT and BT. Choose **Perp.** from the **F3** menu, and construct the perpendicular from B to AT. Label the point of intersection C. Similarly, construct the perpendicular from A to BT, and label the point of intersection D.
b) Choose **Measure/D. & Length** from the **F5** menu, and select AT, BC, BT, and AD. Use these measurements to show that BT + AD is less than AT + BC.

28. a)

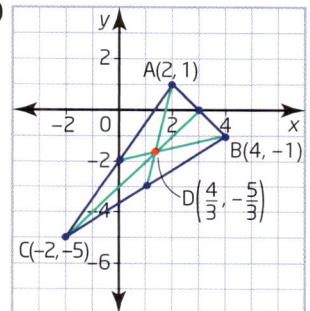

b) Find the point of intersection of two of the medians. Then, verify that the coordinates of this point satisfy the equation for the third median. The centroid is $\left(\frac{4}{3}, -\frac{5}{3}\right)$.

29. The median to the hypotenuse of a right triangle is half as long as the hypotenuse. Methods may vary.
The Geometer's Sketchpad® example: Construct any line and a perpendicular to it. Construct point A where the perpendicular meets the line. Construct point B anywhere on the line and point C anywhere on the perpendicular. Construct line segment BC and the midpoint, D, of BC. Construct line segment AD. Measure and compare the lengths of AD and BC. Observe the ratio of these lengths while dragging point B along the line and point C along the perpendicular.
Cabri® Jr. example: Choose **Line** from the **F2** menu, and construct any line. Choose **Perp.** from the **F3** menu, and construct a line perpendicular to the first line. Choose **Point/Intersection** from the **F2** menu, and construct point A, the intersection of the two lines. Choose **Point/Point on**, and construct point B on the first line and point C on the second line. Choose **Segment** from the **F2** menu, and construct line segment BC. Choose **Midpoint** from the **F3** menu, and construct point D, the midpoint of BC. Construct line segment AD. Choose **Measure/D. & Length** from the **F5** menu, and select BC and AD. Move the cursor to point B, and press ALPHA. Observe the ratio of the lengths of BC and AD while sliding point B along the first line. Slide point C along the other line.

30. a) $\sqrt{41}$
   b) $d = \sqrt{(x_1 - x_2)^2 + (y_1 - y_2)^2 + (z_1 - z_2)^2}$
31. a) Use slopes to show that CE and DF are perpendicular to AB.
   b) 144 m   **c)** (75.5, 45)   **d)** No. CD > CE + DF
32. A
33. C

2.4 Equation for a Circle, pages 92–99

1. a) $x^2 + y^2 = 9$ **b)** $x^2 + y^2 = 64$
   c) $x^2 + y^2 = 100$ **d)** $x^2 + y^2 = 5$
   e) $x^2 + y^2 = 12$ **f)** $x^2 + y^2 = 110$
2. a) 6; points on circle include (6, 0), (0, 6), (−6, 0), and (0, −6)
   b) 12; points on circle include (12, 0), (0, 12, (−12, 0), and (0, −12)
   c) $\sqrt{20}$; points on circle include (2, 4), (−2, 4), (−2, −4), (2, −4), (4, 2)
   d) $\sqrt{50}$; points on circle include (5, 5), (5, −5), (−5, −5), (−5, 5)
   e) 1.3; points on circle include (1.3, 0), (0, 1.3), (−1.3, 0), and (0, −1.3)
3. a) $x^2 + y^2 = 25$ **b)** $x^2 + y^2 = 29$
   c) $x^2 + y^2 = 45$ **d)** $x^2 + y^2 = 193$
4. a) on   **b)** inside   **c)** outside
   d) on   **e)** outside   **f)** on
5. No.
6. $x^2 + y^2 = 25$
7. a) Substituting the coordinates into the equation gives $a^2 = 36$. Therefore, a can be either 6 or −6.
   b) Graph the circle $x^2 + y^2 = 100$. The points (6, 8) and (−6, 8) are both on this circle.
8. a) 50.3 m   **b)** 201 m²
9. a)

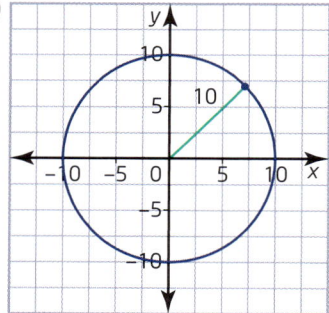

b) The coordinates (−8, 6) and (6, 8) both satisfy the equation of the circle.
   c) $y = -7x$
   d) The coordinates (0, 0) satisfy the equation $y = -7x$.
   e) Answers may vary. For example: Since the endpoints of any chord lie on a circle, they are equidistant from the centre of the circle. All points equidistant from the endpoints of a line segment lie on the right bisector of the line segment. Therefore, the right bisector of any chord of a circle passes through the centre of the circle.

10. a)

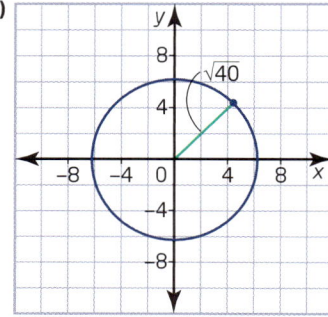

b) The coordinates of points R and S satisfy the equation of the circle.
   c) $y = x$
   d) Since $m_{OM} = 1$ and $m_{RS} = -1$, the line is perpendicular to RS.

11. a)

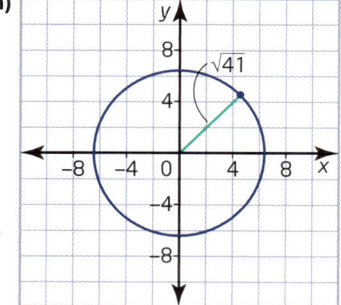

b) The coordinates of points U and V satisfy the equation of the circle.
   c) $y = -\dfrac{1}{9}x$
   d) The midpoint coordinates $\left(-4\dfrac{1}{2}, \dfrac{1}{2}\right)$ satisfy the equation $y = -\dfrac{1}{9}x$.

12. The right bisector of any chord of a circle passes through the centre of the circle. Methods may vary. *The Geometer's Sketchpad®* example: Construct any circle and a line segment between two points on the circle. Construct the right bisector of the line segment. Choose **Animate Point** from the **Display** menu, and animate either endpoint of the line segment. Observe whether the right bisector continues to pass through the centre of the circle. Also, try varying the radius of the circle.
Cabri® Jr. example: Choose **Circle** from the **F2** menu, and construct any circle. Choose **Segment** from the **F2** menu, and construct any line segment with both endpoints on the circumference of the circle. Choose **Perp. Bis.** from the **F3** menu, and select the line segment. Move the cursor to either endpoint of the line segment, and press ALPHA. Drag the endpoint around the circumference of the circle and observe whether the right bisector continues to pass through the centre of the circle. Also, try varying the radius of the circle.

13. a), c), d)

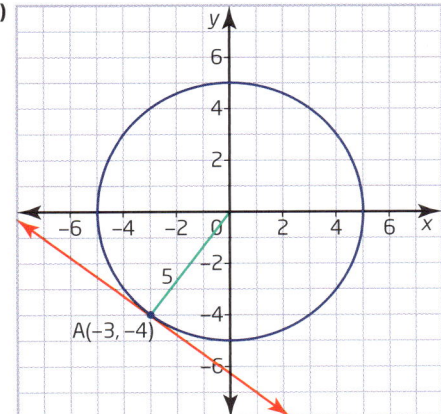

b) The coordinates of point A satisfy the equation $x^2 + y^2 = 25$.

e) $y = -\frac{3}{4}x - \frac{25}{4}$

f) Answers may vary. For example: The tangent touches the circle at point A. Since the circle curves away from the tangent on both sides of point A, the tangent does not touch the circle at any other point.

14. Answers may vary. For example: The point that is equidistant from the three homes is the centre of the circle that passes through all three homes. A line segment joining any two of the homes is a chord of the circle. The point of intersection of the right bisectors of two of these chords is the centre of the circle. Brandon could draw these right bisectors on a city map and then look for a restaurant near the point where they intersect.

15. Yes.

16. The blocks will not fit in the smallest cup.

17. a) $x^2 + y^2 = 250\,000$ **b)** 180 s

c) Answers may vary. For example: Wind or water currents do not move the rowboat or change the shape or speed of the ripple as it travels.

18. a) the region inside the circle centred at (0, 0) with radius 5

b) the region outside the circle centred at (0, 0) with radius 7

c) the region between the circle centred at (0, 0) with radius 5 and the circle centred at (0, 0) with radius 7

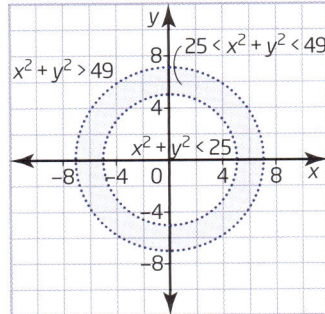

19. $x^2 + y^2 = 8$

20. a) $x^2 + y^2 = 16$ **b)** B(0, 2), D(2, 0)

c) AB, $y = -\frac{1}{2}x + 2$; CD, $y = -2x + 4$

d) $\left(\frac{4}{3}, \frac{4}{3}\right)$ **e)** $4\pi - \frac{16}{3}$, or about 7.2 square units

21. a) 5 m

b)

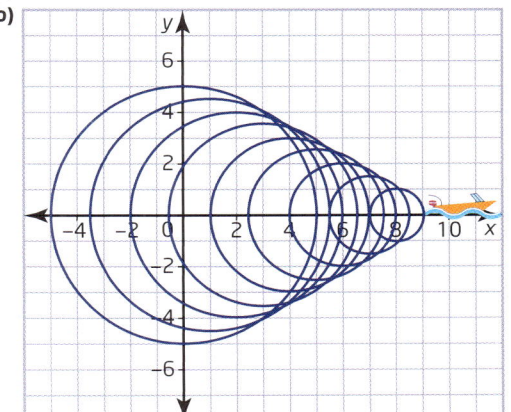

c) At the points of intersection, the waves add together to form a V-shaped wake behind the boat.

22. $(x - 4)^2 + (y - 3)^2 = 25$

23. Answers may vary. For example: No circle with $1 < r < 2$ has any points for which both the x- and y-coordinates are integers.

24. a)

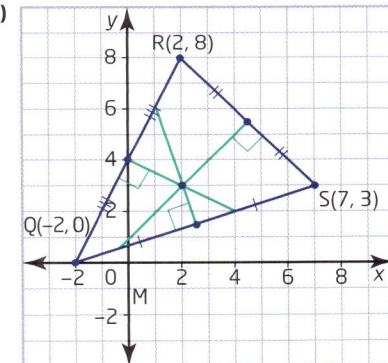

b) The coordinates (2, 3) satisfy the equations of all three of the right bisectors.

c) QC = RC = SC = 5

d) The circle has radius 5 and centre (2, 3).

e) Answers may vary.
The Geometer's Sketchpad® example: Construct △QRS and the right bisector of each side. Construct the point of intersection of the right bisectors and confirm that all three intersect at the same point. Measure the distance from each vertex to the point of intersection of the right bisectors. The distance in part c) is the radius of the circle. Display the coordinates of the point of intersection, which is the centre of the circle. Cabri® Jr. example: Choose **Triangle** from the **F2** menu, and construct △QRS. Choose **Coord. & Eq.** from the **F5** menu, and check the placement of the vertices. Adjust the vertices if necessary. Choose **Perp. Bis.** from the **F3** menu, and select each side of △QRS. Choose **Point/Intersection** from the **F2** menu, and select the three right bisectors. Choose **Measure/D. & Length** from the **F5** menu, and measure the distance from each vertex to the point of intersection of the right bisectors. The distance in part is the radius of the circle. Choose **Coord. & Eq.** from the **F5** menu, and select the point of intersection to display the coordinates of the centre of the circle.

25. $\dfrac{r}{\sqrt{k}}$

26. **a)** ellipse (a type of oval) with its length along the *x*-axis
    b) ellipse with its length along the *y*-axis

Chapter 2 Review, pages 100–103

1. **a)** (1, 2) **b)** (1.5, 2)
   c) (2.5, 4) **d)** (148, 126)
2. **a)** (−1, −5.5) **b)** (4, 3)
3. **a), c)**

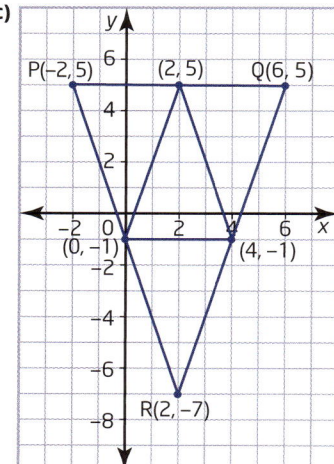

   b) (2, 5), (4, −1), and (0, −1)
   c) The smaller triangle is similar to △PQR and has $\dfrac{1}{4}$ the area.

4. **a)**

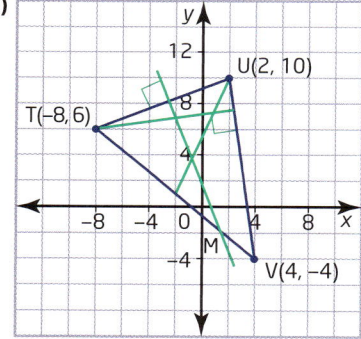

   b) $y = \dfrac{9}{4}x + \dfrac{11}{2}$ **c)** $y = \dfrac{1}{7}x + \dfrac{50}{7}$
   d) $y = -\dfrac{5}{2}x + \dfrac{1}{2}$

5. **a)**

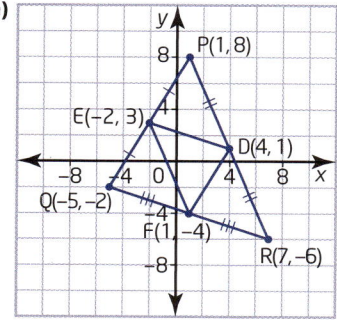

   b) (1, 8), (−5, −2), (7, −6)

c) Answers may vary.
The Geometer's Sketchpad® example: Plot points D, E, and F. Construct line segments DE, EF, and DF. Construct a line through D parallel to EF, a line through E parallel to DF, and a line through F parallel to DE. Construct the points of intersection and display their coordinates.
Cabri® Jr. example: Choose **Point** from the **F2** menu, and construct △QRS. Choose **Coord. & Eq.** from the **F5** menu, and check the placement of the midpoints. Adjust the placement if necessary. Choose **Segment** from the **F2** menu, and construct line segments DE, EF, and DF. Choose **Parallel** from the **F3** menu, and construct a line through D parallel to EF, a line through E parallel to DF, and a line through F parallel to DE. Choose **Point/Intersection** from the **F2** menu, and construct the three points of intersection of the lines. Choose **Coord. & Eq.** from the **F5** menu, and select the points of intersection.

6. **a)** 13 **b)** 10 **c)** $\sqrt{98}$ **d)** $12\dfrac{1}{2}$
7. **a)** 10 **b)** 13 **c)** $\sqrt{128}$
   d) $\sqrt{61}$ **e)** 9 **f)** $\sqrt{65}$
8. **a)** $\sqrt{\dfrac{325}{4}}$ **b)** $\sqrt{117} + \sqrt{73} + \sqrt{82}$, or about 28.4
9. **a)**

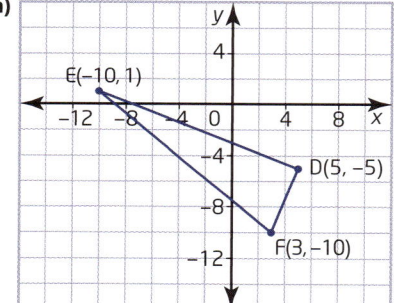

   b) right triangle **c)** $43\dfrac{1}{2}$ square units
   d) Answers may vary.
   The Geometer's Sketchpad® example: Construct △DEF. Measure the angles and side lengths. Select the interior of △DEF, and choose **Area** from the **Measure** menu.
   Cabri® Jr. example: Choose **Triangle** from the **F2** menu, and construct △DEF. Choose **Coord. & Eq.** from the **F5** menu, and check the placement of the midpoints. Adjust the vertices if necessary. Choose **Measure/D. & Length** from the **F5** menu, and select the sides of △DEF. Choose **Measure/Angle**, and select the angles of △DEF. Choose **Measure/Area**, and select △DEF.

10. AC = BC = 5
11. **a)** $m_{DE} = \dfrac{5}{2}$ and $m_{DF} = -\dfrac{2}{5}$; therefore, ∠DEF = 90°.
    b) $\left(2, 2\dfrac{1}{2}\right)$
    c) The distance from the midpoint to each vertex is $\sqrt{\dfrac{145}{4}}$.

12. a) 28.3 km **b)** (55, 50)
   c) No, the coordinates (63, 54) do not satisfy the equation $y = -x + 105$.
   d) From point C, run a straight pipe that meets the main pipeline at a right angle at (57, 48).
13. $\sqrt{10}$
14. a) $x^2 + y^2 = 16$ **b)** $x^2 + y^2 = 34$ **c)** $x^2 + y^2 = 29.16$
15. a) $x^2 + y^2 = \dfrac{81}{4}$ **b)** $x^2 + y^2 = 49$
   c) $x^2 + y^2 = 12$ **d)** $x^2 + y^2 = 65$
16. a) Point A lies on the circle.
   b) $r = \sqrt{(x+2)^2 + (y+6)^2}$
   c) $y = -\dfrac{1}{3}x - \dfrac{20}{3}$
   d)
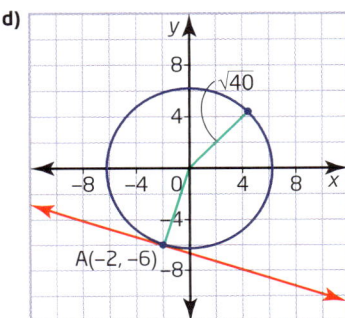
   e) Answers may vary. For example: On either side of point A, the circle curves away from the tangent line.
17. a) Since both $(-3, 1)$ and $(1, 3)$ satisfy the equation $x^2 + y^2 = 10$, the line segment connecting them is a chord of the circle.
   b) $y = -2x$
   c) Since $(0, 0)$ satisfies the equation $y = -2x$, the line passes through the centre of the circle.
18. Yes.

Chapter 2 Practice Test, pages 104–105

1. C
2. C
3. D
4. EF: midpoint $\left(-3, -\dfrac{1}{2}\right)$, length 7; GH: midpoint (1, 4), length 4; IJ: midpoint $\left(\dfrac{1}{2}, -2\dfrac{1}{2}\right)$, length $\sqrt{74}$; KL: midpoint $\left(5, -3\dfrac{1}{2}\right)$, length $\sqrt{13}$
5. **a)** $x^2 + y^2 = 36$
   b) $x^2 + y^2 = 18$
6. Answers may vary. For example: No, any point on the right bisector of BC is equidistant from points B and C.
7. **a)** 11.2 km
   b) (9, 5.5)
   c) Answers may vary. For example: Any point on the perpendicular bisector of PS will be equidistant from the two schools.
   d) $y = -2x + 23\dfrac{1}{2}$

8. a)
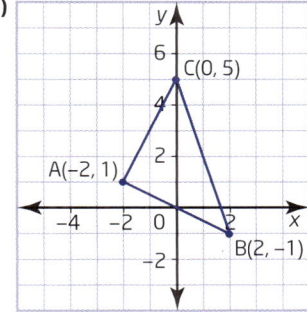
   b) AB = AC = $\sqrt{20}$, BC = $\sqrt{40}$
   c) AB = AC ≠ BC. Since $m_{AC} = 2$ and $m_{AB} = -\dfrac{1}{2}$, AB is perpendicular to AC. Therefore, △ABC is an isosceles right triangle.
   d) 10 square units
   e) Answers may vary.
   The Geometer's Sketchpad® example: Construct △ABC. Measure each side. Compare the lengths of the sides and the measures of the angles. Select the interior of △ABC, and choose **Area** from the **Measure** menu.
   Cabri® Jr. example: Choose **Triangle** from the **F2** menu, and construct △ABC. Choose **Coord. & Eq.** from the **F5** menu, check the placement of the vertices, and adjust them if necessary. Choose **Measure/D. & Length** from the **F5** menu, and select the sides of △ABC. Compare the lengths of the sides. Choose **Measure/Angle**, and select the angles of △ABC. Choose **Measure/Area**, and select △ABC.

9. a)
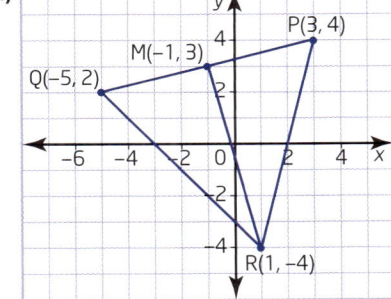
   b) $y = -\dfrac{7}{2}x - \dfrac{1}{2}$
   c) No. Explanations may vary. For example: The slope of PQ is not the negative reciprocal of the slope of the median. Therefore, the median is not perpendicular to PQ and is not an altitude of the triangle.
10. a) $(-3, 5)$ **b)** Yes, (3, 5) also lies on the circle.
   c) $x^2 + y^2 = 34$
   d) Substitute the coordinates (3, 5) into the equation $x^2 + y^2 = 34$ to see if they satisfy the equation.
   e) Answers may vary. For example: $(-3, -5), (-5, 3), (5, 3), (0, \sqrt{34})$
11. a) G(3, 8); H(6, 4)
   b) $m_{GH} = m_{DE} = -\dfrac{4}{3}$; therefore, GH is parallel to DE.
   c) Applying the length formula gives GH = 5 and DE = 10.

12. a) Answers may vary. For example: Since $m_{UV} = 2$ and $m_{WV} = -\frac{1}{2}$, $\angle WVU = 90°$.

b) Use the length formula to show that the length of the median is 5 and the length of the hypotenuse is 10.

c) $x^2 + y^2 = 25$

d) Answers may vary.
The Geometer's Sketchpad® example: Construct △UVW, and measure each angle. Construct the midpoint, M, of side UW. Construct line segment VM. Measure the length of UW and of VM. Construct the circle with centre M and radius 5. Select the circle and choose **Equation** from the **Measure** menu. Cabri® Jr. example: Choose **Triangle** from the **F2** menu, and construct △UVW. Choose **Coord. & Eq.** from the **F5** menu, check the placement of the vertices, and adjust them if necessary. Choose **Measure/Angle** from the **F5** menu, and select the angles of △UVW. Choose **Midpoint** from the **F3** menu, and construct the midpoint, M, of side UW. Choose **Segment** from the **F2** menu, and select points V and M. Choose **Measure/D. & Length** from the **F5** menu, and select UW and VM. Choose **Circle** from the **F2** menu, and construct the circle with centre M and radius 5. Choose **Coord. & Eq.** from the **F5** menu and select the circle.

13. a)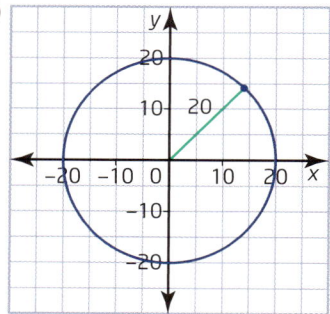

b) $x^2 + y^2 = 400$

c) No, Diane is 20.4 km away from the office.

d) Yes, Diane and Arif are only 12.6 km apart.

Chapter 3

Get Ready, pages 108–109

1. a) $\left(1\frac{1}{2}, 1\frac{1}{2}\right)$ **b)** $(1, -1)$ **c)** $\left(4, 1\frac{1}{2}\right)$ **d)** $(-3, 5)$

2. a) $\sqrt{74}$ **b)** $\sqrt{53}$ **c)** 9 **d)** 10

3. a) $(3, -1)$ **b)** $(-1, 3)$ **c)** $(2, -1)$

4. a) $(-1, -2)$ **b)** $(4, -3)$ **c)** $(-2, -1)$

5. a) $\angle D = 55°$ **b)** $\angle G = 30°$

6. a) $\angle J = \angle K = 70°$ **b)** $\angle P = 80°, \angle R = 50°$

7. a) A rectangle has four sides and four right angles.

b) A parallelogram is a quadrilateral with opposite sides parallel.

c) A trapezoid is a quadrilateral with two sides parallel.

8.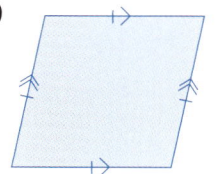

3.1 Investigate Properties of Triangles, pages 110–116

1. 6 square units

2. 30 square units

3. a) JL and KM
b) $\angle MJK = \angle MLK$, $\angle JMK = \angle LMK$, and $\angle JKM = \angle LKM$

4. the bisector of $\angle R$, the altitude from vertex R, and the right bisector of side PQ

5. a) Answers will vary.
b) In an isosceles triangle, the altitude from the vertex between the equal sides bisects the angle at the vertex, bisects the opposite side, and coincides with the median from the vertex.
c) Use compasses or a ruler and protractor to verify that the altitude bisects the opposite side and the angle at the vertex.

6. No. Explanations may vary. For example: The triangle could be isosceles since the median from the vertex between the equal sides is also an angle bisector.

7. a) Answers will vary.
b) The distances are equal.
c) The relationship applies to all right triangles. Methods may vary. For example: Let $A(0, 0)$, $B(x, 0)$, and $C(0, y)$ be the vertices of a right triangle. Find the coordinates of M, the midpoint of the hypotenuse BC. Substitute into the length formula to get expressions for the lengths of AM, BM, and CM. Alternatively, use geometry software to construct two perpendicular lines and their point of intersection. Construct another point on each line. Then, form a right triangle by constructing line segments joining the three points. Construct the midpoint of the hypotenuse. Measure the distance from the midpoint to each vertex. Compare these distances while dragging the vertices of the triangle along the perpendicular lines.

8. Answers may vary. For example: Each median bisects the angle at a vertex. Each median is perpendicular to the opposite side. Each altitude bisects a side. The medians are equal in length. The altitudes are equal in length. Each right bisector of a side passes through a vertex and bisects the angle at the vertex. Congruent triangles or geometry software can be used to show that these properties apply for all equilateral triangles.

9. Alana is correct. Explanations may vary. For example: In an equilateral triangle, the angle bisectors and the right bisectors of the sides coincide. Therefore, the point of intersection of the angle bisectors is also the point of intersection of the right bisectors (the circumcentre and the incentre coincide).
10. **a)** The medians are divided in a 2:1 ratio.
    b) Answers may vary. For example: Draw at least one example of each type of triangle, and measure how the centroid divides all three medians in each triangle. Alternatively, use geometry software to construct a triangle and its medians. Measure from the centroid to either end of each median. Compare these measurements while dragging the vertices of the triangle.
    c) Draw any median. The balance point is on the median two thirds of the way from the vertex to the opposite side.
11. **a)** Answers will vary.
    b) The slopes are equal and DE is half the length of BC.
    c) The relationships apply for any triangle. Methods may vary. For example: Draw at least one example of each type of triangle. In each triangle, compare the slope and length of the line segment joining the midpoints of two sides to those of the third side. Alternatively, use geometry software to construct a triangle and the line segment joining the midpoints of two sides. Measure the slope and length of this segment and of the third side. Compare these measurements while dragging the vertices of the triangle.
12. **a)** Yes.
    b) Yes. Explanations may vary. For example: Angle bisectors drawn in examples of each type of triangle meet at a point in each triangle.
    c) The incentre is the centre of the circle that just touches each side of the triangle.
    d) The incentre is equidistant from each side of the triangle. Explanations may vary. For example: In examples of each type of triangle, a circle that is centred at the incentre and just touches one side of the triangle also just touches the other two sides.
13. Answers may vary. For example: Construct any triangle and the bisector of each of its angles. Observe the point of intersection of the three angle bisectors while dragging the vertices of the triangle. Measure the perpendicular distance from the point of intersection to each side. Compare these distances while dragging the vertices of the triangle. The angle bisectors always meet at a single point, which is equidistant from the sides of the triangle.
14. **a)** Every triangle has a circumcentre. Methods may vary. For example: Draw the right bisectors of the sides in at least one example of each type of triangle. Alternatively, use geometry software to construct a triangle and the right bisectors of its sides. Observe the point of intersection of the right bisectors while dragging the vertices of the triangle.
    b) The circumcentre is equidistant from the vertices. Explanations may vary. For example: The distances from the circumcentre to the vertices are equal in examples of each type of triangle. Alternatively, for a triangle constructed with geometry software, the distances remain equal when the vertices are dragged.
    c) On a map, draw a triangle with Hamilton, Oshawa, and Barrie at the vertices. Then, find the point of intersection of the right bisectors of the sides of the triangle.
15. The altitudes of any triangle meet at a single point. Methods may vary. For example: Draw the altitudes in at least one example of each type of triangle. Alternatively, use geometry software to construct the altitudes of a triangle, and observe their point of intersection while dragging the vertices of the triangle.
16. Answers will vary.
17. **a)** The area of the equilateral triangle on the hypotenuse equals the sum of the areas of the equilateral triangles on the other two sides. Methods may vary. For example: Use the Pythagorean theorem to find an expression for the height of each equilateral triangle. Write an expression for the area of each triangle, and use the Pythagorean theorem to show how the areas are related.
    b) Answers will vary. For example: Use geometry software to construct two perpendicular lines and their point of intersection. Construct another point on each line. Then, form a right triangle by constructing line segments joining the three points. Construct an equilateral triangle on each side. Measure the area of each equilateral triangle, and calculate the sum of the areas of the triangles on the two shorter sides. Compare this sum to the area of the triangle on the hypotenuse while dragging the vertices of the right triangle along the perpendicular lines.
18. **a)** $x = 72°$, $y = 36°$ **c)** about 1.62
    d) The ratio of the sides equals φ.
    e) Yes.
    f) Yes. The ratio of the sides equals φ.
    g) No.
19. Yes. Explanations may vary. For example: The incentre is the centre of the circle that just touches each side of the triangle (see question 12). Since this circle is inside the triangle, its centre also lies inside the triangle.
20. **a)** when the triangle is obtuse
    b) when the triangle is a right triangle
21. The centroid, orthocentre, and circumcentre of a triangle are collinear. Methods may vary. For example: Draw the medians, altitudes, and right bisectors of the sides in at least one example of each type of triangle. Then, check that a line can be drawn through the centroid, orthocentre, and circumcentre. Alternatively, use geometry software to construct a triangle and its centroid, orthocentre, and circumcentre. Construct a line through the centroid, orthocentre, and circumcentre. Drag the vertices of the triangle, and note whether the line continues to pass through all three centres.
22. **a)** when the triangle is obtuse
    b) when the triangle is a right triangle
    Methods may vary. For example: Find the orthocentre in several examples of each type of triangle. Alternatively, use geometry software to construct a triangle and its orthocentre. Then, observe the location of the orthocentre while dragging the vertices of the triangle.

23. Answers may vary. For example: Use similar triangles to show that each median of △ABC passes through the midpoint of a side of △DEF.

3.2 Verify Properties of Triangles, pages 117–127

1. a) $y = \frac{1}{3}x + \frac{4}{3}$ **b)** $y = -\frac{1}{5}x + \frac{11}{5}$ **c)** $x = 2$

2. a) $m_{DE} = m_{BC} = -\frac{2}{5}$
   b) EF is parallel to AB, and DF is parallel to AC.
   c) $DE = BF = \sqrt{29}$
   d) $DE = BF = FC$, $EF = AD = DB$, $DF = AE = EC$

3. $PQ = 2\sqrt{34}$, $ST = \sqrt{34}$

4. a) $AB = BC = 2\sqrt{13}$
   b) The slope of the median is the negative reciprocal of the slope of AC.

5. Answers may vary. For example:
   a) Construct △ABC. Measure and compare the lengths of AB, AC, and BC.
   b) Construct the midpoint, D, of side AC. Construct line segment BD. Measure ∠ADB.

6. a) $DE = \sqrt{80}$, $EF = DF = \sqrt{40}$
   b) $m_{DE} = 2$, $m_{EF} = \frac{1}{3}$, $m_{DF} = -3$
   c) Since $m_{EF} \times m_{DF} = -1$ and $EF = DF$, △DEF is an isosceles right triangle.

7. a) scalene right triangle
   b) $JK = \sqrt{338}$, $KL = \sqrt{104}$, $JL = \sqrt{234}$, and $m_{JL} \times m_{KL} = -1$.
   c) $\sqrt{338} + \sqrt{104} + \sqrt{234}$, or about 43.9
   d) 156 square units

8. Answers may vary. For example:
   a) Construct △JKL.
   b) Measure and compare the lengths and slopes of the three sides.
   c) Calculate the sum of the lengths of the sides.
   d) Measure the area of △JKL.

9. a)

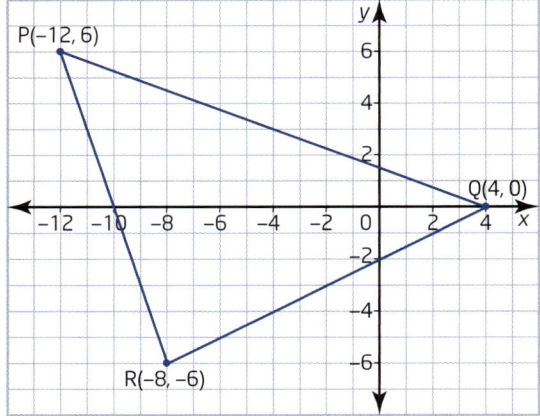

   b) $S(-10, 0)$, $T(-4, 3)$
   c) $m_{ST} = m_{RQ} = \frac{1}{2}$
   d) $ST = 3\sqrt{5}$, $QR = 6\sqrt{5}$

10. a)

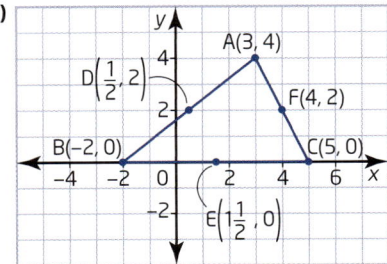

   b) $\frac{ED}{AC} = \frac{EF}{AB} = \frac{FD}{BC} = \frac{1}{2}$
   c) The area of △ABC is 14 square units, and the area of △DEF is 3.5 square units.
   d) The ratio of the areas is the square of the ratio of the lengths of corresponding sides.

11. Answers may vary. For example:
   a) Construct △ABC and the midpoints of its sides. Display the coordinates of the points.
   b) Measure and compare the lengths of the corresponding sides.
   c) Measure and compare the areas of △ABC and △DEF.
   d) Calculate and compare the ratio of the side lengths and the ratio of the areas.

12. a) The medians intersect at (4, 4).
   b) The stress on the support is minimized since the centroid is the balance point of the canopy.

13. a) $JK = KL = 5$, $m_{JK} \times m_{KL} = -1$
   b) Since $JK^2 + KL^2 = JL^2$, △JKL is a right triangle. Since $JK = KL = 5$, △JKL is also isosceles.

14. a) $x = 4$, $y = -x + 4$, $y = x - 4$
   b) (4, 0)
   c) isosceles right triangle since $OA = AB = \sqrt{32}$ and $m_{OA} \times m_{AB} = -1$
   d) the midpoint, (4, 0), of the hypotenuse

15. a) The coordinates $(-4, 4)$ satisfy the equations of all three right bisectors.
   b) $CD = CE = CF = \sqrt{260}$

16. a), c), d)

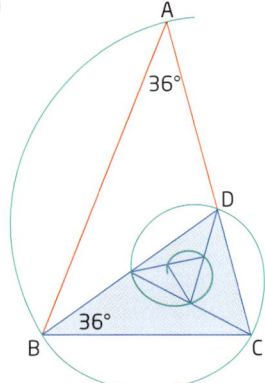

   b) In both triangles, the ratio of the unequal sides is $\frac{1 + \sqrt{5}}{2}$, or about 1.618. △ABC and △BCD are similar because the corresponding angles are equal.
   e) Yes, the curve in each step is similar to and smaller than the curve in the preceding step.

18. a) $S\left(\dfrac{a+c}{2}, \dfrac{b+d}{2}\right)$, $T\left(\dfrac{a+e}{2}, \dfrac{b+f}{2}\right)$

b) $m_{ST} = m_{QR} = \dfrac{f-d}{e-c}$

c) $ST = \dfrac{1}{2}\sqrt{(e-c)^2 + (f-d)^2}$,
$QR = \sqrt{(e-c)^2 + (f-d)^2}$

19. a) Answers will vary.
b) Since each median joins a vertex to the midpoint of the opposite sides, AD = DB, BE = EC, CF = FA, and $\dfrac{AD}{DB} \times \dfrac{BE}{EC} \times \dfrac{CF}{FA} = 1$.
c) Answers may vary. For example: Construct any △ABC and cevians from vertices A and B. Construct the point of intersection of the two cevians. Construct a line segment from vertex C through the point of intersection to side AB. Measure AD, DB, BE, EC, CF, and FA. Calculate $\dfrac{AD}{DB} \times \dfrac{BE}{EC} \times \dfrac{CF}{FA}$, and observe the value of this expression while dragging the vertices A, B, and C.

20. All of the triangles within the pentagon are golden triangles with either two 36° angles and one 108° angle or two 72° angles and one 36° angle.

21. Answers may vary. For example:

L.S. = φ^2
$= \left(\dfrac{1+\sqrt{5}}{2}\right)^2$
$= \dfrac{1 + 2\sqrt{5} + 5}{4}$
$= \dfrac{6 + 2\sqrt{5}}{4}$
$= \dfrac{3 + \sqrt{5}}{2}$

R.S. = $\varphi + 1$
$= \dfrac{1+\sqrt{5}}{2} + 1$
$= \dfrac{1 + \sqrt{5} + 2}{2}$
$= \dfrac{3 + \sqrt{5}}{2}$

L.S. = R.S.

22. C

3.3 Investigate Properties of Quadrilaterals, pages 128–136

1. a) AE = CE, BE = DE **b)** PT = RT, QT = ST
2. a) EF is parallel to HG and EH is parallel to FG.
b) TU is parallel to WV and TW is parallel to UV.
3. a) EF = HG, EH = FG **b)** TU = WV, TW = UV
4. a) AD, EG, and BC are parallel.
b) 10
5. 9
6. Answers may vary. For example: The diagonals of a square bisect one another and are perpendicular. The diagonals also bisect the angles at the vertices.
7. Answers may vary. For example: Use parallel lines to construct a parallelogram. Measure the lengths of the diagonals. Compare these lengths while dragging the vertices. When the diagonals are equal in length, measure and compare the vertex angles.
8. a) Rhombus. Explanations may vary. For example: Since AC and BD bisect each other at right angles, quadrilateral ABCD contains four congruent triangles (side-angle-side). Therefore, the sides of the quadrilateral are all equal in length.
b) Rectangle. Explanations may vary. For example: Since △AEH and △EBF are both isosceles, ∠A + 2∠AEH = 180° and ∠B + 2∠BEF = 180°. So, ∠A + ∠B + 2∠AEH + 2∠BEF = 360°. Since ∠A and ∠B are co-interior angles, ∠A + ∠B = 180°. Substituting into the preceding equation gives ∠AEH + ∠BEF = 90°. The interior angles at E sum to 180°, so ∠FEH = 90°. Similarly, ∠EFG = ∠FGH = ∠GHE = 90°.

9. Answers may vary. For example: Rectangular shapes are easy to make, measure, store, and fit together.
10. No, the quadrilateral could also be a rectangle.
11. Answers may vary. For example:
a) The diagonals of a rectangle are equal in length and bisect each other.
b) The diagonals of a kite are perpendicular and the diagonal joining the vertices between the equal sides bisects the other diagonal.
c) The diagonals bisect each other and are perpendicular.
e)

Shape	Equal Lengths	Perpendicular	Bisect Each Other	Bisect Vertex Angles
square	yes	yes	yes	yes
rectangle	yes	no	yes	no
parallelogram	no	no	yes	no
rhombus	no	yes	yes	yes
kite	no	yes	one	yes

12. Answers may vary. For example:
a) The balance point is at the point of intersection of the diagonals or of the line segments joining the midpoints of opposite sides.
b) Find the balance point of a cardboard rectangle, or show that the distribution of mass around the line segments joining the midpoints of opposite sides is symmetric.
13. Answers will vary.
15. a) when the quadrilateral is a kite or rhombus
b) when the quadrilateral is a square
c) when the quadrilateral is a rectangle
16. a) Yes. Explanations may vary. For example: The point of intersection of the diagonals of a rectangle is equidistant from the vertices.
b) No. Diagrams will vary.
17. Answers may vary. For example: If the fastenings at the corners of a rectangular brace loosen or bend, the brace can shift to a parallelogram shape or even collapse. The shape of a triangular brace cannot change without bending or separating the sides.
18. b) The wide Penrose rhombus is made up of two pairs of golden triangles, and the narrow Penrose rhombus is made up of two congruent golden triangles.

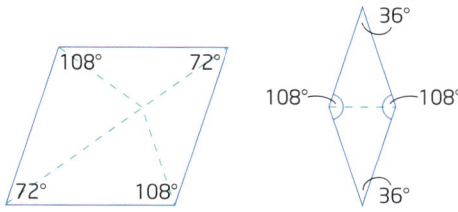

c) Aperiodic tiles can completely cover an infinite plane without any regular repetition of any sequence of the tiles.
d) Answers may vary. For example: Every finite portion of any Penrose tiling is contained infinitely often in every other tiling.
e) The lengths of the sides of both the Penrose dart and the Penrose kite are related by the golden ratio, and each shape can be divided into two golden triangles.

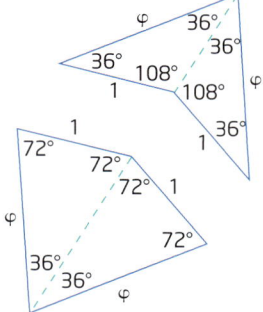

f) Answers will vary.

19. Answers may vary. For example:

L.S. $= \dfrac{1}{\varphi}$

$= \dfrac{2}{1 + \sqrt{5}}$

$= \dfrac{2}{1 + \sqrt{5}} \times \dfrac{1 - \sqrt{5}}{1 - \sqrt{5}}$

$= \dfrac{2 - 2\sqrt{5}}{1 - 5}$

$= \dfrac{2 - 2\sqrt{5}}{-4}$

$= \dfrac{-1 + \sqrt{5}}{2}$

R.S. $= \varphi - 1$

$= \dfrac{1 + \sqrt{5}}{2} - 1$

$= \dfrac{1 + \sqrt{5}}{2} - \dfrac{2}{2}$

$= \dfrac{-1 + \sqrt{5}}{2}$

$= \dfrac{1 - \sqrt{5}}{-2}$

$= \dfrac{-1 + \sqrt{5}}{2}$

L.S. = R.S.

3.4 Verify Properties of Quadrilaterals, pages 137–144

1. $m_{AD} = m_{BC} = \dfrac{1}{3}$
2. EF = FG = GH = EH = 5
3. JK = KL = $\sqrt{10}$, JM = LM = 5
4. a) Since $m_{AB} = m_{CD} = \dfrac{2}{3}$ and

   $m_{BC} = m_{AD} = -\dfrac{3}{2}$, all adjacent sides are perpendicular.

   b) AC = BD = $\sqrt{65}$, and $\left(-\dfrac{1}{2}, -2\right)$ is the midpoint of both AC and BD.

5. a), b)

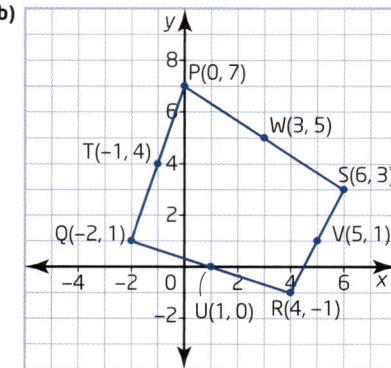

c) $m_{TU} = m_{WV} = -2$, $m_{UV} = m_{TW} = \dfrac{1}{4}$

d) TU = WV = $2\sqrt{5}$, UV = TW = $\sqrt{17}$

6. Answers may vary. For example:
   a) Construct quadrilateral PQRS.
   b) Construct the midpoint of each side and display the coordinates. Construct line segments joining adjacent midpoints.
   c) Measure and compare the slopes of the sides of TUVW.
   d) Measure and compare the lengths of the sides of TUVW.

7. a)

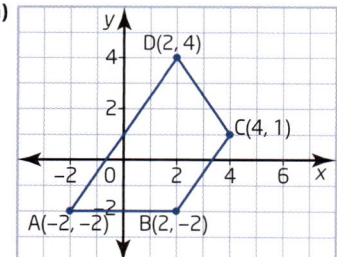

b) $m_{AD} = m_{BC} = m_{EF} = \dfrac{1}{2}$, where E and F are the midpoints of AB and CD, respectively.

8. Answers may vary. For example: Construct trapezoid ABCD and midpoints E and F of AB and CD, respectively. Construct line segment EF. Measure and compare the slopes of AB, CD, and EF.

9. a) (1, 0) is the midpoint of both of JL and MK; $m_{JL} \times m_{MK} = -1$.
   b) No.
   c) The lengths of the sides are equal since the four small triangles formed by the diagonals are all congruent (side-angle-side).

10. a) QT = TS, $m_{PR} \times m_{QS} = -1$
    b) PT ≠ RT

11. a)

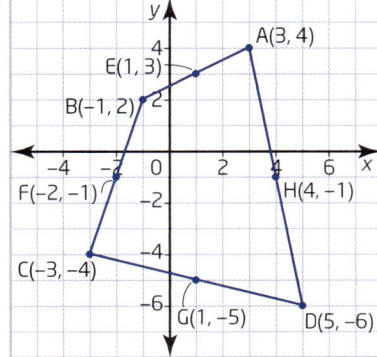

b) EF = FG = GH = EH = 5
c) Answers may vary. For example: Use the length formula to show that two adjacent sides have equal lengths. Since EFGH is a Varignon parallelogram, its opposite sides are equal in length. Therefore, all four sides have equal lengths.

12. a)

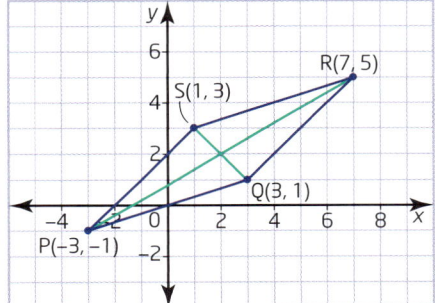

b) (2, 2) is the midpoint of both PR and SQ.
c) PQRS is a parallelogram since $m_{PS} = m_{QR} = 1$ and $m_{SR} = m_{PQ} = \frac{1}{3}$.

13. Answers may vary. For example:
  a) Construct quadrilateral PQRS, the diagonals PR and QS, and their point of intersection, T.
  b) Measure and compare the lengths of PT, QT, RT, and ST.
  c) Measure and compare the slopes and lengths of PQ, QR, RS, and RP.

14. a)

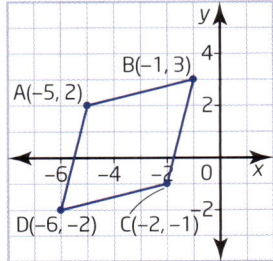

b) The slopes of the adjacent sides are negative reciprocals.

15. Answers may vary. For example:
  a) Construct quadrilateral ABCD.
  b) Construct the midpoint of each side and line segments joining the adjacent midpoints. Measure the angle at each vertex of the new quadrilateral.

16. b) about 1.618:1
  c) about 1.618:1; predictions may vary
  d) about 1.618:1
  e) The ratios are all about 1.618:1.
  f) Yes. Explanations may vary. For example: The smaller rectangle produced in each step is similar to the rectangles in the preceding steps.
  g) Answers may vary. For example: Draw the squares such that the position of each new square relative to the square in the previous step follows a clockwise sequence: right, down, left, up, right, down, and so on. Starting from the vertex farthest away from the second square, draw a smooth curve passing through every second vertex of the nested rectangles.

17. a) $T\left(\frac{a+c}{2}, \frac{b+d}{2}\right)$, $U\left(\frac{c+e}{2}, \frac{d+f}{2}\right)$, $V\left(\frac{e+g}{2}, \frac{f+h}{2}\right)$, $W\left(\frac{a+g}{2}, \frac{b+h}{2}\right)$

  b) $m_{TU} = m_{VW} = \frac{f-b}{e-a}$ and $m_{UV} = m_{TW} = \frac{h-d}{g-c}$

18. $\angle BAD + \angle BCD = 180°$
19. C

3.5 Properties of Circles, pages 145–151

1. a) (4, 8)   **b)** $-\frac{1}{2}$ **c)** $m_{AB} \times m_{OM} = -1$

2. a) CP = CQ = CR = 5
  b)

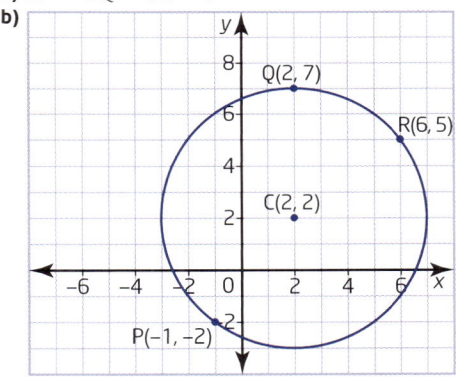

3. a) DA = DB = DC = $\sqrt{40}$ **b)** $2\sqrt{10}$
4. a) EH = FH = GH = $\sqrt{65}$ **b)** $\sqrt{65}$
5. O(0, 0) satisfies $y = -4x$, an equation for the right bisector of PQ.
6. a) Answers may vary. For example: Substituting into the distance formula shows that the distance from the origin to any point that satisfies $x^2 + y^2 = 45$ is $\sqrt{45}$.
  b) The coordinates of points R and S satisfy $x^2 + y^2 = 45$.
  c) $m_{RS} = 3$ and $m_{OM} = -\frac{1}{3}$, so $m_{RS} \times m_{OM} = -1$, where M is the midpoint of RS.
7. Answers may vary. For example: Draw any two chords on the circular part. Then, draw the right bisector of each chord. Mark the point of intersection of the right bisectors as the location for the hole.

8. a) 0.43 m² **b)** 0.56 m² **c)** 0.72 m²
   d) A circular base gives the maximum area for a given perimeter.
9. (−4, 0)
10. Answers may vary. For example: Construct line segments AB and BC. Construct the right bisectors of AB and BC. Construct the point of intersection of the right bisectors, and display its coordinates.
11. Answers may vary. For example: Fold Sudbury onto Toronto, and fold Windsor onto Toronto. Look for a park near the intersection of the two folds.
12. (12, 11)
13. △OMP ≅ △OMQ. Explanations may vary. For example: OP and OQ are equal radii, PM = QM, and OM is common to △OMP and △OMQ. Therefore, the triangles are congruent (side-side-side).
14. Answers may vary. For example: Join point L to point C, the centre of the circle. Since CJ = CL = CK, ∠CJL = ∠CLJ and ∠CKL = ∠CLK. The sum of the angles in △JKL is
∠CJL + ∠CLJ + ∠CLK + ∠CKL = 2∠CLJ + 2∠CLK
= 180°.
Since ∠JLK = ∠CLJ + ∠CLK, ∠JLK = 90°.
15. Answers may vary. For example: Construct a circle with diameter JK. Construct any point L on the circle and measure ∠JLK. Observe this angle measure while dragging or animating point L around the circumference of the circle.
16. Answers may vary. For example:
   a) Distances from the homes to the hospital are minimized, assuming that the homes are evenly spaced within the circle.
   b) The homes may be more spread out in some parts of the town. No suitable site may be available at the centre of the circle. Narrow streets or heavy traffic at the centre of the circle could make travel to a central location take longer than to an outlying location.
   c) Answers will vary.
17. a)

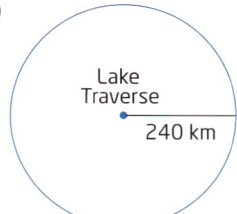

   b) 1.8 × 10⁵ km²
   c) Answers may vary. For example: The area between Lake Traverse and the planned destination should be searched first because the plane was probably still headed in that direction when it went missing.
18. ∠ABC = 180° − $\frac{1}{2}$∠AOC
19. D

Chapter 3 Review, pages 152–153

1. Answers may vary. For example:
   a) a line segment that joins a vertex of a triangle to the midpoint of the opposite side
   b) The medians of a triangle meet at a single point, the centroid. Each median bisects the area of the triangle.
   c) Construct a triangle and the midpoints of its sides. Construct a line segment from each vertex to the midpoint of the opposite side. Construct and measure the areas of the two triangles formed by each median. Observe the point of intersection of the medians and the area measures while dragging the vertices of the original triangle.
2. Answers may vary. For example:
   a) Since AB = AC, ∠MBC = ∠NCB. MB = NC, and side BC is common to △MBC and △NCB. Therefore, △MBC ≅ △NCB (side-angle-side), and MC = NB.
   b) Construct an isosceles △ABC with AB = AC. Construct the midpoints of AB and AC. Construct a line segment joining each midpoint to the opposite vertex. Measure the lengths of these line segments and the lengths of AB and AC. Drag the vertices of the triangle to various locations around the screen, making sure that the lengths of AB and AC remain equal. At each new location, compare the lengths of the medians to AB and AC.
3. Answers may vary. For example:
   a)

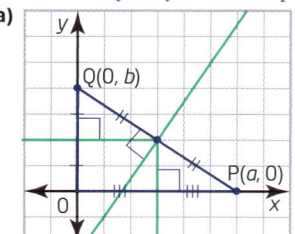

   b) For △POQ with vertices P(a, 0) and Q(0, b), the midpoint of OP is $\left(\frac{a}{2}, 0\right)$ and the midpoint of OQ is $\left(0, \frac{b}{2}\right)$. An equation for the right bisector of OP is $x = \frac{a}{2}$, and an equation for the right bisector of OQ is $y = \frac{b}{2}$. These right bisectors intersect at $\left(\frac{a}{2}, \frac{b}{2}\right)$, which is the midpoint of the hypotenuse. Therefore, the point of intersection of the right bisectors of the sides of any right triangle is the midpoint of the hypotenuse.
   c) Answers may vary. For example: Construct two perpendicular lines, and label the point of intersection A. Construct point B on one of the lines and point C on the other. Construct line segments AB, BC, and AC. Construct the right bisector of each line segment. Observe the point of intersection of the three right bisectors while dragging points B and C along the perpendicular lines.
4. a) Since $m_{DE} = \frac{2}{3}$ and $m_{DF} = -\frac{3}{2}$, $m_{DE} \times m_{DF} = -1$ and ∠D is a right angle.
   b) Calculate the lengths of the sides and show that they satisfy the Pythagorean theorem.

5. Answers may vary. For example:
   a) The midpoint of KL is M(0, 3). Since $m_{KL} = 5$ and $m_{JM} = -\frac{1}{5}$, $m_{KL} \times m_{JM} = -1$ and JM is perpendicular to KL.
   b) Since JK = JL, △JKL is isosceles.
6. Answers may vary. For example:
   a) The diagonals of a square bisect each other and are perpendicular.
   b) The diagonals of a parallelogram bisect each other and bisect the area of the parallelogram.
   c) The diagonals of a kite are perpendicular, and the diagonal joining the vertices between the equal sides bisects the other diagonal.
7. Answers may vary. For example:
   a) Since EF is parallel to AD and BC, AEFD and EBCF are parallelograms. AEFD and EBCF have the same base length as ABCD, but half the height. Therefore, AEFD and EBCF each have half the area of ABCD. Alternative method: Since EF is parallel to AD and BC, all of the corresponding angles in AEFD and EBCF are equal. All of the corresponding sides are also equal since E and F are the midpoints, and opposite sides of a parallelogram have equal lengths. Therefore, AEFD ≅ EBCF, and their areas are equal.
   b) Use geometry software to construct a parallelogram ABCD with the vertices at the points of intersection of two pairs of parallel lines. Construct the midpoints, E and F, of one pair of opposite sides. Construct a line segment EF. Measure the areas of AEFD and EBCF. Compare these areas while dragging the vertices of ABCD.
8. Since $m_{JM} = m_{KL} = \frac{1}{3}$, JM is parallel to KL.
9. a) Rectangle. Explanations may vary. For example: Calculating the slopes shows the adjacent sides are all perpendicular to each other. Calculating the lengths of the sides shows that opposite sides have equal lengths, but adjacent sides do not.
   b) $M\left(4\frac{1}{2}, 1\frac{1}{2}\right)$ is the midpoint of both TV and UW. Therefore, the diagonals of TUVW bisect each other.
10. Answers may vary. For example:
    a) A(−12, −5) and B(12, 5) both satisfy the equation for the circle, and AB = 26, exactly twice the radius of the circle.
    b) (12, −5) or (13, 0).
    c) $m_{AC} \times m_{BC} = -1$, so ∠C is a right angle.
11. a) The coordinates of points P and Q satisfy the equation for the circle.
    b) O(0, 0) satisfies $y = \frac{1}{6}x$, an equation of the right bisector of PQ.
12. Answers may vary. For example: On a map, draw the line segments joining St. Catharines to Hamilton and Hamilton to Oakville. Construct the right bisector of each line segment. The point of intersection of the right bisectors represents the centre of the circle that passes through St. Catharines, Hamilton, and Oakville.

Chapter 3 Practice Test, page 154–155

1. A, B, and E
2. A, B, and E
3. a)  b)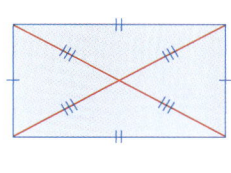
   c) 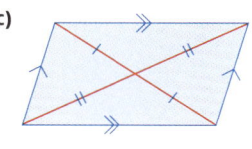 d)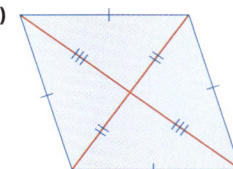
   e) 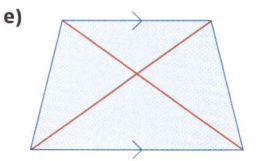 f)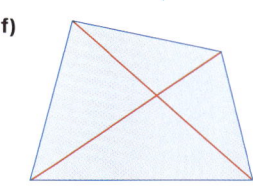
4. Let △ABC be an isosceles triangle with AB = AC and altitudes BP and CQ. ∠QAP is common to △ABP and △ACQ, AB = AC, and ∠APB = ∠AQC = 90°. Therefore, △ABP ≅ △ACQ (angle-angle-side), and PB = QC.
5. a) $AB = BC = \sqrt{60}$
   b) (6, −1) satisfies equations for all three medians ($y = -x + 5$, $x = 6$, and $y = -1$).
6. a) Since $m_{DE} = 2$ and $m_{DF} = -\frac{1}{2}$, $m_{DE} \times m_{DF} = -1$ and ∠D = 90°.
   b) $GD = GE = GF = \sqrt{10}$, where G is the midpoint of EF.
7. a) $JK = KL = LM = JM = \sqrt{29}$
   b) Answers may vary. For example: Construct quadrilateral JKLM. Then, measure and compare the lengths of JK, KL, LM, and JM.
8. a) A(−1, 9), B(3, 8), C(6, 1), and D(2, 2)
   b) $m_{AB} = m_{CD}$ and $m_{AD} = m_{BC}$
9. a) CT = CU = CV = 13
   b) 13
10. AD = BC and $m_{AB} = m_{CD}$
11. Answers may vary. For example: Construct quadrilateral ABCD. Measure and compare the lengths and slopes of the four sides.
12. a) PQ = QR = RS = PS = 5
    b) The midpoints of diagonals PR and SQ are both (6, 0).
    c) Since $m_{PR} = -\frac{1}{2}$ and $m_{SQ} = 2$, $m_{PR} \times m_{SQ} = -1$ and the diagonals are perpendicular.
13. Answers may vary. For example: The point (25, 37) would be a good location because it is equidistant from all four towns.

Chapter 4

Get Ready, pages 162–163

1. **a)** independent variable: time; dependent variable: height
   b)
   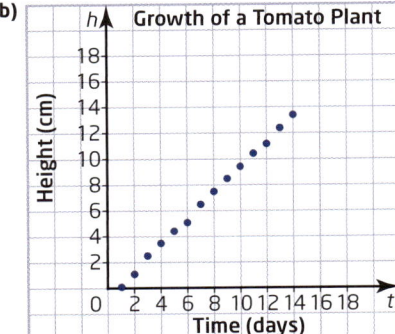
   c) Linear; the points lie on a straight line.
   d) 16.4 cm

2. **a)** independent variable: height; dependent variable: neck circumference
   b)
   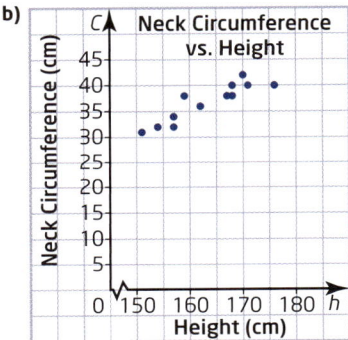
   c) Linear; the points lie on a straight line.
   d) 44 cm

3. The red figure is shifted 4 units left and 1 unit up.

4.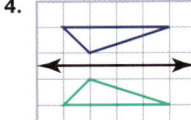

5. **a)** 2^7 **b)** $(-1)^7$ **c)** $\left(\dfrac{1}{2}\right)^5$
   d) 5^5 **e)** $(-3)^3$ **f)** 4^{10}

6. **a)** 2^2 **b)** $(-3)^6$ **c)** 5^5 **d)** 4^2

4.1 Investigate Non-Linear Relations, pages 164–167

1. The scatter plot in part b) could be modelled using a curve because the points do not lie along a line.
2. Non-linear; the points lie on a curve.

3. **a), c)**
   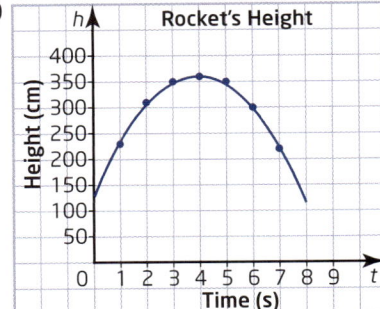
   b) Non-linear; the points lie on a curve.
   d) Answers will vary. For example: 111 m

4. **a), c)**
   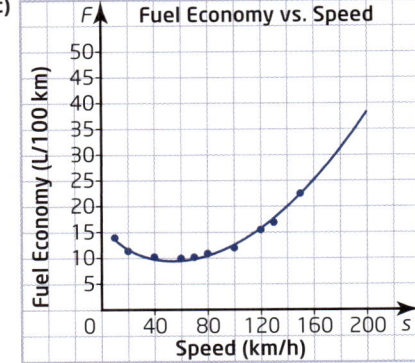
   b) Non-linear; the points lie on a curve.
   d) Answers will vary. For example: 40 L/100 km
   e) The graph for a car with better fuel economy would be translated down compared to the graph in part a).

5. **a), c)**
   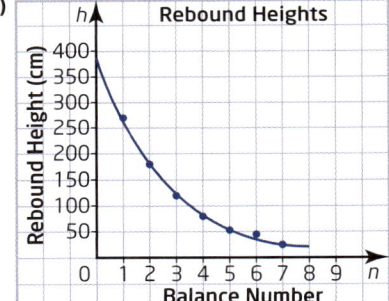
   b) Non-linear; the points lie on a curve.
   d) If the ball were bouncier, the rebound heights would not decrease as fast as in this graph.

6. **a)**

Year	Total Garbage (1000s of tonnes)
2000	200
2001	430
2002	688
2003	975
2004	1292
2005	1639
2006	2015
2007	2421

b)

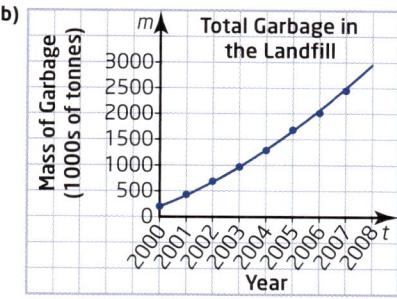

c) Answers will vary. For example: The city will run out of landfill space.

7. a)

Length (cm)	Area (cm²)
2	2
4	8
6	18
8	32
10	50
12	72
14	98
16	128

b), c)

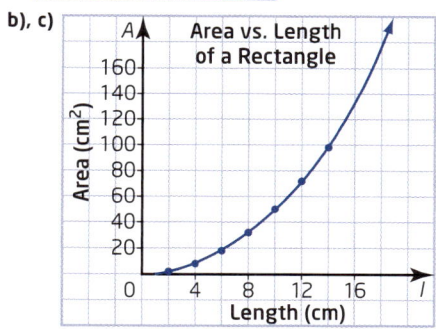

d) Answers will vary. For example: This relation is non-linear because length is a linear measurement but area is a square measurement.

4.2 Quadratic Relations, pages 168–173

1. a)

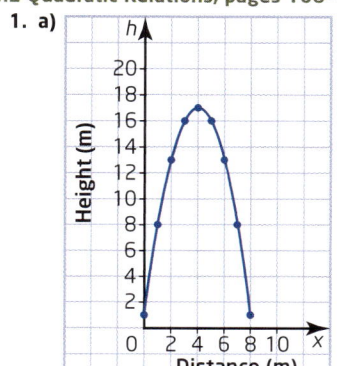

b) The flight path of the ball is parabolic. The axis of symmetry is $x = 4$ and the vertex is (4, 17).
c) The maximum height reached is 17 m.
d) A table of values for $h = -x^2 + 8x + 1$ is the same as the table of values given.

2. a)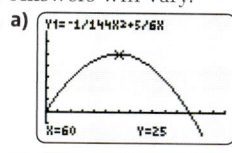

b) The shape of the arch is parabolic.
c) The arch is 10 m tall and 20 m wide.

3. a) linear **b)** quadratic
c) neither **d)** quadratic

4. Answers will vary.

5. a)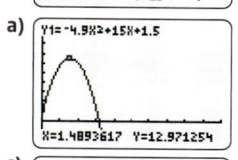

b) 9 m **c)** 120 m
d) The maximum height is 25 m at a horizontal distance of 60 m.
e) $x = 60$

6. a)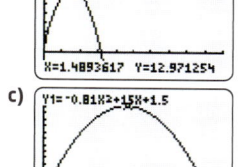

b) There is a quadratic relation between time and height.

c)

$Y1=-0.81X^2+15X+1.5$

There is a quadratic relation.

d)

$Y1=-11.55X^2+15X+1.5$

There is a quadratic relation.

e) All three show a quadratic relation between time and height, but the parabolas have different axes of symmetry and vertices. Since the ball falls to the ground faster on Jupiter than on Earth and the Moon, Jupiter has a stronger force of gravity than Earth and the Moon.

7. The relation is more closely modelled by a quadratic equation because the second differences are very close to being constant.

8. Tables may vary. The arch does not closely resemble a parabola. The second differences are not constant.

x	y	First Differences	Second Differences
−1.5	1.0		
		0.5	
−1.0	1.5		−0.25
		0.25	
−0.5	1.75		0.25
		0.50	
0.0	2.25		−0.35
		0.15	
0.5	2.4		−0.30
		−0.15	
1.0	2.25		0.10
		−0.05	
1.5	2.2		−0.15
		−0.20	
2.0	2.0		−0.05
		−0.25	
2.5	1.75		−1.00
		−1.25	
3.0	0.75		

10. 18 min 31 s

11. $y = \dfrac{n(n + 1)}{2}$

Answers • MHR **527**

4.3 Investigate Transformations of Quadratics, pages 174–179

1.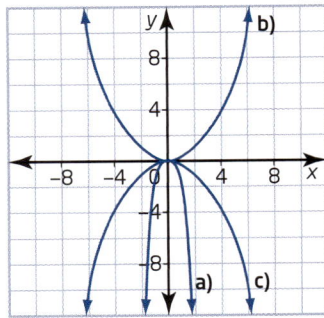

2.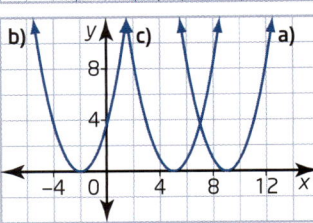

3.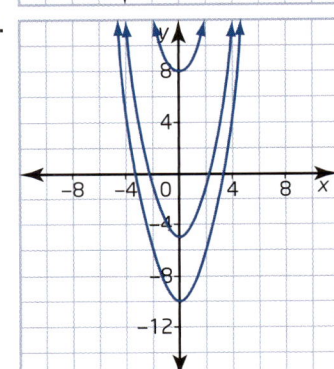

4. a)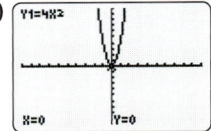

The parabola is vertically stretched by a factor of 4.

b)

The parabola is vertically compressed by a factor of $\frac{2}{3}$.

c)

The parabola is translated 5 units downward.

d)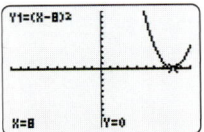

The parabola is translated 8 units to the right.

e)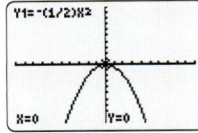

The parabola is compressed vertically by a factor of $\frac{1}{2}$ and reflected in the x-axis.

f)

The parabola is translated 3 units to the left.

g)

The parabola is translated 0.5 units upward.

h)

The parabola is reflected in the x-axis and translated 2 units upward.

5. a)

x	$y = x^2$	$y = 2x^2$	$y = x^2 + 1$	$y = (x-3)^2$
−3	9	18	10	36
−2	4	8	5	25
−1	1	2	2	16
0	0	0	1	9
1	1	2	2	4
2	4	8	5	1
3	9	18	10	0

b) The y-values for $y = 2x^2$ are all twice the y-values for $y = x^2$.
c) The y-values for $y = x^2 + 1$ are all 1 more than the y-values for $y = x^2$.
d) The y-values for $y = (x-3)^2$ are the same as the y-values for $y = x^2$ for x-values that are 3 greater.

6. a) $y = x^2 + 6$ **b)** $y = x^2 - 4$
7. a) $y = (x+7)^2$ **b)** $y = (x-5)^2$
c) $y = (x+8)^2$ **d)** $y = (x-3)^2$
8. a) $y = 8x^2$ **b)** $y = \frac{1}{5}x^2$

9. a)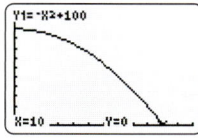

b) The y-intercept is 100. This represents the area of grass if there is no square patio in the centre of the grass. The x-intercept is 10. This represents the side length of the patio, in metres, if the patio completely covers the grass in the backyard.
c) $y = -x^2 + 144$
d) x must be greater than or equal to zero but less than or equal to 10 m and 12 m, respectively.

10. a) 100 m; 400 m
b) When the speed of the car doubles, the length of the skid mark quadruples.
c) s must be greater than 0.
d) Answers may vary. For example: If the pavement were wet, the skid marks would be longer. The equation would have a coefficient greater than 0.04.

11. a)

l	A	First Differences	Second Differences
2	3		
		5	
3	8		2
		7	
4	15		2
		9	
5	24		2
		11	
6	35		

The equation is quadratic. The second differences are constant.
b) $A = l^2 - 1$
c) The transformation is a translation of 1 unit downward.

12. a) Answers will vary. For example: According to the order of operations, multiplying by a or adding k is done after squaring the x-value, so the transformation applies directly to the parabola $y = x^2$. Because the value of h must be added or subtracted before squaring, the shift is opposite to the sign in the bracket and must be the opposite movement to get back to the original y-value for the graph of $y = x^2$.
b) The graph of $y = (2x)^2$ is the graph of $y = x^2$ stretched vertically by a factor of 4.

13. $a = -2$, $k = 5$

14. The graphs of $y = (x - 2)^2$ and $y = (2 - x)^2$ are exactly the same.

15. a) Answers will vary. For example: The graphs are both parabolas; $y = (x - 2)^2 + 5$ opens upward and $x = (y - 2)^2 + 5$ opens to the right. The vertices are (2, 5) and (5, 2), respectively. The equations of the axes of symmetry are $x = 2$ and $y = 2$, respectively. The x and y variables have switched in the equations.
b) $y = 2 \pm \sqrt{x - 5}$

4.4 Graph $y = a(x - h)^2 + k$, pages 180–188

1. a)

Property	$y = (x - 4)^2$
Vertex	(4, 0)
Axis of symmetry	$x = 4$
Stretch or compression factor relative to $y = x^2$	none
Direction of opening	upward
Values x may take	set of real numbers
Values y may take	$y \geq 0$

b)

Property	$y = (x - 2)^2 - 4$
Vertex	(2, −4)
Axis of symmetry	$x = 2$
Stretch or compression factor relative to $y = x^2$	none
Direction of opening	upward
Values x may take	set of real numbers
Values y may take	$y \geq -4$

c)

Property	$y = (x + 3)^2 - 2$
Vertex	(−3, −2)
Axis of symmetry	$x = -3$
Stretch or compression factor relative to $y = x^2$	none
Direction of opening	upward
Values x may take	set of real numbers
Values y may take	$y \geq -2$

d)

Property	$y = \frac{1}{2}(x + 1)^2 + 5$
Vertex	(−1, 5)
Axis of symmetry	$x = -1$
Stretch or compression factor relative to $y = x^2$	$\frac{1}{2}$
Direction of opening	upward
Values x may take	set of real numbers
Values y may take	$y \geq 5$

e)

Property	$y = (x - 7)^2 - 3$
Vertex	(7, −3)
Axis of symmetry	$x = 7$
Stretch or compression factor relative to $y = x^2$	none
Direction of opening	upward
Values x may take	set of real numbers
Values y may take	$y \geq -3$

f)

Property	$y = -(x-1)^2 + 7$
Vertex	(1, 7)
Axis of symmetry	$x = 1$
Stretch or compression factor relative to $y = x^2$	none
Direction of opening	downward
Values x may take	set of real numbers
Values y may take	$y \leq 7$

g)

Property	$y = 2(x-4)^2 - 5$
Vertex	(4, −5)
Axis of symmetry	$x = 4$
Stretch or compression factor relative to $y = x^2$	2
Direction of opening	upward
Values x may take	set of real numbers
Values y may take	$y \geq -5$

h)

Property	$y = -3(x+4)^2 - 2$
Vertex	(−4, −2)
Axis of symmetry	$x = -4$
Stretch or compression factor relative to $y = x^2$	3
Direction of opening	downward
Values x may take	set of real numbers
Values y may take	$y \leq -2$

2. a)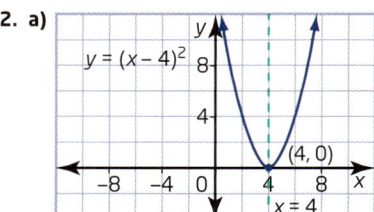

b)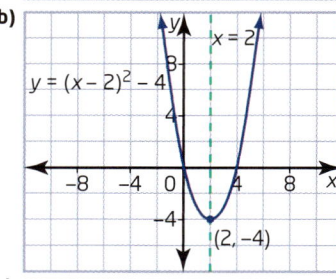

c)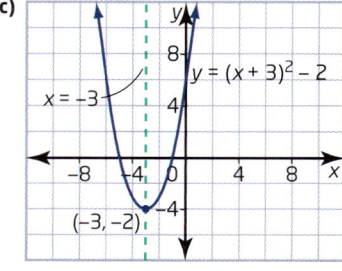

d)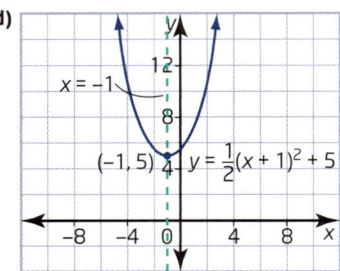

e)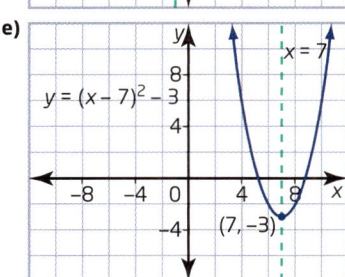

f)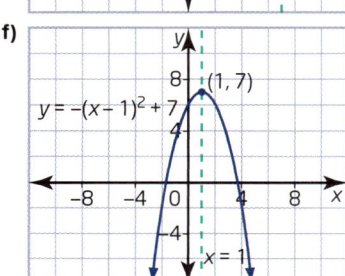

g)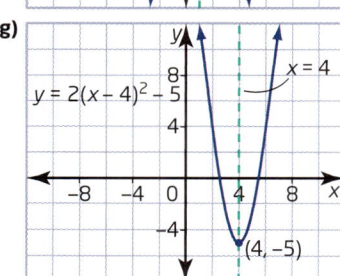

h)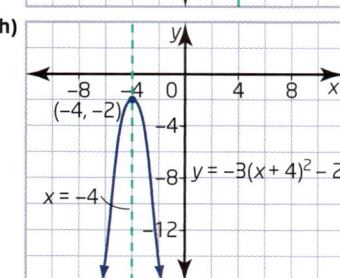

3. $y = (x-2)^2 + 3$
4. $y = -2(x+3)^2$
5. $y = 0.3(x-4)^2 - 1$
6. a) $y = (x-4)^2$ **b)** $y = -(x+3)^2$
7. a) $y = (x-4)^2 - 5$ **b)** $y = -(x+6)^2 + 4$
    c) $y = 5(x-6)^2 - 7$

8.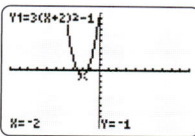

9.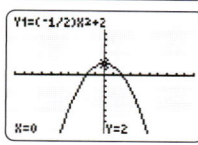

10. a) $y = (x - 1)^2 + 4$ **b)** $y = -(x + 2)^2 + 5$

11. B is correct. The parabola opens downward and has a y-intercept of 20.

12. a)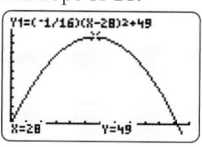

b) 49 m **c)** 28 m **d)** 45 m **e)** 36 m

13. a) $h = -2(d - 4)^2 + 33$ **b)** 25 m **c)** 2 m

14. a) 127 m; 5 s **b)** 2 m

15. a)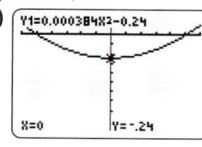

b) $y = 0.000\,384x^2 - 0.24$; $-25 \leq x \leq 25$
c) Answers will vary.

16. a) 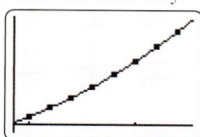 **b)**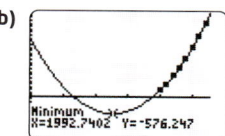

c) $y = 14.6(x - 1992.7)^2 - 576.2$
d) Realistically, $x \geq 2000$ and $y \geq 200$.

17. left parabola: $y = 0.012(x + 100)^2$ for $-100 \leq x \leq -50$;
middle parabola: $y = 0.012x^2$ for $-50 \leq x \leq 50$;
right parabola: $y = 0.012(x - 100)^2$ for $50 \leq x \leq 100$

19. a) $y = -2(x - 4)^2 + 1$ **b)** $y = 2x^2 - 1$
c) $y = -2(x - 4)^2 + 2$ **d)** $y = 2(x + 4)^2 - 1$

20. a) $x^2 + (y - 3)^2 = 25$; $(x - 6)^2 + (y - 1)^2 = 49$;
$(x + 3)^2 + (y - 5)^2 = 64$; $(x - h)^2 + (y - k)^2 = r^2$
b) Answers will vary. For example: A circle with equation $(x - h)^2 + (y - k)^2 = r^2$ has centre (h, k) and a parabola with equation $y = (x - h)^2 + k$ has vertex (h, k).

21. $y = \dfrac{1}{14}x^2 - \dfrac{3}{7}x - \dfrac{6}{7}$

22. C

4.5 Quadratic Relations of the Form $y = a(x - r)(x - s)$, pages 189–193

1.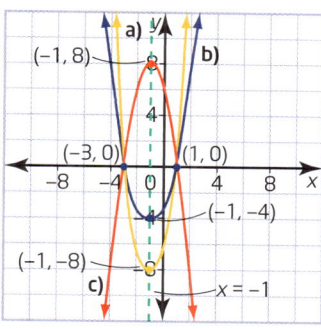

The graphs all have the same x-intercepts and axis of symmetry, but differ in the vertical stretch of the parabola and direction of opening.

2.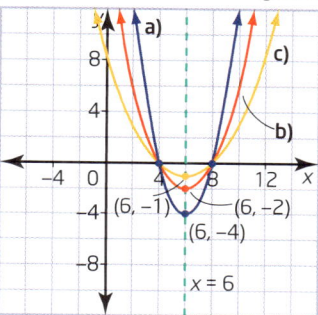

The graphs all have the same x-intercepts, axis of symmetry, and direction of opening, but differ in the vertical stretch of the parabola.

3. a) 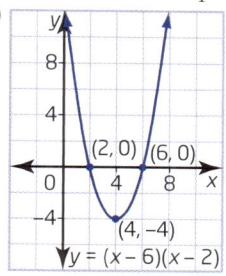 **b)**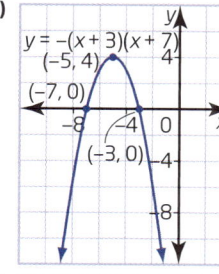

c) 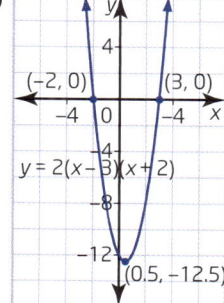 **d)**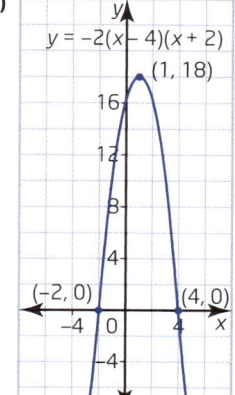

Answers • MHR **531**

4. a)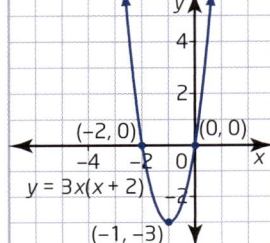

b)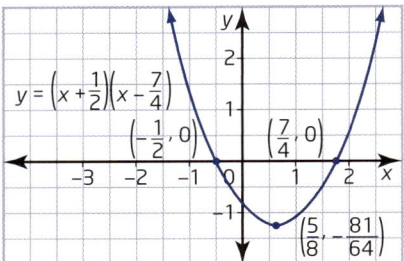

c)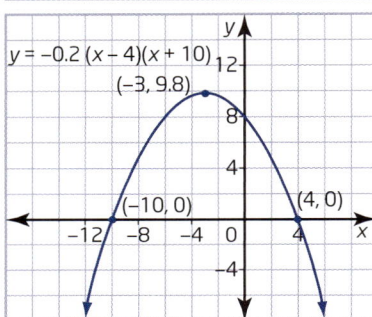

d)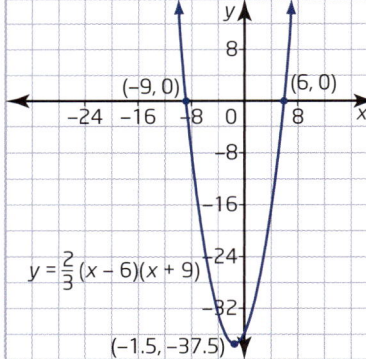

e)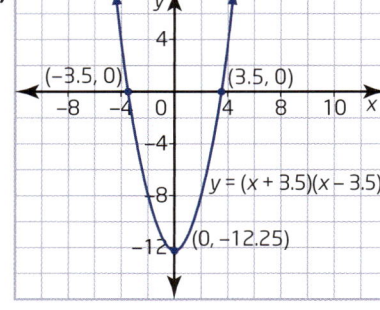

f)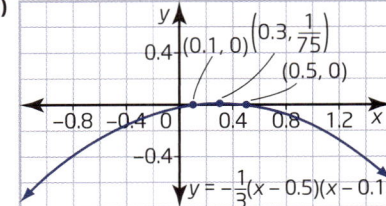

5. a) $y = 0.5(x + 7)(x + 3)$ **b)** $y = -4(x - 2)(x - 4)$
6. a) $(5, 0)$ **b)** 1 **c)** $y = (x - 5)(x - 5)$
7. a) -2 and -2 **b)** $(-2, 0)$
8. a)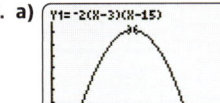

b) 15 m
c) 72 m when it is 9 m from the wall
9. When the x-intercepts are opposite values, the vertex has an x-coordinate of 0.
Answers may vary. For example: $y = 3(x - 2)(x + 2)$
10. a)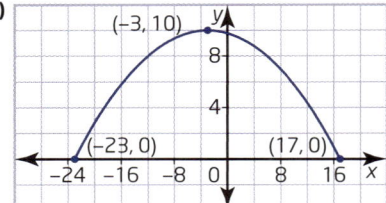

b) $y = -\dfrac{1}{40}(x + 23)(x - 17)$

11. a)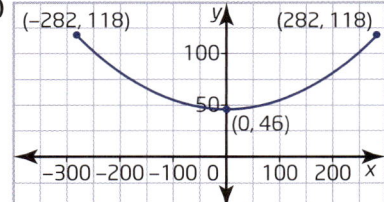

b) It is not possible to write an equation in the form $y = a(x - r)(x - s)$ because the graph has no x-intercepts.

12. a)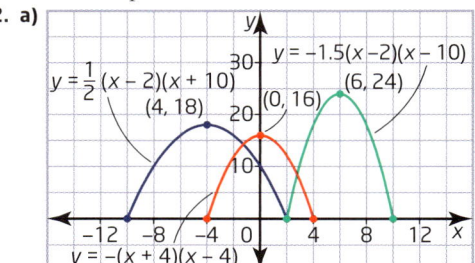

b) 20 m
c) 18 m, 16 m, 24 m

13. a) $R = -10(x - 10)(x + 20)$
b)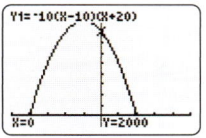
c) The R-intercept represents the current revenue with the current price of a ticket at $20 each. The x-intercepts represent the number of price increases or decreases that would give a revenue of $0.
d) A negative x-value represents a decrease in the ticket price.
e) $15 per ticket

14. a) 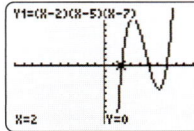 The equation of the relation has three factors. The graph of the relation crosses the x-axis at three points. The three points are the x-intercepts of the relation.
b) 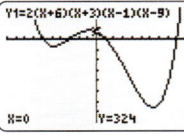 The equation of the relation has four factors. The graph of the relation crosses the x-axis at four points. The four points are the x-intercepts of the relation.
c) 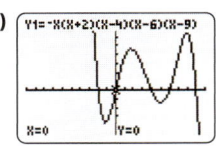 The equation of the relation has five factors. The graph of the relation crosses the x-axis at five points. The five points are the x-intercepts of the relation.

15. $\sqrt{137}$ units

4.6 Negative and Zero Exponents, pages 194–201

1. a) $\dfrac{1}{3^2}$ b) $\dfrac{1}{5^1}$ c) $\dfrac{1}{10^4}$
   d) $\dfrac{1}{7^3}$ e) $\dfrac{1}{(-2)^4}$ f) $\dfrac{1}{(-7)^1}$

2. a) $\dfrac{1}{36}$ b) 1 c) $\dfrac{1}{7}$ d) $\dfrac{1}{1000}$
   e) $-\dfrac{1}{9}$ f) $\dfrac{1}{144}$ g) 1 h) -1

3. a) 9 b) undefined c) -4
   d) $\dfrac{36}{25}$ e) $\dfrac{4096}{81}$ f) $\dfrac{64}{729}$

4. a) $1\dfrac{1}{36}$ b) $7\dfrac{7}{8}$ c) 1 d) 2

5. a) $\dfrac{1}{16}$ b) $\dfrac{1}{64}$ c) $2^{-4}, 2^{-6}$

6. a) 0.125 kg b) 0.015 625 kg
7. a) 2^{-4} b) 0.5 mg
8. a) 3 b) $\dfrac{5}{4}$ c) -2 d) -3
9. Answers will vary.
10. Answers will vary.
11. a) 4000, 8000, 16 000, 32 000
    b) $t = 0$ represents June 1.
    c) $t = -1$ could mean 1 month ago, or May 1.
    d) There were 125 bees 3 months ago on approximately March 1. Let $t = -3$ represent 3 months ago and solve for the number of bees.

12. a) A negative exponent is used because the intensity of light energy is decreasing.
b)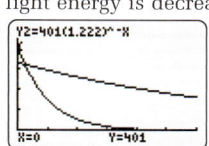
c) The light intensity decreases more quickly in Lake Erie because the base is greater.

14. a) 99.902 343 75 m
b) No, because he will always be walking a distance of half the previous distance. Looking at the graph, the curve will never reach zero, which is the remaining distance needed in order for Chris to reach the end of the track.

Time (min)	Distance Remaining (m)
1	50
2	25
3	12.5
4	6.25
5	3.125
6	1.562 5
7	0.781 25
8	0.396 25
9	0.195 312 5
10	0.097 656 25

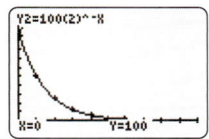

c) $d = 100(2)^{-t}$

15. a) $m = 500(10)^{-t}$ b) 2 h
16. a)–c)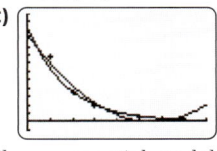
d) The exponential model fits the data better.
17. a), b)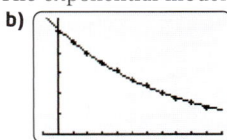
c) An exponential model is better because the atmospheric pressure will never reach 0 millibars.

18.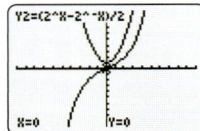

The graph of $y = x^2 + 1$ is a parabola with vertex (0, 1), opening up. When $x < 0$, the graph of $y = \dfrac{2^x - 2^{-x}}{2}$ looks like a parabola that opens downward. When $x > 0$, the graph of $y = \dfrac{2^x - 2^{-x}}{2}$ looks like a parabola that opens upward and is wider than the parabola for $y = x^2 + 1$. The graph of $y = \dfrac{2^x - 2^{-x}}{2}$ crosses the y-axis at the origin and changes direction at this point.

19. a) $x = -4$ **b)** $x = -2$
20. a) 12   **b)** -30

Chapter 4 Review, pages 202–203

1. The graph in part b) can be modelled using a curve because the points lie on a curve.

2. a)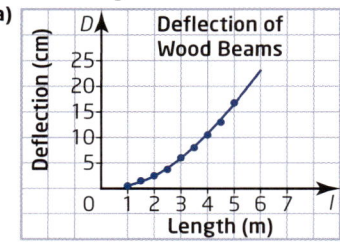

b) There is a non-linear relation between the variables.
c) 23.5 cm

3. a) quadratic   **b)** neither   **c)** linear

4. a)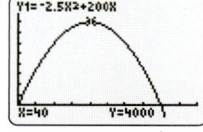

b) 80 min
c) The maximum height of 4000 m is reached after 40 min.

5. a)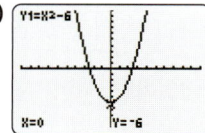

The graph of $y = x^2 - 6$ is the graph of $y = x^2$ translated 6 units downward.

b)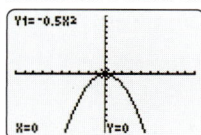

The graph of $y = -0.5x^2$ is the graph of $y = x^2$ reflected in the x-axis and compressed vertically by a factor of 0.5.

c)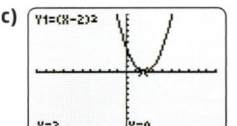

The graph of $y = (x - 2)^2$ is the graph of $y = x^2$ translated 2 units to the right.

d)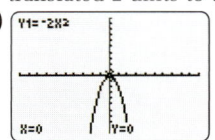

The graph of $y = -2x^2$ is the graph of $y = x^2$ reflected in the x-axis and stretched vertically by a factor of 2.

6. a)

Property	$y = (x - 1)^2 - 4$
Vertex	(1, −4)
Axis of symmetry	$x = 1$
Stretch or compression factor relative to $y = x^2$	none
Direction of opening	upward
Values x may take	set of real numbers
Values y may take	$y \geq -4$

b)

Property	$y = 2(x + 3)^2 + 1$
Vertex	(−3, 1)
Axis of symmetry	$x = -3$
Stretch or compression factor relative to $y = x^2$	2
Direction of opening	upward
Values x may take	set of real numbers
Values y may take	$y \geq 1$

c)

Property	$y = \dfrac{1}{4}(x - 5)^2 + 1$
Vertex	(5, 1)
Axis of symmetry	$x = 5$
Stretch or compression factor relative to $y = x^2$	$\dfrac{1}{4}$
Direction of opening	upward
Values x may take	set of real numbers
Values y may take	$y \geq 1$

d)

Property	$y = -(x + 2)^2 + 6$
Vertex	(−2, 6)
Axis of symmetry	$x = -2$
Stretch or compression factor relative to $y = x^2$	none
Direction of opening	downward
Values x may take	set of real numbers
Values y may take	$y \leq 6$

7. a)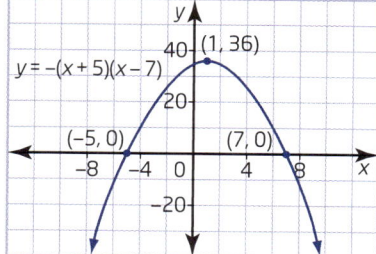

b)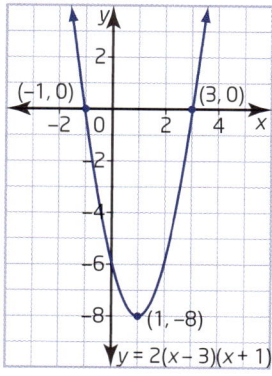

8. a)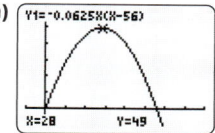

b) 56 m

c) 28 m; 49 m

9. a) $\dfrac{1}{49}$ **b)** 1 **c)** $\dfrac{1}{100\,000}$ **d)** 1

e) $-\dfrac{1}{6}$ **f)** $\dfrac{1}{49}$ **g)** 1 **h)** $-\dfrac{125}{8}$

10. a) $\dfrac{1}{64}$ **b)** $\dfrac{1}{4096}$ **c)** 2^{-6}, 2^{-12} **d)** $244.14

Chapter 4 Practice Test, pages 204–205

1. a)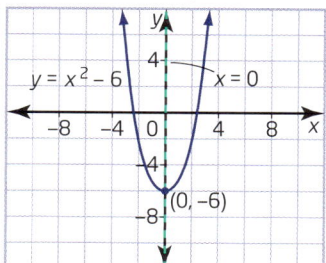

b)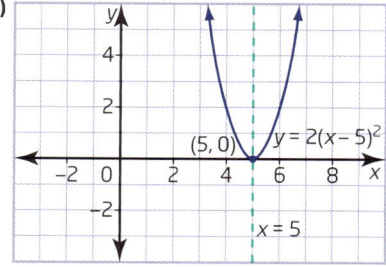

c)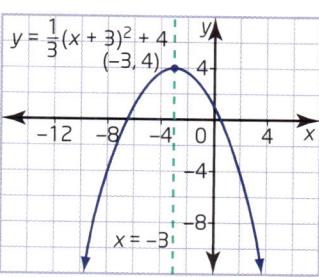

2. a)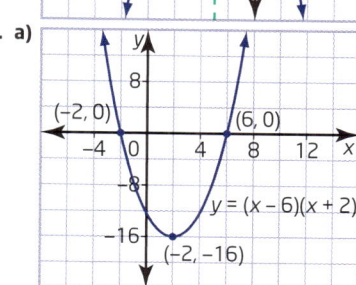

b)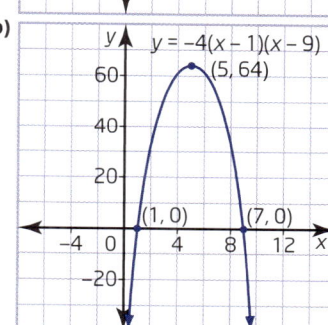

3. a) $y = (x - 5)^2 + 2$ **b)** $y = -\dfrac{1}{6}(x - 2)^2 + 6$

4. a) 1 **b)** $\dfrac{1}{5}$ **c)** $-\dfrac{1}{27}$ **d)** $\dfrac{16}{9}$

5. a) quadratic

b)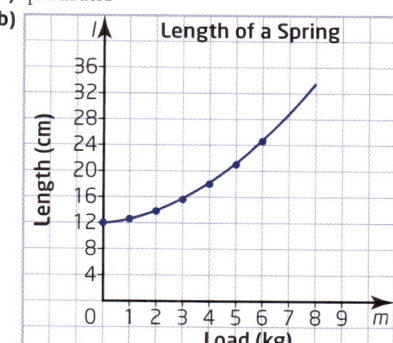

c) 33.6 cm

6. a) 3.71   **b)** 24.185

c), d) Answers will vary.

7. a), b)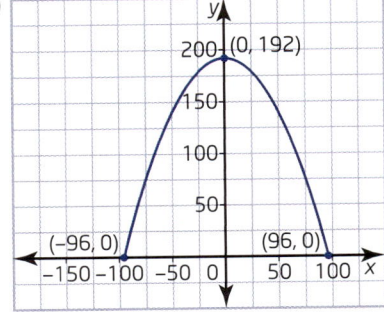

c) $y = -\dfrac{1}{48}x^2 + 192$

8. Answers will vary. For example: If a car uses tires with better grip, then the minimum turn radius will decrease. The value of a will be less than 0.6.
9. a) 46.875 m
   b) If you were standing on a 20-m cliff, you would use the formula $h = \dfrac{3}{40}d^2 - 20$, where h represents the height above the cliff.
10. a)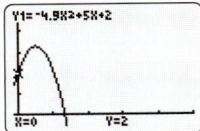
   b) The h-intercept is 2 and it represents the height, in metres, of the volleyball when it was first hit.
   c) 1.3 s; the x-intercept tells you when the volleyball will hit the ground ($h = 0$).
11. a) 20 000, 40 000, 80 000, 160 000
   b) $t = 0$ represents present time, or July 1; $t = -2$ represents 2 years ago.
   c) 3 years ago, because $5000(2)^{-3} = 625$
12.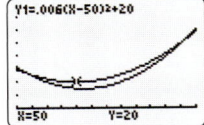

For speeds from 0 km/h to 17.1 km/h, the cost of operating the first car is less than that of the second car. For speeds from 17.1 km/h to 122.9 km/h, the cost of operating the second car is less. The first car is most efficient, at 20¢/km, driving at 50 km/h, and the second car is most efficient, at 15¢/km, driving at 55 km/h.

Chapter 5

Get Ready, pages 208–209

1. a) monomial   b) binomial   c) trinomial
   d) trinomial   e) binomial   f) trinomial
2. a) 5   b) 6   c) 9   d) 5
3. a) $7x - 4$ b) $-3b - 1$ c) $7x^2 + 11x - 1$
   d) $6y^3 - 2y^2 - 2$ e) $15a^2 + a - 19$ f) $3c^2 + 6$
4. a) $15x^2 + 2xy - 3y^2$ b) $3g^2 + 3gh - 10h^2$
   c) $8ab^2 + 2a + 5b$ d) $cd^2 + 10d$
   e) $x + 14$ f) $-4a^2 + 5b - b^2$
5. a) 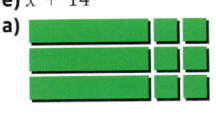   b)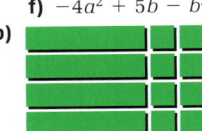

   c) d)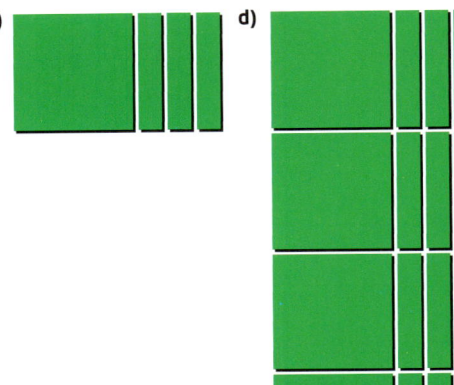

6. a) $21m^2 + 56m$ b) $-4c - 36$
   c) $30a^4 - 40a^3$ d) $2d^2 - 4d + 2$
7. a) $60x^3 - 12x^2$ b) $104x^2 - 16x$
8. a) 1, 2, 5, and 10
   b) 1, 2, 3, 4, 6, 8, 12, and 24
   c) 1, 2, 4, 8, and 16
   d) 1, 2, 4, 8, 16, and 32
9. a) $2 \times 2 \times 2$ b) 2×7
   c) $2 \times 2 \times 7$ d) $2 \times 3 \times 5$
10. a) 3   b) 5   c) 8
    d) 4   e) 3   f) 8

5.1 Multiply Polynomials, pages 210–219

1. a) $(x + 1)(2x + 3) = 2x^2 + 5x + 3$
   b) $(x + 1)(x + 3) = x^2 + 4x + 3$
   c) $(x + 2)(x + 2) = x^2 + 4x + 4$
   d) $(x + 3)(2x + 1) = x^2 + 7x + 3$

2. a)
   b)
   c)
   d)

3. a) $x^2 + 8x + 15$ **b)** $x^2 + 7x + 12$
   c) $y^2 + 6y + 8$ **d)** $r^2 + 6r + 8$
   e) $n^2 + 8n + 7$ **f)** $p^2 + 18p + 81$
   g) $w^2 + 15w + 56$ **h)** $d^2 + 14d + 33$
4. a) $k^2 - 8k + 15$ **b)** $y^2 - 7y + 12$
   c) $x^2 - 6x + 8$ **d)** $q^2 - 6q + 8$
   e) $j^2 - 8j + 7$ **f)** $p^2 - 12p + 27$
   g) $z^2 - 15xz + 56x^2$ **h)** $b^2 - 14bc + 33c^2$
5. a) $x^2 - 2x - 15$ **b)** $y^2 - y - 12$
   c) $c^2 + 2c - 8$ **d)** $w^2 - 2w - 8$
   e) $m^2 + 6m - 7$ **f)** $y^2 - 6y - 27$
   g) $x^2 - xy - 56y^2$ **h)** $a^2 - 4ab - 60b^2$
6. a) $2x^2 + 11x + 12$ **b)** $5y^2 - 22y + 21$
   c) $18c^2 + 27c - 5$ **d)** $14w^2 + 3w - 2$
   e) $25m^2 - 36$ **f)** $18y^2 + 14y - 4$
   g) $56d^2 - 2cd - 30c^2$ **h)** $42q^2 - 37qr - 60r^2$
7. a) $3x^2 + 3x - 90$ **b)** $-2x^2 + 32x - 126$
   c) $-y^2 + 6y + 16$ **d)** $2k^2 + 20k + 42$
   e) $m^3 - 8m^2n + 15mn^2$ **f)** $36a^3 + 90a^2b + 56ab^2$
8. a) $2x^2 + 16x + 17$ **b)** $22x^2 - 51x - 233$
   c) $98x^2 - 51x + 24$ **d)** $5x^2 + 39x + 34$
   e) $16x$ **f)** $105x^2 + 73x - 46$
9. a) $h = -2d^2 + 36d - 90$ **b)** 70 m
10. a) original area: x^2 **b)** new area: $(x + 3)(x + 6)$
   c) $x^2 + 9x + 18$ **d)** increase in area: $9x + 18$
   e) 126 m²

11. a) i) Area: $x(x + 10) = x^2 + 10x$

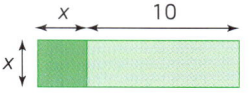

   ii) Area: $x(2x) = 2x^2$

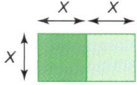

   iii) Area: $(x + 5)(x + 6) = x^2 + 11x + 30$

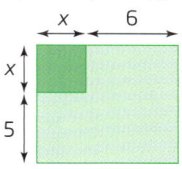

12. a) $-3, 1$
   b) $y = x^2 + 2x - 3$
   c)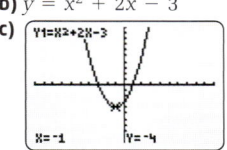

13. a)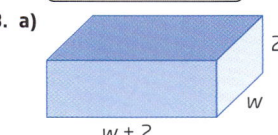
   b) volume: $(w)(w + 2)(2)$ **c)** $2w^2 + 4w$

14. a)

   b) original surface area: $6x^2$
   c) new surface area: $6(x + y)^2$
   d) difference in surface area:
        $6(x + y)^2 - 6x^2 = 12xy + 6y^2$
   e) difference in volume:
        $(x + y)^3 - x^3 = 3x^2y + 3xy^2 + y^3$
15. a) $-3000v^2 + 2100v + 900$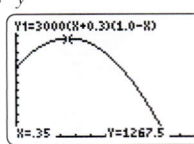
   b) 1200 m
   c) 0.35 m/s

16. Methods may vary. For example:
   a) Area: $4(x + 6) + 5(x) = 9x + 24$
        Alternative method:
        $(x + 4)(x + 6) - x(x + 1) = 9x + 24$
   b) Area: $2(3) + x(x + 4)$; $x^2 + 4x + 6$
        Alternative method:
        $x(x + 7) - 3(x - 2)$; $x^2 + 4x + 6$
17. a) $p = 5 - \dfrac{n}{100}$ **b)** $R = 5n - \dfrac{n^2}{100}$

Answers • MHR **537**

18. $s = n^2 - n + 1$, where s is the number of shaded squares and n is the diagram number.
19. Answers will vary.
20. C

5.2 Special Products, pages 220–227

1. a)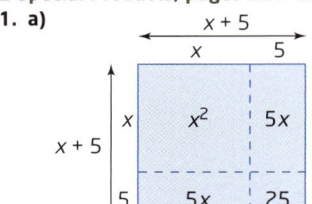

b)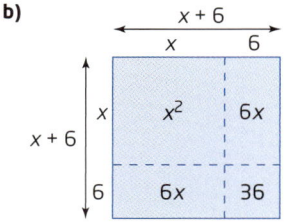

c)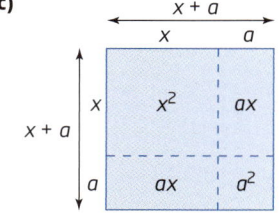

d)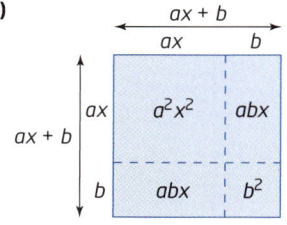

2. a) $x^2 + 10x + 25$ b) $y^2 + 8y + 16$
   c) $w^2 + 12w + 36$ d) $k^2 + 14k + 49$
   e) $m^2 + 22m + 121$ f) $c^2 + 20c + 100$
   g) $g^2 + 18g + 81$ h) $x^2 + 40x + 400$
3. a) $x^2 - 10x + 25$ b) $z^2 - 6z + 9$
   c) $x^2 - 18x + 81$ d) $c^2 - 2c + 1$
   e) $v^2 - 24v + 144$ f) $b^2 - 200b + 10\,000$
   g) $n^2 - 4n + 4$ h) $m^2 - 12m + 36$
4. a) $x^2 + 6xy + 9y^2$ b) $4x^2 - 4xy + y^2$
   c) $25c^2 + 20cd + 4d^2$ d) $9a^2 - 24ab + 16b^2$
   e) $81k^2 + 36km + 4m^2$ f) $16u^2 - 40uv + 25v^2$
5. a) $v^2 - 1$ b) $a^2 - 1$ c) $y^2 - 25$ d) $x^2 - 49$
   e) $e^2 - 81$ f) $z^2 - 36$ g) $x^2 - 144$ h) $y^2 - 9$
6. a) $w^2 - v^2$ b) $9m^2 - n^2$ c) $y^2 - 36x^2$
   d) $9x^2 - 16y^2$ e) $49g^2 - 9h^2$ f) $81x^2 - 64y^2$
7. a) $x^2 - 16$ b) $x^2 - 16x + 64$
   c) $x^2 + 16x + 64$ d) $x^2 - 100$
   e) $x^2 - 121$ f) $x^2 + 24x + 144$
   g) $x^2 - 14x + 49$ h) $x^2 - 900$
8. $A = \pi(r + k)^2$; $A = \pi r^2 + 2\pi rk + \pi k^2$

9. a) 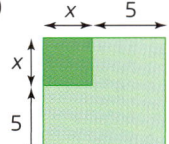 b) $x^2 + 10x + 25$
   c) $10x + 25$

10. a) $(-2, 0)$
    b) $y = x^2 + 4x + 4$
    c) L.S. $= y$ R.S. $= x^2 + 4x + 4$
           $= 0$ $= (-2)^2 + 4(-2) + 4$
                              $= 4 - 8 + 4$
                              $= 0$
       L.S. $=$ R.S.
    Therefore, the point $(-2, 0)$ satisfies the equation $y = x^2 + 4x + 4$.
11. a) area: $(3x + 2y)(3x - 2y) = 9x^2 - 4y^2$
    b) change in area: $(3x + 2y)(3x - 2y) - (3x)^2 = -4y^2$
    c) 476 cm²; 100 cm² less
12. Methods may vary. For example: Area:
    $(x + 2)(x - 2) + (2)(4) = x^2 + 4$
    Alternative method: $(x - 2)^2 + (4)(x) = x^2 + 4$
13. a)

Prism	Surface Area of a Side	Surface Area of Top
bottom	$x(2x + 5)$	$(2x + 5)^2$
middle	$x(2x + 2)$	$(2x + 2)^2$
top	$x(2x - 1)$	$(2x - 1)^2$

   b) $(2x + 5)^2 - (2x + 2)^2 = 12x + 21$
   c) $(2x + 2)^2 - (2x - 1)^2 = 12x + 3$
14. a) $(30 \times 1)(30 + 1) = 899$
    b) $(60 \times 1)(60 + 1) = 3599$
    c) $(100 \times 1)(100 + 1) = 9999$
    d) $(70 \times 1)(70 + 1) = 4899$
15. $32 \times 28 = (30 + 2)(30 - 2)$
              $= 900 - 4$
              $= 896$
    a) $(80 \times 4)(80 + 4) = 6384$
    b) $(30 + 5)(30 - 5) = 875$
    c) $(100 + 4)(100 \times 4) = 9984$
    d) $(80 \times 3)(80 + 3) = 6391$
16. a)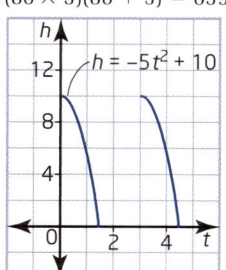

    b) $h = -5(t - 3)^2 + 10$
    c) $h = -5t^2 + 30t - 35$
17. a) $(3264 + x)(2448 + x) = x^2 + 5712x + 7\,990\,272$
    b) 14.7 megapixels
19. a) $x^4 - 8x^3 + 24x^2 - 32x + 16$
    b) $8x^3 - 14x^2 - 109x - 105$
    c) $4x^4 + 20x^3 + 37x^2 + 30x + 9$
    d) $125x^3 - 150x^2 + 60x - 8$

20. a) $\Delta E = \dfrac{1}{2}mv^2 - \dfrac{1}{2}m(v-5)^2$

b) $\Delta E = \dfrac{1}{2}mv^2 - \dfrac{1}{2}m(v-x)^2$

c) $\Delta E = 5mv - 12.5m$; $\Delta E = mvx - 0.5mx^2$

21. a)

n	Sum	Formula
1	$1^3 = 1$	$\dfrac{1^2(1+1)^2}{4} = 1$
2	$1^3 + 2^3 = 9$	$\dfrac{2^2(2+1)^2}{4} = 9$
3	$1^3 + 2^3 + 3^3 = 36$	$\dfrac{3^2(3+1)^2}{4} = 36$
4	$1^3 + 2^3 + 3^3 + 4^3 = 100$	$\dfrac{4^2(4+1)^2}{4} = 100$
5	$1^3 + 2^3 + 3^3 + 4^3 + 5^3 = 225$	$\dfrac{5^2(5+1)^2}{4} = 225$

b) $\left[\dfrac{n(n+1)}{2}\right]^2 = \dfrac{n^2(n+1)^2}{2^2}$

$= \dfrac{n^2(n+1)^2}{4}$

5.3 Common Factors, pages 228–235

1. a) x **b)** $2a$ **c)** x^2
d) k^4 **e)** m **f)** $-3y^2$

2. a)

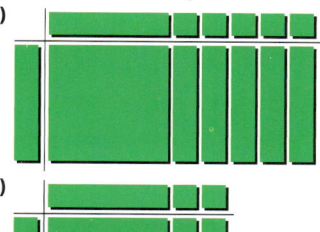

b)

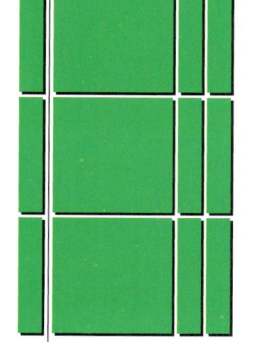

c)

3. a) $5(3w + 5z)$ **b)** not possible
c) $c(17a - 8d)$ **d)** $y(9 - 8y^2)$
e) $6b^2(2b^2 + 3)$ **f)** $2(2g^2 - 4g + 3)$
g) not possible   **h)** $2n^3(n^2 + 6n - 3)$
4. a) $2xy(7x + 8y^2)$ **b)** $2k^2m^2(5k - 3)$
c) not possible   **d)** $22c^2de^2(3c^2 - 1)$
e) not possible   **f)** $5fg(g - 5 + 4f)$
g) $9rs^2(3r - 2r^2 - 4s)$ **h)** $2n^2p^2(2p + 5n^2 - 6n)$
5. a) $(x + 8)(3x + 5)$ **b)** $(b + 1)(a + 9c)$
c) not possible   **d)** $(r + u)(4s - t)$
6. a) $(x + y)(m + 2)$ **b)** $(x + 3)(x + 2)$
c) $(y + 3)(ay + 4)$ **d)** $(2x + 3)(3x - 1)$
e) $(4v - 3)^2$
7. Answers may vary. For example:
a) $12x + 18y$ **b)** $x^3 + x^2 + x$
c) $5y^2 + 10y^3$ **d)** $2a^2b^3 + 4a^3b^4 + 6a^4b^5$
8. a) $P = 2(l + w)$
b) $P = 48$ cm. The perimeters are the same using the original and the factored form of the formula because the formulas are equivalent.
9. a) $SA = 2\pi r(r + h)$
b) $SA = 66\pi$ cm^2, or approximately 207.3 cm^2. The surface areas are the same using the original and the factored form of the formula because the formulas are equivalent.
10. length 1, width $6x^2 + 9x$; length 3, width $2x^2 + 3x$; length x, width $6x + 9$; length $3x$, width $2x + 3$
11. a) $(y - 7)(-5x + 4)$ **b)** $(x - 1)(5y - 2)$
12. a) $(2x - 1)^2 + (2x + 2)^2 + (2x + 5)^2$
b) $12x^2 + 24x + 30$
c) $6(2x^2 + 4x + 5)$
13. a) $8(x^2 - y^2)$ **b)** $\pi(R^2 - r^2)$
14. $y = x(2x - 3)$; x-intercepts are 0 and 1.5.
15. a) $\dfrac{1}{2}(x^2 + 3y^2)$ **b)** $\dfrac{a}{3}(2a^2 - b)$

c) $\dfrac{km^2}{6}(k^3 - 3m + 2k)$; you can wait until the last step to divide.

16. C
17. Let the five consecutive integers be x, $x + 1$, $x + 2$, $x + 3$, and $x + 4$. The sum of their squares is
$x^2 + (x + 1)^2 + (x + 2)^2 + (x + 3)^2 + (x + 4)^2$
$= x^2 + x^2 + 2x + 1 + x^2 + 4x + 4 + x^2 + 6x + 9$
$\quad + x^2 + 8x + 16$
$= 5x^2 + 20x + 30$
$= 5(x^2 + 4x + 6)$
Therefore, the sum is divisible by 5.

5.4 Factor Quadratic Expressions of the Form $x^2 + bx + c$, pages 236–241

1. a)

b)

c) 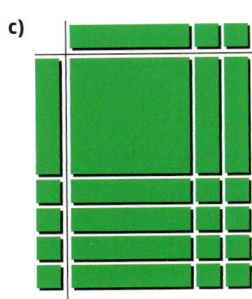 **d)**

2. a) 9, 5   **b)** −3, −2   **c)** 5, −2   **d)** −10, 2
3. a) $(x + 5)(x + 2)$ **b)** $(j + 9)(j + 3)$
   c) $(k + 4)(k + 1)$ **d)** not possible
   e) not possible   **f)** $(d + 6)(d + 4)$
4. a) $(m − 2)(m − 5)$ **b)** not possible
   c) $(y − 4)(y − 1)$ **d)** $(r − 8)^2$
   e) not possible   **f)** $(q − 9)(q − 1)$
5. a) $(a − 5)(a + 2)$ **b)** $(s + 5)(s − 2)$
   c) $(d − 9)(d + 1)$ **d)** not possible
   e) $(g − 7)(g + 2)$ **f)** not possible
   g) $(x + 7)(x − 6)$ **h)** not possible
6. a) $A = (x + 10)(x + 8)$; $A = 575$ cm²
   b) $A = (x − 5)(x − 10)$; $A = 50$ cm²
7. a) $3(x + 3)(x + 1)$ **b)** $2(d − 7)(d − 4)$
   c) $5(z + 6)(z + 2)$ **d)** $4(s − 4)(s + 2)$
   e) $b(x + 12)(x − 2)$ **f)** $x(x + 6)(x + 12)$
8. Answers may vary. For example:
   a) 8, 7   **b)** 5, 4   **c)** 7, 2   **d)** 9, 3
9. Answers may vary. For example:
   a) 5, 9   **b)** −2, −6   **c)** 9, 20   **d)** 3, 8
10. a) $x^2 + 4x + 3$; $x^2 + 4xy + 3y^2$
   b) $x^2 − 2x − 24$; $x^2 − 2xy − 24y^2$
   c) $x^2 + 7x − 18$; $x^2 + 7xy − 18y^2$
   d) $x^2 − 15x + 54$; $x^2 − 15xy + 54y^2$
   The coefficients of corresponding terms in the simplified forms are the same.
11. a) $(a + 8b)(a + 3b)$ **b)** $(k − 9m)(k − 2m)$
   c) $(c + 7d)(c − 3d)$ **d)** $(x − 8y)(x + 2y)$
12. a), b) Answers will vary.
13. a) $y = (x − 6)(x + 2)$ **b)** 6, −2
   c) $x = 2$, (2, −16)

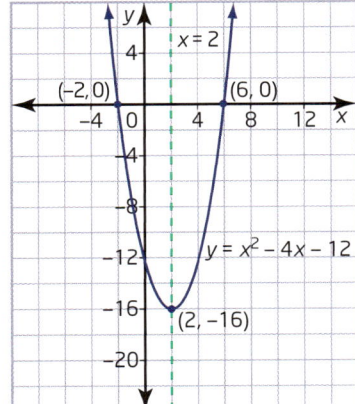

14. a) $h = −5(t + 1)(t − 4)$
   b) The binomial factors can be used to find the t-intercepts, one of which represents when the ball will land on the ground.

15. a) They are alike because the coefficients are the same. They are different because the degrees of the variables are different.
   b) $(x^2 + 5)(x^2 + 4)$
16. a) $(x^2 + 5)(x^2 + 6)$ **b)** $(x^2 − 3y)(x^2 + 4y)$
   c) $(x^3 − 9)(x^3 + 6)$ **d)** $3(x + 6)(x − 7)$
17. a) $x^3 + 6x^2 + 12x + 8$ **b)** $(x + 3)^3$
   c) $(2a + 5b)^3$

5.5 Factor Quadratic Expressions of the Form $ax^2 + bx + c$, pages 242–247

1. a)

$(x + 1)(2x + 3)$

b)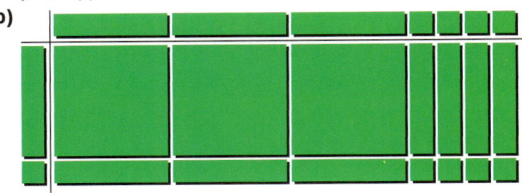

$(x + 1)(3x + 4)$

c)

$(2x + 1)(3x + 1)$

d)

$(2x + 1)(3x + 4)$

2. a) $(2x + 5)(x + 1)$ **b)** $(3y + 8)(2y + 1)$
   c) $(4k + 3)(k + 3)$ **d)** $(3m + 4)(m + 2)$
   e) not possible   **f)** $(3q + 2)(4q + 3)$
3. a) $(x − 2)(4x − 3)$ **b)** $(5n − 6)(n − 1)$
   c) not possible   **d)** $(6a − 1)(a − 1)$
   e) $(3b − 1)(3b − 7)$ **f)** $(5k − 3)(3k − 2)$

4. a) $(3y + 7)(y - 1)$
  b) $(2m - 3)(m + 3)$
  c) $(2k + 1)(4k - 5)$
  d) $(4y - 1)(3y + 1)$
  e) not possible
  f) $(5h + 1)(h - 3)$
5. a) $(3x + y)(x + 2y)$
  b) $(6m + n)(m + 2n)$
  c) $(2p - q)(p - 5q)$
  d) $(c - 2d)(6c + 5d)$
  e) $(3x + y)(3x - 4y)$
  f) $(2d - e)(3d + 2e)$
6. a) $2(2k - 1)(2k - 3)$
  b) $3(3p - 1)(p + 2)$
  c) $2(3m + 2)(m - 3)$
  d) $5(2x - 1)(x + 2)$
  e) $2(5r - 1)(r - 2)$
  f) $2(4y - 3)(y - 2)$
7. a) $(2x + 1)(2x + 5)$; 45
  b) $(7x - 2)(x - 3)$; −12
  c) $(3x + 2)(5x - 4)$; 48
  d) $2(4x - 1)(x + 2)$; 56
  e) $(2x - 3)(3x - 5)$; 1
  f) $(5x - 3)(x + 3)$; 65
  The results are the same because the expressions are equivalent.
8. Answers may vary. For example:
  a) 17, 8 **b)** 28, 20 **c)** 13, 23
9. Answers may vary. For example:
  a) −44, −28 **b)** 24, −60 **c)** 56, 81
10. If there are two integers whose product is $a \times c$ and whose sum is b, then $ax^2 + bx + c$ can be factored over the integers.
11. There will not be as many factors to check.
12. a) $(3x + 8)(2x - 1)$; length $(3x + 8)$, width $(2x - 1)$
  b) $P = 114$ cm; $A = 722$ cm^2
13. $h = -(5t + 2)(t - 5)$; 5 s
14. a) $r = -0.0008(p - 1000)(p - 3000)$
  b) $1000 \leq p \leq 3000$
  c) 2000
15. Answers may vary. For example: number sold: $20 - x$, price per jacket: $36 + 2x$; or number sold: $40 - 2x$, price per jacket: $18 + x$
17. a) $(5x^2 + 3)(x^2 + 3)$
  b) $(7x^2 - 6y^2)(x^2 - y^2)$
  c) $(3x^3 + 8y^3)(2x^3 - y^3)$
  d) $(5m^3 + 4n^2)(2m^3 - 3n^2)$
18. a) $(2x + 2a + 1)(x + a + 1)$
  b) $(2x - 2b + 1)(x - b + 2)$
19. a) Answers may vary. For example: The shape could be a rectangle with dimensions $(2x - 1)$ and $(4x + 7)$, a parallelogram with base $(2x - 1)$ and height $(4x + 7)$, or a triangle with base $(4x - 2)$ and height $(4x + 7)$ or base $(2x - 1)$ and height $(8x + 14)$.
  b) The shape is a square-based prism with side length $(2x - 3y)$ and height x.

5.6 Factor a Perfect Square Trinomial and a Difference of Squares, pages 248–255

1. a) $(x + 4)(x - 4)$
  b) $(y + 10)(y - 10)$
  c) $9(k + 2)(k - 2)$
  d) $(2a + 11)(2a - 11)$
  e) $(6w + 7)(6w - 7)$
  f) $(12p + 1)(12p - 1)$
  g) $(4n + 5)(4n - 5)$
  h) $(10g + 9)(10g - 9)$
2. a) $(m + 7n)(m - 7n)$
  b) $(h + 5d)(h - 5d)$
  c) $(10 + 3c)(10 - 3c)$
  d) $(13a + 7b)(13a - 7b)$
  e) $(5x + 6y)(5x - 6y)$
  f) $(4c + 3d)(4c - 3d)$
  g) $2(9 + 2s)(9 - 2s)$
  h) $3(5h + 3g)(5h - 3g)$
3. a) $x^2 + 12x + 36 = (x)^2 + 2(x)(6) + (6)^2$; $(x + 6)^2$
  b) $k^2 + 18k + 81 = (k)^2 + 2(k)(9) + (9)^2$; $(k + 9)^2$
  c) $y^2 - 6y + 9 = (y)^2 - 2(y)(3) + (3)^2$; $(y - 3)^2$
  d) $m^2 - 14m + 49 = (m)^2 - 2(m)(7) + (7)^2$; $(m - 7)^2$
  e) $x^2 + 20x + 100 = (x)^2 + 2(x)(10) + (10)^2$; $(x + 10)^2$
  f) $64 - 16r + r^2 = (8)^2 - 2(8)(r) + (r)^2$; $(8 - r)^2$

4. a) $4c^2 + 12c + 9 = (2c)^2 + 2(2c)(3) + (3)^2$; $(2c + 3)^2$
  b) $16k^2 - 8k + 1 = (4k)^2 - 2(4k)(1) + (1)^2$; $(4k - 1)^2$
  c) $25x^2 + 70x + 49 = (5x)^2 + 2(5x)(7) + (7)^2$; $(5x + 7)^2$
  d) $9y^2 - 30y + 25 = (3y)^2 - 2(3y)(5) + (5)^2$; $(3y - 5)^2$
  e) $100c^2 - 180c + 81 = (10c)^2 - 2(10c)(9) + (9)^2$; $(10c - 9)^2$
  f) $25 + 80y + 64y^2 = (5)^2 + 2(5)(8y) + (8y)^2$; $(5 + 8y)^2$
5. Answers may vary. For example:
  a) y is not squared.
  b) 107 is not equal to 2(6)(9).
  c) 10 is not a perfect square.
  d) The expression is a sum of squares, not a difference of squares.
6. a) $(2x + 7y)^2$ **b)** $(3k - 4m)^2$
  c) not possible **d)** not possible
  e) $2(a - 7b)^2$ **f)** $4(7n + 6m)(7n - 6m)$
  g) $(5x + 7y)^2$ **h)** $4(5f - 3g)^2$
  i) $100p(2p + 3q)(2p - 3q)$
7. a) area: $(2x + 5)^2 - (x - 3)^2$ **b)** $(3x + 2)(x + 8)$
8. a) 22, −22 **b)** 20, −20
  c) 42, −42 **d)** 25
  e) 25 **f)** 11, −11
9. Answers may vary. For example:
  a) 4, 9 **b)** 1, 25 **c)** 16, 25
10. a) $(3ab - 4cd)^2$ **b)** $(20 + x)(10 - x)$
  c) $(6c)(4)$ **d)** not possible
11. The figure could be a square or a parallelogram with base equal to height.
12. a) $x(x - 1)^2$; height x, length $x - 1$, width $x - 1$
  b) The box is a square-based rectangular prism, so the top and bottom are squares with area $(x - 1)^2$ and the four sides are rectangles with area $x(x - 1)$.
13. a) middle: $(2x + 2)^2 - (2x - 1)^2$;
  bottom: $(2x + 5)^2 - (2x + 2)^2$
  b) middle: $(4x + 1)(3)$; bottom: $(4x + 7)(3)$
  c) middle: 63 cm^2; bottom: 81 cm^2
14. a) 7 cm **b)** $(14\pi r - 49\pi)$ cm^2
15. No. $(x - 1)^2 = (x - 1)(x - 1)$, while $x^2 - 1 = (x - 1)(x + 1)$. The two factored expressions are not equivalent. Alternatively, $(x - 1)^2 = x^2 - 2x + 1$, which is not equivalent to $x^2 - 1$.
16. $y = (x - 2)^2$; the vertex is $(2, 0)$.
17. a) $(15 + 11)(15 - 11) = 104$
  b) $(37 + 27)(37 - 27) = 640$
  c) $(98 + 97)(98 - 97) = 195$
  d) $(28 + 22)(28 - 22) = 300$
18. a) $s = (n + 3)^2 - 4$ **b)** $s = (n + 5)(n + 1)$
  c) 165 **d)** Answers will vary.
19. The figure could be a square-based prism with height πx and base side length $2x + 5$ or a cylinder with radius $2x + 5$ and height x.
20. a) $(x)(x - 8)$ **b)** $(x + 2)^2$
  c) $(5x^2 + 3y^2)(5x^2 - 3y^2)$ **d)** $(k^2 + 4)(k + 2)(k - 2)$
  e) $(a^3 + 10)^2$
  f) $\left(\dfrac{y^2}{9} + \dfrac{x^2}{25}\right)\left(\dfrac{y}{3} + \dfrac{x}{5}\right)\left(\dfrac{y}{3} - \dfrac{x}{5}\right)$
21. a) 72, −72 **b)** 20, −20

22. a) $x^2 - 1 = (x - 1)(x + 1); x^3 - 1 = (x - 1)(x^2 + x + 1);$
$x^4 - 1 = (x - 1)(x + 1)(x^2 + 1);$
$x^5 - 1 = (x - 1)(x^4 + x^3 + x^2 + x + 1)$
b) Answers may vary. For example: $x - 1$ is one of the factors of each of the expressions and the number of terms in the other factor is equal to the degree of the original expression. The terms in the other factor form a sum where the coefficient of each of the terms is one and the terms are the sum of the descending degrees of the variable starting with 1 less than the original expression. The factored form of $x^4 - 1$ does not appear to follow the pattern. When expanded, the last two terms of this factored form result in the expression $x^3 + x^2 + x + 1$, which does follow the pattern.
c) $x^6 - 1 = (x - 1)(x^5 + x^4 + x^3 + x^2 + x + 1)$, which is also $(x - 1)(x + 1)(x^2 + x + 1)(x^2 - x + 1)$.

23. a) By expanding, $(x - 2)(x^2 + 2x + 4) = x^3 - 8$.
b) $(m - 4)(m^2 + 4m + 16)$
c) $(3y - 5z^2)(9y^2 + 15yz^2 + 25z^4)$

24. a) By expanding, $(a + 10)(a^2 - 10a + 100) = a^3 + 1000$.
b) $(k^2 + 6e)(k^4 - 6k^2e + 36e^2)$
c) $(7q^4 + 9r^8)(49q^8 - 63q^4r^8 + 81r^{16})$

25. a) $a^4 + 4a^3b + 6a^2b^2 + 4ab^3 + b^4$
b) $(3x - 2y)^4$

26. D

Chapter 5 Review, pages 256–257

1. a) $x^2 + 13x + 40$ **b)** $x^2 - 5x + 4$
c) $x^2 - 3xy - 18y^2$ **d)** $10a^2 + 33ab - 54b^2$

2. a) $-k^2 + 5k + 14$
b) $w^3 - 10w^2v + 21wv^2$
c) $147x^3 + 504x^2y + 189xy^2$
d) $2y^2 + 2y$
e) $331x^2 + 235x - 204$

3. Area: $x(x + 9) + 7(x); x^2 + 16x$

4. a)
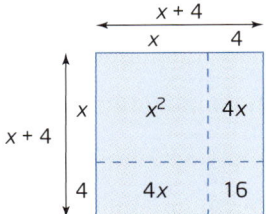

b)
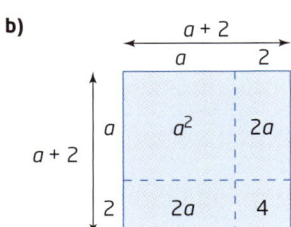

5. a) $x^2 + 12x + 36$ **b)** $k^2 + 16k + 64$
c) $p^2 + 14p + 49$ **d)** $r^2 - 4r + 4$
e) $e^2 - 18e + 81$ **f)** $q^2 - 40q + 400$

6. a) $b^2 - 36$ **b)** $a^2 - 49$
c) $y^2 - 144$ **d)** $x^2 - 225$
e) $e^2 - 100$ **f)** $x^2 - 36$

7. a) $y^2 + 8xy + 16x^2$ **b)** $49m^2 - 14mn + n^2$
c) $4c^2 + 36cd + 81d^2$ **d)** $-50x^2 + 98y^2$
e) $9a^2 - 64c^2$ **f)** $-25x^2 + 64y^2$

8. a)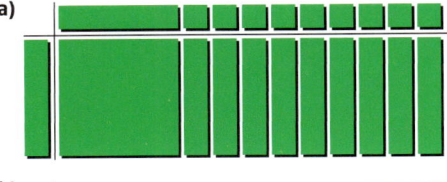

b)

9. a) $12(y + 2z)$ **b)** $x(11y - 9z)$
c) $c(c + 3)$ **d)** $4k(1 - 2k^2)$

10. a) $(m + 3)(4m + 3)$ **b)** $(3k - 2)(3k + 2)$
c) $(x + 2)(8x - 5)$ **d)** $(4x + 3y)^2$

11. a) $4(2m^2 - 4m + 1)$ **b)** $2(9c^3 + 12c^2 - 4c + 3)$
c) $m(15m - 22n + 66n^2)$ **d)** $az(x^2 - z + x)$

12. length $10x^2 + 5x$, width 1; length $2x^2 + x$, width 5; length $10x + 5$, width x; length $2x + 1$, width $5x$;

13. a)

b)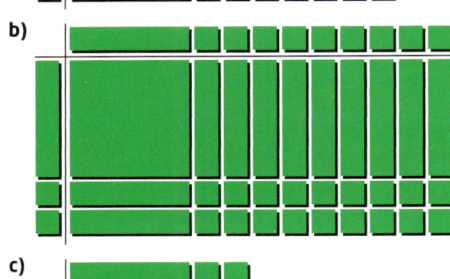

c)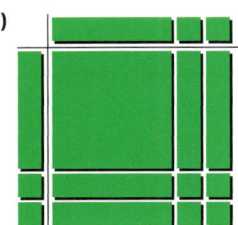

14. a) $(c - 9)(c - 8)$ **b)** $(x - 3)(x - 5)$
c) $(z - 11)(z - 3)$ **d)** $(x + 5)(x - 2)$
e) $(x + 9)(x - 1)$ **f)** $(x - 4)(x + 2)$

15. a) $y = (x - 6)(x + 3)$ **b)** $6, -3$
  c) $x = 1.5$; $(1.5, -20.25)$

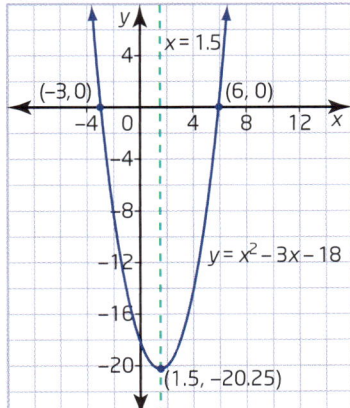

16. a) $(2x + 3)(x + 2)$ **b)** $(2y + 9)(3y + 1)$
  c) $(a - 3)(6a - 5)$ **d)** $(4b - 1)(b - 1)$
  e) $4(3m - 1)(m + 2)$ **f)** $(7k + 2)(2k - 5)$
17. a) $(2x + 3y)(4x - 5y)$ **b)** not possible
  c) $(4m + 3n)(3m + n)$ **d)** not possible
  e) $3(4x + 3y)(2x - y)$ **f)** not possible
18. a) length $4x - 5$, width $2x + 3$
  b) $P = 140$ cm, $A = 1161$ cm^2
19. a) $(x + 7)(x - 7)$ **b)** $(y + 11)(y - 11)$
  c) $(2k + 3)(2k - 3)$ **d)** $16(1 + 3a)(1 - 3a)$
  e) $(3w + 5x)(3w - 5x)$ **f)** $(1 + 9p)(1 - 9p)$
20. a) $x^2 + 14x + 49 = (x)^2 + 2(x)(7) + (7)^2$; $(x + 7)^2$
  b) $k^2 + 8k + 16 = (k)^2 + 2(k)(4) + (4)^2$; $(k + 4)^2$
  c) $y^2 - 10y + 25 = (y)^2 - 2(y)(5) + (5)^2$; $(y - 5)^2$
  d) $25y^2 - 70y + 49 = (y)^2 - 2(y)(7) + (7)^2$; $(5y - 7)^2$
  e) $36c^2 - 108c + 81 = 9(4c^2 - 12c + 9) =$
    $9[(2c)^2 - 2(2c)(3) + (3)^2]$; $9(2c - 3)^2$
  f) $121 + 176y + 64y^2 = (11)^2 + 2(11)(8y) + (8y)^2$;
    $(11 + 8y)^2$
21. a) $120, -120$ **b)** 49
22. a) $(3wx - 4yz)^2$ **b)** $(20 + y)(30 - y)$
  c) not possible **d)** not possible

Chapter 5 Practice Test, pages 258–259
1. a) $(2x + 3)(x + 3) = 2x^2 + 9x + 9$
  b) $(x + 3)(x + 4) = x^2 + 7x + 12$
2. a) $12x^3 - 20x^2y + 32x^2z$
  b) $14m^3 - 7m^2 + 12m - 9$
3. a) $y^2 + 14y + 45$ **b)** $12x^2 - 13x - 14$
  c) $36k^2 - 1$ **d)** $w^2 - 16w + 64$
  e) $16c^2 + 40cd + 25d^2$ **f)** $-318x^2 - 22x + 461$
4. a) $d = 0.006s^2 + 0.012s + 0.006$
  b) The minimum stopping distance is $d = 22.326$ m for both versions of the formula.
5. a) $3d^2e(3e + 2d)$ **b)** $5pqr(3pr^2 - 5p^2q + 1)$
  c) $(x + 6)(3)$ **d)** $(2x + 1)(8x - 3)$
6. a) Surface area: $2(3x + 4)^2 + 4(x)(3x + 4)$
  b) $30x^2 + 64x + 32$
  c) $2(3x + 4)(5x + 4)$
7. a) $(x + 8)(x + 3)$ **b)** $(y - 8)(y - 7)$
  c) $(n - 10)(n + 9)$ **d)** $(x - 7)^2$
  e) $(h + 10)(h - 10)$ **f)** $(d + 8)^2$

8. a) $3(k + 6m)(k - 2m)$ **b)** $(8y + 3)(y + 2)$
  c) $(3w - 7)(3w - 1)$ **d)** $(5a + 6)^2$
  e) $(11w + 12)(11w - 12)$ **f)** $(5x - 6y)(2x + y)$
9. If there are two integers whose product is 9×18 and whose sum is -10, then $9x^2 - 10x + 18$ can be factored over the integers.
10. a) length $x + 15$, width $x - 2$
  b) 3
11. a) $132, -132$ **b)** 4
  c) 36 **d)** 25
12. a) Area: $(x + 9)^2 - (x + 5)(x - 5)$
  b) $2(9x + 53)$
  c) 232 square units; the results are the same because the expressions are equivalent.
13. a) $y = 2x^2 + 24x + 70$ **b)** $y = 2(x + 7)(x + 5)$
  c) Yes, because the three expressions give the same graph when graphed using a graphing calculator.
14. a) height x, side of base $3x - 5$, side of base $3x - 5$
  b) It is a square-based prism, so the top and bottom are squares with side length $3x - 5$ and area $(3x - 5)^2$, and the four sides are rectangles with width $3x - 5$, height x, and area $x(3x - 5)$.
15. Answers may vary. For example:
  a) $4, 9$ **b)** $1, 25$ **c)** $9, 16$
16. a) $(34 + 31)(34 - 31) = 195$
  b) $(127 + 126)(127 - 126) = 253$
  c) $(52 + 48)(52 - 48) = 400$
17. a) The total number of squares, s, in diagram n is $s = 4n^2$.
  b) The total number of shaded squares, S, in diagram n is $S = n + 3$.
  c) The total number of unshaded squares, u, in diagram n is $u = 4n^2 - n - 3$.
  d) $u = (4n + 3)(n - 1)$
  e) $4(15)^2 - 15 - 3 = 882$ unshaded squares
    $(4(15) + 3)(15 - 1) = 882$ unshaded squares

Chapter 6 Answers

Get Ready, pages 262–263
1. a)

b)
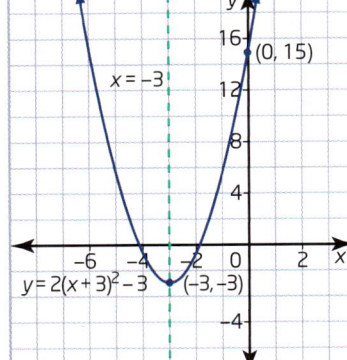

c)
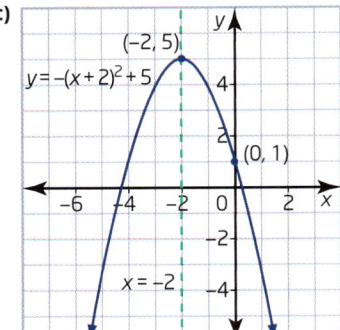

d)
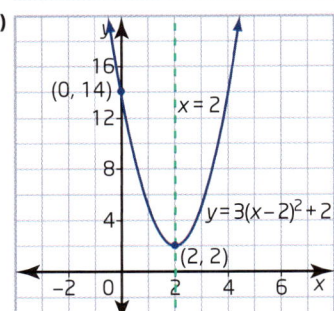

2. a)
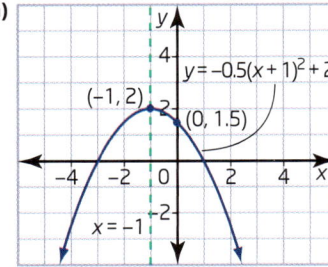

b)
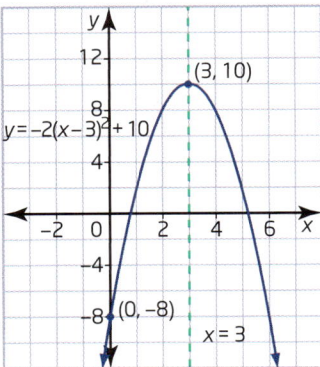

c)
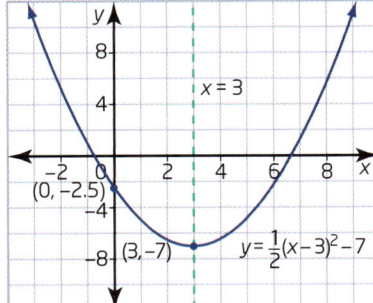

d)
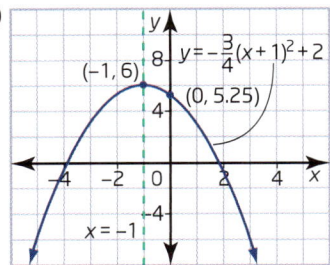

3. a) ± 10 b) ± 6 c) ± 8.7
   d) not possible
4. a) ± 3 b) ± 5 c) ± 5 d) ± 7
5. a) $2(x + 3)(x + 2)$ b) $(x + 14)(x + 2)$
   c) $(x - 9)(x - 7)$ d) $4(x + 3)(x - 3)$
   e) $(9x + 7)(9x - 7)$ f) $3(x - 4)(x + 2)$
   g) $(4x - 1)^2$ h) $(3x + 4)(4x + 1)$
6. a) $(x - 8)(x + 4)$ b) $2(x + 3)^2$
   c) $(8x + 1)(8x - 1)$ d) $(12x - 13)^2$
   e) $(7x + 5)^2$ f) $(2x + 1)(x - 5)$
   g) $(3x - 4)(3x - 2)$ h) $3(2x + 1)(x + 3)$

7. a) The first number is x. The second number is $\frac{1}{2}x$.
   b) The area of the original garden is A. The area of the new garden is $3A$.
   c) The number of price reductions is n. The new price, in dollars, is $12 - n$.
   d) The first number is x. The second number is $x^2 + (x + 1)^2$.
   e) The width is w. The length is $2w - 3$.
8. a) $x + y = 100$ b) $2(l + w) = 50$
   c) $P = 8w$ d) $xy = 4x^2$
   e) $x + y + 3 = 12$

6.1 Maxima and Minima, pages 264–273

1. **a)** $y = (x + 1)^2 + 4$ **b)** $y = (x + 2)^2 + 3$
   c) $y = (x + 3)^2 - 6$
2. **a)** 9 **b)** 49 **c)** 36
   d) 25 **e)** 1 **f)** 1600
3. **a)** $y = (x + 3)^2 - 10$ **b)** $y = (x + 1)^2 + 6$
   c) $y = (x + 5)^2 - 5$ **d)** $y = (x + 1)^2 - 2$
   e) $y = (x - 3)^2 - 13$ **f)** $y = (x - 4)^2 - 18$
   g) $y = (x - 6)^2 - 28$
4. **a)** $(-3, -7)$ **b)** $(-6, -6)$ **c)** $(4, -3)$ **d)** $(3, 8)$
5. **a)** D **b)** A **c)** B **d)** C
6. **a)** $(-5, -5)$

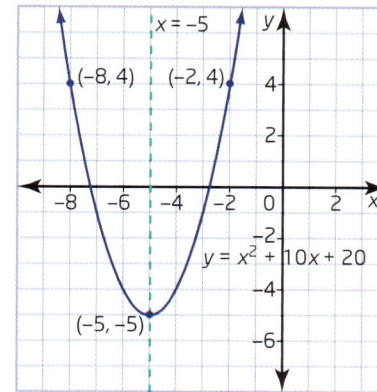

   b) $(8, -4)$

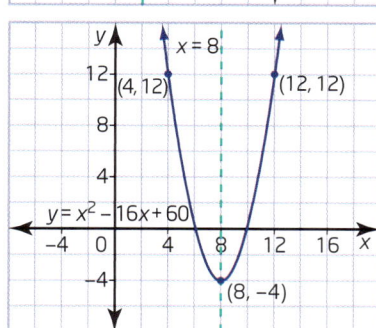

7. **a)** $y = -(x - 40)^2 + 1500$ **b)** $y = -(x + 3)^2 + 13$
   c) $y = 3(x + 15)^2 - 625$ **d)** $y = 2(x - 4)^2 - 17$
   e) $y = -7(x - 1)^2 + 4$
8. **a)** maximum point at $(-5, 16)$
   b) maximum point at $(7, -1)$
   c) minimum point at $(-30, -1725)$
   d) minimum point at $(4, -38)$
   e) maximum point at $(-20, 1880)$
9. **a)** minimum point at $(-3, -10)$
   b) minimum point at $(3.8, 3.5)$
   c) maximum point at $(1.3, -2.3)$
   d) minimum point at $(0.1, 0.5)$
   e) maximum point at $(0.8, 23.3)$
   f) minimum point at $(-0.1, 12.9)$
10. **a)** $(-1, -5)$

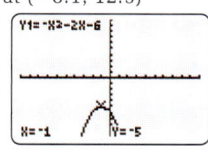

    b) $(-3, 5)$

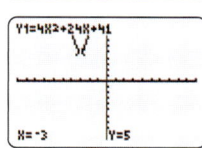

    c) $(3, -4)$

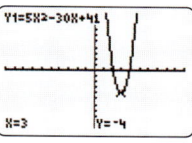

    d) $(2, -1)$

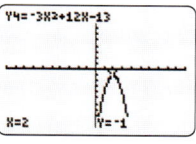

    e) $(-2, -5)$

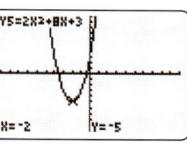

11. **a)** $(-0.75, 8.125)$

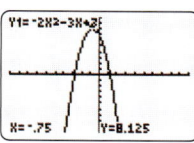

    b) $(1.5, 4.25)$

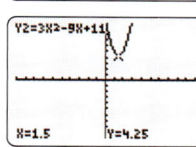

    c) $(4, 6)$

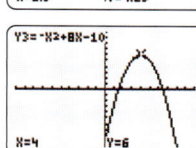

    d) $(2, -5)$

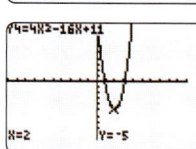

    e) $(-3, -3)$

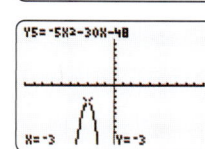

12. The maximum height of 5 m occurs at a horizontal distance of 2 m.
13. For $h = -4.9t^2 + 10t + 1$, the maximum height of 6.1 m occurs at time $t = 1.0$ s, and for $h = -0.0163x^2 + 0.5774x + 1$, the maximum height of 6.1 m occurs at a horizontal distance of $x = 17.7$ m.
14. 4 m
15. The minimum cost of $143 occurs when the machine runs for 21 h.
16. **a)** price of a garden ornament: $4 - 0.5x$; number of garden ornaments sold: $120 + 20x$
    b) $R(x) = (4 - 0.5x)(120 + 20x)$
    c) $R = -10x^2 + 20x + 480$; $R = -10(x - 1)^2 + 490$; to maximize revenue, the artisan should charge $3.50.
    d) Both forms produce the same graph.
17. **a)** minimum point at $(-2, -13)$
    b) maximum point at $(-10, 11)$
    c) minimum point at $(-5, -7.5)$

d) maximum point at (2, 5)
e) minimum point at (6, −6)
f) maximum point at (−15, −4.5)
18. The depth of the half-pipe is 3.2 m.
19. a) $c = 16$, $h = 4$
   b) $b = 12$, $h = 6$ or $b = -12$, $h = -6$
   c) $b = -10$, $c = 27$
20. 30 km/h
21. No.
22. 13.7 h
23. $A = 10x - x^2$, where x represents the width of the rectangle. Since the maximum point of the quadratic relation is (5, 25), a 5 cm by 5 cm square will give a maximum area of 25 cm^2.
24. $A = 200x - 2x^2$, where x represents the width of the field. Since the maximum point of the quadratic relation is (50, 5000), a 50 m by 100 m field will give a maximum area of 5000 m^2.
25.

Angle of Elevation	Maximum Height (m)
20°	0.6
30°	1.3
40°	2.1
50°	3.0
60°	3.8
70°	4.5

26. $\left(\dfrac{47}{26}, -\dfrac{649}{312}\right)$

27. The relation $y = ax^2 + bc + c$ can be expressed as
$y = a\left(x - \dfrac{b}{2a}\right)^2 - \dfrac{b^2}{4a} + c$ by completing the square.
Therefore, the x-coordinate of the vertex is $\dfrac{b}{2a}$.

28. $\sqrt{3}R$
29. D
30. D

6.2 Solve Quadratic Equations, pages 274–281

1. a) −5, −2   b) 3, −4   c) 1, 7   d) 0, −9
   e) $-\dfrac{3}{2}$, 5   f) $\dfrac{1}{2}$, $-\dfrac{4}{3}$ g) $\dfrac{5}{3}$, $\dfrac{3}{4}$
2. a) −2, −6   b) −3, −6   c) 0, −3   d) 14, 4
   e) 0, 2   f) 15, 2   g) 2, −11   h) 0, 11
3. a) $-\dfrac{1}{3}$, −9   b) -1, $-\dfrac{15}{4}$ c) $\dfrac{3}{2}$, $\dfrac{5}{4}$
   d) $\dfrac{1}{4}$, $-\dfrac{1}{4}$ e) 0, −3   f) $\dfrac{3}{2}$
4. a) −1, −4   b) −3, −5   c) 12, 1
   d) −1   e) 10, −30   f) 0, 7
5. a) $-\dfrac{3}{2}$, −2   b) 1, $-\dfrac{8}{9}$ c) $\dfrac{3}{2}$
   d) $-\dfrac{1}{2}$, $\dfrac{5}{8}$ e) $\dfrac{1}{4}$, $-\dfrac{10}{3}$ f) $-\dfrac{1}{3}$, −7
6. a) −8, −2   b) −3, −5
   c) −1, $-\dfrac{3}{2}$ d) $\dfrac{1}{5}$, 3
7. 3 m

8. 3.5 cm
9. a) $(x - 5)(x - 4) = 0$
   b) $(x + 2)(x - 3) = 0$
10. a) $x^2 + x - 42 = 0$
    b) The roots remain the same because the quadratic equation is equivalent to $x^2 + x - 42 = 0$ and will have the same factors.
11. $15x^2 + 2x - 8 = 0$
12. a), b) Answers will vary.
13. Answers will vary.
14. 21 cm and 20 cm
15. $n = 0$ will also satisfy the equation. If Chris wants to divide out a common factor, it should not contain any variables. Chris should subtract $15n$ from both sides of the equation, then divide both sides of the equation by 3, and then solve the equation by factoring.
16. a) For $n = 1$, $S = 1(1 + 1) = 1(2) = 2$. For $n = 2$, $S = 2(2 + 1) = 2(3) = 6$.
    b) 30   c) $n = 17$
17. $n = 4$ or 29
19. The width is 5 m and the length is 12 m.
20. Ralph's shop will lose money during the first 3 years of operation and make a profit during year 4 and year 5 of operation.
21. a) $y = -1$, $y = -2$; the coefficients are the same for the equations, but the solution for the equation $y^2 + 3xy + 2x^2 = 0$ is $y = -x$, $y = -2x$.
    b) i) $y = -x$, $y = -2x$ ii) $y = 2x$, $y = -\dfrac{4}{5}x$ iii) $y = \dfrac{3}{2}x$

6.3 Graph Quadratics Using the x-Intercepts, pages 282–291

1. a) −2, −3   b) 7, 4   c) 0, −9
   d) 3, −8   e) 4, −2   f) 3, −12
2. a) $-\dfrac{1}{2}$, $-\dfrac{9}{2}$ b) $\dfrac{3}{4}$, 0   c) $\dfrac{7}{3}$, $-\dfrac{1}{2}$
   d) $\dfrac{4}{5}$, −2   e) 4, $\dfrac{1}{3}$ f) $\dfrac{5}{2}$
3. a) −7, −2; $\left(-\dfrac{9}{2}, -\dfrac{25}{4}\right)$

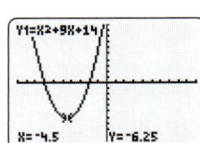

b) 4, 2; (3, −1)

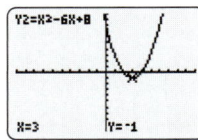

c) −5, 1; (−2, 9)

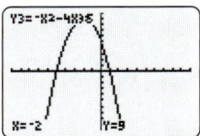

d) −5, 0; $\left(-\dfrac{5}{2}, \dfrac{25}{4}\right)$

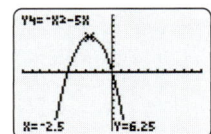

546 MHR • Answers

4. a) 3, −3; (0, −9)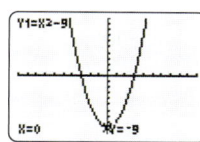

b) 1, 9; (5, 16)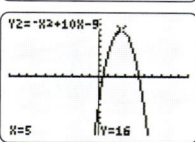

c) 6; (6, 0)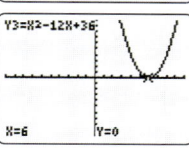

d) 4, −4; (0, 16)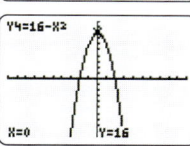

5. a) $-\frac{1}{2}, -7; \left(-\frac{15}{4}, -\frac{169}{8}\right)$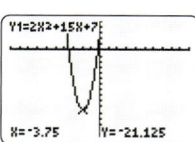

b) $\frac{5}{6}, \frac{1}{2}; \left(\frac{2}{3}, -\frac{1}{3}\right)$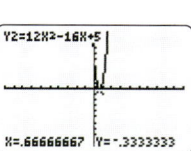

c) $-2, \frac{3}{8}; \left(-\frac{13}{16}, \frac{361}{32}\right)$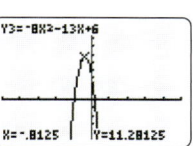

d) $-1, -\frac{9}{8}; \left(-\frac{17}{16}, -\frac{1}{32}\right)$

e) $\frac{3}{4}; \left(\frac{3}{4}, 0\right)$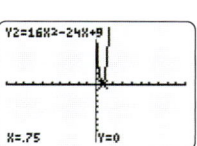

f) $-4, -\frac{1}{2}; \left(-\frac{9}{4}, \frac{49}{4}\right)$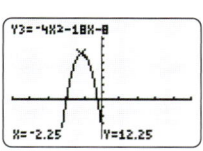

6. a) $y = -x^2 + 6x$ **b)** $y = \frac{1}{5}x^2 - \frac{2}{5}x - \frac{24}{5}$

7. a) $y = 2x^2 + 20x + 32$ **b)** $y = -\frac{3}{4}x^2 - \frac{9}{2}x - \frac{15}{4}$

c) $y = -\frac{1}{2}x^2 + 4x$ **d)** $y = 0.3x^2 - 0.3x - 6$

8. a) width 4 m, height 4 m

b)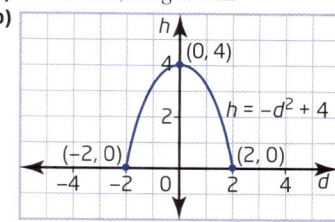

c) $-2 \leq d \leq 2$ so that $h \geq 0$.

9. a) $-\frac{1}{3}, 4$ **b)** $0 \leq x \leq 4$

c) 4 m **d)** maximum height 14.08 m

10. a)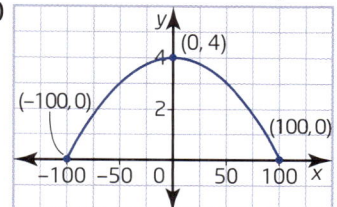

b) 1.44 m

11. x-intercepts −11, 5; y-intercept $\frac{385}{64}$

12. a) −2, 18

b)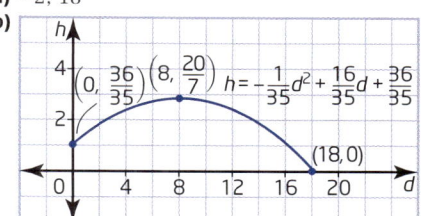

c) $0 \leq d \leq 18$ so that $h \geq 0$.

d) $\frac{36}{35}$ m **e)** 18 m

13. a)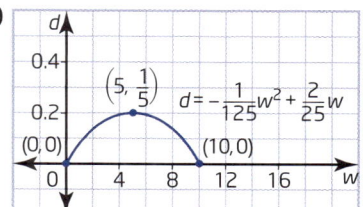

b) $0 \leq w \leq 10$ so that $d \geq 0$.

c) 10 m **d)** 0.2 m

14. If a parabola has only one x-intercept, then the vertex is also the x-intercept.

15. a) 10, −10

b) 6, −6

c) 1

16. a) The Marble Heads' marble travels farther by 1.5 m.
b) 0 m
c) The Marble Heads' marble flies higher.

17. a) 6
b) Yes, because the width of the airplane hangar decreases as the height increases. If the wings of the Bombardier Canadair CRJ-700 are 2 m above the floor, only five airplanes can fit side by side inside the hangar.

18. a) Answers may vary. For example: Parabola A, $y = x^2 - 8x + 18$, Parabola B, $y = -x^2 - 12x - 37$
b) Answers may vary. For example: Parabola A and Parabola B do not intersect the x-axis and thus do not have x-intercepts. Therefore, the equations for these parabolas cannot be factored.

19. −33

20.

There are no x-intercepts for this graph. The vertex of the graph of $y = x^2 + 4$ is (0, 4) and the graph opens upward. The expression $a^2 + b^2$ cannot be factored since the graph of any parabola of the form $y = x^2 + b^2$ does not have any x-intercepts and therefore cannot be solved by factoring.

21. a) 1, 2   **b)** 3, 4

22. a) $\dfrac{3}{8}$ **b)** $\dfrac{1}{2}$

c) The additional information in part b) (John is a boy) changes the situation. For example, only half of the tree diagram of the scenario in part a) needs to be considered.

6.4 The Quadratic Formula, pages 292–303

1. a) $-3, -\dfrac{3}{7}$ **b)** $\dfrac{-4 \pm \sqrt{72}}{4}$

c) $\dfrac{3}{2}$ **d)** $\dfrac{7 \pm \sqrt{17}}{4}$

e) $\dfrac{-5 \pm \sqrt{37}}{6}$ **f)** $-\dfrac{3}{4}$

2. a) $\dfrac{-7 \pm \sqrt{34}}{3}$; −0.39, −4.28

b) $\dfrac{-3 \pm \sqrt{7}}{4}$; −0.09, −1.41

c) $\dfrac{7 \pm \sqrt{65}}{8}$; 1.88, −0.13

d) $\dfrac{45 \pm \sqrt{2305}}{20}$; 4.65, −0.15

e) $\dfrac{-16 \pm \sqrt{216}}{-10}$; 0.13, 3.07

f) $\dfrac{17 \pm \sqrt{409}}{12}$; 3.10, −0.27

3. a) 3, −0.2; (1.4, −12.8); $x = 1.4$

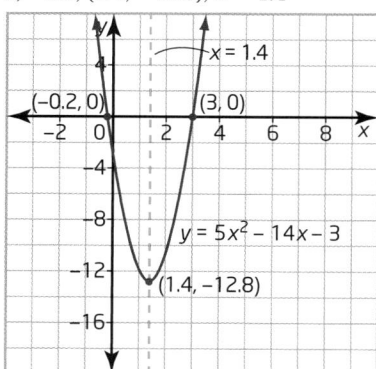

b) 4, −1.5; (1.25, −15.125); $x = 1.25$

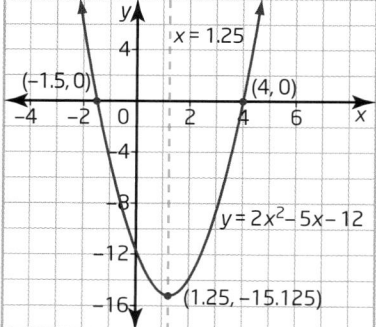

c) −5; (−5, 0); $x = -5$

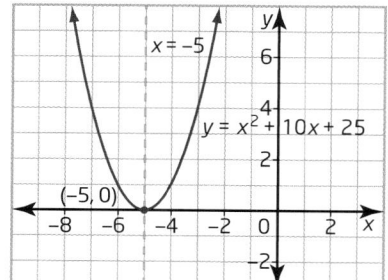

d) $\frac{4}{3}$; $\left(\frac{4}{3}, 0\right)$; $x = \frac{4}{3}$

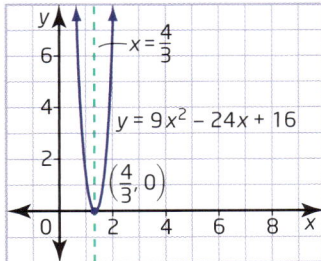

e) no x-intercepts; (1, 2); $x = 1$

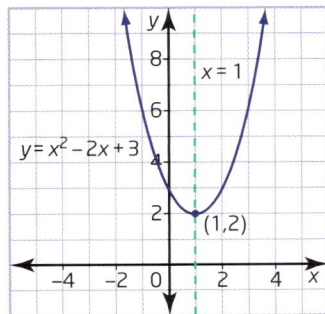

f) no x-intercepts, (−1.5, −0.75); $x = -1.5$

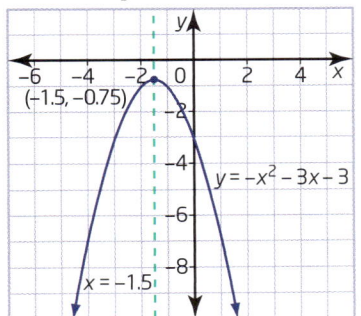

4. a) (3, 2); opens upward; no x-intercepts
b) (2, 4); opens downward; two x-intercepts
c) (−4, −5); opens upward; two x-intercepts
d) (−3, −1); opens downward; no x-intercepts
e) (5, 0); opens upward; one x-intercept

5. a) $y = x^2 - 6x + 11$; since $b^2 - 4ac < 0$, there are no x-intercepts.
b) $y = -x^2 + 4x$; since $b^2 - 4ac > 0$, there are two x-intercepts, 0 and 4.
c) $y = 2x^2 + 16x + 27$; since $b^2 - 4ac > 0$, there are two x-intercepts, $\frac{-16 + \sqrt{40}}{4}$ and $\frac{-16 - \sqrt{40}}{4}$.
d) $y = -2x^2 - 12x - 19$; since $b^2 - 4ac < 0$, there are no x-intercepts.
e) $y = x^2 - 10x + 25$; since $b^2 - 4ac = 0$, there is one x-intercept, 5.

6. a) 10.5 m **b)** 3 m or 7 m
7. a) 1.9 s **b)** 5 m
8. Answers will vary.
9. a) 2.28, −0.56 **b)** 0.75, −4 **c)** 1.5, −0.8
d) 2.54, 0.13 **e)** no real roots **f)** −2.51, 4.51

10. length 139.2 m, height 21.3 m
11. a) 0.56 s **b)** 1.09 s **c)** 0.83 s
12. a) 8 m **b)** 1.55 m
13. 16 m
14. a) Since $\sqrt{b^2 - 4ac} = \sqrt{-0.3072}$, there are no x-intercepts.
b) 100 km/h
16. a) $2x^2 - 14x + 7 = 0$ **b)** $3x^2 + 11x - 2 = 0$
17. a) 3 **b)** 6, 10, 15
c) $\frac{n(n-1)}{2}$ **d)** 46
18. Answers may vary. For example: The quadratic equation $x^2 - 6x + 9 = 0$ has $b^2 - 4ac = 0$. When graphed, the quadratic relation $y = x^2 - 6x + 9$ has one x-intercept, 3, which is also the vertex, (3, 0), so there is only one real root.
19. (3.35, 2.19), (−3.35, 2.19), (−2.41, −3.19), (2.41, −3.19)

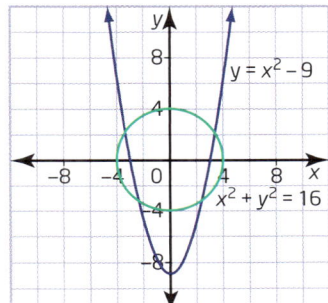

20. The possible numbers of intersection points are 0, 1, 2, 3, and 4; equations will vary.
21. $x = \frac{1 \pm \sqrt{5}}{2}$; $x = 1.618$ or $x = -0.618$;

$$\left(\frac{1 - \sqrt{5}}{2}\right)\left(\frac{1 + \sqrt{5}}{2}\right) = \left(\frac{1 - 5}{4}\right)$$
$$= \left(\frac{-4}{4}\right)$$
$$= -1$$

Therefore, the roots of $x = 1 + \frac{1}{x}$ are negative reciprocals.

22. a) $\frac{157}{68}$
b) converges to the golden ratio, $x = \frac{1 + \sqrt{5}}{2} \doteq 1.618$
23. a) 34, 55, 89; each subsequent term is found by adding the two terms before it.
b) $x = \frac{1 + \sqrt{5}}{2} \doteq 1.618$ (the golden ratio)
24. $a = 2, b = 1, c = -1, d = -2$

6.5 Solve Problems Using Quadratic Equations, pages 304–315

1. a) $h = -4.9t^2 + 45t + 2$ **b)** 9.23 s
2. a) 124 m **b)** $2.79 \leq t \leq 7.21$
3. 1.95 m by 17.95 m
4. 57 and 58 or −57 and −58
5. 17 and 19 or −17 and −19

6. 5 cm, 12 cm, and 13 cm
7. a)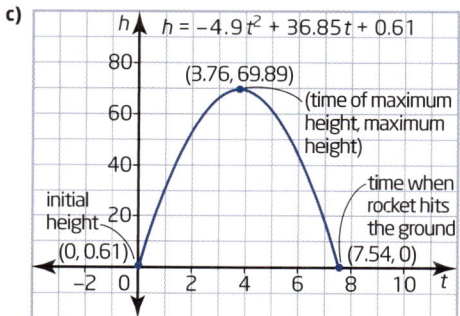
   b) $y = -0.05x^2 + 0.95x + 0.5$
8. 40 mm
9. 46 mm
10. 13 and 14 or −13 and −14
11. 5.5 cm by 6 cm
12. 300 m by 600 m
13. 6 units, 8 units, and 10 units
14. 5.97 m
15. a) $h = -4.9t^2 + 36.85t + 0.61$
    b) Answers may vary. For example: Use a graphing calculator to calculate the total time in the air. When the height is equal to zero, the time is 7.54 s, to the nearest hundredth. Use a graphing calculator to calculate the maximum height of the rocket. When the time is 3.76 s, the height of the rocket is 69.89 m, to the nearest hundredth.
    c)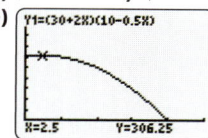
16. a) $h = -4.9t^2 + 15t + 1$ b) 11.1 m   c) 3.1 s
    d) The maximum height of 12.5 m occurs at 1.5 s.
    e) $h = -0.81t^2 + 15t + 1$; 15.2 m; 18.6 s; the maximum height of 70.4 m occurs at 9.3 s.
    f) $h = -11.55t^2 + 15t + 1$; 4.5 m; 1.4 s; the maximum height of 5.9 m occurs at 0.6 s.
17. a) A model for Sherri's revenue, R, in dollars, is $R = (30 + 2x)(10 - 0.5x)$, where x represents the number of $0.50 price reductions.
    b) $2.50   c) $8.75   d) $0
    e)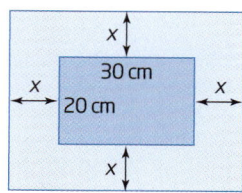
    Part b) is represented by the point (15, 150). Part c) is represented by the vertex (2.5, 306.25), which is the maximum point. Part d) is represented by the x-intercept 20.
18. 28 cm by 38 cm

19. 28.2 cm by 19.2 cm
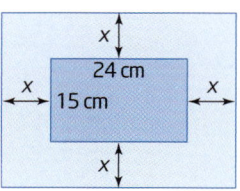
20. 22 m by 68 m
21. a)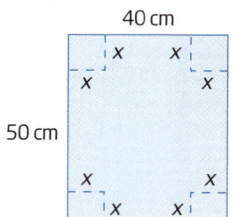
    b) 7.5 cm
    c) 6562.5 cm³
22. 1.5 cm
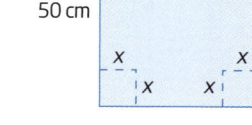
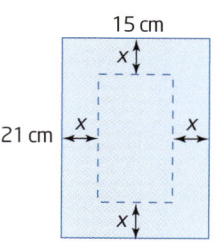
23. 4 cm
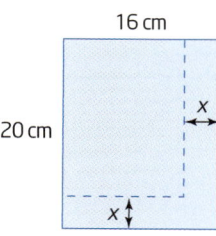
24. 10 m by 15 m
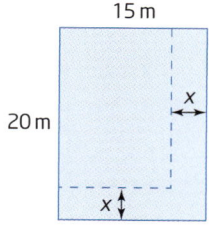
25. Answers will vary. For example: $y = \dfrac{23}{90\,000}x^2 - 23$
26. a)
    b) $y = 0.008x^2 - 0.383x + 8.726$
    c) 61.0 m
    d) 82 km/h, 113 km/h, 183 km/h
    e) Answers may vary. For example: The model does not make sense for speeds less than 24.5 km/h because the stopping distances should be less when the car is going slower.

27. a) one point of intersection because the resulting equation is linear
b) no points of intersection because the resulting quadratic equation does not have any real roots
c) one point of intersection because the resulting quadratic equation has two equal real roots

28. a) $WC = 0.0032w^2 - 0.425w + 6$, where WC represents the wind chill temperature and w represents the wind speed.
b) The QuadReg operation results in a linear relation, since the coefficient of the x^2-term is 0. $WC = t - 13$, where WC represents the wind chill temperature and t represents the air temperature.
c) Answers may vary. For example: The wind chill model from part b) is very good, because the data follow a linear model exactly. The model from part a) is quite good because the result for $w = 60$ is very close to the actual result.

29. Answers will vary.

30. Answers may vary. For example: Solving two equations in two unknowns results in an approximate quadratic model $y = -\dfrac{10}{121}(x - 11)^2 + 14$. Therefore, the pumpkin was at a height of 10 m at horizontal distances of 4 m and 18 m.

31. $f_1 = 1, f_2 = 1, f_3 = 2, f_4 = 3, f_5 = 5$

Chapter 6 Review, pages 316–317

1. a) $y = (x + 4)^2 - 23$ **b)** $y = (x + 1)^2 + 6$
c) $y = (x + 2)^2 + 2$ **d)** $y = (x + 3)^2 - 12$

2. a) $(-6, -6)$

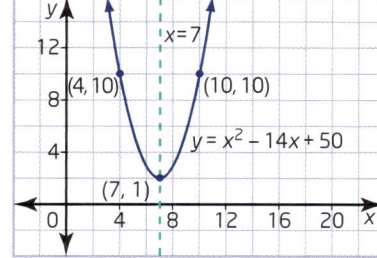

b) $(7, 1)$

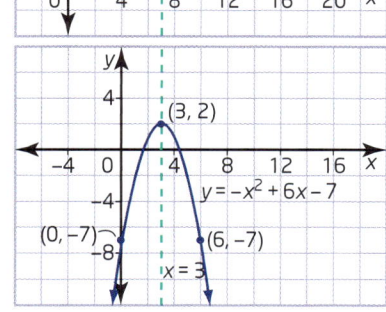

c) $(3, 2)$

d) $(4, -4)$

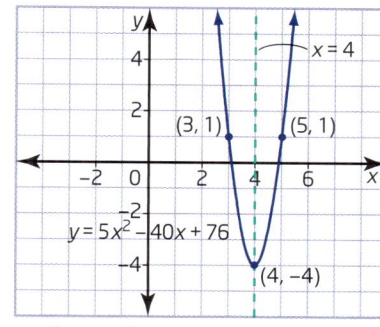

3. a) minimum point at $(0.6, 7.3)$
b) maximum point at $(0.2, -200.1)$
c) minimum point at $(0.2, 0.6)$

4. a) $-3, -7$ **b)** $2, -10$ **c)** $-\dfrac{1}{2}, -3$ **d)** $\dfrac{2}{5}, -3$

5. a) $9, -1$ **b)** $7, 1$ **c)** $-1, -\dfrac{7}{3}$ **d)** $\dfrac{3}{5}$
e) $\dfrac{5}{4}, \dfrac{1}{2}$ **f)** $-\dfrac{2}{3}, -1$

6. 12 cm, 35 cm, 37 cm

7. a) $-2, -6; (-4, -4)$

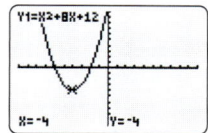

b) $-1, 5; (2, -9)$

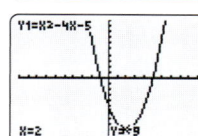

c) $-9, 3; (-3, 36)$

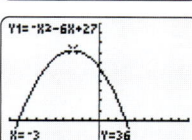

d) $-\dfrac{4}{3}, -2; \left(-\dfrac{5}{3}, -\dfrac{1}{3}\right)$

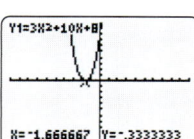

e) $-3, 0; \left(-\dfrac{3}{2}, -\dfrac{9}{4}\right)$

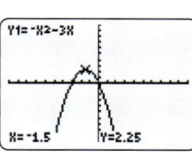

f) $2, -2; (0, -4)$

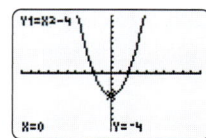

8. They will have the same axis of symmetry because it will pass through the midpoint of the line segment connecting the x-intercepts, or zeros, but the vertex can be different because vertical stretching or compressing will change the y-coordinate of the vertex but not the zeros.
9. a) 20, −20   b) −49
10. a) $-\dfrac{5}{3}, 1$ b) $\dfrac{4 \pm \sqrt{43}}{9}$
    c) $\dfrac{-7 \pm \sqrt{29}}{10}$ d) $-\dfrac{9}{5}$
11. 191.4 km/h
12. a) $h = -4.9t^2 + 4t + 3$ b) 1.29 s
    c) $0.15 \leq t \leq 0.66$
13. 2.4 m
14. a) A model for the Sticker Warehouse's revenue, R, in dollars, is $R = (6 + x)(4 - 0.25x)$, where x represents the number of $0.25 price reductions.
    b) 4 or 6
    c) The maximum revenue of $30.25 occurs with five price reductions.

Chapter 6 Practice Test, pages 318–319

1. a)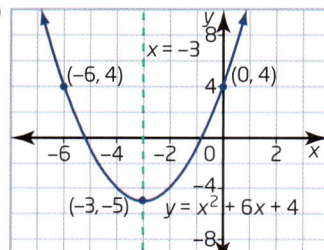

b)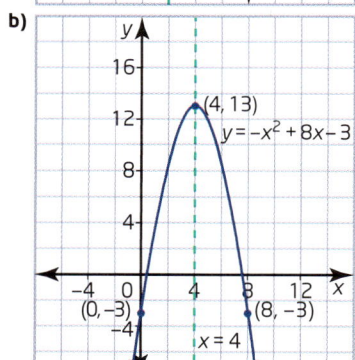

c)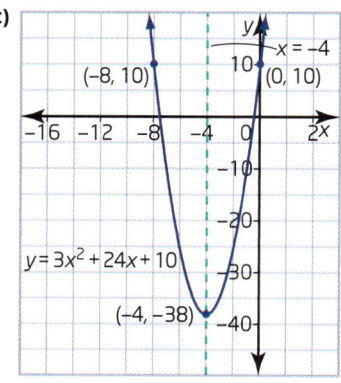

2. a) 4, 1   b) $\dfrac{1}{3}, -\dfrac{1}{3}$ c) 5, −2   d) $\dfrac{2}{3}$
   e) $\dfrac{2}{3}, -5$ f) 0, −5   g) 0, 2   h) $-\dfrac{1}{2}$

3. Answers may vary. For example: Use factoring to find the x-intercepts. Then, find the mean of the x-intercepts to find the x-coordinate of the vertex. Next, substitute this value into the relation to find the corresponding y-coordinate of the vertex. Examples will vary.

4. a) −7, 5; $x = -1$; (−1, −36)

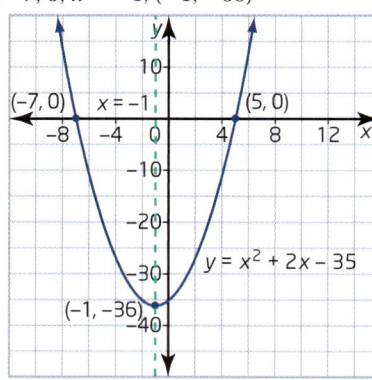

b) −5, 4; $x = -0.5$; (−0.5, 20.25)

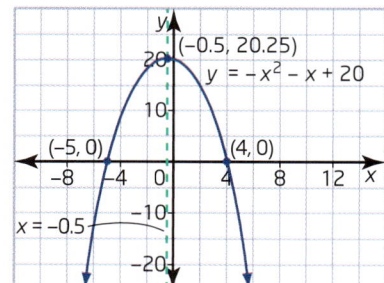

c) 0, −2; $x = -1$; (−1, 3)

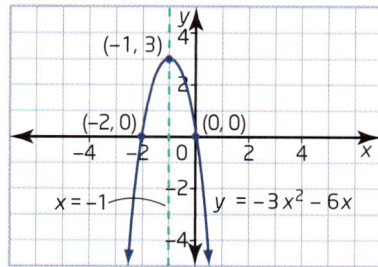

d) 5; $x = 5$; (5, 0)

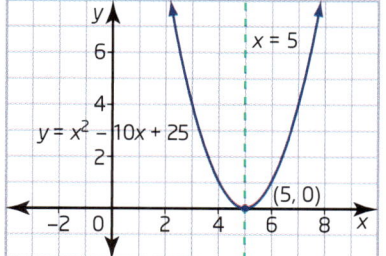

5. a) $3, -\frac{1}{4}$ b) $\frac{-5 \pm \sqrt{53}}{2}$ c) $\frac{5}{3}$
   d) no real roots e) $\frac{9 \pm \sqrt{33}}{8}$ f) $\frac{1 \pm \sqrt{85}}{6}$
6. a) $\frac{-4 \pm \sqrt{8}}{2}$ b) $\frac{8 \pm \sqrt{52}}{2}$ c) $\pm \frac{\sqrt{160}}{8}$
   d) 1 e) 1, 9 f) -1
   g) 0, 7 h) $\frac{-1 \pm \sqrt{309}}{22}$
7. Answers may vary. For example: The axis of symmetry is the same for both because they have the same value for a and b.
8. 21 m
9. a) There will be two x-intercepts because the parabola opens downward and the vertex is above the x-axis.
   b) Let $y = 0$, subtract 18 from both sides, and then divide both sides by -2. Next, take the square root of both sides before subtracting 1. Finally, simplify the results to find the x-intercepts, -4 and 2.
   c) 6 units
10. a) $x^2 - 2x - 15 = 0$
    b) $10x^2 - 11x + 3 = 0$
11. a) width 4 m, height 4 m
    b)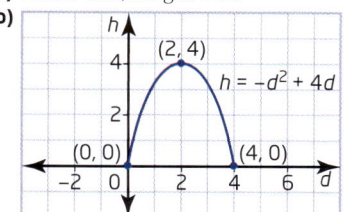
    c) $0 \leq d \leq 4$ so that $h \geq 0$.
12. The minimum cost of $246 occurs when the machine runs for 16 h.
13. 6.34 m
14. 50.8 km/h
15. a) $-1, 4$
    b)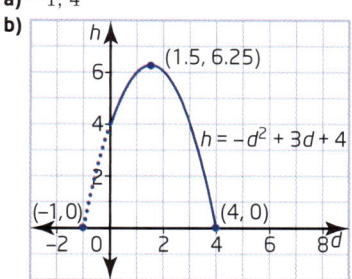
    c) $0 \leq d \leq 4$ since the relation represents Van's height above the surface of the water.
    d) 4 m
    e) 6.25 m
16. a) The maximum height of 12.5 m occurs at 1.4 s.
    b) 3 s
17. 8 cm, 15 cm
18. 24 cm by 24 cm

Chapters 4 to 6 Review, pages 320–321

1. a) linear
   b) quadratic
2. a) 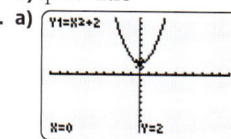 The graph of $y = x^2 + 2$ is the graph of $y = x^2$ translated 2 units upward.
   b) 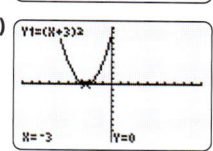 The graph of $y = (x + 3)^2$ is the graph of $y = x^2$ translated 3 units to the left.
   c) 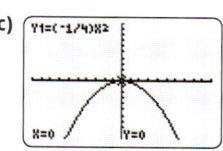 The graph of $y = -\frac{1}{4}x^2$ is the graph of $y = x^2$ vertically compressed by a factor of $\frac{1}{4}$ and reflected in the x-axis.
3. a)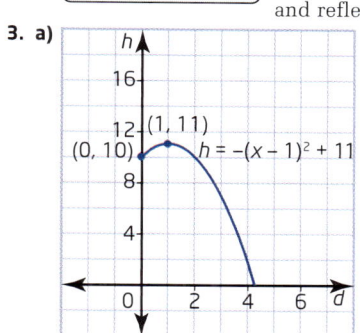
   b) 11 m   c) 4.3 m
4. $y = \frac{1}{4}(x + 3)(x - 5)$
5. a) $\frac{1}{16}$ b) $\frac{1}{9}$ c) 1 d) $\frac{1}{8}$
   e) 1 f) $\frac{64}{27}$
6. a) 1.25 g b) 0.156 25 g
7. Answers may vary. For example: Area: $3x(x + 1) + 2x^2$ or $(3x)(2x + 1) - x^2$; $5x^2 + 3x$
8. a) $n^2 - 9$ b) $h^2 + 10h + 25$
   c) $d^2 - 6d + 8$ d) $m^2 + 10m + 21$
   e) $9t^2 - 25$ f) $x^2 - 14x + 49$
9. a) $6x^3 - 13x^2 - 5x$ b) $3k^2 + 12k + 13$
   c) $24y^2 - 79y - 4$ d) $18a^2 + 15ab - 18b^2$
10.

Width	Length
1	$8x^2 + 4x$
2	$4x^2 + 2x$
4	$2x^2 + x$
x	$8x + 4$
$2x$	$4x + 2$
$4x$	$2x + 1$

11. a) $(y + 9)(y + 3)$ b) $(x + 3)(x - 1)$
    c) $(n + 21)(n + 1)$ d) $(p - 5)(p - 3)$
    e) $(x + 5)(x - 3)$ f) not possible

Answers • MHR 553

12. a) $(p + 6)^2$ **b)** $(3d - 1)^2$
c) $(x + 7)(x - 7)$ **d)** $(2a - 5)^2$
e) $2(2t + 3)(2t - 3)$ **f)** $(a + 2b)(a - 2b)$
13. a) $11, -11, 7, -7$ **b)** $12, -12$
14. $4x + 18$
15. a) $y = (x + 3)^2 - 25$

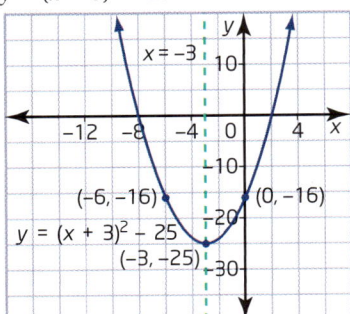

b) $y = (x - 4)^2 - 9$

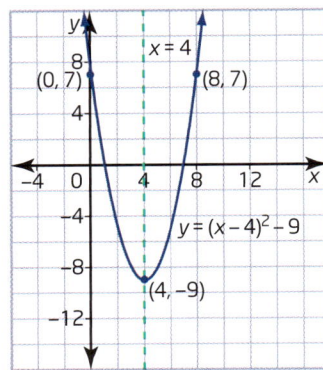

c) $y = (x + 2)^2 + 6$

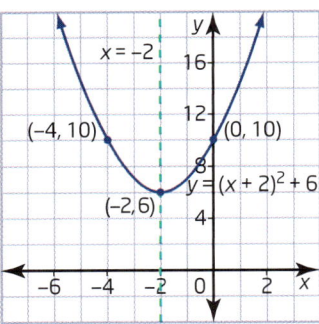

d) $y = -(x - 3)^2 + 1$

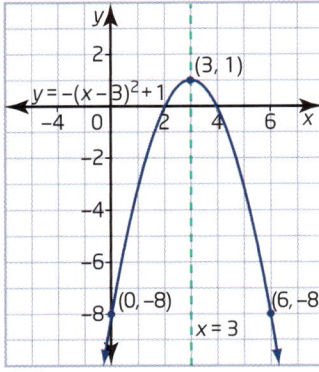

e) $y = 2(x + 2)^2 - 3$

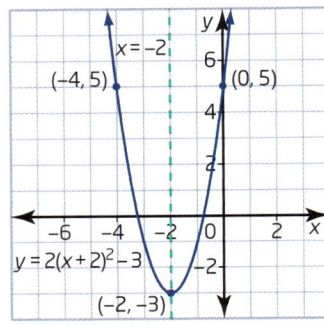

f) $y = -2(x + 3)^2 + 11$

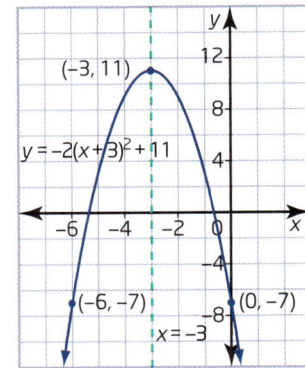

16. a) $12, 2$ **b)** $3, -7$ **c)** $4, -4$
d) $-\dfrac{1}{2}, -2$ **e)** 5

17. a) $2, 1; (1.5, -0.25)$

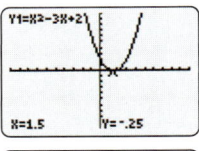

b) $4, -4; (0, -16)$

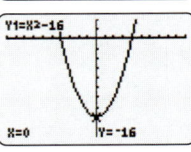

c) $-1.5, 4; (1.25, -15.125)$

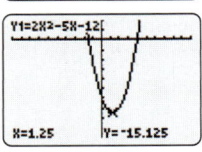

d) $-3, -4; (-3.5, 0.25)$

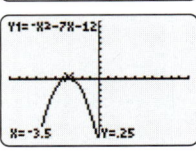

e) $0, 2; (1, 3)$

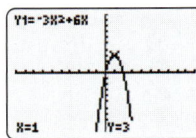

18. $y = -\dfrac{4}{9}x^2 - \dfrac{8}{3}x$

19. a) $\dfrac{6 \pm \sqrt{32}}{2}$ **b)** $\dfrac{5 \pm \sqrt{13}}{6}$

c) $\dfrac{5.6 \pm \sqrt{122.24}}{6.4}$ **d)** $\dfrac{-5 \pm \sqrt{97}}{4}$

e) $\dfrac{8 \pm \sqrt{28}}{6}$

20. 0.6 m, 3.4 m
21. $22.50

Chapter 7

Get Ready, pages 326–329
1. **a)** $c = 25°$, $n = 130°$, $x = 130°$
   b) $a = 150°$, $y = 30°$, $m = 68°$
   c) $e = 45°$, $r = 38°$
   d) $f = 110°$, $u = 70°$, $h = 55°$, $p = 55°$
   e) $k = 72°$, $v = 36°$
2. Answers may vary. For example: The three interior angles of an equilateral triangle are all equal. Let one interior angle be x. Since the sum of the interior angles in a triangle is 180°, $x + x + x = 180°$. Then, $3x = 180°$. This equation can be solved to give $x = 60°$. The three equal interior angles in an equilateral triangle are all 60°.
3. Answers may vary. For example: Since the sum of the interior angles in a triangle is 180°, $x + y + 90° = 180°$. This equation can be solved to give $x + y = 90°$. The two acute angles in a right triangle are complementary.
4. Answers may vary. For example: Let the third interior angle be c. Since the sum of the interior angles in a triangle is 180°, $a + b + c = 180°$. This equation can be solved to give $c = 180° - (a + b)$. Since the angles c and x are supplementary, $c + x = 180°$. Substitute the value for c into this equation to get
   $180° - (a + b) + x = 180°$
   $ 180° - 180° + x = a + b$
   $ x = a + b$
   The exterior angle of a triangle is equal to the sum of the two opposite interior angles.
5. **a)** 18.6 cm **b)** 5.3 m
6. **a)** 7.7 m **b)** 7.4 cm
7. **a)** $\dfrac{2}{3}$ **b)** $\dfrac{5}{22}$
8. **a)** No. **b)** Yes.
9. **a)** $x = 3$ **b)** $y = 4.5$ **c)** $a = \pm 2$
   d) $x = -4$ or $x = 2$
10. Answers will vary.
11. **a)** 1:100 000 000
    b) Answers may vary. For example: 900 km; 2200 km
    c) Answers will vary.
12. **a)** reflection **b)** translation
    c) dilatation **d)** rotation
13. Answers will vary.
14. Answers will vary.

7.1 Investigate Properties of Similar Triangles, pages 330–335
1. Answers will vary.
2. Answers will vary.
3. **a)**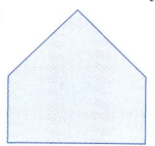

   b) Answers may vary.

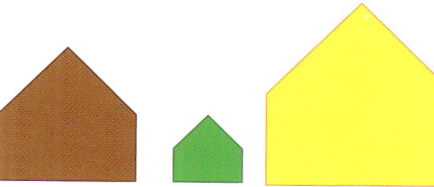

4. Answers may vary. For example:
   a) Congruent figures, because the tiles will be the same, or similar figures if the sides are in proportion.
   b) Similar figures, because the logo on the shoulder would be smaller than the logo on the chest, but the same shape.
   c) Neither, because the door would be rectangular and the window might be a square. The figures could also be similar figures, or congruent figures.
   d) Similar figures, because the three-dimensional model will be smaller than the real building, but the same shape.
5. **a)** △ABC ~ △KLM **b)** △TJP ~ △NGR
   c) △TVX ~ △UVW **d)** △ABC ~ △EDC
6. **a)** $\dfrac{AB}{KL} = \dfrac{BC}{LM} = \dfrac{AC}{KM}$ **b)** $\dfrac{TJ}{NG} = \dfrac{JP}{GR} = \dfrac{TP}{NR}$
   c) $\dfrac{TV}{UV} = \dfrac{VX}{VW} = \dfrac{TX}{UW}$ **d)** $\dfrac{AB}{ED} = \dfrac{BC}{DC} = \dfrac{AC}{EC}$
7. **a)** △PQR ~ △TSR; ∠P = ∠T and ∠Q = ∠S because they are alternate angles. Also, ∠PRQ = ∠TRS because they are opposite angles.
   b) △ABC ~ △ADE; ∠A is common to both triangles; ∠B = ∠D and ∠C = ∠E because they are corresponding angles of parallel lines.
   c) △TUV ~ △WXV; ∠V is common to both triangles, ∠U = ∠X because they are both right angles. Also, ∠T = ∠W because they are corresponding angles of parallel lines.
8. **a)** △ABC ~ △DEF; ratios of corresponding sides are all equal to $\dfrac{1}{3}$.
   b) △DEF ~ △EGF; ratios of corresponding sides are all equal to $\dfrac{1}{3}$.
   c) △JKM ~ △LJM; ratios of corresponding sides are all equal to $\dfrac{1}{2}$.

9. For question 7 a): ∠P = ∠T, ∠Q = ∠S, ∠QRP = ∠SRT;
PQ:TS = QR:SR = PR:TR
b) ∠BAC = ∠DAE, ∠B = ∠D, ∠C = ∠E;
AB:AD = BC:DE = AC:AE
c) ∠T = ∠W, ∠U = ∠X, ∠TVU = ∠WVX;
TU:WX = UV:XV = TV:WV
For question 8 a): ∠A = ∠D, ∠B = ∠E, ∠C = ∠F;
AB:DE = BC:EF = AC:DF
b) ∠D = ∠E, ∠E = ∠G, ∠EFD = ∠GFE;
DE:EG = EF:GF = DF:EF
c) ∠KJM = ∠JLM, ∠JKM = ∠LJM, ∠JMK = ∠LMJ;
JK:LJ = KM:JM = JM:LM
10. Answers will vary.
11. Answers will vary.
12. a) Answers may vary. For example: reflection or translation
b) Answers may vary. For example: rotation or dilatation
13. Answers will vary.
14. Answers may vary. For example: Yes, because the corresponding interior angles will be equal (60°) and the ratios of corresponding side lengths will be equal.
15. Answers may vary. For example: No, because the two equal angles in an isosceles triangle may not equal the two equal angles in a different isosceles triangle.
16. Answers may vary. For example: translation
17. a) $l = 9.0$ cm, $h = 3.6$ cm, $w = 1.8$ cm
b) $l = 27.0$ cm, $h = 10.8$ cm, $w = 5.4$ cm
18. 46.8 kg
19. 48 cm²
20. A

7.2 Use Similar Triangles to Solve Problems, pages 342–351

1. a) [triangle: 3 cm, 4 cm, 5 cm, right angle]
b) 6
c) 18 cm, 24 cm
2. a) area of first triangle 6 cm², area of similar triangle 216 cm²
b) The area of the larger triangle is 36 times as great as the area of the smaller triangle.
c) Answers may vary. For example: 36 is the square of the scale factor, 6.
3. Answers will vary.
4. Answers will vary.
5. a) △PQR ~ △STR because ∠RPQ = ∠RST and ∠PQR = ∠STR because they are corresponding angles of parallel lines, and ∠PRQ = ∠SRT because they are opposite angles.
b) $x = 10$ cm, $y = 18$ cm
6. a) $d = 14$ cm, $f = 8$ cm   b) $s = 6$ cm, $r = 30$ cm
c) $b = 7.5$ cm, $w = 6$ cm   d) $p = 6.75$ cm, $r = 7.5$ cm
e) $d = 12.5$ cm, $e = 15$ cm
7. a) 8 cm   b) 9 cm
8. a) 128 cm²   b) 24 cm²
c) 27 cm²   d) 25.6 cm²
9. 3.1 m
10. 109 m
11. 44 m
12. a) 43.5 cm²   b) $10\frac{7}{8}$ cm²; $32\frac{5}{8}$ cm²
c) 391.5 cm²   d) 29.5 cm

13. a) Answers may vary. For example: 16; 10 × 20, 20 × 20, 20 × 40, 20 × 60, 20 × 80, 20 × 100, 20 × 120, 20 × 140, 20 × 160, 40 × 40, 40 × 60, 40 × 80, 40 × 100, 40 × 120, 40 × 140, 40 × 160
b) 200 cm²   c) 12 800 cm²
d) 3200 cm²   e) 9600 cm²
14. length 22 m, width 8.7 m
15. Answers will vary.
16. 30 cm
17. Answers may vary. For example: Let the first right triangle have base b, height h, and area $A_1 = \frac{1}{2}bh$.
Then the similar right triangle has base kb and height kh, since k is the scale factor that relates the corresponding side lengths. The area of the similar triangle is

$A_2 = \frac{1}{2}$ (base)(height)

$= \frac{1}{2}(kb)(kh)$

$= \frac{1}{2}(k^2)(bh)$

$= k^2\left(\frac{1}{2}bh\right)$

$= k^2 A_1$.

The areas of two similar right triangles are related by the square of the scale factor, k^2.
18. a) Answers will vary.   b) Answers will vary.
c) Answers may vary. For example: The ratio of the areas of the triangles is k^2. $\frac{\text{Area}_{\triangle_1}}{\text{Area}_{\triangle_2}} = k^2$
19. 2:3
20. Answers may vary. For example: Let the second triangle have side lengths a, b, and c. Then, the second triangle has corresponding side lengths of $\frac{3}{5}a$, $\frac{3}{5}b$, and $\frac{3}{5}c$. Then, the two perimeters are

$P_2 = a + b + c$ and
$P_1 = \frac{3}{5}a + \frac{3}{5}b + \frac{3}{5}c$

$= \frac{3}{5}(a + b + c)$

$= \frac{3}{5}P_2$

The ratio of the perimeters is $\frac{3}{5}P_2:P_2$, or 3:5.
21. Answers will vary.
22. Happy Valley/Goose Bay
24. a) 4.8 m   b) 12
25. 150 km²
26. a) Answers may vary. For example: Earth is round and not flat.
b) Answers will vary.
27. D
28. 5.76:1
29. $h = \frac{P}{2} - \frac{A}{P}$
30. 30 m

7.3 The Tangent Ratio, pages 352–365

1. **a)** 0.6667 **b)** 0.7292 **c)** 0.4000
   d) 1.0000 **e)** 0.7500 **f)** 1.8750
2. **a)** 1.5000 **b)** 1.3714 **c)** 2.5000
   d) 1.0000 **e)** 1.3333 **f)** 0.5333
3. **a)** 2.1445 **b)** 0.2679 **c)** 1.8807
   d) 0.0875 **e)** 0.5938 **f)** 7.4947
   g) 0.3739 **h)** 1.0000
4. **a)** 56° **b)** 37° **c)** 31° **d)** 39°
   e) 40° **f)** 41° **g)** 72° **h)** 59°
5. **a)** ∠A = 36°, ∠C = 54° **b)** ∠M = 51°, ∠K = 39°
   c) ∠P = 32°, ∠R = 58° **d)** ∠A = 53°, ∠C = 37°
6. **a)** 6.7 cm **b)** 1.0 m **c)** 10.0 mm **d)** 4.1 cm
7. **a)** 11.0 cm **b)** 6.0 m **c)** 11.2 m **d)** 11.3 m
   e) 5.1 m **f)** 13.1 m
8. **a)** 5.2 m **b)** 23.6 m
9. $\tan 72° = \dfrac{w}{12}$; width is 37 m
10. 8.8 m
11. Rocco's height above the ground: 7 m; Biff's height above the ground: 14 m
12. **a)** 32° **b)** 4.1 min **c)** Answers will vary.
13. 12 m
14. 55°
15. 37°
16. $x = 7.0$ m, $y = 6.3$ m
17. $x = 8.9$ cm, $y = 45°$
18. **a)** Answers may vary.
    b) 18.2 m

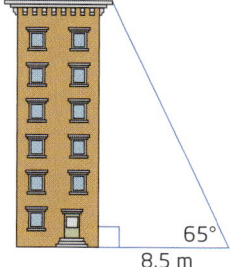

19. **a)** Tables will vary. **b)** $\tan 45° = 1$
    c) Answers will vary. **d)** Answers will vary.
    e) Tangents of angles less than 45° are between 0 and 1; tangents of angles greater than 45° and less than 90° are greater than 1; tangents of angles very close to, but not equal to, 90° are very large, and approach infinity.
    f) Answers may vary. For example: When the angle is less than 45°, the opposite side is shorter than the adjacent side, so the tangent ratio is less than 1. When the angle is greater than 45° but less than 90°, the opposite side is longer than the adjacent side, so the tangent ratio is greater than 1. When the angle gets very close to 90°, the adjacent side gets very small compared to the opposite side, so their quotient becomes very large.
20. **a)** $\tan 0° = 0$; $\tan 90°$ is undefined.
    b) Answers may vary. For example: When the angle is 0°, the opposite side length is zero, so zero divided by any adjacent length equals 0. When the angle is 90°, the adjacent side length is zero, and any opposite side length divided by 0 is undefined.
21. 14°
22. **a)** Answers may vary. For example: He has a slightly larger angle (14.25° compared to 14.04°) being positioned in the middle, but normally a player slaps the puck predominantly in one direction, so positioning in front of a post might be better.
    b) Answers may vary. For example: If he is directly closer to the net, he has a wider angle to work with, so this would be easier. If he is directly farther from the net, he has less of an angle to work with, so this would be more difficult.
23. **a)** Tables will vary. **b)** Answers will vary.

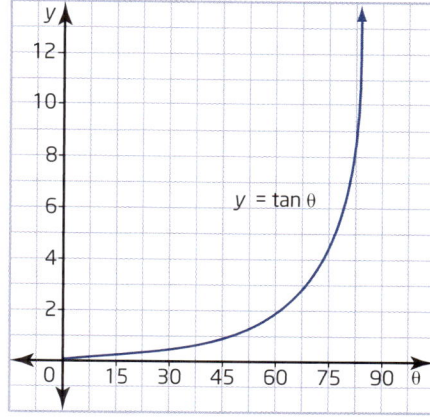

The relationship is non-linear because the graph is not a straight line.
    c) Answers will vary. The graph looks like it increases very quickly as it approaches 90°.
24. 31°
25. 87°
26. **a) i)** $m = 1$ **ii)** $\tan A = 1$ **iii)** The answers are the same.
    iv) ∠A = 45°
    b) i) $m = 2$ **ii)** $\tan B = 2$ **iii)** The answers are the same.
    iv) ∠B = 63°
    c) i) $m = 0.5$ **ii)** $\tan B = 0.5$ **iii)** The answers are the same. **iv)** ∠C = 27°
27. C
28. 15°

7.4 The Sine and Cosine Ratios, pages 366–377

1. **a)** $\sin \theta = \dfrac{4}{5}$, $\cos \theta = \dfrac{3}{5}$, $\tan \theta = \dfrac{4}{3}$
   b) $\sin \theta = \dfrac{12}{13}$, $\cos \theta = \dfrac{5}{13}$, $\tan \theta = \dfrac{12}{5}$
   c) $\sin \theta = \dfrac{60}{67}$, $\cos \theta = \dfrac{30}{67}$, $\tan \theta = 2$
   d) $\sin \theta = \dfrac{89}{120}$, $\cos \theta = \dfrac{2}{3}$, $\tan \theta = \dfrac{89}{80}$
   e) $\sin \theta = \dfrac{4}{9}$, $\cos \theta = \dfrac{8}{9}$, $\tan \theta = \dfrac{1}{2}$
   f) $\sin \theta = \dfrac{10}{27}$, $\cos \theta = \dfrac{25}{27}$, $\tan \theta = \dfrac{2}{5}$
   g) $\sin \theta = \dfrac{25}{54}$, $\cos \theta = \dfrac{8}{9}$, $\tan \theta = \dfrac{25}{48}$
   h) $\sin \theta = \dfrac{11}{17}$, $\cos \theta = \dfrac{13}{17}$, $\tan \theta = \dfrac{11}{13}$

2. a) sin A = 0.5778, cos A = 0.8111, tan A = 0.7123
   b) sin A = 0.5000, cos A = 0.8667, tan A = 0.5769
   c) sin A = 0.7895, cos A = 0.6140, tan A = 1.2857
   d) sin A = 0.8333, cos A = 0.5500, tan A = 1.5152
   e) sin A = 0.7383, cos A = 0.6711, tan A = 1.1000
   f) sin A = 0.7469, cos A = 0.6639, tan A = 1.1250
3. a) 0.5736 **b)** 0.7071 **c)** 0.8660
   d) 0.6018 **e)** 0.4226 **f)** 0.0000
   g) 0.9998 **h)** 0.5000
4. a) 0.1702 **b)** 0.7071 **c)** 0.8660
   d) 0.5000 **e)** 0.0175 **f)** 1.0000
   g) 0.9962 **h)** 0.1219
5. Answers may vary. For example: The results are the same for questions 3 h) and 4 d). sin 30° = cos 60° because the sine and cosine ratios of complementary angles are comparing the same side to the hypotenuse.
6. a) 63° **b)** 30° **c)** 30° **d)** 42°
   e) 49° **f)** 72° **g)** 45° **h)** 24°
   i) 18° **j)** 86° **k)** 7° **l)** 0°
7. a) 63° **b)** 51° **c)** 63° **d)** 70°
   e) 27° **f)** 78° **g)** 80° **h)** 52°
   i) 20° **j)** 89° **k)** 90° **l)** 60°
8. a) sin T = 0.4545; 27° **b)** sin T = 0.2; 12°
9. a) cos T = 0.5; 60° **b)** cos T = 0.3; 73°
10. a) 5.5 cm **b)** 6.1 cm **c)** 13.1 cm
   d) 29.0 cm **e)** 48.1 cm **f)** 15.7 cm
   g) 18.3 cm **h)** 27.4 cm
11. a) 37.1 mm **b)** 8.7 m **c)** 7.6 cm
   d) 13.1 cm **e)** 8.2 cm **f)** 12.2 cm
   g) 6.3 cm **h)** 28.6 cm
12. a) ∠A = 52°, a = 15.4 cm, b = 19.5 cm
   b) ∠D = 75°, d = 15.5 m, f = 4.1 m
   c) ∠G = 45°, ∠I = 45°, i = 5.1 mm
   d) ∠J = 70°, ∠L = 20°, k = 13.1 cm
13. a)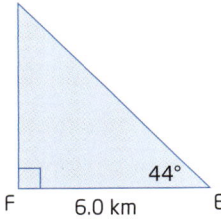
   b) ∠D = 46°, d = 6.2 km, f = 8.6 km
14. a)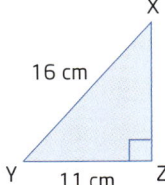
   b) ∠X = 43°, ∠Y = 47°, y = 11.6 cm
15. a) 38 m **b)** 12 m
16. a) 0.76°
   b) For example: Yes. Explanations may vary. If the rise doubles to 40 m, the angle becomes $\tan^{-1}\left(\frac{40}{1.5}\right) = 1.53°$, and 1.53° is about double 0.76°.
17. 13.1 cm
18. 56°
19. 35 m
20. 3.6 cm
21. 4.1 m
22. 21.8 cm
23. 9.3 m
24. 22 m
25. ∠X = ∠Y = 37°, ∠W = 106°
26. a) 53°
   b) 8 min. Explanations may vary. For example: Use the Pythagorean theorem to find the distance along Orchard Avenue, which is 1.6 km. Walking the total distance of 2.8 km at 6 km/h on Rutherford St. and Orchard Ave. would take 28 min, so Enzo saves 8 min by taking the 20-min shortcut. This assumes that Enzo always walks at the same rate.
27. 34 m. Methods may vary. For example: Use the sine ratio to solve for the hypotenuse length.
28. Answers may vary. For example: The sine and cosine ratios of complementary angles are equal. Also, the sum of the square of the sine ratio of a given angle and the square of the cosine ratio of the same angle is one.
29. Answers may vary. For example:
   a) No, because both ratios are with respect to the length of the hypotenuse and since the hypotenuse is always the longest side in a right triangle, the denominator in the ratios will always be larger.
   b) Yes, because the length of the opposite side to an angle can be greater than the length of the adjacent side.
30. Minneapolis
32. x = 7.2 cm, y = 10.8 cm
33. x = 7.4 m, y = 38°
34. a)

Triangle	△ABC	△DEF
tan x	$\frac{3}{4}$	$\frac{5}{12}$
sin x	$\frac{3}{5}$	$\frac{5}{13}$
cos x	$\frac{4}{5}$	$\frac{12}{13}$
tan (90° − x)	$\frac{4}{3}$	$\frac{12}{5}$
sin (90° − x)	$\frac{4}{5}$	$\frac{12}{13}$
cos (90° − x)	$\frac{3}{5}$	$\frac{5}{13}$

   b) Answers may vary. For example: tan x and tan (90° − x) are reciprocals.
   c) Answers may vary. For example: sin x = cos (90° − x)
   d) Answers may vary. For example: cos x = sin (90° − x)
   e) Answers may vary. For example: tan x and tan (90° − x) are reciprocals because when you look at the complementary angle, the opposite sides and adjacent sides switch places. sin x = cos (90° − x) and cos x = sin (90° − x) because in each case the opposite and adjacent sides just switch positions.

35. Answers may vary. For example: Let θ be an acute angle in a right triangle, oriented so that θ is the angle of elevation. Then, the opposite side is the height and the adjacent side is the base of the triangle. Thus, $\sin θ = \dfrac{\text{height}}{\text{hypotenuse}}$. The other acute angle will be $90° - θ$, and for this angle, the adjacent side will be the height of the triangle. Thus, $\cos(90° - θ) = \dfrac{\text{height}}{\text{hypotenuse}}$, which also equals $\sin θ$.

36. Answers may vary. For example:
$$\dfrac{\sin θ}{\cos θ} = \dfrac{\left(\dfrac{\text{opposite}}{\text{hypotenuse}}\right)}{\left(\dfrac{\text{adjacent}}{\text{hypotenuse}}\right)}$$
$$= \dfrac{\text{opposite}}{\text{adjacent}}$$
$$= \tan θ$$

37. a) Examples will vary, but all sums should be 1.
b) Answers may vary. For example:
$(\sin x)^2 + (\cos x)^2 = 1$
c) Answers may vary. For example:
$(\sin x)^2 + (\cos x)^2$
$= \left(\dfrac{\text{opposite}}{\text{hypotenuse}}\right)^2 + \left(\dfrac{\text{adjacent}}{\text{hypotenuse}}\right)^2$
$= \dfrac{(\text{opposite})^2 + (\text{adjacent})^2}{(\text{hypotenuse})^2}$
$= \dfrac{(\text{hypotenuse})^2}{(\text{hypotenuse})^2}$
$= 1$

38. a) N8°W **b)** 202 km/h
39. D
40. 3 m²
41. C

7.5 Solve Problems Involving Right Triangles, pages 378–385

1. 15.4 m
2. a) 16.4 m
b) Answers may vary. For example: Use a different trigonometric ratio or the Pythagorean theorem.
3. a)

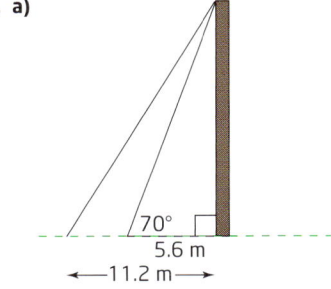

b) 19.0 m, 54°
c) 16°
4. 23 cm

5. 22.7 m
6. 9.2 m apart
7. a) 68°, 53° **b)** 16 m, 10 m
8. a) Answers may vary. For example: Use a different trigonometric ratio or the Pythagorean theorem.
b) 5.2 m
9. Answers may vary. For example: No, because with an angle of 40°, the height of the closest tree is about 25 m tall and Cheryl judges that she can only hit the ball 20 m high. She will hit the tree with the golf ball if she takes this shot.
10. a) 49°
b) Answers may vary. For example: In order for the golf ball to land near A, Cheryl needs to hit the golf ball 46.1 m. Since Cheryl on average hits the golf ball a distance of 50 m with the sand wedge, this is the club she should use.
c) 63°
d) Answers may vary. For example: In order for the golf ball to land near the hole, H, Cheryl needs to hit the golf ball 78.3 m. Since Cheryl on average hits the golf ball a distance of 90 m with the pitching wedge, this is the club she should use.
11. a) 34.6 m **b)** 115.2 m **c)** 40.0 m, 120.3 m
12. Lucy will escape because the trench is 11.9 m wide but she can leap 12 m, which is just enough!
13. a)

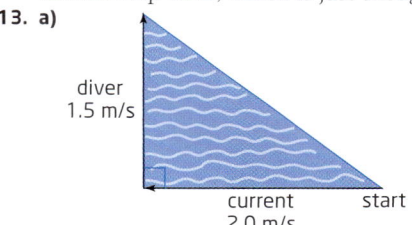

b) 450 m
14. 190 m
15. a) Theresa should tell Branko to look for the yellow bottle.
b) 84 m
16. Answers may vary. For example: Kim lives on the 9th floor and Yuri lives on the 13th floor. Assume every floor has an equal height.
17. $20\sqrt{2}$ cm
18. a) 2.9 km
b) 3.0 km; because the elevation makes the route the hypotenuse of the right triangle with acute angle 15° and adjacent side 2.9 km.
c) 0.8 km
d) 29.7°
19. a) 13 m **b)** 12 m
20. 111 m
21. a) 16.6 km **b)** 27°
22. 68 m
23. 42°
24. Watson Lake
25. Answers may vary. For example: length AB = d. In △ABC, ∠ACB = θ, the hypotenuse is BC, and the opposite side is AB = d. Since $\sin θ = \dfrac{AC}{BC}$, $\sin θ = \dfrac{d}{BC}$.

26. 1.7 m
27. 5°
28. 705.5 km/h
29. 63°
30. 37 m
31. D
32. $x = 2y - z$

Chapter 7 Review, pages 386–389

1. **a)** Answers may vary. For example: Similar figures have the same shape, but congruent figures have the same shape and size. For similar figures, all angles are equal and the corresponding sides have equal ratios; for congruent figures, all angles and all sides are equal.
   b)–e) Answers will vary.
2. Answers may vary. For example: Yes, because they have the same shape.
3. △AXP ~ △NTP because corresponding pairs of angles are equal: ∠AXP = ∠NTP (alternate angles), ∠XAP = ∠TMP (alternate angles), and ∠APX = ∠NPT (opposite angles).
4. △JPW ~ △QBW; $\frac{JW}{QW} = \frac{PW}{BW} = \frac{JP}{QB} = \frac{1}{2}$
5. **a)** e = 10 cm, f = 6 cm
   b) q = 4 cm, w = 18 cm
   c) q = 6 cm, y = 10 cm
6. 2.9 m
7. 23.12 m²
8. 9 m
9. **a)** 69°   **b)** 42°
10. **a)** 10.5 cm   **b)** 14.4 cm
11. 19 m
12. **a)**

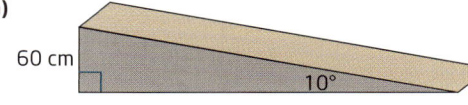

   b) 340 cm   **c)** 350 m
13. **a)** 0, 1, undefined
    b) Answers may vary. For example: tan 0° = 0 because the opposite length is 0; tan 45° = 1 because the opposite and adjacent lengths are equal; tan 90° is undefined because the adjacent length is 0 and you cannot divide by 0.
14. 40.5°
15. **a)** ∠D = 23°, ∠E = 67°
    b) ∠D = 53°, ∠E = 37°
    c) ∠P = 25°, ∠Q = 65°
    d) ∠Q = 35°, ∠R = 55°
16. **a)** 14.8 m   **b)** 97.6 m
    c) 17.8 mm   **d)** 26.4 km
17. f = 7.0 m, ∠F = 49°, ∠H = 41°
18. **a)**

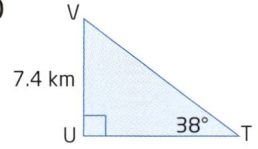

    b) ∠V = 52°, v = 9.5 km, u = 12.0 km

19. 11 m
20. 19°; Answers may vary. For example: Assume that her sailboat's speed and the current's speed are constant.
21. **a)** b = 5.8 m, ∠A = 31°, ∠C = 59°
    b) e = 12 cm, ∠D = 23°, ∠E = 67°
    c) ∠H = 40°, g = 3.1 m, h = 2.6 m
    d) k = 39.2 mm, ∠K = 59°, ∠M = 31°
    e) ∠P = 32°, p = 30 cm, r = 56.6 cm
    f) ∠T = 35°, r = 29.6 km, s = 24.3 km
22. Answers may vary. For example: No, because you need an angle of 9.5° to clear the wires.
23. 68 m
24. Answers may vary. For example: Kathe cannot climb over the fence because the fence is about 2.3 m high and she can only climb 2 m high.
25. 6°
26. 32°
27. 13 m
28. 10°
29. 390 m

Chapter 7 Practice Test, pages 390–391

1. Figures A and G are congruent. Figures D and B are similar.
2. No. Reasons may vary. For example: No, because the ratios of corresponding sides may not be equal.
3. Yes. Reasons may vary. For example: Yes, because the ratio of corresponding sides are always equal.
4. **a)** 0.5543   **b)** 0.2079
   c) 1.0000   **d)** 0.7071
   e) 0.7071   **f)** 11.4301
5. **a)** 63°   **b)** 55°
   c) 69°   **d)** 78°
   e) 79°   **f)** 66°
6. ∠P = 58°, q = 7.3 cm, r = 3.9 cm
7. **a)**

   [Triangle with vertices A, C, B; AB = 19 m, CB = 27 m, right angle at B]

   b) b = 33 m, ∠A = 55°, ∠C = 35°
8. Answers may vary. For example: Yes. He should try to jump the creek because it is about 1.8 m wide and he can jump 2 m.
9. **b)** 34°   **c)** 3.3 km
10. 558.4 m
11. Branko should give the following advice to Theresa. Since Option A will take 78.8 s and Option B will take 77.6 s, Option B is better.
12. 21 m

Chapter 8

Get Ready, pages 394–395

1. **a)** $\sin X = \dfrac{4.0}{8.1}$, $\cos X = \dfrac{7.0}{8.1}$, $\tan X = \dfrac{4.0}{7.0}$
   b) $\angle X = 30°$, $\angle Z = 60°$
2. **a)** $k = 6.5$ cm; $\sin M = \dfrac{3.9}{6.5}$, $\cos M = \dfrac{5.2}{6.5}$, $\tan M = \dfrac{3.9}{5.2}$
   b) $\angle M = 37°$, $\angle B = 53°$
3. Answers may vary. For example: You could use the Pythagorean theorem or apply the trigonometric ratio for sin T.
4. $r = 1.7$ cm, $l = 2.3$ cm, $\angle R = 46°$
5. **a)**

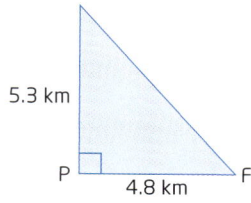

   b) $p = 7.2$ km, $\angle W = 42°$, $\angle F = 48°$
6. **a)** BY = 17.5 m   **b)** 26.6 m
7. 86 m
8. **a)** $b = y - mx$ **b)** $d = st$
   c) $s = \dfrac{P}{4}$ **d)** $b = P - a - c$
9. **a)** $a = \dfrac{b(\sin A)}{\sin B}$ **b)** $b^2 = c^2 - a^2$
   c) $s = \pm\sqrt{\dfrac{A}{6}}$ **d)** $y = \dfrac{x(\sin Y)}{\sin X}$

8.1 The Sine Law, pages 396–404

1. **a)** $a = 4$ cm   **b)** $e = 11$ m
2. **a)** $a = 3.2$ cm   **b)** $e = 5.0$ mm
3. **a)** $\angle Y = 44°$ **b)** $\angle C = 56°$
4. **a)**

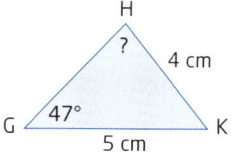

   $\angle H = 66°$
   b)

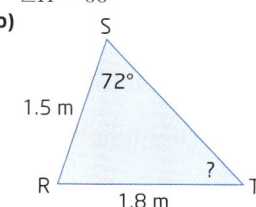

   $\angle T = 52°$

5. **a)** $\angle L = 65°$, $l = 23$ m, $m = 24$ m
   b) $\angle D = 51°$, $d = 16$ cm, $e = 18$ cm
6. **a)** $\angle D = 55°$, $\angle W = 52°$, $w = 28$ cm
   b) $\angle Q = 53°$, $\angle P = 66°$, $p = 13$ m
7. **a)**

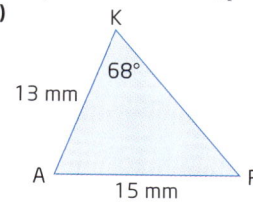

   $\angle R = 53°$, $\angle A = 59°$, $a = 14$ mm
   b)

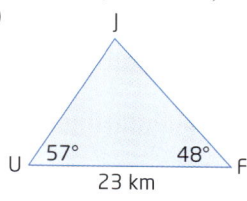

   $\angle J = 75°$, $f = 1.8$ km, $u = 2.0$ km
8. Answers will vary.
9. **a)** 1.8 m   **b)** 2.4 m
10. 7.7 km
11. **a)** 80°   **b)** 14 m   **c)** 12 m, 2 m
    d) Answers may vary. For example: Yes. Use the primary trigonometric ratios.
12. The valley is 115 m deep.
13. 4.7 m
14. Answers may vary. For example: Because $a \neq c$, $\angle A \neq \angle C$. Therefore, since △ABC is an isosceles triangle, either $\angle B = \angle A$ or $\angle B = \angle C$. If $\angle B = \angle A$, then $\angle C = 43°$, and the sine law gives $b = 20.5$ cm, which is impossible, because △ABC is isosceles. If $\angle B = \angle C$, then $\angle A = 43°$, and the sine law gives $b = 15$ cm, which is correct, because if $\angle B = \angle C$, then $b = c$.
15. 52 m
16. **a)** 1 136 610 km²
    b) Answers will vary.
17. 14.4 m²
18. **a)–c)** Answers will vary.
19. No, the sine law does not work if you replace sines with cosines or tangents.
20. **a)** Let △ABC be a right triangle with $\angle B = 90°$ and b the hypotenuse. Then, by the sine law:
    $$\dfrac{\sin A}{a} = \dfrac{\sin B}{b} = \dfrac{\sin C}{c}$$
    $$\dfrac{\sin A}{a} = \dfrac{\sin 90°}{b} = \dfrac{\sin C}{c}$$
    $$\dfrac{\sin A}{a} = \dfrac{1}{b} = \dfrac{\sin C}{c}$$
    So, $\sin A = \dfrac{a}{b}$ and $\sin C = \dfrac{c}{b}$.
    b) Answers may vary. For example: You could, but the sine ratio is faster and already simplified.

21. Substitute $s = \dfrac{a+b+c}{2}$ into
$A = \sqrt{s(s-a)(s-b)(s-c)}$.

$A = \sqrt{\left(\dfrac{a+b+c}{2}\right)\left(\dfrac{a+b+c-2a}{2}\right)\left(\dfrac{a+b+c-2b}{2}\right)\left(\dfrac{a+b+c-2c}{2}\right)}$

$= \sqrt{\dfrac{(a+b+c)(b+c-a)(a+c-b)(a+b-c)}{16}}$

$= \dfrac{1}{4}\sqrt{(a+b+c)(b+c-a)(a+c-b)(a+b-c)}$

$= \dfrac{1}{4}\sqrt{(a+b+c)(a+b-c)(b+c-a)(a+c-b)}$

22. B
23. C

8.2 The Cosine Law, pages 405–411

1. a) 13 cm **b)** 13 mm
2. a) 4.3 m **b)** 1.7 cm **c)** 5.1 mm
3. a)

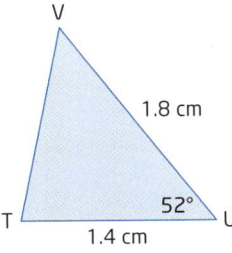

$u = 1.4$ cm

b)

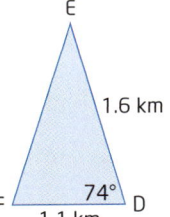

$d = 1.7$ km

4. a) $r = 16$ cm, $\angle P = 48°$, $\angle Q = 62°$
b) $r = 20$ m, $\angle P = 72°$, $\angle K = 61°$
c) $a = 10$ m, $\angle C = 38°$, $\angle B = 51°$
5. a)

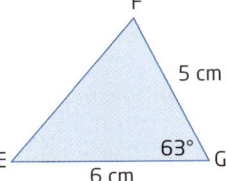

$g = 6$ cm, $\angle F = 63°$, $\angle E = 54°$

b)

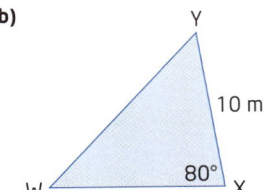

$x = 14$ m, $\angle W = 49°$, $\angle Y = 51°$
6. Answers will vary.
7. 56 m
8. a) 2.6 km **b)** 45°, 65°
9. 39.8 cm
10. a) 7.7 nautical miles
 b) 15.3 nautical miles
 c) Answers will vary.
11. a) 9.8 cm
 b) $\angle B = 84.5°$, $\angle C = 34.0°$
12. a)–c) Answers will vary.
13. a) Diagrams may vary.

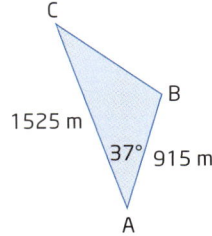

 b) 966 m
14. 12 km
15. Let $\triangle ABC$ be a right triangle with $\angle C = 90°$ and c the hypotenuse. Then, by the cosine law,
$c^2 = a^2 + b^2 - 2ab(\cos C)$
$= a^2 + b^2 - 2ab(\cos 90°)$
$= a^2 + b^2 - 2ab(0)$
$= a^2 + b^2$
17. Answers will vary.
18. a) 15.8 cm **b)** 37.75°
19. Answers may vary. For example: 53 cm, assuming the there is no slack in the drive belt.
20. D
21. Answers may vary.
$(\sin A)^2 + (\cos A)^2$
$= \left(\dfrac{\text{opposite}}{\text{hypotenuse}}\right)^2 + \left(\dfrac{\text{adjacent}}{\text{hypotenuse}}\right)^2$
$= \dfrac{(\text{opposite})^2 + (\text{adjacent})^2}{(\text{hypotenuse})^2}$
$= \dfrac{(\text{hypotenuse})^2}{(\text{hypotenuse})^2}$
$= 1$

8.3 Find Angles Using the Cosine Law, pages 412–419

1. **a)** 49° **b)** 61° **c)** 50°
2. **a)** 51° **b)** 66° **c)** 49°
3. **a)**

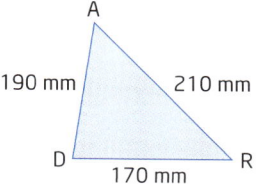

 $\angle D = 71°$

b)

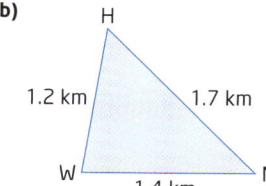

$\angle W = 81°$

4. **a)** $\angle J = 55.5°$, $\angle V = 81.4°$, $\angle M = 43.1°$
   b) Solve for $\angle J$ using the cosine law. Solve for $\angle V$ using the sine law. Then, solve for $\angle M$ using the fact that the sum of the interior angles in a triangle is 180°.
   c) The answers are the same. Explanations may vary. For example: The calculations in my method are easier to complete.
5. **a)** $\angle V = 78.5°$, $\angle T = 57.1°$, $\angle U = 44.4°$
   b) $\angle M = 70.8°$, $\angle P = 59.0°$, $\angle Y = 50.2°$
6. **a)**

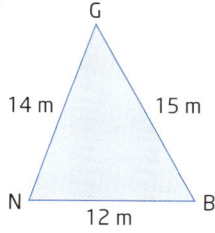

$\angle N = 70.0°$, $\angle B = 61.3°$, $\angle G = 48.7°$

b)

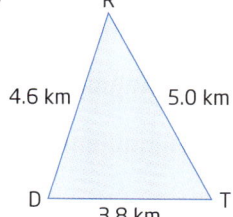

$\angle D = 72.3°$, $\angle T = 61.2°$, $\angle R = 46.5°$

7. Answers will vary.
8. **a)** 78°, 51°, 51° **b)** 14 m²
9. 31°
10. **a)** 82° **b)** 43° **c)** 55°
11. 69.6°, 110.4°, 69.6°, 110.4°
12. Answers will vary.
13. 51.3°, 51.3°, 77.4°. Answers may vary. For example: No, there is only one possible triangle for three given sides.

15. **a)** $\cos A = \dfrac{a^2 - b^2 - b^2}{-2b(b)}$
    $= \dfrac{a^2 - b^2 - b^2}{-2b(b)}$
    $= \dfrac{a^2 - 2b^2}{-2b^2}$
    $= \dfrac{a^2}{-2b^2} - \dfrac{2b^2}{-2b^2}$
    $= \dfrac{a^2}{-2b^2} + 1$
    $= 1 - \dfrac{a^2}{2b^2}$

    b) $\angle A = 30.9°$, $\angle B = \angle C = 74.55°$
16. Answers may vary. For example: For an equilateral triangle, $a = b = c$.
    Substitute into the cosine law.
    $\cos A = \dfrac{a^2 - b^2 - c^2}{-2bc}$
    $\cos 60° = \dfrac{a^2 - a^2 - a^2}{-2a(a)}$
    $\cos 60° = \dfrac{-a^2}{-2a^2}$
    $\cos 60° = \dfrac{1}{2}$

8.4 Solve Problems Using Trigonometry, pages 424–429

1. **a)** cosine law **b)** sine law
   c) primary trigonometric ratios
   d) cosine law
2. **a)** $x = 5.6$ m **b)** Answers will vary.
3. **a)** $x = 4.4$ cm **b)** $x = 4.4$ cm
4. 1.6 km
5. **a)** Diagrams may vary. **b)** 239 360 000 km
   c) Answers may vary. For example: No, because the angle between Earth, the Sun, and Mars is not always the same.
6. **a)** 47 km **b)** $\angle R = 65°$, $\angle D = 74°$, $\angle H = 41°$
7. 9.6 m
8. Yes, because it would take Biff 12 s and Rocco 12.9 s to reach the eucalyptus. Assumptions may vary.
9. 79.8 m. Answers may vary. For example: assume that the bridge is symmetric. Find the unknown angles and sides using triangle laws, the sine law, and the cosine law.
10. 6.4 km. Answers may vary. For example: Assume that the paths are straight.
11. 8.2 cm
12. **a)** The distance is 146 677 195.5 km, which is close to 149 600 000 km.
    b) Answers may vary. For example: Noon, when the Sun appears to be directly overhead.
13. **a)** S51°E **b)** 108 km/h
14. **a)** Javier and Raquel live about 19.7 m vertically apart.
    b) Answers may vary. For example: I assumed that the balconies were equally spaced. Then, I used the tangent ratio with two right triangles formed by drawing a horizontal line between buildings through point H.

15. a) The longest rod fits from the bottom front left corner to the top back right corner. The length of the rod, l, is the hypotenuse of the right triangle, whose legs are the height of the prism and the diagonal of the base of the prism.
$$l = \sqrt{(w^2 + w^2) + (2w)^2}$$
$$= \sqrt{6w^2}$$
$$= \sqrt{6}w$$
b) 35.3° and 54.7°
16. 117 km, S78°E
17. Answers will vary.

Chapter 8 Review, pages 430–431
1. 10 cm
2. 41°
3. **a)** $\angle T = 42°$, $\angle K = 87°$, $k = 36$ km
   b) $\angle C = 53°$, $c = 22$ mm, $n = 20$ mm
4. **a)** 37 cm   **b)** 61° and 37°
5. 20 m
6. **a)** $u = 54$ mm, $\angle D = 59°$, $\angle P = 82°$
   b) $w = 16$ km, $\angle E = 45°$, $\angle Q = 58°$
7. **a)** 33 km   **b)** 53°
8. **a)** 39°
9. **a)** $\angle S = 72.7°$, $\angle F = 54.9°$, $\angle V = 52.4°$
   b) $\angle B = 79.6°$, $\angle S = 62.9°$, $\angle Z = 37.5°$
10. angle to water tower 37°, angle to monument 47°
11. **a)** Diagrams may vary.

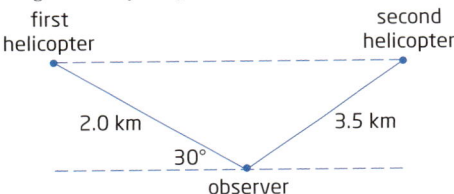

   b) 5.1 km   **c)** 1 km
12. 70 m

Chapter 8 Practice Test, pages 432–433
1. 18 cm
2. 2.5 m
3. 47°
4. 58°
5. **a)** 3.2 m   **b)** 60° and 40°
6. 33.2°
7. $x = 8.7$ m, $\angle Y = 50°$, $\angle Z = 62°$
8. **a)**

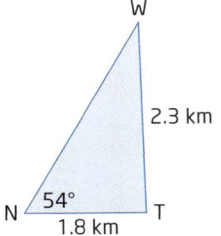

   b) $\angle W = 39°$, $\angle T = 87°$, $t = 2.8$ km
9. 47.5 cm; assume the crest is symmetric.
10. 75 m
11. 40 km

12. 361 m; S74°W
13. **a)** blue jay tree 36.1 m, cardinal tree 25.3 m
    b) 41.4 m
14. 40 min
15. plane's altitude 10 km, jet's altitude 13 km

Chapters 7 and 8 Review, pages 434–435
1. $\angle B = \angle E = 90°$. $\angle ACB = \angle DCE$ (opposite angles). Then, $\angle A = \angle D$ (angle sum of a triangle is 180°). Therefore, $\triangle ABC \sim \triangle DEC$ because corresponding pairs of angles are equal.
2. $h = 14$ cm, $q = 14$ cm
3. **a)** $\angle E = 53°$, $\angle C = 37°$ **b)** $\angle X = 54°$, $\angle Y = 36°$
   c) $\angle U = 33°$, $\angle T = 57°$ **d)** $\angle M = 35°$, $\angle N = 55°$
4. **a)** 6.1 cm   **b)** 29.9 m
   c) 5.4 km   **d)** 99.0 cm
5. **a)** $b = 11.9$ cm, $\angle A = 51°$, $\angle C = 39°$
   b) $\angle H = 31°$, $f = 9.7$ m, $g = 11.3$ m
6. 4.2 m
7. **a)** 20 m   **b)** 59 m
8. 9 cm
9. 3.9 m
10. $\angle P = 51°$
11. $\angle E = 74°$
12. **a)** $\angle B = 65°$, $\angle A = 71°$, $a = 18$ mm
    b) $r = 26$ m, $\angle S = 75°$, $\angle T = 51°$
    c) $x = 30$ cm, $\angle Y = 67°$, $y = 28$ cm
    d) $e = 36$ km, $\angle F = 62°$, $\angle G = 34°$
13. **a)** $\angle C = 75.4°$, $\angle B = 61.3°$, $\angle A = 43.3°$
    b) $\angle V = 70.1°$, $\angle U = 59.0°$, $\angle T = 50.9°$
14. 41 km
15. 1171 m
16. 3 km

Course Review, pages 438–447
1. **a)** Let l represent the length and w represent the width. $2l + 2w = 40$.
   b) If n represents one number and q represents the other number, then $\dfrac{n + q}{2} = 15$.
   c) If q represents the number of quarters and l represents the number of loonies, then $0.25q + l = 37$.
   d) If a represents the number of adult tickets sold and s represents the number of student tickets sold, then $20a + 12s = 9250$.
2. **a)** $(3, -1)$ **b)** $(-2, -5)$ **c)** $(2, 2)$
3. **a)** $x = 2, y = 1$ **b)** $x = 1, y = 3$ **c)** $x = 1, y = 1$
4. **a)** $x = 17, y = 38$ **b)** $a = 4, b = -3$
   c) $k = 1.5, h = 2$ **d)** $a = 3, b = 5$
5. The lines have the same slope, but a different y-intercept. So, the lines are parallel and they have no point in common.
6. **a)** $(6.7, 1.7)$ **b)** $(-4.4, -2.3)$ **c)** $(0.1, -0.9)$
7. $a = 32, b = 20$
8. boat 16 km/h, current 4 km/h
9. 25 mL of 60% hydrochloric acid and 100 mL of 30% hydrochloric acid
10. $x = 5, y = 4$

11. for AB, midpoint is (2, 3), length is $\sqrt{80}$; for CD, midpoint is (−5, 0), length is $\sqrt{80}$; for EF, midpoint is $\left(2, -\dfrac{3}{2}\right)$, length is $\sqrt{65}$

12. a) $y = 6.2x - 2.5$ **b)** $y = 0.2x - 0.4$ **c)** $y = \dfrac{1}{4}x - \dfrac{1}{2}$

13. a) Town B is closer.
b) Answers will vary.

14. DEFG is a kite. Adjacent sides are equal in length: DE = DG = $\sqrt{80}$, and EF = FG = $\sqrt{200}$.

15. a)

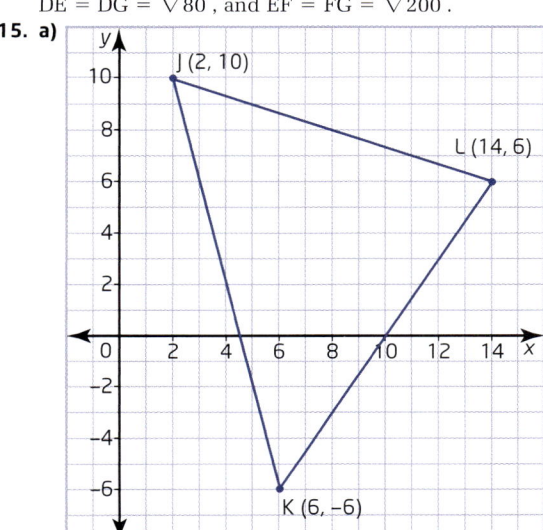

b) M(4, 2), N(8, 8)
c) The length of MN = $2\sqrt{13}$ and length of KL = $4\sqrt{13}$, so MN is half the length of KL.
d) slope MN = slope KL = $\dfrac{3}{2}$

16. No. The equation of the right bisector is $y = \dfrac{3}{2}x + \dfrac{3}{2}$, but the point (−3, −2) does not satisfy this equation.

17. a) Slope AB = slope CD = 1, so AB is parallel to BC. Slope AD = $-\dfrac{2}{7}$ and slope BC = $\dfrac{1}{2}$, so ABCD is not a parallelogram. It is a trapezoid.
b) Answers will vary.

18. a) The shortest pipe will be the perpendicular from H to WM. The equation of WM is $y = 4x - 6$. The equation of the new pipe is $y = -\dfrac{1}{4}x + 28$. These two lines intersect at (8, 26).
b) $2\sqrt{17}$ m, or approximately 8.25 m.

19. a) $x^2 + y^2 = 49$ **b)** $x^2 + y^2 = 61$ **c)** $x^2 + y^2 = 67$

20. The diameter is 16 units; the area is approximately 201 square units.

21. 42 cm

22. a) The centroid is the point where the three medians of a triangle intersect.
b) Determine the equation of two of the medians of the triangle and then find the point of intersection of these two lines.
c) Answers will vary.

23. a) Answers will vary.
b) Answers will vary.

24. AC = BC = $\sqrt{180}$, so △ABC is isosceles.

25. a) Slope DE = $-\dfrac{5}{3}$ and slope EF = $\dfrac{3}{5}$, so DE is perpendicular to EF and △DEF is a right triangle.
b) Show that the side lengths satisfy the Pythagorean theorem.

26. a)

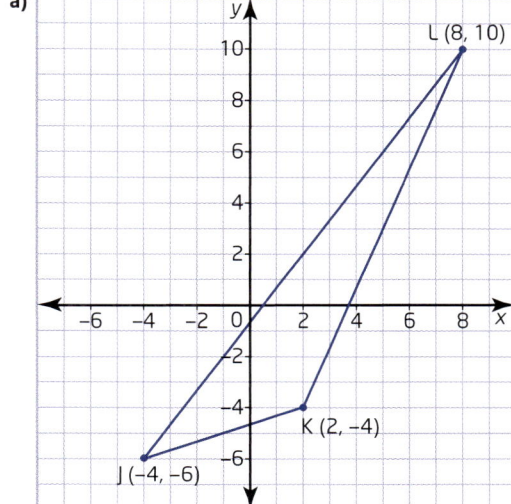

b) Let X, Y, and Z be the midpoints of JL, LK, and KJ. Then the coordinates of these midpoints are X(2, 2), Y(5, 3) and Z(−1, −5). Comparing lengths:
XY = $\sqrt{10}$, JK = $2\sqrt{10}$, YZ = 10, JL = 20,
XZ = $\sqrt{58}$, and KL = $2\sqrt{58}$. Corresponding sides are in proportion, 1:2, so the triangle joining the midpoints of the sides of △JKL is similar to △JKL.

27. a) The equation of the right bisector of JK is $y = \dfrac{3}{4}x + \dfrac{5}{4}$. The equation of the right bisector of JL is $y = 2x - 5$. The equation of the right bisector of KL is $y = -\dfrac{1}{2}x + \dfrac{15}{2}$.
b) (5, 5)
c) The distance from the centroid to each vertex is 5 units.

28. a) squares, rectangles
b) squares, rhombii, parallelograms
c) squares, rhombii, kites

29. a) Answers will vary.
b) Answers will vary.

30. a) All four sides have length $\sqrt{41}$. Slope AB = slope CD = $\frac{5}{4}$ and slope AD = slope BC = $-\frac{2}{3}$, so adjacent sides are perpendicular. Therefore, ABCD is a square.

b) The diagonals intersect at $\left(3, 2\frac{1}{2}\right)$ and the distance from this point to each vertex is $\frac{\sqrt{85}}{2}$. Therefore, the diagonals bisect each other.

31. parallelogram

32. a) An equation for the circle is $(x-4)^2 + (y-2)^2 = 13$. Substitution verifies that points P, Q, and R satisfy this equation and so lie on the circle.

b) An equation for the right bisector of chord PQ is $y = -\frac{2}{3}x + \frac{14}{3}$. The centre (4, 2) satisfies this equation.

33. Answers will vary.

34. a) quadratic **b)** linear **c)** linear

35. a) 2.1 m **b)** 4.43 m **c)** 3.05 m

36. a)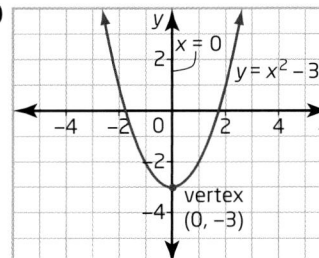

b)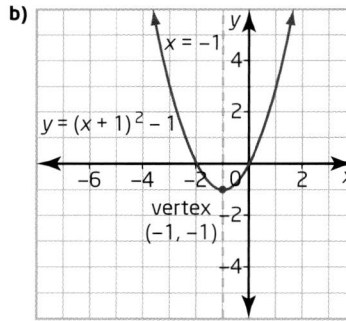

c)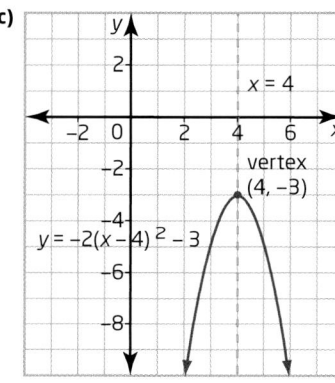

d)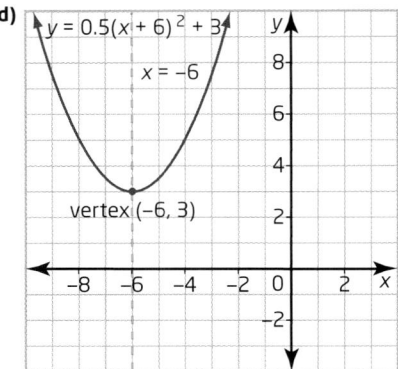

37. a)

b) 151 m **c)** 5.5 s

d) The lava will be ejected away from the crater and so it will probably fall on land that is below the crater. The length of time in the air will probably be more than 11 s.

38. a) $y = -2x^2 + 3$ **b)** $y = x^2 + 2x - 15$

39. -11

40. a) 1 **b)** $\frac{1}{3}$ **c)** $-\frac{1}{32}$ **d)** $\frac{25}{4}$ **e)** 1 **f)** $\frac{3}{4}$

41. a) 1024 s **b)** $\frac{1}{32}$ s

42. a) $8x + 18$ **b)** $4a + 28$ **c)** $2 - 7k$ **d)** $8t^2 - 3t$ **e)** $-3 + 9p$ **f)** $y^3 - 7y$

43. a) $10x^2 + 10x - 10$ **b)** 290 cm²

44. a) $x^2 + 8x + 16$ **b)** $y^2 - 16$ **c)** $a^2 - 10a + 25$ **d)** $9t^2 - 1$ **e)** $25a^2 - 9b^2$ **f)** $18m^2 + 12m + 2$

45. a) $2m^2 - 8m + 7$ **b)** $30t^2 + 12t + 1$ **c)** $-9x^2 + 18xy - 11y^2$ **d)** $9y^2 + 4$ **f)** $18m^2 + 9n^2$ **g)** $68t^2 + 28tz + 98z^2$

46. a) $5(k - 7)$ **b)** $4h(h - 5)$ **c)** $2xy(1 - 4y)$ **d)** $(x - 5)(x + 5)$ **e)** $(1 - 7m)(1 + 7m)$ **f)** $4(a - 2b)(a + 2b)$

47. a) length $n - 2$, width $n - 3$ **b)** perimeter 22 cm, area 30 cm²

48. a) $(x + 3)(x - 4)$ **b)** $(y + 6)(y - 3)$ **c)** $(m + 3)(m + 8)$ **d)** $(t - 3)(t - 5)$ **e)** not possible **f)** $(n - 5)(n - 8)$ **g)** $(w + 5)(w - 6)$ **h)** $(7 - m)(2 + m)$

49. a) $(x + 5)^2$ **b)** $(y - 6)^2$ **c)** not possible **d)** $(2x + 3)^2$ **e)** $(5r - 2s)^2$ **f)** $5(x - 2y)^2$

50. Answers will vary.

51. a) 8, -8 **b)** 9 **c)** 25

52. $m = 5, n = 3$, or $m = 11, n = 10$

53. a) $y = (x + 2)^2 - 3$, vertex $(-2, -3)$, axis of symmetry $x = -2$

b)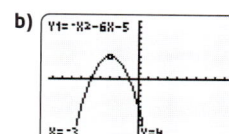
$y = -(x + 3)^2 + 4$,
vertex $(-3, 4)$,
axis of symmetry $x = -3$

c)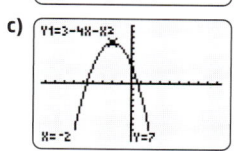
$y = -(x + 2)^2 + 7$,
vertex $(-2, 7)$,
axis of symmetry $x = -2$

54. a) $(-1.5, 0.5)$ **b)** $(0.3, 1.3)$ **c)** $(-0.3, -3.7)$
55. a) $-3, 1$ **b)** $-5, -1$
c) $2, 2$ **d)** $1.5, 1.5$
56. a) $4, -7$ **b)** $-5, -2$ **c)** $-9, 1.5$ **d)** $1, \dfrac{4}{3}$
57. Answers will vary.
58. a) $\dfrac{25}{8}$ **b)** 6 or -6 **c)** 4
59. 9 cm by 4 cm
60. a) $\dfrac{1 \pm \sqrt{17}}{2}$ **b)** $\dfrac{1 \pm \sqrt{15}}{7}$ **c)** $\dfrac{-4 \pm \sqrt{22}}{2}$
d) $\dfrac{-1 \pm \sqrt{6}}{2}$ **e)** $\dfrac{2 \pm \sqrt{7}}{3}$
61. a) 110; $160 **b)** $129; 130
62. 12 cm, 16 cm
63. 2.5 m
64. △ADE ~ △ACB; ∠A is common; ∠ADC = ∠ACB (corresponding angles).
65. 21.5 m
66. a) 33° **b)** 60°
67. 4.6°
68. a) 7.6 m **b)** 5.9 cm
69. a) ∠A = 57°, $a = 47$ cm, $b = 30$ cm
b) ∠F = 49°, $d = 80$ m, $e = 52$ m
c) ∠T = 42°, ∠U = 48°, $u = 11$ m
d) ∠P = 32°, ∠R = 58°, $q = 15$ cm
70. XY = 5.9 cm, ∠X = 54°, ∠Z = 36°
71. 60°
72. a) 16.6 km **b)** 26.9°
73. 60.0 m
74. 30 cm
75. 57°
76. 79.5 cm
77. a) ∠R = 43.4°, ∠Q = 85.6°, $q = 55.2$ cm
b) ∠J = 73°, $k = 20.7$ cm, $l = 11.4$ cm
78. 4.7 cm, 6.0 cm
79. 13.9 m
80. ∠K = 57.3°, ∠L = 48.7°, ∠M = 74.0°
81. 104 m²
82. 41 cm
83. a) 93.6 m **b)** 97.9 m
84. 4.0 km
85. a) ∠F = 69°, $f = 8.8$ cm, $e = 7.5$ cm
b) ∠T = 46°, $s = 7.3$ m, ∠S = 61°
c) $a = 6.9$ cm, ∠B = 42°, ∠C = 70°
d) ∠W = 51°, ∠X = 45°, ∠Y = 84°
86. 68°

Challenge Problems Appendix, pages 448–457

1. Answers will vary.
2. Answers will vary.
3. a) (5, 4) **b)** (4, 5)
c) $(-1, -5)$ **d)** $\left(\dfrac{1}{2}, -\dfrac{1}{2}\right)$
4. 20 cm²
5. $x = 4, y = 6$
6. Answers may vary. For example: $2x + 3y = -3$, $x - 2y = 16$
7. 31, 49
8. a) 1.8 h **b)** 135 km
9. a) 24, 23, 30 **b)** 42, 68, 110 **c)** 37, 50, 65
10. $b = 10, n = 7$
11. $(-4, 0), (4, 0), (0, 6)$
12. a) slope of PS = slope of QR = $\dfrac{1}{2}$; slope of PQ = -3, slope of SR = $-\dfrac{1}{5}$
b) The midpoint of PQ is A$(-2, -2)$, and the midpoint of SR is B(6, 2); the slope of AB = $\dfrac{1}{2}$, which is the same as the slope of the bases PS and QR.
c) PS = $2\sqrt{5}$, QR = $6\sqrt{5}$, AB = $4\sqrt{5}$, so PS + QR = 2AB
13. Answers may vary.

14. 60 square units
15. 32 square units
16. Rohan
17. 30 cm by 20 cm
18. a) linear: $y = 3x - 2$
b) quadratic: $y = -3x^2 + 4$
c) quadratic: $y = x^2 + 6x + 5$
d) neither
19. a) 0.8 m **b)** 8 m **c)** 1.25 m
20. a) $a^2 + b^2 + c^2 + 2ab + 2ac + 2bc$
b) $4x^2 + 9y^2 + 1 + 12xy + 4x + 6y$
21. a) $(x^2 + 1)^2$ **b)** $(x^2 + 3)(x^2 - 2)$
c) $(x^2 - 5)(x^2 + 2)$ **d)** $(x^2 + 9y)(x^2 + y)$
22. a) 8 m **b)** 16
23. 18, 20, 24
24. a) $(2x^2 + 1)(x^2 + 1)$ **b)** $(2x^2 - 1)(x^2 + 3)$
c) $(3x^2 - 4)(x^2 + 1)$ **d)** $(2x^2 - 3)(3x^2 - 2)$
e) $(2x^2 + y)(x^2 + 2y)$ **f)** $(3x^2 - y)(x^2 + 4y)$
25. 20 units, 12 units, 4 units
26. a) $y = m^2 - 2m + 2$ **b)** $y = 8k^2 + 8k - 1$
c) $y = 9t^2 + 6t - 4$ **d)** $y = 12w^2 - 32w + 25$
27. 4 cm by 8 cm by 18 cm
28. b) month 23
c) $P = 100(m - 11)^2 - 12\,100$

29. a) A closed dot is used to show the location of an ordered pair on a graph; an open dot is used to show that an ordered pair is omitted from the graph.
 b) more than 3 h but not more than 4 h
 c) $200
30. 6 cm by 4 cm
31. a) $y = x^2 + 2$ **b)** $y = -x^2 - 1$
 c) $y = 2x^2 - 3$ **d)** $y = -\frac{1}{2}x^2 + 4$
32. a) $y = (x + 4)^2 - 5$ **b)** $y = -(x - 1)^2 + 6$
 c) $y = 3(x + 2)^2 + 3$
33. a) $a = 2, k = 4$ **b)** $a = -1, k = -4$
 c) $a = -2, k = 5$
34. a) $k = -8$ **b)** $k > -8$ **c)** $k < -8$
35. a) $\frac{1}{2^5}$ **b)** $\frac{1}{5^2}$ **c)** 3^4
36. a) $\frac{x^2}{3}$ **b)** $\frac{1}{(3x)^3}$ **c)** $\frac{1}{8y^3}$
37. 20 routes
38. a) $b = 0$ **b)** $x = 0$ always, $x = -b$
39. a) $x^2 - x - 6 = 0$
 b) Yes—any constant multiple of $x^2 - x - 6 = 0$.
40. a) 10 **b)** $-\frac{1}{3}$
41. 31, 32
42. 14 m²
43. 3.2 cm
44. a) no real roots
 b) two real, equal roots
 c) two real, distinct roots
 d) two real, distinct, irrational roots
45. 1:2
46. 60 cm²
47. $x = 3.7$ cm, $\angle A = 38°$
48. 31 cm
49. $a = 6.1, b = 4.1, c = 5.8, \angle A = 73.1°, \angle B = 40.4°, \angle C = 66.5°$
50. These side lengths cannot form a triangle, since $3 + 4 < 8$.
51. $a = 2, b = 3, c = 4$
52. 6
53. a) 1600 m² **b)** 7°
54. base 6 cm, height 8 cm
55. 192.5 cm²
56. 12
57. 60
58. $A = 3, B = 2, C = 4$, or $A = 1, B = 8, C = 3$, or $A = -3, B = -4, C = 2$

Prerequisite Skills Appendix, pages 458–475

Adding Polynomials, page 458
1. a) $7x + 5y + 12$ **b)** $9x - 6y - 12$ **c)** $3x^2 + 2x + 4$
 d) $5a^2 + 3a + 1$ **e)** $-y^2 - 1$ **f)** $-2a - b - 3$

Angle Properties, page 458
1. a) $x = 41°$
 b) $a = 115°, b = 65°, c = 65°, d = 115°, e = 65°, f = 115°, g = 65°$
 c) $w = 74°, x = 70°, y = 36°, z = 70°$
 d) $w = 79°, x = 101°, y = 101°$

Common Factoring, page 459
1. a) $3x + 4y$ **b)** $2x - 5$ **c)** $2c + 5$
 d) $2a - 3$ **e)** $ab + 2c$ **f)** $x - 2$
2. a) $5(y + 3)$ **b)** $8(3x - 2)$
 c) $2a(2b + 3)$ **d)** $3x(x - 6)$
 e) $2x(x^2 + 2x - 3)$ **f)** $3x(2x^2 - x + 3)$
 g) $4ab(2b + 1 + 3a)$ **h)** $10(y^3 - 1)$

Congruent Triangles, page 460
1. a) $\angle P = \angle S, \angle Q = \angle T, \angle R = \angle U$, PQ = ST, PR = SU, QR = TU
 b) $\angle A = \angle K, \angle B = \angle L, \angle C = \angle M$, AB = KL, AC = KM, BC = LM

Evaluating Expressions, page 460
1. a) 13 **b)** 11 **c)** 12 **d)** 6
 e) 18 **f)** 11 **g)** 30 **h)** -2
 i) -3 **j)** -21 **k)** 4 **l)** 0
2. a) 2 **b)** 1 **c)** -25 **d)** 12
 e) -10 **f)** -11 **g)** 12 **h)** 0
 i) 4 **j)** 216 **k)** -36 **l)** -41
3. a) 6, 5, 4, 3, 2 **b)** 1, -1, -3, -5, -7
 c) 3, 4, 5, 6, 7 **d)** 5, 2, 1 2, 5
 e) 8, 3, 0 -1, 0 **f)** 4, 3, 4, 7, 12

Evaluating Radicals, page 462
1. a) 2 **b)** 5 **c)** 0.9 **d)** 1.1
 e) 0.3 **f)** 0.1 **g)** 15 **h)** 1.3
2. a) 6.6 **b)** 11.4 **c)** 58.5 **d)** 4.5
 e) 9.5 **f)** 27.3 **g)** 256.5 **h)** 0.8

Expanding Expressions, page 462
1. a) $2x + 6$ **b)** $3x + 3y - 21$
 c) $5a - 5b + 5c$ **d)** $-10a + 8$
 e) $-2x + y$ **f)** $x^2 + 6x$
 g) $6x^2 + 14x$ **h)** $x^3 - x^2 + 5x$
 i) $-3a^3 - 6a^2 + 3a$

Exponent Rules, page 462
1. a) 2^7 **b)** 3^{10} **c)** 4^7 **d)** 5^6
 e) 2^2 **f)** 3^3 **g)** 4^5 **h)** 2^6
 i) 3^{12} **j)** y^{11} **k)** z^6 **l)** y
 m) z^6 **n)** x^{15} **o)** y^{16} **p)** $6x^7$
 q) $6x^7$ **q)** $8y^7$ **r)** $5m^4$ **s)** $9y^6$
 t) $-8x^9$

First Differences, page 463
1. a) linear **b)** linear **c)** non-linear **d)** linear

Graphing Equations, page 464
1. **a)** line through (0, 4) and (4, 0)
   b) line through (0, −2) and (2, 0)
   c) line through (0, 2) and (−2, 0)
   d) line through (0, 1) and (1, 3)
2. **a)** x-intercept 3, y-intercept 3
   b) x-intercept 4, y-intercept −4
   c) x-intercept 2, y-intercept 8
   d) x-intercept 5, y-intercept −2
3. **a)** slope 1, y-intercept 3
   b) slope −1, y-intercept −4
   c) slope 2, y-intercept 3
   d) slope 3, y-intercept −1
4. **a)** (6, 2) **b)** (2, 5) **c)** (4, −2) **d)** (−1, 4)

Greatest Common Factors, page 465
1. **a)** $2x$ **b)** $4y$ **c)** $5z$ **d)** $10a$
   e) $2x$ **f)** $7ab$ **g)** $6x^2$ **h)** abc
2. **a)** $2a$ **b)** $3y$ **c)** $4x^2$ **d)** $3mn$
   e) $5rt^2$ **f)** 9

Lengths of Line Segments, page 466
1. **a)** 6 **b)** 4 **c)** 6 **d)** 8
   e) 7 **f)** 13 **g)** 4 **h)** 12
   i) 6 **j)** 7 **k)** 14 **l)** 6

Like Terms, page 466
1. **a)** $6x$ **b)** $5y - 14$
   c) $3x - y - 7$ **d)** $4a - 5b + 4c$
   e) $-2x^2 - 9x - 3$ **f)** $-t^2 + t - 4$
   g) $4x + 9y - 8$ **h)** $-y^2 - 18y + 3$
   i) $-2t^2 - 10t + 15$

Number Skills, page 467
1. **a)** 33 **b)** 195 **c)** 108 **d)** $3\frac{4}{15}$
   e) $-\frac{1}{4}$ **f)** $1\frac{1}{2}$ **g)** $-\frac{1}{5}$ **h)** 0.5
   i) 64.4
2. **a)** $\frac{1}{2}, \frac{7}{12}, \frac{3}{5}, \frac{5}{8}, \frac{2}{3}$ **b)** $3\frac{5}{9}, 3\frac{3}{4}, 3\frac{6}{7}, 3\frac{7}{8}$
3. **a)** $\sqrt{9 + 16} = 5, \sqrt{9} + \sqrt{16} = 7$
   b) $(x + y)^2 = x^2 + 2xy + y^2$
   c) $\frac{2}{3} + \frac{5}{6} = \frac{3}{2}$

Percents, page 468
1. **a)** 75%, 0.75 **b)** 50%, 0.5
   c) 840%, 8.4 **d)** $\frac{17}{50}$, 0.34
   e) $\frac{3}{10\,000}$, 0.0003 **f)** $\frac{7}{125}$, 0.056
   g) $\frac{9}{20}$, 45% **h)** $\frac{3}{100}$, 3%
   i) $2\frac{17}{25}$, 269%

Polynomials, page 468
1. **a)** 1 **b)** 3 **c)** 2
   d) 3 **e)** 4 **f)** 5

Pythagorean Theorem, page 469
1. **a)** 5.8 **b)** 7.2 **c)** 4.9
   d) 6.7 **e)** 7.4 **f)** 8.1

Simplifying Expressions, page 469
1. **a)** $7x + 14$ **b)** $9a - 21$ **c)** $2x - 12$
   d) $-5y + 21$ **e)** $5t - 4$ **f)** $7y - 30$
   g) $-6z - 8$ **h)** $17 - 2w$ **i)** $8x - 18$
2. **a)** $5x + 7y$ **b)** $5r + s$ **c)** $-p + 6q$
   d) $20x - 9y$ **e)** $5a + 21b$ **f)** $-c + 19d$
   g) $2a - 3b + 5c$ **h)** $10x + 3y - 6z - 5$
   i) $14x + 17y - 4z$

Slope, page 470
1. **a)** 3 **b)** $\frac{1}{2}$ **c)** 2 **d)** 2
   e) -2 **f)** $\frac{1}{5}$ **g)** 0 **h)** -2
   i) $\frac{3}{2}$
2. **a)** $3, -\frac{1}{3}$ **b)** $-2, \frac{1}{2}$ **c)** $-1, 1$ **d)** $\frac{1}{4}, -4$
   e) $-\frac{2}{3}, \frac{3}{2}$ **f)** $\frac{4}{5}, -\frac{5}{4}$

Solving Equations, page 471
1. **a)** 3 **b)** 6 **c)** -3 **d)** 4
   e) -7 **f)** -2 **g)** 1 **h)** -8
   i) -4
2. **a)** 1 **b)** 5 **c)** 4 **d)** -4
   e) -9 **f)** 18 **g)** 1 **h)** 2
   i) -6
3. **a)** 9 **b)** 1 **c)** 4 **d)** 7
   e) 5 **f)** -2 **g)** -2 **h)** 3
   i) 7

Solving Proportions, page 473
1. **a)** $\frac{12}{5}$ **b)** $\frac{12}{5}$ **c)** $\frac{14}{3}$ **d)** $\frac{8}{3}$
   e) $\frac{10}{3}$ **f)** $\frac{28}{3}$ **g)** $\frac{8}{3}$ **h)** $\frac{16}{5}$
2. **a)** 15.3 **b)** 0.45 **c)** 13.76 **d)** 1.3
   e) 0.27 **f)** 1.25 **g)** 6.98 **g)** 1.04

Subtracting Polynomials, page 474
1. **a)** $2x + 4y + 3$ **b)** $3x - 2y - 1$
   c) $-x^2 - 8x - 9$ **d)** $3a^2 + 6a + 11$
   e) $-7a + 6b + 7$ **f)** $7y^2 - 4y - 2$

Glossary

A

acute angle An angle whose measure is less than 90°.

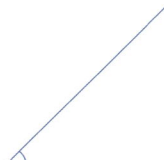

acute triangle A triangle in which each of the three interior angles measures less than 90°.

algebra tiles A collection of squares and rectangles, with different-coloured sides, that are used to represent units and variables.

algebraic expression A mathematical phrase made up of numbers and variables, connected by addition and/or subtraction operators.

$x - 3$, $5y$, and $6 + 2k$ are algebraic expressions.

algebraic modelling The process of representing a relationship by an equation or a formula, or representing a pattern of numbers by an algebraic expression.

alternate angles Pairs of equal angles formed on either side of a transversal crossing a pair of parallel lines.

$b = g$
$c = f$

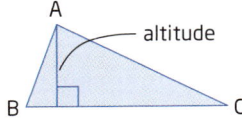

altitude The height of a geometric shape.

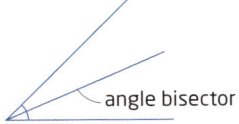

angle bisector A line that divides an angle into two equal parts.

angle of declination Another name for angle of depression.

angle of depression An angle measured below the horizontal.

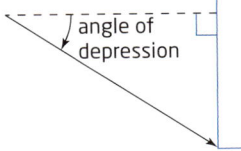

angle of elevation An angle measure above the horizontal.

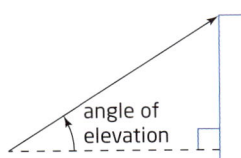

angle of inclination Another name for angle of elevation.

area The number of square units contained in a two-dimensional region.

average Another name for mean. The sum of a set of values divided by the number of values in the set. The mean of 1, 5, and 6 is $\dfrac{1 + 5 + 6}{3}$, or 4.

axis of symmetry A line that divides a figure into two congruent parts.

B

base (of a power) The number used as a factor for repeated multiplication.

In 6^3, the base is 6.

BEDMAS A way of remembering the order of operations. BEDMAS stands for **B**rackets, **E**xponents, **D**ivision, **M**ultiplication, **A**ddition, **S**ubtraction.

binomial A polynomial that has two terms.

$3x + 4$ is a binomial.

bisect Divide into two equal parts.

Cartesian coordinate system The system developed by René Descartes for graphing points as ordered pairs on a grid, using two perpendicular number lines. Also referred to as the Cartesian plane, the coordinate grid, or the xy-plane.

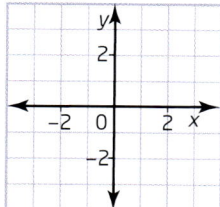

Cartesian grid A grid with perpendicular axes. See Cartesian coordinate system.

centroid The point where the three medians of a triangle intersect.

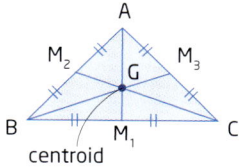

cevian A line segment that joins a vertex of a triangle to any point on the opposite side.

chord A line segment joining two points on a curve.

circle The set of all points in the plane that are equidistant from a fixed point called the centre.

circumcentre The point of intersection of the three right bisectors of the sides of a triangle.

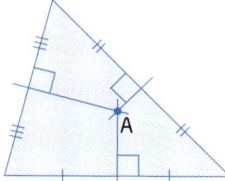

A is the circumcentre.

circumference The perimeter of a circle.

coefficient The number by which a variable is multiplied.

In the term $8y$, the coefficient is 8.

co-interior angles Pairs of supplementary angles formed between a pair of parallel lines crossed by a transversal.

$b + c = 180°$ $f + g = 180°$

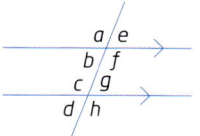

collecting like terms Simplifying an expression containing like terms by adding their coefficients.

collinear Lying on the same line.

common factor A number that is a factor of (divides evenly into) all the numbers in a set.

3 is a common factor of 6, 12, and 15.

complementary angles Angles whose sum is 90°.

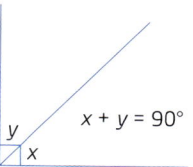

completing the square A process for expressing $y = ax^2 + bx + c$ in the form $y = a(x - h)^2 + k$.

concurrent Meeting at a single point.

congruent figures Figures that are identical in size and shape.

conjecture A general conclusion drawn from a number of individual facts. It may or may not be true.

constant term A term that contains no variables. Its value does not change.

In $2x + 5$, the constant term is 5.

contained angle The interior angle formed at a vertex between two adjacent sides of a polygon.

corresponding angles Pairs of equal angles, in corresponding positions, formed by a transversal crossing a pair of parallel lines.

$a = c$ $b = d$ $e = g$ $f = h$

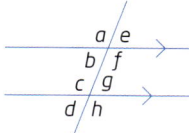

cosine law The relationship between the cosine of an angle and the lengths of the three sides in any acute triangle.

$a^2 = b^2 + c^2 - 2bc(\cos A)$
$b^2 = a^2 + c^2 - 2ac(\cos B)$
$c^2 = a^2 + b^2 - 2ab(\cos C)$

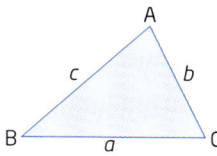

cosine ratio For an acute angle in a right triangle, the ratio of the length of the adjacent side to the length of the hypotenuse.

$$\text{cosine} = \frac{\text{adjacent}}{\text{hypotenuse}}$$

$$\cos \theta = \frac{AC}{AB}$$

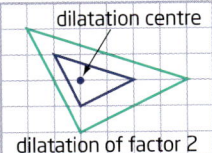

counterexample An example that proves that a hypothesis or conjecture is false.

cube A prism with six congruent square faces.

curve of best fit A smooth curve drawn to approximate the general path or trend in a scatter plot.

cylinder A three-dimensional object with two parallel circular bases.

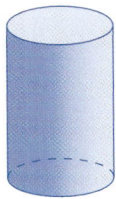

D

degree (of a polynomial) The degree of the greatest-degree term.

$5x^3 + 2x^2 - x + 1$ has degree 3.

degree (of a term) The sum of the exponents on the variables in a term.

The degree of $5x^2y$ is 3.

denominator The number of equal parts in the whole or the group.

$\frac{3}{4}$ has denominator 4.

dependent variable In a relation, the variable whose value depends on the value of the other variable (the independent variable). On a coordinate grid, the values of the dependent variable are on the vertical axis.

In $d = 85t$, d is the dependent variable.

diagonal A line segment joining two non-adjacent vertices of a polygon.

diameter A line segment joining two points on the circumference that passes through the centre of a circle.

difference of squares An expression of the form $a^2 - b^2$ that involves the subtraction of two squares.

dilatation A transformation of a geometric shape that is an enlargement or reduction by a fixed factor.

distributive property $a(x + y) = ax + ay$.

dynamic geometry software Computer software that allows the user to construct two-dimensional shapes, measure them, and transform them by moving their parts.

E

equation A mathematical statement that says two expressions are equal.

$5k - 2 = 3k + 4$ is an equation.

equiangular Having all angles equal.

equidistant The same distance away from a given line or point.

equilateral triangle A triangle with all three sides equal.

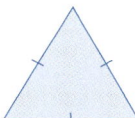

equivalent expressions Algebraic expressions that are equal for all values of the variable.

$7a - 3a$ and $4a$ are equivalent expressions.

equivalent fractions Fractions, such as $\frac{1}{3}$, $\frac{2}{6}$, and $\frac{3}{9}$, that represent the same part of a whole or group.

equivalent linear equations Equations that have the same graph.

equivalent linear systems Two or more linear systems that have the same solution.

equivalent rational numbers Numbers, such as $-1\frac{1}{2}$ and -1.5, that represent the same rational number.

equivalent ratios Ratios, such as 1:3, 2:6, and 3:9, that represent the same division of the whole.

estimate A guess at a measurement based on known comparisons, or a rough calculation using approximate numbers.

evaluate To determine a value for an expression or formula.

expand Multiply, often using the distributive property.

expanded form (of a power) The product of like factors that is equivalent to a power.

$2 \times 2 \times 2 \times 2 \times 2$ is the expanded form of 2^5.

exponent A raised number to denote repeated multiplication of a base.

In 3^4, the exponent is 4.

exponent laws A set of rules that can be used to simplify powers. See product rule, quotient rule, and power of a power rule.

exponential form A shorthand method for writing numbers expressed as repeated multiplications.

3^4 is the exponential form for $3 \times 3 \times 3 \times 3$ or 81.

expression A mathematical phrase made up of numbers and variables, connected by operators.

$3x + 2$ is an expression.

exterior angle An angle contained between one side of a polygon and the extension of an adjacent side.

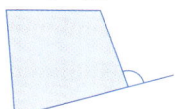

extrapolate Estimate values lying outside the given range of data. To extrapolate from a graph means to estimate coordinates of points beyond those that are plotted.

face A plane surface of a polyhedron.

factor A number and/or variable that divides evenly into a specified product.

For example, $2x$ and $2y$ are factors of $4xy$.

finite differences Differences found from the y-values in a table of values with evenly spaced x-values. See first differences and second differences.

first differences Differences between consecutive y-values in a table of values with evenly spaced x-values.

x	y	First Differences
1	3	
2	5	5 − 3 = 2
3	7	7 − 5 = 2
4	9	9 − 7 = 2
5	11	11 − 9 = 2

formula An algebraic relationship between two or more variables.

fractal A geometric pattern that repeats infinitely with a smaller scale for each repetition.

GCF See greatest common factor.

golden ratio The ratio of two quantities or lengths, a and b, related by the equation $\dfrac{a}{b} = \dfrac{a + b}{a}$.

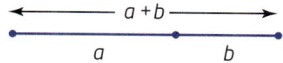

golden rectangle A rectangle whose length, a, and width, b, are in the golden ratio.

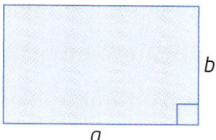

graphing calculator A hand-held device capable of a wide range of mathematical operations, including graphing from an equation and constructing a scatter plot and a line or curve of best fit.

graphing software Computer software that provides features similar to those of a graphing calculator.

greatest common factor (GCF) The greatest number and/or variable that is a factor of two or more numbers or terms.

The GCF of 12 and 8 is 4.
The GCF of $12x^2y$ and $6xy^2$ is $6xy$.

hexagon A polygon with six sides.

hypotenuse The longest side of a right triangle.

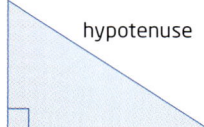

improper fraction A fraction in which the numerator is greater than the denominator, such as $\frac{8}{5}$.

incentre The point at which the three angle bisectors of a triangle meet.

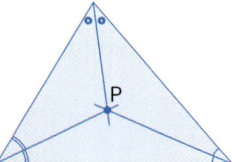

P is the incentre.

independent variable In a relation, the variable that you need to know first. Its value determines the value of the dependent variable. On a coordinate grid, the values of the independent variable are on the horizontal axis.

In $d = 85t$, t is the independent variable.

integer A number in the sequence ..., −3, −2, −1, 0, 1, 2, 3, ...

intercept The distance from the origin of the xy-plane to the point at which a line or curve crosses a given axis.

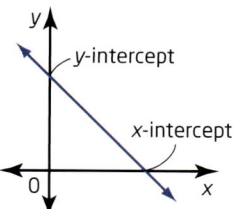

interior angle An angle that is formed inside a polygon by two sides meeting at a vertex.

isometry A transformation that preserves size and shape.

isosceles triangle A triangle with exactly two equal sides.

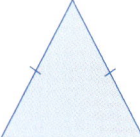

kite A quadrilateral with two pairs of adjacent sides equal.

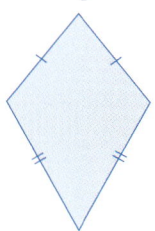

leg (of a right triangle) In a right triangle, either of the sides containing the right angle.

like terms Terms that have the same variable(s) raised to the same exponent(s).

$3xy$, $-xy$, and $2.5xy$ are like terms.

line of best fit The straight line that passes through or as near as possible to the points on a scatter plot.

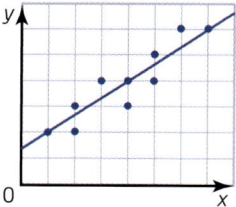

line of symmetry A line that divides a shape into two congruent shapes that are reflections of each other in the line.

line segment The part of a line that joins two points.

linear equation An equation that relates two variables so that ordered pairs satisfying the equation form a straight-line pattern on a graph.

linear regression A mathematical process used by graphing calculators and graphing software to find the line of best fit.

linear relation A relation between two variables that appears as a straight line when graphed on the coordinate plane.

574 MHR • Glossary

linear system A set of two or more linear equations that are considered at the same time.

literal coefficient The variable part of a term.

In $5xy$, the literal coefficient is xy.

lowest terms The form in which the numerator and the denominator of a fraction have no common factors other than 1.

$\frac{3}{5}$ is in lowest terms.

mathematical model A mathematical description of a real situation. The description may be a diagram, a graph, a table of values, an equation, a formula, a physical model, or a computer model.

maximum The greatest value in a set of data.

maximum point The point on the graph of a non-linear relation, such as a parabola, at which the curve changes from increasing to decreasing.

mean The sum of a set of values divided by the number of values in the set.

The mean of 2, 8, 4, 6, and 10 is $\frac{2 + 8 + 4 + 6 + 10}{5}$, or 6.

median (geometry) A line segment that joins a vertex of a triangle to the midpoint of the opposite side.

BM is a median of $\triangle ABC$.

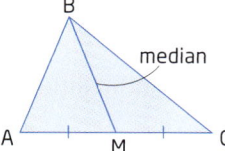

method of elimination A method for solving a linear system by matching the coefficients of one variable and then adding or subtracting the equations to eliminate that variable.

method of substitution A method for solving a linear system by substituting for one variable from one equation into the other equation.

midpoint The point that divides a line segment into two equal segments.

minimum The least value in a set of data.

mimimum point The point on the graph of a non-linear relation, such as a parabola, at which the curve changes from decreasing to increasing.

mixed number A number that is part integer and part fraction, such as $3\frac{1}{2}$.

monomial A polynomial with one term, such as $7x$.

natural number A number in the sequence 1, 2, 3, 4, ….

negative reciprocals Two numbers whose product is −1.

$\frac{3}{4}$ and $-\frac{4}{3}$ are negative reciprocals.

negative slope The ratio of rise to run of a line that rises to the left.

The line shown has slope −1.

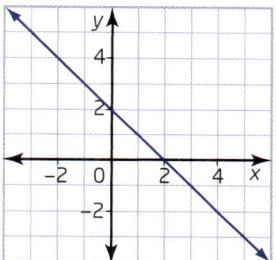

net A two-dimensional (flat) pattern that can be cut out, folded, and taped to form a three-dimensional shape. A net for a cube is shown.

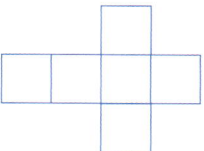

non-linear relation A relationship between two variables that does not follow a straight line when graphed.

numerator The number of equal parts being considered in the whole or the group.

$\frac{3}{4}$ has numerator 3.

numerical coefficient The number factor in a term.

In $7x^2$, the numerical coefficient is 7.

obtuse angle An angle that measures more than 90° but less than 180°.

Glossary • MHR **575**

obtuse triangle A triangle containing one obtuse angle.

octagon A polygon with eight sides.

opposite angles When two lines cross, the pairs of angles formed on either side.

opposite integers Two integers, such as 5 and −5, that are an equal distance either side of 0. Their sum is 0.

order of operations The convention for evaluating expressions containing several operations: **B**rackets, **E**xponents, **D**ivision, **M**ultiplication, **A**ddition, **S**ubtraction (see BEDMAS).

ordered pair A pair of numbers, such as (2, 5), used to locate a point on the coordinate plane.

origin The point of intersection of the x-axis and the y-axis on a coordinate grid. The point (0, 0).

orthocentre The point at which the three altitudes of a triangle meet.

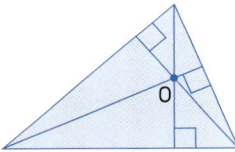

O is the orthocentre.

P

parabola The graph of a quadratic relation, which is U-shaped and symmetrical.

parallel lines Lines in the same plane that never meet. On a graph, parallel lines have the same slope.

parallelogram A quadrilateral with two pairs of opposite sides that are parallel.

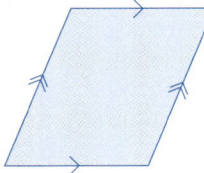

pentagon A five-sided polygon.

percent A fraction whose denominator is 100.

72% means $\frac{72}{100}$.

perfect square A number that can be expressed as the product of two identical factors.

36 is a perfect square, because 36 = 6 × 6.

perfect square trinomial A trinomial of the form $a^2 + 2ab + b^2$ or $a^2 - 2ab + b^2$ that is the result of squaring a binomial.

perimeter The distance around the outside of a shape.

perpendicular bisector See right bisector.

perpendicular lines Two lines that cross at 90°. On a graph, perpendicular lines have slopes that are negative reciprocals (their product is −1).

point of intersection The point where two or more lines cross.

polygon A two-dimensional closed figure whose sides are line segments.

polyhedron A three-dimensional object with faces that are polygons.

polynomial An algebraic expression formed by adding or subtracting terms.

polynomial expression An algebraic expression made up of one or more terms separated by addition or subtraction.

positive slope The ratio of the rise to the run of a line that rises to the right.

The line shown has slope $\frac{2}{3}$.

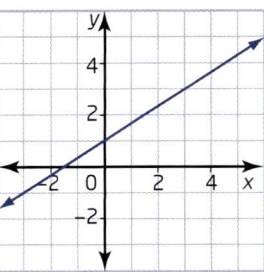

power A short form of writing repeated multiplication of the same number by itself.

5^3, x^2, and 10^7 are powers.

power of a power rule A power of a power can be written as a single power by multiplying the exponents.

$(x^a)^b = x^{ab}$

primary trigonometric ratios The three ratios, sine, cosine, and tangent, defined in a right triangle.

$$\text{sine } \theta = \frac{\text{opposite}}{\text{hypotenuse}}$$

$$\text{cosine } \theta = \frac{\text{adjacent}}{\text{hypotenuse}}$$

$$\text{tangent } \theta = \frac{\text{opposite}}{\text{adjacent}}$$

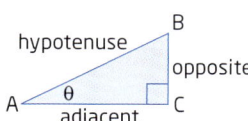

prime number A number with exactly two factors—itself and 1.

2, 5, and 13 are prime numbers.

product The result of multiplication.

product rule To multiply powers with the same base, add the exponents.

$x^a \times x^b = x^{a+b}$

proportion A statement that two ratios are equal. Can be written in fraction form or in ratio form.

$\frac{2}{5} = \frac{4}{10}$ or 2:5 = 4:10.

Pythagorean theorem In a right triangle, the square of the length of the hypotenuse is equal to the sum of the squares of the two shorter side lengths.

$c^2 = a^2 + b^2$

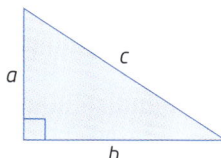

Q

quadratic equation An equation in the form $ax^2 + bx + c = 0$, where a, b, and c are real numbers and $a \neq 0$.

quadratic expression A second-degree polynomial.

$3x^2 + 5x - 1$ is a quadratic expression.

quadratic formula A formula for determining the roots of a quadratic equation of the form $ax^2 + bx + c = 0$.

$$x = \frac{-b \pm \sqrt{b^2 - 4ac}}{2a}$$

quadratic regression A mathematical process used by graphing calculators and graphing software to find the quadratic curve of best fit.

quadratic relation A relation whose equation is in the form $y = ax^2 + bx + c$, where a, b, and c are real numbers and $a \neq 0$.

quadrilateral A polygon that has four sides.

quotient The result of division.

quotient rule To divide powers with the same base, subtract the exponents.

$x^a \div x^b = x^{a-b}$

R

radius A line segment joining the centre of a circle to a point on the circumference, or the length of this line segment.

rate A comparison of two quantities expressed in different units.

60 km/h and $12.95/kg are rates.

ratio A comparison of two quantities with the same units.

rational number A number that can be expressed as the quotient of two integers, where the divisor is not zero.

0.75, $\frac{3}{4}$, and -2 are rational numbers.

ray A part of a line, with one endpoint.

reciprocals Two numbers that have a product of 1.

3 and $\frac{1}{3}$ are reciprocals.

rectangle A quadrilateral with two pairs of equal opposite sides and four right angles.

rectangular prism The mathematical name for a box with six rectangular faces with right angles at every corner.

reflection A transformation in which a point and its image are equidistant from the line of reflection.

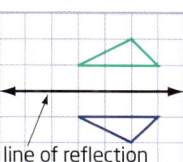

regular polygon A polygon with all sides equal and all interior angles equal.

relation An identified pattern, or relationship, between two variables. It may be expressed as ordered pairs, a table of values, a graph, or an equation.

rhombus A quadrilateral in which the lengths of all four sides are equal.

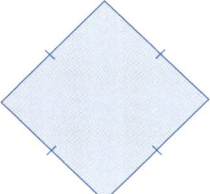

right angle An angle that measures 90°.

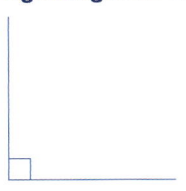

right bisector A line that is perpendicular to a line segment and divides the line segment into two equal parts. Also called a perpendicular bisector.

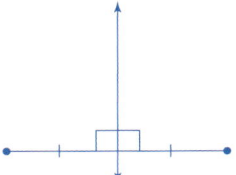

right triangle A triangle containing a 90° angle.

rise The vertical distance between two points.

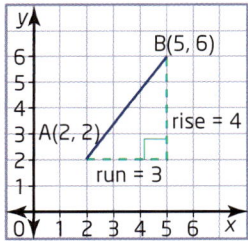

root The value of the variable that makes an equation true. The same as the solution of an equation.

rotation A transformation of a geometric shape in which each point is turned about a centre point, the centre of rotation.

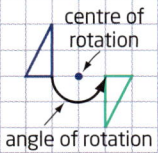

run The horizontal distance between two points. See the diagram for rise.

S

scale factor The factor, often denoted by k, that relates corresponding side lengths of two similar figures.

scalene triangle A triangle with no sides equal.

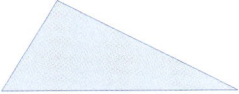

scatter plot A graph showing two-variable data as points plotted on a coordinate grid. See line of best fit and curve of best fit.

scientific notation A method of writing large or small numbers that contain many zeros. The decimal is placed to the right of the first non-zero digit and the exponent on the base 10 tells how the decimal point is moved.

$123\ 000 = 1.23 \times 10^5$
$0.000\ 000\ 085 = 8.5 \times 10^{-8}$

second-degree polynomial A polynomial of the form $ax^2 + bx + c$, where $a \neq 0$.

second differences The differences between consecutive first differences in a table of values with evenly spaced x-values.

x	y	First Differences	Second Differences
1	2		
2	5	5 − 2 = 3	5 − 3 = 2
3	10	10 − 5 = 5	7 − 5 = 2
4	17	17 − 10 = 7	9 − 7 = 2
5	26	26 − 17 = 9	

sector A part of a circle bounded by two radii and an arc of the circumference.

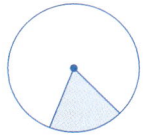

semicircle Half of a circle.

sequence An ordered list of numbers.

similar figures Figures in which corresponding sides are in proportion and corresponding angles are equal.

simplest form (of a ratio) When the terms of the ratio are whole numbers having no common factors other than 1.

simplest form (of an algebraic expression) An expression with no like terms. For example,
$2x + 7$ is in simplest form; $5x + 1 + 6 - 3x$ is not.

simplify Find a simpler and shorter equivalent expression.

sine law The relationship between the sides and their opposite angles in any acute triangle.

$$\frac{a}{\sin A} = \frac{b}{\sin B} = \frac{c}{\sin C}$$

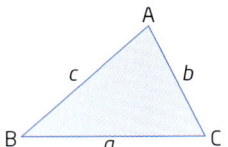

sine ratio For an acute angle in a right triangle, the ratio of the length of the opposite side to the length of the hypotenuse.

$$\text{sine} = \frac{\text{opposite}}{\text{hypotenuse}}$$

$$\sin \theta = \frac{BC}{AB}$$

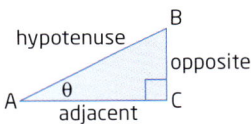

slope A measure of the steepness of a line.

$$\text{slope} = \frac{\text{rise}}{\text{run}}$$

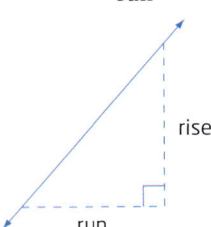

slope angle The angle in a right triangle opposite to the rise and adjacent to the run.

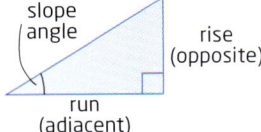

slope formula The slope, m, of a line containing the points $A(x_A, y_A)$ and $B(x_B, y_B)$ is

$$m_{AB} = \frac{\text{vertical change}}{\text{horizontal change}} \text{ or } \frac{\text{rise}}{\text{run}}$$

$$= \frac{y_B - y_A}{x_B - x_A}, x_B \neq x_A$$

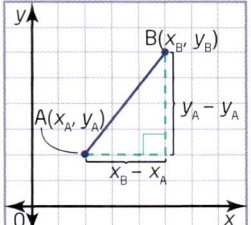

slope y-intercept form of a linear equation The equation of a line in the form $y = mx + b$, where m is the slope and b is the y-intercept.

solution The value of the variable that makes an equation true. The same as the root of an equation.

square A rectangle in which the lengths of all four sides are equal.

square-based prism A prism with two square faces as bases and four rectangular side faces.

square root A number that is multiplied by itself to give another number. The square root of 36 is 6 or -6. The radical sign means the positive square root. For example, $\sqrt{36} = 6$.

standard form of the equation of a line The equation of a line in the form $Ax + By + C = 0$, where A, B, and C are whole numbers, and A and B are not both equal to zero.

straight angle An angle that measures 180°.

180°

substitution Replacing a variable by a value.

supplementary angles Angles whose sum is 180°.

$a + b = 180°$

surface area The number of square units needed to cover the surface of a three-dimensional object.

survey A question or questions asked of a sample of a population.

Glossary • MHR 579

T

table of values A table used to record the coordinates of points in a relation. For example:

$y = x + 3$

x	y
0	3
1	4
2	5

tangent of a circle A line that touches a circle at only one point. It is perpendicular to the radius at that point.

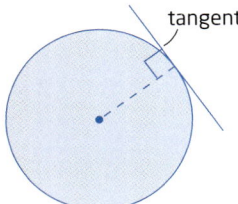

tangent ratio For an acute angle in a right triangle, the ratio of the length of the opposite side to the length of the adjacent side.

$$\text{tangent} = \frac{\text{opposite}}{\text{adjacent}}$$

$$\tan \theta = \frac{BC}{AC}$$

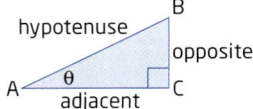

term A number or a variable, or the product of numbers and variables.

The expression $5x + 3$ has two terms: $5x$ and 3.

translation A transformation of a geometric shape in which each point is moved the same distance in the same direction.

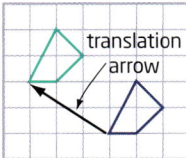

transversal A line that crosses or intersects two or more lines.

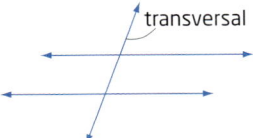

trapezoid A quadrilateral with one pair of parallel sides.

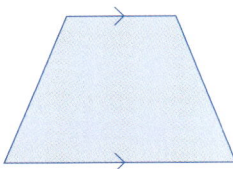

triangle A three-sided polygon.

triangular prism A prism with triangular bases.

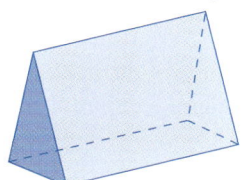

trinomial A polynomial with three terms.

$x^2 + 3x - 1$ is a trinomial.

two-variable data A set of data with two lists of data. Each entry in one list is related in some way to an entry in the other list.

U

unlike terms Terms that have different variables, or the same variable but different exponents.

$2x$, $5y$, and x^2 are unlike terms.

V

variable A letter used to represent a value that can change or vary. For example, t is the variable in the expression $2t + 3$.

variable term A term that contains a variable. Its value changes when the value of the variable changes.

Varignon parallelogram The parallelogram formed by joining the midpoints of adjacent sides of a quadrilateral.

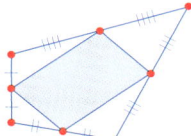

vertex (of a parabola) The point on a parabola where the curve changes direction. It is a maximum point if the parabola opens downward and a minimum point if the parabola opens upward.

vertex (of a polygon) A point at which two sides of a polygon meet.

volume The amount of space that an object occupies, measured in cubic units.

W

whole number A number in the sequence 0, 1, 2, 3, 4, 5, ….

X

x-axis The horizontal number line in the Cartesian coordinate system.

x-coordinate The first number in the ordered pair describing a point in the Cartesian coordinate system.

The point P(2, 5) has x-coordinate 2.

x-intercept The x-coordinate of the point where a line or curve crosses the x-axis. At this point, $y = 0$.

xy-plane A coordinate system based on the intersection of two perpendicular lines called axes. The horizontal axis is the x-axis, and the vertical axis is the y-axis. The point of intersection of the axes is called the origin. Also referred to as the Cartesian coordinate system, the Cartesian plane, or the coordinate grid.

Y

y-axis The vertical number line in the Cartesian coordinate system.

y-coordinate The second number in the ordered pair describing a point in the Cartesian coordinate system.

The point Q(−3, 4) has y-coordinate 4.

y-intercept The y-coordinate of the point where a line or curve crosses the y-axis. At this point, $x = 0$.

Z

zero A value for x, or the independent variable, for which the dependent variable has value 0. It corresponds to the x-intercept of the graph of the relation.

Index

A

Acute triangles, 392
   altitude, 397
   cosine, 405–406
   cosine law, 415–416
   sine law, 415–416
   solving, 415–416
   trigonometry, 434, 435
Addition of polynomials, 208
Alternate angles, 326
Altitude, 88, 90, 201
   acute triangle, 397
   isosceles triangle, 117–119
   triangles, 111–112, 125–127
Angle bisector, 126
Angle of depression, 378, 395
Angle of elevation, 273, 378, 395, 411
Angles
   acute triangle, 412–416
   alternate, 326
   co-interior, 326
   complementary, 326
   corresponding, 326
   cosine law, 412–416, 431
   exterior, 326
   opposite, 326
   properties of, 326
   supplementary, 326
   tangent, 358, 359
   triangle, 109
Arch, 168, 170, 172, 186, 189–191, 287
Area
   circle, 224
   complex figure, 219
   of a region, 252–253
   rectangle, 247, 312
   similar figures, 344–345
   similar rectangles, 345
   similar triangles, 345, 346
   triangles, 111–112, 312
Axis of symmetry, 168, 262
   parabola, 181
   quadratic relations, 189–191

B

Balance point of triangles, 110–112
Base, 163
   reciprocal, 197
Binomial, 208
   common factor, 233
   diagrams, use of, 214
   distributive property, 215, 216
   expanding, 216
   modelling product of, 214
   simplifying, 216
   squaring, 220–222, 223
Binomial factor, 235

C

Cabri Jr.® See Graphing calculator
Carbon-14 dating, 194, 198
Cartesian grid/plane, 50, 56, 70
Centroid, 91, 111, 112, 116
   triangle, 91, 111, 119–121
Cevian, 127
Chord, 97, 145, 146
   right bisector, 98, 157
Circle, 188, 273
   area, 224
   centre, 148–149
   diameter, 67, 89, 105, 145
   equations, 92–95, 102–103, 104
   points on a, 148
   properties of, 145–149, 153
   radius, 67, 224
Circumcentre, 99, 115, 116, 126
Co-interior angles, 326
Collinear, 121
Common factors, 228–233, 256
   binomial, 233
   monomial, 231–232
Complementary angles, 326
   right triangle, 326
Completing the square, 264–269, 292
Compression factor
   parabola, 181
Computer algebra system (CAS), 7
   cosine law, 414–415
   difference of squares, 249
   dimensions of a rectangle, 277–278
   factors of polynomials, 230
   method of elimination, 37
   method of substitution, 24
   perfect square trinomials, 250
   polynomial, multiplication, 212–213
   squaring binomials, 221
Concurrent, 111, 112
   cevians, 127
Congruent
   figures, 330
   parallelograms, 334
   rectangles, 334
   triangles, 55, 117
Contained angle, 407
Corresponding angles, 326

Cosine, 369, 394
   acute triangle, 405–406
   side lengths of triangles, 405–406
Cosine law, 405, 406, 430
   acute triangle, 415–416
   angles, 412–416, 431
   side length of triangle, 407
Cosine ratio, 366, 367, 368, 387
   angle, determining the, 369–370
   right triangle, 370–371
Curve of best fit, 164, 187

D

Degree of a polynomial, 208
Dependent variable, 162
Diagonal, 90
   rectangle, 281
Diameter (of a circle), 67, 89, 105, 145
Difference of squares, 223, 251, 257, 263
   factor, 248–253
   patterns, 248–249
Dilatation (dilation), 329
Distance
   calculating, 70
   comparing, 75
   shortest route, 82–83
   y-coordinate, 84
Distance-speed-time problems, 44
   plots, 165
Distributive property, 4, 209
   binomial, 215, 216
   monomial, 209
   polynomial, 209, 212–213, 256
Division of exponents, 163

E

Elimination, 34–39
   linear systems, 43–45
Equations
   circle, 92–95, 102–103, 104
   equivalent, 29–31
   for a line, 54
   graphing, 182–183
   rearranging, 7
   right bisector, 63–64
   solving, 54
Equidistant, 63
Equilateral triangle, 77, 273, 419
Equivalent
   linear equations, 29
   linear system, 30
   ratios, 328
Evaluation, 4

Exponent laws, 196
Exponential relation, 194
Exponents, 163
   division, 163
   multiplication, 163
   negative, 194–198
   powers, 163
   zero, 194–198
Expressions (simplification), 4
Exterior angle theorem, 326

F

Factor, 209
   difference of squares, 248–253
   grouping, 233
   perfect square trinomial, 248–253
   polynomials, 228–233
   quadratic equation, 282–287
   quadratic expression, 236, 237, 238–239, 242–245, 256, 257, 263
Finite differences, 169, 189–191
First differences, 169
FOIL method, 217
Formula, rearranging, 395
Fractal, 53, 103, 126, 144

G

GCF. *See* Greatest common factor
Golden ratio, 107, 116, 126–127, 136, 144, 153, 302
Graphing, 4, 5, 8–15
   equations, 182–183
   equivalent linear system, 30–31
   linear systems, 43–45
   point of intersection, 11
   quadratic equation, 282–287
   quadratic relation, 170–171
   $y = a(x - h)^2 + k$, 180–184
Graphing calculator, 6, 14–20, 48, 58–60, 67, 72–73, 78, 82, 90, 112, 118, 119, 123, 130–131, 139, 146, 267, 283–284, 305–306, 338–341, 355–356, 420–421
Greatest common factor (GCF), 209, 228–233
   polynomials, 229–230
Grouping (factors), 233

H

Heron's formula, 404
Hypotenuse, 86–87

I

Incentre, 115
Independent variable, 162
Intercepts, 5
Interest, 6
Intersection. *See* Point of intersection
Inverse tangent, 359
Inverse trigonometric operations, 394
Isometry, 341
Isosceles right triangle, 126
Isosceles trapezoid, 155
Isosceles triangle, 419
   altitude, 117–119
   angle bisector, 117–119
   angles of, 326
   congruent, 117
   median, 113, 117–119
   properties of, 117–119

K

Kite, 109, 136

L

Length
   calculating, 74
   formula, 80–87, 102
   line segment, 101, 104, 108
   median, 76
   shortest route, 82–83
Like terms, 208
Line segment, 55
   length of a, 70–76, 101, 104, 108
   midpoint, 100, 104, 108
   right bisector, 55
Linear relations (equivalent), 29–31
Linear systems, 10
   elimination, 34–39, 43–45
   equivalent, 29–31
   graphing, 43–45
   solving problems using, 42–45
   substitution, 20–25, 43–45
Lines
   intersection, 108
   midpoint, 56–64
   parallel, 55
   perpendicular, 21, 55
   point of intersection, 108

M

Maximum, 264–269, 316
   point of a parabola, 181, 262, 267
   revenue, 269
Median, 62
   hypotenuse, 86–87
   isosceles triangle, 113, 117–119
   length, 76
   triangles, 62–63, 67, 78, 89, 111
Method of elimination, 35–39, 35
   linear systems, 34–39
   point of intersection, 37–38
Method of substitution, 20–25
Midpoint, 56
   formula, 80–87, 102
   line segment, 100, 104, 108
   lines, 56–64
   multiple, 158
   parallelogram, 140
Minimum, 264–269, 316
   point of a parabola, 262, 267
Mixtures, 6
Modelling using quadratic expressions, 242–245
Monomial, 208
   common factor, 231–232
   distributive property, 209
   multiplication, 209
   product, 209
Multiplication, 163
   exponents, 163
   monomial, 209
   polynomial, 209, 210–216, 256

N

Natural numbers, 227
Negative exponent, 194–198, 203
Negative reciprocals, 302
Non-linear relations, 164, 202
   curve of best fit, 164
   scatter plot, 164

O

Operations with powers, 163
Opposite angles, 326
Ordered pairs, 168
Orthocentre, 115, 116

P

Parabola, 168, 262
   axis of symmetry, 168, 170, 181
   compression factor, 181
   maximum point, 170, 181, 262, 267
   minimum point, 262, 267
   quadratic formula, 296, 297

stretch factor, 181
vertex, 168, 170, 181
Parallel lines, 55
slope, 55
Parallelogram, 89, 90, 109
midpoints, 140
properties of, 128–131, 137–139, 152
Varignon, 132
Percent, 6
Perfect square
creating, 264–265
Perfect square trinomials, 223, 251, 252, 257, 263
factor, 248–253
Perimeter
rectangle, 32, 235, 312
square, 91, 247
triangle, 77
Perpendicular lines, 21, 55
Platonic solids, 383
Point of intersection, 11, 21, 116
distance, 84
equivalent linear system, 30–31
graphing calculator, 14–15
lines, 108
method of elimination, 37–38
method of substitution, 20–25
The Geometer's Sketchpad®, 15
Polynomial expressions, 206
Polynomials, 208
See also Special products
addition, 208
classifying, 208
distributive property, 209, 212–213, 256
factors, 228–233
greatest common factor (GCF), 229–230
like terms, 208
modelling, 231
multiplication, 209, 210–216, 256
product, 209
simplifying, 208
subtraction, 208
Powers, 163
Primary trigonometric ratios, 367, 368, 394
Prime factors, 209
Product of a monomial and a polynomial, 209
Proportion, 399
Pythagorean theorem, 74, 85–86, 327, 394, 406, 411
length of line segment, 71–72

Q

Quadratic equation, 260, 274, 316
completing the square, 292–293
factor, 274, 275–276, 282–287
graphing, 282–287
roots, 275
solving, 274–278
solving problems, 304–310
x-intercept, 282–287
Quadratic expression, 236, 263
factor, 236, 237, 238–239, 242–245, 256, 257, 263
modelling, 242–245
patterns, 237
Quadratic formula, 292, 293, 294–299, 316, 317
no real roots, 297
parabola, 296, 297
real roots, 294
Quadratic relations, 160, 168, 189–191, 202, 262
axis of symmetry, 189–191
graphing, 170–171
transformations, 174–177
vertex, 189–191
x-intercept, 176–177, 189–191
y-intercept, 176–177
zero, 176–177
Quadrilaterals, 90
midpoints of, 132
properties of, 128–133, 137–141, 152
types of, 109

R

Radius (of circle), 67, 94, 224
Ratios, 328, 399
Real roots, 294
Reciprocal, 197
Rectangle, 90, 109, 167
area, 247, 312
diagonal, 281
dimensions of, 277–278
perimeter, 32, 235, 312
Rectangular prism, 209
surface area, 209
volume, 209, 281
Reflection, 163, 329
Revenue, 193
maximum, 269
Rhombus, 109
diagonals, 141
midpoints, 141
properties of, 141

Right bisector, 55, 63, 89
chord, 98, 157
equations, 63–64
line segment, 55
Right triangle, 78, 85–86, 313
complementary angles, 326
cosine ratio, 370–371
length of legs, 308–309
sine ratio, 370–371
solving problems using, 378–380, 388–389
trigonometry, 434
Rise, 54, 61, 74, 327
Roots of an equation, 275
Rotation, 329
Run, 54, 61, 74, 327

S

Scale factor, k, 343
Scatter plots, 162, 202
non-linear relation, 164
Second differences, 169
Side length in tangent ratio, 360
Similar figures, 330
area, 344–345
triangles, 349–351
Similar rectangles (area), 345
Similar triangles, 55
area, 345, 346
properties of, 330–332, 386
solving problems using, 342–346, 386
Simple interest, 6
Simplification (of expressions), 4
Sine, 369, 394
Sine law, 396, 397, 430
acute triangle, 415–416
angle, finding, 399
side length of triangle, 398
Sine ratio, 366, 367, 368, 387
angle, determining the, 369–370
right triangle, 370–371
Slope, 5, 11–13, 54, 327
formula, 80–87, 102
parallel lines, 55
perpendicular lines, 21, 55
Slope and y-intercept, 5, 11–13, 54
Slope angle, 352, 354, 356
Special products, 220, 256
patterns, 224
Spherical coordinate system, 69
Square, 109
completing the, 264–273
perimeter, 91
side length, 218
Square roots, 262

Strength, 202
Stretch factor
   parabola, 181
Substitution, 4, 20–25
   linear system, 20–25, 43–45
Substitution method, 84
Subtraction of polynomials, 208
Sum and difference of two terms, 221
Supplementary angles, 326
Surface area
   cylinder, 235
   rectangular prism, 209

T

Table of values, 4, 5, 174–175
Tangent, 353, 354, 356, 394
   angle, 358, 359
Tangent of a circle, 98
Tangent ratio, 352–361, 368, 387
   multi-step problem, 360, 361
   side length, 360
Technology. See Graphing calculator; The Geometer's Sketchpad®
Tetrahedron, 383, 429
The Geometer's Sketchpad®, 15–19, 57–58, 67, 71–72, 78, 81, 90, 93–94, 111, 118, 123, 127, 129–130, 138, 144, 146, 211–212, 336–338, 353–355
Three-dimensional problem, 379
Transformations, 202, 329
   quadratic relations, 174–177
Translation, 163, 329
Transversal, 326
Trapezoid, 109
   midpoints, 133
Triangle, 50, 90, 394
   altitude, 88, 111–112
   angles, 109
   areas, 111–112, 312
   balance point, 110–112
   centroid, 91, 111, 119–121
   circumcentre, 115
   congruent, 55
   equilateral, 77
   incentre, 115
   median, 62–63, 67, 78, 89, 111
   midpoints of sides, 122–123
   orthocentre, 115
   perimeter, 77
   properties of, 110–113, 117–123, 152
   right, 78
   similar, 55
   solving, 394, 408
   sum of interior angles, 109
   vertices, 27
Triangular pyramid, 28
Trigonometry, 324, 392
   acute triangles, 434, 435
   right triangles, 434
   solving problems using, 424–427, 431
Trinomial, 208
   perfect square, 223
   two variables, 244

V

Varignon parallelogram, 132, 136
Vertex, 168, 262
   parabola, 181
   perfect square, 266
   quadratic relations, 189–191
Volume, 247
   rectangular prism, 209, 281

W

Word problems, 8–16

X

x-intercept, 190, 316
   quadratic equation, 282–287
   quadratic relations, 189–191

Y

$y = a(x - r)(x - s)$, 189–191
$y = a(x - h)^2 + k$, 180–184
$y = ax^2 + bx + c$, 160–205
$y = mx + b$, 54
y-intercept, 5, 11–13, 54

Z

Zero, 176, 189
   exponents, 194–198, 203

Credits

Photo Credits

piv PhotoLink/Getty Images; pv Bill Ivy/IVY IMAGES; p2-3 B. Lowry/IVY IMAGES; p8 David Tanaka; p10 Photo courtesy of Diamond Aircraft; p20 D. Trask/IVY IMAGES; p25 NASA/Science Photo Library; p34 CORBIS; p43 The McGraw-Hill Companies, Inc., Jill Braaten, photographer; p44 CORBIS; p52-53 Pascal Goetgheluck/Science Photo Library; p56 Kim Steele/Getty Images; p69-70 IVY IMAGES; p80 PhotoLink/Getty Images; p92 Bill Ivy/IVY IMAGES; p103 Creatas/PunchStock; p106-107 Cameraphoto/Art Resource, NY; p110 Bill Lowry/IVY IMAGES; p117 Bill Lowry/IVY IMAGES; p128 CORBIS; p137 Bill Ivy/IVY IMAGES; p145 (left) J. DeVisser/IVY IMAGES; p. 145 (right) Roland W. Meisel; p153 DAJ/Getty Images; p159 Bill Lowry/IVY IMAGES; p160-161 Creatas/PunchStock; p164 (top) Bill Ivy/IVY IMAGES; p164 (bottom) Nick Koudis/Getty Images; p165 Roland W. Meisel; p168 Bill Ivy/IVY IMAGES; p172 (top) Arch Desk and Chair by Roger Heitzman (Photo courtesy of the artist); p172 (bottom) Bill Ivy/IVY IMAGES; p173 Bill Lowry/IVY IMAGES; p174 David Frazier/PhotoEdit; p180 Bill Ivy/IVY IMAGES; p186 Roland W. Meisel; p189 Bill Ivy/IVY IMAGES; p193 Richard Cummins/CORBIS; p194 Nick Koudis/Getty Images; p200 T. O'Keefe/PhotoLink/Getty Images; p205 Photodisc/Getty Images; p206-207 CORBIS; p210 Bill Ivy/IVY IMAGES; p219 ImageState/Punchstock; p220 Judith Nickol/David Tanaka; p227 NASA; p228 IVY IMAGES; p236 PhotoLink/Getty Images; p242 Karl Weatherly/Getty Images; p247 Roland W. Meisel; p260-261 Bill Ivy/IVY IMAGES; p264 Karl Weatherly/Getty Images; p273 David Tanaka; p274 Photodisc/Getty Images; p282 Bill Ivy/IVY IMAGES; p291 Photo Courtesy of Bombardier Aerospace; p298 Doug Menuez/Getty Images; p301 Bill Ivy/IVY IMAGES; p304 Reuters/Corbis; p315 Kevin Fleming/Corbis; p322 Charles Gullung/Zefa/Corbis; p323 Ronnie Kaufman/Corbis; p324-325 Reuters/CORBIS; p328 Clouds Hill Imaging Ltd./CORBIS; p330 Jacob Speijer; p335 Bill Lowry/IVY IMAGES; p352 David Young-Wolff/PhotoEdit; p365 top John Gress/Reuters/CORBIS; PhotoLink/Getty Images; p366 IVY IMAGES; p378 James Shaffer/PhotoEdit; p384 IVY IMAGES; p389 Steve Cole/Getty Images; p390 Geostock/Getty Images; p392-393 J. Dubois/Spectrum/IVY IMAGES; p396 NOAA; p400 NOAA; p405 IVY IMAGES; p412 D. Trask/IVY IMAGES; p424 Digital Vision/Getty Images; p431 J.Dubois/Spectrum/IVY IMAGES; p436 Christopher Covey/Beateworks/Corbis.

Illustration Credits

www.mikecarterstudio.com: p342

Technical Art

Tom Dart, Kim Hutchinson, and Adam Wood/First Folio Resource Group, Inc.